Ethics and Professional Responsibility for Paralegals

Editorial Advisors

ASPEN COLLEGE SERIES

Ethics and Professional Responsibility for Paralegals

Sixth Edition

Therese A. Cannon
Executive Vice President
Western Association of Schools
and Colleges

Wolters Kluwer
Law & Business

Published by Wolters Kluwer Law & Business in New York.

Wolters Kluwer Law & Business serves customers worldwide with CCH, Aspen Publishers, and Kluwer Law International products. (www.wolterskluwerlb.com)

To contact Customer Service, e-mail customer.service@wolterskluwer.com, call 1-800-234-1660, fax 1-800-901-9075, or mail correspondence to:

Wolters Kluwer Law & Business
Attn: Order Department
PO Box 990
Frederick, MD 21705

Printed in the United States of America.

2 3 4 5 6 7 8 9 0

ISBN 978-0-7355-9867-6

Library of Congress Cataloging-in-Publication Data

Cannon, Therese A.
Ethics and professional responsibility for paralegals / Therese A. Cannon. — 6th ed.
p. cm.
Includes index.
ISBN 978-0-7355-9867-6 (perfectbound : alk. paper)
1. Legal assistants — United States. 2. Legal ethics — United States. I. Title.

KF320.L4C37 2011
174′.30973 — dc22 2011009400

About Wolters Kluwer Law & Business

Wolters Kluwer Law & Business is a leading global provider of intelligent information and digital solutions for legal and business professionals in key specialty areas, and respected educational resources for professors and law students. Wolters Kluwer Law & Business connects legal and business professionals as well as those in the education market with timely, specialized authoritative content and information-enabled solutions to support success through productivity, accuracy and mobility.

Serving customers worldwide, Wolters Kluwer Law & Business products include those under the Aspen Publishers, CCH, Kluwer Law International, Loislaw, Best Case, ftwilliam.com and MediRegs family of products.

CCH products have been a trusted resource since 1913, and are highly regarded resources for legal, securities, antitrust and trade regulation, government contracting, banking, pension, payroll, employment and labor, and healthcare reimbursement and compliance professionals.

Aspen Publishers products provide essential information to attorneys, business professionals and law students. Written by preeminent authorities, the product line offers analytical and practical information in a range of specialty practice areas from securities law and intellectual property to mergers and acquisitions and pension/benefits. Aspen's trusted legal education resources provide professors and students with high-quality, up-to-date and effective resources for successful instruction and study in all areas of the law.

Kluwer Law International products provide the global business community with reliable international legal information in English. Legal practitioners, corporate counsel and business executives around the world rely on Kluwer Law journals, looseleafs, books, and electronic products for comprehensive information in many areas of international legal practice.

Loislaw is a comprehensive online legal research product providing legal content to law firm practitioners of various specializations. Loislaw provides attorneys with the ability to quickly and efficiently find the necessary legal information they need, when and where they need it, by facilitating access to primary law as well as state-specific law, records, forms and treatises.

Best Case Solutions is the leading bankruptcy software product to the bankruptcy industry. It provides software and workflow tools to flawlessly streamline petition preparation and the electronic filing process, while timely incorporating ever-changing court requirements.

ftwilliam.com offers employee benefits professionals the highest quality plan documents (retirement, welfare and non-qualified) and government forms (5500/PBGC, 1099 and IRS) software at highly competitive prices.

MediRegs products provide integrated health care compliance content and software solutions for professionals in healthcare, higher education and life sciences, including professionals in accounting, law and consulting.

Wolters Kluwer Law & Business, a division of Wolters Kluwer, is headquartered in New York. Wolters Kluwer is a market-leading global information services company focused on professionals.

This book is dedicated to my father

Summary of Contents

Contents

6. Advertising and Solicitation 237

7. Fees and Client Funds 279

Preface

Approach

This book is written for paralegal students and working paralegals, and for lawyers who use the services of paralegals. It is intended for use primarily as a text but is also used by those in practice as a reference manual.

It has been almost 40 years since the advent of the paralegal profession. What started out as a modest proposal to improve the delivery of legal services has become a reality in the legal profession today. Paralegals are embedded in law practice, serving as integral members of the legal services delivery team. Lawyers in all kinds and sizes of private law firms and those in corporations, government, and the public sector rely heavily on paralegals to accomplish their work. Paralegals are highly educated and competent, engaging in evermore sophisticated work in all areas of law practice.

The paralegal occupation has been one of the fastest growing in the country for 25 years. It is estimated that there are about 200,000 paralegals employed across the country. The career is recognized by the general public, and young people learn of and aspire to it. The roles and functions of paralegals continue to expand into new and exciting areas. The prestige of the occupation has also risen.

The past 30 years have also witnessed tremendous growth and change in the legal profession generally. The forces of change have been many, including the integration of technology, the use of marketing and advertising, greater competitiveness among firms for clients, an influx of new attorneys, increased attorney mobility, the development of megafirms, the impact of a global economy, more complex laws, and legal specialization. These changes have greatly affected legal ethics, in ways that probably no one anticipated.

The role of nonlawyers in providing legal services directly to the public has been the topic of intense debate as the public and the legal profession seek ways to increase access to legal services and to control legal costs. New ethics rules continue to develop in response to this dynamic environment. Paralegals must have a clear understanding of legal ethics — the concepts and rules that guide them in their work. This grounding is essential for paralegals to function competently and with integrity, to be alert to potential ethical dilemmas that occur in their daily work lives, to develop a framework for ethical decision making, and to keep abreast of changes in ethics rules as they develop.

Organization and Coverage of the Fifth Edition

The book is comprehensive and covers all the major areas of legal ethics, placing special emphasis on how the rules affect paralegals. The book begins with a chapter on the regulation of attorneys because paralegals must understand how the legal profession is regulated generally to understand their place in it and the impact that their conduct has on the lawyers who employ them. Chapter 2 contains a brief history of the paralegal career, the ways in which the occupation is regulated, and the growth of voluntary paralegal certification. This chapter examines ethics guidelines for paralegals developed by both bar and paralegal associations. Chapter 3 covers the unauthorized practice of law, introducing the history of UPL and definitions of the practice of law, and explaining the specific functions that either are prohibited outright to nonlawyers or are on the borderline. Chapters 2 and 3 both include material on the provision of legal services directly to clients by nonlawyers. Confidentiality is covered in Chapter 4. In discussing the attorney-client privilege, the work product rule, and the ethics rules regarding confidentiality, the chapter outlines ways to avoid breaches of confidentiality and duties that paralegals have. Special emphasis is given to inadvertent disclosure and technology.

Chapter 5 covers conflicts of interest, a critical concern of paralegals given the mobility of lawyers, clients, and paralegals. This chapter includes an in-depth discussion of conflicts rules and how to avoid conflicts, including the use of screens and conflicts checks. Rules regarding legal advertising and solicitation, with a discussion of the latest cases and trends in marketing of legal services, are covered in Chapter 6. Chapter 7 is devoted to financial matters that arise in the representation of clients and between lawyers and paralegals. It offers a thorough discussion of billing, fees, statutory fee awards that include compensation for paralegal work, fee-splitting, referral fees, partnerships between attorneys and nonlawyers, compensation of paralegals, and handling client funds. Chapter 8 on competence defines the concept of competence specifically in relation to paralegals and includes a discussion of malpractice. Special issues confronted by litigation paralegals and in communications with clients, courts, parties, and witnesses are covered in Chapter 9. Finally, Chapter 10 examines professionalism and issues facing paralegals in today's law firm environment, including titles, overtime, regulation, and pro bono work.

Key Features

Each chapter begins with an overview that describes in a few words the main topics of the chapter. The text body of each chapter is divided topically. Key terms are spelled out in italics when first introduced and are highlighted in the margins. At the end of each chapter are review questions that test each student's memory and understanding of the material. Discussion questions and hypotheticals follow the review questions. These may be assigned to students or used for in-class discussion. Research and outside assignments are also included so that students can be given work to build their knowledge and skills outside of class through legal or factual research or analysis of cases or issues. Cases at the end of the chapters demonstrate how the rules introduced in the chapters are applied specifically to paralegals. Some cases present key principles in professional responsibility with which all paralegals should be familiar. Several new cases are included in the fifth edition, reflecting the rapid changes taking place in unauthorized practice, confidentiality, conflicts of interest, fees, and other areas, as courts address the application of ethics rules to paralegals.

Recognizing that every paralegal program teaches ethics, but each in its own way, I have chosen a comprehensive approach so that professors may use the entire book in full courses on legal ethics or use only selected parts in programs that teach ethics in several courses or across the curriculum. The accompanying Teacher's Manual provides guidance for teachers who want to incorporate ethics material into their substantive courses.

Acknowledgments

I have many people to thank for their support and assistance with this edition of the book. Recognition must go first to the many entities that provided help and information, including the American Association for Paralegal Education, National Association of Legal Assistants,

National Federation of Paralegal Associations, and International Paralegal Management Association.

My heartfelt appreciation also goes to the wonderful people at Aspen, especially Carol McGeehan, Betsy Kenny, and David Herzig, whose patience, warmth, intelligence, and talents made this book possible.

I would like to thank the following copyright holders who kindly granted their permission to reprint from the following materials.

Ethics and Professional Responsibility for Paralegals

1

Regulation of Lawyers

This chapter provides basic background on the regulation of lawyers. Paralegals, who work under the supervision of lawyers, need to understand the rules governing lawyer conduct and how those rules affect them. Chapter 1 covers:

- the inherent power of the courts over the practice of law
- the organized bar's participation in lawyer regulation
- the role of the legislature and statutes in governing the conduct of lawyers
- the American Bar Association and its influence on legal ethics
- sanctions for lawyer misconduct

A. State Courts and Bar Associations

Like other professions that affect the public interest, the legal profession is subject to regulation by the states. Unlike other regulated professions, however, regulation of the legal profession falls mainly to the judiciary rather than the legislature. Because of the function of lawyers in the court system and the separation of powers, the judiciary has historically asserted inherent authority over lawyers.

The highest court in each state and in the District of Columbia is responsible for making rules related to law practice admission and to lawyers' ethical conduct. The codes of ethical conduct promulgated by the states' highest courts include mechanisms for disciplining lawyers who violate the codes. Most state legislatures have also passed statutes that supplement the ethical rules adopted by the courts. Some states consider legislative authority over the practice of law to be concurrent with judicial authority; others consider legislative action to be only in aid of judicial action. A few state supreme courts have allowed the legislature to assert substantial authority over the practice of law. For example, the New York state legislature has the power to regulate the legal profession and has vested the power to impose sanctions on lawyers with the intermediate courts (which are called supreme courts in New York although they are not the highest state courts).

Sometimes the judiciary and the legislature have conflicting ideas about matters affecting the practice of law, and a court will be called on to strike down legislation that attempts to regulate some aspect of the legal profession. Several state supreme courts (including Arizona, Colorado, Idaho, and Washington) have held unconstitutional legislation that would have authorized nonlawyers to engage in conduct that the court considered to be the practice of law. (See the *Bennion* and *UPL Committee* cases at the end of this chapter for examples.) Local court rules also govern attorneys' conduct in matters before the courts.

In practice, many state supreme courts rely heavily on state bar associations to carry out their responsibilities for regulating the practice of law. These courts have delegated authority to the bar to alleviate the burden of handling ethical matters in addition to their caseload.

Integrated bar
A bar association in which the mandatory and voluntary aspects of bar activities are combined, and membership is required

Some state bar associations are ***integrated***, which means that membership is compulsory. In a state with an integrated bar, annual dues to renew the practitioner's law license carry automatic membership in the state bar. Some states have purely voluntary state bar associations; funds to operate the admissions and disciplinary functions in the state are derived from annual licensing or registration fees. Integrated bars generally play a more active role in the admissions and disciplinary functions of the court and in other matters relating to the legal profession. In addition to state bar associations, hundreds of "specialty" bar associations have been established in the last 15 years as a result of the trend away from "general" law practice to practice that is specialized in a few areas of law.

Lawyer disciplinary systems have expanded and reformed in the past 20 years to respond to the growth in complaints about lawyers that has accompanied the growth of the legal profession. Mediation and arbitration are now widely used in disputes between lawyers and clients. Integrated bars and disciplinary authorities also offer or require ethics training for lawyers, conduct random audits of client trust accounts, and some have adopted ethics rules that provide for firm-wide responsibility for ethical breaches. Programs for lawyers with substance abuse problems have expanded into all jurisdictions as it has become clear that unethical conduct is often connected to substance abuse. Disciplinary proceedings and records have been made more transparent and open to the public from their initiation. The courts and the bar understand that to retain control over the legal profession through self-regulation, lawyers must be accountable to the public.

Concerns about the role of lawyers in corporate scandals have resulted in the federal government's adoption of new rules governing the conduct of lawyers in advising corporations in matters relating to securities law. The Sarbanes-Oxley Act of 2002 (15 U.S.C. §7245) led to the Securities and Exchange Commission's adoption of rules that require lawyers to report suspected violations of securities laws up the ladder within the corporate governance structure. Not all attempts of the federal government to regulate lawyers have been successful, however. Some federal cases involve limited application of consumer protection laws to lawyers, in recognition of two important principles: that lawyers are regulated by the states and that lawyers are regulated by the courts. (See *American Bar Ass'n v. F.T.C.*, 430 F.3d 457 (D.C. Cir. 2005).) In 2010, federal legislation designed to reform financial markets exempted lawyers from the authority of a newly created enforcement agency, recognizing that lawyers are subject to discipline by states.

B. American Bar Association

All states but one (California) have patterned their codes of ethics on the models of the American Bar Association (ABA). The ABA is a national voluntary professional association of lawyers, which currently has more than 400,000 members, nearly half of the lawyers in the country. Over 100 years old, the ABA is the chief national professional association for lawyers, asserting a strong voice in matters affecting revision and development of the law, the judiciary, and the administration of justice. Among its many contributions to the profession is the promulgation of model codes of ethics.

The ABA first published the **Canons of Professional Ethics** in 1908. These Canons were patterned after the first code of ethics for lawyers adopted in 1887 by the Alabama State Bar Association. Prior to the adoption of state codes, lawyer conduct was governed largely by common law and some statutes. The 1908 Canons consisted of 32 statements of very general principles about attorney conduct, mainly conduct in the courtroom. Many states adopted these ABA Canons through court rule or statute.

In 1964, the ABA began work on a new set of ethical guidelines at the request of its then-president, Lewis F. Powell, who later served on the U.S. Supreme Court. This new code, called the **Model Code of Professional Responsibility**, was published in 1969. It was designed as a prototype for states to use in developing their own codes. The Model Code, which was adopted at least in part by every state, contained:

- **Canons**, or statements of general concepts;
- **Disciplinary Rules**, or mandatory rule statements; and
- **Ethical Considerations**, or interpretive comments that are aspirational or advisory.

Although the Model Code was quite well received, other events in the legal field led to a call for a revised code within a very short time. Watergate was one of the most pivotal of these events. The misconduct of lawyers in the Watergate scandal damaged the public image of lawyers. Also during this period the U.S. Supreme Court decided several cases relating to the legal profession that struck down rules prohibiting lawyer advertising. Finally, changes in law practice brought about by economic developments and the proliferation of new laws resulted in more and different kinds of ethical problems that were not addressed effectively in the Model Code.

In 1977, the ABA established a new body to revisit the Model Code. The Commission on the Evaluation of Professional Standards, which came to be known as the Kutak Commission after its chair, developed the Model Rules of Professional Conduct, which were adopted by the ABA in 1983. The Model Rules are formatted differently than the Model Code; the difference between mandatory and aspirational language was eliminated and the rules are written as directives and followed by interpretive comments.

Specific amendments have been made many times to the ABA Model Rules since they were adopted, with a major revision completed in 2002. In 2009, the ABA created the Ethics 20/20 Commission, which is examining the rules in view of globalization and the rapidly changing environment for practicing law. Among the topics for review are law firm structures and models of ownership and the continued efficacy of state-by-state regulation.

C. Statutes and Other Forms of Regulation

Although the state codes of ethics contain most of the rules with which we are concerned in this text, attorney conduct is also governed by **statutes**. For example, some states have statutes that prohibit attorneys from engaging in certain conduct in their professional capacity as lawyers and provide for criminal and civil penalties. As we will see in Chapter 3, several states have laws that make the unauthorized practice of law a crime, usually a misdemeanor. Federal securities law, referred to earlier in Section A, is another example of how legislatures govern the conduct of lawyers.

Usually not binding on attorneys but often consulted when ethical issues arise are ***ethics opinions*** of state and local bar associations and the ABA. Bar associations have ethics committees that consider ethical dilemmas posed to them by attorney-members. The committees write opinions that are published in bar journals and on their Web sites to give additional guidance to lawyers facing similar dilemmas. Some state and ABA advisory opinions, especially those that involve paralegals, are cited in this text.

Ethics opinions
Written opinions issued by a bar association interpreting relevant ethical precedents and applying them to an ethical dilemma

D. Sanctions and Remedies

Three main formal sanctions can be imposed on lawyers for ethical misconduct by the state's highest court or other disciplinary body. The most severe sanction is ***disbarment***, in which a lawyer's license to practice law is revoked. Disbarment is only imposed for the most egregious violations or when there is a long-term pattern of serious unethical conduct. Although disbarment is in theory permanent, many admitting authorities allow for re admission of a disbarred lawyer after some period of time if the lawyer demonstrates complete rehabilitation.

Disbarment
Rescinding of a lawyer's license to practice

The second most severe sanction is ***suspension***, in which the attorney is deprived of the right to practice law for a specified period of time. Some disciplinary authorities also exercise the option of imposing ***probation***, under which the disciplined attorney may continue to practice on the condition that certain requirements are met, such as restitution to injured clients, passing an ethics examination, attending ethics "school," or participating in counseling. The suspension is stayed, but the attorney remains on probation for some period during which the disciplinary body may reinstitute the suspension if further ethical violations come to light. Probation may also be imposed following a suspension to allow the disciplinary body ongoing close monitoring of the lawyer.

Suspension
Attorney is deprived of the right to practice law for a specified period of time

Probation
Attorney can practice, but certain requirements must be met

Reprimand or Reproval
Attorney is warned that ethical violations have occurred and further violations will warrant a more severe sanction

The mildest sanction is a ***reprimand***, sometimes called a ***reproval***. This represents a slap on the hand, a warning that the conduct will not be tolerated. Reprimands may be public — placed in the public record — or private — confidentially communicated in writing to the attorney. In either case, the reprimand becomes part of the attorney's record at the court or the state bar. It is considered in determining the appropriate sanction if other violations occur.

In deciding the appropriate sanction, the disciplinary body considers the nature and severity of the offense and whether the attorney has a record of prior misconduct. Other **aggravating and mitigating factors** may be taken into account, such as:

- the extent to which the attorney cooperated in the investigation and appreciates the seriousness of the matter
- the attorney's reputation and contributions to the community through public service and professional activities
- the circumstances surrounding the offense and the extent to which these make the attorney more or less culpable for the conduct
- whether the offense was a one-time incident because of those circumstances or is likely to be repeated
- the degree to which the lawyer is remorseful and willing to remedy the problems that led to the discipline

In addition to direct discipline by the court or state bar, an attorney may be **prosecuted criminally** for violations of statutes governing attorney conduct or conduct that may relate to an attorney's practice, such as laws prohibiting solicitation of clients in hospitals and jails and laws limiting the methods that can be used to collect debts. Civil ***legal malpractice*** lawsuits brought by former clients also constitute a major incentive for conforming to ethical requirements and standards of practice. (See Chapter 8 on Competence for more on legal malpractice.) Judges exercise ***contempt* power** to sanction lawyers appearing before them who engage in improper conduct that affects the administration of justice and the smooth functioning of the courts. (See Chapter 9 on Special Issues in Advocacy.) The courts also play a major role in deciding on matters in conflicts of interest because they rule on **motions to disqualify counsel**, usually brought by the opposing counsel, who claims that a lawyer or law firm has a conflict of interest that jeopardizes client confidentiality. (See Chapter 5 on Conflicts of Interest.)

Legal malpractice
Improper conduct in the performance of duties by a legal professional, either intentionally or through negligence

Contempt
Improper conduct that impairs the administration of the courts or shows disrespect for the dignity or authority of the court

Disqualification
A court order that a lawyer or law firm may not continue to represent a client in a litigated matter before it

REVIEW QUESTIONS

1. What branch of government is primarily responsible for regulating attorney conduct? What level of government? State or federal?
2. What role do state bar associations play in governing lawyer conduct?

3. What role do the state and federal legislatures play in governing the conduct of lawyers?
4. What is an integrated bar? How does it differ from a voluntary bar? What is a specialty bar?
5. What is the American Bar Association? What role, if any, does it play in overseeing attorney conduct? In ethics generally?
6. When did the states first begin to adopt ethics codes?
7. Name and describe the different versions of model ethical rules that have been adopted by the ABA.
8. Why did the ABA decide so soon after the Model Code was adopted to undertake a major revision of it?
9. What are some issues that the ABA is now considering as it reviews the current Model Rules?
10. How many states follow the ABA Model Rules?
11. What are ethics opinions? Who writes them? Are they binding on attorneys?
12. Name and describe the three main direct sanctions for attorney misconduct that are enforced by the highest state court or state bar.
13. Name some other sanctions or remedies for attorney misconduct besides those that are imposed by disciplinary authorities.

DISCUSSION QUESTIONS AND HYPOTHETICALS

1. Look at the ABA Model Code and Model Rules and compare the formats. Which do you find easier to work with?
2. Do you think that lawyers and paralegals should be governed by the states or at the national level? Consider how things have changed since ethics rules were first adopted — in the economy, the practice of law, and the nature of legal work. How does the growing globalization of legal work and law practice affect your thinking?
3. Should there be rules that govern lawyers in international practice? How should these interface with state ethics rules and state and federal laws?
4. It has been said that general practitioners are a dying breed. What does this mean for the regulation of lawyers? Should the ethics rules cover individual lawyers or apply broadly to law firms?

RESEARCH PROJECTS AND ASSIGNMENTS

1. Is your state's bar integrated? Does the legislature share in governing lawyers in some way, such as funding for the courts? Does the judiciary work closely with the bar on matters relating to admission and discipline?

2. Does your state have any laws that govern attorney conduct? What do these laws say? Where are they found in the state statutes?
3. When were the current rules of ethics in your state adopted? Does your state follow the ABA rules exactly or are some of the provisions different? If some are different, which ones and why?
4. Does your state or local bar association publish ethics opinions? If so, where do you find these? Are there any ethics opinions relating to paralegals?
5. Has your state's highest court decided any cases in which the authority of the legislature to regulate attorneys was an issue? If so, what did the court decide?
6. Read the SEC rules adopted pursuant to Sarbanes-Oxley that govern the conduct of lawyers (17 C.F.R. Part 205). Do you think that these provisions impinge on the inherent authority of the courts to govern lawyer conduct?
7. Read *ABA v. FTC,* decided by the U.S. Court of Appeal for the District of Columbia Circuit in December 2005. Do you agree with this decision? Should lawyers be subject to federal law such as this one? What would have been the impact of the decision if it had been decided the other way?
8. Read *Real Estate Bar Ass'n v. Nat'l Real Estate Information Serv.*, decided by the First Circuit U.S. Court of Appeal in June 2010. The facts in this new case are similar to those in *Bennion* below. Has the Supreme Judicial Court of Massachusetts decided the questions referred back to it by the Court of Appeal? If so, did its opinion align with *Bennion*?

CASES FOR ANALYSIS

The Washington Supreme Court case that follows demonstrates how the courts assert their inherent authority over the practice of law. In this case, state legislation that authorized escrow agents and officers to perform duties found by the court to constitute the practice of law was struck down as violating the court's constitutional authority to regulate the practice of law. Later, the Washington Supreme Court adopted the Limited Practice Rules for Closing Officers, which authorize much of the activity described in this statute.

Bennion, Van Camp, Hagen & Ruhl v. Kassler Escrow, Inc.

96 Wash. 2d 443, 635 P.2d 730 (1981)

Defendant petitioner is a registered escrow agent under the Escrow Agent Registration Act . . . and employs licensed escrow officers for closing real estate transactions. Petitioner closed several real estate transactions and in the process prepared documents and performed other services. Two of these transactions involved earnest money agreements specifying that the place of closing was to be the office of the plaintiff respondent, a law firm. Respondent brought suit alleging that the escrow company had engaged in the unauthorized practice of law. . . . Respondent sought a permanent injunction enjoining petitioner from performing any acts constituting the practice of law.

Subsequent to the filing of the action, the legislature enacted RCW 19.62 authorizing certain lay persons to perform tasks relating to real estate transactions. Specifically, the act allows escrow agents and officer to

> select, prepare, and complete documents and instruments relating to such loan, forbearance, or extension of credit, sale, or other transfer of real or personal property, limited to deeds, promissory notes, deeds of trusts, mortgages, security agreements, assignments, releases, satisfactions, reconveyances, contracts for sale or purchase of real or personal property, and bills of sale. . . .

RCW 19.62.010(2).

Petitioner, in reliance upon the statute, moved to dismiss the action for injunctive relief, which motion was denied by the trial court. Respondent moved for, and the trial court granted, a partial summary judgment declaring RCW 19.62 unconstitutional.

The line between those activities included within the definition of the practice of law and those that are not is oftentimes difficult to define. Recently, in *Washington State Bar Ass'n v. Great W. Union Fed. Sav. & Loan Ass'n*, 91 Wash. 2d 48, 586 P.2d 870 (1978), we concluded that preparation of legal instruments and contracts that create legal rights is the practice of law. . . .

The statute in question is a direct response to our holding. We reaffirm that definition. RCW 19.62 authorizes a lay person involved with real estate transactions to "select, prepare, and complete documents and instruments" that affect legal rights. As such the statute allows the practice of law by lay persons. Petitioner requests this court to redefine the practice of law so that the conduct allowed by the statute does not constitute the practice of law. Petitioner asserts that there is a trend allowing lay persons to perform certain services such as those authorized by RCW 19.62 and our holding RCW 19.62 unconstitutional would not protect the public in any way. We disagree. . . .

Petitioner's activities and those activities authorized by RCW 19.62 constitute the practice of law and do not come within any exception. Inasmuch as RCW 19.62 authorizes lay persons to perform services we have defined as the practice of law, it must fall. The statutory attempt to authorize the practice of law by lay persons is an unconstitutional exercise of legislative power in violation of the separation of powers doctrine.

Const. art. 4. §1 provides in pertinent part: "judicial power of the state shall be vested in a supreme court. . . ." An essential concomitant to express grants of power is the inherent powers of each branch. See generally *In re Juvenile Director*, 87 Wash. 2d 232, 552 P.2d 163 (1976). Inherent power is that

> authority not expressly provided for in the constitution but which is derived from the creation of a separate branch of government and which may be exercised by the branch to protect itself in the performance of its constitutional duties.

In re Juvenile Director, at 245, 552 P.2d 163.

It is a well-established principle that one of the inherent powers of the judiciary is the power to regulate the practice of law. The court's powers include the power to admit one to the practice of law and this necessarily encompasses the power to determine qualifications and standards.

The court, in *Graham* [citation omitted], citing to *Sharood v. Hatfield*, 296 Minn. 416, 210 N.W.2d 275 (1973), held that the

> regulation of the practice of law and "'the power to make the necessary rules and regulations governing the bar was intended to be vested exclusively in the supreme court, free from the dangers of encroachment either by the legislative or executive branches.'"

86 Wash. 2d at 633, 548 P.2d 310. "The unlawful practice of law by laymen is a judicial matter addressed solely to the courts." *Washington Ass'n of Realtors*, 41 Wash. 2d at 707, 251 P.2d 619.

Since the regulation of the practice of law is within the sole province of the judiciary, encroachment by the legislature may be held by this court to violate the separation of powers doctrine. The separation of powers doctrine is a fundamental principle of the American political system. For a historical discussion of the doctrine and its importance, see *In re Juvenile Director*, 87 Wash. 2d at 238-43, 552 P.2d 163. We have previously held:

> The legislative, executive, and judicial functions have been carefully separated and, notwithstanding the opinions of a certain class of our society to the contrary, the courts have ever been alert and resolute to keep these functions properly separated. To this is assuredly due the steady equilibrium of our triune governmental system. The courts are jealous of their own prerogatives and, at the same time, studiously careful and sedulously determined that neither the executive nor legislative department shall usurp the powers of the other, or of the courts.

In re Bruen, 102 Wash. at 478, 172 P. 1152.

Thus, the power to regulate the practice of law is solely within the province of the judiciary and this court will protect against any improper encroachment on such power by the legislative or executive branches. In passing RCW 19.62, allowing lay persons to practice law, the legislature impermissibly usurped the court's power. Accordingly, RCW 19.62 is unconstitutional as a violation of the separation of powers doctrine.

We affirm the trial court's summary judgment on the constitutional issue as well as that court's refusal to dismiss the request for injunctive relief. The cause is hereby remanded for trial.

Questions about the Case

1. In your jurisdiction, who handles escrows and real estate closings on residential property — lawyers or licensed agents or brokers? What is the impact on consumers of having only lawyers perform this function?
2. If nonlawyers handle these functions, how are they regulated?
3. Do you think the functions that agents were licensed to perform under the Washington statute are rightfully classified by the court as the practice of law?
4. What is the basis of the court's authority for striking down the statute?
5. Are you convinced by the court's reasoning that it should have exclusive authority over the practice of law?
6. How should proponents of measures that affect the practice of law proceed to avoid having their rules or statutes held unconstitutional?
7. Do you think it is best for the court to have sole authority over the practice of law? Why, or why not? What role, if any, should be played by the legislative and executive branches?

In this case, the state's highest court exercised its exclusive authority over the practice of law to endorse legislation that authorized nonlawyers to assist persons in ways that are typically categorized as the practice of law.

Unauthorized Practice of Law Committee v. State Department of Workers' Compensation

543 A.2d 662 (R.I. 1988)

This case comes before us on appeal by the defendants from a judgment entered in the Superior Court declaring portions of two statutes enacted by the General Assembly (citations omitted) unconstitutional as violative of this court's exclusive power to regulate the practice of law. We reverse. . . .

At its 1985 session the General Assembly enacted a set of comprehensive statutory provisions that created a Department of Workers' Compensation. . . .

The General Assembly, in attempting to implement the scheme of establishing informal hearings within the department as an initial procedure to supplement the formal hearings before the Workers' Compensation Commission, created an office of employee assistants. The function and purpose of these employee assistants are set forth in §42-94-5 as follows:

> The director of the department of workers' compensation shall provide adequate funding for an office of employee assistants and shall, subject to the personnel law, appoint the assistants to the staff of the department. Assistants should, at a minimum, demonstrate a level of expertise roughly equivalent to that of insurance claims analysts or adjusters. The purpose of employee assistants shall be to provide advice and assistance to employees under the workers' compensation act and particularly to assist employees in preparing for and assisting at informal conferences under §28-33-1.1. . . .

In the course of proceedings in the Superior Court, evidence was adduced concerning regulations of the Department of Workers' Compensation and also a position description filed in the department of personnel which defined the duties of employee assistants as follows:

> To provide technical advice and assistance to various parties involving their rights and obligations under the Workers' Compensation Act.
>
> To assist the injured employee in preparation for and at informal Workers' Compensation hearings, and to help in providing the necessary documentation at said hearings.
>
> To provide both routine and technical advice and/or information to the general public regarding rights and responsibilities under the Workers' Compensation Act.
>
> To attempt to settle disputes between injured workers, insurance companies, employers, purveyors of services, and any other interested parties prior to an informal hearing.
>
> To conduct in person interviews; both in office and field.
>
> To gather and prepare information necessary for use at informal hearings.
>
> To do related work as required.

At the conclusion of the presentation of evidence and argument in the Superior Court, the trial justice held that the duties of the employee assistants constituted the practice of law under definitions recognized by this court. . . .

It has long been the law of this state that the definition of the practice of law and the determination concerning who may practice law is exclusively within the province of this court and, further, that the Legislature may act in aid of this power but may not grant the right to anyone to practice law save in accordance with standards enunciated by this court. (Citations omitted.)

However, it should be noted that since 1935 the General Assembly has without interference by this court permitted a great many services that would have come within the definition of the practice of law to be performed by insurance adjusters, town clerks, bank employees, certified public accountants, interstate commerce practitioners, public accountants (other than certified public accountants), as well as employee assistants. The plain fact of the matter is that each of these exceptions enacted by the Legislature constituted a response to a public need. In each instance the Legislature determined that the persons authorized to carry out the permitted activities were qualified to do so. . . .

We must remember that the practice of law at a given time cannot be easily defined. Nor should it be subject to such rigid and traditional definition as to ignore the public interest. . . .

We are of the opinion that the informal hearings, together with lay representation, may well serve the public interest. We concluded from the evidence introduced that the employee assistants will be adequately trained to carry out the relatively simple and repetitive functions which they will be called upon to perform. We do require, however, that in the event an employee is denied compensation at such a hearing the employee be given an opportunity to consult with an attorney of his choice in order to determine whether he or she will appeal to the Workers' Compensation Commission. This consultation should be paid for at state expense at a reasonable fee to be determined by the director. In the event that an attorney chooses to represent the employee before the commission, such attorney would be paid by the employer if the employee prevails as presently provided by law. See G.L. 1956 (1986 Reenactment) §28-35-32.

In authorizing the employee assistants to carry out the functions authorized by §42-94-5, we are dealing with a question of first impression and are relying to a great extent upon the legislative findings that declare the necessity for an informal prompt hearing in the event of controversy. Therefore, this grant of authorization is made upon a somewhat experimental basis. Consequently we shall leave the matter open for the Unauthorized Practice of Law Committee to come again before the court in the event that the public, and particularly employees, are not adequately protected by the services of the employee assistants. Meanwhile the act may be implemented in the form in which it is presently cast, with the single modification set forth in this opinion.

For the reasons stated, the defendants' appeal is sustained. The judgment of the Superior Court is reversed. The papers in the case may be remanded to the Superior Court with directions to enter judgment for the defendants but without prejudice to the plaintiff to bring a new complaint in the event that the public interest shall so warrant in the future, as indicated heretofore in this opinion.

MURRAY, Justice, dissenting.

I respectfully disagree with the majority. I would affirm the trial justice's decision on the basis that the language in G.L. 1956 (1984 Reenactment) §42-94-5, as amended by P.L. 1986, ch. 1, §3, allows a group of nonlicensed employees to perform duties which are equivalent to those reserved for qualified, licensed attorneys. Employee assistants who engage in the unauthorized practice of law serve to the detriment of the public, and this court, by permitting such conduct, compromises established professional standards requisite for the proper administration of justice. . . .

Questions about the Case

1. How did the Rhode Island Supreme Court come to hear this case? What was the lower court's ruling?
2. What system did the Workers' Compensation statute establish that was objectionable to the lower court?
3. Examine the definitions of the practice of law in Chapter 3 and evaluate whether employee assistants functioning under the authority of this statute would be engaging in the "practice of law."
4. What are the reasons that this court decided to endorse the legislation? Are these good reasons? Why was the outcome different from that in *Bennion*, above?
5. What does the court say about other inroads into the practice of law by nonlawyers? Is this important to the court's ruling?
6. Does the court abdicate its exclusive authority over the practice of law?

2

Regulation of Paralegals and Ethics Guidelines for Paralegals

This chapter traces the evolution of the paralegal profession, examines attempts to regulate the profession, and discusses the ways in which paralegals are currently regulated. Chapter 2 covers:

- the development of the paralegal profession since its inception in the late 1960s
- the American Bar Association's involvement in the field
- the role of professional paralegal associations
- past and present efforts to regulate paralegals
- distinctions between certification, licensing, and limited licensing
- liability of paralegals as agents of attorneys
- guidelines on the utilization of paralegal services
- ethics codes promulgated by paralegal associations

A. A Brief History of the Paralegal Profession

1. The Beginnings

The use of specifically educated nonlawyers to assist lawyers in the delivery of legal services is a relatively new phenomenon in the history of American law. The concept is about 50 years old, dating back to the 1960s, when the rapidly rising cost of legal services, combined with the lack of access to legal services for low- and middle-income Americans, caused the government, consumer groups, and the organized bar to take a close look at the way legal services were being delivered.

In response to the unmet need for legal services, the federal government established the Legal Services Corporation to provide funding for legal services to the indigent, low-cost legal clinics started to appear, and prepaid legal plans were developed. Practitioners and the organized bar also attempted to develop alternatives to the traditional practice model that would keep costs down without sacrificing quality. The answers they came up with included better management, increased automation, and the use of **legal assistants** or **paralegals**.

In 1967, the American Bar Association (ABA) endorsed the concept of the paralegal and, in 1968, established its first committee on legal assistants, which later was made a standing committee of the ABA under the name Standing Committee on Legal Assistants. Its name was changed to the **Standing Committee on Paralegals** in 2003 in recognition of the growing preference for the title "paralegal." During the late 1960s and early 1970s, the ABA and several state and local bar associations conducted studies on the use of paralegals. Many studies showed initial attorney resistance to paralegals, but actual use was on the rise.

2. Growth through the 1970s

The first **formal paralegal training** programs were established in the early 1970s. In 1971, there were only 11 programs scattered across the country. In 1974, the ABA adopted guidelines for the paralegal curriculum and, in 1975, began to approve paralegal education programs under those guidelines. There were nine paralegal programs approved that year.

In the mid-1970s, the first professional paralegal associations were formed. Dozens of groups cropped up locally. The **National Federation of Paralegal Associations** (NFPA) and **National Association of Legal Assistants** (NALA) were established. Paralegal educators formed their own organization, the **American Association for Paralegal Education** (AAfPE). In 1976, NALA established its **Certified Legal Assistant** (CLA) program, a voluntary certification program consisting of two days of examinations covering general competencies, such as judgment, communications, ethics, human relations, legal terminology and research, and analysis, and substantive practice areas selected by the candidate from a list of eight.

In 1975, the federal government recognized the existence of this new occupation by creating a new job classification. States, counties, and cities soon followed suit. In 1978, the U.S. Bureau of Labor Statistics predicted that the paralegal career would be one of the fastest growing occupations through the year 2000.

3. New Directions in the 1980s and 1990s

Job opportunities expanded and changed dramatically during the late 1970s and into the 1990s. Although the first paralegals were employed primarily in small law firms and legal aid organizations, large private law firms soon became the biggest employers of paralegals. As a result, large firms and corporate law departments developed paralegal manager and supervisor positions so that the large numbers of paralegals they employed could be effectively deployed. In the 1980s, a group of paralegal supervisors and managers started the **Legal Assistant Management Association** (LAMA), now known as the **International Paralegal Management Association** (IPMA).

During the 1980s, paralegals began freelancing, handling specialized matters for attorneys on an as-needed, independent-contractor basis. Some worked alone in a specialized area of practice, such as probate, and others worked for full-service paralegal support companies.

Since the 1980s the United States has experienced tremendous growth for the paralegal profession. Job opportunities have expanded in all sectors of employment. Clients have come to accept paralegals and even to demand that they be included on the legal services delivery team as a way of keeping costs down. Paralegals, like attorneys, have become more specialized, particularly in large law firms, corporate law departments, and government agencies, where most paralegals work in only one area of practice.

Paralegals have been granted recognition by the organized bar and practitioners. Many state bar associations have guidelines for the use of paralegals and established paralegal committees or divisions.

4. Into the Twenty-first Century

Estimates vary on the number of paralegals employed in the United States. Most sources indicate that there are more than 200,000. About a thousand paralegal educational programs are operating, nearly 300 of which are approved by the ABA, and about 300 of which are members of the American Association for Paralegal Education. Most surveys show that well over half of paralegals hold a baccalaureate degree and even more have some formal paralegal education.

Voluntary certification by one of the paralegal associations has gradually become more common. In addition to NALA's program mentioned above, the National Federation of Paralegal Associations (NFPA) has the **Paralegal Advanced Competency Examination** (PACE), designed to measure the competency of experienced paralegals. The NFPA is an umbrella organization of state and local paralegal associations with more than 50 affiliated local associations, representing about 11,000 paralegals. At the time of this writing, nearly 600 paralegals have earned the Registered Paralegal designation that is granted to those who pass the PACE.

NALA represents more than 18,000 paralegals, including more than 6,500 individual members and about 85 state and local affiliated associations. More than 16,000 paralegals have been certified by NALA. More than 1,900 CLA/CPs have obtained advanced certification.

The International Paralegal Management Association, representing managers and supervisors of paralegals, has about 500 members, local chapters in several major cities across the country, and members in other parts of the world. IPMA leads the way in promoting the expanded and effective utilization of paralegal services.

Another group that includes paralegals is **NALS**, an Association for Legal Professionals. This group was established many years ago as a group for legal secretaries, but in the 1990s changed its name to reflect its changing mission of representing the interests of all people who work in the legal profession. NALS has about 6,000 members but does not track how many of its members are paralegals. It has long offered a certification program for legal secretaries and now also administers a paralegal certification examination called the PP, or Professional Paralegal examination. More than 450 paralegals have passed this examination.

The job market for paralegals vacillates with the ebb and flow of the economy, but overall has continued to grow. Even during the 2009-2010 economic recession, paralegals fared better than lawyers in retaining their jobs or finding new ones. Paralegals have become an expected part of the legal team. Employment opportunities are steady and salaries have increased beyond levels of inflation. However, small law firms still do not employ paralegals to the same degree as large ones, and the ratio of lawyers to paralegals in most firms has stalled at about three or four to one.

Several important trends characterize the paralegal profession at this point in its history. Levels of education for paralegals are increasing every year. Firms often expect a baccalaureate degree and paralegal education. **Certification** and **licensing** and the role of nonlawyer legal service providers continue to dominate the discussion of paralegal professional organizations. Opportunities for growth have been developed in new areas of employment and law practice, and exciting alternative and niche paralegal careers are flourishing. All of these trends point to the maturation and evolution of the paralegal profession.

B. Regulation of Paralegals: Certification and Licensing

1. Definitions of Terms

Certification of an occupation, as used in the context of paralegal regulation, is a form of recognition of an individual who has met specifications of the granting agency or organization. It is usually voluntary, although some proposals for certification of paralegals by courts have been framed as mandatory. NALA's CLA/Certified Paralegal program, NFPA's PACE/RP, and NALS's PP are forms of certification, as are some state bar-sponsored programs, described later in this section.

Certification
A form of recognition of an occupation based on a person's having met specific qualifications, usually undertaken voluntarily

Licensing is a mandatory form of regulation in which a government agency grants permission to an individual to engage in an occupation, to use a particular title, or both. Only a person who is so licensed may engage in this occupation. There is no licensing of paralegals at the present time in the United States. Attorneys are "licensed" by the state or states in which they practice.

Licensing
Mandatory form of regulation in which a government agency grants permission to engage in an occupation and use a title

Typically, both licensing and certification require applicants to meet specified requirements regarding education and moral character and to pass an examination. Additional requirements usually include adoption of an ethics code, a mechanism for disciplining licensed persons who violate ethics rules, and requirements for continuing education.

2. State Regulation of Attorney-Supervised Paralegals

Since the beginning of the paralegal profession, the need for and value of regulating paralegals has been a topic of discussion and debate. The paralegal profession is split, without a clear consensus about regulation. However, the push for regulation has become stronger as paralegals have sought to professionalize the occupation and to distinguish themselves from persons who provide legal services directly to the public.

South Dakota's Supreme Court took a step toward regulation in 1992 when it adopted rules that define legal assistants/paralegals and set qualifications for persons seeking to use that title (South Dakota Supreme Court Rule 92-5, Codified Laws, §16-18-34). Later, Maine became the first state in the country to legislate the use of the titles paralegal and legal assistant. In 1999, **Maine** adopted a state law that defines paralegal or legal assistant as:

> a person qualified by education, training or work experience, who is employed or retained by an attorney, law office, corporation, governmental

> agency or other entity and who performs specifically delegated substantive legal work for which an attorney is responsible.

M.R.S.A. §921.

The Maine law establishes fines for persons using the title legal assistant or paralegal without meeting the terms of the definition. The intention of this law is to deter nonlawyer practitioners from using these titles.

The efforts of California paralegals to get similar protection for the paralegal occupation led to adoption of the **first regulatory scheme for paralegals** in the country. The California statutes create a form of regulation that is neither certification nor licensing. Effective in 2001, **California's law** requires persons who fit the statutory definition of a paralegal to meet certain education or experiential requirements and to engage in specified continuing education. Only persons working under the supervision of a lawyer can use the titles paralegal, legal assistant, and other comparable titles. The statute also makes it unlawful for those not meeting the statutory definition and requirements to hold themselves out as paralegals. Compliance with this law is not monitored by the state in any formal way, as it would be in a full-blown licensing program, but law firms and paralegals in the state generally do comply.

Under the California law, a paralegal, or any other person using one of several similar titles, is defined as:

> A person who either contracts with or is employed by an attorney, law firm, corporation, governmental agency, or other entity and who performs tasks under the direction and supervision of an active member of the State Bar of California . . . that have been specifically delegated by the attorney to him or her. . . .

California Business and Professions Code §6450(a).

It should be noted that one federal court in California has acknowledged this statute is setting the qualifications for paralegal time to be compensated in a fee petition. See *Sanford v. GMRI, Inc.* (CIV-S-04-1535 DFL CMK (E.D. Cal. 2005)), which is excerpted in Chapter 7.

The **Florida Supreme Court** has also limited the use of the titles paralegal, legal assistant, and other similar terms to those persons who work under the direct supervision of a lawyer. It first so defined the terms paralegal and legal assistant when it amended its Rules of Professional Conduct in the year 2000 by adding the definition of paralegal to the general rule on supervision of nonlawyers, which is based on ABA Model Rule 5.3, discussed later (Florida Rule 4-5.3). In 2002, it also added the definition of a paralegal or legal assistant to the Rules Governing the Investigation and Prosecution of the Unlicensed Practice of Law, which now indicate that it constitutes unauthorized practice for someone who does not meet the definition of a paralegal or legal assistant to use that term in providing legal services. Florida has also adopted a registration program for paralegals; see the discussion below.

In 2003, the **Arizona Supreme Court** adopted a definition as part of its newly promulgated rules on the unauthorized practice of law, defining a legal assistant/paralegal as follows:

> a person qualified by education and training who performs substantive legal work requiring a sufficient knowledge of and expertise in legal concepts and procedures, who is supervised by an active member of the State Bar of Arizona, and for whom an active member of the state bar is responsible, unless otherwise authorized by supreme court rule.

Rules of the Supreme Court of Arizona, Rule V.A.

New Mexico court rules define paralegals and set minimum qualifications, and recommend that lawyers not use the designation of paralegal for persons who do not meet these requirements, falling short of prohibiting the use of the title. This may be seen as an interim step toward the kind of "soft" regulation that has been adopted in states like California.

All these initiatives show some acceptance of the idea that paralegals should be regulated, but efforts to regulate paralegals in a more comprehensive way have been met with substantial resistance by the organized bar, which generally holds to the view that paralegal regulation is unnecessary. Lawyers sometimes also express concerns that regulated paralegals would compete for work with lawyers, especially lawyers who are in solo and small practices and serve individuals in areas such as divorce, bankruptcy, and landlord-tenant matters.

Several jurisdictions have seen unsuccessful initiatives to regulate paralegals. A plan in Hawaii to establish mandatory certification of paralegals by the state supreme court was rejected even with strong support among influential leaders on the bench. The state of Wisconsin plan for mandatory licensing of paralegals was finally rejected by the state supreme court in 2008 after having been stalled since 2000. Earlier licensing proposals in Minnesota, Montana, Nevada, New Jersey, Oregon, South Carolina, and Utah were shelved. In Ontario, Canada, where paralegals can perform some functions that would be considered the practice of law in the United States, paralegals have been licensed since 2008. Requirements include formal education at an accredited program and passing an examination. Paralegals are subject to an ethics code and discipline just as lawyers are.

While many paralegals across the country continue to promote regulation, several associations have changed strategy and are working to establish state-sponsored programs of voluntary certification.

3. Voluntary Certification of Paralegals

Early in the profession's evolution, **Oregon** adopted a **voluntary certification program** for legal assistants. It was abolished after a few years because of low participation. The second state to venture into certification, Texas, has been more successful. Texas adopted a voluntary certification program for paralegals in 1994. The program is administered through its Board of Legal Specialization. Certification examinations are given in several practice areas, including family law, civil trial law, criminal law, estate planning and probate, real estate law, and personal injury trial law.

Certification, valid for five years, is renewable on demonstrated participation in continuing education, employment by a Texas attorney, and substantial involvement in the specialty area. There are currently more than 300 certified legal assistants in Texas.

The states of North Carolina, Florida, and Ohio adopted voluntary certification or registration programs in the last few years, North Carolina in 2004 and Ohio and Florida in 2007. The North Carolina and Ohio programs were established by the state bar association and both require applicants to meet entrance standards and pass an examination. Florida's was adopted by the state Supreme Court. North Carolina's certification is designed for paralegals who have met educational requirements or have a specified level of experience, whereas the Ohio plan requires applicants to have designated levels of legal experience in addition to meeting educational criteria. Florida's registration program has two tiers, with paralegals meeting the higher level requirements eligible to call themselves Florida Registered Paralegals.

By all accounts, these programs are very successful. Within two years, North Carolina had certified more than 4,200 paralegals; Ohio has certified 165 paralegals; and Florida's program has produced 4,000 registered paralegals in less than three years of operation. However, other states (for example, Indiana and Oregon) have recently rejected proposals for voluntary certification.

As noted above, the national paralegal associations continue to promote voluntary certification and have increased the numbers of paralegals with these credentials substantially in the last decade. On a national level, these organizations want to be poised for regulation when it comes by having proven examinations in place that can be adopted by states.

At the state level, a growing number of statewide paralegal organizations have developed state-specific certification examinations, usually in connection with NALA and designed for CLAs. California, Florida, and Louisiana have long had paralegal association and sponsored certification, and they have now been joined by Delaware and Pennsylvania.

The ABA Standing Committee on Paralegals continues to hold fast in opposing regulation and maintains a more neutral stance toward voluntary certification, adhering to policy statements on certification and licensing issued in 1975 and 1986. In both instances, the Standing Committee rejected the notion that paralegals need to be licensed, contending that the public is protected by the extensive ethical and disciplinary requirements to which lawyers are subject as the appropriate means to protect consumers. IPMA also opposes licensing of paralegals, asserting that licensing of paralegals who work under lawyer supervision is unnecessary for the protection of the public and would unduly interfere with lawyers' prerogative to hire the best-qualified persons for the job they need done.

The ABA Standing Committee on Paralegals has long had a **definition of legal assistant/paralegal**, which was adopted by the House of Delegates. As revised in 1997, it reads as follows:

> A legal assistant or paralegal is a person, qualified by education, training or work experience, who is employed or retained by a lawyer, law office, corporation, governmental agency or other entity and who performs specifically delegated substantive legal work for which a lawyer is responsible.

4. The Arguments about Regulation of Attorney-Supervised Paralegals

The issues relating to regulation of paralegals who work under the supervision of attorneys are significantly different from those who sometimes call themselves "independent paralegals" or "legal technicians" and who seek to provide legal services directly to the public.

The primary arguments **against licensing** of lawyer-supervised paralegals are that it:

- is unnecessary because attorney-employers are already fully accountable to clients;
- would increase the cost of legal services as the costs of employing paralegals would rise;
- would stifle the development of the profession by limiting the functions that paralegals can perform;
- would inappropriately limit entry into the profession;
- would unnecessarily standardize paralegal education; and
- would limit paralegals from moving into new areas of practice or duties.

In addition, opponents cite the practical difficulty of determining exactly what legal tasks and functions could be assigned exclusively to paralegals through this regulatory process. In other words, what could paralegals be authorized to do that other workers in the legal environment could not do? What would prevent lawyers from having other nonlawyers perform those tasks under different job titles?

Arguments **favoring the licensing** of traditional paralegals center mainly on the benefits to the profession, in terms of establishing it as a separate and autonomous allied legal career, one with its own identity and a concomitant increase in societal status and rewards.

Proponents believe regulation would:

- provide appropriate public recognition for paralegals as important members of the legal services delivery team;
- ensure high standards and quality of work by paralegals;
- expand the use of paralegals, thereby expanding access to legal services and lowering costs;
- provide guidance to clients and to lawyers regarding the paralegal role and qualifications; and
- encourage needed standardization in paralegal education.

The most progressive regulatory models would expand the scope of paralegal work into areas where it might not currently be permitted because of unauthorized-practice-of-law rules and statutes, reinforcing the notion that lawyers could provide general oversight and supervision. This model is based on the idea that paralegals can be used to increase access to legal services by lawyers and nonlawyers working hand in hand as opposed to playing separate but similar roles in the delivery of legal services.

Even among supporters of regulation there are wide differences about the details of a good regulatory plan. Contentious issues relate to what level and kind of formal education should be required; whether experienced paralegals without formal education should be licensed; the necessity for a competency-based examination, a moral character check, continuing education, and a separate ethics code; whether the legislature or court is the most appropriate entity to regulate; how discipline should be handled; and how the entire process should be funded.

A related and much debated concern is whether disbarred or suspended lawyers should be able to work as paralegals. Even without regulation, this is a contentious subject. California Rules of Professional Conduct permit disbarred lawyers to work as paralegals with some specified protections for clients (Rule 1-311). In a recent case, the California court made it clear that it will not condone a disbarred lawyer engaging in work that falls within the definition of the practice of law, including representing clients in administrative hearings. See *Benninghoff v. Superior Court*, 38 Cal. Rptr. 3d 759 (2006). Colorado recently adopted a rule similar to California's but many other states, such as Illinois, Indiana, and Massachusetts, do not allow disbarred lawyers to work in law firms. See, for example, *In the Matter of Scott*, 739 N.E.2d 658 (S. Ct. Ind. 2000).

5. Nonlawyer Legal Service Providers

In the last 20 years, reforming the legal services delivery system to improve **access to legal services** has become a recurring theme. Study after study has demonstrated that the vast majority of Americans do not have access to legal services, cannot afford an attorney when they need one, and do not know how to go about finding an attorney. Persons of modest means need access to the legal system and are more frequently than ever representing themselves with or without the assistance of self-help resources and nonlawyers. Barriers to access include not only inadequate financial resources, but language and physical access. As a result of this diverse array of access barriers, nonlawyer practice has developed in virtually every jurisdiction. More than half the states have considered proposals to regulate nonlawyers who provide legal services directly to the public.

Some consumer groups and nonlawyer practitioners advocate legislation that would authorize nonlawyers to engage in tasks that are otherwise considered the practice of law and therefore within the exclusive domain of licensed attorneys. Although there is substantial resistance to this concept from many practicing attorneys, there has also been support for it going back to the 1970s when the paralegal profession was born. Some commentators favor the idea of **"limited licensing"** of ***nonlawyer legal service providers*** to perform such tasks as handling simple real estate closings and drafting simple wills. However, opposition is strong from those who believe that the system of limited licensure would establish a second tier of legal services that are not as good as those services that lawyers would provide.

Nonlawyer legal service providers
Persons not licensed to practice law who provide legal services directly to the public

Proponents of limited licensure disagree on the appropriate level of regulation. Some favor a simple registration procedure under which practitioners register their names and addresses with an agency or the applicable court. Others want to create higher standards that would protect consumers, favoring educational requirements, a licensing examination, bonding or insurance, and continuing education.

Some states have taken steps to protect consumers from incompetent or unscrupulous providers. In California, ***legal document assistants*** have been required since 2000 to register with the county or counties in which they work. The California law defines and circumscribes their work, specifying that they may not provide legal advice, and sets up minimum education and experience requirements (California Business and Professions Code §§6400, et seq).

Legal document assistants/preparers
Nonlawyer legal service providers who assist persons in preparing legal documents without giving legal advice; called LDAs under California statutes, these persons are called Legal Document Preparers under Arizona court rules

In 2003, Arizona's Supreme Court adopted rules governing the activities of ***legal document preparers,*** defined as nonlawyers who prepare or provide legal documents without lawyer supervision for persons who are representing themselves. Arizona's program sets standards for certification by the court based on education or experience; defines the role of certified LDPs, limiting it to providing and preparing forms, providing information (but not legal advice), filing and arranging for service; and mandates continuing education (Arizona Code of Judicial Administration §7-208).

It is likely that other states will follow the example of California and Arizona as they address the complex issues of increasing access to legal services, while protecting the public from incompetent or unscrupulous service providers. The most progressive plan yet has been made in the state of Washington, where a Limited Practice Rule for Legal Technicians has been proposed to the state supreme court. Under this rule, certified Legal Technicians would be permitted to work directly with the public in family law, interviewing pro se litigants, explaining procedures, providing materials, reviewing and explaining documents, conducting legal research, drafting documents, selecting and completing forms, and the like, without lawyer supervision. Under the plan as now conceived, Legal Technicians would have to meet qualifications for education and work experience and pass a test, and they would be subject to ethics rules under the jurisdiction of the court. At the time of this writing, no action has been taken on this proposal, submitted to the court in January 2008.

C. State Guidelines for the Utilization of Paralegal Services

In an effort to promote the effective and ethical use of paralegals, more than half of the states have adopted **guidelines** to assist attorneys in working with paralegals. At the time of this writing, the following states have some kind of guidelines: Colorado, Connecticut, Georgia, Idaho, Illinois, Indiana, Iowa, Kansas, Kentucky, Michigan, Missouri, Nebraska, New Hampshire, New Mexico, New York, North Carolina, North Dakota, Pennsylvania, Rhode Island, South Carolina, South Dakota, Texas, Utah, Virginia, Washington, and West Virginia.

In Indiana, Kentucky, New Mexico, North Dakota, Rhode Island, and South Dakota, the guidelines have been adopted by the highest court of the state. In other states, the guidelines have been approved by the state bar association, a state bar committee on paralegals, or both.

Some of the states that have adopted guidelines have also prepared accompanying **statements on the effective use of paralegals**. Detailed listings of paralegal job functions accompany the Colorado, Georgia, and New York guidelines.

Nearly all the state guidelines cover several critical areas of ethics that come into play when nonlawyers, not subject to discipline in the way that lawyers are, perform professional-level work and are interacting with clients and the public. These key areas, covered in later chapters of this text, are:

- unauthorized practice of law
- disclosure of status as a paralegal

- confidentiality
- conflicts of interest
- supervision and delegation
- financial arrangements between lawyers and paralegals.

The **ABA Model Guidelines for the Utilization of Paralegal Services**, originally adopted in 1991, serve as a model for states and as a guide to help lawyers use paralegal services effectively and appropriately. Many of the jurisdictions with guidelines have adopted all or part of the ABA guidelines.

D. Paralegal Association Codes of Ethics and Guidelines

The two major national paralegal professional associations both have codes of ethics to guide the conduct of their members. NALA first adopted its **Code of Ethics and Professional Responsibility** in 1975. NFPA adopted its Affirmation of Responsibility in 1977. The current codes of the two organizations are included in Appendix A and Appendix B, respectively. NFPA has also adopted **Model Disciplinary Rules** to establish mechanisms for the enforcement of the ethics rules. The Model Disciplinary Rules set forth procedures for the investigation and prosecution of ethics code violations and for hearings and appeals and institute a system of sanctions.

NALA has both individual members and affiliated local chapters. All members sign a statement of commitment to NALA's code on their membership application. A mechanism is in place at the national level to investigate allegations of code violations and to remove from membership or to remove the CLA designation from any member who has violated the code. In addition to signing the statement of commitment on the membership application, legal assistants who are certified by NALA must reaffirm their commitment to the NALA code every five years when they submit verification that they have completed their continuing education hours, a requirement for continued status as a CLA.

NALA also publishes **Model Standards and Guidelines for the Utilization of Legal Assistants**. The dual purposes of these guidelines are to serve as an educational and informational tool for individual attorneys and state bars and to provide a model for states seeking to develop their own guidelines.

The NFPA issues ethics opinions on current concerns of interest to practicing paralegals. These opinions have addressed such matters as communications over the Internet, the role of paralegals who work in the corporate setting, and outsourcing of legal work.

Both organizations make literature on ethics available. Their addresses, phone numbers, and Web sites are as follows:

The National Association of Legal Assistants
1516 S. Boston, Suite 200
Tulsa, Oklahoma 74119
918-587-6828
http://www.nala.org

The National Federation of Paralegal Associations
P.O. Box 2016
Edmonds, WA 98020
425-967-0045
http://www.paralegals.org

In addition to these two national organizations, some local and regional associations have created and adopted their own ethics rules, borrowing from NALA, NFPA, and the ABA.

E. Liability of Paralegals as Agents of Attorneys

Because paralegals are not attorneys, they are neither bound by state codes of ethics for attorneys nor subject to sanctions for breaches of those codes. Without certification, licensing, or some other form of direct regulation of the paralegal occupation, a paralegal is bound to comply with high standards of professional behavior primarily because the attorney for whom the paralegal works is responsible for any lapses in the paralegal's behavior. Lawyers therefore have a strong **incentive** to ensure that the paralegals they retain and employ are familiar with the state's ethics code and comply with it. Some states specifically require that attorneys take affirmative steps to educate paralegals about ethics and to ensure their compliance.

The ABA Model Rules of Professional Conduct contain an important section on supervision. Rule 5.3 provides as follows:

> With respect to a nonlawyer employed or retained by or associated with a lawyer:
>
> (a) a partner, and a lawyer who individually or together with other lawyers possesses comparable managerial authority in a law firm shall make reasonable efforts to ensure that the firm has in effect measures giving reasonable assurance that the person's conduct is compatible with the professional obligations of the lawyer;

> (b) a lawyer having direct supervisory authority over the nonlawyer shall make reasonable efforts to ensure that the person's conduct is compatible with the professional obligations of the lawyer; and
>
> (c) a lawyer shall be responsible for conduct of such a person that would be a violation of the Rules of Professional Conduct if engaged in by a lawyer if:
>
> (1) the lawyer orders or, with the knowledge of the specific conduct, ratifies the conduct involved; or
>
> (2) the lawyer is a partner or has comparable managerial authority in the law firm in which the person is employed, or has direct supervisory authority over the person, and knows of the conduct at a time when its consequences can be avoided or mitigated but fails to take reasonable remedial action.

Although this rule applies to all nonlawyers in the lawyer's office, it has special application for paralegals, who often work closely with clients and work continuously with sensitive and confidential information. The official **Comments** to this **Model Rule** mandate that lawyers provide appropriate instruction and supervision concerning ethical obligations, highlighting the duty of confidentiality. The Comments also advise managing lawyers to have internal procedures and policies that provide reasonable assurance that nonlawyers will act ethically.

Paralegals have one other very meaningful incentive for complying with high standards of conduct—they are **potential defendants** in civil malpractice suits, which can be brought by clients who believe their attorneys have acted negligently. Paralegals are subject to the same general tort principles that apply to lawyers and other professionals. They are liable for negligent or intentional misconduct that injures a client.

The lawyers for whom they work are also liable under the doctrine of **respondeat superior** or **vicarious liability**. Under this principle of agency law, employers are responsible for the acts of their employees carried out in the course and scope of their employment. This responsibility extends to vendors and others to which lawyers may outsource work, a practice that is the subject of considerable discussion in the last decade as lawyers have outsourced work to vendors at locations outside the country.

Because clients always name their attorneys and rarely name paralegals as defendants in malpractice cases, there is little case law available defining the standards of conduct to which paralegals are held. As a general principle, paralegals would be held to the same standard of care, skill, and knowledge common to other paralegals so long as they do not hold themselves out as attorneys and they perform typical paralegal tasks.

Three cases at the end of the chapter provide examples of attorneys being held responsible for the actions of their nonlawyer staff. The *Musselman* case involves a malpractice action in which a paralegal played a part. In the *Lawless* case, a lawyer is disciplined as a result of the actions of a paralegal. *Struthers* involves the discipline of a lawyer who abdicated his responsibility to nonlawyers who were really running his "practice."

Across the country, the number of lawyers who are disciplined for over-delegating and failing to supervise paralegals is increasing. The gravity of the paralegals' breaches of ethics in these cases ranges from embezzling client funds, to misinforming a client that he did not need to show up for a hearing in a criminal case, to improperly executing documents, to overbilling. In one recent case, a lawyer hired two paralegals in a row who embezzled money from his client trust accounts. Cases like these have arisen in a number of practice areas, including civil litigation, criminal defense, bankruptcy, and estate planning.

REVIEW QUESTIONS

1. When did the paralegal profession begin and what was the impetus for its development?
2. What are the two main professional associations for paralegals?
3. What is certification? What is licensing?
4. What states have some form of direct regulation of paralegals? What entity (court or legislature) adopted the regulation in each case?
5. What states have some form of voluntary certification of paralegals? What entity is responsible for these programs in these states?
6. What are the national associations' programs for paralegal certification called? How do they differ?
7. What is limited licensure? How do nonlawyer legal service providers differ from traditional paralegals who work under lawyer supervision? How do they differ from freelance or independent contractor paralegals?
8. What are the arguments in favor of the licensing of traditional paralegals? The arguments against?
9. What is the ABA's position on paralegal certification and licensing?
10. How many states have guidelines for the utilization of paralegals? What is their purpose?
11. What are the ABA Model Guidelines for the Utilization of Paralegal Services?
12. Do NALA and NFPA have rules on the conduct of paralegals? How are these rules enforced?
13. What are the NALA Model Standards and Guidelines for the Utilization of Legal Assistants? What do they contain? What is their purpose?
14. Can a paralegal assistant who is negligent while working on a client's case be sued by the client for malpractice? Can this paralegal's attorney-employer be sued? If so, on what legal basis?
15. Can a lawyer be disciplined for the unethical conduct of a paralegal whom he or she supervises? Can the paralegal be disciplined?
16. What does ABA Model Rule 5.3 say about attorney responsibility for paralegals?

DISCUSSION QUESTIONS AND HYPOTHETICALS

1. Do you think that paralegals working under the supervision of attorneys should be licensed? Why, or why not?
2. Do you think that nonlawyer legal service providers should be licensed? Should they be permitted to give legal advice as they help "customers" who are representing themselves?
3. If you were creating a licensing scheme for nonlawyer legal service providers, what would it include?
4. If nonlawyer legal service providers were licensed in your state, would you be interested in becoming licensed? Why, or why not?
5. Who is covered and not covered by the ABA definition of a paralegal? Do you like this definition? Why, or why not? How would you change it? How does it compare with some of the other definitions of paralegals in this chapter?
6. What methods can you suggest to improve access to legal services for low- and middle-income persons?
7. Do lawyers have an ethical obligation to delegate work to an employee who has the qualifications to do the work and is the least expensive to the client?
8. Many law firms outsource work to vendors, sometimes even offshore vendors. What is the ethical duty to supervise in that situation? Is it possible to supervise effectively at this distance?
9. What would you do if the lawyer you worked for had a heavy caseload and delegated everything but court appearances to you, including getting clients to sign retainer agreements, conducting intake interviews, and preparing pleadings? Would it make a difference if the lawyer came in late at night and reviewed everything that you did?

RESEARCH PROJECTS AND ASSIGNMENTS

1. Is there a local paralegal association in your area? Is it affiliated with NALA or NFPA, or is it independent? What kinds of activities does it have? What are the benefits of membership? How many members does it have? How many are certified by NALA, NFPA, or another entity? Does it have its own ethics code?
2. Does your state or local bar have a committee that addresses paralegal issues? Can paralegals join it? What does it do?
3. Does your state or local bar have guidelines for attorneys who work with paralegals? Has it considered licensing of traditional paralegals or independent paralegals who provide services directly to the public?
4. Has your state bar or court system conducted any studies on access to legal services or access to justice? If so, read the study and report on

the findings about barriers to access and solutions, proposed or implemented. Does the report discuss how paralegals can contribute to solving the access problem?

5. Can you find any legal malpractice cases in your state in which a paralegal was implicated?
6. Is voluntary certification through the state bar, statewide paralegal association, NALA, NFPA, or NALS popular in your state or local area? How many paralegals in your state are certified?
7. Has your jurisdiction adopted Model Rule 5.3 or some version of it? Are there any disciplinary cases or ethics opinions interpreting this rule? Are paralegal-related issues addressed?
8. What are your state's rules about disbarred lawyers working as paralegals? Do you think that disbarred lawyers should be able to work as paralegals? What are the risks to the client? Does this affect the paralegal profession or the image of paralegals? Read the cases cited in this chapter, check for cases that have cited them, and see where they lead you.
9. As mentioned in this chapter, some law firms outsource work, such as legal research and document management, to vendors outside the country. Is it possible to exercise appropriate supervision under these circumstances? Read ABA Ethics Opinion 08-451 to identify the full array of ethical issues that arise in these circumstances.
10. Research the status of the Legal Technician Rule proposed to the Washington Supreme Court by the Practice of Law Board in January 2008. Study the history of the proposal. How did this proposal come about? What areas of law practice were considered? Do you think this plan would increase access to affordable legal services? What evidence does the proposal provide? Would the public be adequately protected? How?

CASES FOR ANALYSIS

The *Musselman* case demonstrates how a paralegal might become involved in a transaction that results in harm to a client, thus becoming the subject of a malpractice suit.

Musselman v. Willoughby Corp.

230 Va. 337, 337 S.E.2d 724 (1985)

This is an attorney malpractice case arising from a real estate transaction. The lawyer represented a corporate client and employed an untrained paralegal who played a significant role in the closing of the transaction.

The relevant facts mainly are undisputed. Appellee Willoughby Corporation, the plaintiff below, was formed in September 1974. . . .

Appellant Robert M. Musselman, a defendant below, represented the bondholders in formation of the Corporation. He became attorney for the Corporation and also served as its Secretary. He was not a member of the Board of Directors. The daily operations of the Corporation were handled from defendant's law office by defendant's employees. . . .

In 1976, aware that the Board of Directors wished to sell a portion of the Willoughby Tract, defendant contracted Thomas J. Chandler, Jr., a local real estate broker, who obtained an offer to purchase Parcel 9. The offer was made by Charles W. Hurt, a medical doctor who had been a real estate developer in the Charlottesville and Albemarle County area for a number of years. . . .

Subsequently, another standard form purchase contract for $215,000 was completed dated May 6, 1976. The purchaser was shown to be "Charles Wm. Hurt or Assigns." . . . The contract was executed by Hurt, by Musselman on behalf of the Corporation as corporate Secretary, and by the realtor. . . .

[Stanley K. Joynes, III,] had been employed by Musselman in June 1977. Joynes had just graduated from college but had no formal training either as a lawyer or a paralegal. His main responsibility, under Musselman's direction, was to "shepherd the Willoughby Project along." Joynes attended his first Board meeting in July 1977 and was chosen Assistant Secretary of the Corporation.

In the course of the September 1977 Board meeting, defendant was directed to close the Hurt transaction "as soon as possible." Three weeks later, Stuart F. Carwile, Hurt's attorney, notified Musselman by letter dated September 22, 1977 that his client desired to take title to Parcel 9 as follows:

> Stuart F. Carwile and David W. Kudravetz, as trustees for the Fifth Street Land Trust, pursuant to the terms of a certain land trust agreement dated 22 September 1977.

Carwile advised that after Musselman submitted a draft of the deed, Carwile would forward the proposed deed of trust and note for defendant's approval.

The paralegal then prepared the deed, with "some assistance" from other employees of defendant, in accordance with Carwile's request showing the Land Trust as grantee. Joynes arranged for Frankel to execute the deed, dated October 5, 1977, and on that day participated with Carwile in the closing of the transaction. Musselman was out of town on business on both October 4th and 5th. In the course of the closing on October 5th, the paralegal accepted the deed of trust, and other closing documents prepared by Carwile, which specifically exculpated Hurt from personal liability in the transaction as beneficiary under the land trust.

At this point, we note several important undisputed facts. First, the Board of Directors, upon being advised that Hurt, a man of substantial wealth, was to be the purchaser of Parcel 9, intended to rely on Hurt's potential personal liability as a part of the security for payment of the deferred purchase price. Second, Musselman maintained in his trial testimony that he was authorized by the Board to execute the contract of the sale on behalf of the Corporation, and this was not contradicted by any witnesses. In addition, Musselman testified that Joynes, the paralegal, represented the Corporation at the closing, acting within his authority as an employee of defendant. Also, none of the Board members, prior to closing, ever examined either the proposed contract of March 26 or the final contract dated May 6. Moreover, no member of the Board knew before closing that the contract showed the purchaser to be "Hurt or Assigns." In addition, Musselman always was of the opinion that the foregoing language in the contract authorized Hurt to escape personal liability under the contract by assigning his rights in the contract to whomever he chose. Also, Musselman never called the language to the Board's attention or explained its meaning to the Board. Finally, the fact that the closing documents exculpated Hurt from personal liability as beneficiary under the land trust was never revealed or explained to the Board of Directors prior to closing. . . .

The Land Trust defaulted under the terms of the $170,000 note in respect to an interest payment due on April 1, 1978. Subsequently, this action to recover the principal sum plus interest, due under the real estate transaction was filed in September 1978 in numerous counts against Hurt and Musselman. The proceeding against Hurt was severed and he was eventually dismissed by the trial court as a party defendant.

The Corporation's action against Musselman was based on alternative theories. The plaintiff charged that defendant breached certain fiduciary duties in his capacity as an officer of the Corporation. In addition, the Corporation alleged that Musselman, in his capacity as attorney for the Corporation, was negligent and breached his fiduciary duty as counsel to the Corporation.

At the March 1982 trial, the jury was permitted, under the instructions, to find against defendant in his capacity either as attorney, or as an officer of the Corporation, or as both attorney and officer. The jury found against defendant in his capacity as attorney only and fixed the damages, which were not in dispute, at $243,722.99. This sum represented the principal amount due on the obligation, plus interest through the last day of trial. The trial court entered judgment on the verdict in June 1982, and we awarded defendant this appeal in July 1983. . . .

Inexplicably, defendant's main contentions on appeal are based on the faulty premise that he lacked corporate authority to act in executing the contract containing the "or Assigns" language and in completing the conveyance to a land trust, while, in the process, exculpating Hurt from personal liability. This argument is totally inconsistent with defendant's trial testimony that he did, in fact, have authority to execute the contract. It is also at odds with the uncontroverted evidence about defendant's "dominant role" in acting for the Corporation. . . .

There is no merit to this argument. Musselman, being authorized to execute the contract and to close the transaction, had the responsibility as counsel to advise his client, immediately upon discovery of the "problem," that it should attempt to rescind the transaction, if we assume an attempt at rescission would have been successful. Instead, defendant at no time advised the Board of Directors that it should pursue rescission. . . .

For these reasons, the judgment of the trial court will be affirmed.

Questions about the Case

1. What functions did the paralegal Joynes perform in this transaction? Do you think any of these duties were inappropriate functions for a paralegal to perform? Were they carried out competently?
2. What were the mistakes made by the attorney Musselman in this case? What should he have done to fulfill his duty to the client without being negligent?
3. Do you think that Musselman adequately supervised Joynes? Why or why not?
4. Why was Joynes not named as a defendant in this action? Did Joynes act negligently? Did the court hold Musselman liable for Joynes's mistakes?
5. How did the fact that Joynes was "untrained" affect the court's thinking? Does a lawyer have a duty to hire a qualified person? A duty to match the person's skills and knowledge to the work that is delegated?

In the following case, a lawyer is disciplined for failure to supervise his "legal assistants," who, like the paralegal in the *Musselman* case, did not have formal paralegal training and education and breached several aspects of the ethics rules.

Supreme Court of Arizona v. Struthers

179 Ariz. 216, 877 P.2d 789 (1994)

Child Support Collections ("CSC"), a debt collection agency, retained Struthers in December 1989 to work with another lawyer who had been handling CSC's cases. The following day, the first lawyer resigned. . . .

When Struthers started with CSC, the agency was owned by Robert Hydrick and run in large measure by John Star, neither of whom was an attorney. . . .

In 1990, at Struthers' suggestion, Hydrick dissolved CSC. This occurred during an investigation by the State Banking Department into allegations of irregularities in CSC's handling of client funds and that Star was holding himself out as an attorney. Struthers knew about and even represented Star and Hydrick in these matters.

When Hydrick dissolved CSC, Struthers superficially converted its operations into a law practice. In reality, however, CSC simply continued to operate. Star and Hydrick formed a new entity called MIROVI Inc., which was supposed to act as a managing company, providing support personnel and services for Struthers' practice. Star and Hyrick became Struthers' "legal assistants."

From the beginning of Struthers' association with CSC, he had a very large case load. At first he took over from his predecessor about 250 cases, but this number later rose to nearly 750. Although Struthers nominally maintained his status as an independent attorney, CSC (now MIROVI) staff ran his office, his accounting system and performed other tasks, such as conducting client interviews. . . . Under these circumstances, many of the formalities of a law firm were abandoned, giving rise to a number of the violations discussed below. [The violations related to client trust accounts, scope of representation, diligence, communication, fees, safekeeping client property, terminating representation, and professional independence.]

We examine in detail some of the more egregious violations . . . in four categories . . . [including supervision of] nonlawyer assistants. . . .

It is important to note that lawyers are often responsible for the actions of their nonlawyer assistants. Ethical Rule 5.3(a) provides that a lawyer in Struthers' position shall "make reasonable efforts to ensure that the firm has in effect measures giving reasonable assurance" that nonlawyer assistants conduct themselves according to the rules for lawyers. . . .

In the present case, however, Struthers virtually abandoned responsibility for running his office to Star and Hydrick. Although Struthers knew that the Banking Department has charged Star and Hydrick with serious improprieties, he gave them total control of his office and unfettered access to his trust fund. . . .

[H]e knew about Star's dishonesty early in their relationship. Struthers admitted to the Committee that although Star told him he was an attorney licensed in other states, Struthers knew from that start this was not true. . . . Although there may often be some question of what is a reasonable effort to ensure proper conduct by nonlawyer employees, at a minimum the lawyer must screen, instruct, and supervise. [Citation omitted.] Struthers did little but close his eyes.

Moreover, even if Struthers had been unaware that he placed untrustworthy persons in charge of his affairs, he still violated ER 5.3(c) by knowingly ratifying many of their ethical lapses and by failing to mitigate their consequences. For example, although he knew Hydrick had commingled his own funds with those in Struthers' trust account, Struthers did nothing to stop this. . . .

Struthers violated [Rule 43, State Bar Trust Account Guidelines] "when he allowed incompetent and untrustworthy employees to manage his trust account, and then failed to properly supervise them to ensure they were complying with the Trust Account Guidelines." . . . For example, Struthers routinely signed pages of blank checks for his employees to complete in his absence. As a result, Star and Hydrick were free to decide whether and how much to pay clients, and often based their decisions on which clients they favored. . . .

Ethical Rule 5.4(a) provides that a "lawyer . . . shall not share legal fees with a nonlawyer. . . ." Struthers' agreement with MIROVI, however, required him to turn over all fees that he received to MIROVI, with any profit left after paying expenses to be "distributed by the agreement of the parties." . . .

We deal here with a lawyer who, by premeditated scheme, has demonstrated that his practice is not designed to serve the public but, rather, to prey on those most in need of his help. He has demonstrated that he is indeed a danger to the public. To allow him to resume an active practice would be to ignore our obligation to that public. . . .

Accordingly Andrew Leeroy Struthers is disbarred. . . .

Questions about the Case

1. What functions did the nonlawyers perform in the lawyer's office? Can each of these duties be properly delegated to a nonlawyer and supervised?
2. Did these "legal assistants" meet any of the definitions of paralegal or legal assistant in this chapter? If not, what is lacking in their background?
3. Could the lawyer have set up a collections practice with a large caseload and run it in a manner that would comport with ethics rules? Describe how. Note that the court refers to recruiting, delegating, and supervising paralegals. Define each one of these aspects of a lawyer's responsibility for paralegals.
4. Do you think that the lawyer should have been disbarred? What do you think should have happened to Hydrick and Star? Can you use this case to argue for regulation of paralegals?

In the following case, a lawyer faces disciplinary charges for the conduct of a paralegal who runs a business providing services in the immigration area.

The Florida Bar v. Abrams

919 So. 2d 425 (Fla. 2006)

Suzanne Akbas, a paralegal, formed a corporate entity titled U.S. Entry, Inc. to provide legal services to persons with immigration issues who were seeking to gain entry and establish lawful status in the United States. Attorney Daniel Everett Abrams was employed by U.S. Entry as "Managing Attorney" and was paid for "piecemeal legal work," generally at a rate of one hundred dollars per unit of work. Olga Ulershperger and Abdullah Ziya, who were husband and wife, both entered the United States in November 1999 on tourist visas and then in the spring of 2000 sought assistance from U.S. Entry in obtaining further lawful status. Ulershperger was an accomplished gymnast; Ziya was a Turkish Kurd who had suffered persecution, including torture, in his native land.

Akbas told the couple that instead of seeking political asylum based on Ziya's history of persecution, they should apply for employment visas based on Ulershperger's skills as a gymnast. The couple's applications ultimately were denied and their existing visas expired in May 2001. They did not learn of their unlawful status until March or April of 2002, after consulting with an immigration lawyer in California. That lawyer told the couple that they should not have been counseled to seek employment visas but rather should have been counseled to seek political asylum based on Ziya's persecution and torture, but that the one-year time limit for seeking asylum had expired in November 2000. The couple ultimately sought and were granted asylum under an ineffective representation exception to the one-year time limit, which prompted the present proceeding.

Based on the above matters, The Florida Bar filed a two-count complaint against Abrams, and the referee made the following findings of fact:

> . . . [Ulershperger and Ziya] were not notified of the status of their claim or of the lapse of their lawful status. . . . There was no follow-through by the Respondent — not telephone calls, no letters to the INS. . . .
>
> Respondent violated a number of disciplinary rules. . . . Instead of Akbas being employed by and under the Respondent's supervision, it was the other way around. Akbas was the employer and she used Respondent's license to practice law. . . .
>
> The referee recommended that Abrams be found guilty of violating [several sections of] the Rules Regulating the Florida Bar . . . and that the following disciplinary measures be imposed on Abrams: a one-year suspension; restitution in the amount of $2,400; and payment of the bar's costs. . . .
>
> The present record shows that Abrams was listed as the attorney of record on a status extension application submitted by Ziya and was listed as the "Managing Attorney" on the letterhead of a missive used by U.S. Entry in requesting alien labor certification for Ulershperger. The letter was signed, "Suzanne J. Akbas For Daniel E. Abrams, Esq." At the hearing below, [an] immigration lawyer . . . testified . . . that the proper handling of asylum claims requires substantial intake by a lawyer, not a paralegal. . . . Abrams had no contact whatsoever with Ulershperger and Ziya. . . . We approve the referee's recommendation that Abrams be found guilty of violating of rule 4-1.1 [re competent representation]. . . .

> [T]he record shows that even though Akbas worked as a paralegal at U.S. Entry, she actually was the person in control of the corporation's day-to-day operations. She met with clients, conducted client interviews, and made the decisions as to the appropriate course of action for clients. Abrams himself visited the U.S. Entry office only several times a month. Akbas testified that she unsuccessfully tried to get Abrams more involved in the company's operations. We conclude that Abrams's role and course of conduct at U.S. Entry were inconsistent with the title "Managing Attorney," and the title constituted a clear misrepresentation of his status. We approve the referee's recommendation that Abrams be found guilty of violating rule 4-8.4(c) [on dishonesty, fraud, deceit or misrepresentation]. . . .

Based on the foregoing, we approve the referee's findings of fact, recommendations as to guilt, and recommended discipline. . . .

Questions about the Case

1. How would you characterize the relationship of Abrams and Akbas? Who was the employer? Can an employee "supervise" his or her boss?
2. What functions did Akbas perform that might be considered practicing law? Consult Chapter 3 for definitions.
3. Do you think that Abrams should have been held responsible for Akbas's mistakes? Why or why not?
4. Should Akbas have been held responsible for her mistakes? How would this come about?
5. Is there a way for a nonlawyer-run immigration service like U.S. Entry to operate legally and ethically?

Attorneys are responsible for the actions of their employees, including paralegals who work as independent contractors, and may be disciplined when their inaction or neglect results in harm to a client.

Florida Bar v. Lawless

640 So. 2d 1098 (Fla. 1994)

A Canadian couple, Michael and Barbara Seguin, hired Lawless in 1987 to help them acquire permanent residency status in the United States. Lawless initially contracted to acquire residency status for Michael Seguin for a flat fee of $5,000 plus expenses. The Seguins later met with Lawless and paralegal Charles Aboudraah. Although Aboudraah did not work in Lawless's office, Lawless had worked with the paralegal and said he was experienced in immigration cases. Lawless said he would supervise the case, but the Seguins were to contact Aboudraah if they had questions.

From March 19, 1987, through February 11, 1988, the Seguins paid $12,546 to Aboudraah, including $725 to pursue a visa for Barbara Seguin. They thought these payments included the remaining $2,500 of Lawless's flat fee and that Aboudraah gave Lawless a share of these payments. Aboudraah told the Seguins their paperwork had been filed with the Immigration and Naturalization Service and that they were waiting for the INS to send visa cards.

In January 1990 the Seguins received a letter from the INS seeking information about their residency status and indicating that they had not responded to other letters about the matter. When the Seguins asked Lawless and Aboudraah about the letter, they were assured Aboudraah was handling their case.

Soon, however, the Seguins learned that the INS was investigating Aboudraah. Aboudraah became less available to them and he ultimately closed his office. The Seguins contacted Lawless, who discovered that there was no application on file for either Barbara or Michael Seguin. Thus, the Seguins had been living illegally in the United States since 1986.

In April 1990 Lawless told the Seguins he had not received any money from their payments to Aboudraah. He also said he had not been associated with Aboudraah in more than two years. Although Lawless submitted visa applications for the Seguins, they eventually consulted another attorney because they did not think Lawless understood the immigration procedures needed to conclude their case. The Seguins ultimately obtained visas that allowed them to live legally in the United States and operate their business.

The Bar filed a formal complaint against Lawless in 1992. . . .

The Bar argues that given Lawless's disciplinary history, nothing less than a ninety-one-day suspension is an adequate sanction. Lawless contends that a public reprimand is sufficient because this Court has imposed public reprimands in other cases involving a lawyer's failure to supervise nonlawyer employees. . . .

First, we uphold the referee's recommendation that Lawless pay restitution to the Seguins during his probation. We agree with the referee that "had it not been for [Lawless], the Seguins would not have been subjected to Charles Aboudraah's misconduct." Lawless's initial contract with the Seguins called for a $5,000 flat fee plus expenses. After Lawless introduced the Seguins to Aboudraah and assured them he was supervising the case, the Seguins paid $12,546 to Aboudraah. Whether Lawless ever received that money is not the issue: He was responsible for the conduct of his nonlawyer employee and thus must reimburse the Seguins.

Second, we find that the referee's recommendations about supervising paralegals and removing Lawless's name from lawyer referral lists are appropriate in this case. These sanctions will apply during Lawless's suspension and probation. . . .

Accordingly, we suspend Lawless from the practice of law for ninety days, followed by a three-year probationary period. We also impose the other penalties the referee recommended. . . .

Questions about the Case

1. Was the paralegal Aboudraah an employee or an independent contractor? What facts support your conclusion? Does it make any difference in this case?
2. What do Model Rule 5.3 and the definitions of paralegal say about independent contractor paralegals? Is the lawyer's duty any different for them?
3. Did the attorney Lawless supervise the paralegal adequately? What is the basis for your conclusion?
4. Did the attorney Lawless maintain a direct relationship with the clients? What is the basis for your conclusion?
5. Do you believe the sanctions were appropriate?
6. What do you think would have happened if the clients had filed a malpractice suit?

In this interesting case, a paralegal who is the recipient of a gift from an elderly client is held not to be a fiduciary to the client by virtue of her status as a paralegal. This case demonstrates the lack of clear and consistent case law about the liability of legal assistants in their professional capacity.

In re Estate of Divine

263 Ill. App. 3d 799, 635 N.E.2d 581
(Ill. App. 1 Dist. 1994)

Beginning in approximately 1979, Giancola was employed in Chicago by attorney Samuel Poznanovich as a part-time secretary in his law office. Eventually, she became his full-time secretary. Giancola received a paralegal certificate from Roosevelt University in 1980, and took an H & R Block tax course in 1970. Poznanovich employed one other secretary in addition to Giancola.

In 1981, Richard and his wife, Lila, came to Poznanovich's office for income tax services. The Divines did not have any children and both were retired. Giancola estimated that they were in their "early seventies" in 1981. Giancola interviewed the Divines, took tax information from them such as W-2 forms and copies of their previous tax returns, and introduced them to Poznanovich. After this initial meeting, Poznanovich prepared the Divines' tax returns every year until 1986. Each year, Giancola would interview the Divines and gather their tax information. She never prepared their taxes, but simply gathered information for Poznanovich's use. In 1985, Poznanovich also represented Richard in a personal injury case. Giancola was not involved in that case. Additionally, Richard called Poznanovich occasionally for legal advice on other matters. Before 1986, Giancola and Poznanovich saw the Divines only at the law office, although, according to Poznanovich, the relationship became "more and more friendly" each year.

In December 1986, Lila died. Richard called Giancola at the office to tell her about Lila's death. Giancola stated that Richard had "depended on Lila for just about everything" and was very lonely without Lila. Also, he was "unable to do for himself." Giancola went to visit Richard in his apartment on Coles Avenue "within a day or two" of Lila's death. Richard was afraid to leave the apartment alone and could not walk long distances because "his legs were bad." Richard's relatives and Poznanovich also testified that Richard had physical problems with his legs. Giancola stated that for "the most part," Richard was confined to his apartment. After Giancola's first visit, Richard frequently called her, and she visited his apartment once or twice a week. Richard asked her to assist him in getting his groceries and other necessities. Richard gave Giancola money for the groceries and supplies. She testified that he did not give her a "fee" for her services, but admitted that sometimes he gave her "something for [her]self." He did his own cooking while living in the Coles Avenue apartment.

Giancola believed that the neighborhood around Coles Avenue was too dangerous for Richard, and she did not like going there to visit him. She suggested that he move to a safer area; she also mentioned to Poznanovich that Richard's neighborhood was unsafe. Poznanovich's office is located in a building he and his sister own. There are four residential apartments in that building which are rented by Poznanovich and his sister. Giancola occasionally takes the rent checks from tenants for Poznanovich. When an apartment became vacant in Poznanovich's building, Giancola told Richard it "would be easier" if he moved into that apartment. She did not know that Richard's relatives wanted him to move to Michigan City, Indiana. . . .

In addition to getting his supplies and cooking his meals, Giancola cashed checks for Richard and made bank deposits for him. She wrote out the checks for all his bills. She explained that she would write the checks, he would sign them, and she would mail them. All these transactions involved only Richard's personal checking account. Richard would discuss "personal problems" with Giancola, but did not talk to her about legal matters. . . .

In November, 1987, Richard called Poznanovich and asked him to come to his apartment. In the apartment, Richard told Poznanovich that he wanted to "put his affairs in order." First, he handed two bank account passbooks to Poznanovich and said "I want this for my sweetheart." Richard told Poznanovich that his "sweetheart" was Giancola, and that he wanted her to have the two accounts. These two accounts were separate from Richard's personal checking account which Giancola used for his finances. Richard told Poznanovich he did not want to leave the accounts to Giancola in his will because he wanted her "to have them now." Richard explained: "As far as I'm concerned, if it were not for her, I would be dead now." Poznanovich suggested that the accounts be made joint accounts, like the accounts Richard had shared with Lila. When Poznanovich assured Richard that a joint tenancy would allow Giancola to have the money immediately, Richard told Poznanovich to change the two accounts to joint accounts. Giancola was not present during this discussion. Poznanovich testified that he did not receive any direct or indirect financial benefit from this transaction.

Next, Richard asked Poznanovich to draft a will for him. The will made Poznanovich executor of the estate and gave $3,000 each to Giancola and Poznanovich. Poznanovich testified: "I had a problem with [Richard] inserting me as a beneficiary under the will, . . . [and] we agreed that if I were to remain in the will as a beneficiary, I would waive my executor's fee, which I did." The will made one other specific bequest of $2,000, then left one half of the residuary estate to the petitioners and one half to four other family members. After his death, the value of Richard's estate, in addition to the joint accounts, was approximately $150,000.

Poznanovich obtained two signature cards from the bank and had the accounts changed to joint accounts. On November 14, 1987, he asked Giancola to sign these signature cards. Neither Richard nor Poznanovich ever discussed the accounts with Giancola before presenting her with the cards. They also did not discuss the transactions with any members of Richard's family. . . .

At the hearing in the trial court and in this court the petitioners argued that the actions of Poznanovich and Giancola are inextricably intertwined and that because Giancola was a paralegal and an employee of the lawyer, Poznanovich, who was a fiduciary as a matter of law, so also is Giancola a fiduciary as a matter of law. They also repeatedly assert that Poznanovich gained financially from the transactions which benefitted Giancola. Nonetheless, they never requested that Poznanovich or Giancola return the $3,000 bequests and they do not challenge the validity of the will. Additionally, they have never made Poznanovich a party to these proceedings. Essentially, the petitioners argue that Poznanovich's questionable action of drafting a will which gave him a gift and his status as an attorney should be imputed to Giancola and that she should be liable because of his actions.

Under certain circumstances, one person will be charged with liability for the actions of or knowledge given to another person. For example, actions by one partner will be imputed to another partner.

[Citation omitted.] Also, an employer will be held liable for certain actions of his employee. [Citation omitted.] There is no case law holding an employee liable for the acts of his employer, however, and the petitioners cite no law to support their position that Giancola should be accountable for Poznanovich's actions. Unfortunately, there also is no case law in Illinois involving the narrower question of a paralegal's fiduciary duty to his employer's client, making this a case of first impression. In fact, we have found no reported case in the United States involving a paralegal's fiduciary responsibility, as a paralegal, to his attorney's client.

Moreover, there is very little case law from Illinois or any jurisdiction generally discussing paralegals. Two cases address the somewhat analogous issue of a paralegal's possible liability for legal malpractice. A divided Nevada Supreme Court, in *Busch v. Flangas* (1992), 108 Nev. 821, 837 P.2d 438, held that an attorney's law clerk or paralegal who attempts to provide legal services can be liable for malpractice to the client. On the other hand, the *Busch* dissent argued that a law clerk or paralegal, as an employee of an attorney, owes no duty to the attorney's client, but is liable only to the attorney. (*Busch*, 837 P.2d at 441 (Springer, J., dissenting).) The Court of Appeals of Ohio, without extensive discussion, determined that a paralegal could not be sued for legal malpractice because she was not an attorney. *Palmer v. Westmeyer* (1988), 48 Ohio App. 3d 296, 549 N.E.2d 1202, 1209.

On the other hand, the idea that an attorney is liable, in malpractice or as an ethical violation, for his paralegal's acts is well-supported in Illinois. . . .

Several Illinois cases support the idea that paralegals are an extension of their employing attorney. For example, the presence of an attorney's employee, such as a secretary or law clerk, does not destroy the attorney-client privilege for material disclosed to the attorney in the employee's presence. [Citations omitted.] Also, in the majority of Illinois cases discussing paralegals, which involve disputed attorney fee petitions, the courts have held that an attorney may recover reasonable fees for time properly spent by his paralegal. . . .

Based on these cases, we refuse to treat Poznanovich and Giancola as a unit for purposes of Giancola's liability. It is clear that Poznanovich, as a licensed attorney and as an employer, could be held liable for Giancola's actions. Nonetheless, holding Giancola liable as if she were an attorney is not consistent with general *respondeat superior* law or with the decisions discussed above treating paralegals as subordinate employees of attorneys. The theme running through all these cases is that paralegals do not independently practice law, but simply serve as assistants to lawyers. They are not equal or autonomous partners. Thus, while supervisors properly are held liable for paralegals' actions, the subordinate paralegals should not be liable for the actions of these supervisors. Therefore, we refuse to find that Giancola owed Richard a fiduciary duty simply because she worked for

Richard's attorney, and we refuse to hold that paralegals are fiduciaries to their employers' clients as a matter of law. . . .

We also wish to make it clear that we are not saying that the evidence shows that Poznanovich did anything improper. We have discussed his "actions" only in the general sense to illustrate that, while he was a fiduciary to Richard as a matter of law and if he had been the recipient of the joint account funds, the burden of proof would have been on him to show that the transaction was proper, his fiduciary obligations may not be imposed upon Giancola. Nor are we saying that an improper transfer may never be shown under circumstances like those present in this case. If the petitioners had offered evidence from which it could be inferred that collusion existed between Poznanovich and Giancola or that Poznanovich gained financially in any way from the transfer, our holding would be different. But neither the trial judge nor this court may decide a case on speculation, guess, conjecture or suspicion.

For these reasons, the judgment of the circuit court is affirmed.

Questions about the Case

1. What was the paralegal's relationship with the client, and how did it evolve over time? Was it professional or personal?
2. What evidence might show that the paralegal took advantage of the client? Discuss the adequacy of this evidence.
3. Did the petitioners sue the lawyer? Why or why not? On what grounds did they sue the paralegal?
4. Under this case, can a paralegal be held liable for the actions of his or her employing lawyer? Could the lawyer be held liable for the actions of the paralegal?
5. Does a paralegal have a fiduciary duty directly to a client in Illinois? How would you state this principle?
6. Review the rules in Chapter 5 about accepting gifts from clients and determine if either the lawyer or the paralegal in this case violated those rules. What should they have done to protect against a lawsuit like this one?

3

Unauthorized Practice of Law

This chapter covers the limitations on the practice of law, including what acts constitute the practice of law and how these restrictions affect and guide paralegal conduct. Chapter 3 covers:

- the history of the unauthorized practice of law
- definitions of the practice of law
- the effect of restrictions on the practice of law on access to legal services
- the attorney's ethical responsibility to prevent the unauthorized practice of law and to supervise paralegals
- key functions that may constitute the unauthorized practice of law, including:
    - making court appearances and taking depositions
    - preparation and signing of documents and pleadings
    - giving legal advice
    - accepting cases and setting fees
- analysis of functions that may or may not constitute the practice of law
- nonlawyer practice before administrative agencies
- disclosure of the paralegal's nonlawyer status
- paralegals working as independent contractors

A. A Brief History of Unauthorized Practice of Law

1. The Early Years

Limitations on who can practice law in the United States can be traced back to the colonial era. At that time a proliferation of untrained practitioners caused local courts to adopt rules requiring attorneys who appeared before them to have a license granted by the court. Additional rules adopted during this period limited the amount of fees that could be charged by lawyers and mandated that lawyers could not refuse to take a case. The stated purposes of these rules were to prevent stirring up of litigation by unscrupulous "pettifoggers" and "mercenary" attorneys, to stop incompetence that harmed clients and impaired the administration of justice and dignity of the courts, and to prevent exploitive, excessive fees.

These early limitations on the practice of law evolved to their present state incrementally and not always in a smooth and linear way. Many of these rules, along with later rules that governed the training of lawyers and their admission to the bar, were eliminated during an era of deprofessionalization in the early nineteenth century, only to reemerge in the late nineteenth century. State and local bar associations began to gain strength during this period, in part because of concern over the large numbers of lawyers competing with one another for legal work and with newly developing businesses, such as collection agencies, banks and trust companies, and accounting firms, and the establishment of administrative agencies that permitted lay appearances. The first unauthorized practice statutes were passed in several states during the 1850s, prohibiting court appearances by anyone not licensed as an attorney and prohibiting the practice of law by court personnel such as bailiffs. The first unauthorized practice prosecutions were also brought during this period. These cases held it improper for an unlicensed person to hold himself or herself out as an attorney and for a nonlawyer to form a partnership with a lawyer.

The definition of the practice of law that was formulated in early cases gradually broadened to cover activities beyond court appearances. Early cases held that the practice of law also includes the preparation of documents by which legal rights are secured. Gradually new justifications for restricting the right to practice law to licensed attorneys were developed, including the lawyer's professional independence, proven moral character, and special training. Advocates for tight controls over the practice of law also used public protection arguments by pointing out that lawyers are subject to sanctions for breaches of ethics or competence, unlike unlicensed practitioners.

Legal historians believe that the height of unauthorized practice restrictions came during the Depression when lawyers needed most to protect their economic interests from competition. Bar associations became especially powerful trade organizations during this era. Unauthorized practice statutes were passed in virtually all states, making it a crime to practice law without a license. The definition of the practice of law was further expanded to include "all services customarily rendered by lawyers."

In 1930, the American Bar Association created its powerful Special Committee on the Unauthorized Practice of Law, which by the late 1950s had agreements called Statements of Principles with accountants, collection agencies, insurance adjusters, life insurance underwriters, publishers, and realtors, to name a few. These agreements, later rescinded when it became apparent that they would be found illegal under the Sherman Antitrust Act, delineated the legal activities that these other nonlawyer professionals could engage in without stepping into the protected realm of the practice of law. Most state and local bar associations had committees that monitored the activities of competitor organizations, and many also entered into Statements of Principle with nonlawyer legal service providers. The California State Bar, for example, had 20 such agreements, which were rescinded in 1979.

Criminal prosecutions and civil suits to restrain unauthorized practice slowed during the 1960s and 1970s. During this period the sale of legal self-help kits and books began, and soon most courts determined this activity not to constitute the unauthorized practice of law (UPL). These decisions signaled the beginning of a new movement to expand access to legal services by alternative means.

2. Recent UPL History: Nonlawyer Legal Service Providers and Access to Legal Services

The 1980s saw a **resurgence of unauthorized practice prosecutions** because of the increased number of nonlawyer legal service providers providing low-cost legal services directly to the public. Many factors converged to create the great need for alternative legal service providers: the decrease in federal funding for the Legal Services Corporation, which had supplied legal services to low-income persons; the increase in the need for legal services by every socioeconomic group because of the proliferation and complexity of laws; and the rising cost of legal services provided by lawyers, which makes it difficult or impossible for most Americans to employ a lawyer when they need one.

Most nonlawyer legal service providers work in areas of law in which low- and moderate-income people need assistance, such as landlord-tenant matters; family law matters including **divorce**, paternity, domestic violence, and child support; consumer matters including **bankruptcy**;

and **immigration**. Some run "typing services" that assist persons only by typing documents, usually to be filed with the court, after the "customer" fills in the blanks on forms. Others provide more complete information and assistance, helping the customer decide what forms to use, what information to include on the forms, where to file them, and advising the customer on procedural matters and court appearances. Increasingly, these providers use electronic programs to complete standard court forms. Nonlawyer legal service providers call themselves by a variety of titles, including independent paralegals, legal technicians, and document preparers. Some providers are offering their services through We the People (WTP), a national organization that provides help to self-represented persons through offices owned and operated locally. See *In re Finch* at the end of this chapter for a WTP office that crossed the line into UPL.

The unmet need for legal services is well documented, but lawyers are largely opposed to giving up any of their traditional functions to nonlawyers. Clearly, lawyers have both monopolistic, economic reasons for this stance and legitimate professional and societal concerns about the quality of legal services that someone not trained as a lawyer can provide. The debate takes on national proportions as courts throughout the country attempt to address the needs of pro se litigants who attempt to represent themselves.

Prosecutions against nonlawyer legal service providers have been rising. No formal studies document the exact increase in prosecutions; however, starting in the early 1990s most states reported criminal prosecutions for UPL and for injunctive relief against nonlawyer legal service providers after decades of virtually no such cases. Most cases are brought against bankruptcy, landlord-tenant, immigration, and family law practitioners where there has been egregious or incompetent conduct that harmed consumers. But some prosecutions have resulted from lawyer complaints, rather than from complaints from disgruntled consumers.

Defendants in UPL cases sometimes argue, although unsuccessfully, that they are not giving legal advice but are simply assisting lay persons in the preparation of legal documents; that is, giving legal information. Some defendants in unauthorized practice prosecutions have argued unsuccessfully that a statutory power of attorney from a client gives a nonlawyer the authority to represent the client in litigation. (See, for example, *Whitehead v. Town House Equities, Ltd.*, 8 A.D.3d 369, 777 N.Y.S.2d 917 (2004); and *Drake v. Superior Court of San Diego County*, 21 Cal. App. 4th 1826, 26 Cal. Rptr. 2d 829 (1994).) Similarly, it has been consistently held that nonlawyers who are serving as conservators, executors, and other representatives of estates cannot make appearances in court on behalf of these estates. (See, for example, *Hansen v. Hansen*, 114 Cal. App. 4th 618 (2003).)

Some defendants have claimed, to no avail, a public necessity defense based on the lack of availability of legal services for their clients.

For additional justifications on constitutional grounds, see *Board of Commissioners of the Utah State Bar v. Petersen* at the end of this chapter. As we moved into the twenty-first century, several states have increased penalties for unauthorized practice of law. Arizona, which for many years was the only state without a UPL statute or rule, adopted a court rule asserting the state supreme court's authority over anyone who practices law, whether authorized or not. In 2000, the American Bar Association's House of Delegates adopted a resolution calling on the states to vigorously investigate, report, and eliminate incidents of UPL.

The tremendous increase in foreclosures during the economic recession that began in 2008 has given rise to a new form of unauthorized practice, one that has sometimes drawn in lawyers. Foreclosure consultants and loan modification agencies, which seek to negotiate more affordable loans for homeowners with lenders, have been found by courts to be engaged in the unauthorized practice of law. Some of these firms also hire lawyers or use them as outside counsel, which has resulted in disciplinary action against lawyers for a variety of ethics violations, including aiding in unauthorized practice of law, unethical solicitation of clients (see Chapter 6), and fee splitting (see Chapter 7). See *The Cincinnati Bar Ass'n v. Mullaney* for a disciplinary case on lawyers working with a loan modification company.

Another development of note has been the proliferation of electronic resources for persons seeking to represent themselves in various kinds of legal matters. Although one might expect that electronic resources would fall into the protected category of self-help books and materials, some bar associations and courts have challenged this interpretation. For example, in 1997 the Unauthorized Practice of Law Committee of the Supreme Court of Texas investigated the publication of electronic self-help resources, contending that the publication of these resources was tantamount to giving legal advice. These increasingly popular programs guide users to specific options and forms and help them to complete forms by asking them a series of questions that trigger selection and completion of forms. One of the Committee's contentions was that this process constituted legal advice that could only be given in Texas by a lawyer licensed in the state of Texas. The final result of this dispute, after several hearings and much publicity, was that the Texas legislature passed a law allowing self-help companies to publish this material without threat of a UPL prosecution. The use of technology to increase access to legal services through programs like these is growing dramatically despite ongoing controversy over whether it violates UPL rules. See *In re Reynoso*, 477 F.3d 117 (9th Cir. 2007), at the end of this chapter for a recent case in this ongoing debate.

Some states have taken action to regulate nonlawyers who assist persons with **immigration** matters, including Arizona, Illinois, and Oregon. Although federal statutes establish nationwide standards for accredited visa consultants, some immigration "consultants" do not fall within the reach of these federal laws, and widespread abuses of clients have been documented in the immigrant community.

Several states have determined that the preparation of **living trust documents** constitutes the practice of law and have prosecuted nonlawyers running companies that market and prepare living trust plans. These decisions hold that the client's decision about having a living trust, the attendant preparation and execution of documents, and the funding of the trust are functions that require an attorney's judgment and involvement. (See, for example, Florida Bar re: Advisory Opinion on Nonlawyer Preparation of Living Trusts, 613 So. 2d 426 (Fla. 1992); California State Bar Ethics Opinion 97-148; South Dakota Bar Ethics Opinion 91-14; Colorado 90-87; Pennsylvania 90-65; Kansas Advisory Opinion 96-08; and Texas Prof. Eth. Comm. Opinion 95-498.)

In another notable development, in 2009 the Oregon State Bar rejected a proposal that would have provided for paralegals to make court appearances under lawyer supervision in order to increase access to legal services.

3. Other Recent UPL Activity

As noted earlier, lawyers in several jurisdictions have been disciplined for aiding the unauthorized practice of law by participating in businesses that promoted and sold **living trusts**. In most of these cases, nonlawyer living trust marketers had all the client contact, and the lawyer did not counsel the clients about the decision to create a living trust or the provisions and funding of the trust. Courts have found that these lawyers have abdicated their responsibility to advise clients and to exercise independent professional judgment. Many lawyers in these cases failed to supervise the work of their employees in counseling clients or preparing the documents for them. The consequences have been disastrous for many elderly people who thought they were protecting their estates from probate, but were setting up these trusts unnecessarily and paying exorbitant commissions to fund the trusts. One such case is *In re Morin*, found at the end of this chapter. A few others of note are *In re Phillips*, 338 Or. 125, 107 P.3d 615 (2005); *In the Matter of Flack*, 272 Kan. 465, 33 P.3d 1281 (2001); and *Doe v. Condon*, 341 S.C. 22, 532 S.E.2d 879 (2000). (See also Texas Ethics Opinion 95-498 and Arizona Ethics Opinion 98-08.)

Another category of recent UPL cases are those in which lawyers have been disciplined for running **large-volume practices** without adequately supervising their paralegals and other employees. In most of these cases, the firms were set up so that paralegals were accepting cases, having clients sign retainer agreements, preparing legal documents for them, and counseling them about their legal rights with little or no lawyer involvement and no direct relationship between the lawyer and the client. In some cases, these violations were coupled with unlawful solicitation of clients by the nonlawyers and compensation arrangements that violate rules against fee splitting and lawyers and nonlawyers entering into a partnership for the practice of law. Finally, in a few cases, the lawyers have been hired by nonlawyer legal service provider companies to legitimize their work, an arrangement that has repeatedly been found unacceptable by the courts and in advisory opinions. (See, for example, Iowa Ethics Advisory Opinion 96-19 regarding a divorce business and *The Cincinnati Bar Ass'n v. Mullaney* regarding a foreclosure consulting business at the end of the chapter.) Related solicitation and fee-splitting issues are covered, in Chapters 6 and 7, respectively.

The unauthorized practice of law by lawyers who are licensed in one state but practicing in another has been a subject of much discussion within the organized bar in the past decade. Because of the nature of the economy, which does not recognize neatly drawn **jurisdictional lines**, lawyers often engage in legal work in states other than the one(s) in which they are licensed. Sometimes this work takes place in a bordering state and sometimes across the country. States have become more protective of their authority over the practice of law and have been making it more difficult for lawyers to engage in this kind of work. The California Supreme Court in *Birbower, Montalbano, Condon & Frank, P.C. v. Superior Court*, 17 Cal. 4th 119, 949 P.2d 1, 70 Cal. Rptr. 2d 304 (1998), determined that a New York law firm doing some work in California could not collect its fees because the lawyers were not licensed to practice in California and had therefore engaged in unauthorized practice of law, a crime that voided the contract with the clients. Similar cases followed in other jurisdictions. To provide exceptions and clear guidance, the ABA adopted Model Rule 5.5, setting up carefully drawn exceptions for limited out-of-state practice.

Another interesting UPL question is whether a corporate officer who is not a lawyer can represent the corporation in legal matters. Few cases have addressed this issue but most allow this practice in actions in small claims court or in administrative hearings. (See, for example, *Dayton Supply v. Montgomery Bd. of Rev.*, 111 Ohio St. 3d 367 (2006), in which the court allowed a corporate office to appear for the company in a matter concerning the valuation of property.)

Finally, questions have been raised about the rights of nonlawyers and parents to represent their children under the federal Individuals with Disabilities Education Act (IDEA). At least two states have found that nonlawyers cannot represent parents or children in the administrative hearings (see *In re Arons,* 756 A.2d 867 (2000), and Oklahoma Attorney General Opinion 06-27). The law gives parents the right to advocate for their children in administrative hearings, but the courts are split on whether parents can represent their children in federal court judicial reviews of these administrative decisions. Most federal circuits have found that parents cannot represent their children in IDEA actions in federal court as this would constitute unauthorized practice of law. They may, however, represent their own interests in such actions. See *Winkelman v. Parma City School Dist.*, 550 U.S. 516, 127 S. Ct. 1994 (2007), and *Cavanaugh v. Cardinal Local School Dist.*, 409 F.3d 753 (6th Cir. 2005).

B. Practice of Law Defined

No one definitive list of activities captures the meaning of the practice of law. As you can see from the foregoing history, the concept is flexible; it changes over time with the push and pull of economics, political and professional activity, public pressure and consumerism, and the complexity of laws. The oft-quoted ABA Model Code of Professional Responsibility (ABA Model Code) EC 3-5 states: "It is neither necessary nor desirable to attempt the formulation of a single, specific definition of what constitutes the practice of law." Efforts to build a national consensus for a definition of the practice of law have been unsuccessful. For example, in 2003, an ABA Task Force on the Model Definition of the Practice of Law had to withdraw its proposed definition when it was met with harsh criticism from the Department of Justice, the Federal Trade Commission, and other organizations that believed that it was overly broad and illegally noncompetitive. States continue to establish their own definitions in statutes and court rules and rely on court decisions that provide tests for determining what defines the practice of law. The traditional tests for determining if an act constitutes the practice of law are found in Charles W. Wolfram's treatise Modern Legal Ethics (1986):

1. *The professional judgment test:* whether the activity at issue is one that requires the lawyer's special training and skills. Wolfram suggests that a better version of this test would be "whether the matter handled was of such complexity that only a person trained as a lawyer should be permitted to deal with it." Id. at 836.
2. *The traditional areas of practice test:* whether the function in question is one that would traditionally be performed by an attorney or is commonly understood to be the practice of law. Id.
3. *The incidental legal services test:* whether the activity is essentially legal in nature or is a law-related adjunct to some business routine or transaction, that is, completing a simple legal document incidental to a banking or real estate transaction, for which no separate fee is charged, would not constitute the practice of law under this definition. Id.

Some scholars add other tests, such as whether the activity in question is characterized by a personal relationship between lawyer and client or whether the activity is one for which the public interest would best be served by limiting it to licensed attorneys.

Examples of definitions of the practice of law in a few major UPL cases may be instructive.

> [I]t embraces the preparation of pleadings and other papers incident to actions of special proceedings, and the management of such actions and proceedings on behalf of clients before judges in courts. However, the practice of law is not confined to cases conducted in court. In fact, the major portion of the practice of any capable lawyer consists of work done outside of the courts. The practice of law involves not only appearance in court in connection with litigation, but also services rendered out of court, and includes the giving of advice or the rendering of any service requiring the use of legal skill or knowledge, such as preparing a will, contract, or other instrument, the legal effect of which under the facts and conclusions involved must be carefully determined.

Davies v. Unauthorized Practice Committee of State Bar of Texas, 431 S.W.2d 590, at 593 (Tex. Civ. App. 1968).

> [O]ne is deemed to be practicing law whenever he furnishes to another advice or service under circumstances which imply the possession and use of legal knowledge and skill. . . . Practice of law includes the giving of legal advice and counsel, and the preparation of legal instruments and contracts of which legal rights are secured. . . . Where the rendering of services for another involves the use of legal knowledge or skill on his behalf—where legal advice is required and is availed of or rendered in connection with such services—these services necessarily constitute or include the practice of law.

In re Welch, 185 A.2d 458, 459 (Vt. 1962).

> [The] definition of law practice has two aspects: exercise of professional judgment and application of legal principles to individual cases. An exercise of professional judgment occurs any time there is "informed or trained discretion exercise in the selection or drafting of a document to meet the [legal] needs of persons being served"; "an intelligent choice between alternative methods of drafting a legal document"; or advice given that "involves the application of legal principles." [Citations omitted.]

Oregon State Bar v. Taub, 190 Or. App. 280, 78 P.3d 114 (2003). Also see the definitions offered by other courts in each of the cases at the end of this chapter.

States have adopted some definitions that are more specific than those commonly adopted in the past. For example, the Arizona Supreme Court defines the practice of law as follows:

> "Practice of law" means providing legal advice or services to or for another by:
>
> (1) preparing any document in any medium intended to affect or secure legal rights for a specific person or entity;

> (2) preparing or expressing legal opinions;
> (3) representing another in a judicial, quasi-judicial, or administrative proceeding, or other formal dispute resolution process such as arbitration and mediation;
> (4) preparing any document through any medium for filing in any court, administrative agency or tribunal for a specific person or entity; or
> (5) negotiating legal rights or responsibilities for a specific person or entity.

Arizona Supreme Court Rule 31(a)(2)A.

Hundreds of published opinions on UPL help to define the practice of law. UPL cases come to the courts by a variety of paths:

- criminal prosecutions of a nonlawyer or out-of-state lawyer (UPL is a misdemeanor in more than 30 states and a felony in a few)
- civil contempt proceedings brought when a nonlawyer appears in court on behalf of a client (a remedy in more than 25 states)
- actions for injunctive relief, usually brought by bar associations or courts (a remedy in at least 40 jurisdictions)
- contempt proceedings brought against nonlawyers appearing before a court (a proper remedy in every jurisdiction)

Additional deterrents to unauthorized practice include liability for negligent performance, unenforceability of the contract for legal services, court dismissal of an action brought by a nonlawyer for a client, and a court's voiding of a judgment in which a nonlawyer represented the prevailing party.

C. The Lawyer's Responsibility to Prevent the Unauthorized Practice of Law

Rules that prohibit the unauthorized practice of law affect lawyers and nonlawyers alike. Lawyers engage in UPL if they practice in a state in which they are not licensed or practice while they are suspended or after they have been disbarred. Nonlawyers engage in UPL when they perform services for the public that fall under the definition of the practice of law. As you will see in the next sections, some of the prohibited activities are absolutely prohibited, whereas others may be done with **lawyer supervision**. In a traditional legal setting where paralegals are supervised by lawyers, paralegals may engage in UPL by overstepping the accepted boundaries.

Lawyers are obligated by various rules not to aid the unauthorized practice of law. In many states, a statute prohibits a lawyer from aiding unauthorized practice. In others, the ethical codes contain such a restriction. See ABA Model Code DR 3-101(A) and ABA Model Rule 5.3(b), also discussed in Chapter 2.

Under ethics rules, lawyers are responsible for the training and supervision of paralegals and for the proper delegation of work to paralegals. The obligation of adequate supervision runs to all areas of ethics — such as confidentiality, conflicts, and competence — but carries special force in the area of unauthorized practice. Cases interpreting ethics rules make clear that lawyers are responsible for the actions of their nonlawyer assistants, including actions that constitute UPL. Further, lawyers must maintain professional independence and may not form partnerships with nonlawyers or divide legal fees with nonlawyers (ABA Model Rule 5.4). Chapter 7 discusses the financial restrictions on the lawyer-nonlawyer relationship.

As discussed in Chapter 2, Rule 5.3(b) of the ABA Model Rules requires lawyers to make "reasonable efforts to ensure that the [nonlawyer assistant's] conduct is compatible with the professional obligations of the lawyer" and makes lawyers accountable for the conduct of their paralegals. Guideline 1 of the ABA Model Guidelines for the Utilization of Paralegal Services (ABA Model Guidelines) and all state guidelines on paralegal utilization state that lawyers are responsible for all the professional actions that their paralegals perform at the lawyer's direction. Guidelines typically note the attorney's duty to employ and delegate work to paralegals who are competent for the task.

Guideline 2 of the Model Guidelines provides an expansive definition of permissible paralegal functions and notes that lawyers are prohibited from delegating to paralegals those tasks proscribed to one not licensed as a lawyer by statute, administrative rule or regulation, or controlling authority.

See also Guidelines IV, V, and VII of the NALA Model Standards and Guidelines for the Utilization of Legal Assistants, Canons 1 through 5 of the NALA Code of Ethics and Professional Responsibility, and Section 1.8 of the NFPA Model Code of Ethics and Professional Responsibility. NALA and NFPA codes are found in this book's Appendices.

D. What Constitutes the Practice of Law

1. Court Appearances

The one function that is universally considered to be the exclusive province of licensed attorneys is the representation of a client in court proceedings. Recall from the brief history of unauthorized practice at the beginning of this chapter that this was the first kind of restriction placed on nonlawyer practitioners in the early days of the United States.

The rationale for this rule is strongly supported by the avowed purposes of unauthorized practice rules generally. Presumably, a court appearance, especially an adversarial one such as a pretrial motion or a trial, requires knowledge and skills that only a lawyer possesses by virtue of specialized education, training, and experience. Many would say that appearing in court on behalf of a client represents the highest use of an attorney's professional judgment and skills. In addition to benefiting from an attorney's special competence, the client is protected by ethics and related rules to which only an attorney is bound on matters relating to attorney-client privilege, conflicts of interest, and confidentiality. A court appearance is an event that decides a client's rights and responsibilities. The client should have the best representation possible at this critical moment. Further, incompetent representation in a hearing or trial may not only damage the client, but may also impair the administration of justice.

Despite the clear rules and strong rationale for these prohibitions on the nonlawyer's role in court-related matters, a few notable exceptions do exist. Perhaps most important is the general principle of self-representation. The **right of self-representation** in federal courts is guaranteed by statute (28 U.S.C. §1654 (1948)). Any doubt about the constitutional right to represent oneself in state court was resolved in *Faretta v. California*, 422 U.S. 806 (1975). However, cases in federal and several state courts have determined that the right to self-representation does not encompass a right to be represented by a nonlawyer.

Some states have carved out narrow exceptions for the **marital relationship**. A California statute, for instance, permits one nonlawyer spouse to represent the other if both are joined as defendants in the same case and are appearing pro se. Cal. Code of Civ. Proc. §371. However, parents cannot generally represent their children in actions before the courts (e.g., cases brought under the federal IDEA, discussed above). And nonlawyer plaintiffs cannot represent other nonlawyer co-plaintiffs.

All jurisdictions have rules permitting **law students** to engage in limited practice under lawyer supervision, and nearly all allow law students to represent clients in court. This exception has been created for the dual purposes of providing practical training for law students and increasing the availability of legal services. Rules governing law student practice vary from jurisdiction to jurisdiction. Most states' rules identify specific qualifications that the law student must meet, require certification of the student by the law school dean and attorney-sponsor, and impose strict limitations on the kind of court appearances that the law student may make without being accompanied by the supervising attorney.

In some local jurisdictions, **paralegals are allowed to make appearances** for their attorney-employers in uncontested matters. Some enlightened courts permit such appearances under local court rules, including courts in the states of Indiana and Washington. For example, Seattle-King County, Washington, has a court rule that permits paralegals who are registered with the local bar association to present stipulated, *ex parte,* and uncontested orders in court when such orders are based solely on the documents in the record. Paralegals must have six months of work experience with an attorney, must devote at least half their work time to paralegal tasks, and must have a certificate from an ABA-approved program or the equivalent.

The rationale for prohibiting nonlawyer representation in court appearances extends to another aspect of the litigation process: the **taking of depositions**. In a ***deposition***, one of the key discovery tools, the attorney asks questions in person of an opposing or a third party. The responses are given orally under oath and are recorded by a court reporter or stenographer, who then produces a transcript of the questions and answers. A deposition may be introduced in court. It carries the same weight as testimony given under oath in court. This testimony may be used at trial to impeach the credibility of the deponent or in lieu of direct testimony if the deponent is no longer available.

Deposition
Method of discovery in which a witness or party makes statements under oath, in question-and-answer form

The attorney's role in representing a client being deposed includes making objections to questions on evidentiary grounds and preserving these objections for the record. Typically, objections are based on relevancy or privilege. The attorney who is deposing a party or witness is performing a task similar to that of direct examination in a trial and therefore must be familiar with the complex rules of evidence.

During a deposition, the attorney wants to learn about the facts of the case and to assess the credibility of the deponent as a potential witness. This work requires not only a full understanding of the factual and legal issues but highly developed skills in phrasing questions that will elicit candid and thorough responses, perhaps beyond those the party intends to reveal.

For the foregoing reasons, paralegals may not conduct a deposition. Although rarely challenged, two states have issued an ethics opinion on the question. In Opinion 87-127 (1987), the Pennsylvania state bar ethics committee said that a lawyer may not allow a paralegal to conduct a deposition even when she or he has a series of attorney-approved questions. The basis for this opinion was that the paralegal would not be qualified to answer any questions that might arise and may be called on to give legal advice. In 1996, the Iowa Bar issued a similar opinion indicating that paralegals may not ask questions at a deposition even when supervised by an attorney. (Iowa Bar Ethics Opinion 96-3.) See *State v. Foster*, 674 So. 2d 747 (1996) at the end of this chapter for a case involving nonlawyers who were prosecuted for taking depositions.

Almost three-quarters of the paralegals in the country work in litigation. Paralegals are involved in all phases of the litigation process, from legal research and drafting of pleadings and motions through the discovery process (including preparing and answering interrogatories, and handling subpoenas *duces tecum* and document productions) and trial preparation to settlement, trial, and post-judgment matters. Paralegals play an active role in the discovery and trial phases of the litigation process. They are often the factual experts in cases and, as such, work with attorneys in preparing for depositions by assisting in identifying areas of questioning. Many also help to prepare clients for the experience of being deposed or testifying at trial. Some accompany clients to independent medical examinations. It is common for paralegals to attend depositions and trials, taking notes, assisting with the introduction of evidence, and otherwise handling a variety of details, functions that generally have been supported by the courts and the organized bar.

Pleading
A written document filed with a court that sets forth the facts of a party's case or the defendant's grounds for defense

Related is the prohibition on paralegals signing a pleading or other document filed with the court on behalf of the client. A ***pleading*** constitutes a written "appearance" in court that only a licensed attorney can make. The lawyer's failure to sign a pleading may also imply that the lawyer has not properly reviewed the document before it was filed. A few ethics opinions address this matter. See, for example, Florida State Bar Ethics Opinion 87-11, warning against allowing a nonlawyer to sign pleadings and notices with the nonlawyer's initials. One state may allow a narrow exception: the North Carolina State Bar Ethics Council issued an ethics opinion that allows a lawyer to delegate the signing of a pleading in "exigent circumstances" for the protection of the client (N.C. Formal Ethics Opinion 2006-13).

2. Giving Legal Advice

The largest and most complex category of conduct that constitutes the practice of law is giving legal advice. (See ABA Model Guideline 3(c).) Like representing a client in court, formulating a substantive legal opinion to guide a client's conduct is a core lawyer function that cannot be delegated. A lawyer's legal advice lies at the heart of his or her value because it requires the application of the attorney's knowledge of law; judgmental and analytical abilities; and understanding of the client's situation, context, and goals.

The cases and advisory opinions about what constitutes "giving legal advice" can be summed up as follows:

- recommending a course of conduct or a particular action to a client;
- evaluating the probable outcome of litigation, negotiations, or other proposed action for or with a client;
- outlining legal rights or responsibilities to a client;
- interpreting and applying statutes, decisions, or legal documents to a client.

In practice, many paralegals have frequent **contact with clients**, which creates the potential for the paralegal to give legal advice. Paralegals generally get considerable satisfaction from working with clients and have an important role as liaison between the lawyer and clients. The benefits to the firm and the client are countless. Paralegals are often easier to reach than attorneys, who may often be in court or meetings. Paralegals are sometimes more patient with clients and may use less legal jargon. It is also more cost-efficient for the client and the lawyer to have the client speak with a paralegal.

Clients frequently develop good rapport with paralegals and eventually may ask a paralegal a question that requires a response that would amount to giving legal advice. That the paralegal knows the answer to the question further exacerbates this dilemma. To avoid giving legal advice, the paralegal must first consult with the attorney before relaying the lawyer's advice to the client. The paralegal may then communicate the lawyer's legal advice, so long as it is the exact legal opinion of the attorney, delivered without expansion or interpretation. Attorneys can delegate to a paralegal the function of conveying legal advice so long as the paralegals are not formulating and giving advice without lawyer approval and the lawyer still maintains a direct relationship with the client, exercising independent professional judgment.

One exception to the prohibition against nonlawyers giving legal advice has been created for so-called ***jailhouse lawyers***. In *Johnson v. Avery*, 393 U.S. 484 (1969), the Supreme Court held that a state may not bar inmates from helping one another to prepare post-conviction writs unless the state provides a reasonable alternative. This opinion was upheld and expanded in *Wolff v. McDonnell*, 418 U.S. 539, 94 S. Ct. 2963 (1974), in which the court specifically held that prisons could not prohibit inmates from giving or receiving legal assistance to other inmates without providing a reasonable alternative. The Board of Corrections of the State of Arizona decided to hire paralegals to help inmates with their appeals and writs after a similar opinion in *Lewis v. Casey*, 518 U.S. 343, 116 S. Ct. 2174 (1996). However, there has been a trend toward restricting the exercise of these rights. See *Shaw v. Murphy*, 532 U.S. 223, 121 S. Ct. 1475 (2001).

Jailhouse lawyers
Inmates who help other inmates to prepare post-conviction writs

The prohibition against nonlawyers giving legal advice has been challenged by persons seeking to aid those representing themselves in legal matters. As noted above, ***self-representation*** aids such as do-it-yourself legal kits and books, typing services, and most electronic resources do *not* constitute the unauthorized practice of law as long as they are not sold in conjunction with direct personalized assistance in completing the forms or procedures. Whether or not electronic programs that pro se litigants use to fill out legal forms does amount to UPL is something of an open question. (See, for example, *In re Reynoso,* at the end of this chapter.)

Self-representation
The act of representing oneself in legal proceedings before a tribunal

A related concern is the advent of court-sponsored resources to help pro se litigants without the use of an intermediary or adviser. User-friendly **computer programs** have been set up in courthouses in several states, including California, Colorado, Florida, and Arizona, enabling users to prepare court-approved forms in domestic relations, small claims, and landlord-tenant matters. Users answer a series of questions, and forms and instructions are filled in automatically and printed out for filing.

There is a nationwide trend toward expanding the role of nonlawyers in providing legal assistance to pro se litigants despite the unauthorized practice prohibitions. Most of the progress in this area has come about as the result of legislation that narrowly circumscribes the role of the nonlawyer within a particular area of practice where there is a great need for access to the civil legal system by persons who cannot afford attorneys and seek to represent themselves. In California, government-employed small claims advisers are authorized by statute to assist litigants in filling out and filing forms and preparing for trial. Legislation in California, Maryland, and a few other states permits private nonlawyer practitioners to assist litigants in unlawful detainer and summary ejection proceedings. In Washington and other jurisdictions, court facilitators assist pro se litigants in child support and family law proceedings.

As noted in Chapter 2, two states, California and Arizona, have officially recognized the role of nonlawyer legal service providers in assisting consumers to prepare and file documents. Under California statutes, **legal document assistants** (LDA)are required to meet certain educational or experiential requirements and to register with the county in which they do business. Similarly, but in a more comprehensive system, an Arizona Supreme Court Rule created the category of **legal document preparers** (LDP), who are certified by the court on payment of minimal fees and proof of meeting educational or experiential requirements. LDAs and LDPs are required to comply with legal and ethical restrictions. In both states, provisions prohibit them from giving legal advice. In California the related statute on unlawful detainer assistants (UDAs) has been used to prosecute UDAs who failed to register, did not meet the requirements of the law concerning written contracts with clients, and committed UPL. (See *Brockey v. Moore* at the end of this chapter.)

As described in Chapter 2, the state of Washington has adopted a court rule that creates a practice of law board, the purpose of which is to establish licensing of nonlawyers who will be authorized to provide legal services in designated areas of law. This rule, which went into effect in 2001, has not yet been effectuated.

Another emerging area of interest concerns the dispensing of **legal advice on the Internet**. Whether on a legal Web site, electronic bulletin board, or in a chat room, nonlawyers are prohibited from giving legal advice on the Internet. Lawyers must take care as well when operating in this medium not to establish an attorney-client relationship inadvertently and not to give legal advice. It is important in this context to keep in mind the distinction between legal information and legal advice. Providing general legal information, such as that given in a self-help book or program, or in a newspaper column about the law, is encouraged. However, legal advice that is specific to a person's case cannot be given by a person who is not licensed to practice law, including a lawyer who is licensed in one state but gives the advice to someone about a legal matter in another state.

One final word of warning about nonlawyers who assist persons with their legal matters directly, whether as a legal document preparer or as a jailhouse lawyer: communications between persons and their non-lawyer advisers are not protected by the ***attorney-client privilege.*** This rule applies to all nonlawyer representatives. Courts have consistently refused to extend the privilege to communications between nonlawyers of all kinds and their "clients" or "customers." As you will learn in Chapter 4, if a communication is not protected by the privilege, a court can require the persons involved to testify about the contents of the conversation, even if the "customer" or client believed that the communication was privileged.

Attorney-client privilege
Rule of evidence that protects confidential communications between lawyer and client during their professional relationship

3. Establishing the Attorney-Client Relationship and Setting Fees

The last main category of conduct that is reserved exclusively for lawyers is establishing the lawyer-client relationship and setting the fees to be charged for the legal services. As stated in ABA Model Guideline 3, a lawyer may not delegate responsibility for establishing an attorney-client relationship or the amount of a fee to be charged for a legal service.

The attorney-client relationship and fee arrangements between attorney and client are considered sacrosanct. A lawyer should establish a **direct relationship** with a client and not allow a paralegal to make the decision independently about whether or not to undertake the representation. The related matter of what fee to charge for the service should be determined by the lawyer.

This prohibition does not prevent a paralegal from communicating standard or specific fee information to a client at the lawyer's instruction, drafting retainer agreements or engagement letters, or presenting lawyer-approved documents for the client's signature. It should be noted that there are cases and ethics opinions that dictate against a paralegal's signing such a document on behalf of the lawyer. (See, for example, *Attorney Grievance Commission of Maryland v. Hallmon*, 343 Md. 390, 681 A.2d 510 (1996), and Pennsylvania Bar Association Formal Opinion 98-75.)

In addressing the question of establishing the lawyer-client relationship and the fee agreement, courts look at the facts of the case to see if the lawyer has a direct relationship with the client, has met with the client, has properly reviewed documents, and has exercised **independent**

professional judgment on behalf of the client. If the lawyer has abdicated the exercise of judgment to the nonlawyer employee, the lawyer may be found in breach of ethical obligations and the paralegal may be seen as engaging in unauthorized practice of law.

The ABA Model Rules and the predecessor Model Code both emphasize early on the importance of the attorney-client relationship. (See ABA Model Rule 5.4.) NALA Model Standards and Guidelines and most state guidelines on working with paralegals also make reference to these matters. See NALA Guideline VI.1; NALA Code of Ethics Canon 3.

E. Paralegal Tasks That May Constitute the Unauthorized Practice of Law

Throughout this chapter, a number of legal tasks have been discussed as falling within or outside the boundaries of the practice of law. Because the concept of unauthorized practice is vague and changes with time and place, creating a definitive list of functions that fall on either side of the boundary is not really possible. Such a list is likely to be quickly outdated or to be inaccurate for one locale or another.

1. Common Paralegal Functions

The following is a short list of generic paralegal functions, not specific to any particular area of practice, that are commonly performed by paralegals under the supervision of a lawyer:

- conduct legal and factual research and investigation
- draft memoranda, pleadings, and other legal documents
- prepare standard form documents
- prepare correspondence for attorney and paralegal signature
- interview clients and witnesses
- act as liaison with clients and others outside the firm
- organize, analyze, and summarize legal documents
- file documents with courts and government agencies
- handle procedural, administrative, and scheduling matters

There is little dispute over the propriety of paralegals performing the above functions under attorney supervision; however, other, very specialized tasks present special ethical challenges for paralegals and the lawyers who utilize their services, as the rest of this section describes.

2. Will Executions

A ***will execution*** is a relatively simple but critical step in the process of estate planning. Whether by case law or statute, very specific rules exist in every state about the signing and witnessing of wills, including the number of witnesses, their relationship to the person(s) making the will, and their presence during the signing. Few states have addressed this issue. In an early ethics opinion, the New York State Bar Association recommended against paralegals handling these proceedings on their own. NYSBA Ethics Opinion 74-343 concluded that the delegation of the task of supervising a will execution is "tantamount" to "counseling a client" and constitutes the practice of law. Iowa guidelines, adopted in 1988, indicate that "generally, a lawyer should be present for the execution of legal documents." However, newer guidelines, such as those in Connecticut, specifically allow paralegals to attend and supervise will executions so long as the paralegal does not give any legal advice.

Will execution
The formal process of signing and witnessing a will

Rhode Island and Colorado list witnessing the execution of documents or wills as permissible functions for paralegals. See *In re Morin* at the end of this chapter for an example of the problems that arise when wills are not properly executed.

3. Real Estate Closings and Related Matters

The role of paralegals and other nonlawyers in the real estate industry in handling ***real estate closings*** has been the subject of ongoing controversy. The jurisdictions that have issued opinions are split. For example, the Illinois State Bar Association reaffirmed its opinion on the subject in a 1984 position paper with the following language:

Real estate closing
The consummation of the sale of real estate by payment of the purchase price, delivery of the deed, and finalizing collateral matters

> Attorney assistants may attend real estate closings of all types, but only in the company of the employing attorney and at such closings prepare computations, revisions of agreements and perform similar tasks, but only at the direction of, and under the supervision of, the employing attorney.

Position Paper of the Illinois State Bar Association Real Estate Section Council and Unauthorized Practice of Law Committee Re: Use of Attorney Assistants in Real Estate Transactions, Approved by the State Bar Board of Governors, May 16, 1984.

Georgia, Pennsylvania, and some of the bar associations in New York have issued comparable advisory opinions. (See, for example, Georgia's Formal Advisory Opinions 86-5 and 00-3.) North Carolina Advisory Opinion 00-13 (July 12, 2000) recommends that although a nonlawyer can oversee the execution of documents, a lawyer should be available to confer with clients. Pennsylvania's guidelines, found in Formal Opinion

98-75, state that the closing may involve the "legal interpretation of documents, . . . and advice to the clients as to the course of action to be taken. . . ." Others entities, like the Federal Trade Commission and the U.S. Department of Justice, have advocated allowing nonlawyers a greater role in real estate closings to increase competition and lower the cost of services.

As noted in the Pennsylvania opinion, the rationale for this prohibition is that the client might need or want legal advice, particularly an explanation of the meaning and legal consequences of the various legal documents that must be signed. In addition, there is always the potential for last-minute disputes that may require the services of the attorney. A paralegal who explains the legal consequences of documents or attempts to resolve a dispute over terms would likely be giving the kind of legal advice that constitutes the unauthorized practice of law.

These concerns are addressed by bar association opinions that endorse the use of paralegals to attend real estate closings unaccompanied by a lawyer. For example, a Florida Bar advisory opinion states that "[a] law firm may permit a paralegal or other trained employee to handle a real estate closing at which no lawyer in the firm is present if certain conditions are met." The conditions listed in the opinion include attorney supervision and review up to the time of the closing; attorney availability to give advice during the closing if needed; client consent; a determination that the closing will be purely ministerial and that the client understands the documents in advance; and a prohibition against the legal assistant giving legal advice or making legal decisions during the closing. Imposing these limitations on the paralegal role protects the client's interests adequately and prevents the unauthorized practice of law (Florida Professional Ethics Committee Advisory Opinion 89-5 (1989)).

Several states have followed this reasoning and adopted similar opinions. See, for example, Virginia State Bar Unauthorized Practice of Law Committee Opinion No. 91-47, New York State Bar Association Ethics Opinion 95-677, Wisconsin Ethics Opinion 95-3, Connecticut Bar Association Ethics Opinion 96-14, and Vermont Bar Association Formal Opinion 99-3.

4. Negotiating Settlements

Special mention also needs to be made about one paralegal function that is fairly common in personal injury practices—negotiating settlements. Paralegals in many personal injury firms handle client contact and documentation of cases. "Working up" the case typically involves collecting medical bills, assisting the client with medical insurance claims, and discussing the case with insurance claims adjusters. Paralegals handling these matters often have ongoing communications with adjusters, providing information about the nature and extent of the client's injuries, treatment, and property damage. Adjusters may make offers to settle to the paralegal, who, of course, must convey the offer to the attorney, who in turn is ethically obligated to discuss the offer to settle with the client.

Few jurisdictions have addressed the matter of paralegals negotiating settlements. South Carolina Ethics Advisory Opinion 89-24 indicates that permitting a nonlawyer to do the "actual negotiation, even without authority to settle the case, may be an inappropriate delegation of responsibility by the attorney." Georgia Bar Guidelines for Attorneys Utilizing Paralegals, found in the State Bar of Georgia Advisory Opinion 77-21, indicate that "[n]egotiation with opposing parties or their counsel on substantive issues in expected or pending litigation" and "[c]ontacting an opposing party or his counsel in a situation in which legal rights of the firm's client will be asserted or negotiated" are both tasks that should not be delegated to paralegals. An early Florida ethics opinion also endorses this view, indicating that lawyers may not delegate to nonlawyers the handling of negotiations with insurance company adjusters (Op. 74-35).

These opinions are very limiting and in practice are not followed in many firms. As long as the paralegal does not commit the client to a particular settlement without lawyer approval or argue the legal merits of a case with opposing counsel, the rationale for prohibiting this task is weak. Paralegals who work in this area, however, must take special care to act as the conduit for information in the negotiations, and not to interpret the law or value of a case in a way that would affect the client's position. (See *The Florida Bar v. Neiman*, 816 So. 2d 587 (2002), for a case where a paralegal's involvement in settlement negotiations crossed the line into the practice of law.) Finally, the cases that are starting to be decided about nonlawyer loan modification services hold that some aspects of negotiating a loan modification do constitute the practice of law. (See *Cincinnati Bar Ass'n v. Mullaney* at the end of this chapter.)

REVIEW QUESTIONS

1. When were the first rules limiting the practice of law passed in the United States? What did the rules limit? What were the purposes of these rules?
2. What was the role of bar associations in limiting the practice of law to licensed attorneys? Describe the ABA's Statements of Principle entered into with other professional associations. What happened to these agreements?
3. What kinds of legal functions do most nonlawyer legal service providers perform? Whom do they serve? What areas of law do they work in? How do UPL rules circumscribe their work? What titles do nonlawyer legal service providers use?

4. Give the most complete and accurate definition of the practice of law that you can.
5. What are the potential consequences of engaging in the unauthorized practice of law? Are prosecutions for unauthorized practice of law increasing or decreasing? Why?
6. What are an attorney's responsibilities to prevent the unauthorized practice of law? What might happen to an attorney whose paralegal engages in the practice of law?
7. Make a list of the specific functions that constitute the practice of law and may not be performed by paralegals. What rationale lies behind each prohibition?
8. What are the exceptions to the general rule against a nonlawyer appearing in court on behalf of a client? Describe each exception and the rationale.
9. Give your best definition of what constitutes giving legal advice. Why are nonlawyers prohibited from giving legal advice? What is the difference between giving legal advice and giving legal information?
10. What are the exceptions to the general prohibition against giving legal advice?
11. Does selling a self-help divorce kit constitute giving legal advice? What about developing and selling electronic programs that help someone to prepare a will or complete the forms required to file for divorce?
12. Does answering someone's questions about legal matters constitute giving legal advice? Why, or why not? If a lawyer does this, is an attorney-client relationship formed?
13. What kinds of work can legal typing services perform without engaging in the unauthorized practice of law?
14. Why are paralegals prohibited from setting legal fees? From accepting a case? Can a paralegal quote a fee to a prospective client over the phone? Sign a retainer agreement with a client?
15. Should a paralegal supervise a will execution without an attorney present? Why, or why not?
16. Should a paralegal supervise a real estate closing without the supervising attorney present? Why, or why not?
17. Should a paralegal negotiate a settlement in a case? What steps should the paralegal take to be sure that he or she does not practice law unethically when negotiating?
18. Can parents represent their children in court cases? Are there any statutes that allow parents to represent their children in administrative agencies?
19. Can a nonlawyer set up a service to help people to renegotiate their bank loans and avoid foreclosure? Can a lawyer work for such a company?

DISCUSSION QUESTIONS AND HYPOTHETICALS

1. Do you agree that only licensed attorneys should be able to give legal advice and represent clients in court? Why, or why not? What are the consequences of limiting these functions to lawyers only?
2. Do you think that a sole practitioner lawyer who has ten paralegals working in her or his office can adequately supervise that many paralegals adequately? Is the answer the same for every area of law practice? What office procedures and policies might ensure adequate supervision under these conditions? What if the lawyer is in court every day and only spends a few hours a week in the office?
3. Do you think that a lawyer who hires a paralegal without any formal paralegal training is violating his or her duty to supervise? Why, or why not? Might this be appropriate or inappropriate depending on the circumstances? What factors would you consider in deciding? Glance back at the *Musselman* case from Chapter 2 for some insight.
4. How can a lawyer engage in the unauthorized practice of law? How has multijurisdictional practice affected UPL?
5. Why should law students, and not paralegals, be permitted to represent clients in court?
6. Based on *Faretta v. California*, do you think a constitutional argument could be made that citizens should be able to choose their representative in court, even if that person is a nonlawyer? Try to formulate that proposition and then develop the arguments against it.
7. Because it is essential for lawyers to have a direct relationship with their clients, and paralegals are prohibited from giving legal advice, why are paralegals allowed to have any client contact?
8. Which of the following acts by a paralegal would be permissible and which prohibited under the definitions of legal advice given in this chapter?
   a. interviewing a client to obtain the facts relating to an automobile accident
   b. telling the client that the firm probably would be able to get a $10,000 recovery
   c. explaining to the client what happens at a deposition
   d. discussing the questions that the opposing counsel might ask at the deposition
   e. attending a deposition without the lawyer present
   f. explaining to the client the meaning of an affidavit given to the client for signature
   g. telling a client that his or her case is likely to settle
   h. telling a client that the best course of action would be to file a small claims action

i. answering a client's questions about the meaning of terms in a contract
j. giving a client the legal opinion that she or he knows the lawyer would give
k. relaying a message from the attorney to the client, which tells the client that it is okay to sign a contract
l. talking with opposing counsel about the legal grounds for the client's case
m. attending a real estate closing without the lawyer present and explaining the purpose of each document to be signed

9. Could you use *Johnson v. Avery* to make an argument that poor people who do not have access to legal services have a right to legal advice from whomever they choose unless the state provides an alternative? Is this argument convincing? Why, or why not?
10. The cases that hold self-help kits not to be prohibited by unauthorized practice of law statutes also hold that helping customers to use those kits does violate unauthorized practice of law statutes. Do you think this an appropriate place to draw this line? Do any of the cases in this chapter help you to draw this line?
11. What are the policy reasons for permitting nonlawyers to give legal advice in small claims or unlawful detainer cases, or to serve as family court facilitators for pro per litigants? Why do these reasons not apply to other kinds of legal matters? How do you reconcile this exception with the policy reasons for prohibiting nonlawyers from giving legal advice?
12. In a personal injury law firm that takes every case that comes to it and that charges the same contingency fee, why should it be necessary for the lawyer to set the fee and establish the relationship with the client? Should this be an ethical rule, or is it really a matter of good practice? Suppose the initial contact between the attorney and client is a five-minute meeting to formalize the relationship and the client never speaks to the attorney again because the paralegal "works up" the case, negotiates the settlement, and has all the client contact. Is the attorney maintaining a direct relationship with the client? Does the *Lawless* case in Chapter 2 help you to decide?
13. What kinds of prohibited tasks might be made permissible for paralegals in the future?
14. Legal Documentation Company, also known as Divorce Documentation Service, prepares documents for persons representing themselves in all kinds of legal transactions. The company's owner interviews a person who wants to file for divorce; asks this customer questions about the length of the marriage, children, property, whether or not the customer wants support; and then fills in the blanks on the forms and provides sample testimony for uncontested divorces. Is this UPL?

What facts do you need to make this analysis? See *Statewide Grievance Committee v. Zadora*, 772 A.2d 681 (Conn. 2001).

15. An insurance company distributes to claimants a flyer entitled "Do I Need an Attorney?" that apparently attempts to advise claimants about the efficacy and costs of hiring a lawyer. Is this UPL? Is it speech that should be protected under the First Amendment? For an interesting analysis, see *Allstate Ins. Co. v. W. Virginia State Bar*, 233 F.3d 813 (U.S.C.A. 4th Cir. 2000).
16. Hanna is a family law paralegal with ten years of experience. She works very independently and really knows the process well. Her friend, Isabel, wants to file for divorce. Isabel and her husband, Jim, did not have any children; both work and have good benefits and own a couple of pieces of property. Isabel asks Hanna to help her do the divorce papers because Isabel and Jim don't want to pay a lawyer to do it. It seems that the situation is not contentious and that the couple will be able to end the relationship without a fight. What should Hanna do? Can she help them fill out the paperwork? Can she fill it out for them? Can she draft a settlement agreement for them? If she helps them and the court finds an error in her work, what are the consequences? If she helps them and the situation becomes contentious between them, what happens? Can Hanna be called to testify about what she knows?
17. Paralegal Joan Johnson works for the corporate department of a large law firm. The partner in charge, Susan Smith, always introduces Joan to clients and encourages them to call her directly for updates and information. Joan values this client contact and the trust that Susan has placed in her. Joan has developed a good relationship with a client, Ken Kaplan, who owns several small companies. Ken calls Joan frequently to check on the status of matters that the firm is handling for him. One day, Ken calls asking Joan about a new corporate entity that he wants formed. He is trying to decide in what jurisdiction the corporation should be formed. Joan knows that it would be most favorable to form the corporation in Delaware. Can Joan answer? What might be the consequences of her different actions? How should she handle this situation?
18. Lon Lane is a business litigation paralegal for a firm that handles construction litigation. A prospective client, Cathy Connor, who is also a friend of Lon's, comes in to see the lawyer, Mat Moore, who is unexpectedly called away. Mat asks Lon to interview Cathy. Cathy tells a detailed story about the faulty construction on her major house-remodeling job. Cathy asks Lon, "Do I have a good case? Can you represent me? How much do you think I will get?" Lon is 100 percent certain that Mat will want to take the case and that Cathy will get some compensation for damages. How should Lon answer each of the three questions? Can Lon get Cathy to sign an agreement for Mat to represent her? Can Lon tell Cathy what kind of fee agreement

Mat would normally make with a client in a case like this? Does it make any difference that Cathy and Lon are friends?

19. Fran Francis has just gone to work for Georgia Graham, who is genius litigator and fiery advocate but is notoriously disorganized and hard to get along with. Fran is the third in a series of paralegals who have worked for Georgia in a year. Georgia is away on vacation for two weeks, giving Fran time to get organized and situated. Among other tasks, Fran has taken it upon herself to straighten Georgia's office. While Fran is going through Georgia's desk, she finds a file in the back of the bottom drawer. It appears to relate to a case on which the statute of limitations will run out the next day, and it looks like nothing has been filed. On top of her worries about this the case, Georgia did not give permission to Fran to go through her desk. Fran knows how to prepare the complaint and file it and also realizes that it could be amended later. What should Fran do? Can she prepare the complaint? Sign it? File it?

RESEARCH PROJECTS AND ASSIGNMENTS

1. Interview five litigation paralegals in your area and ask them what kinds of tasks they perform. Find out if they attend trials and depositions with the attorneys for whom they work. Ask them if they have client contact and if they are ever asked questions that elicit "legal advice."
2. Contact the local legal aid organization in your area and find out how many paralegals and other nonlawyers they employ and use as volunteers and what these persons do. Do any of the functions they perform cross the line into unauthorized practice under the definition used in this book? If so, why do you think that this situation is permitted?
3. What are the rules governing will executions in your state? Does the state or local bar association have an advisory opinion about paralegals supervising will executions without the presence of an attorney? Interview three probate/estate-planning paralegals and find out what the practice is in their firms.
4. Do parties to residential real estate transactions in your state usually utilize the services of lawyers? If not, who does? If so, are paralegals who work for real estate lawyers permitted to handle closings without an attorney present? Is it common practice? Does the state or local bar have an opinion about it? Do you find the Illinois or the Florida rules most appropriate? Why?
5. Has your state bar or supreme court studied the problem of increasing access to legal services? What are the nature and extent of the problem in your state? What are some of the solutions that have been proposed in your state?

6. Research cases and disciplinary actions in your jurisdiction concerning loan modification services and foreclosure consultants. Have any nonlawyers been prosecuted for UPL in doing this work? Have any lawyers been disciplined? Has an ethics opinion been issued? Given the legitimate need of many homeowners for help in dealing with these issues, what kinds of services should be available and what should be the role of the legal community in providing them? (See *The Cincinnati Bar Ass'n v. Mullaney* at the end of this chapter for an example.)
7. Research the ABA and your state bar's Web site for information on "unbundling of legal services." What is this concept and how does it work? Do you see a role for paralegals in unbundling?
8. Research the questions of UPL and technology-based programs designed for the self-represented in law reviews and report on some these articles and their views. See, for example, Lanctot, C. "Scriveners in Cyberspace: Online Document Preparation and the Unauthorized Practice of Law" 30 Hofstra L. Rev. 811 (2002); French, S. "When Public Policies Collide . . . Legal 'Self-Help' Software and the Unauthorized Practice of Law" 27 Rutgers Computer & Tech L.J. 93 (2001); Fountaine, C. "When Is a Computer a Lawyer?: Interactive Legal Software, Unauthorized Practice of Law, and the First Amendment" 71 U. Cin. L. Rev. 147 (2001).
9. What do you think of disbarred lawyers working as paralegals? Is this practice permitted in your state? Is it more likely that a disbarred lawyer would engage in unauthorized practice of law than a paralegal? Why do you think this? Research cases in your state. For a start, see *In re Scott*, 739 N.E.2d 658 (Ind. 2000), where a lawyer is disciplined for hiring a disbarred lawyer and allowing him to serve as the main contact with clients and to prepare and file various legal documents without adequate supervision.
10. Read *Ohio State Bar Ass'n v. Burdzinski, Brinkman, Czarzasty & Lanwehr, Inc.*, 112 Ohio St. 3d 107, 858 N.E.2d 372 (2006), which addresses the question of nonlawyer consultants providing advice and counsel in labor election campaigns. What did the court decide? How does this fit with the definitions of UPL in this chapter?
11. If you are interested in the use of paralegals in criminal cases, read and brief *Mississippi Bar v. Thompson*, 5 So. 3d 330 (Miss. 2008), a disciplinary case about a lawyer who hired a former inmate who then engaged in UPL.

F. Practice before Administrative Agencies

Administrative agency
A government body responsible for the control and supervision of a particular activity or area of public interest

Administrative agencies are created by state and federal legislatures to provide for the regulation of certain highly **specialized** fields. A few examples of administrative agencies are the Environmental Protection Agency, the National Labor Relations Board, and the Patent Office at the federal level, and workers' compensation, unemployment insurance, public utility, and disability boards at the state level. Many administrative agencies handle an extremely large volume of cases that do not require much more than a mechanical application of rules. The volume of cases and the specialized non-legal subject matter make it impractical and inefficient to adjudicate disputes in these fields through regular court procedures.

Administrative agencies are **quasi-judicial** in nature, meaning that disputes before these agencies are resolved through a hearing similar to although less formal than a trial, before an administrative law judge or hearing officer or examiner, with advocates representing the parties. Procedures typically include the issuance of subpoenas, testimony under oath, admission of evidence, and oral and written arguments.

Someone representing a client before an administrative agency requires legal skills that are comparable to those needed by a lawyer representing a client in a trial. The advocate must have knowledge of the law and of the procedures used by the agency; be able to apply this knowledge to the specific facts and context of the case, using the proper analytical and judgmental abilities in doing so; and be able to advocate the client's case competently in an adversarial setting. Although the area of law might be narrower and the rules of evidence and procedure more informal than in a court, the functions of the advocate and the skills necessary for success in this setting are similar to a trial lawyer's.

Despite the similarities just described, many administrative agencies do not require advocates to be lawyers. The federal government has long permitted nonlawyer practice before many of its administrative agencies. The purpose of doing so is twofold: to allow easy **access** to these agencies and to make the process as informal, efficient, and inexpensive as possible. The Administrative Procedure Act, 5 U.S.C. §555(b) (1994), specifically authorizes individual federal administrative agencies to permit nonlawyer practice. It states that persons appearing before an agency may be "accompanied, represented, and advised by counsel or, if permitted by the agency, by other qualified representative."

This provision leaves the decision about nonlawyer practice to the agency itself. Some agencies require a J.D. degree or a license as a lawyer or certification as a public accountant, or recommendations of others admitted to practice, or passing an exam. A few such federal agencies are the U.S. Patent Office, Internal Revenue Service, and Interstate Commerce Commission. Other agencies allow all nonlawyer representatives without requiring them to meet any specific standards. Examples of these agencies include the Small Business Administration, Social Security Administration, and Bureau of Indian Affairs.

There is no consistency among the states about nonlawyer practice before administrative agencies. Some state statutes authorize representation by nonlawyers before many or all state administrative agencies, and some do not. In states that have a strong judicial history supporting the inherent power of the court to oversee the practice of law, legislation authorizing nonlawyer practice before state administrative agencies has been struck down. See, for example, *Denver Bar Association v. P.U.C.*, 154 Colo. 273, 391 P.2d 467 (1964), and an opinion of the Illinois State Bar Association, which holds that employers cannot utilize non-attorney representatives in termination hearings held before the Illinois Department of Employment Security. Another way of limiting nonlawyer representation without actually banning it is by prohibiting nonlawyers from collecting fees. (See, for example, California Labor Code §§4903 and 5710.) Also recall the case in Chapter 1, *UPL Committee v. State Department of Workers' Compensation*, in which the court upheld legislation that created a job for nonlawyer advisers to assist persons filing claims.

Some debate revolves around whether paralegals employed by attorneys may represent clients before state administrative agencies that allow nonlawyer representation. Most states allow it. For example, the State Bar of California opines that "a law firm may delegate authority to a paralegal employee, provided that the employee is adequately supervised, to make appearances at Workers' Compensation Appeals Board hearings." Advisory Opinion 88-103 (1988). For another example, see Michigan Ethics Opinion RI-125 (1992).

There is also periodic conflict between the states' authority to regulate the practice of law and the federal government's authority over its administrative agencies. The key case of *Sperry v. Florida*, 373 U.S. 379 (1963), would seem to have resolved this conflict when it held that the U.S. Patent Office regulations authorizing nonlawyer practice supersede state law by virtue of the U.S. Constitution's Supremacy Clause. However, unauthorized practice charges are still brought occasionally against nonlawyer practitioners who appear before federal agencies. See, for example, *Unauthorized Practice Committee, State Bar of Texas v. Cortez*, 692 S.W.2d 47 (Tex. 1985).

G. Disclosure of Paralegal Status and Job Titles

Many paralegals act as the liaison to persons outside the law firm — clients, witnesses, co-counsel, opposing law firms, courts, and so forth. This contact may take the form of telephone conversations, e-mail communications, correspondence, and meetings in person. A key ethical aspect of the liaison role is ensuring that the person with whom the paralegal is dealing is fully aware that the paralegal is not a lawyer.

Disclosure of status fits in this chapter on unauthorized practice of law for two reasons. First, a nonlawyer **may appear to be engaging in unauthorized practice** if he or she seems to others to be a lawyer. Not clearly identifying one's status may mislead the other person into believing that the paralegal is a lawyer. It is not difficult to see how someone, especially a lay person such as a client or witness, might misconstrue the paralegal's status because he or she "sounds" like an attorney. To the other person, a paralegal's inadvertent lack of disclosure may appear to be intentional. A severe consequence is that the paralegal could be charged with holding himself or herself out as an attorney, which in many states is considered unauthorized practice of law and is a misdemeanor. Disciplinary action against the attorney may also result, as many states have rules prohibiting attorneys from aiding in the unauthorized practice of law.

The second reason that disclosure fits into the context of unauthorized practice of law is that a paralegal who is mistaken for a lawyer may be called upon **to give legal advice**. If a client mistakenly believes that a paralegal is an attorney, the client may ask questions that require the paralegal to respond with legal advice. This situation places the paralegals in the uncomfortable position of having to refrain from responding to clients and to backtrack by explaining their nonlawyer status and why it would be unethical to give a legal opinion.

ABA Model Guideline 4 and similar state guidelines hold lawyers responsible for **informing clients** and others that the paralegal is not licensed to practice law. Some state guidelines on paralegal utilization advise "routine, early disclosure" or disclosure at the "outset" of the communication with the third party. Using a proper **title** for a paralegal is an important aspect of disclosure. The title must reflect that the person is not a lawyer, but should also accurately designate the role that the person has on the legal services delivery team. The title "associate," for example, is not appropriate for paralegals as it is commonly used for lawyers who are working for a firm but have not achieved partnership status.

The preferred and proper titles for paralegals have been the subject of some debate over the years. In the last several years, many firms started to call legal secretaries legal assistants. This usage accelerated the trend toward use of the title paralegal. It is noteworthy that this title cannot be used for legal secretaries in California unless they meet the statutory requirements to qualify as a legal assistant and maintain their continued education.

Although the titles **legal assistant** and **paralegal** have usually been used interchangeably, they carry different connotations in some regions of the country, and one or the other appellation may be preferred within the local paralegal community. Frequently, a legal specialty is attached to a title to indicate the area of practice in which the paralegal works, for instance, probate or litigation paralegal. As more firms have developed career paths for paralegals, new titles have been created, such as senior paralegal and litigation support specialist. As a general rule, any title that does not potentially mislead a third party into believing that the paralegal is a lawyer is permissible.

Paralegals are permitted to use their certification designations with their titles, e.g., Certified Paralegal or Registered Paralegal. Iowa, Mississippi, and New York have opinions that support this practice. (See, for example, Mississippi Ethics Opinion 95-223 and New York State Bar Association Ethics Opinion 97-695.) In another twist on titles, New York issued an opinion endorsing the terms *paralegal* and *senior paralegal*, but finding unacceptable and ambiguous the terms *paralegal coordinator, legal associate, public benefits advocate, family law advocate, housing law advocate, disability benefits advocate*, and *public benefit specialist*. New York State Bar Ethics Opinion 640 (54-92) (1992).

Paralegals are also permitted to **sign correspondence** with their job titles. Many states have ethics opinions or guidelines that endorse the signing of correspondence by paralegals so long as the paralegals use an accurate job title that is not misleading. Early in the development of the paralegal occupation, the ABA issued an informal ethics opinion that supported this practice:

> The lawyers' use of assistants to perform specialized tasks . . . is becoming increasingly common, and, indeed essential to the efficient practice of law. The Committee is of the opinion that it is appropriate for Legal Assistants to sign correspondence which is incident to the proper conduct of his or her responsibilities but care should be taken to identify accurately the capacity of the person who signs the letter so that the receiver is not misled.

ABA Comm. on Ethics and Professional Responsibility, Informal Op. 1367 (1976).

A more problematic practice is communicating legal advice in correspondence signed by the paralegal. In theory, this practice is not different from a paralegal relaying legal advice orally from the lawyer to the client, with the added benefits of the advice being spelled out in writing. The e-mail or letter documents the advice being issued by the lawyer through the paralegal. However, some states have opinions that indicate that allowing a paralegal to sign a letter containing legal advice or threatening legal action constitutes the unauthorized practice of law. (See, for example, Georgia Formal Advisory Opinion 00-2 and the Utah State Bar Legal Assistant Guidelines, which state that paralegals may "[a]uthor and sign letters provided the legal assistant's status is clearly indicated and the correspondence does not contain independent legal opinions or legal advice." Guideline D.8.) Care should be taken in wording letters that might contain legal advice to ensure that the client will understand that the advice was formulated by the lawyer and is only being communicated by the paralegal.

State rules on the use of business cards by paralegals and listing of paralegals on law firm letterhead have not been uniform across the country. Some bar associations were concerned that **business cards** might be misused to solicit clients (discussed in Chapter 6). Most states have balanced the benefits of disclosure about a paralegal's status in favor of having business cards. The ABA has long supported the use of business cards by paralegals, as indicated in a 1971 opinion:

> The term "legal assistant" appears to be coming into general use as connoting a lay assistant to a lawyer, as evidenced by its use in the title of the American Bar Association's Special Committee on Legal Assistants. . . . Informal Opinion 909 permits the designation on a business card of an employee of a law firm who does investigation work for the firm as an "Investigator." By the same reasoning, it would appear to be proper to designate a legal assistant as such on a business card, provided that the designation is accurate, and the duties involved are properly performed under the direction of the lawyer. . . .

ABA Comm. on Ethics and Professional Responsibility, Informal Op. 1185 (1971).

Related is the question of listing paralegals' **names and titles on law firm letterhead**. The ABA Model Code (in effect from 1969 to 1980), which had been adopted in whole or in part by nearly all jurisdictions, originally prohibited the listing on an attorney's letterhead of virtually anything other than attorneys' names and the firm's address and phone numbers. ABA Model Code DR 1-102(A)(4) (1969, amended 1980).

The decision of *Bates v. State Bar of Arizona*, 430 U.S. 350 (1977), raised questions about the constitutionality of these restrictions. This case, which appears in Chapter 6, held that the state could not impose blanket restrictions on lawyer advertising. In its opinion, the Supreme Court emphasized that consumers need information about legal services to make legal services more accessible and to help consumers to select a lawyer.

Because of this case and several that followed it, all states and the ABA revised the ethics rules that limited the kind of information that may appear on lawyers' letterhead, in announcements, and the like. Several states that prohibited the listing of paralegals on letterhead adopted new rules permitting this practice. All but a few states that have opinions on the subject permit the listing of paralegals on letterhead.

The ABA ethics opinion, adopted after *Bates*, reads in part:

> The listing of nonlawyer support personnel on lawyers' letterheads is not prohibited by these [Model Rules 7.1 and 7.5] or any other Rules so long as the listing is not false or misleading. In order to avoid being misleading, the listing must make it clear that the support personnel who are listed are not lawyers. The listing of support personnel, such as the law firm administrator or office manager, administrative assistants, paralegals or others,

> appropriately designated may furnish useful information to the public in determining whether to engage the firm and in learning the status of members of the support staff with whom they have contact.
>
> A law firm also may list nonlawyer personnel on business cards, written advertisements and the like, provided the designation is not likely to mislead those who see it into thinking that the nonlawyers who are listed are lawyers or exercise control over lawyers in the firm.

ABA Comm. on Ethics and Professional Responsibility, Informal Op. 1527 (1989).

The ABA Model Guidelines also conform to this policy. Guideline 5 states that a lawyer "may identify paralegals by name and title on the lawyer's letterhead and on business cards identifying the lawyer's firm."

Hence the general practice permits paralegals to be listed with appropriate job titles on business cards and letterhead, in firm announcements, in firm newsletters, in telephone directory advertisements or listings, in print advertisements, on firm Web sites, and so forth. In practice, most law firms provide paralegals with business cards but do *not* list them on the firm letterhead or on the door. Practice regarding paralegal listings on letterhead and on Web sites varies with the locale, the size of the firm, and the nature of its practice. Small and midsized firms are more likely to list paralegals than are large firms for both practical and firm-culture reasons. However, many firms provide paralegals with customized stationery that has the firm name and the paralegal's name and title.

The NFPA Model Code addresses the issue of disclosure in Section 1.7, which requires that titles be fully disclosed. Canon 5 of the NALA Code also requires disclosure "at the outset of any professional relationship. . . ."

H. Paralegals Working as Independent Contractors

Many paralegals offer their services as *independent contractors*, handling projects for attorneys on an as-needed basis. In the 1970s, the first ***freelance paralegals*** worked in the probate area, which lends itself well to effective paralegal use because the probate process is highly structured and procedural. In addition, many firms handle only a small amount of probate work, not enough to warrant having a full-time paralegal on staff. Gradually, freelance paralegals came to offer their services in other areas of practice, especially litigation. Many work as litigation support specialists, focusing on trial preparation, usually in large civil lawsuits. They assist law firms in organizing and managing the sometimes massive numbers of documents in large cases and assisting in discovery.

Freelance paralegals
Legal assistants who work as independent contractors providing services to lawyers on an as-needed basis

The use of independent contractors in the legal field is not limited to paralegals. Contract attorneys and a wide array of support services are now provided to firms in this fashion. Outsourcing to vendors and the growing use of part-time and freelance workers constitute a major trend in the economy. This practice gives businesses more flexibility in meeting their needs. It appears to be growing into all sectors of the economy and is now firmly a part of the legal landscape.

Many paralegals find that working as an independent contractor is an attractive career path. Many freelance paralegals work for themselves, running their own businesses. Paralegals with an entrepreneurial spirit often find this kind of work more rewarding than working 9 to 5 (or longer) for a paycheck. They enjoy the added responsibility of working for themselves, the freedom and flexibility of choosing their own hours, the power to decline an assignment if they choose, and the earning potential.

Working as a freelance paralegal presents special ethical concerns in many areas—such as confidentiality and conflicts of interest—and issues are also present in the area of unauthorized practice of law. One concern is to distinguish the independent paralegal who is supervised by a lawyer from a nonlawyer legal service provider who works directly with the public and sometimes uses the title of independent paralegal. The confusion between these two categories of nonlawyers has resulted in legislation and court rules in some states that prohibit nonlawyer legal service providers from calling themselves paralegals. (See more on this earlier and in Chapter 2.)

ABA Model Rules of Professional Conduct allow attorneys to use the services of all kinds of independent contractors, including paralegals. Rule 5.3, which outlines attorneys' ethical responsibilities regarding nonlawyer assistants, specifically includes nonlawyers "retained by" a lawyer as well as those employed by a lawyer, and the accompanying comment to Rule 5.3 emphasizes that assistants may be "independent contractors."

The 30-year history of the paralegal profession is characterized by a tremendous expansion in the nature and extent of legal tasks that paralegals perform. The trend is toward continued growth into new areas and functions that neither attorneys nor paralegals might have expected when the profession was just beginning. The pressures to expand the functions performed by supervised paralegals and to allow some legal services to be delivered directly to the public by nonlawyers will undoubtedly continue. In the coming years, social and economic forces will change the way we view the practice of law and will redefine the rules prohibiting the practice of law by nonlawyers.

REVIEW QUESTIONS

1. Why are nonlawyers allowed to practice before some administrative agencies?
2. Name five federal agencies that permit nonlawyer practice.
3. Do states allow nonlawyers to represent clients before their administrative agencies? Discuss.
4. Can paralegals who work under the supervision of a lawyer represent clients before administrative agencies for their attorney-employers? Discuss.
5. Can a state court prohibit a nonlawyer from practicing before a federal administrative agency within the state on grounds that such representation constitutes the unauthorized practice of law? Why, or why not?
6. Why must paralegals be careful to disclose their status as a paralegal/nonlawyer?
7. Name three job titles that are appropriate for paralegals to use in identifying their status. Name some titles that are not acceptable.
8. May paralegals sign correspondence on firm letterhead? What limitations might be placed on the form and content of such correspondence?
9. May paralegals have business cards? How should a card read? How might it be misused?
10. May paralegals' names be listed on law firm letterhead? Why, or why not? Why have policies about this changed? Is this practice common?
11. Are freelance paralegals who work for lawyers engaging in the unauthorized practice of law? How might they be more susceptible to allegations that they have engaged in UPL?

DISCUSSION QUESTIONS AND HYPOTHETICALS

1. How can the prohibition against nonlawyers representing clients in court be reconciled with nonlawyer representation of clients before administrative agencies? Do you think that the differences in these two settings are substantial enough to warrant the difference in policy?
2. How can independent paralegals who work under the supervision of lawyers distinguish themselves from those who serve the public directly? Do different job titles make a difference? For example, nonlawyer direct service providers are called legal document assistants in California and legal document preparers in Arizona. Will this solve the problem in those states?

3. Do you think freelance paralegals who provide services to attorneys are engaged in the practice of law? Might lawyers who use the services of independent contractors be more likely to fail in their responsibility to select, train, supervise, and review the work of these paralegals than those who are employed full-time by a firm? What about other independent contractors who serve lawyers, for example, process servers, investigators, accountants, and experts?
4. A lawyer hires an independent paralegal who will (1) conduct initial interviews of clients that have requested estate planning services, and (2) supervise execution of estate planning portfolios prepared by the lawyer. Is this UPL? What do you need to know to decide? See State Bar of Arizona Ethics Opinion 98-08 (1998) for one state's analysis.

RESEARCH PROJECTS AND ASSIGNMENTS

1. Are there any state administrative agencies in your jurisdiction that permit nonlawyer practice? Do nonlawyers appear before these agencies frequently or infrequently? What about paralegals working under the supervision of lawyers? Are there any state or local bar ethics opinions on this matter?
2. Do any statutes in your state disallow fees for nonlawyer representatives in administrative agencies? Which ones? Do lawyers represent clients in these agencies or do most people represent themselves?
3. Contact ten local law firms, five large and five small, and find out:
   a. if their paralegals have business cards;
   b. if their paralegals are listed on the law firm letterhead;
   c. if their paralegals have individualized letterhead;
   d. if their paralegals' names appear in advertisements, firm brochures, or newsletters;
   e. if their paralegals' names are listed on the door to the firm;
   f. if their paralegals' names are listed in the directory to the firm in the lobby of the building;
   g. if their paralegals' names and credentials are on the law firm Web site;
   h. if their paralegals sign correspondence to clients; and
   i. what job titles their paralegals use.
4. Contact your local paralegal association and find out if independent contractor or freelance paralegals are widely used in your area. Interview five freelance paralegals and the attorneys who utilize their services. Ask them what special ethical problems they face. Does the freelance paralegal work in the attorney's office or elsewhere? How does the attorney select an independent contractor? How does the attorney supervise and review the work of the independent contractor?

5. Contact the paralegal managers of five large law firms in your area and ask if they outsource any paralegal work. If they do, find out if the work is done locally or overseas and what measures are in place to guard against ethical violations.
6. Is it UPL for a company to represent a debtor in negotiations with a creditor's lawyer? See the Supreme Court of Georgia In re UPL Advisory Opinion 2003-1 (2005) or *Cincinnati Bar Ass'n v. Telford*, 85 Ohio St.3d 111, 707 N.E.2d 462 (1999).
7. Is it UPL for a financial service company to prepare loan documents and charge a fee for their preparation in connection with a mortgage transaction? See *King v. First Capital Financial Services Corp.*, 828 N.E.2d 1155 (Ill. 2005).
8. Read Johnstone, Q. "Unauthorized Practice of Law and the Power of the State Courts: Difficult Problems and Their Resolution" 39 Willamette L. Rev. 795 (2003) for an interesting discussion of UPL issues facing state courts and proposals for more effective resolution of these matters.
9. Read and brief *The Florida Bar v. Neiman*, 816 So. 2d 587 (Florida 2002), for a compelling example of a paralegal engaged in the unauthorized practice of law while in the employ of lawyers.

CASES FOR ANALYSIS

The following is the most well known of the early unauthorized practice cases involving nonlawyer legal service providers. Like the *Brumbaugh* case cited by the court, it involves a secretarial service that prepared legal documents for laypersons.

The Florida Bar v. Furman

376 So. 2d 378 (Fla. 1979)

PER CURIAM.

The Florida Bar has petitioned this Court to enjoin Rosemary W. Furman, d/b/a Northside Secretarial Service, from unauthorized practice of law in the State of Florida. . . . We find the activities of the respondent to constitute the practice of law and permanently enjoin her from the further unauthorized practice of law.

The Florida Bar alleged . . . that Furman, a non-lawyer, engaged in the unauthorized practice of law by giving legal advice and by rendering legal services in connection with marriage dissolutions and adoptions in the years 1976 and 1977. The bar specifically alleges that Furman performed legal services for at least seven customers by soliciting information from them and preparing pleadings in violation of Florida law. The bar further contends that through advertising in the *Jacksonville Journal*, a newspaper of general circulation, Furman held herself out to the public as having legal expertise in Florida family law and sold "do-it-yourself divorce kits." The bar does not contend that Furman held herself out to be a lawyer, that her customers suffered any harm as a result of the services rendered, or that she has failed to perform the services for which she was paid.

In describing her activities, Furman states that she does not give legal advice, that she does prepare pleadings that meet the desires of her clients, that she charges no more than $50 for her services, and that her assistance to customers is in aid of their obtaining self-representative relief from the courts. In general, the respondent alleges as a defense that the ruling of this court in *Florida Bar v. Brumbaugh*, 355 So. 2d 1186 (Fla. 1978), violates the first amendment to the United States Constitution by restricting her right to disseminate and the right of her customers to receive information which would allow indigent litigants access to the state's domestic relations courts. She alleges that our holding in Brumbaugh is so narrow that it deprives citizens who are indigent of equal protection of the laws as provided by the Florida and United States constitutions. . . .

. . . The Respondent admits that the customer returns with the intake sheet not completed, because the people are unfamiliar with the legal terms and some are illiterate and, of course, she then proceeds to ask questions to complete the intake sheet for preparing the Petition for Dissolution of Marriage. Then after she types the Petition for Dissolution of Marriage, she advises the customer to take the papers for filing to the Office of the Clerk of Circuit Court, and Respondent follows the progress of the case every step of the way until it is at issue. She then notifies the customer to come in for a briefing session preferably the day before the date set for trial. In the course of briefing Respondent furnishes the customer with a diagram of the Court chambers and where to find the Judge to which that particular case has been assigned. . . . She also explains the full procedure that will take place before the Judge, including the questions the customer should ask. . . . The facts in the record of this case establish very clearly that the Respondent performs every essential step in the legal proceedings to obtain a dissolution of marriage, except taking the papers and filing them in the Clerk's office and going with the customer to the final hearing and interrogating the witness.

Respondent admitted that she could not follow the guidelines as set forth in the *Florida Bar v. Brumbaugh*, for the reason that the customers who come to obtain her services are not capable for various and sundry reasons, mainly not being familiar with legal terminology or illiterate, and were unable to write out the necessary information. Therefore, she was compelled to ask questions and hold conferences with her customers. . . .

We do not write on a clean slate in this case. Last year we took the opportunity to clearly define to non-lawyers the proper realm in which they could operate without engaging in the unauthorized practice of law.

In *Brumbaugh*, we clearly stated what services a similar secretarial business could lawfully perform. . . .

Before the referee and before this court, Furman admitted that she did not abide by the dictates of *Brumbaugh*. She says that it is impossible for her to operate her "do-it-yourself divorce kit" business in compliance with this court's ruling in that case. The bar alleges that Furman has engaged in the unauthorized practice of law as previously defined by this court. The referee so found. She so admits. We believe the referee's findings are supported by the evidence.

In other portions of the referee's report, he urges that as part of our disposition in this case we require the bar to conduct a study to determine how to provide effective legal services to the indigent. . . .

Therefore, we direct The Florida Bar to begin immediately a study to determine better ways and means of providing legal services to the indigent. We further direct that a report on the findings and conclusions from this study be prepared and filed with this court on or before January 1, 1980, at which time we will examine the problem and consider solutions.

Accordingly, we find that Rosemary Furman, d/b/a Northside Secretarial Service, has been guilty of the unauthorized practice of law by virtue of the activities recited herein and she is hereby permanently enjoined and restrained from further engaging in the unauthorized practice of law in the State of Florida.

It is so ordered.

Questions about the Case

1. Did Furman ever hold herself out as an attorney? Did any of her customers believe she was an attorney? Did her customers complain about her services? Who brought this action against her, and what relief was sought?
2. Make a list of the services Furman performed for her customers. Do these functions fall under the definitions of the practice of law cited in this chapter?
3. Do you think that nonlawyers should be prohibited from performing these tasks? Why, or why not?
4. What does the effective delivery of legal services to the indigent have to do with this case? What did the referee recommend to the court about this? How did the court respond?

In this more recent Florida case, the court is faced once again with constitutional arguments about the UPL statute, this time in a prosecution involving two paralegals who took depositions.

State v. Foster

674 So. 2d 747 (Fla. 1996)

The State of Florida appeals from orders issued in separate cases (1) dismissing charges against Scott E. Foster, Jr., and his wife, Martha J. Foster, purportedly arising from the unauthorized practice of law and (2) finding [the Florida UPL statute] vague and violative of federal constitutional protections or unconstitutional in its application to the appellees. . . .

Mr. Foster was charged with four counts of unauthorized practice of law for his participation in four depositions by questioning four witnesses in two different cases. . . . [T]he state likewise charged Mrs. Foster for her participation in one deposition by questioning a witness.

The applicable statute provides:

> Any person not licensed or otherwise authorized by the Supreme Court of Florida who shall practice law or assume or hold himself out to the public as qualified to practice law in this state, or who willfully pretends to be, or willfully takes or uses any name, title, addition, or description implying that he is qualified, or recognized as qualified, to act as a lawyer in this state, and any person entitled to practice who shall violate any provisions of this chapter shall be guilty of a misdemeanor of the first degree. . . .

Neither of the appellees disputes the fact that each participated in the respective depositions by questioning one or more witnesses. The Fosters are paralegals who own a business that performs paralegal functions. Neither one is a licensed attorney. . . .

The first issue to be resolved is whether taking a deposition constitutes the practice of law. . . . The Supreme Court of Florida considered an analogous question in *Florida Bar v. Riccardi*, 304 So. 2d 444 (Fla. 1974). . . . The court held that Mr. Riccardi's conduct constituted the unauthorized practice of law. . . . [W]e agree that appellee's questioning of witnesses in depositions likewise constituted the unauthorized practice of law in violation of [the Florida statute].

The second issue is whether the lower courts correctly found the statute to be unconstitutionally vague. . . . The Supreme Court of Arizona has described the practice of law as follows: "We believe it sufficient to state that those acts, whether performed in court or in the law office, which lawyers customarily have carried on from day to day through the centuries must constitute 'the practice of law.' " [Citation omitted.]

. . . [T]he definition of the practice of law in Florida is not confined to the language of [the statute], but rather is shaped by decisional law and court rules as well as common understanding and practices. . . . The Supreme Court of Florida has defined various acts as constituting the practice of law, including "appearing in Court or in proceedings which are part of the judicial process," [citation omitted] and, specifically, active participation in depositions, the conduct for which appellees were charged. *Riccardi*, 304 So. 2d at 445. . . . The appellees have not pointed out, nor have we found, any instance where [the statute] has been found unconstitutional on any of the grounds argued at trial or set forth on appeal. We note that foreign courts that have reviewed comparable "unlicensed practice of law" provisions consistently have found no unconstitutional vagueness. [Citations omitted.] . . .

In supporting its ruling . . . , the trial court noted the Supreme Court of Florida's statement in the *Florida Bar v. Brumbaugh*, 355 So. 2d 1186 (Fla. 1978) that "it is somewhat difficult to define exactly what constitutes the practice of law in all instances." In its very thorough opinion, the trial court reasoned that, if Florida's highest court cannot "define exactly" the practice of law, then the statute addressing the unauthorized practice of law must necessarily be unconstitutionally vague. We respectfully disagree, finding that the quoted language in *Brumbaugh* must be considered within the factual context of that case. . . . We agree that "any attempt to formulate a lasting, all encompassing definition of 'practice of law' is doomed to failure 'for the reasons that under our system of jurisprudence such practice must necessarily change with the ever changing business and social order.'" *Id.* at 1191-92. . . .

The quoted comment was not intended, and should not be construed, to suggest that the practice of law cannot be defined or that an attempt to interpret [the Florida statute] must involve guesswork and chance. Were we to adopt the appellees' suggestion that . . . renders a statute void for vagueness, the State would be effectively precluded from establishing minimum qualifications for practice in the regulated and licensed professions and occupations. . . .

We think that in determining whether the giving of advice and counsel and the performance of services in legal matters for compensation constitute the practice of law it is safe to follow the rule that if the giving of such advice and performance of such services affect[s] important rights of a person under the law and if the reasonable protection of the rights and property of those advised and served requires that the persons giving such advice possess legal skill and a knowledge of the law greater than that possessed by the average citizen, the giving of such advice and the performance of such services by one for another as a course of conduct constitute the practice of law. *State ex rel. The Florida Bar v. Sperry*, 140 So. 2d 587 (Fla. 1962). . . .

A deposition is an important, formal, recorded proceeding in which lawyers must observe the Florida rules of court and must rely on their training and skills to question witnesses effectively. The activities and services involved . . . often implicate ethical questions and strategic considerations of utmost importance. The effectiveness of a person deposing a witness can have a significant impact on whether objectionable information is identified and addressed or waived, whether a case is made, and how the evidence therefore is used in any subsequent proceeding.

Depositions are transcribed by a court reporter for possible use later in court. . . .

We conclude that, lacking adequate legal training, a nonattorney participating in the examination of a witness poses . . . dangers of "incompetent, unethical, or irresponsible representation." [Citations omitted.]

The third question is whether [the Florida statute], although facially constitutional, is unconstitutional in its application to the appellees' particular conduct. . . . [W]e decline to apply the overbreadth doctrine to the instant case, where the appellees' active participation in depositions does not lie at the fringe of conduct constituting the practice of law. . . . Reversed. . . .

Questions about the Case

1. What do you think of the language in the Arizona case cited in this case? Does it give notice to the public about what functions fall under the Florida statute?
2. How persuasive is the appellees' argument that if the court cannot define the practice of law it is necessarily vague?
3. Is a definition in a court opinion sufficient to give notice to nonlawyers who are involved in providing legal services? How might such persons find out about the rule?
4. Did you find the *Sperry* case formulation of the practice of law useful? How might you break down the long sentence cited here into more useful components?

In the following case, a "paralegal" who is prosecuted for the unauthorized practice of law raises multiple defenses.

Board of Commissioners of the Utah State Bar v. Petersen

937 P.2d 1263 (Utah 1997)

Petersen, a nonattorney, has worked in Manti, Utah, since 1991. During that time, he has prepared wills, divorce papers, and pleadings and conducted legal research on behalf of clients for a fee. Petersen also advertised his services in local publications. Just prior to moving to Manti, Petersen had completed a nine-month correspondence course through the N.R.I. Paralegal School. Petersen subsequently registered as a paralegal through the National Paralegal Association, the Pennsylvania organization which offered the correspondence course. However, Petersen was never employed by an attorney, and none of his law-related work was supervised by an attorney. Petersen's activities were brought to the attention of the Board of Bar Commissioners of the Utah State Bar, and the Bar filed a formal complaint in 1993. The Bar claimed that Petersen has engaged in the unauthorized practice of law in violation of section 78-51-25 of the Utah Code and sought a permanent injunction against him. Section 78-51-25 of the Utah Code states in relevant part as follows:

> No person who is not duly admitted and licensed to practice law within this state . . . shall practice or assume to hold himself out to the public as a person qualified to practice or carry on the calling of a lawyer within the state.

Petersen filed two pretrial motions to have section 78-51-25 declared unconstitutional. . . . The trial court denied both motions.

The case was tried to a jury. . . . The jury returned a verdict in favor of the Bar and against Petersen, and the court ordered Petersen to stop the unauthorized practice of law. . . .

On appeal, Petersen argues that section 78-51-25 is constitutionally vague, . . . overbroad, . . . [and that it] violates the separation of powers doctrine . . . by purporting to authorize the legislature to pass a law that regulates the unauthorized practice of law. . . .

Petersen claims that an ordinary reader would not understand . . . section 78-51-25 to prohibit the kinds of activities in which he was engaged. He asserts that the obvious reading of the statute is that a non-lawyer is prohibited from either claiming to be or working as a lawyer, neither of which Petersen did. . . . We disagree. . . . The obvious reading of the statute is that unless a person is licensed to practice law within the state, he cannot practice as a lawyer, act as a lawyer, or even *present himself to the public as a person qualified* to act as a lawyer. . . .

Although "the practice of law" has not been exactly defined, an "ordinary reader" would understand that certain services, when performed on someone else's behalf, are part of such practice. Such services would include not only appearing in court, but also drafting complaints, drafting or negotiating contracts, drafting wills, counseling or giving legal advice on matters, and many other things. . . .

Further, when such services are performed for a fee, it is even more likely that they constitute the practice of law. . . .

Petersen's conduct falls within the clear sanction of section 78-51-25. Although not licensed to practice law, he met with and counseled clients on how best to proceed in their particular cases; with the aid of forms he selected, he drafted such things as complaints, summonses, motions, orders, and findings of fact and conclusions of law for pro se clients; he drafted wills; and he advertised his services in local publications. Thus Petersen held himself out to the public as a person qualified to provide, for a fee, services constituting the practice of law.

Petersen claims that section 78-51-25 is unconstitutionally overbroad . . . because it would make it "illegal for anyone to aid in the legal process" and thus would deprive many individuals, including Petersen, of their right to employment . . . [including] police officers who inform individuals in custody of their *Miranda* rights, nonattorney justice court judges when rendering a judgment, and court clerks who assist in the filing of court documents. . . . Petersen's arguments are without merit. . . . He may work under the supervision of an attorney. In addition, it is absurd to argue that the statute prohibits the activities of policemen, justice court judges, and clerks of court. None of these individuals offer legal advice, draft legal documents, or in any way represent clients for a fee. . . .

Petersen also claims that it is a violation of the . . . Utah Constitution to treat him any differently . . . than a paralegal working under the supervision of an attorney. . . . The legislative objective of section 78-51-25 was to protect the public. . . . As Petersen himself concedes, it is certainly a legitimate objective to want to protect the public from people claiming to be qualified to practice law even though they are not so qualified. . . . [I]t is reasonable to classify individuals based on a license to practice law. There are many safeguards built into the licensing process that offer protection to the public . . . including those laws which hold attorneys responsible for the actions of their paralegals. . . .

Petersen next claims that section 78-51-25 . . . violates the separation of powers doctrine. . . . This court's power over the regulation of the practice of law is a power over "members of the legal profession as officers of the Court." [Citation omitted.] The scope of article VIII, Section 4, does not extend to the unauthorized practice of law. Therefore, section 78-51-25 does not encroach on any exclusive jurisdiction of the Utah Supreme Court and does not violate the separation of powers doctrine. . . .

Therefore, we affirm the trial court's judgment and injunction. . . .

Questions about the Case

1. What were the paralegal's educational credentials? Was Mr. Petersen a paralegal as that term is commonly understood in your state? Did he work under lawyer supervision?
2. What was Mr. Petersen charged with, and what sanction was imposed by the trial court?
3. What were the three arguments with which he defended himself against the UPL charge? Set forth each argument and the response of the court to each argument. Do you agree with the court's analysis or Mr. Petersen's?
4. Think back to the separation of powers discussion in Chapter 1. Does it make sense to you that the court has authority over the practice of

law and the legislature over the "unauthorized" practice of law? Note the recent court rules about unauthorized practice that are referenced in this chapter. Do most states embrace this distinction?

In this case, a bankruptcy court considers the conduct of the owner-operators of an office of We the People, a company that provides services to people who are representing themselves in court, usually in bankruptcy and family law matters. The case addressed statutory violations as well as negligence, contract, and UPL.

In re Finch

(Bankr. M.D. Tenn. 2004)

All of the debtors involved in these matters consulted We the People [WTP] to prepare bankruptcy petitions. In each case, Chapter 7 petitions were filed, and Vincent Gould was listed as the petition preparer. . . . The trustee found inaccuracies and omissions in the Statements and Schedules of the debtors in *Finch, Toalson*, and *Smith*. Accordingly, the trustee filed dischargeability actions pursuant to 11 U.S.C. §727 seeking to deny the debtors' discharges for omitting or providing inaccurate information on their petitions, Statements, and Schedules.

Each of these debtors filed their petitions *pro se*, but following the dischargeability complaints filed by the Chapter 7 trustee, each debtor retained counsel to defend the adversary proceedings. In all three cases, the debtors filed third-party actions against Vincent and Shannon Gould and WTP alleging that the negligence, breach of contract, and/or violations of 11 U.S.C. §110 led to the omissions and inaccuracies in their bankruptcy filings. Accordingly, in the *Finch, Toalson*, and *Smith* cases, the debtors seek a judgment over Vincent and Shannon Gould and WTP. . . .

Harry David Finch is a former contractor who is in the process of obtaining disability. His wife died in 2001, and he has had no steady income since that time. He has a 10th grade education and difficulty reading. The debtor had been on medication for his multiple medical problems for more than two years prior to filing bankruptcy. He contacted WTP after his friend, Felicia Stevens, saw their advertisement on a bus stop. Stevens testified that she told Finch that WTP advertised bankruptcy filings for $199. Finch remembered WTP's phone number as having "LEGAL" in the number and contacted them. At his WTP meeting, he signed a "Contract for Services" provided by WTP, received information about bankruptcy, and received a "workbook" to fill out and return to WTP.

Finch testified that a WTP employee named Sandy or Cindy told him that they would file everything, and that he thought WTP was representing him. When Finch got to a question asking about real property, he explained to Sandy/Cindy that he had owned some real property, but had sold it and gotten some money for it. The debtor testified that Cindy/Sandy told him that he did not have to list the property.

Finch's friend, Felicia Stevens, helped Finch finish filling out the workbook at his house. She testified that when they got to the question concerning ownership of real property, the question had been marked through. Stevens thought maybe it should have been filled out, and she testified that she heard the debtor call WTP to confirm that the question should be blank. Although she did not hear the entire conversation, she heard Finch call WTP, and Finch then told her that WTP said it should be left blank. The debtor left the real property question blank, and it was left blank on the bankruptcy petition that WTP filed. The debtor paid WTP $199 for their services, and another $199 for the filing fee.

WTP filed the debtor's voluntary petition under Chapter 7 of the Bankruptcy Code on October 9, 2003. The debtor signed his petition, Statements and Schedules indicating that the information contained therein was correct. However, at the 11 U.S.C. §341 Meeting of Creditors, when asked by the trustee, the debtor indicated that he had owned and sold property located at 1066 Chestnut Road, Ashland City prior to filing. Finch indicated he received $15,000.00 from the sale. Upon request of the trustee, the debtor provided bank records showing that the debtor used the money to pay bills from January 2003 until July 2003. The property had not been disclosed in the debtor's Statements and Schedules because Finch had relied on WTP's advice to leave the question blank. . . .

[Finch] hired an attorney after the trustee filed a §727 action against him seeking to deny his discharge. The debtor's attorney then helped him amend his Statements and Schedules to include the property transfer and a pending consumer protection lawsuit that the debtor had brought against Nissan. The debtor testified that he would have told the trustee about the lawsuit if he had been asked about it at the Meeting of Creditors, and he did not know he should have listed it until consulting his attorney.

The trustee's dischargeability action seeks to deny the debtor's discharge based on the omission of the property transfer and the omission of the lawsuit. The debtor counters that the property transfer was not listed based on advice given by WTP, and that he did not know to list the pending lawsuit until meeting with an attorney. No money is or was remaining from the sale of the property as of the filing of bankruptcy or the Meeting of Creditors.

Michael Scott Toalson has not worked for several years except for a few months in the summer of 2003. He testified that he is disabled due to health issues including cardiovascular problems, back troubles, and foot problems. In 1999, he lived in Fulton, Kentucky on his late parents' property he owned jointly with his brother and sister. He and his brother took out a loan to buy out his sister's 1/3 interest, and Toalson lived in the Fulton, Kentucky home until it was sold in November of 2002 for $45,000. He and his brother divided the sale proceeds evenly after repaying the loan.

Toalson used the sale proceeds to pay living expenses. Although the debtor had receipts documenting some of the expenses paid, he could not account for every dollar received from the sale proceeds. Toalson's testimony was credible, however, that all of the proceeds had been expended on reasonable living expenses. When he was down to his final $200, he decided to file bankruptcy.

Toalson explained that he saw WTP's advertisement in a "Sensible Shopper" flyer stating that if he called "44-LEGAL," he could file bankruptcy for $200. He called WTP and spoke to Cindy and made an appointment. At the first meeting, he met with Cindy for about 10-15 minutes. She gave him a packet of information containing informational brochures about bankruptcy, a WTP Contract for Services, and a bankruptcy "workbook." Toalson testified that Cindy went through some of the workbook highlights, but that Shannon Gould took over when he needed help with Question 10 asking about real property. Toalson explained that Shannon Gould marked through questions that did not pertain to him. . . . Toalson stated that Mrs. Gould told him that because he did not transfer the Fulton, Kentucky property to a creditor or family member, he did not have to list the transfer. This advice was given after Mrs. Gould consulted with Mr. Vincent Gould, who in turn referenced a book source and confirmed the omission. . . .

The debtor returned to WTP to sign his petition, Statements, and Schedules and on October 7, 2003 paid an additional $215 to Mr. Gould to cover the filing fee and copy fee. He was told where to sign, and was not offered an opportunity to compare his workbook with his finalized papers. In fact, under questioning by the UST, the debtor identified several instances where WTP had made changes, such as: (1) WTP marked out questions; (2) WTP inserted corrections without the debtor's permissions; (3) WTP added information without asking the debtor; (4) WTP suggested to Toalson to include such things as exemption statutes; (5) WTP recommended assigning a "yard sale" value for personal property and exemptions; and (6) WTP "helped" with whether a claim was priority, secured, or unsecured. WTP filed the debtor's voluntary petition under Chapter 7. . . . The debtor signed his petition, Statements, and Schedules indicating that the information contained therein was correct. However, the debtor disclosed at his Meeting of Creditors, when asked by the trustee, that he had sold his parents' house seven months prior to filing. The property had not been disclosed in the debtor's Statements and Schedules because Toalson had relied on WTP's advice to leave the question blank.

The trustee told the debtor after his Meeting of Creditors that he might need to consult an attorney because of the omissions in the

Toalson testified that Mr. Gould told him that he could do an amendment for $30, and when Toalson stated he had no money, Mr. Gould said he would take care of it, but Toalson never heard from WTP again. . . .

The trustee's dischargeability action seeks to deny the debtor's discharge based on the omission of the property transfer. The debtor counters that the property transfer was not listed based on advice given by WTP. No money is or was remaining from the sale of the property as of the filing of bankruptcy or as of the Meeting of Creditors. . . .

In 2003, Linda Smith and her husband decided to divorce. In the divorce negotiations, Smith quitclaimed her interest in the marital residence in exchange for expediting the divorce. Smith testified that there was no equity in the house, and she received nothing in return for giving up her interest. She got her divorce in June, 2003, but continued to suffer from financial problems.

In July of 2003, Smith lost her job at Shoney's Restaurant and testified that five minutes after leaving the restaurant, she called WTP at "44-LEGAL" and talked to a man about how to file bankruptcy. At WTP, she paid the $199 fee, and was given a workbook by Shannon Gould. Smith testified that she had difficulties with the workbook and took it back twice to ask questions. Specifically, she asked about Question 10 regarding transfer of property. According to Smith, Vincent Gould told her that the property transfer "wouldn't matter" and therefore, she left Question 10 blank. Smith testified that she told WTP about her divorce, and that she had left Question 4a, asking for suits or administrative proceeding to which she had been a party within one year, blank as well.

Smith explained that Shannon Gould later called her to discuss the exemptions and the valuation of her car. Mrs. Gould told her Tennessee had a "wildcard exemption." Smith asked her what value to place on the car, and was told by Mrs. Gould that she could not advise her on that issue. When Smith then asked if $3,000 would work because she did not understand what Gould was talking about, she was told by Gould that it would.

When Mrs. Smith went back to sign her bankruptcy petition, she told WTP that she had obtained a job making about $1,400 per month. She thought this information was in the petition, Statements, and Schedules that she signed. Smith paid Mr. Gould $200 for the filing fee and asked WTP to file her petition.

WTP filed the debtor's voluntary petition under Chapter 7. . . . The debtor signed her petition, Statements, and Schedules indicating that the information contained therein was correct. However, at the 11 U.S.C. §341 Meeting of Creditors, upon questioning by the trustee, the debtor indicated that: (1) she had recently divorced; (2) that she had owned and quitclaimed her interest in real property to facilitate her divorce; (3) that she was employed at the time of filing her petition; and (4) that she did own an engagement ring (later valued at $1,000) that was not listed in the petition. Smith thought that she had properly filled Statements and Schedules. The debtor returned to WTP with his brother.

out her petition, and she testified that she was completely cooperative with the trustee once she realized the errors and omissions contained in her original petition. . . .

The debtor hired an attorney after the trustee filed a §727 action against her seeking to deny her discharge. The debtor's attorney then refiled her entire petition to accurately reflect the property transfer, her divorce, her employment, and her engagement ring. The debtor provided all information requested of her to both the UST and the chapter 7 trustee. . . .

The trustee contends that these debtors' discharges should be denied pursuant to 11 U.S.C. §§727(a)(2), (a)(3), (a)(4), and/or (a)(5). [These provisions relate to providing false information in the documents filed with the court.] . . . The Section 727 provisions are to be construed liberally in favor of debtor and strictly against the movant. [Citation omitted.] In these cases, the court finds that the trustee is unable to show by a preponderance of the evidence that their discharges should be denied based upon any of the §727 provisions relied upon. Accordingly, the court dismisses all of the trustee's §727 complaints against all three debtors in the *Finch, Toalson*, and *Smith* cases. . . .

Section 110 provides for monetary sanctions and injunctive relief against bankruptcy petition preparers who violate the specific provisions of the statute. For most of these requirements, the statute allows the court to impose a $500 fine for each violation. 11 U.S.C. §§110(b)(2), (c)(3), (d)(2), (e)(2), (f)(2), and (g)(2). The court may also disallow and order the turnover of any petition preparer fee found to be excessive. 11 U.S.C. §110(h)(2). In addition, the Bankruptcy Court shall certify all violations of this section to the District Court, and a debtor, trustee, or creditor may then move that court for actual damages, a penalty of $2,000 or twice the fees paid to the petition preparer, whichever is greater, and attorneys' fees and costs. 11 U.S.C. §110(i)(1). The Bankruptcy Court may enjoin the petition preparer from engaging in further violations of the statute, or may permanently enjoin a petition preparer from preparing any petitions in the future. 11 U.S.C. §110(j)(1). . . .

A bankruptcy petition preparer is defined in section 110(a)(1) to be a "person, other than an attorney, who prepares for compensation a document for filing." In this case, Mr. Vincent Gould testified that he and his wife were co-owners of the franchise "We the People" in Nashville, Tennessee. Mr. Gould explained that he and his wife were "partners with each other" in operating the business they called "We the People Nashville." They owned and operated WTP Nashville for approximately 11 months from April 2003 until March 2004. Both Mr. and Mrs. Gould testified that they accepted compensation for their role as "glorified secretaries" for preparing bankruptcy petitions. Although Mrs. Gould testified that only her husband had actually signed the petitions, the proof was uncontradicted and even acknowledged by the Goulds, that both Mr. and Mrs. Gould prepared documents for filing with the anticipation of compensation.

The court finds that Vincent Gould, Shannon Gould, and We the People Nashville are all bankruptcy petition preparers within the meaning of section 110(a)(1). All of the debtors independently testified that the phone number for WTP was "44-LEGAL." Section 110(f) prohibits a bankruptcy petition preparer from using the word "legal" or "any similar term" in an advertisement. Each violation subjects WTP to a fine of not more than $500 for each violation. This is a strict liability provision. [Citation omitted.] In other words, there is no "reasonable cause" exception, and proof of each violation results in a fine of not more than $500 per violation. . . . Accordingly the court finds that the third-party defendants should be fined $500 for each violation of section 110(f) in each of the three bankruptcy cases. The court finds a total fine of $1,500 shall be assessed jointly and severally among Vincent Gould, Shannon Gould, and WTP Nashville.

Section 110(g) prohibits WTP from collecting or receiving any payment from the debtor for the court fees in connection with filing a petition. Although there is minor disagreement about the scope of this provision, it is clear that a petition preparer accepting money, that is later used to pay court filing fees, is a violation. . . . In all three cases, however, these debtors testified that they paid WTP either in cash or money order made payable to Vincent Gould. Mr. Finch had receipts showing that he had paid WTP's fee and later paid WTP for the filing fee. His receipt shows $215 paid for "chapter 7 BK filing fee plus copy fee," and is signed by Vincent Gould. Likewise, Mr. Toalson paid WTP's fee on his first visit, and testified that he later paid the filing fee by a money order payable to Mr. Gould. Ms. Smith also paid the WTP fee of $199 and testified that she later made payment to Mr. Gould for the court costs and filing fees at the time of filing the petition. . . .

[T]he court finds that Vincent Gould and WTP violated section 110(g). There was absolutely no attempt to comply with the statutory requirements of section 110(g), and therefore, the court finds that a $500 fine for each of the three violations should be imposed. A total fine of $1,500 shall be assessed jointly and severally among Vincent Gould, Shannon Gould, and WTP Nashville.

Section 110(h)(2) prohibits a preparer from charging an excessive fee. This section allows the court to disallow and order the immediate turnover of any fee received within 12 months immediately prior to the filing of the case that is found to be excessive. . . . In deciding whether fees are excessive, the Court must determine the reasonable value of the services rendered. Courts have found bankruptcy petition preparers' services to be of no value or negative value where those services accomplished little benefit and, in some instances, harmed the debtor or put his or her bankruptcy discharge at risk. [Citations omitted.] . . .

The fee charged by WTP in all three cases was at least $199, exclusive of the filing fee. Because WTP cannot engage in the unauthorized practice of law, the type of services for which WTP is eligible for compensation under state law is limited to its "typing service." . . . Based on the proof in this case, the value of services provided to these debtors is unquestionably negative. WTP's involvement with the debtors has created incredible problems in these debtors' cases. All debtors had dischargeability actions brought against them by the chapter 7 trustee caused by inconsistencies and omissions in the petitions, and all of the debtors were forced to hire bankruptcy counsel to defend the dischargeability actions and to prosecute the third-party actions. Accordingly, the Court finds that the services rendered to these debtors by the Goulds and WTP had no value to the debtors. Pursuant to 11 U.S.C. §110(h)(2), the Court will disallow and order the immediate turnover by Vincent Gould and WTP to the trustee of all fees paid by the debtors. . . .

Section 110(i) provides that if a bankruptcy petition preparer violates this section or commits any fraudulent, unfair, or deceptive act, then this court shall certify the findings of such to the district court. Fraudulent, unfair, or deceptive acts cover a broad spectrum of conduct. . . . [U]nfair acts and deceptive practices include such conduct or omissions that are likely to mislead a reasonable consumer. . . . The proof in all three cases before the court is replete with evidence demonstrating unfair and deceptive practices by the third-party defendants.

All three debtors allege that the third-party defendants' "advice" caused the section 727 actions to be brought by the trustee, and made it necessary to hire counsel to defend those actions and prosecute WTP. The court finds that WTP's "assistance" to these debtors constituted unfair acts and deceptive practices, negligence, and a breach of their contract to provide "typing services." Mr. and Mrs. Gould's testimony was unhelpful in their defense of the section 110(i) allegations. Mrs. Gould had no recollection of dealings with any of the debtors. Mr. Gould remembered only his dealings with Mr. Finch and his testimony was inconsistent with Mr. Finch's version of events. Mr. Gould testified that he would never provide legal advice to the debtors. He explained that based on his WTP cultural training, that he and his wife were provided "scripts" of what to say to the debtors, and that it was office policy not to provide legal advice. Mr. Gould testified that if a debtor had a question, he simply re-read the question to them, and then if a debtor still did not understand, it was office policy to refer the clients to the "supervising attorney." Mr. Gould testified that he does not think he has ever deviated from that office policy.

Mrs. Gould also testified that everything that was said to the debtors was "scripted." She also followed office policy of referring clients to the supervising attorney if they had a question. Although she did not remember any of the debtors specifically, Mrs. Gould testified that she had never provided valuation information. She explained that she and her husband bought the business to help people and making a judgment call might hurt someone; so, she did not do it.

Each of the debtors did have specific recall of their dealings with WTP, Mr. and Mrs. Gould. All three debtors assert that their recollections demonstrate negligence, breach of contract, the unauthorized practice of law, and unfair and deceptive conduct by the third-party defendants. . . .

In Tennessee, a claim of common law negligence requires proof of the following elements: a duty of care owed by the defendant to the plaintiff; conduct falling below the applicable standard of care that amounts to a breach of that duty; an injury or loss; cause in fact; and proximate or legal cause. [Citation omitted.] Non-attorneys who attempt to practice law will be held to the same standards of competence demanded of attorneys and will be liable for negligence if these standards are not met. *See Tegman v. Accident & Medical Investigations, Inc.*, 30 P.3d 8, 13 (Wash. Ct. App. 2001), *rev. granted in part*, 43 P.3d 21 (Wash. 2002), *and remanded*, 75. P.3d 497 (Wash. 2003). In all three of these cases, all of the negligence elements are plainly met. If WTP is required to meet the same standard of competence demanded by attorneys, the conduct of the Goulds and WTP fell substantially below that bar.

Examples of the negligence by the third-party defendants are numerous, including instructing Mr. Finch to omit a recent property transfer. Likewise, Mr. Toalson was told by WTP to omit the sale of the Kentucky real property. WTP also marked out questions, suggested property valuations, added exemption statutes, and suggested how to classify claims for Mr. Toalson. In Mrs. Smith's case, WTP instructed her to leave out the recent quitclaim of her marital residence to her soon-to-be ex-husband, excluded her new employment from the petition after being informed of such by Smith, and "helped" the debtor with the valuation of her vehicle for exemption purposes. This course of conduct is actionable as negligence, breach of contract, the unauthorized practice of law, and/or violations of 11 U.S.C. §110(i) as unfair and deceptive.

When the third-party plaintiffs "helped" these debtors by filling in unsolicited answers, supplying relevant code sections, suggesting valuations, determining what court the petitions should be filed in, providing advice on how to answer certain questions, and crossing out questions that should have been answered, they did so negligently. As a direct result of that negligence, all of these debtors had their discharges challenged by the chapter 7 trustee, and were forced to hire counsel to defend themselves and prosecute the third-party defendants. The court finds the third-party defendants were negligent in their conduct as it relates to these debtors, and that negligence was the proximate cause of these debtors' losses. . . .

Several courts have found that the unauthorized practice of law constitutes a fraudulent, unfair, or deceptive act under section 110(i). [Citations omitted.] The Tennessee Attorney General has spoken on the unauthorized practice of law by document preparation services in Tenn. Op. Atty. Gen. No. 94-101, 1994 WL 509446 (Tenn. A.G. 1994). The Opinion provides in relevant part: . . . (a) The "practice of law" is defined to be and is the appearance as an advocate in a representative capacity or the drawing of papers, pleadings, or documents or the performance of any act in such capacity in connection with proceedings pending or prospective before any court, commissioner, referee or any body, board, committee, or commission constituted by law or having authority to settle controversies. (b) The "law business" is defined to be and is the advising or counseling for a valuable consideration of any person, firm, association, or corporation, as to any secular law, or the drawing or the procuring of or assisting in the drawing for a valuable consideration of any paper, document, or instrument affecting or relating to secular rights, or the doing of any act for a valuable consideration in a representative capacity, obtaining or tending to secure for any person, firm, association, or corporation any property or property rights whatsoever.

The provisions of T.C.A. §23-3-101 are mirrored in rules regulating the practice of law adopted by the Tennessee Supreme Court. . . . The purpose of the aforementioned provisions regulating the practice of law is "to prevent the public's being preyed upon by those who, for valuable consideration, seek to perform services which require skill, training and character, without adequate qualifications." [Citations omitted.] . . .

In these cases, WTP stepped over the line. Mr. and Mrs. Gould's general denials that they followed office policy of referring all questions to the supervising attorney are not only self-serving, but pale under the weight of the specific and credible testimony of all three debtors. "Section 110 itself proscribes virtually all conduct falling into the category of guidance or advice, effectively restricting 'petition preparers' to rendering only 'scrivening/typing' services." [Citation omitted.] The court finds that under even the most generous definition of "unauthorized practice of law," WTP has engaged in the practice of law without a license. Whether the court characterizes their conduct as negligent, unauthorized practice of law, or otherwise, the result is the same — "unfair and deceptive" within the meaning of section 110(i). The credible testimony of the debtors amply supports a finding that the third-party defendants have committed unfair and deceptive acts.

The debtors also assert that the third-party defendants breached their services contract by providing legal advice. WTP's obligation to the debtors, as outlined in the Contract for Services, was to "complete a BANKRUPTCY form with information supplied by [the debtor] for the purpose of filing Pro Se (For Self) in the appropriate court." The contract further states that WTP are not attorneys and "will not provide legal advice in any form whatsoever." Clearly this contract was breached by the outpouring of "assistance" given by the Goulds and WTP in all three cases. For all of the same reasons that the third-party defendants were negligent, they also breached their contract. Anything more than the promised scrivener service was a breach of contract. . . .

This matter is CERTIFIED to the United States District Court for the Middle District of Tennessee. Under section 110, upon motion of the debtor, trustee, or a creditor, the district court shall order the payment of damages following a hearing. . . .

Questions about the Case

1. What kinds of activities are bankruptcy preparers allowed to perform and what kinds are they prohibited from performing under the statute? What specific provisions were violated by these preparers? What were the remedies or sanctions?
2. What did the court find about the petitioners' claims of fraud? Breach of contract? Negligence?
3. What definition of the practice of law was used? Which aspects of this definition applied to the facts here?
4. What did WTP say in its defense? Did this defense comport with the claims of Finch and others? How did the court handle this matter?

In this case of first impression, an online program designed for consumers to use in preparing forms to file for bankruptcy was found by a court to be the practice of law.

In re Reynoso

477 F.3d 1117 (9th Cir. 2007)

This appeal arises from an adversary proceeding initiated by the United States Trustee ("Trustee"), during the bankruptcy proceeding of Debtor Jayson Reynoso, against Henry Ihejirika, d/b/a Frankfort Digital Services, Ltd. and Ziinet.com (collectively "Frankfort"). . . .

The United States Bankruptcy Court for the Northern District found that Frankfort . . . acted as a "bankruptcy petition preparer" within the meaning of 11 U.S.C. 110 . . . [and concluded that] Frankfort had committed fraudulent, unfair or deceptive conduct, and had engaged in the unauthorized practice of law. . . . [The decision was affirmed by the Bankruptcy Appellate Panel.]

Frankfort sold access to websites where customers could access browser-based software for preparing bankruptcy petitions and schedules, as well as informational guides promising advice on various aspects of relevant bankruptcy law.

. . . Reynoso accessed one of Frankfort's websites . . . , [which] represented to potential customers, like Reynoso, that its software system offered expertise in bankruptcy law:

> Ziinet is an expert system and knows the law. Unlike most bankruptcy programs that are little more than customized word processors the Ziinet

> engine is an *expert system*. It knows bankruptcy law right down to the state in which you live. . . .

It explained that its program would select bankruptcy exemptions for the debtor and would eliminate the debtor's "need to choose which schedule to use for each piece of information."

The site also offered customers access to the "Bankruptcy Vault" — a repository of information regarding "loopholes" and "stealth techniques." For example, according to the site, the Vault would explain how to hide a bankruptcy from credit bureaus and how to retain various types of property.

Reynoso paid $219 for a license to access the Ziinet Engine, including the Vault. . . . The online software prompted Reynoso to enter his personal information, debts, income, assets, and other data into dialog boxes. The program then used the data to generate a complete set of bankruptcy forms. . . .

Reynoso printed the forms and filed his chapter 7 bankruptcy petition. . . . During the first meeting with creditors, the chapter 7 trustee noticed errors in the petition and, upon questioning Reynoso, learned that he had paid for the assistance of an "online bankruptcy engine." . . .

Frankfort argues that the creation and ownership of a software program used by a licensee to prepare his or her bankruptcy forms is not preparation of a document for filing under the statute. Whether a software provider may qualify as a bankruptcy preparer under 11 U.S.C. 110(a)(1) is a question of first impression in the Ninth Circuit. We hold that the software at issue in this case qualifies as such.

Frankfort charged fees to permit customers to access web-based software. Frankfort's software solicited information from the customers. Critically, it then translated that information into responses to questions on the bankruptcy forms, and prepared the bankruptcy forms for filing using those responses. . . .

In sum, for a fee, Frankfort provided customers with complete bankruptcy petitions. . . . This is materially indistinguishable from other cases in which individuals or corporations have been deemed bankruptcy preparers. . . .

Since "bankruptcy petition preparers" are — by definition — not attorneys, they are prohibited from practicing law. [Citations omitted.] . . .

Several features of Frankfort's business, taken together, lead us to conclude that it engaged in the unauthorized practice of law. To begin, Frankfort held itself out as offering legal expertise. Its websites offered customers extensive advice on how to take advantage of so-called loopholes in the bankruptcy code, promised services comparable to those of a "top-notch bankruptcy lawyer," and described its software as an "expert system." . . .

The software did, indeed, go far beyond providing clerical services. It determined where (particularly, in which schedule) to place information provided by the debtor, selected exemptions for the debtor and supplied relevant legal citations. Providing such personalized guidance has been held to constitute the practice of law. [Citations omitted.] . . .

The judgment of the Bankruptcy Appellate Panel of the Ninth Circuit is affirmed.

Questions about the Case

1. Did the court say that a software program can engage in the practice of law? What do you think of this idea?
2. Do you think that the outcome would have been different if the advertising for the software had not made claims about its expertise? Was this an important factor?
3. Under the bankruptcy statutes, petition preparers are required to include their names on petitions. Why do you think that this provision was included in the bankruptcy law?
4. What would a court decide if a bankruptcy petition preparer used another company's software to help petitioners fill in forms? For one court's view of this unsettled area, see *In re Gross*, Bankr. E.D. Va. 8-27-2009, where the court said, "Even though [the preparer] may have relied on a computer program rather than her own knowledge or analysis, she, rather than the debtor, effectively chooses which exemptions [to claim]. The act of selecting exemptions requires 'the exercise of legal judgment.' . . ."
5. What are the ramifications of this decision for other legal software providers? How is this different from software to prepare a will or a divorce? What might companies that provide this software do to protect against UPL claims?

Landlord-tenant law is another area in which nonlawyer legal service providers commonly work. In the following case an eviction service is prosecuted under the state unauthorized practice and consumer protection statutes.

People v. Landlords Professional Services

215 Cal. App. 3d 1599, 264 Cal. Rptr. 548 (1989)

In 1982 the Orange County Apartment News carried an advertisement for the eviction services provided by LPS. The ad stated "Evictions as low as $65" and showed the picture of a purposeful and authoritative looking man, arms folded across his chest, stating: "One low price $65 plus costs uncontested or contested in pro per. Attorney for trial extra if needed." Below the picture were the words "Time to Act!" and "Call & talk to us." The advertisement ended with an address and telephone number.

In 1982 Roberta Spiegel decided to evict the tenants of an apartment she owned. A friend recommended LPS. Roberta spoke to Bill Watts, an employee of LPS, who told her to come to the LPS office and bring all documentation related to the rental. On arrival Roberta was given a booklet with Mr. Watts's business card attached. The card was imprinted with the words "Landlord's Professional Services" and the name Bill Watts. Beneath Mr. Watts's name was the word "Counselor."

The booklet begins with a chronology of an unlawful detainer action as carried out by the eviction service. The chronology was generally factual. However, at the end of the chronology, this bit of advice is imparted concerning what to do after the tenants have been evicted: "*You must change the locks at that time.* If you do not change the locks you may have a problem. The defendant may re-enter and take possession, and the ball game starts from the beginning."

The following pages of the booklet contain examples of the types of forms used in an unlawful detainer action and provide a guide for how those forms should be completed. Often the guidance is purely factual, i.e., where a form requires the name of the city in which the subject property is located the guide states "enter city." The advice given, however, can be more useful. In discussing the "Notice to Pay Rent or Quit," for example, the guide states: "Acceptance of any money after service may void notice. You don't have to accept money after notice expires."

Bill Watts reviewed the normal routine in an unlawful detainer action with Roberta, who was unfamiliar with eviction procedures. Roberta asked questions about the procedure and Bill answered them. Roberta told Bill she had already mailed the tenants a three-day notice. Bill told her this was insufficient and she would have to take another notice to the apartment. Bill asked Roberta questions and completed the documents and forms necessary for the unlawful detainer action and eventually filed them.

On December 7, 1982, Ralph Lopes, an investigator with the Orange County District Attorney's Office, called LPS and stated he was a property owner who was interested in eviction services. . . . The procedure for commencing and carrying through an unlawful detainer action was explained by Jacqueline Sutake, an LPS employee. . . . Lopes asked what it meant in the LPS ad when it stated "pro per." Sutake explained LPS was not an attorney and Lopes would be representing himself. Sutake stated LPS could not represent him in court. If an answer was filed by the tenant, LPS would type up Lopes's testimony and he could read it in court. Lopes asked if he would need an attorney. Sutake stated if an answer is filed by an attorney, LPS recommends its client obtain one as well but that it is possible to prevail without the assistance of counsel.

Lopes asked if he could turn off the utilities at the rental property. Sutake stated he could not. Lopes asked what would occur if he needed an attorney during the process. Sutake stated he could use his own attorney or "we have attorneys here."

Ms. Sutake testified she did not advise her clients on questions of law. She did, however, explain the unlawful detainer procedure and would share with clients her personal experiences as a landlord. If the case presented was more complex than the routine uncontested unlawful detainer action, she would suggest the client contact an attorney. Ms. Sutake explained her activities were always supervised by an attorney. When an unfamiliar situation arose she would ask an attorney for help and the attorney would determine if the complexity of the case required the services of a lawyer. In most cases her work was reviewed by an attorney before being filed.

In February 1983, the Orange County District Attorney filed a civil complaint against LPS and five other eviction services, alleging the unauthorized practice of law. (Bus. & Prof. Code. §§6125, 6126.) The complaint sought monetary penalties . . . and injunctive relief. At the conclusion of the hearing below the trial court ordered LPS to pay $8,000 in civil penalties for eight violations of Business and Professions Code section 17200 and $9,000 for nine violations of Business and Professions Code section 17500. . . .

The trial court also granted the following permanent injunction: "Defendants, their agents, officers, employees and representatives are enjoined from engaging in or performing directly or indirectly any and all of the following acts: '1. the preparation, other than at the specific and detailed direction of a person in propria persona or under the direct supervision of an attorney, of written instruments relating to evictions such as: three day notices, summons and complaints, at issue memoranda, judgments, writs of execution or other legal documents relating to evictions.

'2. Explaining orally or in writing, except under the direct supervision of an attorney, to individual clients: (A) the effect of any rule of law or court; (B) advising such persons as to the requirements for commencing or maintaining a proceeding in the Courts of this state; or (C) advising or explaining to such clients the forms which are legally required or how to complete such forms.

'3. Holding themselves out or allowing themselves to be held out to newspapers, magazines, or other advertising, or representing themselves as being able to provide, except through an attorney, any of the following: legal advice, the preparation of legal documents (other than as a secretarial service), or any explanation of any rules of law or court in relation to evictions or as being qualified to do any of the above activities.

'4. Any employee, agent, officer, or representative of L.P.S., not a licensed member of the California Bar, is prohibited from practicing law in any form or holding themselves out as having the right to practice law in any form.' " . . .

Business and Professions Code section 6125 states: "No person shall practice law in this State unless he is an active member of the State Bar." Business and Professions Code section 6126, subdivision (a), provides: "Any person advertising or holding himself or herself out as practicing or entitled to practice law or otherwise practicing law who is not an active member of the State Bar, is guilty of a misdemeanor."

The code provides no definition for the term "practicing law." In *Baron v. City of Los Angeles* (1970) 2 Cal. 3d 535, 542 [86 Cal. Rptr. 673, 469 P.2d 353, 42 A.L.R.3d 1036], our Supreme Court noted that as early as 1922, before the passage of the State Bar Act, it had adopted a definition of "practice of law" used in an Indiana case: "[A]s the term is generally understood, the practice of law is the doing and performing services in a court of justice in any manner depending therein throughout its various stages and in conformity with the adopted rules of procedure. But in a larger sense it includes legal advice and counsel and the preparation of legal instruments and contracts by which legal rights are secured although such matter may or may not be depending in court." [Citations omitted.] . . .

The eviction service offered by LPS was designed to assist clients in the preparation, filing and resolution of unlawful detainer actions. LPS, therefore, offered to assist clients in advancing their legal rights in a court of law. We believe general California law and the approach taken by other states with respect to divorce services teach that such services do not amount to the practice of law as long as the service offered by LPS was merely clerical, i.e., the service did not engage in the practice of law if it made forms available for the client's use, filled the forms in at the specific direction of the client and filed and served those forms as directed by the client. Likewise, merely giving a client a manual, even a detailed one containing specific advice, for the preparation of an unlawful detainer action and the legal incidents of an eviction would not be the practice of law if the service did not personally advise the client with regard to his specific case.

With these principles in mind, we conclude LPS was engaged in the unauthorized practice of law. The advertisement used by LPS implies its eviction services were not limited to clerical functions. The tenor of the advertisement was that the service accomplished evictions. The advertisement's statement "Call & talk to us" was a general invitation for clients to discuss the matter of eviction with LPS. Bill Watts's LPS business card listed his title as "Counselor." In short, LPS cast about itself an aura of expertise concerning evictions.

While an eviction may not be the most difficult of procedures, it is, nonetheless, a legal procedure carried out before a court with specific legal requirements for its accomplishment. As we have seen, some courts have held that providing advice as to which forms to use, which blanks to fill in with what information or in which courts an action must be filed is itself the practice of law. Here, of course, LPS's eviction advice went further. It provided specific information to its clients concerning eviction procedure. This it did in the context of personal interviews where it was able to provide additional information and advice addressed to the specific problems and concerns of its clients. . . . Given the aura of expertise created by the business practices of LPS such advice would undoubtedly be relied upon by its clients, perhaps to their serious detriment. . . .

The judgment is affirmed.

Questions about the Case

1. What specific conduct by LPS constituted unauthorized practice of law? What conduct constituted false or misleading advertising?
2. What definition of the practice of law does this court use? How does it compare to other definitions cited in this chapter?
3. How did the prosecutor's office investigate LPS?
4. Does it make any difference that an eviction is simple and many nonlawyers could file the appropriate papers without any help?
5. Did the court cite any instances where LPS customers were given bad advice or were harmed?

In this California landlord-tenant matter, plaintiffs seek damages and an injunction against a nonlawyer legal service provider who should have been registered under state law as an Unlawful Detainer Assistant. Related UPL and false advertising claims are also covered in the case.

Brockey v. Moore

107 Cal. App. 4th 86, 131 Cal. Rptr. 2d 746 (2003)

In adopting the Unlawful Detainer Assistants Act (Bus. & Prof. Code 6400 et seq.) the Legislature found in part that "there currently exist numerous unscrupulous individuals . . . who purport to offer protection to tenants from eviction. They represent themselves as legitimate tenants' rights associations, legal consultants, professional legal assistants, paralegals, attorneys or typing services. . . . The acts of these unscrupulous individuals . . . are particularly despicable in that they target low-income and non-English-speaking Californians as victims for their fraudulent practices." [Citation omitted.]

Under names such as "Legal Aid" and "Legal Aid Services" defendant Walter Moore operates a business which purports to offer typing services, particularly in eviction cases. Victims of Moore's deception Brockey [and others] were eventually directed to Legal Services of Northern

California's Redding office and obtained representation in the underlying cases and in this action seeking monetary and injunctive relief.

A jury found [that] Moore practiced law in violation of the State Bar Act (Bus. & Prof. Code 6125), violated the Consumer Remedies Act (Civ. Code 1750, et seq.) and awarded damages of $150 to each of the plaintiffs. . . .

Plaintiffs lived in a mobile home park . . . [T]hey received unlawful detainer summonses they wanted to fight. None had the means to hire a lawyer and they tried to obtain free legal help.

The Judicial Council summons form for unlawful detainer actions states . . . "if you do not know an attorney, you may call an attorney referral services or a legal aid office. . . ." The Judicial Council information sheet on waiver of costs states "If you have any questions and cannot afford an attorney, you may wish to consult the legal aid office, legal services office, or lawyer referral services in your county. . . ."

Brockey (who lived with Gayler) looked in his local telephone directory under "Legal Aid" . . . and found a local number which he called. That number was forwarded to Moore's Modesto business. . . . [Moore using the name Jay] told Brockey that he had to wire money. . . . Brockey did not tell [Moore] which boxes to check, that he wanted each party to bear its own fees, or that he wanted to raise an affirmative defense by talking to the judge at the time of trial. Gayler thought that they had contacted a law office "that offered services to low income people, [maybe on] a sliding scale of some sort." . . .

Plaintiff Pavloff called "411" information to get the number for free "Legal Aid Services," which he had used before, and was given Moore's number by the operator. He was told to wire $85, which he did. He did not tell [Moore] how to fill out the forms. . . .

The plaintiffs had to sign an "agreement & disclosure" form for the "Legal Aid Services Processing Center" in Modesto after paying money but before receiving their answers. The form states that "[t]his office is a professional document preparation and typing service only," that is not a law office and "will not provide any legal advice." It suggests that clients contact an attorney. . . .

[Six other persons not participating as plaintiffs had similar experiences in seeking free or low-cost legal services.]

Moore's former employee . . . testified he was told not to tell callers where the company was, to use aliases, and not to refer callers to the "real" legal aid. . . . When [he] worked there . . . , the company received from 60 to 200 calls a day. . . . [Testimony from various nonprofit groups and Legal Aid confirmed Moore's practices. An instruction was given to the jury indicating that the reference to Legal Aid on the Judicial Council forms and instructions refers to a "publicly funded nonprofit law corporation, which provides free legal services to low-income eligible clients."]

Moore was the owner and manager of "Legal Aid" and "Legal Aid Services" and "Premiere Marketing." He was not a lawyer or paralegal, but claimed to have an attorney "on staff," though he did not [at the time that he performed services for the plaintiffs.] [He claimed that he had a business license as Legal Aid and that he only typed what people told him to. Various discrepancies in his testimony came to light, including false statements about his Web site and the availability of a 900 number. Moore had been sanctioned by the local Bankruptcy Court for using the word "legal" in his advertisements and ordered to disgorge fees.] Moore . . . admitted that he was not registered under the UDAA and had not posted the required bond. . . .

The judgment recites that the jury found Moore practiced law without a license, violated the UDAA and acted with fraud, oppression or malice. The annexed injunction prohibits Moore in part from using names "Legal Aid Services" or "Legal Aid" or "Legal Services" because these three names signify a non-profit law office providing free legal services to low-income persons and families; using the term "legal" except as a paralegal; and using "local" telephone numbers which forward to his Modesto business. The injunction requires Moore to change his website, tell his customers he is not an attorney, place newspaper advertisements regarding the lawsuit and so forth.

In our view, the way Moore words his telephone book listings is calculated to mislead and is likely to mislead consumers. . . . [The court dismissed various grounds for appeal and affirmed.]

Questions about the Case

1. If Moore had been registered as an Unlawful Detainer Assistant, would the outcome have been different?
2. Which of Moore's acts appear to constitute UPL?
3. Why was the court at trial and on appeal concerned about the use of the word "legal" in the name of Moore's business?
4. Describe the background of the people that were Moore's "clients." Did this make a difference in the court's analysis?
5. Do you find it troubling that the court does not prohibit Moore from calling himself a "paralegal"? Remember that other California legislation prohibits the use of the term "paralegal" by anyone who is not working for a lawyer and does not meet the qualifications set forth in the statute.

In recent years, preparing living trusts for consumers has become a popular business for lawyers and nonlawyer practitioners alike. In this case, an attorney working with paralegals was found to have violated several ethics rules in the conduct of his living trust practice.

In re Morin

319 Or. 547, 878 P.2d 393 (1994)

The facts relating to this case are undisputed. The accused was licensed to practice law in California in 1974 and was admitted to practice law in Oregon in 1984. During the spring of 1988, the accused began conducting "living trust" seminars and selling "living trust packages," which included pour-over wills and directives to physicians.

The accused and two of his employees, who were paralegals, travelled throughout Oregon and northern California, conducting seminars and preparing the living trust packages. If a person at a seminar indicated that he or she was interested in discussing a living trust package, the accused or one of the paralegals would make an appointment and return to meet with the client. The accused or the paralegal would gather information from the client and then prepare the documents for the living trust package in the accused's Medford office.

At trial, Monnett, a paralegal employed by the accused, testified that he usually travelled alone, conducted seminars before groups, collected information from prospective clients, and assisted clients in executing the documents contained in the trust packages. He testified that the questions that he answered at the seminars were general and did not apply to individual clients' problems.

Monnett also testified that, during meetings with individual clients, he read their wills and explained to them the operative parts of the will. He also testified that he inquired into the clients' assets and advised them whether or not they needed a trust. He reviewed the trusts and other legal documents with the clients. Some of the clients never met the accused and dealt only with Monnett throughout the process. Both Monnett and the other paralegal employed by the accused, Pesterfield, testified that the accused instructed them to call him if they had legal questions. Both also testified that they believed that the accused reviewed all the documents that were prepared because he signed all of them and because occasionally he discussed the contents of the documents with Monnett.

Ordinarily, after the documents were prepared, the accused or one of the paralegals scheduled an additional appointment with the client to execute the documents. . . .

The accused testified that clients in the Medford and Ashland area ordinarily executed the documents in the living trust packages in the accused's office, where the accused's office staff members served as witnesses. When the accused or the paralegals executed documents at seminar sites, however, it was difficult for them to have the wills and directives to physicians witnessed.

The accused and the paralegals began a practice of taking the wills and directives to physicians back to the accused's office in Medford after they were signed by the clients at the seminar sites and directing the office staff to sign the documents as witnesses. The signatures of the "witnesses" on the wills were notarized either by the accused or by one of his employees. The signatures on the directives to physicians were not notarized. The accused then mailed the signature pages back to the clients. . . .

[T]he accused admitted that he had caused the wills and directives to physicians of approximately 300 clients to be executed outside the presence of the witnesses, who later signed the wills and directives to physicians.

The accused stated before the trial panel that he knew that a will is invalid unless it is either executed or affirmed by the testator in the presence of two witnesses. He also testified that part of the fee he charged his clients was for a valid will and that he understood that his clients believed that they were receiving valid wills as part of the living trust packages. . . . Here, the accused charged his clients a fee for the performance of certain services, including the preparation and execution of a *valid* will and a valid directive to physicians. The accused intentionally failed to provide his clients with the valid documents for which they had paid. The accused intentionally charged clients for services that he knew he would not provide. Accordingly, the fee was excessive and the accused violated DR 2-106(A). . . .

There is insufficient evidence for us to conclude that the paralegals engaged in the unlawful practice of law by giving the seminars on living trusts and by answering general questions about the living trust packages. Disseminating information that is "directed to the general public and not to a specific individual" is not the practice of law. *Oregon State Bar v. Gilchrist*, 272 Or. 552, 558, 538 P.2d 913 (1975). Apparently, the seminars and questions answered by the paralegals in the seminars went to general information about the advantages of living trusts and about the contents of the packages. The dissemination of that information did not involve the practice of law.

It appears, however, that at least Monnett went beyond the mere dissemination of general information to the public. The Bar alleges that it was Monnett's interactions with individuals that constituted the practice of law. In *Gilchrist*, this court held that advertising and selling do-it-yourself divorce kits did not constitute the practice of law. 272 Or. at 557-60, 538 P.2d 913. This court also held, however:

> [A]ll personal contact between defendants and their customers in the nature of consultation, explanation, recommendation or advice or other assistance in selecting particular forms, in filling out any part of the forms, or suggesting or advising how the forms should be used in solving the particular customer's marital problems does constitute the practice of law. . . .

Id. at 563-64, 538 P.2d 913. . . .

This court set forth the test for ascertaining what conduct constitutes the practice of law in *State Bar v. Security Escrows, Inc.*, 233 Or. 80,

89, 377 P.2d 334 (1962): "[T]he practice of law includes the drafting or selection of documents and the giving of advice in regard thereto any time an informed or trained discretion must be exercised in the selection or drafting of a document to meet the needs of the persons being served."

In *State Bar v. Miller & Co.*, 235 Or. 341, 347, 385 P.2d 181 (1963), this court held that an insurance salesperson that assisted people in preparing estate plans could:

> explain to his prospective customer alternative methods of disposing of assets . . . which are available to taxpayers *generally*. . . . He cannot properly advise a prospective purchaser with respect to his *specific* need for life insurance as against some other form of disposition of his estate, unless the advice can be given without drawing upon the law to explain the basis for making the choice of alternatives. [Emphasis in original.]

In this case, Monnett examined wills and interpreted them for clients of the accused. Moreover, Monnett discussed clients' individual assets with them to determine whether a living trust would be an appropriate device for the particular client to use. Monnett also told the accused's clients his opinion of the usefulness of another trust format, telling them that it "didn't do much." In short, Monnett advised clients and potential clients of the accused on legal decisions specific to them, and he used discretion in selecting between using a trust and a will and among trust forms. Accordingly, Monnett, a nonlawyer, practiced law.

The accused argues that, even if Monnett practiced law, he did not assist Monnett. He argues that he "took pains to tell these paralegals not to practice law at the seminars." He also told them to call him at the office or at home "[i]f any legal questions arose." Furthermore, the accused argues that he did not know of Monnett's conduct nor did he aid in that conduct: therefore, he did not violate the rule.

This court's decision in *In re Jones*, 308 Or. 306, 779 P.2d 1016 (1989), is instructive. In that case, the accused allowed a nonlawyer to use pleading paper and a letterhead stamp with the lawyer's name on it in the nonlawyer's dissolution-processing business. . . . The accused knew that the nonlawyer had been warned by the Bar not to practice law. . . . The accused instructed her to bring any legal questions that she had to him. . . . This court held that the accused aided a nonlawyer in the practice of law because he "took no steps to enforce his instruction or to test her ability to determine when legal help was needed." . . . This court also found it to be important that the clients were never required to speak with the accused. . . .

Here, as in *Jones*, although the accused told his paralegals not to practice law, he did not tell them the precise contours of what constituted the practice of law. Moreover, the accused created the situation in which at least one of his paralegals had the opportunity to practice law. The accused sent the paralegals to meet with clients alone, and he failed to supervise them properly. Thus, even if the accused did not intend for the paralegals to practice law, he assisted in that unlawful practice by allowing them too much freedom in dealing with clients, thereby allowing at least Monnett to provide legal advice to those clients. Accordingly, we conclude that the accused assisted in the unlawful practice of law. . . .

Accordingly, considering the ABA Standards and the prior decisions of this court, we conclude that the trial panel's decision of disbarment is correct.

Questions about the Case

1. What exactly did the paralegals do in this case that constitutes unauthorized practice of law?
2. Could the attorney have run his practice in a way that avoided the ethical violations cited? How?
3. What was wrong with the way the wills were executed? What was the result for the client? Is this legal malpractice? (See Chapter 8.)
4. What did the court say about the attorney charging fees for the invalid wills?
5. Did the court condemn the activities of the paralegals as unauthorized practice of law?
6. What definition of the practice of law did this court use?

The following case illustrates what can happen when lawyers affiliate with an organization of nonlawyers. This specific scenario involves a foreclosure consulting company and a law firm. Similar cases could be found throughout the country during the economic recession that started in late 2007.

Cincinnati Bar Ass'n v. Mullaney

119 Ohio St. 3d 412 (2008)

Respondents Brooking and Moeves are principals in Brooking, Moeves & Halloran, P.L.L.C. ("the Brooking firm"), a law firm established in September 2004. . . . Respondent Mullaney was employed as an associate of the Brooking firm and its predecessors . . . from May 2004 until May 2006. Foreclosure Solutions, L.L.C., is a company located in Ohio that purports to serve homeowners threatened with foreclosure by helping them set up a savings plan, so that after the homeowners follow the plan, Foreclosure Solutions can use the money saved to negotiate with the lenders to reinstate the loan and avoid foreclosure.

In 2003, Moeves . . . worked out a deal with Timothy Buckley, president of Foreclosure Solutions, agreeing to represent Foreclosure

Solutions' customers in Kentucky courts. Pursuant to their agreement, Moeves began accepting clients from Foreclosure Solutions, who routinely obtained a limited power of attorney to hire an attorney for its customers, and Moeves collected a flat fee from Foreclosure Solutions of $125 for each client. With the formation of the Brooking firm in the fall of 2004, Moeves and Buckley extended their agreement to include representation of Foreclosure Solutions' customers in Ohio courts. . . .

Foreclosure Solutions' customers paid between $700 and $1,100 for the company's services, the goal of which was to stall pending foreclosure proceedings while trying to negotiate a settlement with the lender. The company is not a licensed or accredited consumer-credit-counseling agency. Nor is Buckley or any of his employees, to the respondents' knowledge, licensed to practice law in any jurisdiction.

Foreclosure Solutions advertised to attract customers and often sent advertisements to defendants listed on court foreclosure dockets. Agents of the company told prospective customers that an attorney and legal services would be furnished to them as part of their fee. The company then hired a lawyer for the customer-client to respond in court to the recently filed foreclosure action. The client had no choice in the lawyer's selection, and after the lawyer was hired, Foreclosure Solutions' agents continued to negotiate directly with the foreclosing creditors.

Foreclosure Solutions' agents met with customers to collect the company's fee and had the customer sign a standardized contract, the "Work Agreement," containing the basic terms and conditions of the engagement. The agent also had the customer sign a standardized limited power of attorney appointing Foreclosure Solutions as the customer's attorney-in-fact, which, in addition to authorizing the hiring of an attorney, allowed company agents to negotiate on the customer's behalf with creditors. Neither the Work Agreement nor the limited power of attorney identified any particular lawyer, established when a lawyer was to be hired, or informed the client of the amount of the lawyer's fee.

As the solution to a customer's foreclosure troubles, the Work Agreement provided for the customer to set up a savings account and deposit a certain amount of money into it on a regular basis; Foreclosure Solutions would then use that money as a bargaining chip in negotiations with the creditor. Foreclosure Solutions determined the amount the client was to periodically deposit in the savings account. The Work Agreement specified that bankruptcy was considered a last resort.

Once the Foreclosure Solutions customer had signed the Work Agreement and limited power of attorney, the agent completed a financial worksheet and determined the savings recommendation. The agent then collected Foreclosure Solutions' fee, none of which was designated as attorney fees. From this $700 to $1,100 fee, Foreclosure Solutions paid the lawyers their flat fee. . . .

Under the arrangement with Foreclosure Solutions, the Brooking firm represented approximately 2,000 clients in Ohio foreclosure proceedings during 2005 and 2006, at first accepting $125 and later $150 for each case. . . . Brooking represented Foreclosure Solutions' customers during the spring and summer of 2006. . . . Respondents did not oversee solicitations or have any other involvement with Foreclosure Solutions' customers before the company sent its customers' files to the Brooking firm. When received by the firm, the files typically contained the Work Agreement, the limited power of attorney, an intake sheet that had been completed by a Foreclosure Solutions' agent, and a copy of the complaint in foreclosure. The intake sheet, another standardized form, contained the client's financial information. The Brooking firm often received several client files at a time, together with one check for all the fees.

When it accepted a new case, the Brooking firm routinely sent the client an informational brochure entitled "The Nuts and Bolts of an Ohio Foreclosure" that Moeves and Mullaney had prepared. As the foreclosure actions went forward, Mullaney, Brooking, or Moeves responded in court with standardized pleadings and other filings, sending copies to the clients. Cases rarely if ever went to trial, and if the parties could not negotiate a resolution, trial courts granted judgment to the lenders and ordered the sale of the property. At that time, Mullaney, Brooking, or Moeves notified the client of the sale date and sent a standardized letter recommending that the client contact a bankruptcy lawyer. . . .

In following its typical procedure, the Brooking firm lawyers did not as a rule meet with the Foreclosure Solutions clients to determine their particular objectives or complete financial situation or to discover facts that could be defenses to foreclosure. The lawyers generally communicated with the clients through boilerplate correspondence, which the lawyers had no indication that the clients understood. As an example, one standard Brooking firm letter asked whether the client knew of any defenses to the foreclosure, relying on the client to guess what factors might be useful in his or her case.

In this way, Mullaney, Brooking, and Moeves failed to determine what action, including filing bankruptcy immediately, was in any one particular client's best interest. Respondents instead simply followed the Foreclosure Solutions "savings plan" strategy and allowed the foreclosure action to proceed until either a settlement could be negotiated with the lender or the court granted judgment in favor of the lender and ordered the property to be sold, with the lawyers filing routine pleadings and motions at critical stages to delay the process. Only when a sale was imminent did Mullaney, Brooking, and Moeves advise the clients to consider another remedy by contacting a bankruptcy attorney. . . .

In restricting a lawyer's use of referral services to those that serve the public interest and otherwise comply with the rule, DR 2-103(C) prohibits lawyers from using "a person or organization to recommend or promote the use of the lawyer's services or those of the lawyer's partner or associate, or any other lawyer affiliated with the lawyer or the lawyer's firm, as a private practitioner." Foreclosure Solutions is not a referral service as described by the rule, yet Mullaney, Brooking, and Moeves accepted clients from that company. We therefore find that respondents violated DR 2-103(C).

DR 3-101(A) prohibits lawyers from aiding nonlawyers in the unauthorized practice of law. We have held that by advising debtors of their legal rights and the terms and conditions of settlement in negotiations to avoid pending foreclosure proceedings, laypersons engage in the unauthorized practice of law. *Cincinnati Bar Assn. v. Telford* (1999), 85 Ohio St. 3d 111, 707 N.E.2d 462. Here, Mullaney, Brooking, and Moeves facilitated nonlawyers' negotiations with the creditors of debtors facing foreclosure by doing business with Foreclosure Solutions. We therefore find that respondents violated DR 3-101(A).

Except in circumstances not relevant here, DR 3-102(A) prohibits lawyers from sharing legal fees with nonlawyers. By accepting a portion of the compensation that the customers paid Foreclosure Solutions for legal services, Mullaney, Brooking, and Moeves shared legal fees with nonlawyers. We therefore find that respondents violated DR 3-102(A).

DR 3-103(A) prohibits a lawyer from forming a partnership with a nonlawyer if any activities of the partnership consist of the practice of law. Brooking and Moeves, principals in the Brooking firm, partnered with Foreclosure Solutions in representing debtors facing foreclosure. We therefore find that these two respondents violated DR 3-103(A).

DR 6-101(A)(2) prohibits a lawyer from handling a legal matter without preparation adequate under the circumstances. DR 7-101(A)(1) prohibits a lawyer from intentionally failing to seek a client's lawful objectives. These rules prohibited Mullaney, Brooking, and Moeves from surrendering their professional judgment to Foreclosure Solutions.

Counseling debtors in financial crisis as to their best course of legal action requires the attention of a qualified attorney. *Columbus Bar Assn. v. Flanagan* (1997), 77 Ohio St. 3d 381, 383, 674 N.E.2d 681. Expert testimony in this case discredited respondents' approach to their foreclosure clients' cases. John Rose, an experienced bankruptcy attorney, explained a few of the adverse consequences that the tactics used by Foreclosure Solutions and respondents could have.

Rose first pointed out that stall tactics usually result in mounting arrearages for the debtor and increased legal fees for the creditor, lessening the debtor's chances of getting ahead financially and of reaching an agreement with the creditor. Moreover, delay in seeking bankruptcy relief may result in lost opportunities to obtain maximum relief. . . . [I]n keeping with Brooking-firm practice, Mullaney did not explore . . . any other legal remedy for the clients referred by Foreclosure Solutions. . . .

Mullaney, Brooking, and Moeves failed to evaluate their clients' situations and develop a strategy to meet their individualized needs, and instead stuck to Foreclosure Solutions' single strategy to obtain relief. By not investigating and evaluating each client's debts and assets and other potential resources in order to assess the opportunities presented by existing law, respondents were inadequately prepared to represent their clients and failed to seek the clients' lawful objectives. We therefore find that respondents violated DR 6-101(A)(2) and 7-101(A)(1). . . .

When imposing sanctions for attorney misconduct, we consider relevant factors, including the duties violated and sanctions imposed in similar cases. . . . Regarding similar cases, we find respondents' misconduct most analogous to that of attorneys sanctioned for providing legal services in affiliation with nonlawyers marketing living trusts and related products to consumers. . . .

Respondents engaged in a pattern of misconduct and committed multiple offenses. . . . The vulnerability of respondents' clients also weighs against these lawyers. . . . "Many, if not all, of the clients harmed by the respondents' misconduct were in desperate financial circumstances, about to lose their homes and vulnerable to purveyors of a scheme to save their homes and assets. Respondents' participation as lawyers lent an aspect of legitimacy to the sale of a plan of otherwise dubious value. . . .

A number of mitigating factors are also common to all respondents. None of the respondents has a prior disciplinary record . . . ; the Brooking firm stopped accepting Foreclosure Solutions clients shortly after relator filed the formal complaint, . . . and respondents cooperated with disciplinary authorities and established their good character and reputation apart from their misconduct. . . .

As a new attorney, Mullaney devoted many hours trying to assist the clients assigned to him; however, practices in place at the Brooking firm necessarily constrained his efforts. For his part in representing Foreclosure Solutions customers, a public reprimand is appropriate. Brooking, on the other hand, is a seasoned practitioner. . . . [A] one-year suspension of Brooking's license to practice, all stayed on the condition that he commit no further misconduct, is appropriate. Moeves is also a seasoned practitioner but is not admitted to the Ohio bar. Moeves entered into the agreement with Foreclosure Solutions and then put into place the practices that led to all the charges against him and the other respondents. For his integral role in this ill-advised undertaking, an injunction prohibiting his pro hac vice practice in this state for two years is appropriate. . . .

Questions about the Case

1. What were the individual ethics violations, and what facts support the court's findings for each violation?
2. What specific conduct by Foreclosure Solutions constituted the practice of law?
3. What kinds of services could this company have provided to help people in danger of losing their homes without violating the UPL rules?

4. Could this law firm have worked out an arrangement with a foreclosure consulting firm that would be acceptable under the ethics rules? What might this arrangement look like?
5. Also see *Cincinnati Bar Ass'n v. Foreclosure Solutions*, 123 Ohio St. 3d 107 (2009), in which the company and the individuals who established it were found to have violated unauthorized-practice-of-law rules, were enjoined from engaging in further unethical conduct, and were fined $50,000.

4
Confidentiality

This chapter covers confidentiality and the attorney-client privilege, which comprise one of the most fundamental elements of legal ethics. The principles of confidentiality and the privilege are explained and good practices to protect confidentiality are discussed. Chapter 4 covers:

- the foundations and basic principles of confidentiality
- the attorney-client privilege and the difference between the evidentiary privilege and the ethics rules on confidentiality
- information that is privileged or protected by the rule of confidentiality
- conditions under which the privilege and the duty of confidentiality may be broken or waived
- the work product rule
- applications of the principles and rules of confidentiality for paralegals
- methods to protect confidentiality of information and records
- special problems in maintaining confidentiality with technology

A. The Principle of Confidentiality

Confidentiality is one of the oldest and most honored precepts of legal ethics, one that is unquestioned in its importance. Issues relating to confidentiality and situations that jeopardize confidentiality face paralegals daily. Ethical dilemmas concerning confidentiality arise in all kinds of law practices from the smallest to the largest law firm, in corporate law settings, and in government.

The principle of confidentiality is based on the notion that a lawyer must know all the facts about a matter to best serve the client and that a client is not likely to provide full disclosure without assurance that incriminating and embarrassing information will not be revealed. The principle of confidentiality is also based on agency law. A lawyer has a fiduciary relationship with the client that requires the lawyer's highest trust, which includes confidence, loyalty, and good faith.

Attorney-client privilege
The rule of evidence that protects confidential communications between a lawyer and client made in the course of the professional relationship

The general duty of confidentiality encompasses both ethics rules and evidentiary rules relating to ***attorney-client privilege*** and **work product**. The attorney-client privilege is a rule of evidence that protects confidential information from being divulged in litigation by way of discovery or testimony. The ethics rules on confidentiality are much broader than the attorney-client privilege, and require a lawyer not to divulge virtually any information about a client in any context.

B. Attorney-Client Privilege

1. Defined Generally

All jurisdictions make provision for the attorney-client privilege by statute, court rule, or common law. The general rule is that a client who seeks a lawyer's advice or assistance may invoke an unqualified privilege not to testify and to prevent the lawyer from testifying as to communications made by the client in confidence to the lawyer. The client is the holder of the privilege; only the client may waive it, by consenting to the disclosure of confidential communications. And although the client is the holder of the privilege, the attorney must advise the client of the existence and protection of the privilege.

Case law and statutes have clarified the meaning of the attorney-client privilege: The privilege covers confidential communications between lawyer and client—whether oral or written—so long as the advice sought by the client is **legal**; other kinds of advice—personal or business, for instance—are not covered. **Initial consultations** are protected by the privilege even if the lawyer does not undertake representation, as are matters in which the lawyer does not charge a fee. The privilege does not cover material or information that is not classified as a communication, such as physical evidence. The privilege lasts indefinitely. It continues after the representation of the client ends. In most states, the privilege is considered to exist even after the death of the client; however, some states, like California, extinguish the privilege upon the final resolution of the client's estate. (See *HLC Properties, Ltd. v. Superior Court*, 35 Cal. 4th 54 (2005).) There are very limited reasons for which the privilege will be waived, as noted later.

2. How the Privilege Applies to Paralegals

One of the key aspects of the privilege for paralegals is that it covers communications made directly to or in the presence of the lawyer or the lawyer's agents, a category that includes colleagues and employees in the law firm who are working or may be working on the client matter. This principle extends to experts, investigators, vendors, and outside agencies working with counsel on a case. For example, the privilege covers contracted companies that provide services to lawyers, such as data processing or management firms that store confidential information.

Some state statutes on the privilege specifically extend its scope to employees of attorneys. Even without such statutory language, the privilege would be defeated were it not extended to persons who work with lawyers on clients' matters as members of the legal services delivery team. In an important case, the Arizona Court of Appeals confirmed this principle in unequivocal language:

> We hold that a lawyer does not forfeit the attorney-client privilege by receiving otherwise privileged client communications through the conduit of a properly supervised paralegal employee.

Samaritan Foundation v. Superior Court, 844 P.2d 593 (Ariz. App. Div. 1 1992) at 599. This case is excerpted at the end of this chapter.

After this decision was handed down in 1992, the Arizona attorney-client privilege statute was amended to include paralegals along with other named law office personnel, such as secretaries and clerks. The publicity surrounding the case caused a heightened awareness about paralegals being covered by the privilege. All state and federal courts that have addressed the issue since that time have held that the privilege extends to paralegals and other nonlawyer employees. For an example of an ethics opinion on the subject, see Michigan Opinion Number RI-123, which held that information collected by a paralegal in an interview with a prospective client is protected.

A patent case, *HPD Laboratories, Inc. v. Clorox Co.*, 202 F.R.D. 410 (2001), found at the end of this chapter, raises concerns about the application of the privilege to paralegals working in corporations. In that case, the internal memoranda prepared by an experienced paralegal who worked very autonomously were found not to be protected by the privilege. Paralegals must be cognizant that the privilege derives from the attorney-client relationship and does not exist independently from it.

Paralegals working with lawyers must be distinguished from nonlawyer legal service providers. Because the privilege applies only to the attorney-client relationship, it does not cover nonlawyer legal service providers, even those authorized by states to work as legal document assistants or preparers, or to jailhouse lawyers. Both these categories of nonlawyers conduct their work without lawyer involvement or supervision.

3. How the Protection of the Privilege Can Be Lost

Disclosure of confidential information to another person who is not essential to the representation may result in a court's finding that the information has lost the privilege. The client can waive the privilege by implication by repeating the communication to non-confidential third parties or otherwise by intentionally making the confidential information public. For example, if a client tells friends about otherwise protected communications, the privilege covering the information that is revealed may be lost. Likewise, if a lawyer or paralegal does not treat information as privileged, a court may find that it is not privileged.

Rules on whether disclosure to third persons results in the loss of the privilege vary from jurisdiction to jurisdiction and depend to a large extent on the status of the person to whom the information was revealed and the purpose of the disclosure. Generally if the disclosure is made for the purpose of furthering the representation, it will be protected.

Communications must be made in a **confidential setting** to merit the protection of the privilege. This means that the setting must be private—that is, one in which others cannot overhear—and there should not be any other persons present who would not otherwise be covered by the privilege. The presence of a colleague, family member, or friend of the client, for example, can negate the privilege. See *People v. Mitchell* later in this chapter for a case in which the setting is determinative of the privilege. Under contemporary rules, an eavesdropper who listens in on a confidential communication will not destroy the privilege unless of course the setting was such that the lawyer and client could expect the conversation to be overheard.

Some disclosures are specially protected and do not result in a waiver of the privilege. For example, information disclosed during plea bargaining or settlement negotiations cannot later be admitted at trial to prove guilt or liability.

An interesting issue concerning whether or not a waiver has taken place arises in the context of federal investigations and related civil lawsuits. During the last decade, the Department of Justice adopted a policy that it would consider the cooperation of a corporation in deciding whether or not to indict it on criminal charges, and in making this determination it considered whether the corporation had waived its privilege during the investigation and produced documents that would otherwise be privileged. The plaintiffs in a related action moved to compel production of the documents involved, but the court found that the privilege had not been waived because the disclosure had been coerced. *Regents of the Univ. of California v. Superior Court*, 165 Cal. App. 4th 672, 81 Cal. Rptr. 3d 186 (2008). Since this decision was rendered, the Department of Justice has revised its policy to prohibit forced disclosures.

4. Matters Not Covered by the Privilege

The privilege usually does not extend to the **identity of a client** or to **a client's whereabouts.** In one well-known case, *Baird v. Koerner*, 279 F.2d 623 (9th Cir. 1960), the court held the identity of a client to be privileged when the attorney sent a payment to the Internal Revenue Service anonymously on the client's behalf for underpayment of federal taxes. Because revealing the identity of the client could have led to conviction of a federal crime, the client's identity was protected. A few other cases have followed this reasoning, generally only when revealing the client's identity would lead to a criminal prosecution. Protection of confidential communications about a client's whereabouts is almost never extended. Usually in such cases, the client is a fugitive, so that the attorney's nondisclosure of the client's location would amount to assisting the client in committing a future crime.

The **fee arrangement** between a lawyer and client has historically not been privileged. Exceptions to this rule are triggered when details of the fee arrangement would reveal privileged information, such as the identity of a client when the identity itself is privileged. Government prosecutors, grand juries, and the Internal Revenue Service have subpoenaed information about fee agreements to identify and seize legal fees paid to attorneys with money or assets obtained through illegal activity, such as the drug trade and money laundering. Criminal defense attorneys often challenge the government on the basis of the privilege. They contend that fee arrangements and records as well as client names should be privileged and that the government's actions interfere with the right to counsel.

A client cannot bring a **preexisting document** within the protection of the privilege simply by giving it to his or her attorney. For example, in the Microsoft antitrust litigation, internal e-mails that had been copied to a lawyer were found not to be privileged and were ordered to be produced. If a preexisting document is covered by another privilege, such as the spousal privilege, it will continue to be privileged while in the attorney's possession.

Physical evidence of a client's crime is not protected by the privilege, and an attorney who comes into possession of such evidence is probably required under law to turn it over to the prosecutor. The attorney may or may not be compelled to testify about the source of the evidence, depending on the attorney's role in obtaining the evidence — if the lawyer obtained the evidence illegally, the court would be more inclined to force such testimony.

5. Inadvertent Disclosure of Privileged Information

In addition to actual client consent to waiver of the privilege and consent implied from the actions of the client, inadvertent disclosure might destroy the privilege. For example, if a protected document is accidentally given to opposing counsel in a document production, a dispute may arise over whether the privilege is lost. The cases across the country are not uniform; a few states consistently hold that such conduct constitutes a waiver of the privilege and the majority finds that inadvertent disclosure does not automatically constitute a waiver. Most cases hold that the disclosure is not tantamount to waiver so long as reasonable good-faith measures to prevent disclosure were made. Some courts also look at the extent of the disclosure, the timeliness of attempts to rectify it, and the issue of fairness. Most courts acknowledge that inadvertent disclosure by the attorney should not result in waiver of the privilege because the client is the holder of the privilege and would not actually or impliedly consent to the revealing of damaging protected information. Often counsel enter into agreements, called non-waiver or claw-back agreements, concerning the inadvertent disclosure of privileged information, whereby they agree in advance that they will not review and will return any obviously privileged documents that are disclosed by mistake during discovery.

In 2008 a new Federal Rule of Evidence was signed into law to protect against the loss of the privilege when documents are inadvertently produced during discovery. This section states in part:

> (b) INADVERTENT DISCLOSURE. When made in a Federal proceeding or to a Federal office or agency, the disclosure does not operate as a waiver in a Federal or State proceeding if:
>
> (1) the disclosure is inadvertent;
>
> (2) the holder of the privilege or protection took reasonable steps to prevent disclosure; and

(3) the holder promptly took reasonable steps to rectify the error, including (if applicable) following Federal Rule of Civil Procedure 26(b)(5)(B).

Federal Rule of Evidence Section 502.

Fed. R. Civ. P. 26(b)(5)(B) provides:

> If information produced in discovery is subject to a claim of privilege or of protection as trial-preparation material, the party making the claim may notify any party that received the information of the claim and the basis for it. After being notified, a party must promptly return, sequester, or destroy the specified information and any copies it has; must not use or disclose the information until the claim is resolved; must take reasonable steps to retrieve the information if the party disclosed it before being notified; and may promptly present the information to the court under seal for a determination of the claim. The producing party must preserve the information until the claim is resolved.

See *Victor Stanley, Inc. v. Creative Pipe, Inc.* at the end of this chapter for a court's analysis of whether the privilege was waived when otherwise protected documents were disclosed in a document production.

Receiving inadvertently disclosed privileged material creates ethical duties for the recipient. For more on this issue, see Section E.4.

6. Exceptions to the Privilege/ Permissive Disclosure

Privileged information may be disclosed by a lawyer when the client calls into question the attorney's **professional competence** through criminal charges, a malpractice suit, disciplinary action, or a contention of ineffective counsel on appeal from a criminal conviction.

When an attorney represents **two clients** who later become adversaries, otherwise privileged communications relating to the joint matter are not protected. However, pooled information shared by counsel who represent different clients with common interests generally is protected, although it may be used by the parties in later litigation in which the interests of the parties are adverse.

Also, confidential communications about a **future crime or fraud** a client is planning are not protected. The basis for this exception is that a lawyer's services should not be used to assist a client in committing a crime. (Note in the discussion of the ethical rules in Section D that the rules provide more protection for this kind of information than does the privilege.) Under the important crime-fraud exception, privileged communications can be disclosed if they were made in furtherance of a crime or fraud. What communications fall into this exception varies from jurisdiction to jurisdiction, but the trend seems to be toward more court-ordered disclosure for plaintiffs in civil lawsuits and prosecutors in criminal cases. For example, in the major tobacco litigation of the 1990s, the crime-fraud exception was used successfully in several cases to gain access to incriminating documents sent between the companies and their lawyers. See, for example, *Haines v. Liggett Group Inc.*, 975 F.2d 81 (3d Cir. 1992), and *American Tobacco Co. v. State of Florida*, 697 So. 2d 1249 (4th Fla. Dist. Ct. App. 1997).

7. The Privilege in the Corporate Setting

Special problems in applying the attorney-client privilege inhere in the representation of corporations. Who is the client and what communications are protected? Different jurisdictions use different tests to determine the application of the privilege. On one end of the spectrum is the ***control group test***, which limits the privilege to confidential communications between the attorney and the management personnel responsible for acting on behalf of the corporate entity in the legal matter at issue. The broader ***subject matter test***, now followed in most jurisdictions, was formulated in *Upjohn Co. v. United States*, 449 U.S. 383 (1981). The Supreme Court in that case extended the privilege to all corporate employees who communicate in confidence with the attorney for the purpose of enabling the attorney to render legal services to the corporation. Some states continue to follow the control group test in state litigation.

Control group test
Limits attorney-client privilege to confidential communications between the attorney and top management personnel

Subject matter test
Applies attorney-client privilege to all corporate employees who communicate in confidence with the attorney for the purpose of enabling the attorney to render legal services

Another issue that arises in corporate representation relates to the **holder of the privilege.** The corporation, not the employee, is the client and thus the holder of the privilege; only the corporation may waive it. The employee who communicates the information may object to the corporation's waiver of the privilege because the information implicates or embarrasses the employee, but the corporation is the client and the holder of the privilege. See, for example, *U.S. v. Martin*, 278 F.3d 988 (9th Cir. 2002), for a case where a lawyer who represented a corporation revealed information about the criminal activities of a corporate officer to a government agency.

Paralegals must take great care in discussing legal matters with employees of a corporate client. Employees often believe that the corporation's lawyers and paralegals represent their individual interests, which is not strictly true. The lawyer represents the interests of the corporation, which may or may not be aligned with those of the employee in any given case. In some situations, the corporation may waive the privilege to protect its own interests, with the result that the employee becomes the target of an investigation. See *U.S. v. Nicholas*, 606 F. Supp. 2d 1109 (C.D. Cal. 2009), at the end of Chapter 5 for a case in point.

Another issue that arises in the corporate setting is whether an **internal audit or investigation** conducted by a corporation's attorneys is protected under the attorney-client privilege. Whether a court will extend the protection of the privilege to such audits varies from state to state and depends to a large extent on how carefully the lawyers and their client constructed the audit to preserve the privilege.

Finally, the **Sarbanes-Oxley Act** (15 U.S.C. §7201) resulted in the adoption of Securities and Exchange Commission regulations concerning lawyers who practice securities law. The key provisions of this code require lawyers to report evidence of a material violation "up the ladder" to the chief legal counsel or chief executive officer; require reporting to the audit committee if no action is taken; and allow lawyers to reveal confidential information to prevent the corporation from committing a material violation that is likely to cause financial injury or to rectify such an action or to prevent an illegal action. Many lawyers and bar associations fought the adoption of these provisions as compromising the attorney-client privilege and setting up different ethics rules from those of the states in which they practice. The notion of the federal government having authority over the ethical responsibilities of lawyers is contrary to the basic principle that lawyers are governed by the courts, not the legislature.

8. Court-Ordered and Other Legal Disclosure

If protected communications are sought in a court proceeding, the attorney must respond to the court and **invoke the privilege**. If the court orders the lawyer to testify or to produce documents, he or she may do so or may refuse and appeal the ruling. Often, a court will order an ***in camera*** examination to determine whether to order disclosure in open court.

In camera
Proceedings held in the judge's chambers without the jury or public present

If an attorney breaks the privilege without client consent or court order, the client may seek to enjoin or suppress the attorney's testimony or seek dismissal of the case. And, of course, the client may sue the attorney for malpractice and file a complaint with the appropriate disciplinary authorities.

Finally, some states have statutes or cases that allow limited disclosure of confidential information for specific purposes, such as a challenge to the validity of a will. In such a case, the lawyer's notes of conversations with a deceased may be sought to prove or disprove the testator's capacity.

C. Work Product

Federal and state rules of evidence and discovery provide for the protection of materials prepared by lawyers in anticipation of litigation. This

Work product doctrine
Protects the work done by a lawyer and his or her employees and agents in the process of representing a client in litigation

work product doctrine was set forth in the 1947 case of *Hickman v. Taylor*, 329 U.S. 495, in which the Court created a qualified immunity from discovery for a lawyer's trial preparation so as to allow each side to prepare fully and in private. Under this case and subsequent cases and statutes, the work product rule encompasses two kinds of trial preparation material: informational material and mental impressions. **Mental impressions**, which are covered by an unqualified privilege, are the lawyer's ideas on how to conduct the case — that is, strategies and theories, including research. **Informational material**, which is protected by a qualified privilege, covers factual research such as witness statements.

When the opposition finds informational material critical to its case and does not have an effective substitute, it may ask the court to break the privilege and force the opposing counsel to disclose the material. The work product doctrine as enunciated in *Hickman* is codified in the Federal Rules of Civil Procedure and provides the model for most state rules as well.

Because only material prepared in **anticipation of litigation** is protected under the work product doctrine, some material, such as investigator's reports, prepared before there was a clear indication that a lawsuit would be filed, may be discoverable. This aspect of the rule creates special problems in litigation with insurance companies. Cases in this area vary widely, some lending protection whenever an insurance investigation is made, some only after an attorney becomes involved and orders the investigation or reports.

The life of the work product protection varies with the jurisdiction. Some states hold that the protection terminates with the litigation; others continue it indefinitely; still others terminate it with the end of the litigation except as to future related litigation.

The work product doctrine has special application in **electronic discovery**. Discovery of the opposition's electronic databases under the information prong of the rule is generally permitted if documents are input verbatim. However, paraphrased or summarized documents, selectively input documents, and documents sorted topically by means of an index of issues prepared by an attorney and staff generally are protected because such information relates to case preparation, usually representing both strategic and legal theories the lawyer is developing. See the *Bloss* case at the end of this chapter for an example of a dispute over an index.

Related is the matter of claiming the privilege for documents that the opposing party seeks in discovery. In cases with massive numbers of documents, lawyers can declare a **blanket privilege** for large categories of documents. Most judges will not allow this; a document-by-document basis for the privilege must be shown. When a paralegal prepares a **log of documents** that are claimed as privileged, the log should state the grounds for the privilege, for example, "Letter seeking advice re merger discussions," not simply "Letter re merger." Also, a log should indicate all the senders and recipients. If a document was sent to a number of persons who do not fall within the privilege, the court may find that it is not privileged.

As with the attorney-client privilege, work product protection can be waived by actual or implied consent of the client.

REVIEW QUESTIONS

1. What is the basis for the principle of confidentiality?
2. Define the attorney-client privilege. How does it differ from the ethics duty of confidentiality?
3. A client seeks advice from an attorney. Give three examples of advice that would be covered by the attorney-client privilege. Give three examples of advice that would not. What's the difference?
4. Are initial consultations covered by the privilege if the attorney does not undertake representation?
5. Are conversations that take place between nonlawyer employees and a client covered by the privilege? Under what circumstances?
6. Do privileged communications that are relayed to outside vendors hired by a lawyer retain the protection?
7. Does the privilege cover communications in cases in which the attorney does not charge a fee, such as pro bono matters?
8. Are conversations protected by the privilege if they take place in the reception areas? Lobby? Elevator? A restaurant? A cocktail party?
9. Is a nonlawyer who helps a friend prepare divorce papers covered by the privilege? What about a jailhouse lawyer? A legal document preparer/assistant, such as those in California and Arizona?
10. Name three ways in which a privilege may be destroyed.
11. Does the privilege cover information about a client's identity? A client's whereabouts? The fee arrangement made with the attorney?
12. When are a client's written papers protected by the privilege? When are they not?
13. What does an attorney do when a court requests disclosure of information that the attorney believes to be privileged?
14. What happens when privileged information is inadvertently disclosed to opposing counsel?
15. Name three general kinds of circumstances under which an attorney may disclose privileged information.
16. What complications in applying the privilege arise when an attorney's client is a corporation?
17. Define the work product doctrine. What is the reasoning behind this rule? What are the two kinds of information covered by the rule, and what kind of privilege attaches to each one?
18. Is the database in a computerized litigation support program protected as work product? Explain why or why not.

19. Does the privilege apply to a paralegal who works in a corporate setting? In what ways might the privilege be jeopardized in this setting?
20. Who is the holder of the privilege in the corporate setting? Who can waive the privilege?
21. In a federal court case in which privileged material is inadvertently disclosed in discovery, is the privilege waived? What factors might a court consider in deciding?
22. What does Sarbanes-Oxley require of lawyers who work in securities law?

DISCUSSION QUESTIONS AND HYPOTHETICALS

1. Do you think that the government should be able to access information about clients' identities and their fee arrangements with lawyers? If not, what principles and arguments do you have for your opinion? If so, what is the basis and rationale for your opinion?
2. You discover that opposing counsel has included clearly privileged documents in a document production. What would you do? What rule does your state follow in deciding whether an inadvertent disclosure results in a waiver of the privilege?
3. A distressed client comes running into your reception area and demands to see her lawyer. The lawyer is unavailable and you are the assigned paralegal. You greet the client and she begins to tell her story in a loud voice in front of other people waiting in the reception area. What should you do? What might happen if you allow the client to continue?
4. What kind of steps might you take in your office to protect against inadvertent disclosure of privileged information?
5. Why is the privilege not extended to nonlawyer legal service providers who may be assisting clients with legal matters? Is this a good policy?
6. A subpoena comes in seeking the following documents. Which are protected by the privilege?

   a. Notes of your meeting with a client.
   b. The database of documents that you have compiled in a case.
   c. The database of case law that you have compiled in a case.
   d. Notes of your meeting with a witness.
   e. Notes of your meeting with a witness who is no longer available.

7. What would you suggest if your supervising lawyer instructed you to have all the information on a litigated matter input verbatim in full text?

8. Jan is a litigation paralegal in a large full-service law firm. Many of the clients are wealthy individuals and corporations. One morning a client named Adam, who is a famous actor, comes into the office unannounced. His lawyer, John, is not in, but the receptionist asks Jan to talk to Adam in the reception area. When Jan sees Adam, she knows something is wrong: he is disheveled and wild-eyed. He immediately erupts in a loud whisper about someone dying the night before. He is incoherent, but Jan hears the words "argument" and "gun." What should Jan do? What if Jan cannot get Adam to stop, and he tells the whole story in the reception area? Is this information privileged? Why or why not? What if one of the paparazzi following Adam overhears the conversation with his ear to the door?

RESEARCH PROJECTS AND ASSIGNMENTS

1. Find the source of the attorney-client privilege in your state. Is it in the statutes? A case or series of cases? A court rule? How does it compare with the general definition of the privilege given in this chapter?
2. Are there any cases in your state relating to paralegals and the privilege? What do they say?
3. Find the rule for the work product doctrine in your state. How does it compare with the provision in the Federal Rules of Civil Procedure?
4. Courts have historically allowed the privilege to stand in situations in which a confidential communication is relayed to a lawyer by a nonlawyer such as an accountant (*United States v. Kovel*, 296 F.2d 918 (2d Cir. 1961)) or a lawyer's public relations firm (*In re Grand Jury Subpoenas*, 2003 U.S. Dist. LEXIS 9022, S.D.N.Y. (2003)). However, in another case, communications between the client's lawyer and an investment adviser about a client's prospective transaction were held not to be privileged (*United States v. Ackert*, 169 F.3d 136 (2d Cir. 1999)). Read and compare these cases. What conclusions can you draw?
5. There are many cases in which the government has tried to find the identity of a client, sometimes one who is seeking tax advice. Read some of these cases, starting with *United States v. BDO Seidman*, 225 F. Supp. 2d 918 (2002). Check for other cases on this issue and formulate a rule.
6. Read these cases about the protection of fee agreements between lawyers and clients and write a report that summarizes and compares the various rulings: *In re Grand Jury Subpoena for Attorney Representing Reyes-Requena*, 926 F.2d 1423 (5th Cir. 1991); *In re Grand Jury Matter*, 969 F.2d 995 (11th Cir. 1992); *U.S. v. Ellis*, 90 F.3d 447 (11th Cir.

1996); *U.S. v. Ritchie*, 15 F.3d 592 (6th Cir. 1994); *Whitehouse v. U.S. Dist. Ct.*, 53 F.3d 1349 (1st Cir. 1995); *United States v. Goldberger & Dubin*, 935 F.2d 501 (2d Cir. 1991).

7. Read *In re Grand Jury Subpoena Duces Tecum*, 112 F.3d 910 (8th Cir.), *cert. denied*, 521 U.S. 1005 (1997), in which the court held that the presence of White House lawyers during conversations between Hillary Clinton and her lawyers destroyed the privilege. Debate the merits of this decision.
8. Read *Swidler & Berlin v. United States*, 524 U.S. 399, 118 S. Ct. 2081 (1998), in which the Supreme Court held that the privilege survives the death of the client. In this case, Independent Counsel Kenneth Starr sought the notes of the lawyer for Vincent Foster, who committed suicide during the investigation into Whitewater and other matters relating to President Bill Clinton. On what grounds does the Court base its decision? Do you agree with the decision?
9. Does your state provide for permissive disclosure of privileged information in the case of a will contest? Under what other circumstances is disclosure permitted under your state law?
10. Legislation adopted to implement the federal government's "war on terrorism" has resulted in compromises to the privacy of all Americans. Some lawyers who are representing clients accused of terrorist activities have claimed that their phones are being tapped. Research federal laws on terrorism and find out if this kind of activity is legal under the statutes. If so, what procedures must be followed to engage in wiretapping? What do you think about this?
11. A lawyer is seeking to substitute himself for a party that got a default judgment against the lawyer's former client. Should this be allowed? How is the rule of confidentiality implicated? See *Styles v. Mumbert*, 164 Cal. App. 4th 1163, 79 Cal. Rptr. 3d 880 (2008).
12. Should e-mails among several lawyers in a law firm concerning the threat of a malpractice action by a client be protected by the privilege if the client later does sue for malpractice? See *Koen Boo Distributors v. Powell, Trachtman, et al.*, 212 F.R.D. 283 (E.D. Penn. 2002)
13. Can opposing counsel depose a certified paralegal who is also a nurse about her observation of an independent medical examination? Do her observations fall under the work product rule? If so, which prong? See *Black-Dienes v. Markey*, 40 Pa. D. & C.4th 571, 1999 Pa. D. & C. LEXIS 134 (1999).

D. Ethics Rules of Confidentiality

Broad protection for client confidentiality was included in the earliest codes governing attorney conduct and is included in the ethics rules in every state. In addition to requiring lawyers to protect client confidences, these rules also provide the most important components of the foundation for conflict of interest rules, discussed in Chapter 5.

Rule 1.6 of the ABA Model Rules of Professional Conduct contains a broad statement obligating the lawyer not to reveal "information relating to the representation of a client. . . ." The rule does not make a distinction between confidences and secrets, as did the former ABA Model Code. This language means that virtually all information is covered, regardless of when and how it was learned by the attorney. No private setting is required; the information need not have been communicated directly by the client; information learned before or after the representation is covered. Further, the client need not request confidentiality for the attorney to protect against disclosure.

Section (a) of Rule 1.6 provides for disclosure with the client's informed consent or if implied to carry out the representation. There are four exceptions allowing permissive (i.e., allowing but not requiring) disclosure under 1.6(b): (1) to prevent reasonably certain death or substantial bodily harm; (2) to prevent the client from committing a crime or fraud that is reasonably certain to result in substantial injury to the financial or property interests of another; (3) to prevent, mitigate, or rectify such injury; (4) to secure legal advice about the lawyer's compliance with ethics rules; (5) to establish an attorney's claim or defense in a dispute between the lawyer and client; and (6) to comply with a court order or law.

Not all states have adopted this version of the rule verbatim, and jurisdictions vary significantly in the way that they approach permissive disclosure related to crime, fraud, and other actions that may harm persons. More than half the states allow disclosure of confidential information to prevent any crime; a few mandate disclosure and a few prohibit disclosure. Some states allow disclosure only if the crime would likely result in death or substantial bodily harm. Some states permit disclosure to prevent a fraud that would result in substantial loss to a person.

Comment 16 to Rule 1.6 reiterates the principles of Rule 5.3 indicating that lawyers must act competently to safeguard confidential information against inadvertent or unauthorized disclosure by persons subject to the lawyer's supervision, which, of course, includes paralegals.

E. Paralegals and the Rules on Confidentiality

1. Application of the Rule to Paralegals

Virtually every state that has guidelines on paralegal utilization requires attorneys to ensure that paralegals preserve client confidences.

The ABA Model Guidelines for the Utilization of Paralegal Services (ABA Model Guidelines) cover confidentiality in Guideline 6. Most state guidelines speak in terms of the attorney "instructing" the paralegal to preserve client confidences or to "exercise care" to ensure that paralegals preserve client confidences. One state, Illinois, is more detailed in its statement, calling on the lawyer to ensure that the paralegal's work product "does not benefit the client's adversaries." Illinois State Bar Association Recommendations to Attorneys for the Use of Legal Assistants, Recommendation (A)(3) (1988). The Iowa guidelines remind attorneys that the confidentiality duty covers "casual disclosure (for example, by common gossip) as well as intentional misuse (for example, by such things as insider trading)." Ethical Guidelines for Legal Assistants in Iowa, V.A. (1988).

Finally, at least one state has issued an opinion endorsing the use of freelance paralegals' services so long as the supervising attorney exercises care to prevent disclosure or use of client confidences. Maryland Ethics Opinion 86-83 (1986). The ABA reached a similar conclusion about attorney supervision of freelance lawyers in its Formal Ethics Opinion 88-356 (1988).

NALA Model Guideline IV requires paralegals to preserve confidences and secrets, using the terminology of the ABA Model Code. Canon 7 of the NALA Code calls on paralegals to protect client confidentiality and to uphold the laws on the attorney-client privilege. NFPA Model Code Section 1.5 requires paralegals to "preserve all confidential information" and in several subsections details rules prohibiting paralegals from using confidential information to the client's disadvantage or advantage of the paralegal or a third person and warning against "indiscreet communications" about clients.

More than other nonlawyer employees in the law firm, paralegals have access to confidential information about clients. They are frequently included in client conferences in which privileged information is revealed, are privy to confidential written communications from and to clients, and are working on highly sensitive and private matters for clients.

2. Protecting Confidentiality in Daily Practice

Law firms need to have and follow well-established policies and procedures to prevent inadvertent disclosure of confidential information. Some firms include these in their written manuals, orientation programs, or training videos.

Policies should deny unauthorized personnel **access to files** and to the file room. **Code numbers** can be used on client files instead of names. Access to extremely sensitive confidential information should be limited to as few employees and vendors as possible.

Old files and papers (even scratch paper) concerning clients should be disposed of properly, preferably by shredding. Stories of carelessness in disposing of papers abound. One firm was horrified to learn that its confidential drafts of documents had been turned into scratch paper. In one case, the files of a lawyer with financial problems were about to be auctioned off with his other personal assets when another lawyer came to the rescue.

Computer screens should not be visible to those walking through the office. Conversations over the **intercom and speaker phone** should be limited to nonconfidential matters to prevent unauthorized personnel, clients, or others visiting the office from overhearing.

Privileged documents should be **labeled** as such when they are created to reduce the risk that they will not be handled carefully. Privileged documents should also be segregated from nonconfidential documents in **separate files** whenever possible. Procedures should limit who has access to any privileged documents.

The most common kind of disclosure of confidential information takes place in casual **conversation** about work outside the office. Like everyone else, lawyers and paralegals talk with friends and family about their work. Casual conversations concerning clients that are held with coworkers and people outside the firm are potentially serious breaches of ethics. Participants in these conversations may repeat what they learn to others and conversations may be overheard. Improper disclosures like this are not uncommon and rarely result in sanctions; however, the consequences—losing a client, having a court deny protection to the information, having opposing counsel learn confidential information through the grapevine, or having a client bring a malpractice suit or initiate a disciplinary complaint—are quite serious and should provide a major incentive to exercise great discretion when discussing client matters.

There are many commonsense practices that paralegals should live by to prevent disclosure. One set of practices centers on the importance of keeping communications between the client and the lawyer and staff sufficiently private to withstand a challenge under the attorney-client privilege by demonstrating that the communication was intended to be confidential. Lawyers and paralegals must not carry on a conversation in the **presence of persons** who are not necessary to the representation. Conversations with clients should take place in the privacy of a **closed office or conference room**, not the reception or secretarial area, lunchroom, hallway, elevator, or restaurant. Cell phones present special risks as many people talk in public places on cell phones even though their side of the conversation can be overheard. As noted later in the technology section, e-mail recipients should be carefully limited to those within the scope of the privilege and privilege statements should be included on all e-mails that pertain to protected information.

The presence of others during confidential discussions should be limited to those attorneys and nonlawyer employees who are working on the client's case. This automatically excludes such law firm employees as receptionists, file clerks, and mailroom personnel. Although these people are covered by the privilege, it is wise to limit the staff members who have confidential information to as few people as possible. Paralegals should not take calls from a client while meeting with another client because the client present might learn confidential information by hearing part of the conversation. Likewise, when seeing a client or anyone else from outside the firm, paralegals should not have any other clients' files or an active computer screen visible to the visitor.

The work product rule is the primary means of protecting information in databases, especially those used for litigation support. To ensure that a **database** is protected, lawyers must be involved in the design and planning of the database. Headnotes should include their legal theories, opinions, conclusions, and strategies. Clients, witnesses, and others should not have access to the database. Full-text databases are most likely to be found discoverable. To prevent this, only selected material should be included and headings or annotations to assist with searches should be developed cooperatively by attorneys and legal assistants. See *Bloss v. Ford Motor Co.* at the end of this chapter for an example of an index that was found to be discoverable.

Confidentiality agreement
An agreement entered into between a law firm and an employee or other agent in which the employee or agent agrees to keep client information confidential

Confidentiality agreements are another means to guard against disclosure of protected information. A confidentiality agreement should require the signer not to disclose and to prevent any disclosure of confidential information. It should require the signer to return all documents acquired or developed during the course of work and admonish the signer not to remove any documents from the workplace. Such agreements should be signed by all employees, independent contractors, vendors, and outside agencies with access to privileged information.

Finally, steps should be taken to prevent anyone in the law firm from using confidential information **for their own gain**. For example, if a paralegal learns that a real estate development being handled by a firm will result in dramatic increases in property values in the surrounding areas, she or he may not misuse this information to buy property. Similarly, using confidential information to benefit on the stock market is forbidden by insider trading rules. In addition to the individual's liability under securities law, the firm is also liable. Fines may be levied against a law firm whose employee uses confidential or inside information to engage in unlawful securities transactions if the firm did not exercise appropriate supervision to prevent the unlawful trading.

In one case, a paralegal at a prominent New York law firm turned in a lawyer from another firm who tried to bribe her to obtain inside information on mergers and acquisitions that the firm was working on. In another, a stock trader who learned about a big merger from a friend who was a second-year associate at a San Francisco law firm reaped more than

$40,000 in profits before he pleaded guilty to felony charges. In another recent case, a summer intern and paralegal at a large New York plaintiff's firm was arrested when he stole the firm's 400-page trial plan in a large asbestos case and tried to sell the plan to the defendants' lawyers for $2 million.

3. Special Issues Relating to Technology

The use of technology has changed the practice of law dramatically in the past 30 years and has created new challenges related to the protection of confidential client information. Electronic records are more portable and accessible than paper; are easier to retrieve, copy, and transmit; are easier to alter and intercept; and are more difficult to delete. Firms must take special security measures to preserve confidentiality and to protect against potential claims that the privilege has been waived because communications were not treated as private and confidential.

Most firms no longer use freestanding **fax** machines because the fax function is built into an integrated technology system. However, faxing documents still poses risks. When faxing confidential material, steps should be taken to ensure that the client is on the receiving end and to guard against third parties who are not covered by the privilege of having access to the communication, which could give rise to a claim that the communication was not treated as privileged. An appropriate notice of the privileged or confidential nature of the material should accompany the transmission and the word *confidential* or *privileged* should appear on every page.

Calls made on some **cellular and cordless telephones** can be intercepted by special scanners, making them less secure for sensitive conversations than ordinary land-based telephone lines. Under the Federal Electronic Communications Privacy Act and state statutes, an interception of any kind of communication made through these media does not destroy the privilege if the communication is otherwise protected by the attorney-client privilege. Despite these statutes, caution must be exercised when using cordless and some cellular telephones for privileged communications. Remember that a breach of the duty of confidentiality can take place even if the privilege is not lost.

Some state and local bar associations have issued opinions recommending that lawyers not use such telephones for confidential communications because of the risk of interception and the lowered expectation of privacy. Many of these opinions were rendered before the current technology developed. Now risk of interception on most cell phones is slim; however, it is still good practice to be especially careful about sensitive conversations on cell phones. It is wise for lawyers to inform clients of the risks involved and to obtain their consent to use this means of communication to discuss confidential matters. The safest practice is obviously to limit the conversations on such phones and to communicate about especially sensitive privileged matters only on a secure land-based phone.

Special protections must be in place to ensure that privileged material stored electronically is not vulnerable. Physical security of computers and network servers is essential. Servers should be in a secure, locked room and should be secured to the furniture or floor. New concerns about security relate to the increased use of "cloud computing," where data is stored by vendors at remote locations, resulting in multiple copies of the data, sometimes in multiple locations.

Passwords should be carefully chosen so that they are not obvious (i.e., do not use initials, birthdates, and the like) and are regularly changed. Passwords should not be written down and left in an accessible place and employees should be admonished not to reveal their passwords to anyone except their supervisor. Users should log out when they leave their offices for any period of time. Some firms use **electronic identification cards** ("smart cards") in conjunction with passwords. Some firms restrict what passwords can log on at remote locations. A list of who logged on and when should be maintained.

Security systems, **antivirus software**, and regular **backups** should be in place. Disks and backup tapes should be kept in secure locations. Special software must be used to **delete material;** otherwise it may be subject to retrieval. The number of persons serving as network administrators should be small, and these persons should be especially screened and trained; policies that prohibit their access to materials except to service the network should be adopted. **Laptop** computers and smart phones should require passwords and protective software so that if they are stolen confidential information and the firm network cannot be accessed.

Electronic mail communications are protected by federal and state statutes, in the same way that telephone conversations are. In other words, if a communication is privileged, it does not lose the privilege simply by being made through e-mail. In the early days of e-mail, some state bars issued advisory opinions warning lawyers not to communicate by e-mail with clients. Many people did not trust the technology and believed that e-mail was not secure and did not meet their duty to protect confidentiality. However, in 1999, the ABA issued an advisory opinion that endorsed the use of unencrypted e-mail "because the mode of transmission affords a reasonable expectation of privacy from a technological and legal standpoint." This opinion recommends that lawyers consult with clients about transmitting highly sensitive information by e-mail and warns lawyers to follow their clients' instructions about the appropriate method of transmission (ABA Formal Opinion 99-413). This opinion effectively put an end to the debate about the ethics of e-mailing with clients.

To guard against inadvertent disclosure of confidential information and to meet the duty of confidentiality, firms must take steps to ensure security of these communications. Many firms have **firewalls** and **closed**

networks with key clients, which make messages less vulnerable to interception. Some use **encryption** software that encodes messages at the sending end so that they can be opened at the receiving end only with a matched decoding program. Some companies offer **digital courier** service that provides secure document delivery services.

Firms should take special steps when sending documents electronically to opposing counsel. Embedded **metadata** can be tracked so that earlier drafts of documents can be accessed, including the names and dates of revisions and comments that may have been included on earlier drafts. An ABA opinion (Ethics Opinion 06-442) recommends that electronic documents be scrubbed or sent by a method that ensures that metadata cannot be revealed, such as scanning the document to create a PDF. Importantly, this opinion indicates that metadata can be used by the recipient. See more on this later under the discussion of inadvertent disclosure.

Finally, programs are available to **track e-mail** that is forwarded to others. For example, opposing counsel who sends an e-mail can see what happens to the e-mail after it is received, for example, if it is forwarded to the client or someone else, including the cover e-mail that accompanies it. Good practice thus dictates that such e-mails not be directly forwarded but be transferred in other ways.

Firms need good procedures and practices to protect the confidentiality and privileged status of e-mail communications. Paralegals should follow these practices:

- Do not use e-mail for highly sensitive communications with clients.
- Inform clients about the risks involved in electronic communications and obtain their written consent to use electronic mail.
- Label all confidential communications as privileged and include a statement telling the reader what to do if the communication is inadvertently sent to the wrong person (i.e., not to read it and to contact the sender).
- Limit the recipients of a privileged e-mail to those who are absolutely essential to the privileged communication and warn recipients not to send such communications on to other persons.
- Do not send e-mail to a client mailbox that can be accessed by persons not covered by the privilege.
- Do not send documents that have been drafted electronically to opposing counsel without "scrubbing" them through software or the creation of a PDF.
- Do not forward e-mails directly if they are received from opposing counsel or others outside the individuals covered by the privilege.
- Be especially careful about "replying to all" when responding to e-mail; check to be sure that all of the recipients are covered by the privilege.
- Beware of misdirecting an e-mail when you use the "auto-fill" function, which automatically fills in the e-mail address once you type in the first few letters.

In addition, firms should have internal policies that employees are informed of and agree to in writing. Policies should:

- prohibit employees from misusing e-mail to send personal, sexually explicit, or harassing material
- prohibit accessing another person's e-mail
- stress the importance of sending confidential material only to those who need to have it
- remind employees not to leave their e-mail access open and unattended or to share their passwords
- establish procedures for sending and storing privileged material
- establish the rights of the employer and employee regarding e-mail, including when the employer has the right to review an employee's e-mail messages

Finally, the dramatic increase in the use of various forms of electronic social networking has created new risks to client confidentiality. The widespread use of Facebook, MySpace, Twitter, and blogs poses serious threats to the privilege and has implications in other areas of ethics as well. A few examples illustrate some of the potential problems. An experienced public defender in Illinois was terminated recently when she was found to have described clients in her blog in a way that allowed their identification, through her use of first names or derivatives of first names or jail identification numbers. She revealed, among other things, that clients had lied to the court. Another lawyer was sanctioned by a court after posts on Facebook that showed him partying when he was supposed to be at a family funeral. Lawsuits have been brought against lawyers and others who are alleged to have defamed lawyers or criticized judges in their blogs or on their social networks. Other risks relate to client conduct, such as clients claiming to have injuries who post photos or videos of themselves engaging in activities that would not be possible if their claims were true. Finally, the police and prosecutors routinely search YouTube and other sites for evidence of crimes (e.g., videos of riots and illegal auto racing). Sound firm-wide policies regarding social networking and blogs are a must.

4. More on Inadvertent Disclosure

Lawyers and paralegals have a duty to guard against inadvertent disclosure of confidential information to unintended recipients. Under ABA Model Rule 1.6, comment 17 indicates that lawyers do not need to take special security precautions if the method of transmission affords a reasonable expectation of privacy, but warns lawyers to consider several factors, including the sensitivity of the information and the extent to which its privileged status might be protected by the law or an agreement.

Unfortunately, incidents of inadvertent disclosure are not uncommon. Large-scale discovery, the discovery of electronically stored information, the extensive use of e-mail, and the spread of e-discovery all contribute to the ease with which information can be disclosed in error.

Examples of inadvertent disclosure are everywhere in the legal media and cases. For example, a lawyer in a large law firm accidentally released sealed documents to a magazine; another firm inadvertently placed sealed records in an appellate file to find them later published in a magazine; a staff member accidentally sent a long, detailed memorandum outlining legal strategy to the plaintiff's lawyer; and a lawyer accidentally handed over to opposing counsel a memorandum from a paralegal to witnesses in a case when the memo was stuck to another document with a paper clip. A trial judge in a Baltimore dismissed a panel of prospective jurors in a major asbestos case when a staffer working for a defense firm inadvertently faxed a privileged document on jury selection strategy to the plaintiff's firm. Recently a lawyer in a prominent firm accidentally released a confidential internal memo about opposing counsel to more than a dozen reporters. Another common error is sending confidential information by mistake to a listserv. In more than a few cases, a lawyer has hit the wrong e-mail address in his or her mailbox and sent a confidential client communication to hundreds of people.

Paralegals often have extensive responsibility for discovery, including responding to subpoenas duces tecum and handling **document productions**. When thousands of pages of documents are requested by opposing counsel, the paralegal is usually the one to review, organize, and examine these documents, to prepare privileges logs, and to see that the documents are purged of privileged material before they are copied and provided to the opposing counsel. In addition to needing guidance from the supervising attorney as to what documents to look for, the paralegal needs a clear understanding of the privilege so that he or she can flag documents that may be protected and bring them to the attorney's attention. Increasingly important are the methods by which electronically stored documents are screened for removal before a document production. See *Victor Stanley, Inc. v. Creative Pipe, Inc.* at the end of this chapter for a case in which the lawyers' actions resulted in waiver of the privilege because of their failure to conduct an adequate review of electronically stored information.

In addition to the ethical breach involved in inadvertently disclosing documents, paralegals need to know how to meet ethical obligations when they come into possession of privileged documents through the error of the opposition. The ABA Model Rules were amended in 2002 to address this issue. Model Rule 4.4(b) states that a lawyer who receives a document that was inadvertently sent should promptly notify the sender. This rule stops far short of the ABA ethics opinions that had been issued earlier; with the adoption of this rule, these opinions were withdrawn.

ABA Formal Ethics Opinions 92-368 and 94-382, superseded by Ethics Opinion 06-440, stated that the lawyer who receives privileged material should:

> 1. upon recognizing the privileged or confidential nature of the materials,
>   a. either refrain from reviewing such materials or
>   b. review them only to the extent required to determine how appropriately to proceed . . .
> 2. notify her adversary's lawyer that she has such materials and . . .
> 3. either
>   a. follow instructions of the adversary's lawyer with respect to the disposition of the materials, or
>   b. refrain from using the materials until a definitive resolution of the proper disposition of the materials is obtained from a court.

Although these opinions have been withdrawn, several cases still in force cite them and several states have adopted similar opinions that have not been withdrawn. Courts have held that lawyers are obligated not to examine such materials and either to return them to the lawyer who disclosed them or to go to court for a resolution. See, for example, *Rico v. Mitsubishi Motors Corp.* at the end of this chapter. This opinion endorses the earlier appellate court case of *State Compensation Insurance Fund v. Telanoff*, 70 Cal. App. 4th 644, 82 Cal. Rptr. 2d 799 (1999), which follows the reasoning of the earlier ABA Formal Opinions. Similarly, some ethics opinions warn against exploiting unsolicited breaches of confidentiality. New York State Bar Ass'n Comm. on Professional Ethics, Op. 98-700. Finally, as noted above, state and federal rules on discovery may protect against waiver of the privilege and allow a claim of privilege to be made after inadvertent production of a privileged document in discovery (see Federal Rule of Evidence 502(B) and Federal Rule of Civil Procedure 26(b)(5)).

The disclosure of privileged information by sending out documents with embedded **metadata** is an unsettled area of legal ethics. As noted above, ABA Formal Ethics Opinion 06-442 indicates that the sending lawyer has a duty to prevent such disclosure, but it does not provide definitive guidance on whether the receiving lawyer is required to give notice to opposing counsel, as would be required in other kinds of inadvertent disclosures under Model Rule 4.4(b). The opinion does indicate that the recipient is not prohibited from examining and using the embedded information. Other bar association ethics opinions differ considerably. See Alabama Bar Association Ethics Opinion 07-02, which prohibits use of the metadata; Florida Bar Ethics Opinion 06-02; Arizona Bar Ethics Opinion 07-03, which prohibits examination of the metadata and advises the recipient to notify the sender; Colorado Bar Ethics Opinion 08-119; District of Columbia Ethics Opinion 2007-341; Maine

Ethics Opinion 08-196; Maryland Ethics Opinion 07-09, which aligns with the ABA opinion allowing examination and use of the metadata; New Hampshire Bar Ethics Opinion 08-09/4, advising lawyers not to search for metadata; New York City Bar Ass'n Ethics Opinion 08-738; New York Ethics Opinion 01-749, which advises against mining for metadata; Pennsylvania Bar Ethics Opinion 07-500; and Vermont Bar Ethics Opinion 2009-01, which indicates that searching for data is acceptable but notification upon finding it is required.

Paralegals are often the first ones to discover that a document has been inadvertently disclosed. The safest approach for the paralegal is to refrain from examining the documents and to communicate the situation to the supervising attorney to handle.

REVIEW QUESTIONS

1. Under what circumstances may an attorney reveal protected information pursuant to the ethics rules?
2. What are a lawyer's responsibilities in preventing the disclosure of confidential information by his or her employees?
3. What do the state guidelines on paralegal utilization say about the paralegal's role in client confidentiality? What do the ABA Guidelines for the Utilization of Paralegal Services say? What about the paralegal associations' rules? Are these sources in accord?
4. Name ten procedures or policies that would help a firm prevent disclosure of confidential information.
5. How can inadvertent disclosure of confidential information be avoided? What should you do if you receive privileged information in error?
6. What procedures and practices should be in place to guard against disclosures of confidential information via faxes, cellular phones, and computer databases?
7. What are the risks of disclosure through e-mail communications? How should these communications be protected?
8. What are confidentiality agreements? Who should use them? What provisions should they contain?
9. What is metadata? How might it reveal privileged client information? What are a lawyer's or paralegal's duties concerning metadata? What are the duties if one receives a document with metadata in it? Can the paralegal look for metadata? Use it? Does the lawyer have to notify the sender?
10. What is "misuse" of confidential information? Give examples of how confidential information can be misused. What might be the ramifications of such misuse?
11. What conduct should lawyers and paralegals be wary of when blogging or posting to social networks?

DISCUSSION QUESTIONS AND HYPOTHETICALS

1. What would you do as a paralegal if an attorney at your firm introduced you during a social event to a client, who then proceeded to tell you the whole sordid story that led to his being represented by the firm?
2. What would you do if while attending a local paralegal association meeting you overheard a group of paralegals talking about a case on which you worked for opposing counsel? Would your answer be any different if you weren't working on the opposite side of the case?
3. What would you do if you overheard a paralegal in your firm discussing confidential information about a client with a person in another firm? Would your answer be different if an attorney were doing the talking?
4. You happen to know that on Tuesdays and Fridays the file room personnel always have their friends eat lunch with them in the file room. What should you do? Would your answer be different if the friends were employees of another firm?
5. What would you do if you caught a client going through other clients' files on your desk while you were momentarily out of the room?
6. What should you do with handwritten notes of a confidential conversation once they have been typed up and put into a client's file?
7. What would you do if you were assigned to respond to a document production but knew nothing about the case?
8. Lawyers from opposing firms were on a conference call. Lawyers from the ABC firm hung up and lawyers from the XYZ firm remained on the line talking. The call was recorded through an automatic conference call system and the ABC lawyers got a recording of the conversation. Can they listen to it? What should they do about it? What if the conversation reveals that the ABC lawyers were planning something fraudulent with their client? For one court's opinion, see *Jasmine Networks, Inc. v. Marvell Semiconductors, Inc.*, 117 Cal. App. 4th 794, 12 Cal. Rptr. 3d 13 (2004).
9. A law firm finds a document produced by opposing counsel that is marked privileged but is not privileged. Should the privilege attach to the document? What should the recipient do about this? See *In re Asousa Partnership*, 202 F.R.D. 410 (Bankr. E.D. Pa. 2005) for one court's opinion.

RESEARCH PROJECTS AND ASSIGNMENTS

1. Find the ethics rule of confidentiality in your state. Does it vary from the ABA model? How? Which do you think is the best formulation of the rule?

2. Does your state mention confidentiality in its guidelines for paralegals? In any ethics opinions?
3. Contact five local law firms and find out what written policies they have to protect the confidentiality of information. Be sure to ask about confidentiality agreements and protections for e-mail and metadata.
4. Research the kinds of electronic software available to protect the confidentiality and security of documents and e-mail, including software used for encryption, deletion, couriers, scrubbing of documents, and prevention of e-mail tracking. Evaluate the value of these in protecting client confidentiality.
5. Have any cases on inadvertent disclosure been decided in your jurisdiction? What about ethics opinions issued by the bar? What are the rules in your jurisdiction about waiver and about receipt of inadvertently disclosed information?
6. Does your jurisdiction have an opinion about metadata? What do you think the rules on metadata should be? Should recipients be permitted to mine these data? Use them in discovery? Should the recipient be required to notify the sender upon receiving metadata?
7. Research the policies of law firms concerning social networking sites and blogs. You may want to contact some large law firms to see if they have policies, and/or research model policies available through state or local bars or included in legal ethics publications. Draft a model policy.
8. In Chapter 3 you read about lawyers entering into relationships with nonlawyer service companies that prepared living trusts and sold insurance policies to "clients" to fund the trusts. Read the case of *In re Phillips*, 338 Or. 125, 107 P.3d 615 (2005), to see how this scenario results in a breach of client confidentiality.
9. Can a lawyer or paralegal use privileged information that has been obtained illegally and then passed on by someone else? To start your research, see Florida Bar Ethics Opinion 07-01 and District of Columbia Bar Ethics Opinion 02-318.
10. If a paralegal sues her employer, can she take any or all of the e-mails and other documents that relate to her employment? See *Bedwell v. Fish & Richardson P.C.*, Case No. 07-CV-0065-WQH (S.D. Cal. 12-3-2007).
11. Assuming that the attorney-client privilege and work product rule apply to paralegals, under what circumstances might a court allow a paralegal to be deposed? See *Wal-Mart Stores, Inc. v. Dickinson*, 29 S.W.3d 796 (2000).
12. For an example of how the California courts apply the work product rule to witness statements, see *Coito v. Superior Court*, 182 Cal. App. 4th 758, 106 Cal. Rptr. 3d 342 (2010). In this wrongful death action, the plaintiff sought statements of four juveniles who were interviewed by state investigators after the drowning that led to the action.

13. For a high-profile case on waiver of the privilege, see *U.S. v. Stewart*, 03 Cr. 717 (MGC) (S.D.N.Y. 2003). This decision involves the prosecution of Martha Stewart for securities law violations. Ms. Stewart had forwarded to her daughter an otherwise privileged e-mail that she had sent to her lawyer. The court had to decide if the e-mail was privileged.

CASES FOR ANALYSIS

In the following case, statements that would otherwise have been protected by the attorney-client privilege were held to be admissible because of the setting in which they were made and the persons present. As you read, think about what you would have done as the paralegal.

People v. Mitchell

86 A.D.2d 976, 448 N.Y.S.2d 332 (1982)

Defendant appeals from his conviction for murder, second degree. The autopsy of the victim's body revealed 11 stab wounds on the face, chest, and back, four of which penetrated the aortic arch, liver, and heart. While the charge to the jury that "a person is presumed to intend the natural and probable consequences of his act, and, accordingly, if the consequences are natural and probable, he will not be heard to say that he did not intend them" was an error, we find the error to have been harmless. The evidence of defendant's guilt was overwhelming, and the question of intent was not a "vital issue at trial."

There was no error in the court's finding admissible the testimony of two secretaries and a paralegal concerning statements made by defendant to them in the common waiting room shared by defendant's attorney with another lawyer. Defendant made the statements while his attorney was away from his office and before defendant had had an opportunity to consult with him on this matter. Under the circumstances, defendant could not reasonably have expected that the communication would be confidential nor could the communication have been for the purposes of securing legal advice or assistance. We have considered defendant's other arguments and find them to be without merit.

Judgment affirmed.

All concur, except CALLAHAN, J., who dissents and votes to reverse and grant a new trial in the following Memorandum:

I view existing precedent to mandate reversal and a new trial. . . .

Furthermore, I disagree with the majority that there was no error in the trial court's ruling with respect to the admission of certain statements made by defendant to personnel in the waiting room of his attorney's office.

The record reveals that defendant telephoned the office of an attorney who was representing him on another pending charge and went to the office at their request. The trial court erroneously concluded that the attorney-client relationship did not exist until defendant's attorney arrived at his office. Contrary to the majority's view, it appears to be clear that defendant had gone to the attorney's office for the purpose of securing legal advice or assistance. Since the attorney-client privilege applies to "a confidential communication made between the attorney or *his employee* and the client in the course of professional employment" (CPLR 4503, subd. [a], emphasis added), I would remit for a further in camera hearing to determine (1) whether the two secretaries and a paralegal were, in fact, "employees" of defendant's attorney and (2) whether such statements were made in the "presence of strangers" (there being unsubstantiated claims that an unnamed third party was present) which would take the statements outside the privilege. Although the burden of proving each element of the claimed privilege rests upon the defendant, the trial court's erroneous ruling precluded defendant from offering proof to support his claim of privilege.

Questions about the Case

1. Where did the defendant make the statements in question? Who was present?
2. What is the basis for the court's decision that the statements were admissible? Do you agree or disagree? Why?
3. What does the dissenting justice say? Do you find his reasoning convincing?
4. What would you do if you were the paralegal in such a law office, and a client came in and began telling his whole "story" to you and the staff in the reception area?

This well-known case clearly confirms the extension of the attorney-client privilege to paralegals who work on litigated matters. It should be noted that this Court of Appeals opinion was vacated in part on other grounds in *Samaritan Foundation v. Goodfarb*, 862 P.2d 870 (Ariz. 1993).

Samaritan Foundation v. Superior Court

844 P.2d 593, 173 Ariz. 426 (App. 1992)

In February of 1988, a child suffered a cardiac arrest in surgery and emerged revived but neurologically impaired. This special action arises from discovery disputes in the medical malpractice suit brought by the child and her parents against the hospital and two physicians.

Shortly after surgery, at the direction of the hospital's legal department, a nurse paralegal interviewed four operating room witnesses. The witnesses now claim at depositions to recall little or nothing of the event. Though the paralegal's summaries might refresh the witnesses' recollection, the hospital declines to provide these summaries to the witnesses or release them to plaintiffs' counsel.

Plaintiffs (real parties in interest) moved to compel disclosure. The hospital and its fellow petitioners responded that the summaries are absolutely protected by the attorney-client privilege and immune from discovery under the work product doctrine. The trial court ordered the summaries to be produced for inspection *in camera*, found only portions to be privileged, and ordered the remainder — "the functional equivalent of a witness statement" — disclosed. . . .

Petitioners and amici argue that, even if work product immunity might yield to plaintiffs evidentiary needs, the attorney-client privilege absolutely bars disclosure of communications by Samaritan or PCH employees to a member of Samaritan's legal staff. This argument poses several subordinate issues:

> (1) Does the attorney-client privilege apply when, as here, the conduit of communications is a paralegal? . . .

Arizona's attorney-client privilege statute provides that

> an attorney shall not, without the consent of his client, be examined as to any communication made by the client to him, or his advice given thereon in the course of professional employment. An attorney's *secretary, stenographer or clerk* shall not, without the consent of his employer, be examined concerning any fact the knowledge of which was acquired in such capacity.

Ariz. Rev. Stat. Ann. ("A.R.S.") §12-2234 (1982) [emphasis added]. Paralegals are not mentioned in the statute.

Plaintiffs argue that paralegals are an omitted and, therefore, unprotected conduit for attorney-client communications. See *Church of Jesus Christ*, 159 Ariz. at 29, 764 P.2d at 764 ("Privilege statutes, which impede the truth-finding function of the courts, are restrictively interpreted."). Although we accept the precept of restrictive construction and will have more to say about it later in this opinion, we find plaintiffs' construction too restrictive in this instance.

. . . [O]ur legislature recognized that lawyers often communicate with clients through agents. . . . We believe that the legislature intended by reference to "secretary, stenographer or clerk" to list a representative, not exclusive, group of agents through whom a lawyer and client might confidentially confer.

The law has recognized in other contexts that an attorney may properly and efficiently act through a paralegal. This Court, for example, has found paralegal services compensable in attorneys' fee awards, reasoning that lawyers should not devote time to tasks more economically assigned to legal assistants, "solely to permit that time to be compensable [in a fee award]." *Continental Townhouses East Unit One Ass'n v. Brockbank*, 152 Ariz. 537, 544, 733 P.2d 1120, 1127 (App. 1986); accord *Missouri v. Jenkins*, 491 U.S. 274, 288 & n.10, 109 S. Ct. 2463, 2471 & n.10, 105 L. Ed. 2d 229 (1989). Similarly, lawyers should not retain information-gathering tasks more efficiently delegated to paralegals, solely to protect the client's privilege. We hold that a lawyer does not forfeit the attorney-client privilege by receiving otherwise privileged client communications through the conduit of a properly supervised paralegal employee.[8]

We caution that this holding does not create an automatic "paralegal-client privilege." There may be circumstances in which a nominal paralegal serves an investigative function independent of the attorney-client relationship. . . . Such circumstances, however, are not established here. Ms. Fraiz was an employee of Samaritan's Legal Department, acting solely at its direction, in anticipation of litigation against PCH. Her paralegal status did not strip the communications she received of whatever attorney-client privilege might otherwise attach. . . .

Although the interview summaries are protected by both the work product doctrine and by a qualified attorney-client privilege, plaintiffs have made the requisite showing that their need for disclosure outweighs the corporation's interest in confidentiality. Because the trial court did not abuse its discretion in ordering limited disclosure, the relief that petitioners have requested is denied.

Questions about the Case

1. Why are the plaintiffs seeking the nurse-paralegal's interview summaries?
2. Does the Arizona attorney-client privilege statute cover paralegals?
3. What are the arguments for and against paralegals being covered by the privilege?
4. What does footnote 8 in the case remind us about?
5. Did the court provide full protection for the paralegal interview summaries? What did the court protect and not protect, and why?

8. An attorney is ethically responsible for the conduct of a nonlawyer employed by, retained by, or associated with the lawyer. 17A A.R.S. Sup. Ct. Rules, Rules of Professional Conduct, Rule 42, ER 5.3 (1988). The Rules of Professional Conduct require the lawyer with direct supervisory control over the nonlawyer to "make reasonable efforts to ensure that the [nonlawyer's] conduct is compatible with the professional obligations of the lawyer." *Id.* Those obligations include client confidentiality. *Id.* ER 5.3 cmt.

This next case involves the application of the attorney-client privilege to a paralegal who works in the legal department of a corporation. As an experienced and highly specialized paralegal, she functions very autonomously. The court must decide if the nature of her work takes her communications with other employees out of the attorney-client privilege.

HPD Laboratories, Inc. v. Clorox Co.

202 F.R.D. 410 (2001)

This discovery dispute presents an interesting question about the scope of the attorney-client privilege. Plaintiff, HPD Laboratories, Inc. ("HPD"), seeks to compel defendant, The Clorox Company ("Clorox") to turn over documents that contain statements to and from Karen Peeff ("Ms. Peeff"), a longtime paralegal in Clorox's in-house legal department. Clorox objects and contends that the documents are covered by the attorney-client privilege, as defined by California law. HPD disagrees and reasons that, under federal law, the attorney-client privilege does not encompass Ms. Peeff's communications because she acted independently rather than in conjunction with or at the discretion of an attorney. . . .

To facilitate its operations, Clorox maintains an in-house legal team. Karen Peeff has been a part of the team since 1985. She currently serves as a "legal specialist" for advertising and regulatory matters. Her duties include (1) reviewing prospective product labels, packages, and advertisements; (2) assessing whether those items comply with apposite state and federal statutes and regulations; and (3) advising Clorox's marketing department on compliance issues. Ms. Peeff's immediate supervisor is Patrick Meehan, an attorney. Notably, Ms. Peeff admits that she does not regularly consult with her supervisor, or other in-house counsel, prior to dispensing advice. . . .

HPD filed this suit. . . . It accused Clorox of . . . infringing the 330 Patent by selling Bleach & Blue . . . ; falsely advertising Rain Clean . . . ; committing unfair competition . . . and tortious interference with business relations. . . . Discovery ensued. . . .

Ms. Peeff is an important source of information at Clorox, no doubt due to her longevity and experience. Employees routinely confer with her on marketing and other issues. Notably, Ms. Peeff took part in many discussions concerning Rain Clean. She raised several questions for consideration and provided advice in her capacity as a Legal Specialist on advertising and regulatory matters. Her statements are embodied in several documents. . . .

Strictly speaking, none of the documents in controversy reflect communications between attorney and client. That fact is not determinative however, as statements to and from non-attorneys may warrant protection on occasion. The question is, thus, whether Ms. Peeff's statements deserve attorney-client protection even though she is not an attorney. . . .

To varying degrees, each of the subject documents contains statements from Clorox employees to Ms. Peeff. Those employees clearly sought legal advice on a variety of issues associated with labeling and marketing Rain Clean. . . .

These communications are not protected merely because they solicited legal advice or because they were directed to a paralegal. To invoke the attorney-client privilege, a client's statement must at minimum "be made in confidence for the purpose of obtaining legal advice *from the lawyer.*" [Citation omitted.] Clorox proffers no evidence that its employees approached Ms. Peeff to obtain advice from in-house or outside counsel. In fact, the opposite is true. The disputed documents convey statements and questions to Ms. Peeff herself. They do not, on their face, seek anything from Clorox's team of lawyers. This is not an oversight. In her more than fifteen years at Clorox, Ms. Peeff developed significant familiarity with marketing and regulatory matters. Recognizing her expertise, Clorox employees often sought out her opinions. Indeed, one of Clorox's project leaders averred that he routinely reviews all of his legal and substantiation issues with Ms. Peeff even though he knows that she is not a lawyer.

While there is nothing wrong with Clorox employees using Ms. Peeff as a legal resource, there is also nothing privileged about their communications to her in this instance. . . . Moreover, although not dispositive, Clorox has provided no evidence that its employees thought that their statements were privileged and that they would not have spoken to Ms. Peeff otherwise. . . .

The record also lacks evidence that Ms. Peeff relayed these statements to her supervisors in order to obtain legal advice for interested employees. In fact, Ms. Peeff actually admits that she did not discuss or pass on the disputed documents — or the concerns raised in them to in-house counsel. This admission confirms that she did not function as a conduit of information for Clorox's lawyers. . . .

Ms. Peeff's statements are not privileged simply because she expressed legal advice or works in Clorox's legal department. Federal courts expand attorney-client privilege to third-party communications for one reason: to facilitate the attorney's provision of legal advice to the client. . . . Moreover, federal law does not recognize a freestanding "paralegal privilege." . . .

A paralegal's statements may assist an attorney because they pass on that attorney's advice to the client. In this instance, however, Ms. Peeff did not function as a go-between. . . .

A paralegal's statements may also be privileged because they convey advice formulated "under the supervision and at the direction of an attorney." [Citation omitted.] Courts do not, however, safeguard advice that paralegals develop and disseminate on their own. . . . Ms. Peeff admits that she did not consult with the lawyers before answering questions about Rain Clean. This admission, standing alone, constitutes a sufficient basis for concluding that her statements are not privileged because it shows that she acted independently. . . .

Clorox has not presented any evidence . . . that would even suggest that Ms. Peeff acted either at the direction or under the actual supervision of a lawyer. Given the absence of such evidence, the Court finds that Ms. Peeff conveyed her own advice. That advice, while legal in nature, is not privileged. . . .

Clorox attempts to avoid this conclusion by pointing out that Ms. Peeff works within its legal department under attorney supervision. It further highlights that, over time, she received training from lawyers to deal with diverse legal and regulatory issues and used the basic knowledge she acquired to provide the specific advice in question. Finally, Clorox notes that Ms. Peeff meets with attorneys when "unusual or novel" compliance issues arise. . . .

Clorox's position is flawed for several reasons. First, although Ms. Peeff may function under theoretical direction of an attorney, she did not receive any discernible supervision or guidance. . . . Second, Ms. Peeff's statements are not inherently privileged merely because she is a legal employee. . . . Her activities, not her job title, determine whether protection is warranted. . . . Third, the documents at issue are not protected simply because Ms. Peeff received generalized legal training, which she subsequently used to advise Clorox's employees. A non-lawyer's statements do not automatically become privileged simply because, at some point, that person interacted with or learned from an attorney. . . .

ORDERED that HPD's discovery application to compel Clorox to produce statements to and from Ms. Peeff is GRANTED. . . .

Questions about the Case

1. What was the title used by the paralegal in this case? Did this make a difference?
2. What kind of supervision and direction did the lawyers in the Clorox legal department give to the paralegal Peeff? How did this factor into the court's reasoning?
3. What should a paralegal in this employment situation do to ensure that communications she has with employees are protected by the attorney-client privilege?
4. Do you agree with the court's decision? What does it mean for the concept of lawyers having "general" instead of "direct" supervision over paralegals? What impact would this decision have on paralegal utilization in the corporate sector if it were widely known?

5. Did the paralegal engage in the unauthorized practice of law in carrying out her duties at Clorox? Did the lawyers to whom she reported assist in UPL?

This next case involves the discoverability of a set of document indexes. As you read, remember what was said in the text about the work product rule protection of trial preparation materials.

Bloss v. Ford Motor Co.

126 A.D.2d 804, 510 N.Y.S.2d 304 (1987)

HARVEY, Justice.

Appeal from an order of the Supreme Court at Special Term (Walsh, Jr., J.), entered January 24, 1986, in Fulton County, which denied defendant's motion to strike plaintiffs' demand for discovery and granted plaintiffs' cross motion to compel discovery.

In May 1981, plaintiffs commenced this action against defendant seeking damages caused when the jeep plaintiff Edward Bloss was driving, while employed by the United States Army, overturned. Defendant allegedly designed, manufactured and sold the jeep to the Army. In preparation for the instant lawsuit, and others pending against it, defendant retained a law firm in Detroit, Michigan, to review and index the approximately 76 boxes of documents relating to the design and development of the vehicle in question. An attorney from the Detroit firm, along with two or three paralegals, spent approximately a month reviewing the documents. As part of this review, two indexes of the documents were prepared.

In January 1985, Jeffrey Anderson, an attorney from the law firm representing plaintiffs, traveled from Troy, New York, to Dearborn, Michigan, to review the aforementioned documents. . . . Anderson's cursory review of the documents revealed that they had been indexed. He was subsequently informed that between 25 to 30 boxes of documents had been removed as defendant claimed they were either attorney's work product or contained confidential attorney-client information.

Plaintiffs subsequently served a discovery notice upon defendant seeking production of its indexes. Defendant moved for a protective order and plaintiffs cross-moved to compel production of the indexes. Special Term granted plaintiffs' cross motion and ordered defendant to produce the indexes in question. The court permitted defendant to redact any information which it, in good faith, believed to contain conclusions or opinions of its attorney. Defendant appealed.

Defendant asserts that the indexes are privileged matter (CPLR 3101[b]), attorney's work product (CPLR 3101[c]) or material prepared for litigation (CPLR 3101[d]). . . .

Turning first to whether the indexes constituted attorney's work product, the term "work product" has been narrowly construed to include only material prepared in an attorney's professional capacity and which necessarily involved professional skills. Documents which could have been prepared by a layman are not covered. [Citations omitted.] Here, plaintiffs seek only indexes of the documents relating to the design and development of the subject vehicle. No opinions, strategy or legal conclusions are sought. Defendant has not shown that the indexing of the documents was accomplished by using any particular legal skills.

Nor has defendant shown that the indexes are immune from disclosure under CPLR 3101(b). To be immune under that section, defendant must establish that the information sought would divulge confidential attorney-client communications. There is no indication in the record that the indexes contained confidential communications between defendant and its attorneys. In any event, Special Term specifically allowed defendant to redact any legal opinions from the indexes.

Defendant's further contention that the indexes are protected from discovery as material prepared for litigation has been considered and found meritless. We conclude that it was within Special Term's discretion to order defendant to produce redacted copies of the indexes.

Order affirmed, with costs.

Questions about the Case

1. What was it that the plaintiff's attorney Anderson was seeking in this case? What were the defendant's grounds for not producing this material?
2. What was the paralegals' involvement in this case?
3. Why did the court deny the defendant's assertion that the index was protected by the work product rule?
4. Why did the court deny the defendant's assertion that the index was protected by the attorney-client privilege?
5. Based on your reading of the material on work product in this chapter, under what conditions could the rule protect an index? Could the defendants in this case have created such a protected index?

In the following case, the court has to decide whether the disclosure of electronically stored information in a document production resulted in a waiver of the privilege. The opinion sets forth the three tests that have been used by the courts and applies the intermediate test to the facts. The opinion provides guidance for lawyers and paralegals seeking to guard against disclosure of protected electronically stored information.

Victor Stanley, Inc. v. Creative Pipe, Inc.

250 F.R.D. 251 (D. Md. 2008)

The plaintiff, Victor Stanley, Inc. ("VSI" or "Plaintiff"), filed a motion seeking a ruling that five categories of electronically stored documents produced by defendants Creative Pipe, Inc. ("CPI") and Mark and Stephanie Pappas ("M. Pappas," "S. Pappas" or "The Pappasses") (collectively, "Defendants") in October, 2007, are not exempt from discovery because they are within the protection of the attorney-client privilege and work-product doctrine, as claimed by the Defendants. VSI argues that the electronic records at issue, which total 165 documents, are not privileged because their production by Defendants occurred under circumstances that waived any privilege or protected status. . . . Defendants acknowledge that they produced all 165 electronic documents at issue to VSI during Rule 34 discovery, but argue that the production was inadvertent, and therefore that privilege/protection has not been waived. . . .

The following facts are not subject to dispute. The Defendants' first Rule 34 response was a "paper production," not ESI [electronically stored information], made in May 2007. Plaintiff objected to its sufficiency, and following a hearing, the court ordered the parties' computer forensic experts to meet and confer in an effort to identify a joint protocol to search and retrieve relevant ESI responsive to Plaintiff's Rule 34 requests. This was done and the joint protocol prepared. The protocol contained detailed search and information retrieval instructions including nearly five pages of keyword/phrase search terms. It is noteworthy that these search terms were aimed at locating responsive ESI, rather than identifying privileged or work-product protected documents within the population of responsive ESI. After the protocol was used to retrieve responsive ESI, Defendants reviewed it to locate documents that were beyond the scope of discovery because of privilege or work-product protection. Counsel for Defendants had previously notified the court on March 29, 2007, that individualized privilege review of the responsive documents "would delay production unnecessarily and cause undue expense." To address this concern, Defendants gave their computer forensics expert a list of keywords to be used to search and retrieve privileged and protected documents from the population of documents that were to be produced to Plaintiff. However, Defendants' counsel also acknowledged the possibility of inadvertent disclosure of privileged/protected documents, given the volume of documents that were to be produced, and requested that the court approve a "clawback agreement" fashioned to address the concerns. . . . However, on April 27, 2007, Defendants' counsel notified the court that because Judge Garbis recently had extended the discovery deadline by four months, Defendants would be able to conduct a document-by-document privilege review, thereby making a clawback agreement unnecessary. Accordingly, Defendants abandoned their efforts to obtain a clawback agreement and committed to undertaking an individualized document review. Following their privilege review, Defendants made their ESI production to Plaintiff in September 2007. . . . [B]y the time of this production, Defendants had discharged their local attorneys . . . and brought in new counsel. . . . Plaintiff's counsel began their review of the materials. They soon discovered documents that potentially were privileged or work-product protected and immediately segregated this information and notified counsel for Defendants of its production, following this same procedure each time they identified potentially privileged/protected information. Defendants' Counsel, Mr. Schmid, responded by asserting that the production of any privileged or protected information had been inadvertent. Defendants also belatedly provided Plaintiff with a series of privilege logs, purportedly identifying the documents that had been withheld from production pursuant to Fed. R. Civ. P. 26(b)(5).

The parties disagree substantially in their characterization of how Defendants conducted their review for privileged and protected documents before the ESI productions were made to Plaintiff. Defendants contend that after the joint ESI search protocol was implemented and the responsive ESI identified, their computer forensics expert, Ms. Genevive Turner, "conducted a privilege search using approximately seventy different keyword search terms . . . [that] had been decided upon previously by Mr. Pappas, his former attorney, Christopher Mohr, and another attorney, F. Stephen Schmid. . . . All documents which were returned during the keyword search were segregated and provided to one of Mr. Pappas' attorneys, John G. Monkman, Jr. for the first phase of the pre-production privilege review." This characterization, however, is somewhat misleading. In actuality, after the joint retrieval protocol had been executed, Ms. Turner determined that there were some ESI files (4.9 gigabytes) that were in text-searchable format and others (33.7 gigabytes) that were not. Turner conducted a search for privileged material on the text-searchable files using the seventy keywords developed by M. Pappas, Mohr and Schmid. As to the non-text-searchable files, she produced them to Monkman for manual privilege review. Monkman reviewed each of the files identified as privileged/protected by Turner based on her keyword searches. Additionally, Monkman and M. Pappas teamed up to begin doing a "page-by-page" manual privilege review of the non-text-searchable ESI files. "[D]ue to the compressed schedule and time constraints in reviewing these tens of thousands of documents within the time permitted, this review was undertaken by reviewing the page titles of the documents. Documents whose page titles indicated that the privilege might be applicable were reviewed in their entirety by Mr. Pappas or me. This was the only way for us to complete the unwieldy review of these documents within the time permitted." . . .

The implied conclusion that the court is invited to draw, from the limited information provided by the Defendants, is that the 165 documents that are the subject of the present motion were contained within the population of non-text-searchable ESI files that were produced by the Defendants to the Plaintiff, making their production inadvertent. However, this inference is not so easily drawn.

First, the Defendants are regrettably vague in their description of the seventy keywords used for the text-searchable ESI privilege review, how they were developed, how the search was conducted, and what quality controls were employed to assess their reliability and accuracy. While it is known that M. Pappas (a party) and Mohr and Schmid (attorneys) selected the keywords, nothing is known from the affidavits provided to the court regarding their qualifications for designing a search and information retrieval strategy that could be expected to produce an effective and reliable privilege review. As will be discussed, while it is universally acknowledged that keyword searches are useful tools for search and retrieval of ESI, all keyword searches are not created equal; and there is a growing body of literature that highlights the risks associated with conducting an unreliable or inadequate keyword search or relying exclusively on such searches for privilege review. Additionally, the Defendants do not assert that any sampling was done of the text-searchable ESI files that were determined not to contain privileged information on the basis of the keyword search to see if the search results were reliable. Common sense suggests that even a properly designed and executed keyword search may prove to be over-inclusive or under-inclusive, resulting in the identification of documents as privileged which are not, and non-privileged which, in fact, are. The only prudent way to test the reliability of the keyword search is to perform some appropriate sampling of the documents determined to be privileged and those determined not to be in order to arrive at a comfort level that the categories are neither over-inclusive nor under-inclusive. There is no evidence on the record that the Defendants did so in this case. Rather, it appears from the information that they provided to the court that they simply turned over to the Plaintiff all the text-searchable ESI files that were identified by the keyword search Turner performed as non-privileged, as well as the non-text-searchable files that Monkman and M. Pappas' limited title page search determined not to be privileged. . . .

VSI vigorously disputes Defendants' assertion that the text-searchable ESI received by Defendants' computer forensic expert, Turner, following the execution of the joint search and retrieval protocol was in a format that was difficult to search for privileged or protected materials. Plaintiff contends that it was able to do a keyword search of the text-searchable ESI produced by Defendants in about one hour using a "readily-available desktop search tool." VSI further contends that the non-text-searchable files that Monkman and M. Pappas reviewed by looking at the title pages consisted primarily of image files, such as photographs, catalogs, and drawings, which are not likely to contain privileged or protected information. Most importantly, however, the Plaintiff argues that the Defendants' complaint—that they could not effectively conduct a privilege review of the non-text-searchable files because there were so many of them—is a red herring because "the privileged materials [that are the subject of this motion] were all in text and thus were all searchable using standard text search tools. Contrary to Mr. Pappas' assertion, a majority of the .PDF files in the ESI were searchable using readily available search tools. The ESI contained 9008 .PDF files, the majority of which were searchable and the remaining could have been made searchable using readily available OCR software and/or the native OCR Text Recognition tool within Adobe Acrobat."

Thus, according to the Plaintiff, the Defendants have waived any claim to attorney-client privilege or work-product protection for the 165 documents at issue because they failed to take reasonable precautions by performing a faulty privilege review of the text-searchable files and by failing to detect the presence of the 165 documents, which were then given to the Plaintiff as part of Defendants' ESI production. . . .

As this court discussed in some detail in *Hopson*, 232 F.R.D. at 235-38, courts have taken three different approaches when deciding whether the inadvertent production to an adversary of attorney-client privileged or work-product protected materials constitutes a waiver. Under the most lenient approach there is no waiver because there has not been a knowing and intentional relinquishment of the privilege/protection; under the most strict approach, there is a waiver because once disclosed, there can no longer be any expectation of confidentiality; and under the intermediate one, the court balances a number of factors to determine whether the producing party exercised reasonable care under the circumstances to prevent against disclosure of privileged and protected information, and if so, there is no waiver. As also noted in *Hopson*, the Fourth Circuit Court of Appeals has yet to decide which approach it will follow, although individual district courts within the circuit have adopted the intermediate balancing approach. [Citations omitted.] . . .

The intermediate test requires the court to balance the following factors to determine whether inadvertent production of attorney-client privileged materials waives the privilege: (1) the reasonableness of the precautions taken to prevent inadvertent disclosure; (2) the number of inadvertent disclosures; (3) the extent of the disclosures; (4) any delay in measures taken to rectify the disclosure; and (5) overriding interests in justice. [Citations omitted.] The first of these factors militates most strongly in favor of a finding that Defendants waived the privilege in this case. . . .

Defendants, who bear the burden of proving that their conduct was reasonable for purposes of assessing whether they waived attorney-client privilege by producing the 165 documents to the Plaintiff, have failed to provide the court with information regarding: the keywords used; the rationale for their selection; the qualifications of M. Pappas and his attorneys to design an effective and reliable search and information retrieval method; whether the search was a simple keyword search, or a more sophisticated one, such as one employing Boolean proximity operators; or whether they analyzed the results of the search to assess its reliability, appropriateness for the task, and the quality of its implementation. While keyword searches have long been recognized as appropriate and helpful for ESI search and retrieval, there are well-known limitations and risks associated with them, and proper selection and implementation obviously involves technical, if not scientific knowledge. [Citations omitted.] . . .

Use of search and information retrieval methodology, for the purpose of identifying and withholding privileged or work-product protected information from production, requires the utmost care in selecting methodology that is appropriate for the task because the consequence of failing to do so, as in this case, may be the disclosure of privileged/protected information to an adverse party, resulting in a determination by the court that the privilege/protection has been waived. Selection of the appropriate search and information retrieval technique requires careful advance planning by persons qualified to design effective search methodology. The implementation of the methodology selected should be tested for quality assurance; and the party selecting the methodology must be prepared to explain the rationale for the method chosen to the court, demonstrate that it is appropriate for the task, and show that it was properly implemented. . . .

Further, the Defendants' attempt to justify what was done, by complaining that the volume of ESI needing review and time constraints presented them with no other choice is simply unpersuasive. Defendants were aware of the danger of inadvertent production of privileged/protected information and initially sought the protections of a non-waiver agreement. . . . Had they not voluntarily abandoned their request for a court-approved non-waiver agreement, they would have been protected from waiver. . . . According to Defendants' version of the facts, when they undertook an individualized review of the non-text-searchable ESI and determined that they could only review the title pages, they neither sought an extension of time from the court to complete an individualized review nor reinstated their request for a court-approved non-waiver agreement. . . . In these circumstances, Defendants' protests that they did their best and that their conduct was reasonable rings particularly hollow.

The remaining factors to be assessed under the intermediate test may be quickly disposed of. The Defendants produced 165 asserted privileged/protected documents to the Plaintiff, so this case does not present an instance of a single document slipping through the cracks. Further, the court's *in camera* review of the documents reflects that many of them are email and other communications between the Defendants and their various attorneys, as well as draft discovery responses, documents relating to settlements in unrelated litigation, comments from M. Pappas to counsel regarding discovery responses, and email correspondence between M. Pappas and Ms. Turner, the ESI forensic expert retained by Defendants. Thus, the disclosures were substantive — including numerous communications between defendants and their counsel. . . . [A]ny order issued now by the court to attempt to redress these disclosures would be the equivalent of closing the barn door after the animals have already run away. [Citations omitted.] And, while the precise dates of the disclosures of the documents at issue are not clear, . . . it is noteworthy that the Defendants did not discover the disclosure, but rather the Plaintiff made the discovery and notified the Defendants that potentially privileged/protected ESI had been produced. Therefore, this is not an instance in which a party inadvertently produced privileged information to an adversary, discovered the disclosure promptly, and then took immediate steps to inform the adversary that they had received the information inadvertently, thus demanding that it be returned.

While Defendants' counsel did assert privilege and inadvertent production promptly after being notified by the Plaintiff of the production of possible privileged/protected information, the more important period of delay in this case is the one-week period between production by the Defendants and the time of the discovery by the Plaintiff of the disclosures — a period during which the Defendants failed to discover the disclosure. Finally, the Defendants have pointed to no overriding interests in justice that would excuse them from the consequences of producing privileged/protected materials. The Plaintiff is blameless, but the Defendants are not, having failed to take reasonable precautions to prevent the disclosure of privileged information, including the voluntary abandonment of the non-waiver agreement that the Plaintiff was willing to sign. Every waiver of the attorney-client privilege produces unfortunate consequences for the party that disclosed the information. If that alone were sufficient to constitute an injustice, there would never be a waiver. The only "injustice" in this matter is that done by Defendants to themselves. [Citations omitted.] . . .

For the reasons stated, the court finds that the Defendants waived any privilege or work-product protection for the 165 documents at issue by disclosing them to the Plaintiff. Accordingly, the Plaintiff may use these documents as evidence in this case, provided they are otherwise admissible. . . .

Questions about the Case

1. What kind of information was contained in the documents that were inadvertently produced by the defendants' counsel? Would this information have ordinarily been protected by the attorney-client privilege?

2. What kind of review did the defendants' lawyers perform to guard against privileged documents being produced to opposing counsel? What did the court say about the adequacy of this review?
3. What is a "clawback" agreement? Why did the parties not have one? Would the outcome have been different if there had been one?
4. What are the three kinds of tests that courts can use when deciding whether the privilege has been waived when there has been an inadvertent disclosure? Which test did this court use? What are the factors that will be considered under this test?
5. Federal Rule of Evidence 502 provides that a disclosure "does not operate as a waiver . . . if (1) the disclosure is inadvertent; (2) the holder of the privilege or protection took reasonable steps to prevent disclosure; and (3) the holder promptly took reasonable steps to rectify the error, including (if applicable) following Federal Rule of Civil Procedure 26(b)(5)(B)." Would the outcome have been different if this rule had been in effect at the time of the disclosure? See *Amobi v. Dist. of Columbia Dep't of Corrections*, 262 F.R.D. 45 (D.C. 2009), where the court found waiver for inadequacy of precautions after the adoption of Fed. R. Evid. 502.

The following case involves a paralegal who reviewed inadvertently disclosed confidential information. The firm for which he worked was disqualified for this serious breach of ethics.

Richards v. Jain

F. Supp. 2d 1195 (U.S.D.C. W.D. Wash. 2001)

[This case involves discovery in a lawsuit by a former employee against his employer. Hagens Berman represented the plaintiff and this decision arose from a motion to disqualify the Hagens Berman firm.] Hagens Berman came into possession of a Jaz Disk containing copies of privileged documents in mid to late August 2000. The Disk was provided by Plaintiff John Richards in response to a request by Hagens Berman for any documents supporting Richards' legal claim. Hagens Berman was aware at the time it received the Disk that it contained a copy of every email stored on Richards' computer's hard drive. . . .

In mid September 2000, a paralegal with Hagens Berman, Mr. Haegele, ran searches on the email files and viewed all documents that contained at least one of the following terms in either the subject line or the message body: "Naveen", Jain, "YPI", "stock", or "options". The search produced "thousands of emails." Among those emails were documents clearly marked "Attorney-Client Privileged" that contained information subject to Defendants' attorney-client privilege and were relevant to this case. . . . Mr. Haegele reviewed all of the documents and sorted them into two groups: "relevant" and "not relevant." . . . The relevant documents were printed out and then sent to Hagens Berman attorney Sean Matt who reviewed all of the "relevant" documents in September 2000. . . .

This lawsuit was filed in December 2000, several months after Hagens Berman's in-house review of the privileged emails. . . . Mr. Haegele ran further searches on the files . . . and produced thousands of additional emails all of which were printed and given to Mr. Matt without being reviewed by Mr. Haegele. Matt reviewed the emails. . . . The relevant documents were produced to Defendants.

Richards was deposed on June 7, 2001. At his deposition, Richards confirmed that in or around August 2000, he had provided Hagens Berman with the Disk. . . . Thereafter defense counsel sent a letter to attorney Steve Berman asserting that . . . Defendants were now aware that Hagens Berman had in its possession a CD-ROM containing attorney-client privileged information. Mr. Berman send a responsive letter to Defendants . . . asserting that Defendants ought to have been aware for four months that Hagens Berman possessed copies of Richards' emails and, further, that no attorney at Hagens Berman had reviewed any privileged information or was aware that the Disk contained privileged information. In mid-June, Mr. Haegele was instructed by Mr. Matt to stop running searches on the emails and to insure that the Disk was in a secure location. . . .

Disqualification may be necessary where a party has had access to privileged information such as where an attorney has a conflict of interest due to a prior representation. The rule also applies equally to support staff that had access to privileged information due to former employment. [Citations omitted.]

The undisputed facts in this case make it clear that disqualification of Hagens Berman is necessary to remedy the substantial taint placed on any further proceedings by the possession and review of the Disk. Disqualification is justified under three alternate theories. First, nonlawyers and lawyers are bound by the same ethical duties. Mr. Haegele's review of privileged material was an ethical violation regardless of his status as a paralegal. Secondly, Hagens Berman failed to fulfill its duties under RPC 5.3(b) when it did not take reasonable measures to ensure the ethical conduct of a nonlawyer. Lastly, Mr. Haegele's conduct in reviewing the privileged material and the knowledge gained by that review are imputed to the Hagens Berman firm under RPC 5.3(c). . . .

An attorney who receives privileged documents has an ethical duty upon notice of the privileged nature of the documents to cease review of the documents, notify the privilege holder, and return the documents. See ABA Formal Ethics Opinion 94-382. A failure to abide by these rules is grounds for disqualification. [Citations omitted.] . . .

Courts have interpreted the Washington RPC regarding confidential information to apply equally to paralegals as to attorneys. . . . For purposes of disqualification, courts have therefore treated paralegals and other non-attorneys as having the same ethical responsibilities regarding confidential information as attorneys. [Citations omitted.] . . . Accordingly, as this Court would without question disqualify Hagens Berman had it been Mr. Berman or Mr. Matt that conducted the full review of the Disk, the Court must come to the same conclusion based on Mr. Haegele's review of the privileged materials. . . .

Mr. Berman and Mr. Matt had a duty under the RPC to ensure the ethical behavior of staff members under their supervision. . . . A reasonably diligent attorney would have at the very least inquired, prior to requesting the Disk, if Richards [a corporate vice president] was privy to privileged information or if Richards had exchanged emails with counsel. It does not appear that anyone at Hagens Berman made this inquiry. The court finds Mr. Matt's and Mr. Berman's statements that they "never once considered that the emails provided us could contain information subject to InfoSpace's attorney-client privilege" to be a failure of reasonable care approaching recklessness. . . . [U]pon instructing Mr. Haegele to perform searches on the contents of the emails, Mr. Haegele ought to have been told to cease reviewing documents if any question arose as to whether the Disk contained privileged information. Mr. Haegele reviewed literally hundreds of documents that were on their face privileged and informed no one and did not stop reviewing the documents. Mr. Haegele stated at oral argument that he simply ignored the privilege banners. The Court concludes that Hagens Berman did not make "reasonable efforts to ensure that [Mr. Haegele's] conduct [was] compatible with the professional obligations of the lawyer." This is a violation of RPC 5.3(b). . . .

Mr. Berman's and Mr. Matt's failure to take any reasonable measures to protect the attorney-client privilege through proper supervision of a paralegal creates an appearance of impropriety . . . that justifies disqualification. . . . Under RPC 5.3(b), as soon as Mr. Berman or Mr. Matt knew of the unethical conduct, . . . they were required to take remedial action to mitigate the effects of the conduct. Failure to do so makes the attorneys responsible for the actions of the nonlawyer and thereby imputes the conduct and the knowledge of the paralegal to the attorneys. . . .

Questions about the Case

1. When did the paralegal know that privileged documents had been disclosed on the disk? What should he have done?
2. Which of the two rules on receipt of inadvertently disclosed privileged information does the court follow? Do you think the court would have decided differently if the case had come after withdrawal of the ABA opinions in question?

3. What should Mr. Matt have done to attempt to remedy this matter earlier?
4. Do you think that the lawyers supervised the paralegal properly? Take a look at Chapter 2 on supervision again and consider Ethics Rule 5.3.
5. Would a paralegal who had taken an ethics course in school be likely to make this same mistake?

In the following case, a lawyer tried to use a copy of the inadvertently disclosed notes of opposing counsel to impeach experts at a deposition. The notes were prepared in part by a paralegal.

Rico v. Mitsubishi Motors Corp.

42 Cal. 4th 807, 171 P.3d 1092,
68 Cal. Rptr. 3d 758 (2007)

Here we consider what action is required of an attorney who receives privileged documents through inadvertence and whether the remedy of disqualification is appropriate.

Two Mitsubishi corporations (collectively Mitsubishi or defendants), and the California Department of Transportation (Caltrans), were sued by various plaintiffs after a Mitsubishi Montero rolled over while being driven on a freeway. Subsequently, Mitsubishi representatives met with their lawyers, James Yukevich and Alexander Calfo, and two designated defense experts to discuss their litigation strategy and vulnerabilities. Mitsubishi's case manager, Jerome Rowley, also attended the meeting. Rowley and Yukevich had worked together over a few years. Yukevich asked Rowley to take notes at the meeting and indicated specific areas to be summarized. The trial court later found that Rowley, who had typed the notes on Yukevich's computer, had acted as Yukevich's paralegal. At the end of the six-hour session, Rowley returned the computer and never saw a printed version of the notes. Yukevich printed only one copy of the notes, which he later edited and annotated. Yukevich never intentionally showed the notes to anyone, and the court determined that the sole purpose of the document was to help Yukevich defend the case.

The notes are written in a dialogue style and summarize conversations among Yukevich, Calfo, and the experts. They are dated, but not labeled as "confidential" or "work product." The printed copy of these compiled and annotated notes is the document at issue here.

Less than two weeks after the strategy session, Yukevich deposed plaintiffs' expert witness, Anthony Sances, at the offices of plaintiffs' counsel, Raymond Johnson. Yukevich, court reporter Karen Kay, and Caltrans counsel Darin Flagg were told that Johnson and Sances would be late for the deposition. After waiting in the conference room for some time, Yukevich went to the restroom, leaving his briefcase, computer, and case file in the room. The printed document from the strategy session was in the case file. While Yukevich was away, Johnson and Sances arrived. Johnson asked Kay and Flagg to leave the conference room. Kay and Flagg's departure left only the plaintiffs' representatives and counsel in the conference room. Yukevich returned to find Kay and Flagg standing outside. Yukevich waited approximately 5 minutes, then knocked and asked to retrieve his briefcase, computer, and file. After a brief delay, he was allowed to do so.

Somehow, Johnson acquired Yukevich's notes. Johnson maintained that they were accidentally given to him by the court reporter. Yukevich insisted that they were taken from his file while only Johnson and plaintiffs' team were in the conference room. As a result, Mitsubishi moved to disqualify plaintiffs' attorneys and experts. The trial court ordered an evidentiary hearing to determine how Johnson obtained the document.

The court reporter was deposed and denied any specific recollection of the Sances deposition. She could not testify what she had done with the deposition exhibits that night and could only relate her general practice. She said she generally collects exhibits and puts them in a plastic covering. She did not remember ever having given exhibits to an attorney. She also testified that she had never seen the document in question. If documents other than exhibits remain on a conference table, she leaves them there. The trial court found that the Sances deposition took place over approximately eight hours. It was a document-intense session and documents were placed on the conference table.

Another member of plaintiffs' legal team submitted a declaration supporting Johnson's assertion that he received the document from the reporter. The court ultimately concluded that the defense had failed to establish that Johnson had taken the notes from Yukevich's file. It thus ruled that Johnson came into the document's possession through inadvertence.

The court found the 12-page document was dated, but not otherwise labeled. It contained notations by Yukevich. Johnson admitted that he knew within a minute or two that the document related to the defendants' case. He knew that Yukevich did not intend to produce it and that it would be a "powerful impeachment document." Nevertheless, Johnson made a copy of the document. He scrutinized and made his own notes on it. He gave copies to his co-counsel and his experts, all of whom studied the document. Johnson specifically discussed the contents of the document with each of his experts.

A week after he acquired Yukevich's notes, Johnson used them during the deposition of defense expert Geoffrey Germane. The notes purportedly indicate that the defense experts made statements at the strategy session that were inconsistent with their deposition testimony. Johnson used the document while questioning Germane, asking about Germane's participation in the strategy session.

Defense Counsel Calfo defended the Germane deposition. Yukevich did not attend. Calfo had never seen the document and was not given a copy during the deposition. When he asked about the document's source, Johnson vaguely replied . . . , "It was put in Dr. Sances' file." Calfo repeatedly objected to the "whole line of inquiry with respect to an unknown document." He specifically said that, "I don't even know where this exhibit came from."

Only after the deposition did Johnson give a copy of the document to Calfo, who contacted Yukevich. When Yukevich realized that Johnson had his only copy of the strategy session notes and had used it at the deposition, he and Calfo wrote to Johnson demanding the return of all duplicates. The letter was faxed the day after Germane's deposition. The next day, defendants moved to disqualify plaintiffs' legal team and their experts on the ground that they had become privy to and had used Yukevich's work product. As a result, they complained, Johnson's unethical use of the notes and his revelation of them to co-counsel and their experts irremediably prejudiced defendants.

The trial court concluded that the notes were absolutely privileged by the work product rule. The court also held that Johnson had acted unethically by examining the document more closely than was necessary to determine that its contents were confidential, by failing to notify Yukevich that he had a copy of the document, and by surreptitiously using it to gain maximum adversarial value from it. The court determined that Johnson's violation of the work product rule had prejudiced the defense and "the bell cannot be 'unrung' by use of in limine orders." Accordingly, the court ordered plaintiffs' attorneys and experts disqualified.

Plaintiffs appealed the disqualification order. The Court of Appeal affirmed. . . .

Plaintiffs contend that the Court of Appeal erred by holding that the entire document was protected as attorney work product. We reject that contention. The Legislature has protected attorney work product under California Code of Civil Procedure section 2018.030, which provides, "(a) A writing that reflects an attorney's impressions, conclusions, opinions, or legal research or theories is not discoverable under any circumstances. (b) The work product of an attorney, other than a writing described in subdivision (a), is not discoverable unless the court determines that denial of discovery will unfairly prejudice the party seeking discovery in preparing that party's claim or defense or will result in an injustice." . . .

Thus, the codified work product doctrine absolutely protects from discovery writings that contain an "attorney's impressions, conclusions, opinions, or legal research or theories." [Citations omitted.] The protection extends to an attorney's written notes about a witness's statements. [Citations omitted.] "[A]ny such notes or recorded statements taken by defendants' counsel would be protected by the absolute work product privilege because they would reveal counsel's 'impressions, conclusions, opinions, or legal research or theories' within the meaning of [the work product doctrine]." [Citation omitted.] When a witness's statement and the attorney's impressions are inextricably intertwined, the work product doctrine provides that absolute protection is afforded to all of the attorney's notes.

Plaintiffs urge that the document is not work product because it reflects the statements of declared experts. They are incorrect. The document is not a transcript of the August 28, 2002 strategy session, nor is it a verbatim record of the experts' own statements. It contains Rowley's summaries of points from the strategy session, made at Yukevich's direction. Yukevich also edited the document in order to add his own thoughts and comments, further inextricably intertwining his personal impressions with the summary. [Citation omitted.] In this regard, the trial court found: "As to the content of the document, although it doesn't contain overt statements setting forth the lawyer's conclusions, its very existence is owed to the lawyer's thought process. The document reflects not only the strategy, but also the attorney's opinion as to the important issues in the case. Directions were provided by Mr. Yukevich as to the key pieces of information to be recorded, and Mr. Yukevich also added his own input as to the important details, by inserting other words in the notes. The attorney's impressions of the case were the filter through which all the discussions at the conference were passed through on the way to the page." . . .

Although the notes were written in dialogue format and contain information attributed to Mitsubishi's experts, the document does not qualify as an *expert's* report, writing, declaration, or testimony. The notes reflect the *paralegal's* summary along with *counsel's* thoughts and impressions about the case. The document was absolutely protected work product because it contained the ideas of Yukevich and his legal team about the case. (§2018.030, subd. (a).)

Because the document is work product we consider what ethical duty Johnson owed once he received it. Plaintiffs rely on *Aerojet-General Corp. v. Transport Indemnity Insurance* (1993), 18 Cal. App. 4th 996 (*Aerojet*), to argue that because the document was inadvertently received, Johnson was duty bound to use the nonprivileged portions of it to his clients' advantage. This argument fails. *Aerojet* is distinguishable because there are no "unprivileged portions" of the document. . . .

In *State Fund, supra,* 70 Cal. App. 4th 644, the plaintiff sent defendant's attorney (Telanoff) three boxes of documents that were identical to the documents provided during discovery. Inadvertently, plaintiff also sent 273 pages of forms entitled, "Civil Litigation Claims Summary," marked as "ATTORNEY-CLIENT COMMUNICATION/ ATTORNEY WORK PRODUCT," and with the warning, "DO NOT CIRCULATE OR DUPLICATE." In addition, "[t]he word 'CONFIDENTIAL' [was] repeatedly printed around the perimeter of the first page of the form." When counsel discovered the mistake and demanded return of the documents, Telanoff refused. The trial court, relying on American Bar Association (ABA) Formal Ethics Opinion No. 92-368 (Nov. 10, 1992), imposed monetary sanctions.

The Court of Appeal framed the issue as follows: "[W]hat is a lawyer to do when he or she receives through the inadvertence of opposing counsel documents plainly subject to the attorney-client privilege?" [Citation omitted.] . . . The *State Fund* court went on to articulate the standard to be applied prospectively: "When a lawyer who receives materials that obviously appear to be subject to an attorney-client privilege or otherwise clearly appear to be confidential and privileged and where it is reasonably apparent that the materials were provided or made available through inadvertence, the lawyer receiving such materials should refrain from examining the materials any more than is essential to ascertain if the materials are privileged, and shall immediately notify the sender that he or she possesses material that appears to be privileged. The parties may then proceed to resolve the situation by agreement or may resort to the court for guidance with the benefit of protective orders and other judicial intervention as may be justified." [Citation omitted.] To ensure that its decision was clear in setting forth the applicable standard in these cases, the court explicitly stated that it "declared the standard governing the conduct of California lawyers" in such instances.

The existing *State Fund* rule is a fair and reasonable approach. The rule supports the work product doctrine [citation omitted], and is consistent with the state's policy to "[p]reserve the rights of attorneys to prepare cases for trial with that degree of privacy necessary to encourage them to prepare their cases thoroughly and to investigate not only the favorable but the unfavorable aspects of those cases" and to "[p]revent attorneys from taking undue advantage of their adversary's industry and efforts." . . .

The *State Fund* rule also addresses the practical problem of inadvertent disclosure in the context of today's reality that document production may involve massive numbers of documents. A contrary holding could severely disrupt the discovery process. As amicus curiae The Product Liability Advisory Council, Inc. argues, "Even apart from the inadvertent disclosure problem, the party responding to a request for mass production must engage in a laborious, time consuming process. If the document producer is confronted with the additional prospect that any privileged documents inadvertently produced will become fair game for the opposition, the minute screening and re-screening that inevitably would follow not only would add enormously to that burden but would slow the pace of discovery to a degree sharply at odds with the general goal of expediting litigation."

Finally, we note that "[a]n attorney has an obligation not only to protect his client's interests but also to respect the legitimate interests of fellow members of the bar, the judiciary, and the administration of justice." [Citation omitted.] The *State Fund* rule holds attorneys to a reasonable standard of professional conduct when confidential or privileged materials are inadvertently disclosed.

Here, it is true that Yukevich's notes were not so clearly flagged as confidential as were the forms in *State Fund*. . . . But, as the Court of Appeal observed, "[T]he absence of prominent notations of confidentiality does not make them any less privileged." The *State Fund* rule is an objective standard. In applying the rule, courts must consider whether reasonably competent counsel, knowing the circumstances of the litigation, would have concluded the materials were privileged, how much review was reasonably necessary to draw that conclusion, and when counsel's examination should have ended. . . .

The standard was properly and easily applied here. Johnson admitted that after a minute or two of review he realized the notes related to the case and that Yukevich did not intend to reveal them. Johnson's own admissions and subsequent conduct clearly demonstrate that he violated the *State Fund* rule. . . .

The next question is whether disqualification was the proper remedy. . . .

The *State Fund* court held that " '[m]ere exposure' " to an adversary's confidences is insufficient, standing alone, to warrant an attorney's disqualification. (*State Fund, supra*, 70 Cal. App. 4th at p. 657.) The court counseled against a draconian rule that " '[could] nullify a party's right to representation by chosen counsel any time inadvertence or devious design put an adversary's confidences in an attorney's mailbox.' " However, the court did not "rule out the possibility that in an appropriate case, disqualification might be justified if an attorney inadvertently receives confidential materials and fails to conduct himself or herself in the manner specified above, assuming other factors compel disqualification."

After reviewing the document, Johnson made copies and disseminated them to plaintiffs' experts and other attorneys. In affirming the disqualification order, the Court of Appeal stated, "The trial court settled on disqualification as the proper remedy because of the unmitigable damage caused by Johnson's dissemination and use of the document." Thus, "the record shows that Johnson not only failed to conduct himself as required under *State Fund*, . . . but also acted unethically in making full use of the confidential document." The Court of Appeal properly concluded that such use of the document undermined the defense experts' opinions and placed defendants at a great disadvantage. Without disqualification of plaintiffs' counsel and their experts, the damage caused by Johnson's use and dissemination of the notes was irreversible. Under the circumstances presented in this case, the trial court did not abuse its discretion by ordering disqualification for violation of the *State Fund* rule.

Plaintiffs attempt to justify Johnson's use of the document by accusing the defense experts of giving false testimony during their depositions.

Plaintiffs allege that the statements attributed to the experts in the document contradicted their deposition statements and that the experts lied about the technical evidence involved in the case. As an initial matter, we are not persuaded that any of the defense experts ever actually adopted as their own the statements attributed to them. The document is not a verbatim transcript of the strategy session, but Rowley's summary of points that Yukevich directed him to note. Yukevich then edited the document, adding his own thoughts and comments. As the trial court observed, the document was an interpretation and summary of what others thought the experts were saying.

Moreover, we agree with the Court of Appeal that, "when a writing is protected under the absolute attorney work product privilege, courts do not invade upon the attorney's thought processes by evaluating the content of the writing.

. . . We also reject plaintiffs' argument that the crime or fraud exception should apply to privileged work product in this civil proceeding. Under the work product doctrine "[a] writing that reflects an attorney's impressions, conclusions, opinions, or legal research or theories *is not discoverable under any circumstances.* (§2018.030, subd. (a), italics added.) . . . By its own terms, the crime or fraud exception does not apply here.

We affirm the Court of Appeal's judgment.

Questions about the Case

1. What was the nature of the document at issue? Who prepared it? What was it to be used for? What was the role of the paralegal in preparing this document? Was this important?
2. Why did the court decide that the document did not fall strictly into the attorney-client privilege, but was instead protected by the work product rule?
3. What did the plaintiff's lawyer do that was unethical? What should he have done?
4. What would have happened if California followed the current Model Rule on receipt of inadvertently disclosed documents? Would the outcome have been the same? Does the court seem to know that the ABA has reversed its stance on this issue? Does the court care?

5

Conflicts of Interest

This chapter explains the rules concerning conflicts of interest that may arise in the representation of clients, how those rules apply to paralegals, and why paralegal conflicts are increasingly common in today's dynamic legal environment. Chapter 5 covers:

- the foundation on which conflict of interest rules rest
- the rules governing simultaneous and successive representation and their application to paralegals
- special conflict situations and their application to paralegals
  - being called as a witness
  - business transactions with clients
  - publication rights
  - financial assistance to clients
  - lawyer's interest in litigation
  - gifts from clients
  - agreements with clients limiting lawyer malpractice liability
  - payment of attorney's fees by third persons
  - conflicts involving family members or relatives
- disqualifications caused by conflicts of interest that are imputed to a firm
- client consent to representation despite a conflict
- screens to protect against disqualification
- conflicts checks and a paralegal's responsibility to maintain records

A. Introduction

Conflicts of interest constitute one of the most troublesome areas of ethics for lawyers, paralegals, and clients. The growth in the size of law firms, the development of branch offices, mergers of firms, the mobility of lawyers and paralegals from firm to firm, and practice specialization have made the potential for conflicts of interest an ever-present concern. Traditional restrictive rules governing conflicts are being modified and adjusted to adapt to the changing environment of law practice and to new kinds of conflicts. Strict conflicts rules can pose an undue hardship on law firms, law firm employees, and clients, as we will see in some cases in this chapter. Avoiding conflicts remains one of the critical ethical obligations of lawyers and paralegals.

The principles underlying conflicts of interest are loyalty and confidentiality. Both of these duties are threatened when a lawyer or paralegal has an interest that is adverse to a client's. This is true whether the adverse interest is a personal or business one, or relates to the current or past representation of another client. For example, an attorney who has received confidential information from one client that may help another client may feel obligated by the duty of loyalty to divulge that confidential information to help the second client. A lawyer who represents two clients, even if in different matters, may not represent them both with equal zeal, especially if one is a favored client (perhaps because this client brings more business to the lawyer).

Ethics rules governing conflicts of interest have existed since the first codes of lawyer conduct came into being, and conflicts are covered in the ethics rules, cases, and opinions of every jurisdiction. The ethics rules provide the basis for attorney discipline and are supplemented by court interpretations in cases in which a party has moved to disqualify a law firm because of a conflict of interest. The courts have seen many more conflict dilemmas than have disciplinary bodies and have built a considerable body of law as they interpreted and applied the rules to increasing numbers and kinds of conflict situations.

The ABA Model Rules of Professional Conduct and state and local rules cover several categories of conflict situations, including:

- simultaneous representation of adverse interests
- representation that is adverse to a former client
- representation of clients whose interests are aligned
- lawyer's financial, personal, or business interests that are or may be adverse to a client

A critically important aspect of the conflicts rules for paralegals is the principle of imputed or vicarious disqualification, a general rule under which the conflict of interest of one person in a firm is imputed to the entire firm, causing the firm to be subject to disqualification from representing the client in question. Some kinds of conflicts are imputed, and others are not. Most states apply the rules of imputation for lawyers to paralegals.

Guideline 7 of the ABA Model Guidelines for the Utilization of Paralegal Services (ABA Model Guidelines) advises attorneys to take measures to prevent conflicts resulting from a paralegal's other employment or interests. The comment to this guideline makes it clear that personal and financial interests are covered, as well as interests related to the representation of a client. The comment also discusses the screening of a paralegal from any case in which a conflict exists, a matter covered later in this chapter in Section F. About half the states that have paralegal guidelines refer to paralegal conflicts of interests and call on the lawyer generally to ensure against conflicts impinging on the services rendered to the client. See, for example, Indiana Guideline 9.10(g); Kansas Guideline X; Michigan Guideline 5; New Mexico Guideline VI; North Carolina Guideline 7; South Dakota Guideline 9. Virginia Guideline IX prohibits a paralegal directly from participating in matters where there "may be" a conflict of interest. A few states, such as New Mexico and Connecticut, identify the kinds of conflicts that may "impinge" on services to a client, including "personal, social, business" and "relationship" interests, whereas other states refer only to conflicts arising out of the paralegal's employment (New York State Bar Association Guideline IV). Some state guidelines mention the availability of screening for paralegals (e.g., Pennsylvania), which has been almost universally accepted by the courts, as we will see later in this chapter.

The NFPA Model Code includes an extensive section on conflicts of interest (Section 1.6), which acknowledges the different kinds of conflicts that may face paralegals, calls on paralegals to maintain records so that conflicts checks can be conducted, and requires paralegals to adhere to the requirements of screens. The NALA Code of Ethics and Professional Responsibility does not refer directly to conflicts of interest although general language about confidentiality and adherence to ethical codes for lawyers would cover conflict situations. (See Canon 3(c) and Canon 7.) The NALA Model Guidelines refer to conflicts under Guideline I.

B. Simultaneous or Concurrent Representation

The most clear-cut case of a conflict of interest is ***simultaneous or concurrent representation*** of two clients whose interests are adverse to one another in a lawsuit. It seems absurd to suggest that a lawyer could adequately represent both the plaintiff and the defendant in the same case.

Simultaneous or concurrent representation conflict
Where an attorney represents two clients whose interests are adverse to one another

However, simultaneous representation problems do arise in situations that are less obvious than a lawyer serving both clients in a contested matter. Many matters that are not litigated have clients with opposing interests, as the following section demonstrates.

ABA Model Rule 1.7(a) prohibits concurrent conflicts, which it defines as "directly adverse" interests or "a significant risk that the representation of one or more clients will be materially limited by the lawyer's responsibilities to another client, a former client or a third person or by a personal interest of the lawyer." The conflict can be avoided if "(1) the lawyer reasonably believes that [she or he] will be able to provide competent and diligent representation . . . ; (2) the representation is not prohibited by law; (3) the representation does not involve . . . a claim by one client against another client . . . in the same litigation . . . ; and (4) each affected client gives informed consent, confirmed in writing."

To represent the clients in question, the lawyer would have to have both an assurance of **adequate representation** of both clients and **client consent**. Adequate representation of two adverse clients is no small hurdle; it is often quite difficult for an attorney to demonstrate objectively how he or she can be equally loyal to and zealous on behalf of two clients who oppose each other. Even if the lawyer believes that this is possible, it is easy to see how clients would question a lawyer's loyalty if the same firm or lawyer were opposing their interests in another case.

To avoid conflicts, lawyers should have good procedures for **checking for conflicts** when they undertake representation of a new client or hire or retain new personnel. They should decline representation when a conflict is presented that cannot be waived by the clients involved or for which they cannot obtain a consent or establish a screen that will withstand judicial scrutiny. Finally, they should withdraw from representation promptly when an irremediable conflict is discovered after the representation is undertaken. (See more on conducting conflict checks later in this chapter.)

The courts generally have treated simultaneous representation as improper on its face and start with the presumption that disqualification is required. The more remote the adverseness, however, the less strictly the rule is applied. For example, it is not considered a conflict of interest per se for an attorney to represent business competitors simultaneously in unrelated matters.

Determining whether there has been valid client **consent** (or "waiver" of the client's right to assert the conflict of interest) is also critical. The ABA Model Rules require informed written consent. The Model Rules formulation mandating the consent in writing is relatively recent and most jurisdictions have adopted it. Some states require consultation for consent to be valid. Consultation means that the lawyer seeking the consent has provided the client with sufficient information to permit the client to appreciate the significance of the conflict. The Model Rules require "informed consent," which means that the lawyer must disclose the "facts and circumstances" giving rise to the conflict, information about the "material advantages and disadvantages" for the client, and the client's "options or alternatives" (Comment 22 to ABA Model Rule 1.7). For some kinds of conflicts, the lawyer may recommend that the client consult with independent outside counsel.

General open-ended consents will not ordinarily be upheld. Whether a court honors a client's consent depends on a number of circumstances, including:

- whether the conflict is one that is "consentable"; that is, the lawyer can provide adequate representation
- the extent of the lawyer's disclosure and discussions with the client about the implications of the dual representation
- whether the consent was truly voluntary and not given under pressure from the attorney or others
- when in the course of the representation the lawyer raised the issue with the client
- the capacity of the client to understand fully the implications of the dual representation and consent
- whether the client consulted with and relied on independent counsel before giving consent
- whether the consent is in writing and signed

These factors suggest some guidelines that should be followed to ensure that consents will be upheld. Thorough **written disclosures**, which are highly recommended, should state the circumstances giving rise to the potential conflict and the actual and reasonably foreseeable consequences to the client if the lawyer undertakes or continues the representation. If the client consults with **independent counsel**, the independent must be truly independent, that is, not from the same firm or recommended by the firm seeking the consent. The written consent should also include:

- consideration for the consent (i.e., future or continued representation)
- procedures to screen appropriately to protect confidentiality
- procedures to follow if a client decides to withdraw consent

Some firms ask clients to consent to **future conflicts**, which is the subject of considerable debate. Whether such consent will be upheld depends on the same factors set forth earlier, especially on whether the particular conflict is "consentable." Other factors include whether the client is an experienced user of legal services, was well informed about the conflict, and got assistance from independent counsel.

In general, a lawyer cannot withdraw from representing one client to represent the other, more favored client. A court reviewing this situation will ordinarily disqualify the lawyer if representation was concurrent at any time. Improper simultaneous representation generally results in disqualification from representing *either* client unless, of course, there is proper consent.

Imputed disqualification
A conflict of interest involving one person that is attributed to the entire law firm, which is disqualified from representing the party at issue

Imputed disqualification rules are usually applied strictly in cases of simultaneous representation involving lawyers. In other words, if one lawyer in a firm has a conflict in an ongoing case without client consent, the entire firm is disqualified. These rules apply to branch offices of the same firm. A screen to protect against improper access to confidential information will not ordinarily remedy the conflict, as it would in cases involving former clients. Fortunately for paralegals, most courts have been more lenient in applying the conflict rules to situations in which the paralegal carries a concurrent conflict to a new firm. See Sections C and F and the cases in this chapter.

Issue conflicts
Occurs when an attorney argues opposing sides of a legal issue, the result of which may be that one client's interests are harmed

Related to direct conflicts in active matters involving clients are what is called ***issue or positional conflicts***. An issue conflict occurs when a lawyer is representing two clients in unrelated cases and urging a legal position in one case that would have negative consequences for the other client if the lawyer prevails. It is usually not considered unethical for lawyers to take inconsistent positions but this scenario can rise to the level of a concurrent conflict if the representation in one case would "materially impair" the representation of other client. If this situation arises, the lawyer may seek consent or need to withdraw from one or both matters. (See Comment 24 to ABA Model Rule 1.7.)

Although the Model Rules do not prohibit representation of competitors, some firms have policies against representing direct competitors in the same industry. Obviously, clients may have concerns about both loyalty and protection of confidential information if a firm represents competitors. In addition, the potential for being "conflicted out" of representing a client in the case of litigation between competitors is a practical deterrent to law firms. Although not prohibited, lawyers should be especially wary of this potential conflict if the industry is known for cut-throat competition or if the lawyer possessed confidential information about one client that will damage the other client.

The Model Rules prohibition of simultaneous representation when the lawyer's responsibilities to one client may "materially limit" representation covers a wide range of situations. For example, a lawyer representing two criminal defendants with conflicting trial dates might have to delay one trial to the detriment of that client.

Concurrent conflicts of interests arise in litigation in many ways. One of the most common is dual representation of a husband and wife in a **marital dissolution**. Many marital dissolution matters begin amicably and seem to lend themselves to resolution by one attorney, for reasons of cost and efficiency, but end up in court. Although the courts are not unanimous, many bar associations and experts advise against an attorney representing both parties to a marital dissolution. Sometimes one of the spouses later becomes dissatisfied with the property settlement agreement and challenges it in court on the basis that the lawyer had a conflict of interest and favored the other spouse.

Similar problems can arise in representation of **co-parties** in civil litigation. Although aligned initially, co-parties may become adversaries during the course of litigation if cross-claims are filed or another party seeks to realign the parties. One problem area is serving as joint defense counsel in mass litigation, where the interests of all parties may not align perfectly and confidentiality is difficult to maintain. Similarly, a passenger and driver who sue a third party may find themselves adversaries if the passenger learns that the driver was partially at fault and sues the driver. Some jurisdictions, such as California, have decided cases that prohibit any joint representation of a driver and a passenger as an inherent conflict of interest.

ABA Model Rule 1.8(g) prohibits a lawyer who is representing multiple clients from making an **aggregate settlement** of civil claims or a collective plea in a criminal case without informed written consent. Representing seemingly aligned **defendants in criminal cases** is especially risky, as the interests of the defendants are often potentially adverse. In addition to the ethical issues, multiple representation may deprive one or both of the defendants of effective assistance of counsel, which constitutes grounds for appeal in a criminal conviction.

Other less obvious conflict traps arise in litigation. For example, a firm may be disqualified for retaining an **expert witness** who was previously interviewed by the opposing counsel if confidential information was disclosed to the expert during the course of the interview. Representing both present and future **claimants in class action** suits may also result in an allegation of a conflict if a settlement seems to favor one group over another. Generally a lawyer may not serve as both named plaintiff and counsel in a class action suit, a conflict that will be imputed to the firm.

Although litigation is the most obvious setting for conflicts of interest, many other kinds of legal matters pose potential conflicts. A lawyer may represent more than one party to a **negotiation** if the parties' interests seem aligned but should be aware of the potential for a conflict if negotiations fail or if the resulting contract becomes the subject of a dispute. If litigation is the result, the attorney may not represent either of the parties against the other and may be subject to suit by a former client for malpractice because of the conflict. For example, entertainment law firms that represent producers, directors, writers, and actors have been accused of favoring wealthier or more prestigious clients in negotiations on film deals, resulting in less advantageous positions for other clients. Clients of these firms usually consent in writing to the multiple representation; however, when deals fall apart, parties to the contracts may complain that there was not full disclosure or that they were pressured into signing consents, as they would have been frozen out of deals if they had sought independent counsel.

A conflict of interest may arise in the **drafting of estate plans** for members of the same family, especially if the family members are not in agreement about the disposition of the estate. Similarly, conflicts between an **estate and the heirs** of the estate may prohibit representation of both parties. For other conflicts in a probate setting, see Section E.5, on gifts from clients.

A lawyer who represents a **corporation** may be invited to serve on its board of directors. The ABA Rules advise that lawyers not serve as directors if there is a "material risk that the dual role will compromise the lawyer's independence of professional judgment." (See ABA Model Rule 1.7 Comment 34, and Model Rule 1.13.) Serving on a corporate board increases a lawyer's risk of being sued and threatens the attorney-client privilege as well—remember from Chapter 4 that information that is not treated as confidential and is not communicated for the purpose of obtaining legal advice is not protected. The interests or positions of the board, management, and shareholders may at times diverge. Lawyers serving on boards find themselves in serious conflict situations in shareholder derivative suits, especially when there are allegations of self-dealing or fraud by the board or management. Increasingly, law firms restrict or limit service on corporate boards, not only because of the potential for conflicts, but because of the heightened liability of directors under Sarbanes-Oxley. Conflicts may also occur in the corporate setting if an attorney represents several entities within the corporate family (e.g., parent, subsidiary, "sister" companies) and these entities find themselves in an adversarial position with one another. Finally, as is also noted in Chapter 4, lawsuits against corporations often result in potential confidentiality and conflict issues when employees are represented by the same lawyer. See *U.S. v. Nicholas* at the end of this chapter for a case in point.

A lawyer may be representing multiple clients whenever he or she represents more than one party to a **transaction** such as a real estate sale, a mortgage, a loan, or a contract—for example, representing both a school district and the underwriters in a school bond issuance. Several states have advisory opinions on the issue of representing both sides in a real estate transaction, most of which recommend against dual representation except in purely ministerial matters. Some states prohibit dual representation in any complex commercial real estate transaction because of the great potential for conflicts.

A lawyer who has acted as a **judge, law clerk to a judge, mediator**, or other **third-party neutral** in a matter cannot later represent any of the parties involved without informed written consent under Model Rule 1.12. Some cases have held that this kind of conflict is imputed to the law firm where the lawyer works, thereby prohibiting the representation of the client by any lawyer in the firm.

An area of practice in which there has been an increase in serious conflicts is **bankruptcy.** The bankruptcy code requires that lawyers for the debtor be "disinterested" and not represent or hold an interest that is adverse to the bankrupt (11 U.S.C. §327(a)). Lawyers are required to disclose related interests on standard forms. A lawyer representing a debtor cannot have pre-existing relationships with others who might be involved in the bankruptcy, such as investment bankers involved with a bankrupt corporation or shareholders of the debtor corporation. Such representation would constitute not only an ethical breach, but a violation of federal bankruptcy law, which may result in criminal penalties, as one lawyer learned when he was sent to prison for 15 months and disbarred. Another firm was not awarded fees for its work after it failed to disclose services for another client that conflicted with the interests of the bankrupt (*In re Prince*, 40 F.3d 356 (11th Cir. 1994)).

C. Successive Representation

The ethics rules also govern the conduct of lawyers who represent a client in a matter that may be adverse to a former client — called ***successive representation***. The ability of clients to be represented by the counsel of their choice and the increasing mobility of lawyers have been significant factors in recent court decisions that apply the conflict rules in cases of successive representation with a good deal more flexibility than ever before.

Successive representation conflict
Situation involving a current client whose interests conflict with those of a former client

The general rule is that an attorney cannot undertake successive representation if the interests of the former and current clients are **truly adverse** and if the past and current matters are **substantially related**. This formulation presupposes an attorney-client relationship with the former client in which the attorney would have learned confidential information about the new matter. If the current representation relates to the same or a closely related matter, the lawyer would be in a position to breach his or her duty of confidentiality to the former client by revealing the confidential information to assist the current client. (Remember from Chapter 4 that the duty of confidentiality continues after the termination of the attorney-client relationship.) Some commentators also cite the duty of loyalty to the former client as a basis for the rule, but others contend that the duty of loyalty, unlike the duty of confidentiality, does not continue after the termination of the lawyer-client relationship. Informed written consent to successive representation is permitted as a way to cure the conflict.

Prior to the provision for successive representation in the Model Rules and in states that used to follow the Model Code, some courts came to rely on Canon 9 of the ABA Model Code in deciding whether to disqualify an attorney or firm from successive representation. Canon 9 calls on lawyers to avoid even the **appearance of impropriety**. Most circuits and states, however, do not order disqualification solely on the basis of an appearance of impropriety, but determine whether the former client's rights of confidentiality are in jeopardy. Most ethics experts disfavor disqualification predicated solely on the appearance of impropriety; such a finding does not mean that confidential information has been revealed, and the disqualification could severely harm the interests of the client, who loses the right to choose his or her own lawyer.

The ABA Model Rules provide specifically for successive conflicts. Rule 1.9(a) states the general rule that has been followed by most courts: A lawyer may not represent a person in a matter that is "the same or substantially related" to the representation of a former client in which the interests of the potential client are "materially adverse" to the former client except with informed written consent of the former client.

Paragraph (b) of Rule 1.9 covers the situation in which a lawyer changing firms is faced with the question of whether to represent a new client in a matter that is adverse and substantially related to a matter of a former client of the attorney's former firm. Such representation is prohibited if the attorney learned confidential information about the former client in his or her past employment except with the former client's informed written consent. Rule 1.9(c) reiterates the lawyer's duty not to reveal confidential information of a former client under any circumstances, unless other rules permit or require it or the information has become generally known.

A separate ABA Model Rule applies to **government lawyers**. Model Rule 1.11 allows a former government lawyer to represent a private client in a matter in which the lawyer previously "participated personally and substantially" only with the government agency's informed written consent. It also allows screening to avoid firm disqualification in such a representation. A lawyer who moves to private practice from government service is prohibited from switching sides or from negotiating for private employment with a party or an attorney with whom the lawyer is dealing on a matter. The more flexible approach for government lawyers who wish to move into private practice is predicated on policy reasons: Without this rule lawyers would be effectively discouraged from entering government and civil service, which is far less lucrative than private practice can be. The general acceptance of screening for government lawyers with conflicts is important to paralegals as these principles have been applied by some courts to allow screening for paralegal conflicts. See, for example, the *Hayes* case at the end of this chapter.

As the courts rule on an increasing number of motions for disqualification, they face the challenge of applying conflicts rules consistently and fairly to complex fact situations. The courts have been somewhat inconsistent in deciding the question of whether a **substantial relationship** exists between the former and current clients' matters. Most courts examine the *facts* of the two matters to see whether it is likely that the attorney would have learned confidential factual information that relates to both matters. The ABA and other ethics experts favor this approach. A few courts look to the *legal issues* and require a clear or even identical congruence of the issues before ordering disqualification. In either case, if a court finds that the matters are not substantially related, the lawyer and the lawyer's firm will not be disqualified. If the matters are found to be substantially related, a presumption that confidential information was disclosed arises. Some courts have held that this presumption is irrebuttable, precluding evidence to the contrary, such as evidence that the attorney did not learn any confidential information on the prior matter or that the lawyer has been screened. The trend is for the court to find the presumption rebuttable and to allow the lawyer to provide evidence to overcome the presumption that confidential information has been or will be revealed.

D. Attorney as Witness

Another kind of conflict of interest arises when a lawyer or someone in the lawyer's firm is called on to testify in a case in which the lawyer is acting as an advocate.

The rationale for prohibiting a lawyer from testifying in a case in which he or she is an advocate is to protect the client's interest because the potential exists for such testimony to harm the client's case. This harm may come about in a variety of ways, depending on the nature of the attorney's testimony. If the testimony is in the client's favor, opposing counsel could discredit it by making the argument that the lawyer is biased in the client's favor. The attorney may also have an unfair advantage as a witness because a jury may give the lawyer undue credibility. Some courts and commentators express concern that opposing counsel will not examine a colleague attorney-witness vigorously out of professional courtesy. Finally, the harm to the client is clear if the lawyer's testimony is not in the client's favor.

Ethics rules prohibit **advocate-witness conflict**, and lawyers have been disqualified in cases where such conflicts were present. ABA Model Rule 3.7 prohibits a lawyer from acting as an "advocate at a trial in which the lawyer is likely to be a necessary witness" unless the testimony relates to an uncontested matter or relates to the value or nature of legal services in the case or disqualification would cause a hardship to the client. The meaning of **necessary witness** is crucial in deciding whether the lawyer can continue as counsel. If testimony would be useful but is not critical to the client's case, or if other credible evidence could be used to prove the same point, the lawyer's testimony is not "necessary." This rule also limits its application to trial situations, which enables the lawyer to represent the client in non-litigated matters as well as in pretrial and post-trial matters.

Paralegal as Witness

The rules prohibiting witness-advocate conflicts are applicable to paralegals, who are sometimes potential witnesses in litigation. The rationale stated earlier for this prohibition is not as compelling when a paralegal would be called to testify, as it is based on the advantage that a lawyer has because of his or her professional status and role as an advocate. The advocate role cannot be attributed personally to a paralegal, who does not argue the client's case in court. A more convincing argument could be made for disqualification if the paralegal's testimony would harm the client's case. Because the conflict would not be imputed to the paralegal's firm, it is unlikely that a court would force disqualification of the whole firm but the firm may decide that the paralegal should not continue to work on the case. An Ohio Ethics Opinion, 87-7 (1987), states that in-house counsel is not required to withdraw because the corporation's paralegal is called as a witness. The opinion specifically cites as a reason that the paralegal's role is not that of advocate.

REVIEW QUESTIONS

1. On what principles are the conflicts of interest rules based?
2. Why are conflicts problems so common?
3. What is the general rule about simultaneously representing two clients whose interests are adverse?
4. Can clients consent to a simultaneous conflict of interest? Under what circumstances may a client consent? What factors would a court consider in deciding whether to honor a consent?
5. What are the requirements for a client consent? What should be disclosed in a letter to a client regarding the potential conflict?
6. What do the NALA and NFPA ethical rules say about conflicts?
7. What is an issue conflict? What do the ABA Model Rules say about handling cases that present issue conflicts?
8. Is it a conflict of interest for an attorney to represent two clients whose interests were not adverse but whose trial dates conflict? Would it be a conflict of interest at all if the attorney could successfully obtain a postponement of one of the trials? Why, or why not?
9. Is it ethical for a lawyer to represent both the husband and the wife in an amicable uncontested divorce? Why, or why not? Is it wise to undertake this kind of representation?
10. Is it ethical for an attorney to represent the passenger and the driver in a lawsuit against another driver? Why, or why not?
11. Is it ethical for an attorney to represent codefendants in a criminal case? Why, or why not?
12. Can a firm represent more than one party to a business transaction?
13. Can a lawyer serve on the board of directors of a corporate client? Why or why not? Can a firm represent both a corporation and its officers?

14. Can a firm represent all the family members in creating an estate plan?
15. Can a lawyer with a conflict withdraw from representing one client and continue representing the other client?
16. What is the general rule about representing a client whose interests may be adverse to a former client?
17. What do the ABA Model Rules say about successive conflicts?
18. How and why has Canon 9 been applied in cases of successive representation? Why are courts moving away from this basis for disqualification?
19. How does a court decide if matters in successive representation are "substantially related"? If a court finds that matters are substantially related, is the lawyer or firm automatically disqualified? In what two ways might the lawyer rebut a presumption that the confidentiality of information is at risk?
20. Why is a lawyer generally prohibited from handling a litigated matter in which he or she will be called to testify? Name the exceptions to the general rule.
21. Do the rules applied to lawyer-witnesses apply equally to paralegals? Explain any differences.

DISCUSSION QUESTIONS AND HYPOTHETICALS

1. If you worked in a law firm and were getting a divorce, would you find it acceptable to have two different lawyers in your firm represent you and your spouse? What if you were getting married and needed a prenuptial agreement?
2. Do you think firms should refuse to handle matters in which there are issue conflicts? Explain your reasoning.
3. Do you think firms should have policies that prevent lawyers from representing clients who are competitors in the same industry? What are the costs and benefits of such a policy? Should a defense firm have a policy that it will not hire paralegals who have worked for plaintiffs' firms?
4. What would you do if you worked for an attorney who had such a heavy court calendar that she or he was constantly rescheduling court dates and delaying motions and trials? What does this have to do with conflicts of interest?
5. Should a firm be disqualified because one of its paralegals might be called on to testify against a client in a case? What else might the firm do besides withdrawing from representation?
6. What would you do if you knew that your firm had a conflict of interest problem that it was not addressing internally? Would it make any difference in your actions if the firm was knowingly ignoring the problem?

7. Do you think that clients should be asked to consent in advance to future conflicts that might arise? Research this area and see what ethics commentators think.

RESEARCH PROJECTS AND ASSIGNMENTS

1. Draft a letter to a client explaining a recently discovered potential conflict based on your previous employment and prepare a consent form for the client to sign.
2. Contact five local law firms and ask them to provide you with a model client consent form.
3. Locate the federal bankruptcy law that prohibits lawyers from representing a debtor in bankruptcy if the lawyer has preexisting relationships with other possible parties in the bankruptcy matter. How often has this provision been used against lawyers?
4. Check your state's ethics rules and see if they follow the ABA Model Rules exactly or if they deviate from these rules.
5. Check your state and local bars' ethics opinions to see if there are any that concern conflicts arising from the employment of nonlawyers or paralegals.
6. Firm ABC represented Jones Corporation. A lawyer in a branch office filed a lawsuit against a subsidiary of Jones. Is this a conflict? What should a court do when faced with a disqualification motion in such a matter? For one court's analysis, see *J.P. Morgan v. Liberty*, 189 F. Supp. 2d 24 (S.D.N.Y. 2002).
7. Can a lawyer represent a debtor filing for bankruptcy and one of the debtor's creditors? For a case on point, see *U.S. v. Gellene*, 182 F.3d 578, in which the offending lawyer was found guilty of fraud and disbarred.
8. An attorney represents a family. The grandmother wants to disinherit her wayward granddaughter. Can the lawyer do the estate plan? See ABA Ethics Opinion 05-432 for an analysis of "conflicting economic interests" and "expectant legal rights."

E. Other Conflicts in Relationships with Clients

1. Business Transactions with Clients

Business transactions between a lawyer and client have tremendous potential for creating serious conflicts in which a lawyer's interests differ from those of the client and with the lawyer's duties to represent the client. Further, clients rely on the lawyer's superior legal knowledge and are generally in a weaker bargaining position on the business deal. The lawyer's duties of loyalty, trust, and zealous representation are implicated whenever a lawyer enters into a business transaction with a client. If the business transaction is personal to the lawyer involved, it is not generally imputed to the firm.

The ABA Model Rules prohibit business transactions between lawyers and clients but provide for an exception with client consent. ABA Model Rule 1.8(a) prohibits a lawyer from entering into a business transaction with a client or acquiring an interest adverse to a client unless "(1) the transaction and terms . . . are fair and reasonable . . . [and] are fully disclosed . . . in writing . . . ; (2) the client is advised in writing of the desirability of seeking and is given a reasonable opportunity to seek independent legal counsel . . . ; and (3) the client gives informed consent, in a writing signed by the client, to the essential terms of the transaction and the lawyer's role. . . ."

A client's consultation with independent counsel is of utmost importance. Lawyers must allow the client a reasonable amount of time within which to obtain the opinion of independent counsel and to reflect on whether to sign the consent. Independent counsel must be truly independent; that is, not recommended by or associated with the lawyer.

In practice, lawyers and clients have many opportunities to enter into business transactions, not all of which are prohibited. Commercial transactions in which clients provide service in their business capacities, such as banking, medical services, products, and utilities, are not prohibited. In these transactions, the attorney has no advantage over the client.

Examples of business transactions that are generally prohibited include: (1) a lawyer purchasing real estate from a client while also drafting the documents relating to the sale; (2) a lawyer advising clients to make investments in businesses in which he or she has an interest; (3) a lawyer borrowing money from a client while failing to advise the client how to perfect the client's security interest; and (4) a lawyer going into business with a client, forming a corporation for the business that gives the lawyer an ownership interest and continuing to represent the corporation as its lawyer.

One interesting variation of a lawyer-client business relationship is found in firms representing start-up companies with little capital. The firms sometimes take an interest in the new company in exchange for legal services. This kind of arrangement has been upheld as long as the client consented in writing after full disclosure and an opportunity to seek independent legal advice.

Business Transaction Conflicts Involving Paralegals

Conflicts based on business transactions with clients may arise for paralegals as well as lawyers. For example, a paralegal may be invited to invest in a client's business or may own stock in a client's company. Such conflicts are more easily curable for a paralegal than they are for a lawyer because clients rely on the lawyer, not the paralegal, for legal advice, giving the lawyer a potentially unfair advantage over the client. However, paralegals should be aware of the general prohibition on business transactions with clients and take care to avoid dual roles that might create a conflict. Finally, paralegals who purchase stock in client companies must be careful to honor laws prohibiting the use of inside information in buying and selling stock, which were discussed in Chapter 4. Many law firms have rules prohibiting lawyers and paralegals from buying stock in corporations that they represent in securities work.

2. Publication, Literary, and Media Rights

A variation of the prohibition on business relationships with clients is the restriction on lawyers entering into an agreement that grants the attorney publication, literary, or media rights relating to the subject matter of his or her employment prior to the conclusion of the representation, which is found in ABA Model Rule 1.8(d). This rule protects against conflicts that might arise concerning what is best for the client as opposed to what would enhance the value of the "story," that is, the value of the lawyer's interests in the literary or media rights.

In addition to disciplinary action for violation of this rule (which is rare), this kind of conflict may be the basis of a motion to disqualify counsel or of an appeal in a criminal case based on ineffective counsel.

3. Financial Assistance to Clients

Whenever a lawyer loans funds to a client, a new dimension — that of creditor and debtor — is imposed on the attorney-client relationship. Because of the inherent conflict in both representing the client and being the client's creditor, the ABA Model Rules prohibit most kinds of financial assistance to clients. ABA Model Rule 1.8(e) permits lawyers to advance court costs and expenses, allowing repayment to be contingent on the outcome of the litigation and allowing lawyers to pay litigation costs outright for indigent clients. Some states have not adopted these two aspects of the ABA rules.

Advancing a client funds for living expenses is not allowed under the exception allowing advances for "costs." Doing so is generally regarded as unethical conduct; however, a loan from attorney to client for living expenses may be evaluated separately under the rules relating to business transactions, rather than under the rules about advancing costs.

4. Lawyer's Interest in Litigation

Lawyers are prohibited from acquiring a proprietary interest in litigation in which they are involved under ABA Model Rule 1.8(i). Contingency fees in civil cases and liens to secure fees or expenses are excepted.

The rule prohibiting an attorney from obtaining an interest in litigation derives from the old prohibitions on maintenance, ***champerty***, and ***barratry***. Under English common law these were crimes relating to "stirring up litigation." Champerty was obtaining a financial interest in the litigation. It was long felt that such conduct encouraged unmeritorious litigation and dishonesty in the courtroom.

Obviously, these old rules have changed; all jurisdictions allow contingency fees (discussed in Chapter 7) and lawyer advertising (discussed in Chapter 6). The contemporary rules on holding an interest in litigation are founded not so much on concerns about "stirring up litigation," but on the conflict that arises when an attorney "owns" a lawsuit and may be tempted to favor his or her own financial interests in the outcome over the best interests of the client.

Champerty
An old common law agreement between a lawyer and a client under which the lawyer undertakes representation and pays costs and is reimbursed and paid out of the recovery; such agreements were outlawed in most states

Barratry
The common law crime of stirring up lawsuits and disputes

5. Gifts from Clients

A long-standing rule strongly disfavors gifts made from clients to their lawyers. This rule is especially pertinent when a lawyer drafts a document under which he or she receives a gift, such as in a will or trust. This scenario is rife with potential for undue influence, fraud, and overreaching, especially because clients in such cases are frequently elderly and may be more vulnerable to overreaching by their attorneys.

Courts frequently void both inter vivos and testamentary gifts in such cases, even without an affirmative showing of undue influence. Some courts allow the attorney-beneficiary to present evidence showing the legitimacy of the gift. To do so, the attorney usually must show that the gift was fair and fully intended by the client, who had the requisite capacity and was not subject to undue influence by the lawyer. One serious additional problem sometimes results from such a gift: It may raise the question of the client's testamentary capacity, potentially voiding the entire estate plan including the gift to the attorney.

In addition to the voiding of a gift, an attorney may be subject to discipline under the state's ethics rules. ABA Model Rule 1.8(c) prohibits a lawyer from soliciting a substantial gift from a client or preparing a document in which the lawyer or a person related to the lawyer is given a gift unless the lawyer is related to the client. "Simple gifts" from clients, such as holiday presents or tokens of appreciation, are permitted under Comment 6.

One potential area for abuse arises when a lawyer drafts the documents that appoint him or her to perform additional services, such as those of executor or trustee. Although this practice is common, more questionable is the lawyer's drafting of the document nominating him or her to serve as executor or trustee and as counsel. Some states prohibit this arrangement unless the court approves it upon a finding that it is in the best interests of the estate. Comment 8 to Rule 1.8 indicates that a conflict will be found if the lawyer cannot exercise independent professional judgment in the dual role.

Gifts from Clients to Paralegals

Paralegals also have a potential conflict when a client gives them a gift, especially a valuable gift. As with business transactions, there is less risk of the appearance of undue influence when a gift is bestowed on a paralegal than on a lawyer, but the appearance of impropriety may be present nonetheless. In the case of a substantial gift, especially by an elderly or otherwise vulnerable client, it is advisable for the paralegal's supervising attorney to recommend that the client consult with independent counsel and for the paralegal to refrain from working on the gift document in any way. For example, see the *Estate of Divine* case in Chapter 2.

6. Agreements with Clients Limiting the Attorney's Malpractice Liability

Both case law and the ethics rules prohibit attorneys from attempting to limit their liability for malpractice. In this situation, the lawyer is seeking to protect his or her own interests at the expense of the client. Lawyers cannot attempt to limit their liability by asking clients to sign a disclaimer before representation or pressure a client into signing a release after the malpractice has taken place.

ABA Model Rule 1.8(h) prohibits a lawyer from attempting to limit his or her liability prospectively unless the client is represented by independent counsel. It also prohibits a lawyer from settling a malpractice claim unless the client is given the advice in writing and time to seek independent counsel.

Lawyers cannot circumvent the rule against limiting liability by including in an engagement letter or retainer agreement provisions that relieve them from responsibility. For example, a provision that attempted to relieve the attorney from further responsibility if the client failed to inform the lawyer of a new address or phone number has been held to violate ethics rules. Both case law and bar ethics opinions have consistently disallowed such provisions. Equally unacceptable is an endorsement on a check that purports to release the lawyer from liability.

7. Payment of Attorney's Fees by a Third Party

If someone other than the client pays the attorney's fees, a conflict may arise over who is guiding the representation, the client or the payor. The lawyer's loyalty and sense of responsibility may be divided and judgment clouded if the person paying the fee wants to be involved in making decisions about the case. The potential for harm to the client is greatest when the interests of the client and the one paying for the representation diverge. Some common instances of third-party payments are a parent paying the fees for a child, a spouse for another spouse, a corporation for a director, and an employer for an employee.

A related questionable situation arises when the legal fees for the representation of a criminal defendant are paid by an unknown third party, who may be the operator of the criminal enterprise for which the defendant worked. In more than one such case, the unnamed third-party payor sought to guide the defense by keeping the client quiet about matters that may have mitigated guilt or lessened the sentence imposed. This situation could not only result in an ethical breach, subjecting the attorney to a civil suit and disciplinary action, but constitutes grounds for appeal based on ineffective assistance of counsel.

Generally, the ethics rules permit third-party payment of attorney's fees so long as the third party does not interfere with the exercise of the attorney's independent professional judgment or does not otherwise interfere with the attorney-client relationship and the duties of the attorney that arise from the relationship.

ABA Model Rule 1.8(f) prohibits an attorney from accepting compensation from a third party unless the client gives informed consent, the arrangement does not result in the third party's interference with the attorney's exercise of independent judgment, and the lawyer honors the confidentiality of client information. Related is Model Rule 5.4(c), which states that lawyers shall not permit the one who pays their fees "to direct or regulate" their professional judgment. In a recent ABA Ethics Opinion, the rule was further clarified as follows: "[W]hen the lawyer recognizes the necessity of revealing confidential information relating to one client in order to effectively carry out the representation of another, . . . the lawyer would be required to withdraw from representing one or both of her clients" (ABA Formal Opinion 08-450).

These rules have been applied in employment settings in which paralegals might find themselves. For example, the salary of a lawyer in a public defender's office is paid by a government entity, not by the indigent client who the attorney represents. The courts have upheld this arrangement so long as those who have interests that may conflict with a client's do not influence the lawyer's professional judgment and conduct or compensation. The issue is more complicated when a legal advocacy organization that has a political agenda is representing a client whose personal interests may at some time clash with those of the organization. The U.S. Supreme Court has endorsed the activities of such organizations and struck down the application of state statutes and ethics regulations that attempted to limit their activities. See *NAACP v. Button*, 371 U.S. 415 (1963), which was based on the First Amendment right of free association. The Court held in *NAACP* that only a compelling state interest could justify regulation that would limit activities of the organization in bringing lawsuits to redress grievances.

8. Relatives and Close Friends

The face of the legal profession has changed dramatically in the last 30 years. The number of women entering law school has increased from less than 10 percent in 1970 to about 50 percent now. Women now make up about 35 percent of the lawyers in the country, and the percentage shifts upward a bit every year as more women graduate from law school and more older lawyers (mainly men) retire. As women lawyers have entered what used to be a male-dominated profession, the potential for conflicts based on family relationships has greatly multiplied. When married or other closely related attorneys represent adverse interests, the possibility of a conflict that may harm a client clearly exists. Spouses naturally discuss their work with one another, giving rise to the risk of disclosure of confidential information, which can be especially harmful if the spouse who learns the information represents the opposing side in a matter. Duties of loyalty and zealous representation are also implicated; an attorney-spouse may not fight as zealously for a client when the opposing counsel is his or her spouse. Because spouses have a financial interest in one another's income, the potential to increase the marital funds from a large fee may also influence an attorney-spouse's sense of loyalty or independent judgment.

Conflicts based on family or other close relationships are not covered explicitly in the language of the rule; however, Comment 11 to Model Rule 1.7 states that lawyers who are closely related (e.g., "parent, child, sibling, or spouse") may not ordinarily represent opposing clients in the same matter without informed consent. Family conflicts are not imputed to the lawyer's firm.

Some states have more specific prohibitions in this kind of situation, listing the specific relatives who are affected and expanding the scope of the rule to specified nonrelatives. For example, the California rule covers persons who live with the lawyer or have an intimate personal relationship with the lawyer.

Relatives of Paralegals

The ethical rules governing conflicts based on family relationships are also applicable to paralegals. The potential for disclosure of protected information is just as great when the conflict involves a paralegal as when it involves a lawyer. Law firms should consider family conflicts when conducting conflicts checks. Paralegals who are related by blood or marriage to someone working in the legal community must be certain to inform their firms fully of their family relationships so that potential conflicts can be identified and addressed.

Two state ethics opinions have addressed the problems created when a paralegal is related to another person involved in a representation. Vermont Ethics Opinion 87-15 (1987) recommended that a law firm could represent clients in a real estate transaction in which the adverse party was the spouse of one of the firm's paralegals so long as the situation was fully disclosed to the client, the paralegal did not work on the matter, and the paralegal was admonished not to reveal client confidences or secrets. Similarly, Michigan Ethics Opinion CI-1168 (1986) found that a legal services organization could represent a plaintiff in an action in which a potential defendant was about to be married to the organization's paralegal and in another action in which the fiancé's father (and paralegal's future father-in-law) was a defendant. The opinion advised full disclosure and consent by the client-plaintiffs. Absent consent, the opinions advised that the organization would be required to withdraw from representation or to terminate the paralegal's employment.

F. Imputed Disqualification

1. Introduction

As mentioned throughout the previous sections, the conflict of one person in a firm may cause the entire firm to be disqualified from representing a client. ***Vicarious or imputed disqualification*** is based mainly on the somewhat outdated idea that all the lawyers in a firm know everything about all the clients and cases being handled by the firm. Particularly, the partners in a firm (rather than other employees, whether lawyers or nonlawyers) are believed to share confidential information about clients. Although sharing of information to this extent no longer characterizes large law firms, other grounds for imputing conflicts lie in conflicting financial incentives. Even if confidential information can be protected by

Vicarious or imputed disqualification
The imputation of a conflict to others in a firm so that the entire firm is disqualified from undertaking the representation

careful screening, it may not be possible to protect against the actual or perceived pressure to handle a case in a manner that will most benefit the firm and not necessarily be the most beneficial for the client.

When a firm is disqualified by a court, it may be required to **disgorge fees** paid for the legal services during the representation. This remedy is most often applied when the firm knew or should have known of the conflict and failed to disclose it to the client. A disqualification may also be the basis for a **malpractice** case against the lawyer and firm for breach of fiduciary duty.

The strict application of imputed disqualification rules has created severe problems for law firms, individual lawyers, and clients. Today lawyers do not stay in one law firm for their whole careers as they did 20 years ago, and clients choose lawyers on a matter-by-matter basis. Law firms merge and dissolve, creating great potential for conflicts. Vicarious disqualification also poses special concerns for paralegals, whose job mobility is threatened by an overly rigid application of the rules.

2. ABA and State Rules on Imputation of Conflicts and Screening

ABA Model Rule 1.10 does not apply the imputed disqualification rule equally to all kinds of conflicts. It does not prohibit the firm or lawyer from representing the client if the conflict is personal to the lawyer, such as those conflicts covered in Rule 1.8, such as business transactions and gifts from clients. Part (b) of the Rule covers conflicts that may be created when a **lawyer leaves a firm**. The firm may represent a client whose interests are adverse to those of a former client of the lawyer who left unless the matter is the same or substantially the same, or unless any remaining lawyer has confidential information related to the matter. The rule allows for informed written client consent to conflicts that are imputed to a firm.

In an important revision adopted in 2009, screening is allowed in situations covered by Rule 1.9, that is, when lawyers change firms. Lawyers must assert that no confidential information will be communicated to the new firm. The screening must be timely, notice of the screening procedures must be given to the former client, and certification of compliance must be given "at reasonable intervals" upon request. This change was considered for several years before it was adopted. Support was not unanimous either within the ABA or among the states. About half of the states allow screening in scenarios like this one, and about half do not.

As noted earlier in this chapter, the Model Rules also have specific provisions for **government lawyers**. Rule 1.11(a) allows a former government lawyer to represent a client in a matter in which the lawyer participated while employed by the government, with the agency's informed written consent. It further allows another lawyer in the firm to undertake representation when such a conflict exists, provided the former government lawyer is screened from the case and receives no part of the fee, and written notice is given to the government agency. The rule also prohibits a former government lawyer from representing a client against a person about whom the lawyer has damaging confidential information obtained while the lawyer was in government service. Screening and disallowing fee participation in the matter are permitted to enable another lawyer in the former government lawyer's firm to represent such a client. Rule 1.11(d) covers lawyers who are currently employed by the government. It prohibits them from participating in matters in which they were previously involved in private practice and from negotiating for private employment with an opposing attorney or party in a current case.

3. Court Rulings on Imputed Disqualification

Most court decisions on vicarious disqualification were made during the time that the ABA Model Code was followed by nearly all jurisdictions. As a result, the courts have frequently applied a per se rule of imputed disqualification. The trend, however, is toward a more flexible approach, under which the presumption of imputed disqualification may be rebutted by evidence that the disqualified lawyer did not have access to confidential information or that the disqualified lawyer is being properly screened from any involvement in the matter in question. See, for example, *People ex rel. Dept. of Corp. v. Speedee Oil Change Systems, Inc.*, 20 Cal. 4th 1135 (1999). Not all courts are in favor of this trend. Some continue to follow "bright-line" rules requiring disqualification of lawyers and nonlawyers in all simultaneous conflicts where there is not client consent.

4. Use of Screens to Avoid Disqualification

The use of **screening** to overcome disqualification of the entire firm first arose in cases involving former government lawyers. Although the risk of conflicts involving former government lawyers is especially high because of their perceived inside knowledge, connections, and influence, the legal community has been concerned about the ability of government lawyers to move into private practice. If disqualification rules are strictly applied, and screens are not allowed to overcome them, government lawyers' employment options are quite limited. Going into government service would become a "permanent" career choice, a significant deterrent to entering government service, in which salaries are substantially lower than in private practice.

Screen or cone of silence
Isolates a disqualified person by setting up law office procedures to prevent the affected person from any involvement with or communication about the matter

Screening in private law firms, in cases involving attorney and nonlawyer employees not previously in government service, has become common practice. A screen (which used to be called a *Chinese wall* and is sometimes also called a ***cone of silence*** or ethical wall) isolates the disqualified attorney or paralegal by setting up office procedures to prevent the disqualified person from having access to information about the matter and from being involved in any way in the matter. Screens are often a requirement for a client consent or waiver and are sometimes used when consent cannot be obtained in an attempt to avoid disqualification.

For a court to find that a screen is effective, careful procedures should be followed:

- A **memorandum** concerning the affected matter and person involved should be sent to the entire firm, including lawyer and nonlawyer staff, spelling out the restrictions on access to confidential information and on communicating about the matter.
- **Files and documents** should be marked to indicate the limitations on access. Hard copy files should be stored separately in a place that cannot be accessed by the affected person. Programmed computer warnings or blocks should be employed to prevent the screened employee from having access to documents on the firm's computer network.
- Firm and department e-mails and voice mails concerning the matter in question should not be communicated to the affected lawyer or paralegal.
- The wall must be erected in a **timely** manner, for example, before the affected person begins employment with the firm or as soon as the conflict is discovered.
- **Physical separation** of the disqualified person from those working on the case is also advisable. In other words, the affected person should not share the same or proximate workspace with others working on the case.
- The affected person should sign an **agreement** vowing not to disclose any confidential information about the matter and not to discuss the matter with anyone at the firm.
- An attorney who is disqualified should agree not to **share fees** generated by the matter, so accounting procedures should be set up to ensure that fees are not shared.
- If the matter extends over a long period of time, the announcements of the screen should be **republished** periodically as a reminder and for the benefit of new employees.

Proving the effectiveness of a screen can be challenging. For the most part, a court evaluating the procedures expects to review affidavits and testimony about the thoroughness and care of the measures taken and the extent to which they are observed. Screening procedures should be routine and careful records must be kept. A court will examine not only the specific procedures in place, but the context of the situation. Is the firm large or small? Does the disqualified attorney or paralegal work in the same department or physical area of the office as the team representing the client in question? Where are the files relating to the case kept? Do the disqualified person and the staff handling the representation work on other matters together? Does the firm have sanctions for breaking the rules relating to the wall? How many other persons in the firm have access to the confidential information?

Firms sometimes use disqualification motions as a **strategy**, to delay a case from proceeding to trial even if they do not reasonably believe that confidential client information has been compromised. Courts look askance at such motions, especially if they are not made as early as possible in the proceedings or are based more on appearance of impropriety than on any real danger of harm to a client or a likely breach of confidentiality or loyalty. Firms have also been known to use the disqualification rules to prevent another firm from being able to represent a client on a specific matter. For example, a large corporate client may refer minor matters to all the competitor firms in town so that, in the event of litigation, no other qualified attorney without a conflict is available to represent the opposing party—that is, all the attorneys are "conflicted out."

As noted above, the ABA Model Rules now support the use of screens, and the trend among states is to endorse this practice as well. At the present time, more than 25 states allow screens, which is a substantial increase since the last revision of this text. (For a recent court decision exemplifying this trend, see *Kirk v. First American Title Ins.*, 183 Cal. App. 4th 776, 108 Cal. Rptr. 3d 620 (2010).) Advocates of screens as a means to cure an imputed conflict believe not only that the rules are antiquated and impair lawyer mobility and client choice of counsel, but that they discriminate unfairly against private lawyers in favor of government lawyers.

Screening Paralegals and Other Nonlawyer Employees

Many cases in the last decade have addressed the application of the conflict rules to paralegals. The crux of many of these cases is whether a screen can protect a firm from being disqualified because of a conflict of a paralegal. In 1988, the ABA issued Informal Opinion 88-1521, which endorsed the screening of paralegals and which has been followed in most cases decided since that time.

> A law firm that employs a nonlawyer who formerly was employed by another firm may continue representing clients whose interests conflict with the interests of clients of the former employer on whose matters the nonlawyer has worked, as long as the employing firm screens the nonlawyer from information about or participating in matters involving those clients and strictly adheres to the screening process described in this

> opinion and as long as no information relating to the representation of the clients of the former employer is revealed by the nonlawyer to any person in the employing firm. In addition, the nonlawyer's former employer must admonish the nonlawyer against revelation of information relating to the representation of clients of the former employer.

The opinion distinguishes between using a screen for a lawyer's conflicts and using one for those of a paralegal. At the time this opinion was written, a conflict occasioned by a lawyer's move to another firm would usually result in the disqualification of the new firm, and a screen would not protect the firm from disqualification in most states. However, this advisory opinion found that a paralegal with a similar conflict can be screened, thereby preventing the paralegal's firm's disqualification. The rationale for the more flexible application of screens in cases involving paralegals is expressed in the opinion as follows:

> It is important that nonlawyer employees have as much mobility in employment opportunity as possible consistent with the protection of clients' interests. To so limit employment opportunities that some non-lawyers trained to work with law firms might be required to leave the careers for which they are trained would disserve clients as well as the legal profession. Accordingly, any restrictions on the nonlawyer's employment should be held to the minimum necessary to protect confidentiality of client information.

The ABA Model Guidelines for the Utilization of Paralegal Services also endorse the use of screens for conflicts involving paralegals. The American Law Institute Restatement early on endorsed the principle that disqualification rules for lawyers should not limit paralegal job mobility. Comment 4 to Rule 1.10 was added in 2001, stating that imputed disqualification does not apply to nonlawyers, including paralegals, legal secretaries, or law clerks. It also states:

> Such persons, however, ordinarily must be screened from any personal participation in the matter to avoid communication to others in the firm of confidential information that both the nonlawyers and the firm have a legal duty to protect.

Several important state cases decided in the 1990s demonstrate the complexities of this issue and the range of opinions expressed by courts. In an early and influential California case, *In re Complex Asbestos Litigation*, the plaintiff's attorney, a sole practitioner, was disqualified from a number of asbestos cases because his paralegal had previously worked for a firm representing several of the defendants in the case, and he had made no attempt to screen this paralegal. The California Court of Appeal clearly endorsed the use of a screening procedure for paralegals to rebut the presumption that confidential information was shared (even though the paralegal in this case was not screened). See this case at the end of this chapter.

Several Texas cases have fleshed out the rules about paralegal conflicts. The Texas Supreme Court endorsed the use of screens for paralegals in ongoing litigation in the case of *Phoenix Founders, Inc. v. Marshall*, 887 S.W.2d 831 (Tex. 1994), presented later in this chapter. In other cases, courts approved the use of screens but found the procedures employed by the firms to be inadequate. See, for example, *Grant v. Thirteenth Court of Appeals*, 38 Tex. Sup. Ct. J. 12 (1994). In a more recent decision, the Texas Court of Appeals denied a disqualification, citing careful procedures put in place to screen the paralegal from participation in the case (*Rubin v. Enns*, 23 S.W.3d 382 (2000)). In *In re American Home Products Corp.*, 985 S.W.2d 68 (1998), the Court applied the precedents to a complicated situation involving a freelance paralegal and co-counsel. The Texas Supreme Court disqualified a lawyer, holding that the paralegal (who protested that she was not a paralegal and did not have confidential information) did have a conflict and that she was not properly screened. The Texas appellate courts have also addressed a conflict that arose when a lawyer worked for opposing counsel as a paralegal prior to becoming a lawyer. Although the court affirmed that the presumption of shared confidences is rebuttable for paralegals, it applied an irrebuttable presumption to these facts and disqualified the firm. *In re TXU U.S. Holdings Co.*, 110 S.W.3d 62 (2002). Finally, in a recent appellate court case, a firm was disqualified despite having screened the paralegal. See *In re Guaranty Ins. Serv., Inc.*, No. 03-09-00640-CV (Tex. App. 2010).

Cases involving paralegal conflicts have been decided at the appellate level in Florida, but the judicial districts there do not share a single formulation of a rule. See *Koulisis v. Rivers*, 730 So. 2d 289 (Fla. App. 4th Dist. 1999); *Stewart v. Bee-Dee Neon & Signs, Inc.*, 751 So. 2d 196 (Fla. App. 1st Dist. 2000); *First Miami Securities, Inc. v. Sylvia*, 780 So. 2d 250 (Fla. App. 3d Dist. 2001); *Lansing v. Lansing*, 784 So. 2d 1254 (Fla. App. 5th Dist. 2001); *Matluck v. Matluck*, 825 So. 2d 1071 (Fla. App. 4th Dist. 2002); *Sultan v. Earing-Doud*, 852 So. 2d 313 (Fla. App. 4th Dist. 2003); *Eastrich No. 157 Corp. v. Gatto*, 868 So. 2d 1266 (Fla. App. 4th Dist. 2004).

Arizona addressed the issue in *Smart Industries Corp. v. Superior Court*, 876 P.2d 1176 (Ariz. App. Div. 1 1994), and Oklahoma recently set its standards in *Hayes v. Central State Orthopedic Specialists, Inc.*, 2002 Okla. 30, 51 P.3d 562 (Okla. 2002). The Ohio Supreme Court has established an analysis for deciding when a nonlawyer conflict will result in the disqualification of a law firm in *Green v. Toledo Hosp.*, 94 Ohio St. 3d 480, 764 N.E.2d 979 (2002). The Nevada Supreme Court overruled its 1997 decision disallowing screens for paralegals in the case of *Leibowitz v. Dist. Ct.*, 119 Nev. Adv. Op. No. 57, 78 P.3d 515 (2003), overruling in part *Ciaffone v. District Court*, 113 Nev. 1165, 945 P.2d 950 (1997). See this case at the end of the chapter.

Kansas is the only state whose supreme court has taken a more restrictive view. See *Zimmerman v. Mahaska Bottling Co.*, 270 Kan. 810, 19 P.3d 784 (2001), included at the end of this chapter.

Several bar association ethics opinions have also addressed the issue. See, for example, Alabama Ethics Opinion 89-94 (1989); Florida Advisory Opinion 86-5 (1986); Kentucky Bar Association Ethics Opinion E-308 (1985), which imposes eight steps (including an effective screen) on the former and employing firm to ensure against breaches of confidentiality; North Carolina Ethics Opinions 74 (1989) and 176 (1994); Philadelphia Ethics Opinion 80-77 (1980); Vermont Bar Association Opinion 78-2 (1978); New Jersey Ethics Opinion 665 (1992) reversing an earlier opinion; and Michigan Ethics Opinions RI-115 (1992) and RI-284 (1996). The Nebraska State Bar continues to retain its Ethics Opinion 94-4 in which it states that a "law firm must avoid the present representation of a cause against a client of a law firm with which any present lawyer, law clerk, paralegal, secretary or other ancillary staff-member was formerly associated, and which cause involves a subject matter which is the same as or substantially related to that handled by the former firm while such person was associated with that firm." Citing to Nebraska court cases, the opinion states, "a Chinese wall does little or nothing to erase the appearance of impropriety."

As the courts are faced with more cases involving paralegal conflicts, it seems likely that most of them will apply the conflicts rules with some flexibility. As is evident from the cases in this chapter, the courts have shown sensitivity to the different roles of the lawyer and paralegal and to the problems of job changing in an increasingly mobile legal business.

G. Conflicts Checks

Conducting a conflicts check when a firm is considering hiring a new employee, representing a new client, or undertaking a new matter is necessary to identify potential and real conflicts. Comment 3 to ABA Model Rule 1.7 calls for every lawyer to "adopt reasonable procedures, appropriate for the size and type of firm and practice, to determine in both litigation and non-litigation matters the persons and issues involved" so that a determination can be made as to whether a conflict or potential conflict exists.

When a **prospective client** seeks representation by a firm, the lawyer or paralegal who has the initial contact with the person should obtain information necessary to conduct the conflicts check before the prospective client reveals confidential information about the matter for which representation is sought. This early detection process gives greater protection of the confidential information in the event that the firm does not undertake representation and prevents the law firm from inadvertently placing itself in a conflict situation that would require disqualification. New client information obtained should relate to the client's activities and the nature of representation sought. If the client is a business client, such as a corporation or partnership, the information should include the names of subsidiaries and other related businesses as well as principal shareholders, officers, directors, partners, and the like. The lawyer and client should discuss the nature of the legal services sought — for instance, whether representation is needed for a single matter such as a lawsuit or negotiation of a business deal or is needed for an array of ongoing legal matters. If a lawsuit is contemplated, the names of potential adversaries should be obtained. Finally, if the client has other legal matters pending, basic information about these matters (such as the names of adversaries and counsel) should be obtained. When an existing client seeks representation on a new matter, information relating to the nature of this matter and potential adversaries should always be obtained. Finally, it is good practice to update client information on existing clients regularly — names of officers and directors and the nature of business activities, for instance — to ensure the accuracy and currency of all information.

Similarly, prospective employees, including both lawyers and nonlawyers, must provide the firm with basic information about matters on which they worked in previous employment, major business or financial interests that have the potential to create conflicts, and personal and family relationships that may give rise to conflicts. It is critical in providing this information not to reveal any confidences and to supply the minimum amount of information needed to conduct a conflicts check. ABA Formal Ethics Opinion 09-455 provides guidance to lawyers and paralegals who are changing firms and to the firms that hope to hire them. It states in part:

> Any disclosure of conflicts information should be no greater than reasonably necessary to accomplish the purpose of detecting and resolving conflicts and must not compromise the attorney-client privilege or otherwise prejudice a client or former client. A lawyer or law firm receiving conflicts information may not reveal such information or use it for purposes other than detecting and resolving conflicts of interest. Disclosure normally should not occur until the moving lawyers and the prospective new firm have engaged in substantive discussion regarding a possible new association.

The firm must process the information to determine if any conflicts or potential conflicts exist that would preclude representation or would require consents or the erection of a screen to isolate the disqualified employee. Many firms have computer software programs to conduct conflicts checks quickly and thoroughly. Although a database is an important tool, many firms are finding that using a database alone is not sufficient to identify all potential conflicts. To provide further screening, firms are communicating with daily e-mail alerts about new client matters and using in-house conflicts specialists to follow through on all checks.

Firms also need an established procedure for evaluating conflicts that have been identified through the conflicts check. They need to decide how the firm should address a potential conflict: How serious is the conflict? Is it the kind of conflict that would be imputed to the firm? Can the firm provide adequate representation under the circumstances? Can client consent be obtained? Will a screen be allowed? Some firms have an ethics or conflicts committee or an ethicist-lawyer to advise on these matters. Prompt action on new clients and matters is essential to prevent a client or prospective client from delay in securing counsel. The conflicts committee should evaluate each new client, new matter, and new prospective employee — along with any potential conflicts they carry with them — applying the relevant ethics rules, case law, and firm policies that may have an impact on their decision.

Another way firms are protecting themselves against conflicts is to send very clear and detailed letters to parties with whom they have some contact but are not representing, for example, prospective clients, parties in joint litigation, and peripheral parties in transactions. These letters explain that the firm is not representing the party. Likewise, engagement letters for clients should be clear about the scope of the representation to keep the firm from being conflicted out of representing another client in a different matter that may come up later.

Avoiding conflicts of interest is a critical matter for paralegals. Like lawyers, paralegals have an ethical responsibility to keep good records of the matters on which they work and to be forthcoming with this information when appropriate. When a paralegal prepares to change jobs, begins work on a new matter, or engages in freelance work, the record of client matters on which the paralegal worked will be needed. At least one state, New York, requires lawyers to keep records of client matters for this purpose.

For freelance and independent contractor paralegals, every new assignment is a job change; freelancing greatly increases the potential for greater numbers of conflicts. Although it has become common practice for freelance paralegals and lawyers to handle assignments on a temporary, as-needed basis, this practice does necessitate careful monitoring. ABA Formal Opinion 88-356 (1988) endorses the use of temporary lawyers and the agencies that place them in firms but warns that special care is required to ensure against conflicts and breaches of confidentiality. These same principles apply to the increasingly common practice of outsourcing legal work.

The NFPA Model Code recognizes the importance of conflicts checks by calling on paralegals to "create and maintain an effective record keeping system" to enable the paralegal to identify conflicts, to reveal such information as is necessary to evaluate the existence of an actual conflict, and to comply with screening procedures. NFPA Model Code EC-1.6(d).

REVIEW QUESTIONS

1. What is the general rule about business transactions between lawyers and clients? Give an example of a business transaction between a lawyer and a client. Why do ethics rules prohibit them? Name two conditions necessary for a business transaction to override the ethics rules' prohibitions.
2. What is the general rule about an attorney being granted publication and media rights? What is the rationale behind it?
3. Are attorneys prohibited from paying clients' costs in a matter? Loaning a client money? Why? What are the circumstances under which a lawyer may cover a client's costs?
4. Why are lawyers prohibited from obtaining an ownership interest in a lawsuit they are handling? How does this rule square with the idea of contingency fees?
5. Under what circumstances are gifts from clients prohibited? Explain the rationale. What steps should be taken to legitimize a gift to an attorney? Do some states have statutes that cover this situation? How and why?
6. May an attorney attempt to limit his or her malpractice liability to a client in advance of the representation? Why or why not? May a lawyer get a client to settle a malpractice claim in writing? Under what conditions?
7. What potential conflicts arise when a third party pays a client's legal fees? Give two examples of how this can commonly come up. How can an attorney accept the fee and guard against the conflicts that might arise from it? How do these rules affect legal aid organizations? Public defenders' offices?
8. What do the ethics rules say about closely related attorneys representing adverse interests? What family or other relationships are covered? Do these rules apply to paralegals? Do any state's rules cover relationships outside of blood or marriage? Are these conflicts imputed to a paralegal's firm?
9. What is imputed disqualification? What is the basis for this rule? How does the rule apply to paralegals?
10. What do the ABA Model Rules say about imputed disqualification?
11. What is the basis for screens being used to prevent disqualification in the case of former government lawyers?
12. What do the new ABA rules say about screens for lawyers? Why is this position changing?
13. What are the elements of a screen that will withstand judicial scrutiny?
14. Why might a court look with disfavor on disqualification motions?
15. What does the ABA say about the use of screens in conflicts cases involving paralegals? Is this policy more flexible than that applied to attorneys? Why?

16. How do the states stand on the use of screens in cases involving paralegals?
17. How should a conflicts check be conducted when a firm has a new client? A new matter or case? A new employee? On an ongoing basis?
18. Describe a paralegal's obligation to avoid conflicts when changing positions. How does this differ from the requirements for freelance paralegals?
19. What do the ABA Model Guidelines for the Utilization of Paralegal Services say about screening of paralegals? What do the state guidelines say? How do NALA and NFPA address paralegal conflicts in their ethics codes?

DISCUSSION QUESTIONS AND HYPOTHETICALS

1. Do you think paralegals should be subject to the same rules on conflicts as lawyers? Why, or why not? Make a list of the reasons on each side of this argument.
2. Do you think the rules on conflicts of interest are antiquated? Why, or why not? How would you change them to make them more responsive to the current and future legal environment?
3. Do you think that it is fair for former government lawyers to be able to avoid conflicts with screens, but not lawyers who have worked only in the private sector? Be sure to state the rationale for this exception for government lawyers and either support or refute it. Should the rules for government lawyers also apply to those who work for nonprofits, such as political advocacy groups and legal aid providers? Why or why not?
4. What would you do if a client of an attorney with whom you work asked you to invest in his or her business? Buy property from him or her? Do you think that entering into these transactions would create a conflict of interest? Why or why not? How could you remedy the conflict?
5. Do you think that a paralegal obtaining the rights to a current client's story creates a conflict of interest? Why or why not?
6. Would you loan a client money for living expenses? Why or why not? Would your answer be different if lending the money would keep your client from accepting a low settlement offer because of the client's dire financial condition?
7. What would you do if an elderly client wanted to leave you a substantial gift in his or her will? Would it make any difference if the client had no other living relatives? If the client wanted to do this because she was estranged from her children?

8. What would you do if a client gave you a valuable piece of jewelry? Would it make a difference if the gift were in thanks for your work on a case? What if the client promised to give you a personal "bonus" if your firm prevailed in the case?
9. What would you do if you worked for a firm that had all new clients sign an engagement agreement limiting the firm's malpractice liability?
10. Do you think the rules prohibiting conflicts among relatives should be limited to parents, children, siblings, and spouses? What about roommates? Long-term live-in relationships? In-laws? Civil partnerships that are recognized in some states for gay couples? Is it any "safer" for closely related lawyers and paralegals to work in the same firm? What kinds of ethical and other problems might this create? Should these conflicts be imputed to the firm?
11. List all the reasons you can think of to justify imputed disqualification. Do these reasons also apply to paralegals? Should the same rules of imputed disqualification apply to paralegals?
12. Knowing how people love to talk about their work, do you think an internal memorandum telling the staff not to discuss a particular case with a certain employee is really an effective method to protect confidentiality? What other measures or sanctions would be more effective?
13. Do you think it is possible to screen an employee in a small law firm, for example, a firm with one lawyer, one paralegal, and one secretary? What if the firm had two lawyers, two paralegals, and two secretaries?
14. Make a list of all the information you would want to conduct a conflicts check on the following: (1) a new client; (2) a new matter for an existing client; (3) a prospective paralegal employee; (4) a prospective attorney employee; (5) a prospective partner.
15. Who do you think should conduct conflicts checks and decide how to handle conflicts matters within a law firm? Does it make a difference if the firm is a national, multi-branch firm or a small, local firm?
16. What kinds of conflicts policies (going beyond the legal ethics rules) do you think a law firm should ideally have? Consider the economic implications of policies that may impose limits on a firm's accepting cases.
17. What kind of information should a paralegal keep on his or her own career conflict list? When should a paralegal give this information to prospective employers? Does supplying this information in itself violate confidentiality rules? What should you do if a firm that has offered you a job does not request this information?
18. Should agencies that place paralegals in temporary or freelance jobs do conflicts checks before they send a paralegal to a law firm? Why or why not? Should a paralegal work for an agency that fails to do this? What would you do if you went out on a freelance job and

discovered after two days that you had worked on the opposing side of the case the previous week?

19. Bill Brown is a paralegal who works for a large law firm handling the defense in some major products liability litigation. Bill knows that the cases are settling and that he may therefore lose his job. During his employment for this firm, he met a solo lawyer, Mary Maynard, a plaintiff's lawyer who was on the opposition in a few of the products liability cases. He really respected Mary's work. She does family law cases in addition to the litigation that Bill worked on. Can he contact Mary about employment with her? If she offers him a position, can he take it? Are there any restrictions on his work for her firm? Can he check the computer files of the firm to see what cases Mary and his firm have in common? Can he work for Mary on other cases? If so, what measures must be taken to guard against a conflict? Can he go to work for Mary after the products liability cases settle?

RESEARCH PROJECTS AND ASSIGNMENTS

1. What are your state's ethics rules on conflicts of interest? Does your state or local bar have any special guidelines or ethics opinions on the application of conflict rules to paralegals? Are there any cases in your state involving firm disqualification because of a paralegal conflict of interest?
2. Interview paralegals at five local law firms of different sizes and ask them about their policies and procedures for establishing screens and conducting conflicts checks. Ask the paralegal manager or a senior paralegal if they believe that screens are effective.
3. Draft a form to use for conflicts checks of paralegals and the related policies on how and when checks are done and follow-up procedures.
4. Draft an "I'm not your lawyer" letter to a prospective client that your firm interviewed but decided not to represent.
5. The question of what to disclose when interviewing for a position is sometimes challenging because it pits two ethics principles — avoiding conflicts of interest and protecting client confidences — against each other. For one local bar's guidance on what to do when interviewing with a new firm, see D.C. Ethics Opinion 2002-312. Summarize this opinion for the class.
6. What happens when a paralegal becomes a lawyer? Which rules apply? See *In re TXU U.S. Holdings Company*, 110 S.W.3d 62 (2002), for one court's application of the rules.
7. Do the rules about nonlawyer employees apply when a former employee of the opposing party is hired by a law firm? See *In re Bell Helicopter Textron*, 87 S.W.3d 139 (2002).

8. In the *Lamb* case at the end of this chapter, the court found that the screen had been effective in preventing confidences from being revealed. For another recent case, where the court found that the screen was not adequate, see *In re Guaranty Ins. Serv., Inc.*, No. 03-09-00640-CV (Tex. App. 2010), and be sure to read the strong dissent, which contends that the court applied the wrong standard.

CASES FOR ANALYSIS

In this California case of first impression, a sole practitioner was disqualified from handling several asbestos cases when a paralegal who had previously worked for the defense firm involved came to work for him.

In re Complex Asbestos Litigation

232 Cal. App. 3d 572, 283 Cal. Rptr. 732 (1991)

Attorney Jeffrey B. Harrison, his law firm, and their affected clients appeal from an order disqualifying the Harrison firm in nine asbestos-related personal injury actions. The appeal presents the difficult issue of whether a law firm should be disqualified because an employee of the firm possessed attorney-client confidences from previous employment by opposing counsel in pending litigation. We hold that disqualification is appropriate unless there is written consent or the law firm has effectively screened the employee from involvement with the litigation to which the information relates. . . .

Michael Vogel worked as a paralegal for the law firm of Brobeck, Phleger & Harrison (Brobeck) from October 28, 1985, to November 30, 1988. Vogel came to Brobeck with experience working for a law firm that represented defendants in asbestos litigation. Brobeck also represented asbestos litigation defendants, including respondents. At Brobeck, Vogel worked exclusively on asbestos litigation.

During most of the period Brobeck employed Vogel, he worked on settlement evaluations. . . .

Vogel also monitored trial events, received daily reports from the attorneys in trial, and relayed trial reports to the clients. . . .

In 1988, Vogel's duties changed when he was assigned to work for a trial team. With that change, Vogel no longer was involved with the settlement evaluation meetings and reports. Instead, he helped prepare specific cases assigned to the team. Vogel did not work on any cases in which the Harrison firm represented the plaintiffs. . . .

Brobeck gave Vogel two weeks' notice of his termination, though his termination date was later extended to the end of November.

Vogel contacted a number of firms about employment, and learned that the Harrison firm was looking for paralegals. The Harrison firm recently had opened a Northern California office and filed a number of asbestos cases against respondents. Sometime in the second half of November 1988, Vogel called Harrison to ask him for a job with his firm.

In that first telephone conversation, Harrison learned that Vogel had worked for Brobeck on asbestos litigation settlements. Harrison testified that he did not then offer Vogel a job for two reasons. First, Harrison did not think he would need a new paralegal until February or March of 1989. Second, Harrison was concerned about the appearance of a conflict of interest in his firm's hiring a paralegal from Brobeck. Harrison discussed the conflict problem with other attorneys, and told Vogel that he could be hired only if Vogel got a waiver from the senior asbestos litigation partner at Brobeck.

Vogel testified that he spoke with Stephen Snyder, the Brobeck partner in charge of managing the Northern California asbestos litigation. Vogel claimed he told Snyder of the possible job with the Harrison firm, and that Snyder later told him the clients had approved and that Snyder would provide a written waiver if Vogel wanted. In his testimony, Snyder firmly denied having any such conversations or giving Vogel any conflicts waiver to work for Harrison. The trial court resolved this credibility dispute in favor of Snyder.

While waiting for a job with the Harrison firm, Vogel went to work for Bjork, which represented two of the respondents in asbestos litigation in Northern California. Vogel worked for Bjork during December 1988, organizing boxes of materials transferred from Brobeck to Bjork. While there, Vogel again called Harrison to press him for a job. Vogel told Harrison that Brobeck had approved his working for Harrison, and Harrison offered Vogel a job starting after the holidays. During their conversations, Harrison told Vogel the job involved work on complex, nonasbestos civil matters, and later would involve processing release documents and checks for asbestos litigation settlements. Harrison did not contact Brobeck to confirm Vogel's claim that he made a full disclosure and obtained Brobeck's consent. Nor did Harrison tell Vogel that he needed a waiver from Bjork.

Vogel informed Bjork he was quitting to work for the Harrison firm. Vogel told a partner at Bjork that he wanted experience in areas other than asbestos litigation, and that he would work on securities and real estate development litigation at the Harrison firm. Initially, Vogel's work for the Harrison firm was confined to those two areas.

However, at the end of February 1989, Vogel was asked to finish another paralegal's job of contacting asbestos plaintiffs to complete client questionnaires. The questionnaire answers provided information for discovery requests by the defendants. Vogel contacted Bjork and others to request copies of discovery materials for the Harrison firm. Vogel also assisted when the Harrison firm's asbestos trial teams needed extra help.

In March 1989, Snyder learned from a Brobeck trial attorney that Vogel was involved in asbestos litigation. In a March 31 letter, Snyder asked Harrison if Vogel's duties included asbestos litigation. Harrison responded to Snyder by letter on April 6. In the letter, Harrison stated Vogel told Snyder his work for the Harrison firm would include periodic work on asbestos cases, and that Harrison assumed there was no conflict of interest. Harrison also asked Snyder to provide details of the basis for any claimed conflict. There were no other communications between Brobeck and the Harrison firm concerning Vogel before the disqualification motion was filed.

In June, a Harrison firm attorney asked Vogel to call respondent Fibreboard Corporation to see if it would accept service of a subpoena for its corporate minutes. Vogel called the company and spoke to a person he knew from working for Brobeck. Vogel asked who should be served with the subpoena in place of the company's retired general counsel. Vogel's call prompted renewed concern among respondents' counsel over Vogel's involvement with asbestos litigation for a plaintiffs' firm. On July 31, counsel for three respondents demanded that the Harrison firm disqualify itself from cases against those respondents. Three days later, the motion to disqualify the Harrison firm was filed; it was subsequently joined by all respondents.

The trial court held a total of 21 hearing sessions on the motion, including 16 sessions of testimony. During the hearing, several witnesses testified that Vogel liked to talk, and the record indicates that he would volunteer information in an effort to be helpful.

A critical incident involving Vogel's activities at Brobeck first came to light during the hearing. Brobeck's computer system access log showed that on November 17, 1988, Vogel accessed the computer records for 20 cases filed by the Harrison firm. On the witness stand, Vogel at first flatly denied having looked at these case records, but when confronted with the access log, he admitted reviewing the records "to see what kind of cases [the Harrison firm] had filed." At the time, Vogel had no responsibilities for any Harrison firm cases at Brobeck. The date Vogel reviewed those computer records was very close to the time Vogel and Harrison first spoke. The access log documented that Vogel opened each record long enough to view and print copies of all the information on the case in the computer system.

Vogel, Harrison, and the other two witnesses from the Harrison firm denied that Vogel ever disclosed any client confidences obtained while he worked for Brobeck. However, Harrison never instructed Vogel not to discuss any confidential information obtained at Brobeck. Vogel did discuss with Harrison firm attorneys his impressions of several Brobeck attorneys. After the disqualification motion was filed, Harrison and his office manager debriefed Vogel, not to obtain any confidences but to discuss his duties at Brobeck in detail and to assess respondents' factual allegations. During the course of the hearing, the Harrison firm terminated Vogel on August 25, 1989.

The trial court found that Vogel's work for Brobeck and the Harrison firm was substantially related, and that there was no express or implied waiver by Brobeck or its clients. The court believed there was a substantial likelihood that the Harrison firm's hiring of Vogel, without first building "an ethical wall" or having a waiver, would affect the outcome in asbestos cases. The court also found that Vogel obtained confidential information when he accessed Brobeck's computer records on the Harrison firm's cases, and that there was a reasonable probability Vogel used that information or disclosed it to other members of the Harrison firm's staff. The court refused to extend the disqualification beyond those cases where there was tangible evidence of interference by Vogel, stating that on the rest of the cases it would require the court to speculate.

The trial court initially disqualified the Harrison firm in all 20 cases Vogel accessed on November 17, 1988, which included 11 cases pending in Contra Costa County. However, on further consideration, the trial court restricted its disqualification order to the 9 cases pending in San Francisco. . . .

Our statutes and public policy recognize the importance of protecting the confidentiality of the attorney-client relationship. . . . The obligation to maintain the client's confidences traditionally and properly has been placed on the attorney representing the client. But nonlawyer employees must handle confidential client information if legal services are to be efficient and cost-effective. Although a law firm has the ability to supervise its employees and assure that they protect client confidences, that ability and assurance are tenuous when the nonlawyer leaves the firm's employment. If the nonlawyer finds employment with opposing counsel, there is a heightened risk that confidences of the former employer's clients will be compromised, whether from base motives, an excess of zeal, or simple inadvertence.

Under such circumstances, the attorney who traditionally has been responsible for protecting the client's confidences — the former employer — has no effective means of doing so. The public policy of protecting the confidentiality of attorney-client communications must depend upon the attorney or law firm that hires an opposing counsel's employee. Certain requirements must be imposed on attorneys who hire their opposing counsel's employees to assure that attorney-client confidences are protected. . . .

Hiring a former employee of an opposing counsel is not, in and of itself, sufficient to warrant disqualification of an attorney or law firm. However, when the former employee possesses confidential attorney-client information, materially related to pending litigation, the situation implicates " 'considerations of ethics which run to the very integrity of our judicial process.' " [Citations omitted.] Under such circumstances, the hiring attorney must obtain the informed written consent of the former employer, thereby dispelling any basis for disqualification. [Citations omitted.] Failing that, the hiring attorney is subject to disqualification unless the attorney can rebut a presumption that the confidential attorney-client information has been used or disclosed in the new employment. . . .

An inflexible presumption of shared confidences would not be appropriate for nonlawyers, though, whatever its merits when applied to attorneys. There are obvious differences between lawyers and their nonlawyer employees in training, responsibilities, and acquisition and use of confidential information. These differences satisfy us that a rebuttable presumption of shared confidences provides a just balance between protecting confidentiality and the right to chosen counsel.

The most likely means of rebutting the presumption is to implement a procedure, before the employee is hired, which effectively screens the employee from any involvement with the litigation, a procedure one court aptly described as a "cone of silence." (See *Nemours Foundation v. Gilbane, Aetna, Federal Ins.* (D. Del. 1986) 632 F. Supp. 418, 428.) Whether a potential employee will require a cone of silence should be determined as a matter of routine during the hiring process. It is reasonable to ask potential employees about the nature of their prior legal work; prudence alone would dictate such inquiries. Here, Harrison's first conversation with Vogel revealed a potential problem — Vogel's work for Brobeck on asbestos litigation settlements. . . .

Two objectives must be achieved. First, screening should be implemented before undertaking the challenged representation or hiring the tainted individual. Screening must take place at the outset to prevent any confidences from being disclosed. Second, the tainted individual should be precluded from any involvement in or communication about the challenged representation. To avoid inadvertent disclosures and to establish an evidentiary record, a memorandum should be circulated warning the legal staff to isolate the individual from communications on the matter and to prevent access to the relevant files. . . .

We decline to adopt the broader rule urged by respondents and applied by other courts, which treats the nonlawyer employee as an attorney and requires disqualification upon the showing and standards applicable to individual attorneys. . . .

Respondents' alternative formulation, that a substantial relationship between the type of work done for the former and present employers requires disqualification, presents unnecessary barriers to employment mobility. Such a rule sweeps more widely than needed to protect client confidences. We share the concerns expressed by the American Bar Association's Standing Committee on Ethics and Professional Responsibility: "It is important that nonlawyer employees have as much mobility in employment opportunity as possible consistent with the protection of clients' interests. To so limit employment opportunities that some nonlawyers trained to work with law firms might be required to leave the careers for which they are trained would disserve clients as well as the legal profession. Accordingly, any restrictions on the nonlawyer's employment should be held to the minimum necessary to protect confidentiality of client information." (ABA Ethics Opinion 88-1526.) Respondents' suggested rule could easily result in nonlawyer employees becoming "Typhoid Marys," unemployable by firms practicing in specialized areas of the law where the employees are most skilled and experienced.

Absent written consent, the proper rule and its application for disqualification based on nonlawyer employee conflicts of interest should be as follows. The party seeking disqualification must show that its present or past attorney's former employee possesses confidential attorney-client information materially related to the proceedings before the court. The party should not be required to disclose the actual information contended to be confidential. However, the court should be provided with the nature of the information and its material relationship to the proceeding. [Citations omitted.]

Once this showing has been made, a rebuttable presumption arises that the information has been used or disclosed in the current employment. The presumption is a rule by necessity because the party seeking disqualification will be at a loss to prove what is known by the adversary's attorneys and legal staff. [Citations omitted.] To rebut the presumption, the challenged attorney has the burden of showing that the practical effect of formal screening has been achieved. The showing must satisfy the trial court that the employee has not had and will not have any involvement with the litigation, or any communication with attorneys or coemployees concerning the litigation, that would support a reasonable inference that the information has been used or disclosed. If the challenged attorney fails to make this showing, then the court may disqualify the attorney and law firm. . . .

There can be no question that Vogel obtained confidential attorney-client information when he accessed the Harrison firm's case files on Brobeck's computer. . . .

The Harrison firm also argues that there was no evidence that Vogel disclosed any confidences to any member of the firm, or that any such information was sought from or volunteered by Vogel. Harrison testified that he never asked Vogel to divulge anything other than impressions about three Brobeck attorneys. Harrison and his office manager also testified that Vogel was not involved in case evaluation or trial tactics discussions at the Harrison firm. However, this evidence is not sufficient to rebut the presumption that Vogel used the confidential material or disclosed it to staff members at the Harrison firm. Moreover, there was substantial evidence to support a reasonable inference that Vogel used or disclosed the confidential information.

Despite Harrison's own concern over an appearance of impropriety, Harrison never told Vogel not to discuss the information Vogel learned at Brobeck and did not consider screening Vogel even after Brobeck first inquired about Vogel's work on asbestos cases. The evidence also amply supports the trial court's observation that Vogel was "a very talkative person, a person who loves to share information." Further, Vogel's willingness to use information acquired at Brobeck, and the Harrison firm's insensitivity to ethical considerations, were demonstrated when Vogel was told to call respondent Fibreboard Corporation and Vogel knew the person to contact there. . . .

The order of the trial court is affirmed. . . .

Questions about the Case

1. Did Vogel actually work on any of the cases from which his employer Harrison is being disqualified? Did Vogel possess any confidential information about these cases? How did he obtain it and why?
2. Did Harrison do a conflicts check on Vogel? Did he attempt to screen Vogel from working on cases that he had worked on at Brobeck? Did he admonish Vogel not to reveal any confidential information about these cases?
3. Did Vogel get consent from the clients involved? From the Brobeck firm?
4. Was Vogel cautious in accepting assignments to work on cases he may have worked on previously at Brobeck? Was he careful about what he said to other employees about his previous employment?
5. Does the court provide guidance to lawyers who hire paralegals who may carry potential conflicts? How would you state this rule?
6. Did the court's flexible application of screening rules to paralegals help Vogel? Why, or why not?
7. What should Vogel have done to guard against this disqualification? What about Harrison?

The following case is another example of the trend in the courts to permit the use of screens in matters involving a job-changing paralegal.

Phoenix Founders, Inc. v. Marshall

887 S.W.2d 831 (Tex. 1994)

In this original proceeding, we consider whether a law firm must be disqualified from ongoing litigation because it rehired a legal assistant who had worked for opposing counsel for three weeks. We hold that disqualification is not required if the rehiring firm is able to establish that it has effectively screened the paralegal from any contact with the underlying suit. Because this standard had not been adopted in Texas prior to the trial court's disqualification order, we deny mandamus relief without prejudice to allow the trial court to reconsider its ruling in light of today's opinion.

The present dispute arises from a suit brought by Phoenix Founders, Inc. and others ("Phoenix") to collect a federal-court judgment against Ronald and Jane Beneke and others. The law firm of Thompson & Knight represented Phoenix in the original federal-court suit, which began in 1990 and ended in 1991, and has also represented them in the collection suit since its commencement in 1992. The Benekes have been represented in the latter suit by the firm David & Goodman.

In July of 1993, Denise Hargrove, a legal assistant at Thompson & Knight, left her position at that firm to begin working for David & Goodman as a paralegal. While at David & Goodman, Hargrove billed six-tenths of an hour on the collection suit for locating a pleading. She also discussed the case generally with Mark Goodman, the Benekes' lead counsel.

After three weeks at David & Goodman, Hargrove returned to Thompson & Knight to resume work as a paralegal. At the time of the rehiring, Thompson & Knight made no effort to question Hargrove in regard to potential conflicts of interest resulting from her employment at David & Goodman.

Three weeks after Hargrove had returned, counsel for the Benekes wrote to Thompson & Knight asserting that its renewed employment of Hargrove created a conflict of interest. The letter demanded that the firm withdraw from its representation of Phoenix.

Hargrove resigned from Thompson & Knight the next week, after having been given the option of either resigning with severance pay or being terminated. The firm itself, however, refused to withdraw from the case. The Benekes then filed a motion to disqualify. . . .

The disqualification order states that Hargrove possesses confidential information relating to the Benekes, and that all such confidential information was imputed to the firm of Thompson & Knight at the time she was rehired.

This Court has not previously addressed the standards governing a disqualification motion based on the hiring of a nonlawyer employee. With respect to lawyers, however, this Court has adopted a standard requiring disqualification whenever counsel undertakes representation of an interest that is adverse to that of a former client, as long as the matters embraced in the pending suit are "substantially related" to the factual matters involved in the previous suit. [Citation omitted.] This strict rule is based on a conclusive presumption that confidences and secrets were imparted to the attorney during the prior representation. [Citation omitted.]

The Benekes argue that the standards applied to the hiring of lawyers should also apply to the hiring of paralegals. . . . [T]he Benekes urge that the entire firm of Thompson & Knight must be automatically disqualified because of the confidences Hargrove obtained while working at David & Goodman.

We agree that a paralegal who has actually worked on a case must be subject to . . . a conclusive presumption that confidences and secrets were imparted during the course of the paralegal's work on the case. . . .

We disagree, however, with the argument that paralegals should be conclusively presumed to share confidential information with members of their firms. The Disciplinary Rules require a lawyer having direct supervisory authority over a nonlawyer to make reasonable efforts to ensure that the nonlawyer's conduct is compatible with the professional obligations of the lawyer. Tex. Disciplinary R. Prof. Conduct 5.03(a). If the supervising lawyer orders, encourages, or even permits a nonlawyer to engage in conduct that would be subject to discipline if engaged in by a lawyer, the lawyer will be subject to discipline. R. 5.03(b). Thus, to the extent that the Disciplinary Rules prohibit a lawyer from revealing confidential information, R. 1.05(b)(1), they also prohibit a supervising lawyer from ordering, encouraging, or permitting a nonlawyer to reveal such information.

This view is consistent with the weight of authority in other jurisdictions. The American Bar Association's Committee on Professional Ethics has considered whether a law firm that hires a paralegal may continue representing clients whose interests conflict with interests of the former employer's clients on whose matters the paralegal has worked. ABA Ethics Informal Op. 1526 (1988). After surveying case law and ethics opinions from a number of jurisdictions, the Committee concluded that the new firm need not be disqualified, as long as the firm and the paralegal strictly adhere to the screening process set forth in the opinion, and as long as the paralegal does not reveal any information relating to the former employer's clients to any person in the employing firm. Id. A number of courts have since relied on the ABA's opinion to allow continued representation under similar conditions. [Citations omitted.]

Underlying these decisions is a concern regarding the mobility of paralegals and other nonlawyers. A potential employer might well be reluctant to hire a particular nonlawyer if doing so would automatically disqualify the entire firm from ongoing litigation. This problem would be especially acute in the context of massive firms and extensive, complex litigation. Recognizing this danger, the ABA concluded that "any restrictions on the nonlawyer's employment should be held to the minimum necessary to protect confidentiality of client information." ABA Op. 1526 at 2. [Citations omitted.]

We share the concerns expressed by the ABA, and agree that client confidences may be adequately safeguarded if a firm hiring a paralegal for another firm takes appropriate steps in compliance with the Disciplinary Rules. See ABA Op. 1526 at 3. Specifically, the newly-hired paralegal should be cautioned not to disclose any information relating to the representation of a client of the former employer. The paralegal should also be instructed not to work on any matter on which the paralegal worked during the prior employment, or regarding which the paralegal has information relating to the former employer's representation. Additionally, the firm should take other reasonable steps to ensure that the paralegal does no work in connection with matters on which the paralegal worked during the prior employment, absent client consent after consultation. See id.

Each of these precautions would tend to reduce the danger that the paralegal might share confidential information with members of the new firm. Thus, while a court must ordinarily presume that some sharing will take place, the challenged firm may rebut this presumption by showing that sufficient precautions have been taken to guard against any disclosure of confidences.

Absent consent of the former employer's client, disqualification will always be required under some circumstances, such as (1) when information relating to the representation of an adverse client has in fact been disclosed, or (2) when screening would be ineffective or the nonlawyer necessarily would be required to work on the other side of a matter that is the same as or substantially related to a matter on which the nonlawyer has previously worked. . . .

In reconsidering the disqualification motion, the trial court should examine the circumstances of Hargrove's employment at Thompson & Knight to determine whether the practical effect of formal screening has been achieved. The factors bearing on such a determination will generally include the substantiality of the relationship between the former and current matters; the time elapsing between the matters; the size of the firm; the number of individuals presumed to have confidential information; the nature of their involvement in the former matter; and the timing and features of any measures taken to reduce the danger of disclosure.

The ultimate question in weighing these factors is whether Thompson & Knight has taken measures sufficient to reduce the potential for misuse of confidences to an acceptable level. As with any disqualification motion, the trial court must adhere to an exacting standard so as to discourage any use of a disqualification motion as a dilatory tactic. . . .

Because we have modified the controlling legal standard, the writ of mandamus is denied without prejudice to allow the trial court to reconsider the disqualification motion in light of today's opinion. The stay order previously issued by this Court remains in effect only so long as necessary to allow the trial court to act.

Questions about the Case

1. Was the paralegal Hargrove aware of the potential conflict of interest? Did she work on the Phoenix Founders matter at Thompson & Knight either before she went to David & Goodman or after?
2. Did David & Goodman do a conflicts check?
3. Did Thompson & Knight attempt to screen Hargrove from the Phoenix Founders matter on her return to the firm?

4. What is the standard applied to lawyers in disqualification motions in Texas courts? Does the court apply this same standard to paralegals?
5. What authority does the Texas Supreme Court rely on to make this new rule?
6. What specific steps does the court prescribe to establish an acceptable safeguard against the disclosure of client confidences?
7. Did the Texas Supreme Court here decide whether to disqualify Thompson & Knight?

In this case, the firm knew that the paralegal who had joined the firm had conflicts and attempted to establish an adequate screen.

Lamb v. Pralex Corp.

333 F. Supp. 2d 361 (D.V.I. 2004)

The plaintiff in this case is represented by Lee J. Rohn. . . . Defendants are represented by Kevin Rames, Esq. . . . This motion revolves around Eliza Combie, who worked as a paralegal at the Rames law office from October 30, 2000 to March 26, 2004. Her work at Rames' office involved working with several litigation matters, including this case.

On March 26, 2004, Combie began work with the Rohn law firm. Combie, Rohn and K. Glenda Cameron, Esq., an associate at the firm, assert that they discussed the possible conflicts raised by Combie's possible employment. They also aver that at the initial interview, Combie acknowledged that there were cases in which she was conflicted, at which time she was informed that, should she accept employment with the Rohn firm, she would be barred from contact with those cases.

Rohn and Cameron also state that on Combie's first day of work with Rohn, she submitted the list of cases. The list was circulated to all employees and a memo informing employees to refrain from discussing those cases in her presence was circulated and posted in common areas of the office. Combie, Rohn and Cameron all aver that no one in the office has discussed any of the relevant matters with Combie. They also state that Combie is locked out of the electronic files and does not work in close proximity to them or to Rohn.

Rames invokes ABA Rules of Professional Conduct 5.3, 1.9, 1.16, and 1.10 to argue that Rohn and her entire law firm must be disqualified because during Combie's previous employment with Rames she obtained confidential information regarding pending matters which she may divulge to Rohn. Rohn denies any impropriety and assures the court that no confidences have been disclosed, and that a "scrupulous" screening procedure has been implemented to shield Combie from contact with the conflicted cases. Rames argues that such "self-serving" statements and are insufficient to stave off disqualification.

A motion to disqualify counsel requires the court to balance the right of a party to retain counsel of his choice and the substantial hardship which might result from disqualification as against the public perception of and the public trust in the judicial system. . . .

Disqualification issues must be decided on a case by case basis and the party seeking disqualification of opposing counsel bears the burden of clearly showing that the continued representation would be impermissible. [Citation omitted.] Courts are required to "preserve a balance, delicate though it may be, between an individual's right to his own freely chosen counsel and the need to maintain the highest ethical standards of professional responsibility." [Citation omitted.] This balance is essential if the public's trust in the integrity of the Bar is to be preserved. The Court was unable to find a Third Circuit decision on this precise issue. However, several courts have addressed it.

ABA Rule 5.3 addresses the responsibilities of attorneys who employ nonlawyer assistants. It encompasses the protection of client confidences communicated to a nonlawyer assistant, such as a paralegal or secretary. [Citation omitted.] The rule imposes a duty on the supervising attorney to ensure that the non-lawyer adheres to professional obligations. Thus, a trial court has the authority, in a litigation context, to disqualify counsel based on the conduct of a nonlawyer assistant that is incompatible with the lawyer's ethical obligations. *Smart Industries Corp. Mfg. v. Superior Court in and for County of Yuma*, 876 P.2d 1176, 1181 (Ariz. App. Div. 1994). Moreover, such disqualification may be imputed to the entire law firm. *Leibowitz v. The Eighth Judicial District Court of the State of Nevada*, 78 P.3d 515, 523 (Sup. Ct. Nev. 2003).

The issue is whether plaintiff's counsel should be disqualified because a paralegal formerly employed by defendants' attorney and who was involved in litigation concerning defendants is now employed by plaintiff's counsel. The Standing Committee on Ethics and Professional Responsibility, pursuant to the ABA Model Rules of Professional Conduct, hold that a law firm that hires a paralegal formerly employed by another law firm may continue to represent clients whose interests conflict with the interests of clients of the former employer on whose matters the paralegal has worked, so long as the employing firm screens the paralegal, and as long as no information relating to said clients is revealed to the employing firm. *Informal Opinion 88-1526*. . . .

A Court faced with such a motion must first determine whether confidential information has been divulged. Rames claims that Combie participated in all of the cases in which his firm was litigation counsel; that he "shared with Combie litigation strategies and tactics"; and that Combie was "privy to the firm's entire case load as she worked on the vast majority of cases that were and are pending in the Rames law office." Rames maintains that Combie's possession of confidential client information gives Rohn an unfair advantage, and violates the notions of fairness and integrity in the judicial process, requiring disqualification of Rohn and her entire law firm. Combie's affidavit, annexed to Rohn's opposition, counters that Combie "never participated in any discussions or meetings with Attorney Rames," and was never privy to any strategy and tactical deliberation with regard to any opposing counsel. Combie avers that her duties revolved around filing of pleadings and correspondence and that information was transmitted to her on an "as needed" basis. Rames dismisses these statements as self-serving and untrue.

The Court finds that Combie was exposed to confidential information at the Rames law firm. It is reasonable for paralegals to handle confidential client information in order for the law firm employer to render efficient and cost-effective service. Combie is described as an experienced and competent worker. Therefore, it is conceivable that based on her skills, she was given substantial responsibility with the cases, including this case. By virtue of her working on the cases, it is also conceivable that she and Rames shared confidential information regarding them.

However, the fact that Combie has acquired confidential information in a former job is not sufficient by itself to require disqualification of her new employer. [Citations omitted.] . . . The hiring of a nonlawyer who possesses confidential information of an adversary puts such confidential information at risk. As a result, a rebuttable presumption arises that the information will be disclosed to the new employer. [Citations omitted.] The presumption serves to strike a balance between protecting confidentiality and the right to counsel of one's choice. A party is able to rebut the presumption that confidential client information has been used or disclosed, by presenting evidence of effective screening mechanisms to shield the employee from the cases. [Citation omitted.] In other words, the challenged attorney has the burden of showing that the practical effect of formal screening has been achieved and that the employee has not had and will not have any involvement with the litigation or any communication concerning the litigation. [Citation omitted.] In this jurisdiction, the erection of a "Chinese Wall" is recognized in this regard. [Citations omitted.]

Rohn states, and Combie and Cameron aver, that during her interview the parties discussed the fact that she was previously employed with Rames, who is an adversary of Rohn and is opposing counsel in this case. They further state that upon Combie's disclosure of the conflicted cases, "they advised her that were an offer of employment extended, she would be prohibited from and have no access to the electronic or physical files for those cases on which she would be conflicted." A list of the cases was circulated to all employees and posted in common areas; Combie has not been near the files and does not know their location; the employees have been instructed not to discuss the cases in her presence; and she has been locked out of the electronic filing system with regard to those cases.

The evidence of screening provided by Rohn was not directly contradicted by Rames. Although the Court understands his chagrin, more is required before a court will be forced to relieve a litigant of his counsel of choice. A majority of courts have endorsed screening procedures similar to the ones implemented in this case, under similar circumstances. Additionally, Rohn's office employs several individuals and there is little likelihood that Combie will be required to work on the conflicted cases. The Court is satisfied that the procedures employed by Rohn's office to shield Combie from the files, supports a finding that any information obtained at the Rames law firm will not be disclosed.

In light of the foregoing, disqualification is not warranted. In addressing ethical problems created by nonlawyers changing employment from a law firm representing one party to a law firm representing an adverse party, courts must fashion rules which strike a balance between the public policy of protecting the confidentiality of attorney-client communications and a party's right to representation by chosen counsel. [Citations omitted.] Accordingly, any restrictions on the nonlawyer's employment should be held to the minimum necessary to protect confidentiality of client information.

A prophylatic rule which requires the employing firm to establish procedures which ensure that confidential information has not and will not be disclosed to the employing firm safeguards the competing interests. The Court finds that plaintiff's counsel has rebutted the presumption of improper disclosure by presenting evidence of the "Chinese Wall" implemented in that regard. Accordingly, disqualification is not warranted and the defendants' motion will be denied at this time.

Questions about the Case

1. Did the lawyers who hired the paralegal in question conduct a conflicts check? When?
2. Did the lawyers screen the paralegal? How? Did the screen have all the components of a screen that are described in this chapter?
3. What reasoning did the court apply in deciding if a disqualification was warranted?
4. Was the screen found to be adequate by the court? Why?
5. How did the court decide? What rule did it establish for the future?

In this case of first impression in Oklahoma, the state's highest court endorses the principle of screening nonlawyer employees and providing an opportunity for the firm being challenged to show that the screen is effective and that no confidences have been revealed.

Hayes v. Central States Orthopedic Specialists, Inc.

2002 Okla. 30, 51 P.3d 562 (Okla. 2002)

From August 1999 until June 2000 April Mendoza worked in Tulsa as a secretary for the firm of Norman Wohlgemuth Chandler & Dowdell, as secretary for John Dowdell and Christina Little . . . , the lawyers primarily responsible for the litigation between Mark Hayes, M.D. and Central States Orthopedic Specialists, Inc. . . . In May Ms. Mendoza gave notice to Norman Wohlgemuth that she was taking a job as secretary for Mr. Frank Hagedorn, a partner in the Tulsa firm of Estill, Hardwick, Gable, Golden & Nelson.

There is significant disagreement between plaintiff and Ms. Mendoza as to the nature and extent of Ms. Mendoza's involvement in the Hayes litigation. Dr. Hayes claims that Ms. Mendoza works on documents containing attorneys' work product and was "intimately familiar" with documents relating to settlement negotiations between the parties. But Ms. Mendoza stated in an affidavit that her duties were purely administrative and she had no recollection of any confidential information relating to the Hayes case. . . .

Dr. Hayes' lawyers sent a letter to Hall Estill requesting that the firm withdraw from the case but Hall Estill declined to do so, and . . . Dr. Hayes filed a motion asking the trial court to require Hall Estill to withdraw. . . .

[T]he trial court filed a written order . . . granting Dr. Hayes' motion and disqualifying Hall Estill. . . .

We begin our discussion of this issue by observing "*Legal practitioners are not interchangeable commodities.*" . . . [Citation omitted.]

A recurring theme in the cases that have recognized waiver as the basis for denying motions to disqualify is that need to insure that such motions are not used for strategic purposes. . . . [D]isqualification is such a drastic measure that it should be invoked if, and only if, the court is satisfied that real harm is likely to result from failing to invoke it.

The undisputed facts here reveal that Dr. Hayes and Mr. Dowdell discussed what to do . . . but decided to take no action whatever for eight months. . . . Although they attempted to explain their inaction on the basis that they were involved in settlement negotiations, it seems to us that this stage of the litigation would have been the very point at which they should have been most worried about Ms. Mendoza's knowledge. . . .

We hold that . . . Dr. Hayes . . . through delay of eight months . . . waived any right he might have had to insist on the harsh remedy of disqualifying Hall Estill. . . . [T]he hardship on Central Orthopedic . . . would likely be significantly greater than any hardship Dr. Hayes will likely suffer. . . .

As a result of our holding, . . . it is not strictly necessary for us to address the screening issue. We shall do so, however, because it presents an important question of first impression. . . . The importance of the issue is demonstrated by the *amici curaie* brief filed on behalf of several groups who represent non-lawyers who work as legal assistants in law firms. . . .

The trial court's order relied on *Zimmerman v. Mahaksa Bottling Co.*, 19 P.3d 784 (Kan. 2000), which held, "Screening devices are prohibited under the [Rules of Professional Conduct.]" Thus, despite the undisputed evidence that Ms. Mendoza has not revealed any confidences and was screened from doing so by Hall Estill, the trial court, based on

Zimmerman, nevertheless disqualified Hall Estill without any inquiry into the effectiveness of the screening. We hold that this was error.

Most authorities recognize that the considerations going into whether screening is proper for lawyers are entirely different than those involving non-lawyer employees. . . .

Rule 1.11 of the Rules of Professional Conduct expressly provide for the use of screening to prevent disqualification of firms who hire former government lawyers, judges, arbitrators, or law clerks. . . .

Contrary to the conclusion of the *Zimmerman* and *Ciaffone* courts, we have found no opinion from any jurisdiction criticizing *Smart Industries* other than *Zimmerman* and *Ciaffone*. . . .

In *Ciaffone*, 945 P.2d at 953, the court relied on an article by M. Peter Moser, *Chinese Walls: A Means of Avoiding Law Firm Disqualification When a Personally Disqualified Lawyer Joins the Firm*, 3 Geo. J. Legal Ethics 399, 403, 407 (1999), to support its conclusion that screening for non-lawyer employees has been "roundly criticized." . . . Moser suggested, "Greater use of screening mechanism[s such as] so called 'Chinese walls,' should be permitted to protect former clients' confidences from disclosure." [Citation omitted.] Thus, far from showing that the use of devices for non-lawyers had been "roundly criticized," the Moser article stands for the proposition that screening devices for non-lawyers are "generally permitted" and such devices should be more widely used than they are now. . . .

We hold that a *per se* rule that would prohibit a court's examination of the effectiveness of a screening device for a non-lawyer is not appropriate under Oklahoma law. Thus before being disqualified for having hired the non-lawyer employee from its opponent, the hiring firm should be given the opportunity to prove that the non-lawyer employee has not revealed client confidences to the new employer and has been effectively screened from doing so. . . .

ORDER OF THE TRIAL COURT REVERSED AND MATTER REMANDED WITH INSTRUCTIONS TO DENY PLAINTIFF'S MOTION TO DISQUALIFY DEFENDANT'S COUNSEL.

Questions about the Case

1. Did the nonlawyer in this case have a conflict? Did the hiring firm know it? What did the firm do about it?
2. Why did the firm seeking disqualification wait so long to file the motion to disqualify? Was this important in the case?
3. Why did the court act on the matter of screens after finding that it did not need to?
4. Why did a paralegal association (NALA) file an amicus brief?
5. This state is geographically close to which other states that have opinions about screens? What do these other states say? Why did the court

not follow Nevada and Kansas? (See later for a Nevada case that overturned the Nevada case cited in this opinion.)

The Kansas Supreme Court here follows the Nevada case of *Ciaffone v. District Court* (which has since been overturned) in refusing to allow screening of paralegals carrying conflicts. Prior to this ruling, most lawyers in Kansas had held this view based on the two Kansas cases cited and an influential Kansas Bar Association ethics opinion.

Zimmerman v. Mahaska Bottling Co.

270 Kan. 810, 19 P.3d 784 (2001)

This is an interlocutory appeal from the district court's order disqualifying the law firm of Fisher, Patterson, Sayler & Smith (Fisher Patterson) from representing the appellants in this suit. The district court found that Kay French, a legal secretary, acquired material and confidential information regarding this personal injury lawsuit while employed at Dickson & Pope, the firm retained by the appellee, and that her current employment with Fisher Patterson required disqualification of the firm. . . .

The district court's findings of fact were based upon the *in camera* testimony and also upon the testimony taken in open court. Suffice it to say that French has knowledge of particular facts which are material and confidential regarding the Zimmerman matter. . . .

The provisions of the KRPC specifically set forth disciplinary rules for lawyers. The provisions of the KRPC apply equally, however, to nonlawyer employees. . . . KRPC requires nonlawyers to be treated in the same manner as lawyers when considering confidentiality issues under KRPC 1.10.

We next address whether a "screening device" or "Chinese wall" is an appropriate remedy where the person in question is a nonlawyer who has switched sides by moving from one firm to another. This court has twice held that the use of "screening devices" or a "Chinese wall" is unavailable as a remedy when faced with a KRPC 1.10 problem. See *Lansing-Delaware Water District*, 248 Kan. at 573, 808 P.2d 1369 . . . ; *Parker v. Volkswagenwerk Aktiengesellschaft*, 245 Kan. 580, 589, 781 P.2d 1099 (1989). . . . This court has never addressed whether the use of a screening device or Chinese wall is appropriate for nonlawyer employees of a firm.

Although not binding on this court, KBA Ethics Opinion No. 90-05 addresses whether screening is available for nonlawyer employees. . . . "A screening wall imposed unilaterally is inappropriate to meet this burden under our case law." . . .

The Nevada Supreme Court rejected the use of a Chinese wall for the nonlawyer employee in *Ciaffone*. . . .

The appellant cites *Smart Industries* in support of their argument that a screening device or "Chinese wall" is an appropriate remedy when faced with a nonlawyer who has switched sides by moving from one firm to another. . . .

The appellant suggests that there are several policy reasons to treat nonlawyers differently than lawyers and that screening devices can be effectively used to prevent communication of material and confidential information. They are: (1) screening devices adequately protect the former client's confidentiality concerns; (2) screening balances the interest of the current client in maintaining his or her choice of counsel throughout the proceedings; (3) screening would protect the interests of the nonlawyer employee in allowing them greater flexibility to change jobs; and (4) screening is allowed under the rules when a government attorney leaves employment with the government and moves to a private firm.

Screening devices, however, are prohibited under the KRPC. There is no provision or exception which allows them for lawyers. Because the provisions of KPRC apply to nonlawyers as well, we decline to create a screening exception in this case. The need for confidentiality, the trust of the client, and the public's respect for the legal system all support the rule in Kansas prohibiting the use of screening devices. . . .

[N]onlawyers are privy to a great deal of confidential information regarding litigation in the office they work in. They are also often involved in legal strategy and planning. The client expects and our legal system requires the client's confidences to be protected. To treat nonlawyers in a different manner than lawyers would seriously erode the foundation of KRPC and place at risk the public trust in the legal system. . . .

Our holding today does not mean that disqualification is mandatory whenever a nonlawyer moves from one private firm to another where the two firms are involved in pending litigation and represent adverse parties. A firm may avoid disqualification if (1) the nonlawyer employee has not acquired material and confidential information regarding the litigation or (2) if the client of the former firm waives disqualification and approves of the use of a screening device or Chinese wall.

The . . . order disqualifying Fisher Patterson from the Zimmerman case is affirmed.

Questions about the Case

1. Did the legal secretary in this case know that she possessed confidential information about the case at issue from her former employment? Did this matter to the court?

2. On what precedents did the court rely in making its decision?
3. The majority of state courts that have addressed this issue have found that screening is acceptable. What did this court say about those decisions? What was the basis for this court's deciding against screening?
4. What were the reasons stated to the court to persuade it that screening is the best solution?
5. How can a firm avoid disqualification if it wants to hire a paralegal who has worked at a firm that is opposing counsel in a case?
6. What would it take in the state of Kansas for the courts to recognize screening?

The following case overrules one part of the *Ciaffone* case mentioned in the previous decision and sets a new rule in the state of Nevada. The case shows the trend to allow screening of paralegals where a state might not allow screening for lawyers in the same situation.

Leibowitz v. District Court

119 Nev. 523, 78 P.3d 515 (2003)

The law firm of Ecker & Standish was disqualified from representing petitioner Steven Leibowitz pursuant to our decision in *Ciaffone v. District Court*, which addressed imputed disqualification based upon employment of a nonlawyer employee who had access to confidential or privileged information of an adverse party during the course of the employee's prior employment. For the reasons set forth below, we determine that screening is permissible for nonlawyer employees, clarify in part and overrule in part our decision in *Ciaffone* and grant the petition.

This petition for a writ of mandamus arises out of a divorce proceeding. Steven and Deena Leibowitz were married in 1986. The parties later separated, and Deena filed a complaint for divorce in February 2000. Deena hired the law firm of Dickerson, Dickerson Consult & Pocker (DDCP) to represent her. Steven retained the law firm of Ecker & Standish (ES) to represent him in the divorce proceeding. . . .

[T]he district court entered a final judgment resolving all the parties' property, custody, and other divorce issues. . . . Both Steven and Deena appealed the final judgment. . . .

Later in the summer of 2001, while the appeal was pending, Steven filed a motion seeking to modify child custody and visitation. The district court certified its inclination to consider the motion. . . . Steven filed a motion to remand the issues to the district court. Deena opposed the motion.

After filing the motion to remand, ES advised DDCP that ES had hired Haunani Magalianes, a former DDCP employee, as a legal assistant. . . . During discussion regarding possible disqualification, ES discovered that one of its former employees, Pollie J. Baker, worked at DDCP for periods of time between June 2001 and April 2002.

On February 14, 2002 attorney Howard Ecker advised DDCP via letter that ES had hired Magalianes. With respect to the Leibowitz case, Ecker indicated that Magalianes advised Ecker that she did not believe that she had obtained any privileged information as a result of her work in the Leibowitz matter.

DDCP employed Magalianes in its domestic division until May 26, 2000. Thereafter Magalianes transferred to DDCP's civil division until approximately April 2001. According to Magalianes, . . . she had three contacts with the Leibowitz case. First, [she] took the initial phone call from Deena regarding potential representation by DDCP. . . . Second, [she] prepared a short memorandum to attorney Robert P. Dickerson that contained the initial information obtained. . . . Lastly, [she] prepared a substitution of attorney for and a transmittal letter to Deena's former attorney. . . . DDCP asserts Magalianes also participated in a meeting involving a child custody dispute. . . . [She] denies participating in this meeting. DDCP's billing records do not reflect [her] attendance at the meeting, although one of the attorneys present filed an affidavit indicating that [she] was present during a phone call with opposing counsel and at a conference among Deena's counsel after the telephone conversation. . . .

As a condition of her employment, and in the course of her employment with ES, Magalianes was screened from any contact with the Leibowitz case. Specifically, [she] had no access to actual or computer files and was prohibited from conversing with law firm personnel regarding the Leibowitz matter.

ES employed legal assistant Pollie J. Baker from October 2000 until mid-January 2001. Baker worked primarily for ES attorney Ed Kainen. During the period of [her] employment, ES represented Steven in the divorce proceedings. Attorney Thomas J. Standish testified that he did the majority of work on the Leibowitz divorce, but he had some help from Kainen. Baker had access to the Leibowitz files, but Baker averred that she did not have any contact with the Leibowitz case while employed at ES. ES presented evidence that [she] had actual involvement with the case.

Around June 2001, Baker went to work for DDCP and . . . worked there for several months. She left DDCP for a short time and returned in late 2001. Baker ended her relationship with DDCP on April 24, 2002. DDCP indicated that it did not inform ES about Baker's employment at the time because it was unaware of Baker's previous employment with ES. [Her] resume did not disclose her employment with ES. . . .

The district court concluded that *Ciaffone* mandated automatic disqualification whenever a nonlawyer employee had access to an adverse part's privileged or confidential information during employment by that party's attorneys. . . . The district court disqualified ES but declined to disqualify DDCP. . . .

[T]he facts in *Ciaffone* infer that mere exposure to a client's file is sufficient to warrant disqualification. In *Ciaffone*, the nonlawyer's involvement with the prior client's case was limited to some work in a secretarial, word processor capacity. The opinion is silent on whether or not this exposure related to privileged or confidential information. Instead the opinion seems to suggest that any exposure to a client's file is sufficient to invoke imputed disqualification. We there take this opportunity to clarify that the imputed disqualification standards . . . do not apply simply because a nonlawyer employee was exposed, or had access to, a former client's file. The rule only applies when the nonlawyer employee acquires privileged, confidential information.

[In *Ciaffone*, we] concluded that screening was not permitted under the rule for attorneys, and therefore, it should not be permitted for nonlawyers.

Petitioners and amici urge us to overrule that portion of *Ciaffone* and permit nonlawyer screening. They respectfully assert that this court misapprehended the weight of authority on this issue. We agree.

In *Ciaffone*, . . . we rejected [the reasoning of the relevant ABA Ethics Opinion] and said that it was "roundly criticized." We also inferred that a majority of courts had rejected nonlawyer screening and cited a law review article by M. Peter Moser in support of these statements. In fact, Mr. Moser did not criticize nonlawyer screening. He pointed out that a majority of jurisdictions permit nonlawyer screening and argued that screening should also be permitted for lawyers.

As pointed out by the amici's briefs, the majority of professional ethics commentators, ethics tribunals, and courts have concluded that nonlawyer screening is a permissible method to protect confidences held by nonlawyer employees who change employment. Nevada is in the minority of jurisdictions that do not allow screening of nonlawyers moving from private firm to private firm.

Imputed disqualification is considered a harsh remedy that "should be invoked if, and only if, the court is satisfied that real harm is likely to result from failing to invoke it." [Citations omitted.] This stringent standard is based on the client's right to counsel of the client's choosing and the likelihood of prejudice and economic harm to the client when severance of the attorney-client relationship is ordered. It is for this reason that the ABA opined in 1988 that screening is permitted for nonlawyers. . . .

We are persuaded that *Ciaffone* misapprehended the state of the law regarding nonlawyer imputed disqualification. We therefore overrule *Ciaffone* to the extent it prohibits screening of nonlawyer employees.

When a law firm hires a nonlawyer employee, the firm has an affirmative duty to determine whether or not the employee previously had access to adversarial client files. If the hiring law firm determines that the employee had such access, the hiring law firm has an absolute duty to screen the nonlawyer employee from the adversarial cases irrespective of the nonlawyer employee's actual knowledge of privileged or confidential information.

Although we decline to mandate an exhaustive list of screening requirements, the following provides an instructive minimum:

1. The newly hired nonlawyer must be cautioned not to disclose any information relating to the representation of a client of a former employer.
2. The nonlawyer must be instructed not to work on any matter on which he or she worked during the prior employment, or regarding which he or she has information relating to former employer's representation.
3. The new firm should take reasonable steps to ensure that the nonlawyer does not work in connection with matters on which he or she worked during the prior employment, absent client consent . . . after consultation.

In addition, the hiring law firm must inform the adversarial party, or their counsel, regarding the hiring of the nonlawyer employee and the screening mechanism utilized. The adversarial party may then: (1) make a conditional waiver (i.e., agree to the screening mechanisms); (2) make an unconditional waiver (eliminate the screening mechanisms); or (3) file a motion to disqualify counsel.

However, even if the new employer uses a screening process, disqualification will always be required — absent unconditional waiver by the affected client — under the following circumstances:

1. When information relating the representation of the adverse client has been disclosed to the new employer; or, in the absence of disclosure to the new employer,
2. When screening would be ineffective or the nonlawyer necessarily would be required to work on the other side of the matter that is the same or substantially related to a matter on which the nonlawyer has previously worked. . . .

To determine whether screening has been or may be effective, the court should consider: (1) the substantiality of the relationship between the former and current matters, (2) the time elapsed between matters, (3) the size of the firm, (4) the number of individuals presumed to have confidential information, (5) the nature of their involvement with the former matter, (6) the timing and features of any measured taken to reduce the danger of disclosure, and (7) whether the old firm and the new firm represent adverse parties in the same proceeding, rather than in different proceedings. . . .

As to Baker, the record supports the . . . finding that she did not obtain confidential information about Steven's case while employed by

ES. . . . [W]e conclude the district court did not err in refusing to disqualify DDCP. . . .

Balancing Deena's interest in preventing possible disclosure of confidential information with Steven's interest in retaining the attorney who has presented him for two years, and the entirety of the divorce proceedings, we conclude that ES should not be disqualified. Magalianes' contacts with Deena were brief and, according to the record, consisted mainly of routine information with some possible confidential information. . . . [T]here is no indication in the record that any confidential information discussed at the conference related to anything but the weekend custody dispute. Although ES is a small firm, there is no evidence that Magalianes would be, by the nature of the firm, forced to work on the Leibowitz matter. Moreover, given the length of time ES represented Steve, the fact that a final judgment has been issued and Magalianes' involvement occurred early in the proceedings, the public's interest in the administration of justice is not significantly impacted. . . . Finally, Steve would suffer extreme prejudice if he had to retain a new attorney this late in the proceedings. . . .

[W]e overrule Ciaffone's prohibition against screening for nonlawyer employees, clarify that mere opportunity to access confidential information does not merit disqualification and conclude that the district court erred in disqualifying the law firm of ES from representing Steven Leibowitz. . . .

LEAVITT, J., with whom AGOSTI, C.J., agrees, dissenting:

I would deny the petition because the district court properly disqualified the law firm of ES.

I would follow the reasoning in *Ciaffone v. District Court* . . . [in which] we held that screening was ineffective to prevent disqualification. . . . [W]e noted . . . "the uncertainty regarding the effectiveness of the screen, the monetary incentive involved in breaching the screen, the fear of disclosing privileged information in the course of proving an effective screen, and the possibility of accidental disclosures."

Questions about the Case

1. What were the facts about the two paralegals in this case? What degree of access did they each have to confidential information in this matter? What was the extent of their work on this matter? Did it make a difference?
2. The court's decision has a clarification of part of the *Ciaffone* case and overrules part of the *Ciaffone* case. What are these two holdings?
3. What should a firm do when it discovers a conflict carried by a new paralegal?
4. What factors will a court look at in deciding whether to disqualify a firm based on a paralegal's conflict?

5. Did the court indicate why it had so misinterpreted the state of the law when it issued the *Ciaffone* opinion?
6. What do you think of the points raised by the dissent?

This case illustrates what can happen in the corporate setting when a law firm represents both the corporation and its corporate officers. Not only is a conflict of interest at issue, but an additional danger is the disclosure of confidential client information that would harm the individual and help the corporation in pending civil and criminal cases.

United States v. Nicholas

606 F. Supp. 2d 1109 (C.D. Cal. 4-1-2009)

In May 2006, Irell & Manella LLP ("Irell") undertook three separate, but inextricably related, representations of Broadcom Corporation ("Broadcom") and its Chief Financial Officer, Defendant William J. Ruehle. More specifically, Irell represented Broadcom in connection with the company's internal investigation of its stock option granting practices. At the same time, Irell also represented Mr. Ruehle in connection with two shareholder lawsuits filed against him regarding those same stock option granting practices. . . .

In June of 2006, Irell lawyers met with Mr. Ruehle at his office to discuss the stock option granting practices at Broadcom. . . . Subsequently, Broadcom directed Irell to disclose statements Mr. Ruehle made to the Irell lawyers about Broadcom's stock option granting practices to Broadcom's outside auditors, Ernst & Young, as well as to the Securities and Exchange Commission ("SEC") and the United States Attorney's Office (the "Government"). . . . The Government now argues that it can use Mr. Ruehle's statements to the Irell lawyers against him at the trial in this criminal case. . . .

In the spring of 2006, after a series of articles related to the stock option granting practices both at Broadcom and other corporations, Broadcom was aware that it might be investigated by the Government or sued on the basis of its stock option granting practices. In mid-May 2006, Broadcom retained Irell to investigate its stock option granting practices on behalf of the corporation. Shortly thereafter, on May 25, 2006, a group of shareholders filed a derivative action against Mr. Ruehle and other current and former officers of Broadcom ("Derivative Action") concerning the corporation's stock option granting practices. On May 26, 2006, an amended complaint was filed in *Jin v. Broadcom Corp., et al.* ("Jin Action"), naming Mr. Ruehle personally and asserting substantially similar claims regarding stock option practices at Broadcom. In addition to its representation of Broadcom in connection with the internal investigation, Irell accepted individual representation of Mr. Ruehle in both the Jin Action and the Derivative Action, accepting service on his behalf and appearing as counsel of record until September 2006. During the entire period of these representations, Irell never obtained Mr. Ruehle's informed written consent to its dual representation of him and the company as required by Rule 3-310I of the Rules of Professional Conduct.

In late May of 2006, Mr. Ruehle received several emails regarding Irell's representation of him and Broadcom in connection with stock option practices at the company. . . . The [first] email provided information about the nature of the Jin Action and the Derivative Action and assessed the relative strengths and weaknesses of the judge assigned to the case. Confirming Mr. Ruehle's understanding that Irell would represent Broadcom's officers individually as they had in past litigation, Mr. Dull directed "anyone who has any concerns" to "contact me or any of the Irell lawyers." . . . In the [second] email, Mr. Heitz updated Mr. Ruehle about the progress of Irell's interviews of other witnesses with knowledge of the stock option granting practices at Broadcom and requested a time to discuss these issues with Mr. Ruehle.

On May 31, 2006, the day before his first interview with the Irell lawyers, Mr. Ruehle received three emails from Mr. Heitz. The first . . . updated Mr. Ruehle on the Irell lawyers' progress in their interviews of witnesses with knowledge of the stock option granting practices at Broadcom. The next asked Mr. Ruehle to review his personal records for information related to a stock option grant in 2000 and advised him of the relevance of such information to Irell's investigation. In the final email . . . Mr. Heitz provided a further update on Irell's fact-gathering with respect to Broadcom's stock option granting practices. On June 1, 2006, Mr. Heitz and Mr. Lefler met with Mr. Ruehle and interviewed him regarding Broadcom's stock option granting practices. The Irell lawyers did not tell Mr. Ruehle that they were not his lawyers. The Irell lawyers did not suggest that Mr. Ruehle might want to consult with his own lawyer before speaking with them. After their meeting, Mr. Heitz had subsequent conversations with Mr. Ruehle in June 2006 about Broadcom's stock option granting practices and never disclosed to Mr. Ruehle in any of these conversations that his statements to him would be disclosed to third parties.

On June 13, 2006, the SEC commenced its investigation of the stock option granting practices at Broadcom. Throughout June and July 2006, Mr. Ruehle continued to receive legal advice from Irell. On June 13, 2006, Mr. Ruehle sent an email to Mr. Siegel . . . seeking legal advice regarding the SEC's investigation. On the same day, Mr. Lefler sent an email to Mr. Ruehle asking him to consent to Irell's acceptance of process on his behalf in the Jin Action. On June 28, 2006, Mr. Ruehle received an email from Mr. Siegel that offered detailed strategic advice regarding the SEC investigation. Finally, on July 25, 2006, Mr. Dull forwarded an email to Broadcom's board of directors from Mr. Lefler that detailed Irell's strategy for the Derivative Action and the Jin Action. Mr. Lefler's memorandum assessed the merits of the actions, considered the strengths and weaknesses of the judge assigned to the case, and outlined the specific litigation tactics Irell planned to employ in these actions.

In August of 2006, at Broadcom's direction, Irell disclosed the substance of Mr. Ruehle's interviews with Mr. Heitz and Mr. Lefler to Broadcom's outside auditors, Ernst & Young. Thereafter, again at Broadcom's direction, Irell disclosed the same information to the SEC and the United States Attorney's Office in connection with their investigations of stock option granting practices at Broadcom. . . . Ruehle did not consent to any of these disclosures.

Mr. Ruehle first learned that the Government intended to use his statements to Irell against him when the FBI Form FD302 memoranda were produced to him in December 2008 in connection with the Government's criminal case. Mr. Ruehle promptly objected and asserted that his conversations with Irell were privileged communications. Mr. Ruehle previously litigated the issue in the Derivative Action before a Special Master, who found Mr. Ruehle's communications were, in fact, privileged. Nonetheless, the Government contended that Mr. Ruehle's assertion of the privilege was not well taken and filed an *ex parte* application for an evidentiary hearing in this Court to determine the applicability of the privilege. . . .

The attorney-client privilege protects "[c]onfidential disclosures by a client to an attorney made in order to obtain legal assistance." [Citation omitted.] To sustain a claim of privilege, the party seeking to assert the privilege must first establish the existence of an attorney-client relationship. Determining whether an attorney-client relationship exists depends on the reasonable expectations of the client. [Citation omitted.] . . . To determine the reasonable expectations of a client, courts look to "circumstantial evidence, taking into account all kinds of indirect evidence and contextual considerations that appear relevant to determining whether it would have been reasonable for the person to have inferred that she was the client of the lawyer." [Citation omitted.] Second, the party seeking to assert the privilege must demonstrate that the communication was made in order to obtain legal advice. When a lawyer consults with a client for purposes of "fact finding" in order to provide legal advice, the discussion between the lawyer and client qualifies as one undertaken for the purpose of seeking legal advice. [Citation omitted.] . . . As the Supreme Court of the United States observed, "the privilege exists to protect not only the giving of professional advice to those who can act on it but also the giving of information to the lawyer to enable him to give sound and informed advice. The first step in the resolution of any legal problem is ascertaining the factual background and sifting through the facts with an eye to the legally relevant." *Upjohn Co. v. United States*, 449

U.S. 383, 390-91, 101 S. Ct. 677, 66 L. Ed. 2d 584 (1981). Finally, in order for the privilege to apply, the communication must be intended to remain confidential. CAL. EVID. CODE §952. Under California law, communications made in the course of an attorney-client relationship are presumed confidential. CAL. EVID. CODE §917(a).

There is no serious question in this case that when Mr. Ruehle met with the Irell lawyers on June 1, 2006, Mr. Ruehle reasonably believed that an attorney-client relationship existed, he was communicating with his attorneys in the context of this relationship for the purpose of obtaining legal advice, and that any information he provided to Irell would remain confidential. Mr. Ruehle testified that he understood Irell would be representing him in both the Jin Action and the Derivative Action. Prior to his initial meeting with the Irell lawyers, Mr. Ruehle received an email from Broadcom's General Counsel . . . confirming that Irell would be representing him personally in both litigations. In the days leading up to their June 1, 2006 interview, the Irell lawyers frequently updated Mr. Ruehle on the progress of their investigation of the stock option practices at Broadcom. But more than mere progress reports, Mr. Heitz discussed his strategy for defending the corporation and its directors and summarized the fact-finding that would be necessary to support that strategy. In these emails, which were sent to Mr. Ruehle individually as opposed to the entire board of directors, Mr. Heitz asked Mr. Ruehle to review and obtain specific information and advised him how this information would be relevant to preparing a defense. The evidence establishes that Mr. Ruehle had a reasonable belief that an attorney-client relationship existed prior to his initial interview with the Irell lawyers on June 1, 2006.

Second, Mr. Ruehle testified that he believed that the interviews were being conducted to gather information in preparation for the litigations and for the purpose of obtaining legal advice. Mr. Ruehle was first asked by the Irell lawyers to schedule a meeting with them in an email that he received 4 minutes after he received an email from Mr. Dull informing Mr. Ruehle that Irell would be representing him personally in the pending litigations. Mr. Heitz and Mr. Lefler requested a time to discuss Broadcom's stock option granting practices, the exact same subject matter of the two pending civil lawsuits in which Irell represented Mr. Ruehle individually. Mr. Ruehle was never advised that he should have another lawyer present at the meeting to represent his interests. Based on these communications, Mr. Ruehle reasonably understood the Irell lawyers to be gathering facts and information for his defense against the claims asserted against him as well as for the company's own internal investigation.

Finally, Mr. Ruehle intended his statements to be confidential, and he had no reason to suspect that his conversations with the Irell lawyers would be disclosed to third parties. Mr. Ruehle testified that had he understood that the Irell lawyers might disclose his statements to third parties, "at a minimum [he] would have stopped and asked some very serious questions at that time." Mr. Ruehle was an experienced corporate officer and had substantial prior experience with civil litigation. He knew he was being personally investigated regarding Broadcom's stock option granting practices, and he would never have agreed to provide information that Irell could then turnover to the Government should it commence a criminal investigation of him.

The Government nevertheless suggests that because the Irell lawyers supposedly gave Mr. Ruehle an *Upjohn* warning, his statements to the Irell lawyers are not privileged communications. A so-called *Upjohn* warning or "Corporate Miranda" is ordinarily given to inform a "constituent member or an organization that the attorney represents the organization and *not* the constituent member." . . . The warning is intended to make clear to the individual being interviewed that the corporation, and not the individual employee, is the client and therefore "controls the privilege and the confidentiality of the communication." An *Upjohn* warning apprises a corporate employee that no attorney-client relationship exists, and any communication between the lawyer and the individual may be disclosed to third parties at the corporation's discretion. In this case, the Government's reliance on the alleged *Upjohn* warning is misplaced.

As an initial matter, the Court has serious doubts whether any *Upjohn* warning was given to Mr. Ruehle. Mr. Ruehle did not remember being given any warning, no warning is referenced in Mr. Lefler's notes from the meeting, and no written record of the warning even exists. But even if an *Upjohn* warning were provided to Mr. Ruehle, the substance of the warning Mr. Heitz testified he gave is woefully inadequate under the circumstances. . . . [H]e never told Mr. Ruehle that he and Mr. Lefler were not Mr. Ruehle's lawyers or that Mr. Ruehle should consult with another lawyer. Most importantly, neither Mr. Heitz nor Mr. Lefler ever told Mr. Ruehle that any statements he made to them could be shared with third parties, including the Government in a criminal investigation of him. . . . [H]ad he comprehended the substance of the admonition that Mr. Heitz testified he gave, Mr. Ruehle would never have agreed to the interview and would have sought the advice of another lawyer before providing any information.

Perhaps most critically, however, whether an *Upjohn* warning was or was not given is irrelevant in light of the undisputed attorney-client relationship between Irell and Mr. Ruehle. An *Upjohn* warning is given to a non-client to advise the employee that he is not communicating with his personal lawyer, no attorney-client relationship exists, and any communication may be revealed to third parties if disclosure is in the best interest of the corporation. Here, Mr. Ruehle was represented by Irell in litigations related to the identical subject matter as Irell's internal investigation on behalf of Broadcom. An oral warning, as opposed to a written waiver of the clear conflict presented by Irell's representation of both

Broadcom and Mr. Ruehle, is simply not sufficient to suspend or dissolve an existing attorney-client relationship and to waive the privilege. An oral warning to a current client that no attorney-client relationship exists is nonsensical at best — and unethical at worst. . . .

The most fundamental aspect of the attorney-client relationship is the duty of undivided loyalty owed by a lawyer to his client, and ultimately all of the ethical rules are derived from this fundamental principle. [Citation omitted.] The duty of loyalty requires a lawyer "to protect his client in every possible way, and it is a violation of that duty for him to assume a position adverse or antagonistic to his client." [Citation omitted.] . . . Simply put, a lawyer cannot, consistent with the duty of loyalty, "jettison one client in favor of another." [Citation omitted.] All clients are equal under the Rules of Professional Conduct, and no lawyer can sacrifice the interests of one client for those of another.

In this case, Irell committed at least three clear violations of its duty of loyalty to Mr. Ruehle. First, Irell failed to obtain Mr. Ruehle's informed written consent to Irell's simultaneous representation of Mr. Ruehle individually in the Jin Action and Derivative Action, on the one hand, and Broadcom in its internal investigation, on the other hand. Under the Rules of Professional Conduct, a lawyer may not simultaneously represent two clients whose interests actually or potentially conflict without each client's informed written consent. . . . CAL. RULES OF PROF'L CONDUCT R. 3-310I. . . . The disclosure and consent must be in writing so that the client understands the seriousness of the decision and to avoid disputes or ambiguities.

By the spring of 2006, Broadcom was acutely aware of the possibility that it might be investigated or sued on the basis of its stock option granting practices. At the time Irell accepted representation of Broadcom and Mr. Ruehle in May 2006, Irell knew or should have known that Broadcom's interests and Mr. Ruehle's interests conflicted and were adverse to each other. If there were any wrongdoing committed in connection with Broadcom's stock option practices, Broadcom might contend that Mr. Ruehle was responsible for it and that he acted without the knowledge and approval of the company. In these circumstances, Irell had a clear duty to disclose to Mr. Ruehle the potential conflict of interest created by the dual representation and obtain Mr. Ruehle's informed written consent to that conflict. Irell readily admits, however, that it did not apprise Mr. Ruehle of that conflict nor did it obtain his written waiver of the conflict.

Second, Irell breached its duty of loyalty to Mr. Ruehle, a current client, by interrogating him for the benefit of another client, Broadcom. The duty of loyalty requires every lawyer "to protect each of his or her clients in every possible way." [Citation omitted.] Thus, "[i]t is a clear violation of that duty for the attorney to assume a position adverse or antagonistic to the client without the latter's free and intelligent consent, given with full knowledge of all the facts and circumstances." [Citation omitted.] By attempting to mine information from one client to that client's possible detriment in order to help another client, the court concluded that the lawyer "violated his duty of loyalty." . . .

Absent informed written consent and waiver of the conflict of interest, Irell should not have interviewed Mr. Ruehle on behalf of Broadcom alone. In effect, Irell was interrogating one client to benefit another client. The Rules of Professional Conduct simply do not allow for such subordination. When Irell interviewed Mr. Ruehle about the stock option granting practices at Broadcom, it should have known that in the course of the interview, Mr. Ruehle might provide incriminating evidence about his role in those practices. Irell should never have permitted Mr. Ruehle, let alone encouraged him, to disclose his role without full knowledge of the consequences. . . . By sacrificing the interests of Mr. Ruehle in favor of those of Broadcom, Irell breached its duty of loyalty to him.

Finally, Irell disclosed Mr. Ruehle's privileged communications to third parties without his consent. An attorney has a duty to "maintain inviolate the confidence, and at every peril to himself or herself to preserve the secrets, of his or her client." CAL. BUS. & PROF. CODE §6068(e). Only with a client's permission may a lawyer disclose confidential communications. CAL. EVID. CODE §954; CAL. RULES OF PROF'L CONDUCT R. 3-100. A lawyer's duty to preserve confidences persists beyond the end of the attorney-client relationship. CAL. BUS. & PROF. CODE §6068(e). . . . Mr. Ruehle never gave Irell permission to jettison his rights for those of Broadcom and disclose the confidential information that he shared with Irell to the Government and other third parties. For Irell to have done so without Mr. Ruehle's consent was wrong and a clear breach of its duty of loyalty to him.

Irell's ethical breaches of the duty of loyalty are very troubling. Mr. Ruehle's confidential and privileged information has been disclosed to numerous third parties, most notably the Government in connection with its criminal prosecution against him. The Government's case against Mr. Ruehle is a serious one, and Mr. Ruehle faces a significant prison sentence if convicted on all counts charged in the indictment. . . . The Government's burden is not an easy one, as it has to prove the charges against Mr. Ruehle beyond a reasonable doubt. Suppressing relevant evidence is obviously not helpful to the Government in that regard, but more importantly, it hinders the adversarial process and the jury's search for the truth. Irell should not have put the parties and the Court in this position. The Rules of Professional Conduct are not aspirational. The Court is at a loss to understand why Irell did not comply with them here. Because Irell's ethical misconduct has compromised the rights of Mr. Ruehle, the integrity of the legal profession, and the fair administration of justice, the Court must refer Irell to the State Bar for discipline. Mr. Ruehle, the Government, and the public deserve nothing less. . . .

For the foregoing reasons, all evidence reflecting Mr. Ruehle's statements to Irell regarding the stock option granting practices at Broadcom is suppressed. Irell is hereby referred to the State Bar for appropriate discipline.

Questions about the Case

1. Who were the clients of Irell in this case? What is the evidence that Irell represented Ruehle?
2. Describe the conflict of interest that existed in this case. Could this conflict have been cured with a consent or waiver? See the tests set forth in the Model Rules and discussed in this chapter.
3. Describe the confidential information that was revealed. How was it obtained? To whom was it revealed? Was this a breach of the ethics rules? What were the possible consequences to Ruehle of having this information revealed?
4. Once Irell obtained the evidence that might mitigate Broadcom's liability and implicate Ruehle, what should it have done? Could it continue to represent both clients? Could it have selected one client over the other?
5. Do you think the lawyers involved should be disciplined? Would Ruehle have a cause of action for malpractice or some other breach of duty?

6

Advertising and Solicitation

This chapter covers the rules governing lawyer advertising and direct solicitation of clients, tracing the continued development of these rules since restrictions on advertising were banned by the U.S. Supreme Court nearly 30 years ago. Chapter 6 covers:

- key U.S. Supreme Court cases on the regulation of advertising and solicitation
- current state of legal advertising and marketing
- ethics rules governing advertising
- application of rules to paralegals
- ethics rules prohibiting direct solicitation of clients
- application of the rules in the dynamic environment of the Internet

A. Advertising

1. Background and History

In 1977, the landmark case of *Bates v. State Bar of Arizona*, 433 U.S. 350, upset decades of ethics rules prohibiting lawyer advertising, which dated back to the first state codes and first American Bar Association (ABA) model rules, the 1908 Canons. The early rules prohibited virtually every form of advertising except business cards. Later, inclusion of biographical information on approved lists of lawyers was permitted.

The political and social environment surrounding the *Bates* decision was one of growing consumer protectionism. In this climate, it was recognized that most citizens did not have access to legal services while the cost of legal services was rising dramatically. During the late 1960s and throughout the 1970s, new nontraditional methods of increasing access to legal services were being developed. Legal aid clinics and public interest law firms began opening their doors. The first prepaid legal insurance plans were established. Storefront legal clinics handled common legal problems at lower cost than traditional firms. The organized bar and the public shared the realization that citizens of modest incomes were unable to afford an attorney and did not know how to find one.

The ABA Code of Professional Responsibility (ABA Model Code) adopted in 1969 contained the traditional restrictions on lawyer advertising. Only business cards, announcements of attorney personnel changes within the firm or new locations or addresses, and Christmas cards to existing clients were permitted. The ABA made some slight modifications in these rules in the mid-1970s to accommodate the special needs of legal aid organizations and prepaid legal insurance plans. However, it was not until *Bates* that sweeping changes were made in the ethics codes of every jurisdiction.

In the *Bates* case, two Arizona lawyers advertised low-cost legal services in a local newspaper and were disciplined by the state bar. Their challenge to restrictions on lawyer advertising was ultimately heard by the U.S. Supreme Court, which struck down the restrictions as violative of the First Amendment. The Court held that lawyer advertising—like other forms of commercial speech—was protected, and states could prohibit advertisements only in limited ways—for example, for false, misleading, or deceptive ads and by means of reasonable time, place, and manner restrictions.

The *Bates* case (included at the end of this chapter) outlines very clearly the arguments on both sides of the lawyer advertising issue. The legal profession's resistance to lawyer advertising at the time was tremendous, because lawyers believed that advertising would de-professionalize and commercialize law practice. Although strong opposition to advertising still exists, most lawyers in the country engage in some form of advertising that would have been prohibited before *Bates*.

Legal advertising and marketing have become pervasive. Firms have strategic marketing plans that include advertising and often try to create a firm image or "brand." Studies also show that, although many lawyers attribute the declining image of the legal profession to advertising, the public does not. The public considers advertising as a source of information and only begins to perceive it as objectionable when it becomes "invasive." Studies also show that advertising works — increasing numbers of people find a lawyer through advertising. The growth in the use of the Internet for marketing of legal services has expanded dramatically and created new ethical issues. Studies show that millions of people have used the Internet to find legal services. All large law firms, and even most smaller ones, have their own Web sites.

Some firms are using nonlawyer "sales" and business development personnel to help them reach prospective clients. Many firms have glossy brochures or press kits that describe the backgrounds of attorneys, explain the nature of their services, and highlight prominent matters that they have handled. Many also issue regularly published newsletters for clients, updating them on the latest firm triumphs and informing them of changes in the law that may encourage them to have legal work done. Many hold social events and educational seminars for clients and send press releases to the media to announce significant events in the firm, for example, when the firm wins an important case or a prestigious new partner joins the firm.

Firms publish daily, weekly, or monthly newsletters on industry issues, such as banking or corporate securities; sponsor blogs; offer Web seminars; and post videos or podcasts on their blogs or Web sites. Web sites dedicated to illnesses or medical conditions that have resulted in class action suits against pharmaceutical companies are common. Online legal referral services, lawyer-client matching sites, legal advice sites, chat rooms, sponsored links, and even mass e-mail marketings have been tried. (See Section A.4 or more on the ethics of using various forms of Web-based communications.)

Law firms place a high value on lawyers who can bring in business. "Rainmakers" who attract work, work well with clients, and keep them satisfied are essential to the success of a firm. Many law firms try to establish a high public profile by donating funds to worthy causes, participating in community and civic activities, taking pro bono cases that will generate favorable publicity, and encouraging lawyers to participate in a wide variety of community and civic activities outside the firm. Some firms sponsor in-house seminars to train lawyers how to better market their services and to enhance client relations. Many firms give seminars at trade shows sponsored by industries from which they draw clients.

Some large firms use client surveys to assess the attitudes, needs, and levels of satisfaction of their clients. Surveys, conducted either orally through structured interviews or in writing, aim to identify the importance of various factors in meeting clients' needs and to find out how the firm's responsiveness, communication, services, and fee structure are perceived. Some firms find that client relations are improved simply by virtue of conducting the survey, and the information gained may be used to enhance services and to remedy weaknesses. Sophisticated research is used to identify issues and trends in an area of practice or industry. Firms use the results to develop events, articles, blog posts, and webinars to provide legal information to clients and prospective clients.

Smaller firms also engage in advertising. The more traditional firms use the same kinds of marketing activities as large firms. But many small firms are specialized, handling one or two kinds of legal matters and seeking a clientele that might not otherwise have a ready referral to an attorney. Personal injury firms have led the way in lawyer advertising, most visibly with television and radio spots, but also with billboards, flyers placed on cars or doorknobs, posters on telephone poles, and even ads on the back of grocery store receipts. Firms that handle immigration, family law, workers' compensation, Social Security matters, and bankruptcy frequently utilize these techniques. Direct-mail and e-mail advertising is used to target persons who may need specific kinds of legal services, such as foreclosure prevention. Some lawyers use 900 numbers to dispense legal advice, and others include catchy 800 numbers in their print, radio, or television ads. A growing number of small firms and solos advertise in directories published by the local churches they belong to.

Paralegals play an important role in marketing by serving clients efficiently, emphasizing the cost savings to the client from the use of paralegals, identifying sources for referrals, alerting attorneys to opportunities for rainmaking, and working with attorneys to develop marketing plans and client surveys.

2. Case Law on Advertising

Several Supreme Court decisions that followed *Bates* made it clear that the Court will not look favorably at restrictions on lawyer advertising. In *In re R.M.J.*, 455 U.S. 1991 (1982), the Court held that a practitioner could advertise the areas of law in which he practiced in language other than that specified in the state ethics code because the language the lawyer used was not misleading and the code was unnecessarily restrictive. The court also allowed the lawyer to state in the ads the jurisdictions in which he was licensed to practice. In *Zauderer v. Office of Disciplinary Counsel of Supreme Court of Ohio*, 471 U.S. 626 (1985), the Supreme Court reversed the state supreme court's ruling that disciplined a personal injury attorney for placing a newspaper ad that pictured the intrauterine device that was the subject of litigation. The Court held that the attorney had the right to publish ads directed at readers with specific legal problems so long as the ads were accurate and not misleading. In 1988, the Supreme Court in *Shapero v. Kentucky Bar Association*, 486 U.S. 466, held that state ethics codes could not prohibit truthful and nondeceptive direct-mail advertising. The language it found unconstitutional in the Kentucky code was identical to ABA Model Rule 7.3, which has since been extensively revised. Prior to this case, ethics rules had classified direct-mail advertising with telephone and in-person solicitation and had prohibited it. In *Peel v. Attorney Registration and Disciplinary Commission of Illinois*, 496 U.S. 91 (1990), the Court struck down state prohibitions on statements carried on a lawyer's letterhead that indicated the lawyer's certification as a specialist. Although the certifying agency here — the National Board of Trial Advocacy — was not one authorized by the state, it had objective and verifiable criteria for the certification of a civil trial specialist. This ruling resulted in changes in several state codes that had restrictions similar to those of Illinois.

Peel was followed by another case endorsing the use of a designation by an organization not approved by a state agency. In *Ibanez v. Florida Dept. of Business and Professional Regulation*, 512 U.S. 136 (1994), the Court held that an attorney/certified public accountant who advertised her certified public accountant (CPA) and certified financial planner (CFP) designations could not be reprimanded by the Florida Board of Accountancy for false, deceptive, and misleading advertising because the ad was truthful and the designations were publicly recognized by potential clients.

The pattern of the court striking down state prohibitions on lawyer advertising was finally broken in 1995 in the case of *Florida Bar v. Went For It, Inc.*, 515 U.S. 618 (1995). In this landmark case, the Supreme Court upheld restrictions on targeted direct mail advertising sent to accident and disaster victims. The Florida Bar, like the bars in many other jurisdictions, had adopted a rule prohibiting such ads from being sent within 30 days of the incident. In upholding the prohibition, the Court cited heavily to bar studies that showed how negatively such letters were viewed by the public, which saw the lawyers' conduct as an invasion of privacy designed to take advantage of vulnerable people in tragic circumstances. The case could be viewed as marking a change in the way that restrictions on lawyer advertising are treated by the Court or as one in a series of cases that are defining permissible limits since the *Bates* decision. The case appears at the end of this chapter.

Since that case, a number of states have attempted, with varying degrees of success, to impose specific kinds of restrictions on lawyer advertising. Cases challenging new restrictions have been brought in many states, including Florida, Louisiana, New York, and South Carolina. In most of these cases the plaintiffs, who are usually local practitioners and often are members of Public Citizen, a national group that represents more than 100,000 lawyers, challenge an array of new rules. The results have been split. For example, in *Public Citizen, Inc. v. Louisiana Att'y Disciplinary Bd.*, 642 F. Supp. 2d 539 (E.D. La. 2009), the court found 12 subsections of the rules to be constitutional and only one to fail the test. That rule required a spoken and written disclosure identifying a spokesperson in an ad as a spokesperson, with an indication that he or she is not a lawyer and is being paid, if that is in fact the case. In *Alexander v. Cahill*, 598 F.3d 79 (2d Cir. 2010), the court struck down "content-based" restrictions with the exception of portrayals of fictitious law firms and imposed a 30-day moratorium on targeted advertising following a specific incident. Also see *Harrell v. Florida Bar*, 09-11910 (11th Cir. 2010), which sent the matter back to the lower court after finding the issues justiciable.

3. Ethics Rules on Advertising

The ABA Model Code was amended after *Bates* to comply with that decision, but now all states have adopted rules more like the ABA Model Rules. ABA Model Rule 7.1 prohibits lawyers from making false or misleading communications about themselves or their services. A communication is considered "false or misleading if it contains a material misrepresentation of fact or law, or omits a fact necessary to make the statement considered as a whole not materially misleading." Comment 3 to the rule indicates that facts that create unjustified expectations and unsubstantiated comparisons with other lawyers can be misleading, and suggests that appropriate disclaimers may "preclude a finding" that the ad is false or misleading.

Testimonial advertisements
Ads in which a client or person acting as a client explains how valuable the lawyer's services were

Many states have variations on this rule. Some states specifically prohibit ***testimonials***, contending that they are inherently misleading, create unjustified expectations, or are self-laudatory. A growing number of jurisdictions allow testimonials, usually with the requirement that they include information about payment to the endorser or the status of the endorser as a client, or have disclaimers to avoid unjustified expectations. The U.S. Supreme Court has twice refused to review a case in which a California lawyer was disciplined for using a testimonial. Dramatizations in radio and television ads are also disfavored by many in the organized bar, but are becoming increasingly common and have generally been tolerated. Several states permit them, usually with disclaimers that advise the viewers that the ad is a dramatization and does not guarantee similar results.

The ABA Model Rules do not require ads to be "dignified." The evaluation of what is "dignified" is completely subjective and would not meet the tests established by *Bates* and its progeny. Some state bars encourage dignity in lawyer advertising through aspirational goals that recommend against "the use of inappropriately dramatic music, unseemly slogans, hawkish spokespersons, premium offers, slapstick routines or outlandish settings," which undermine public confidence in the legal profession. But the number of ads that employ these techniques is growing.

Some states prohibit all lawyer comparison advertising. Other states prohibit statements regarding past performance on the grounds that they are inherently misleading and create false expectations. Several states specifically prohibit predictions of success; these claims would probably be found to be misleading even without a specific prohibition in the code. Claims about quality are generally prohibited, as they are incapable of objective measurement. Fee information and comparisons are generally permissible, although some states have adopted specific language that may or may not be used to describe fees.

ABA Model Rule 7.2(a) permits lawyers to advertise through written, recorded, or electronic media. Rule 7.2(b) prohibits payment to a person for recommending legal services except for the cost of ads, charges for legal service organizations or lawyer referral services, or payment when a lawyer buys another lawyer's practice. Rule 7.2(c) adds the requirement that at least one lawyer's name and office address must be included in the ads.

Related ABA Model Rule 7.3(c) requires lawyers to include the words "Advertising Material" at the beginning and end of targeted direct-mail and recorded communications and on the outside of the envelope of a direct-mail ad. Most states have similar rules about labeling on direct-mail advertising pieces. Many states require lawyers to keep copies of ads and records on when and where they were used, whatever the method of advertising, for two years or for longer periods, and some require copies of ads to be sent to a specific state agency. Others require specifically worded disclaimers in ads. A few states have a review committee that passes on ads before they are used. Rule 7.3 has also been interpreted to allow counsel for plaintiff and defense in class actions to contact putative members of the class (ABA Formal Op. 07-445).

Some states have restrictions on contacting accident victims within a 30- to 60-day period after an accident. Federal law also prohibits lawyers and their agents from making unsolicited communications concerning possible causes of action to victims or their relatives for 45 days after an accident involving an air carrier (49 U.S.C. §1136(g)(2)). This ban covers both advertising (e.g., by direct mail) and in-person or phone solicitation.

ABA Model Rule 7.4 allows lawyers to communicate the fact that they practice in a particular field of law and to advertise their certification by an organization approved by a state regulatory authority or the ABA. Lawyers may also indicate that they are licensed as patent attorneys or are engaged in admiralty practice. Most jurisdictions have adopted Rule 7.4, but some jurisdictions prohibit the use of the word "specialize" to describe an attorney's area of expertise and allow terms such as "limited to" or "concentrated in" in particular areas of practice.

Finally ABA Model Rule 7.5 covers firm names and letterheads. Under this rule, a lawyer's letterhead must meet the standards set forth in Model Rule 7.1, that is, not be false or misleading. Trade names are permitted under this rule so long as they do not imply a connection to a government agency or legal services organization. Some states have strict limits on the use of trade names. Firms with multi-jurisdictional practices may use the same firm name but must show limits on listed lawyers' licenses to practice. Lawyers in public office cannot be listed in the firm name or on its letterhead unless the lawyer is actively and regularly practicing with the firm. Finally, lawyers cannot state or imply that they practice with a partnership or organization unless they do this in fact. For example, lawyers who share office space but are not partners cannot hold themselves out as partners by means of their firm name or letterhead.

An interesting debate has arisen about whether lawyers can advertise their designation as a "Super Lawyer" or "Best Lawyer," a designation usually made by a publication based on the votes of peers. The question is whether there should be a total ban on these designations as inherently misleading, or whether narrower restrictions can be applied. Arizona, Connecticut, Iowa, Michigan, and Arizona have ethics opinions that allow the designation within carefully drawn parameters, such as requirements that the ratings be peer-based and not predicated on the lawyer advertising in the publication; New Jersey adopted an amendment to its rules in 2009 to allow this kind of designation if the name of the organization is included, the basis for the title is substantiated, and a disclaimer indicating the ad was not approved by the state bar is included (New Jersey Rule of Professional Conduct 7.1(a)(3)). This change was made after the New Jersey Supreme Court vacated an earlier ethics opinion that found such designations inherently misleading (see *In re Opinion 39*, 197 N.J. 66, 961 A.2d 722 (2008).

As indicated in Chapter 3, paralegals' names and titles may be listed on letterhead and business cards in most jurisdictions. Earlier restrictions on nonlawyers being listed on letterhead and having business cards have been revised because of changes in the rules on lawyer advertising brought about by *Bates* and the cases that followed it. For example, Indiana and South Dakota guidelines adopted in the early 1990s and an opinion of a 1994 New Jersey Committee on Attorney Advertising condone the use of paralegals' names and titles on letterhead and in newspaper advertisements (Opinion 16 issued in 1994). Two ethics opinions specifically endorse the use of "CLA" and "CLAS" on letterhead and business cards. (Mississippi Bar 95-223 and New York State Bar Association 97-695.)

New York State Bar Association Committee on Professional Ethics Opinion 640 (1992) issued an opinion about titles that may be used by paralegals. Whereas the committee endorsed the use of "paralegal" and "senior paralegal," which unambiguously convey nonlawyer status, it recommends against the use of several other titles: legal associate, paralegal coordinator, public benefits specialist, legal advocate, family law advocate, housing law advocate, disability advocate, and public benefits advocate. The committee objected to these titles on the ground that they are likely to be confusing to the public, which would be misled about the nonlawyer status of someone with one of these titles. No other jurisdiction has issued such an opinion.

A final concern about letterhead and business cards relates to their use, which should be carefully monitored by the law firm. Several ethics opinions advise against allowing clients to use lawyers' letterhead to send correspondence without attorney review. Business cards, of course, must not be used for unethical solicitation.

Ethics rules on advertising and solicitation continue to be among the most hotly debated issues in legal ethics. At one end of the opinion spectrum are attorneys who favor a wide-open and unrestricted environment to demystify the legal profession, to promote greater access to legal services, and to encourage a more competitive climate among lawyers. At the other end are more traditional lawyers who believe that strong prohibitions are essential to preserve the good reputation and status of the legal profession and to protect the public from unscrupulous practitioners.

4. Application of the Rules to Electronic Communications

Lawyers in all legal settings use various kinds of Web-based communications to reach prospective clients. Most firms have Web sites, which, like firm brochures, provide background information on lawyers in the firm and areas in which the firm practices and may include newsworthy articles about legal issues of interest to clients. Some lawyers have blogs, participate in chat groups, use social networking, advertise on Craigslist and similar sites, and use direct e-mail to reach prospective clients. Some lawyers post advertisements and articles to bulletin boards and newsgroups and participate in online trade group seminars.

Several companies operate "matching" services, in which prospective clients prepare a form explaining their legal problem, providing the locality and time frame for retaining counsel, and sometimes indicating the fee that they are willing to pay. The network of lawyers registered with the service can then communicate with the client and offer their services. Some firms attract and serve clients entirely over the Internet in a virtual law practice.

The use of Web-based communications has raised ethical issues that fall in many areas of the ethics rules. Is direct e-mail to prospective clients advertising or solicitation, and which rules apply? Is a Web site more like a television ad or a firm brochure? If an attorney states a legal opinion in a chat group, is the attorney forming an attorney-client relationship with the person posing the question? Is the attorney violating unauthorized practice rules in states in which he or she is not licensed to practice but where the opinion is read? Is it inherently misleading to advertise on the

Internet when the attorney is not licensed in all the states where the ad may be read? Can a lawyer pay a referral fee to an Internet service that matches lawyers and clients?

Concerns about confidentiality and conflicts of interest also arise in the online environment. In communicating with a prospective client, the duty of confidentiality is triggered once the lawyer has a discussion with the client about representation. So what is the duty of the lawyer when a prospective client sends unsolicited confidential information to the lawyer? When does a prospective client have a reasonable expectation that the lawyer would be willing to discuss representation? Can this expectation arise from the nature of the lawyer's Web site or other electronic communication? What happens if the lawyer already represents the other side? Once the confidential information is given to the lawyer, is the lawyer prohibited from representing the opposing party? Most experts indicate that the lawyer is conflicted out of representing the opposing party if the lawyer has obtained information that would be significantly harmful to the person who revealed it.

The ABA and the state ethics authorities are gradually addressing the many issues related to Web-based communications through ethics opinions applying the ethics rules to advertising and solicitation on the Internet. A few early opinions found it ethical to operate a firm **Web site** and to post ads to electronic newsgroups so long as the material complies with existing rules on advertising, including those prohibiting false and misleading statements and requiring the lawyer to maintain copies of the material for review by disciplinary authorities. Some states require lawyers with Web sites to file a copy with the bar and to pay a filing fee, just as they would with any other lawyer advertisement, and other states have review committees that examine Web sites before they are posted.

The ethics opinions on participation in social networking media, such as **blogs, Twitter, and chat groups**, are not consistent. Most authorities, including the ABA, find that they are akin to in-person solicitation and are subject to the restrictions that apply to that kind of communication, whereas others find that they are not solicitation, as they are not "in person" as required by the ethics rules. Even in states that do not regard them as solicitation, lawyers are warned to guard against inadvertently forming an attorney-client relationship or giving legal advice in a jurisdiction where they are not licensed to practice.

Some bars have considered **direct e-mail advertising** and found that it is not direct solicitation because it is not "live"; the reader can choose not to read it and can reflect on its contents before responding. Direct e-mail marketing lacks the immediacy and confrontational aspects of in-person and telephone communication. However, some states have disciplined lawyers for "soliciting" clients on the Internet, in part because potential clients located in jurisdictions where the lawyers were not licensed to practice could read the ads and be misled about the lawyer's authority to practice in that jurisdiction.

A few states prohibit lawyers from being listed in lawyers' **directories** on the Internet. Several states classify fee-charging directories as profit-making **referral services** that lawyers are prohibited from using unless they are approved by the state bar. Generally, the ethical concern with such referral services is that the lawyer is paying a referral fee to a nonlawyer or is fee splitting with a nonlawyer. (See more on these prohibitions in Chapter 7.) Most states allow online matching services. As noted earlier, these services invite a prospective client to submit a form that indicates the nature of the legal problem; lawyers who are members of the service in the relevant jurisdiction can respond. A few states prohibit lawyers from participating on these sites, considering them to be unapproved lawyer referral services, but others (New York, Rhode Island, North Carolina, and South Carolina) allow them as a form of advertising. Texas allows participation as long as the matching is automated and not done by nonlawyers running the service. The Federal Trade Commission supports these sites as an effective method for providing access to affordable legal services.

The use of the Internet to communicate about legal services is evolving and dynamic and regional differences in applying the ethics rules are quite evident. A few generalizations can be made about the ethics of electronic advertising and solicitation:

- It is not unethical for a lawyer or law firm to have a **Web site** providing information about the firm so long as the ethics rules on advertising are followed, including those prohibiting false and misleading statements, requiring that lawyers maintain copies of the material for review, specifying language about certifications, and mandating that the lawyer's name and address be included in the advertisement.
- A lawyer's Web site must state the **jurisdiction(s)** in which the lawyers in the firm are licensed to practice law and should contain disclaimers to warn prospective clients that they can practice only in those states to prevent the communication from being misleading and to guard against UPL.
- In most jurisdictions, Internet advertising, including direct e-mail advertising, constitutes **advertising**, not solicitation, so that lawyers can utilize the Internet to advertise so long as the existing ethics rules on advertising are followed. Presumably, this advertising also permits sponsored links and the use of "pay per click" services.
- Services that match up lawyers with clients may be classified as **referral services**, which must have relevant approvals, or as advertisements, which are permitted as long as other ethics rules on advertising are honored.
- Jurisdictions are split on whether **blogs and chat groups** or chat rooms are akin to in-person solicitation, and therefore subject to the more rigorous restrictions that apply to that kind of communication, or should be classified as advertising. Some states, including California,

find that chat rooms are not the same as solicitation as the contact is not "in person." Blogs may be subject to ethics rules on advertising if they are found to constitute advertising, which is generally determined by their content.

- Lawyer **directories on the Internet** are generally permitted, even if lawyers pay for the entries, just as regular hard copy directories would be permitted.

Disclaimers
A statement denying a person's claim or right

Disclaimers associated with Web-based communications are increasingly important in protecting lawyers against ethical pitfalls. Most lawyers have disclaimers on their Web sites, indicating that information provided therein is not "legal advice" and that no attorney-client relationship is established by virtue of the prospective client sending a lawyer an e-mail. Disclaimers should also warn that such communications are not privileged and should ask that prospective clients not send confidential information to the firm's mailbox. Disclaimers should state the jurisdictional limits of the lawyer's practice. Such disclaimers should also be included on electronic ads and other forms of Web-based communications like e-newsletters. Disclaimers should be written in simple English so that nonlawyer prospective clients can understand them. Good practice suggests that the prospective clients be required to sign off that they have read the disclaimers before they proceed to send any information to the lawyer. Disclaimers should be placed where they will be seen by users and not buried several clicks away from the page where the e-mail contact link is provided. See ABA Formal Ethics Opinion 10-457 for more advice on ensuring that the use of Web sites does not lead to ethical violations.

Through disclaimers and careful site construction, lawyers can discourage prospective clients from providing confidential information in unsolicited e-mails. Sites can invite the prospective client to first send his or her name, the nature of the claim, and the names of other possible parties so that the lawyer can conduct a conflicts check before any confidential information is revealed. This protects both the prospective client and the lawyer.

Some commentators have called for uniform national ethics rules concerning Internet communications although little progress has been made to achieve uniformity. The great variation among states in their handling of advertising and solicitation exacerbates this already difficult new area of ethics. A lawyer may be in compliance with the local jurisdictional rules but will clearly be in violation of the rules in another state where the communication is read. Further, the lawyers in states with more restrictive advertising rules believe that they are at a competitive disadvantage because they are more limited in what they can say, how they can say it, and where they can say it. Differences in rules on advertising in directories, how one's areas of expertise can be described, whether testimonials can be used, and whether extensive disclaimers are required make advertising on the Internet especially challenging for lawyers in restrictive jurisdictions.

B. Solicitation

The changes in ethics rules and practice relating to advertising have not had much impact on the rules restricting the conduct of lawyers in soliciting clients directly, either in person or by telephone. The foundation for these restrictions is strong and virtually unquestioned by the profession. The rules related to ***solicitation*** reflect concerns about the intimidation, undue influence, and unfair bargaining position that lawyers may have when they confront a prospective client face-to-face, on the phone, or otherwise in "real time." The legal profession has a long-standing prohibition against "ambulance chasers" or ***runners and cappers*** — agents of lawyers who prey on accident victims by soliciting them directly at the scene of an accident or while they are in a hospital as the result of an accident. This kind of overreaching conduct, especially when it is directed toward clients who are vulnerable and not in a position to make a rational or well-thought-out choice about selecting counsel, clearly offends most lawyers and the public.

Solicitation
Direct unrequested contact with a prospective client for the purpose of obtaining employment

Runners and cappers
Agents of lawyers who solicit clients in violation of ethics rules

Several cases have addressed this issue. The leading case upholding restrictions on direct solicitation is *Ohralik v. Ohio State Bar Association*, 436 U.S. 447 (1978), included at the end of this chapter. This case involved an attorney who solicited an accident victim both by telephone and in person. Aggravating the solicitation violation was the attorney's refusal to stop the solicitation after the potential "client" refused representation.

The U.S. Supreme Court case of *Edenfield v. Fane*, 507 U.S. 761 (1993), caused speculation that the Court might strike down some of the restrictions against direct solicitation by lawyers. In that case, a Florida certified public accountant sought relief from regulations that prohibited direct solicitation of clients. The Court held that such restrictions are a violation of free speech in a business context where prospective clients are sophisticated and experienced business executives.

An exception to rules against direct solicitation of clients is made in cases involving organizations that seek to represent plaintiffs in cases that further a specific political principle, such as freedom of speech or association, or civil rights. Examples of such organizations are the National Association for the Advancement of Colored People and the American Civil Liberties Union. The leading cases in this area are *NAACP v. Button*, 371 U.S. 415 (1963), and *In re Primus*, 436 U.S. 412 (1978).

ABA Model Rule 7.3 prohibits direct solicitation in person, by live telephone, or by real-time electronic contact. This last category of direct solicitation was added to address concerns about solicitation over the Internet. Exceptions are carved out for contact with other lawyers, family members, close personal relationships, and prior professional relationships. A lawyer must cease solicitation if someone in the excepted categories objects or if the solicitation of that person involves "coercion, duress or harassment." The public interest exception to the ABA Model Rule appears in the comments.

Some states have adopted additional provisions that prohibit any direct or written solicitation of persons who are in a vulnerable physical, emotional, or mental state. California, for example, adds that communications transmitted at the scene of an accident or en route to a health care facility are presumed to violate rules against solicitation.

There is a split in the jurisdictions over the use of prerecorded telephone messages. Some states classify these messages as direct telephone solicitation and prohibit them, whereas others find this method to be more like direct-mail advertising and do not per se prohibit them.

The application of the advertising and solicitation rules to class actions also poses some interesting questions. Before a class is certified, lawyers for both plaintiffs and defendants can communicate with prospective members of the class who are not represented by counsel. Once the class is certified, defense counsel cannot communicate with putative members of the class. (See ABA Formal Opinion 07-445.)

A lawyer who attempts to use agents or intermediaries to circumvent rules against solicitation will be held responsible in a disciplinary action for the conduct of his or her agents, under general principles of agency law as well as ethics rules. ABA Model Rule 8.4(a). Despite these very clear rules, instances of unethical solicitation are not that uncommon, especially by lawyers using agents. For example, agents of lawyers, including accident investigators, have been found soliciting business at the scene of airline crashes and industrial accidents. Some states are attempting to overcome the difficulties inherent in stopping unlawful solicitation by creating disaster response teams of volunteer and staff lawyers who go the scenes of major accidents and disasters to warn victims about unlawful solicitation and to deter lawyers from engaging in such conduct. The most recent rash of unlawful solicitation involves foreclosure consultants and loan modification agencies, which solicit clients who are in danger of losing their homes and then contract with or refer clients to lawyers to handle their cases. (See *Cincinnati Bar Ass'n v. Mullaney* in Chapter 3 for an example.)

A few ethics opinions address situations in which nonlawyers solicited legal work for lawyers. The Illinois State Bar Association found it improper for an attorney's employee, designated a "tax representative," to conduct work independently, referring back to the attorney clients that he believed needed further assistance from a lawyer (Illinois State Bar Association 94-8). And the Rhode Island Bar found fee-splitting and unlawful solicitation in a collection agency owned by a nonlawyer who sold forms and legal services, paying the attorney who provided the legal services a percentage of the fees collected (Rhode Island Bar 95-47). Some personal injury lawyers offer a referral fee to anyone who brings a new case to the firm, often accomplished through the agent's unethical in-person or telephone solicitation. In this scenario, the violation is often coupled with the unethical practice of paying a fee for the referral (see Chapter 7).

The NALA and NFPA ethics codes do not address advertising and solicitation directly but prohibit a legal assistant from engaging in any act that is unethical. (See NALA Canon 3(c), NALA Guidelines 1.3, and NFPA 1.3.) Likewise, the ABA Model Guidelines for the Utilization of Paralegal Services require the lawyer to ensure that the paralegal's conduct is compatible with ethical rules. (See Guidelines 1 and ABA Model Rule 5.3.)

REVIEW QUESTIONS

1. When were prohibitions on lawyer advertising lifted? Under what leading U.S. Supreme Court case? What was the ruling in the case?
2. How did the recognition in the 1960s and 1970s that many Americans do not have access to legal services affect the movement toward acceptance of lawyer advertising?
3. What kinds of restrictions may states place on lawyer advertising after the *Bates* case?
4. Why do many lawyers dislike lawyer advertising?
5. What kinds of advertising do lawyers most commonly use?
6. What are some of the new ways that lawyers are using the Internet to reach prospective clients?
7. What do the key court decisions since *Bates* say about lawyer advertising?
8. What are the general provisions about advertising found in the ABA Model Rules?
9. What kinds of restrictions do some states have that the ABA Rules do not have?
10. Do lawyer ads have to be "dignified"? Is this restriction constitutional?
11. List the media in which lawyers may advertise under the ABA Model Rules.
12. What are the rules governing lawyer advertising of specializations and certifications?
13. Are states permitted to place time restrictions or moratoriums on direct-mail ads to accident victims?
14. Are law firms allowed to use trade names? Under what circumstances?
15. What information about paralegals may law firms include on their letterhead? Their business cards? Web sites?

16. Are lawyers prohibited from soliciting clients in person? On the telephone? Why?
17. What are the exceptions to the direct solicitation rule?
18. May lawyers use paralegals to solicit clients directly?
19. How common are violations of the ban on direct solicitation?
20. What job titles for paralegals are and are not acceptable?
21. What role can a paralegal play in marketing?
22. What do ethics rules say about various forms of electronic communication, such as e-newsletters, matching sites, blogs, chat rooms, and Web sites? Is the use of these media considered advertising or solicitation?
23. Under what circumstances might a lawyer use the designation "Super Lawyer"?
24. What do NALA's and NFPA's ethics codes say about advertising and solicitation?

DISCUSSION QUESTIONS AND HYPOTHETICALS

1. Using the *Bates* case, make a list of the reasons that support banning lawyer advertising and of those that support little restriction of lawyer advertising. Which side of the argument do you find more persuasive?
2. Do you think advertising has hurt or helped the public image of lawyers? Has it made legal services more accessible?
3. Do you think that dramatizations should be restricted? Why, or why not? How?
4. Do you think testimonials should be prohibited? Why, or why not?
5. Is there anything objectionable about an ad that states that an attorney is an experienced trial attorney and an expert in personal injury cases when the attorney has only been in practice a year and all her cases have settled out of court?
6. An ad says, "No recovery, no fee." The fact is that the client is liable for the costs even if he loses. Is this objectionable? Under what rule?
7. May an ad say that an attorney is an "expert"? "Highly qualified"? "Competent"? Why, or why not? What about buying an ad in a special magazine called *Super Lawyers* and getting an entry as a "Super Lawyer" as a result?
8. May an ad say that a firm specializes in "quickie divorces"? "Guaranteed visas"? Why or why not?
9. May an ad say the fee is $150 an hour without any additional information? Why or why not?
10. May a firm in a jurisdiction that allows trade names have the name "Public Law Firm"? "Legal Defenders"? "Foreclosure Recovery Center"?

11. May a law firm print its name and phone number on pens that are given out to clients? On shirts donated to the local Little League team? On city maps sent to new residents?
12. Consider the following communications and see how they measure up under the ethics rules and guidelines in this chapter:

    a. Spam e-mail that says in the subject line, "Retain top-notch attorneys for pennies a day."
    b. An e-mail ad that says in the body, "Whether it's a simple speeding ticket or an extensive child custody case, we cover ALL areas of the legal system."
    c. An e-mail that says, "Legal Services for Less than a Penny a Day" and goes on to offer "a top law firm in your area" to produce a "will for you, absolutely FREE, with your membership."
    d. What if the ad in c above also indicated, "Why pay $200 or more an hour when you can get the same first-rate service for less than $1 per day?"
    e. A television ad that has a lawyer called "Action Jackson" talking about his services.
    f. A television ad with a well-known actor saying, "Call the Johnson law firm, RIGHT NOW."
    g. A television ad with O. J. Simpson suggesting that people call a lawyer referral service.
    h. A mailing of realistic-looking black plastic grenades with business cards saying that the prospective business client needs to be "armed" against lawsuits.
    i. A television ad with a personal injury plaintiff lawyer in a boxing ring fighting against "insurance defense firms."
    j. A URL for a lawyer Web site that reads, "topcorporatelawyer.com."
    k. A TV commercial featuring a pit bull in a spiked collar and a telephone number that spells PIT-BULL.
    l. Television and phone book ads that say, "Don't settle for less than you deserve."
    m. A 10-second Spanish-language radio ad that says, "If you have had an automobile accident, by law you have the right to receive at least $15,000 for your case."

13. How is in-person solicitation different from advertising? How is telephone solicitation different from advertising? Is targeted, personalized, direct-mail advertising more like a newspaper print ad or a telephone call? Why, or why not?
14. Should political and public interest organizations be excused from restrictions on in-person solicitation? Why, or why not?
15. Suppose a corporation called "Foreclosure Fighters" was organized to represent people (for a fee) whose homes were being foreclosed on. Would it be allowed to solicit clients directly under the exception

for public interest causes? What if it is nonprofit? Is the name acceptable?

16. What would you do if you were asked to go to the hospital to visit a friend who had been in a car accident to try to get the friend to hire your firm to represent him or her?
17. Can a criminal defense lawyer have flyers about her services handed out at the courthouse?
18. A television ad says, "It's not your fault you were hurt on the job, but I know you're afraid to file a job injury claim. You're afraid your boss won't believe you're really hurt—or worse, that you'll be fired. We'll protect you against these threats—these accusations—and work to protect your job. I'm not an actor, I'm a lawyer. I'm Joe Smith. Call me and we'll get you the benefits you deserve." Is this ad acceptable under the ABA Model Rules? See *In re Anonymous Members of the S.C. Bar*, 385 S.C. 283, 684 S.E.2d 560 (2009).

RESEARCH PROJECTS AND ASSIGNMENTS

1. Locate the rules governing advertising and solicitation in your jurisdiction. Compare them with the ABA Model Rules.
2. Collect examples of as many different kinds of lawyer ads as you can find in your area. Check the Internet, Yellow Pages, billboards, television, radio, and so on. Rate these ads according to their (1) usefulness and information value; (2) effectiveness in recruiting clients to a firm; and (3) degree of dignity or offensiveness. Present to the class.
3. Call five local law firms and find out what they are doing to bring in clients, including what methods of advertising they use. Collect their firm brochures, newsletters, Web site home pages, Internet ads, and other advertising materials and rate them the same way you did the ads in question 2.
4. Does your jurisdiction have any ethics opinions on advertising and solicitation on the Internet? Find and summarize them, comparing them to the ethics rules and leading cases in this chapter.
5. Write an ethics rule that covers advertising and solicitation on the Internet and is constitutional under *Bates* and its progeny.
6. Search the Internet for a site that matches lawyer services with prospective clients. How does it work? What kinds of disclaimers does it have? Are lawyers who use it operating ethically within the rules of your jurisdiction?
7. Search the Internet for a law firm site that offers information about a drug that has been the subject of class action litigation. What kinds of disclaimers and other information are provided to ensure that the lawyers are acting within the bounds of the ethics rules?

8. A client submits a form on the lawyer's Web site indicating that she needs a divorce and is seeking a property settlement agreement and sole custody of her child. She sends financial information and asks if an extramarital affair that she had will affect the settlement. The statement at the bottom of the form indicates that by sending this information the prospective client is not forming an attorney-client relationship. The lawyer who receives the form already represents the other spouse. What are the issues presented by this scenario? How should they be resolved under the rules set forth in this chapter? See California State Bar Ethics Opinion 2005-168 for guidance.
9. Since the 1980s, California has seen repeated insurance fraud rings that involved staged car accidents and were run by groups of doctors, chiropractors, and lawyers filing and settling the claims. Many cases have involved allegations of "capping" and unauthorized practice of law. See *People v. Zanoletti*, 173 Cal. App. 4th 547 (2009). How was this ring organized? What crimes were committed? What ethics rules are implicated?

CASES FOR ANALYSIS

In the following landmark case, the U.S. Supreme Court struck down restrictions on lawyer advertising under the First Amendment. As you read, take note of the arguments for and against such restrictions and how the Court deals with each one.

Bates v. State Bar of Arizona
433 U.S. 350, 97 S. Ct. 2691 (1977)

Justice BLACKMUN delivered the opinion of the Court.

As part of its regulation of the Arizona Bar, the Supreme Court of that State has imposed and enforces a disciplinary rule that restricts advertising by attorneys. This case presents two issues: whether §§1 and 2 of the Sherman Act, 15 U.S.C. §§1 and 2, forbid such state regulation, and whether the operation of the rule violates the First Amendment, made applicable to the States through the Fourteenth.

Appellants John R. Bates and Van O'Steen are attorneys licensed to practice law in the State of Arizona. As such, they are members of the appellee, the State Bar of Arizona. After admission to the bar in 1972, appellants worked as attorneys with the Maricopa County Legal Aid Society.

In March 1974, appellants left the Society and opened a law office, which they call a "legal clinic," in Phoenix. Their aim was to provide legal services at modest fees to persons of moderate income who did not qualify for governmental legal aid. In order to achieve this end, they would accept only routine matters, such as uncontested divorces, uncontested adoptions, simple personal bankruptcies, and changes of name, for which costs could be kept down by extensive use of paralegals, automatic typewriting equipment, and standardized forms and office procedures. More complicated cases, such as contested divorces, would not be accepted. Because appellants set their prices so as to have a relatively low return on each case they handled, they depended on substantial volume.

After conducting their practice in this manner for two years, appellants concluded that their practice and clinical concept could not survive unless the availability of legal services at low cost was advertised and, in particular, fees were advertised. Consequently, in order to generate the necessary flow of business, that is, "to attract clients," appellants placed an advertisement (reproduced in the Appendix to this opinion, infra, [at 221]), in the Arizona Republic, a daily newspaper of general circulation in the Phoenix metropolitan area. As may be seen, the advertisement stated that appellants were offering "legal services at very reasonable fees," and listed their fees for certain services.

The issue presently before us is a narrow one. First, we need not address the peculiar problems associated with advertising claims relating to the *quality* of legal services. Such claims probably are not susceptible of precise measurement or verification and, under some circumstances, might well be deceptive or misleading to the public, or even false. Appellee does not suggest, nor do we perceive, that appellants advertisement contained claims, extravagant or otherwise, as to the quality of services. Accordingly, we leave that issue for another day. Second, we also need not resolve the problems associated with in-person solicitation of clients — at the hospital room or the accident site, or in any other situation that breeds undue influence — by attorneys or their agents or "runners." Activity of that kind might well pose dangers of overreaching and misrepresentation not encountered in newspaper announcement advertising. Hence, this issue also is not before us. Third, we note that appellee's criticism of advertising by attorneys does not apply with much force to some of the basic factual content of advertising: information as to the attorney's name, address, and telephone number, office hours, and the like. . . . We recognize, however, that an advertising diet limited to such spartan fare would provide scant nourishment.

The heart of the dispute before us today is whether lawyers also may constitutionally advertise the *prices* at which certain routine services will be performed. Numerous justifications are proffered for the restriction of such price advertising. We consider each in turn:

1. *The Adverse Effect on Professionalism.* Appellee places particular emphasis on the adverse effects that it feels price advertising will have on the legal profession. The key to professionalism, it is argued, is the sense of pride that involvement in the discipline generates. It is claimed that price advertising will bring about commercialization, which will undermine

the attorney's sense of dignity and self-worth. The hustle of the marketplace will adversely affect the profession's service orientation, and irreparably damage the delicate balance between the lawyer's need to earn and his obligation selflessly to serve. Advertising is also said to erode the client's trust in his attorney: Once the client perceives that the lawyer is motivated by profit, his confidence that the attorney is acting out of a commitment to the client's welfare is jeopardized. And advertising is said to tarnish the dignified public image of the profession.

We recognize, of course, and commend the spirit of public service with which the profession of law is practiced and to which it is dedicated. . . . But we find the postulated connection between advertising and the erosion of true professionalism to be severely strained. At its core, the argument presumes that attorneys must conceal from themselves and from their clients the real-life fact that lawyers earn their livelihood at the bar. We suspect that few attorneys engage in such self-deception. And rare is the client, moreover, even one of modest means, who enlists the aid of an attorney with the expectation that his services will be rendered free of charge. In fact, the American Bar Association advises that an attorney should reach "a clear agreement with his client as to the basis of the fee charges to be made," and that this is to be done "[a]s soon as feasible after a lawyer has been employed." [Citation omitted.] . . .

Moreover, the assertion that advertising will diminish the attorney's reputation in the community is open to question. Bankers and engineers advertise, and yet these professions are not regarded as undignified. In fact, it has been suggested that the failure of lawyers to advertise creates public disillusionment with the profession. The absence of advertising may be seen to reflect the profession's failure to reach out and serve the community: Studies reveal that many persons do not obtain counsel even when they perceive a need because of the feared price of services or because of an inability to locate a competent attorney. Indeed, cynicism with regard to the profession may be created by the fact that it long has publicly eschewed advertising, while condoning the actions of the attorney who structures his social or civic associations so as to provide contacts with potential clients.

It appears that the ban on advertising originated as a rule of etiquette and not as a rule of ethics. Early lawyers in Great Britain viewed the law as a form of public service, rather than as a means of earning a living, and they looked down on "trade" as unseemly. Eventually, the attitude toward advertising fostered by this view evolved into an aspect of the ethics of the profession. But habit and tradition are not in themselves an adequate answer to a constitutional challenge. In this day, we do not belittle the person who earns his living by the strength of his arm or the force of his mind. Since the belief that lawyers are somehow "above" trade has become an anachronism, the historical foundation for the advertising restraint has crumbled.

2. *The Inherently Misleading Nature of Attorney Advertising.* It is argued that advertising of legal services inevitably will be misleading (a) because such services are so individualized with regard to content and quality as to prevent informed comparison on the basis of an advertisement, (b) because the consumer of legal services is unable to determine in advance just what services he needs, and (c) because advertising by attorneys will highlight irrelevant factors and fail to show the relevant factor of skill.

We are not persuaded that restrained professional advertising by lawyers inevitably will be misleading. Although many services performed by attorneys are indeed unique, it is doubtful that any attorney would or could advertise fixed prices for services of that type. The only services that lend themselves to advertising are the routine ones: the uncontested divorce, the simple adoption, the uncontested personal bankruptcy, the change of name, and the like — the very services advertised by appellants. Although the precise service demanded in each task may vary slightly, and although legal services are not fungible, these facts do not make advertising misleading so long as the attorney does the necessary work at the advertised price. . . .

The second component of the argument — that advertising ignores the diagnostic role — fares little better. It is unlikely that many people go to an attorney merely to ascertain if they have a clean bill of legal health. Rather, attorneys are likely to be employed to perform specific tasks. Although the client may not know the detail involved in performing the task, he no doubt is able to identify the service he desires at the level of generality to which advertising lends itself.

The third component is not without merit: Advertising does not provide a complete foundation on which to select an attorney. But it seems peculiar to deny the consumer, on the ground that the information is incomplete, at least some of the relevant information needed to reach an informed decision. The alternative — the prohibition of advertising — serves only to restrict the information that flows to consumers. Moreover, the argument assumes that the public is not sophisticated enough to realize the limitations of advertising, and that the public is better kept in ignorance than trusted with correct but incomplete information. We suspect the argument rests on an underestimation of the public. . . .

3. *The Adverse Effect on the Administration of Justice.* Advertising is said to have the undesirable effect of stirring up litigation. The judicial machinery is designed to serve those who feel sufficiently aggrieved to bring forward their claims. Advertising, it is argued, serves to encourage the assertion of legal rights in the courts, thereby undesirably unsettling societal repose. There is even a suggestion of barratry.

But advertising by attorneys is not an unmitigated source of harm to the administration of justice. It may offer great benefits. Although advertising might increase the use of the judicial machinery, we cannot accept the notion that it is always better for a person to suffer a wrong silently than to redress it by legal action. As the bar acknowledges, "the middle 70% of our population is not being reached or served adequately by the legal profession." ABA, Revised Handbook on Prepaid Legal Services 2 (1972). Among the reasons for this underutilization is fear of the cost, and an inability to locate a suitable lawyer. Advertising can help to solve this acknowledged problem: Advertising is the traditional mechanism in a free-market economy for a supplier to inform a potential purchaser of the availability and terms of exchange. The disciplinary rule at issue likely has served to burden access to legal services, particularly for the not-quite-poor and the unknowledgeable. A rule allowing restrained advertising would be in accord with the bar's obligation to "facilitate the process of intelligent selection of lawyers, and to assist in making legal services fully available." ABA Code of Professional Responsibility EC 2-1 (1976).

4. *The Undesirable Economic Effects of Advertising*. It is claimed that advertising will increase the overhead costs of the profession, and that these costs then will be passed along to consumers in the form of increased fees. Moreover, it is claimed that the additional cost of practice will create a substantial entry barrier, deterring or preventing young attorneys from penetrating the market and entrenching the position of the bar's established members.

These two arguments seem dubious at best. . . . The ban on advertising serves to increase the difficulty of discovering the lowest cost seller of acceptable ability. As a result, to this extent attorneys are isolated from competition, . . . the incentive to price competitively is reduced. Although it is true that the effect of advertising on the price of services has not been demonstrated, there is revealing evidence with regard to products: where consumers have the benefit of price advertising, retail prices often are dramatically lower than they would be without advertising. It is entirely possible that advertising will serve to reduce, not advance, the cost of legal services to the consumer.

The entry-barrier argument is equally unpersuasive. In the absence of advertising, an attorney must rely on his contacts with the community to generate a flow of business. In view of the time necessary to develop such contacts, the ban in fact serves to perpetuate the market position of established attorneys. Consideration of entry-barrier problems would urge that advertising be allowed so as to aid the new competitor in penetrating the market.

5. *The Adverse Effect of Advertising on the Quality of Service*. It is argued that the attorney may advertise a given "package" of service at a set price, and will be inclined to provide, by indiscriminate use, the standard package regardless of whether it fits the client's needs.

Restraints on advertising, however, are an ineffective way of deterring shoddy work. An attorney who is inclined to cut quality will do so regardless of the rule on advertising. And the advertisement of a standardized fee does not necessarily mean that the services offered are undesirably standardized. Indeed, the assertion that an attorney who advertises a standard fee will cut quality is substantially undermined by the fixed-fee schedule of appellee's own pre-paid Legal Services Program. Even if advertising leads to the creation of "legal clinics" like that of appellants' — clinics that emphasize standardized procedures for routine problems — it is possible that such clinics will improve service by reducing the likelihood of error.

6. *The Difficulties of Enforcement.* Finally, it is argued that the wholesale restriction is justified by the problems of enforcement if any other course is taken. Because the public lacks sophistication in legal matters, it may be particularly susceptible to misleading or deceptive advertising by lawyers. After-the-fact action by the consumer lured by such advertising may not provide a realistic restraint because of the inability of the layman to assess whether the service he has received meets professional standards. Thus, the vigilance of a regulatory agency will be required. But because of the numerous purveyors of services, the overseeing of advertising will be burdensome.

It is at least somewhat incongruous for the opponents of advertising to extol the virtues and altruism of the legal profession at one point, and, at another, to assert that its members will seize the opportunity to mislead and distort. We suspect that, with advertising, most lawyers will behave as they always have: They will abide by their solemn oaths to uphold the integrity and honor of their profession and of the legal system. For every attorney who overreaches through advertising, there will be thousands of others who will be candid and honest and straightforward. And, of course, it will be in the latter's interest, as in other cases of misconduct at the bar, to assist in weeding out those few who abuse their trust.

In sum, we are not persuaded that any of the proffered justifications rise to the level of an acceptable reason for the suppression of all advertising by attorneys. . . .

In holding that advertising by attorneys may not be subjected to blanket suppression, and that the advertisement at issue is protected, we, of course, do not hold that advertising by attorneys may not be regulated in any way. We mention some of the clearly permissible limitations on advertising not foreclosed by our holding.

Advertising that is false, deceptive, or misleading of course is subject to restraint. [Citation omitted.] . . . For example, advertising claims as to the quality of services — a matter we do not address today — are not susceptible of measurement or verification; accordingly, such claims may be so likely to be misleading as to warrant restriction. Similar objections might justify restraints on in-person solicitation. We do not foreclose the possibility that some limited supplementation, by way of warning or disclaimer or the like, might be required of even an advertisement of the kind ruled upon today so as to assure that the consumer is not misled. In sum, we recognize that many of the problems in defining the boundary between deceptive and nondeceptive advertising remain to be resolved, and we expect that the bar will have a special role to play in assuring that advertising by attorneys flows both freely and cleanly.

As with other varieties of speech, it follows as well that there may be reasonable restrictions on the time, place, and manner of advertising. [Citation omitted.] Advertising concerning transactions that are themselves illegal obviously may be suppressed. And the special problems of advertising on the electronic broadcast media will warrant special consideration.

The constitutional issue in this case is only whether the State may prevent the publication in a newspaper of appellants' truthful advertisement concerning the availability and terms of routine legal services. We rule simply that the flow of such information may not be restrained, and we therefore hold the present application of the disciplinary rule against appellants to be violative of the First Amendment.

The judgment of the Supreme Court of Arizona is therefore affirmed in part and reversed in part. It is so ordered.

APPENDIX TO OPINION OF THE COURT

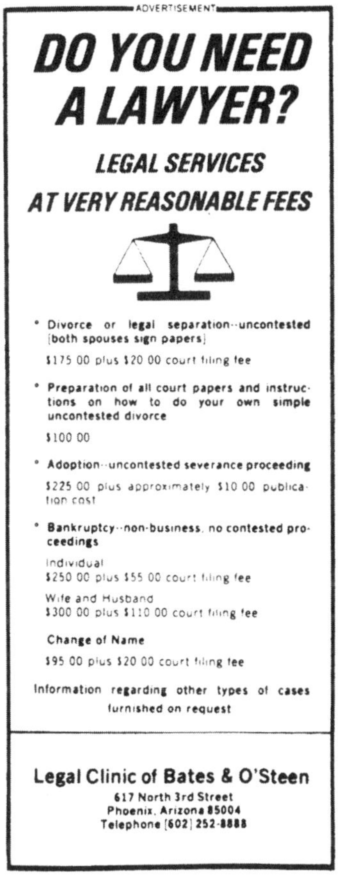

Questions about the Case

1. Examine the ad that is the subject of this litigation and evaluate whether it:
   a. is false or misleading;
   b. is undignified;
   c. is offensive to you personally;
   d. denigrates the image of the legal profession;
   e. would be helpful to someone seeking a lawyer.
2. Make a list of the bar's justifications for prohibiting advertising and summarize how the court refutes each one. Do you agree with the bar's arguments or the Court's rationale on each?
3. What kinds of restrictions may be placed on lawyer advertising after *Bates*?
4. What kind of guidance does this opinion give about other forms of advertising, such as e-mail and television?

The following is the most recent case decided by the Supreme Court on lawyer advertising. Note the difference in the approach to these ethical restrictions and to those in the previous cases in which the restrictions were struck down.

Florida Bar v. Went For It, Inc.
515 U.S. 618, 115 S. Ct. 2371 (1995)

In 1989, the Florida Bar completed a 2 year study of the effects of lawyer advertising on public opinion. After conducting hearings, commissioning surveys, and reviewing extensive public commentary, the Bar determined that several changes to its advertising rules were in order. In late 1990, the Florida Supreme Court adopted the Bar's proposed amendments with some modifications. *The Florida Bar: Petition to Amend the Rules Regulating the Florida Bar—Advertising Issues*, 571 So. 2d 451 (Fla. 1990). Two of these amendments are at issue in this case. Rule 4-7.4(b)(1) provides that "[a] lawyer shall not send, or knowingly permit to be sent, . . . a written communication to a prospective client for the purpose of obtaining professional employment if: (A) the written communication concerns an action for personal injury or wrongful death or otherwise relates to an accident or disaster involving the person to whom the communication is addressed or a relative of that person, unless the accident or disaster occurred more than 30 days prior to the mailing of the communication." Rule 4-7.8(a) states that "[a] lawyer shall not accept referrals from a lawyer referral service unless the service: (1) engages in no communication with the public and in no direct contact with prospective clients in a manner that would violate the Rules of Professional Conduct if the communication or contact were made by the lawyer." Together, these rules create a brief 30-day blackout period after an accident during which lawyers may not, directly or indirectly, single out accident victims or their relatives in order to solicit their business.

In March 1992, G. Stewart McHenry and his wholly owned lawyer referral service, Went For It, Inc., filed this action for declaratory and injunctive relief in the United States District Court for the Middle District of Florida challenging Rules 4.7-4(b)(1) and 4.7-8 as violative of the First and Fourteenth Amendments to the Constitution. McHenry alleged that he routinely sent targeted solicitations to accident victims or their survivors within 30 days after accidents and that he wished to continue doing so in the future. Went For It, Inc. represented that it wished to contact accident victims or their survivors within 30 days of accidents and to refer potential clients to participating Florida lawyers. In October 1992, McHenry was disbarred for reasons unrelated to this suit, *The Florida Bar v. McHenry*, 605 So. 2d 459 (Fla. 1992). Another Florida lawyer, John T. Blakely, was substituted in his stead. . . .

The District Court . . . entered summary judgment for the plaintiffs. . . . The Eleventh Circuit affirmed. . . . We granted certiorari. . . .

In *Bates v. State Bar of Arizona, supra*, the Court struck a ban on price advertising for what it deemed "routine" legal services: "the uncontested divorce, the simple adoption, the uncontested personal bankruptcy, the change of name, and the like." Id., at 372. Expressing confidence that legal advertising would only be practicable for such simple, standardized services, the Court rejected the State's proffered justifications for regulation.

Nearly two decades of cases have built upon the foundation laid by *Bates*. It is now well established that lawyer advertising is commercial speech and, as such, is accorded a measure of First Amendment protection. [Citations omitted.] . . .

Such First Amendment protection, of course, is not absolute. We have always been careful to distinguish commercial speech from speech at the First Amendment's core. " '[C]ommercial speech [enjoys] a limited measure of protection, commensurate with its subordinate position in the scale of First Amendment values,' and is subject to 'modes of regulation that might be impermissible in the realm of noncommercial expression.' " . . .

Mindful of these concerns, we engage in "intermediate" scrutiny of restrictions on commercial speech, analyzing them under the framework set forth in *Central Hudson Gas & Electric Corp. v. Public Service Comm'n of N.Y.*, 447 U.S. 557 (1980). Under *Central Hudson*, the government may freely regulate commercial speech that concerns unlawful activity or is misleading. Id., at 563-564. Commercial speech that falls into neither of those categories, like the advertising at issue here, may be regulated if the government satisfies a test consisting of three related prongs: first, the government must assert a substantial interest in support of its regulation;

second, the government must demonstrate that the restriction on commercial speech directly and materially advances that interest; and third, the regulation must be " 'narrowly drawn,' " id., at 564-565.

The Florida Bar asserts that it has a substantial interest in protecting the privacy and tranquility of personal injury victims and their loved ones against intrusive, unsolicited contact by lawyers. . . . This interest obviously factors into the Bar's paramount (and repeatedly professed) objective of curbing activities that "negatively affec[t] the administration of justice." . . . Because direct mail solicitations in the wake of accidents are perceived by the public as intrusive, the Bar argues, the reputation of the legal profession in the eyes of Floridians has suffered commensurately. . . . The regulation, then, is an effort to protect the flagging reputations of Florida lawyers by preventing them from engaging in conduct that, the Bar maintains, " 'is universally regarded as deplorable and beneath common decency because of its intrusion upon the special vulnerability and private grief of victims or their families.' " . . .

We have little trouble crediting the Bar's interest as substantial. On various occasions we have accepted the proposition that "States have a compelling interest in the practice of professions within their boundaries, and . . . as part of their power to protect the public health, safety, and other valid interests they have broad power to establish standards for licensing practitioners and regulating the practice of professions." [Citations omitted.] Our precedents also leave no room for doubt that "the protection of potential clients' privacy is a substantial state interest." [Citations omitted.] . . .

Under *Central Hudson*'s second prong, the State must demonstrate that the challenged regulation "advances the Government's interest 'in a direct and material way.' " [Citations omitted.] . . . The Florida Bar submitted a 106-page summary of its 2 year study of lawyer advertising and solicitation to the District Court. That summary contains data—both statistical and anecdotal—supporting the Bar's contentions that the Florida public views direct mail solicitations in the immediate wake of accidents as an intrusion on privacy that reflects poorly upon the profession. . . . A survey of Florida adults commissioned by the Bar indicated that Floridians "have negative feelings about those attorneys who use direct mail advertising." . . . Fifty-four percent of the general population surveyed said that contacting persons concerning accidents or similar events is a violation of privacy. . . . A random sampling of persons who received direct mail advertising from lawyers in 1987 revealed that 45% believed that direct mail solicitation is "designed to take advantage of gullible or unstable people"; 34% found such tactics "annoying or irritating"; 26% found it "an invasion of your privacy"; and 24% reported that it "made you angry." . . . Significantly, 27% of direct mail recipients reported that their regard for the legal profession and for the judicial process as a whole was "lower" as a result of receiving the direct mail. [Citations omitted.]

The anecdotal record mustered by the Bar is noteworthy for its breadth and detail. . . . In light of this showing — which respondents at no time refuted, save by the conclusory assertion that the rule lacked "any factual basis," [citation omitted] we conclude that the Bar has satisfied the second prong of the *Central Hudson* test. . . .

Passing to *Central Hudson's* third prong, we examine the relationship between the Florida Bar's interests and the means chosen to serve them. [Citation omitted.] With respect to this prong, the differences between commercial speech and noncommercial speech are manifest. . . . "What our decisions require" . . . "is a 'fit between the legislature's ends and the means chosen to accomplish those ends' . . . that represents not necessarily the single best disposition but one whose scope is 'in proportion to the interest served,' that employs not necessarily the least restrictive means but . . . a means narrowly tailored to achieve the desired objective." [Citations omitted.] . . . We find little deficiency in the ban's failure to distinguish among injured Floridians by the severity of their pain or the intensity of their grief. . . . Rather than drawing difficult lines on the basis that some injuries are "severe" and some situations appropriate (and others, presumably, inappropriate) for grief, anger, or emotion, the Florida Bar has crafted a ban applicable to all postaccident or disaster solicitations for a brief 30-day period. Unlike respondents, we do not see "numerous and obvious less burdensome alternatives" to Florida's short temporal ban. [Citation omitted.] The Bar's rule is reasonably well tailored to its stated objective of eliminating targeted mailings whose type and timing are a source of distress to Floridians, distress that has caused many of them to lose respect for the legal profession. . . .

We believe that the Florida Bar's 30-day restriction on targeted direct mail solicitation of accident victims and their relatives withstands scrutiny under the three part *Central Hudson* test that we have devised for this context. The Bar has substantial interest both in protecting injured Floridians from invasive conduct by lawyers and in preventing the erosion of confidence in the profession that such repeated invasions have engendered. The Bar's proffered study, unrebutted by respondents below, provides evidence indicating that the harms it targets are far from illusory. The palliative devised by the Bar to address these harms is narrow both in scope and in duration. The Constitution, in our view, requires nothing more.

The judgment of the Court of Appeals, accordingly, is *reversed*.

Questions about the Case

1. Why does the Court open its opinion with the recitation of the bar study of lawyer advertising and the resulting changes in the code? What does this tell you about where the Court is going to go?

2. Does the Court in any of the previous cases on lawyer advertising use the *Central Hudson* analysis that the Court uses here? How does this analysis affect the decision? What is the three-pronged test of *Central Hudson*?
3. Do you find the Florida bar study on lawyer advertising persuasive? Could the bar have adopted a different and less restrictive approach to addressing the problem of lawyers preying on accident and disaster victims?
4. What is the primary interest of the state in adopting this restriction? Do you think it is an adequate justification to restrict commercial speech?

The following is an example of the role a paralegal can play in lawyer advertising, but in this instance the paralegal is not familiar with the restrictions on lawyer advertising that have been set forth in this chapter.

In the Matter of Cartmel

676 N.E.2d 1047 (Ind. 1997)

The Disciplinary Commission alleges that the respondent, Thomas O. Cartmel, violated the *Rules of Professional Conduct for Attorneys at Law*. . . .

The Commission's *Verified Complaint* is in three counts. Pursuant to Count II, the parties agree that on May 1, 1994, the respondent's then-legal assistant placed an advertisement in the *Indianapolis Star*. The advertisement read as follows:

PAST CREDIT PROBLEMS

> Our law firm will have incorrect, obsolete or unverifiable negatives removed from your credit report! Our attitude is this: If you are wanting the cheapest fee in town, . . . call our "Competitors"! (We don't accept everyone we talk to. . . . We don't have to!) If you are wanting:
>
> - 29 years in practice
> - 100% results
> - Reestablished credit
> - The absolute best company to deal with your personal needs
>
> Call us to set up an appointment. . . . If we take your case, you'll be among the numerous individuals we've given a second chance to!

Upon learning of the advertisement (after it had been published approximately five times), the respondent promptly cancelled it, realizing that its contents were objectionable.

Pursuant to our *Rules of Professional Conduct*, lawyers are responsible for the professional actions of a legal assistant performing legal assistant services at the lawyer's direction and should take reasonable measures to insure that the legal assistant's conduct is consistent with the lawyer's obligations. . . . We find that the legal assistant's placement of the advertisement violated Prof. Cond. R. 7.1(b). . . .

The advertisement contained misleading, unfair and self-laudatory language prohibited by the rule.

We also find that the placement of the advertisement violated Prof. Cond. R. 7.1(d)(2) and (4). . . .

The advertisement contained a prediction of future success and a statement as to the quality of services offered. . . .

[The court also found that the lawyer violated obligations to hold client funds separately to complete work on a client matter in Count II.]

. . . [A] client hired the respondent to clear her negative credit history and paid him his quoted fee of $600. During the ensuing year, the client dealt exclusively with one of the respondent's legal assistants, Jeff. Between May 1993 and early 1995, the client periodically spoke with Jeff about the status of her pending credit repair. He informed her several times that he was working to clear her credit history. In early 1995, the client began dealing with the respondent's new legal assistant, Dan, who informed the client that Jeff had done little work on her file. Thereafter, the client contacted Dan once or twice a month regarding the status of her credit. . . . [T]he client wrote the respondent and requested that her case be completed. Dan responded to the letter, stating that his review of her credit report revealed that she has successfully applied for credit and that, therefore, the respondent's obligation to her was terminated. . . .

By failing to ensure that his nonlawyer staff's conduct was compatible with the respondent's professional obligation to diligently pursue client matters and keep the client accurately informed about the status of her affairs, the respondent violated Prof. Cond. R. 5.3(b). . . .

We accord some extenuating weight to the agreed mitigating factors. However, it is clear that the respondent abdicated many of the day-to-day functions of his legal practice to legal assistants without adequately supervising their work product or activities. Lawyers should give their legal assistants appropriate instruction and supervision concerning legal aspects of their employment, taking into account the fact that they do not have legal training. . . . The respondent's failure to take such steps resulted in the publishing of a clearly inappropriate legal advertisement. . . .

It is therefore ordered that the respondent be suspended from the practice of law for a period of sixty (60) days. . . .

Questions about the Case

1. What did the paralegal do in this case concerning the ad? What did the paralegal do concerning the client?
2. What should the lawyer have done to meet his ethical duties here?

3. What was objectionable about this ad? Do you think it would fail the requirements of the current ABA Model Rules?
4. Do you think it is common for a paralegal to have the responsibility for writing and placing an ad?
5. Do you think the discipline was appropriate?
6. What did the court say about paralegals' education? Do you agree?

The following case was decided just after *Bates*. In it, the Court addresses the question of restrictions on in-person solicitation of clients by attorneys. Pay close attention to the Court's reasons for the distinction between advertising and solicitation.

Ohralik v. Ohio State Bar Association

436 U.S. 447, 98 S. Ct. 1912 (1978)

Justice POWELL delivered the opinion of the Court.

In *Bates v. State Bar of Arizona*, 433 U.S. 350 (1977), this Court held that truthful advertising or "routine" legal services is protected by the First and Fourteenth Amendments against blanket prohibition by a State. The Court expressly reserved the question of the permissible scope of regulation of "in-person solicitation of clients — at the hospital room or the accident site, or in any other situation that breeds undue influence — by attorneys or their agents or 'runners.'" Id., at 366. Today we answer part of the question so reserved, and hold that the State — or the Bar acting with state authorization — constitutionally may discipline a lawyer for soliciting clients in person, for pecuniary gain, under circumstances likely to pose dangers that the State has a right to prevent.

Appellant, a member of the Ohio Bar, lives in Montville, Ohio. . . . On February 13, 1974, while picking up his mail at the Montville Post Office, appellant learned from the postmaster's brother about an automobile accident that had taken place on February 2 in which Carol McClintock, a young woman with whom appellant was casually acquainted, had been injured. Appellant made a telephone call to Ms. McClintock's parents, who informed him that their daughter was in the hospital. Appellant suggested that he might visit Carol in the hospital. Mrs. McClintock assented to the idea, but requested that appellant first stop by at her home.

During appellant's visit with the McClintocks, they explained that their daughter had been driving the family automobile on a local road when she was hit by an uninsured motorist. Both Carol and her passenger, Wanda Lou Holbert, were injured and hospitalized. In response to the McClintocks' expression of apprehension that they might be sued by Holbert, appellant explained that Ohio's guest statute would preclude such a suit. When appellant suggested to the McClintocks that they hire a lawyer, Mrs. McClintock retorted that such a decision would be up to Carol, who was 18 years old and would be the beneficiary of a successful claim.

Appellant proceeded to the hospital, where he found Carol lying in traction in her room. After a brief conversation about her condition, appellant told Carol he would represent her and asked her to sign an agreement. Carol said she would have to discuss the matter with her parents. She did not sign the agreement, but asked appellant to have her parents come to see her. Appellant also attempted to see Wanda Lou Holbert, but learned that she had just been released from the hospital. He then departed for another visit with the McClintocks.

On his way appellant detoured to the scene of the accident, where he took a set of photographs. He also picked up a tape recorder, which he concealed under his raincoat before arriving at the McClintocks' residence. Once there, he re-examined their automobile insurance policy, discussed with them the law applicable to passengers, and explained the consequences of the fact that the driver who struck Carol's car was an uninsured motorist. Appellant discovered that the McClintocks' insurance policy would provide benefits of up to $12,500 each for Carol and Wanda Lou under an uninsured-motorist clause. Mrs. McClintock acknowledged that both Carol and Wanda Lou could sue for their injuries, but recounted to appellant that "Wanda swore up and down she would not do it." The McClintocks also told appellant that Carol had phoned to say that appellant could "go ahead" with her representation. Two days later appellant returned to Carol's hospital room to have her sign a contract, which provided that he would receive one-third of her recovery.

In the meantime, appellant obtained Wanda Lou's name and address from the McClintocks after telling them he wanted to ask her some questions about the accident. He then visited Wanda Lou at her home, without having been invited. He again concealed his tape recorder and recorded most of the conversation with Wanda Lou. After a brief, unproductive inquiry about the facts of the accident, appellant told Wanda Lou that he was representing Carol and that he had a "little tip" for Wanda Lou: the McClintocks' insurance policy contained an uninsured-motorist clause which might provide her with a recovery of up to $12,500. The young woman, who was 18 years of age and not a high school graduate at the time, replied to appellant's query about whether she was going to file a claim by stating that she really did not understand what was going on. Appellant offered to represent her, also, for a contingent fee of one-third of any recovery, and Wanda Lou stated "O.K."

Wanda's mother attempted to repudiate her daughter's oral assent the following day, when appellant called on the telephone to speak to Wanda. Mrs. Holbert informed appellant that she and her daughter did not want to sue anyone or to have appellant represent them, and that if they decided to sue they would consult their own lawyer. Appellant insisted that Wanda had entered into a binding agreement. A month later Wanda confirmed in writing that she wanted neither to sue nor to be represented by appellant. She requested that appellant notify the insurance company that he was not her lawyer, as the company would not release a check to her until he did so. Carol also eventually discharged appellant. Although another lawyer represented her in concluding a settlement with the insurance company, she paid appellant one-third of her recovery in settlement of his lawsuit against her for breach of contract.

Both Carol McClintock and Wanda Lou Holbert filed complaints against appellant with the Grievance Committee of the Geauga County Bar Association. The County Bar Association referred the grievance to appellee, which filed a formal complaint with the Board of Commissioners on Grievances and Discipline of the Supreme Court of Ohio. After a hearing, the Board found that appellant had violated Disciplinary Rules (DR) 2-103 (A) and 2-104 (A) of the Ohio Code of Professional Responsibility. The Board rejected appellant's defense that his conduct was protected under the First and Fourteenth Amendments. The Supreme Court of Ohio adopted the findings of the Board, reiterated that appellant's conduct was not constitutionally protected, and increased the sanction of a public reprimand recommended by the Board to indefinite suspension.

The decision in *Bates* was handed down after the conclusion of proceedings in the Ohio Supreme Court. We noted probable jurisdiction in this case to consider the scope of protection of a form of commercial speech, and an aspect of the State's authority to regulate and discipline members of the bar, not considered in *Bates*. 434 U.S. 814 (1977). . . .

The solicitation of business by a lawyer through direct, in-person communication with the prospective client has long been viewed as inconsistent with the profession's ideal of the attorney-client relationship and as posing a significant potential for harm to the prospective client. It has been proscribed by the organized Bar for many years. . . .

Appellant contends that his solicitation of the two young women as clients is indistinguishable, for purposes of constitutional analysis, from the advertisement in *Bates*. Like that advertisement, his meetings with the prospective clients apprised them of their legal rights and of the availability of a lawyer to pursue their claims. . . .

In-person solicitation by a lawyer of remunerative employment is a business transaction in which speech is an essential but subordinate component. While this does not remove the speech from the protection of the First Amendment, as was held in *Bates* and *Virginia Pharmacy*, it lowers the level of appropriate judicial scrutiny.

As applied in this case, the Disciplinary Rules are said to have limited the communication of two kinds of information. First, appellant's solicitation imparted to Carol McClintock and Wanda Lou Holbert certain information about his availability and the terms of his proposed legal services. In this respect, in-person solicitation serves much the same function as the advertisement at issue in *Bates*. But there are significant differences as well. Unlike a public advertisement, which simply provides information and leaves the recipient free to act upon it or not, in-person solicitation may exert pressure and often demands an immediate response, without providing an opportunity for comparison or reflection. The aim and effect of in-person solicitation may be to provide a one-sided presentation and to encourage speedy and perhaps uninformed decision-making; there is no opportunity for intervention or countereducation by agencies of the Bar, supervisory authorities, or persons close to the solicited individual. The admonition that "the fitting remedy for evil counsels is good ones" is of little value when the circumstances provide no opportunity for any remedy at all. In-person solicitation is as likely as not to discourage persons needing counsel from engaging in a critical comparison of the "availability, nature, and prices" of legal services, cf. *Bates*, 433 U.S., at 364; it actually may disserve the individual and societal interest, identified in *Bates*, in facilitating "informed and reliable decisionmaking." Ibid.

It also is argued that in-person solicitation may provide the solicited individual with information about his or her legal rights and remedies. In this case, appellant gave Wanda Lou a "tip" about the prospect of recovery based on the uninsured-motorist clause in the McClintocks' insurance policy, and he explained that clause and Ohio's guest statute to Carol McClintock's parents. But neither of the Disciplinary Rules here at issue prohibited appellant from communicating information to these young women about their legal rights and the prospects of obtaining a monetary recovery, or from recommending that they obtain counsel. DR 2-104 (A) merely prohibited him from using the information as bait with which to obtain an agreement to represent them for a fee. The Rule does not prohibit a lawyer from giving unsolicited legal advice; it proscribes the acceptance of employment resulting from such advice. . . .

The substantive evils of solicitation have been stated over the years in sweeping terms: stirring up litigation, assertion of fraudulent claims, debasing the legal profession, and potential harm to the solicited client in the form of overreaching, overcharging, underrepresentation, and misrepresentation. . . .

The State's perception of the potential for harm in circumstances such as those presented in this case is well founded. The detrimental aspects of face-to-face selling even of ordinary consumer products have been recognized and addressed by the Federal Trade Commission, and it hardly need be said that the potential for overreaching is significantly greater when a lawyer, a professional trained in the art of persuasion, personally solicits an unsophisticated, injured, or distressed lay person. Such an individual may place his trust in a lawyer, regardless of the latter's qualifications or the individual's actual need for legal representation, simply in response to persuasion under circumstances conducive to uninformed acquiescence. Although it is argued that personal solicitation is valuable because it may apprise a victim of misfortune of his legal rights, the very plight of that person not only makes him more vulnerable to influence but also may make advice all the more intrusive. Thus, under these adverse conditions the overtures of an uninvited lawyer may distress the solicited individual simply because of their obtrusiveness and the invasion of the individual's privacy, even when no other harm materializes. Under such circumstances, it is not unreasonable for the State to presume that in-person solicitation by lawyers more often than not will be injurious to the person solicited.

The efficacy of the State's effort to prevent such harm to prospective clients would be substantially diminished if, having proved a solicitation in circumstances like those of this case, the State were required in addition to prove actual injury. Unlike the advertising in *Bates*, in-person solicitation is not visible or otherwise open to public scrutiny. Often there is no witness other than the lawyer and the lay person whom he has solicited, rendering it difficult or impossible to obtain reliable proof of what actually took place. This would be especially true if the lay person were so distressed at the time of the solicitation that he could not recall specific details at a later date. If appellant's view were sustained, in-person solicitation would be virtually immune to effective oversight and regulation by the State or by the legal profession, in contravention of the State's strong interest in regulating members of the Bar in an effective, objective, and self-enforcing manner. It therefore is not unreasonable, or violative of the Constitution, for a State to respond with what in effect is a prophylactic rule.

On the basis of the undisputed facts of record, we conclude that the Disciplinary Rules constitutionally could be applied to appellant. . . . Under our view of the State's interest in averting harm by prohibiting solicitation in circumstances where it is likely to occur, the absence of explicit proof or findings of harm or injury is immaterial. The facts in this case present a striking example of the potential for overreaching that is inherent in a lawyer's in-person solicitation of professional employment. They also demonstrate the need for prophylactic regulation in furtherance of the State's interest in protecting the lay public. We hold that the application of DR 2-103(A) and 2-104(A) to appellant does not offend the Constitution.

Accordingly, the judgment of the Supreme Court of Ohio is affirmed.

Questions about the Case

1. Why do you think the Court felt compelled to decide this case?
2. What exactly did attorney Ohralik do to break the ethics rules? Did you find his conduct objectionable?

3. What is the basis for the different rules on in-person solicitation and advertising? Do you find this reasoning convincing?
4. What general rule can you derive from this case? Do the ethics rules in your state comport with this decision? Do they carve out any exceptions?

In this case, a lawyer challenged a law passed in the District of Columbia to prevent abuses related to the solicitation of accident victims.

Bergman v. Dist. of Columbia

986 A.2d 1208 (D.C. 2010)

Scott N. Bergman, a member of the District of Columbia Bar, brought this action against the District of Columbia and the Members of the Council of the District of Columbia, challenging the validity of the White Collar Insurance Fraud Prosecution Enhancement Amendment Act of 2006 ("the Act"), D.C. Law 16-144 (Act 16-340), 53 D.C. Reg. 2828 (effective July 25, 2006), codified at D.C. Code §22-3225.14 (2009 Supp.). Bergman asserted that the Act unconstitutionally restricts his freedom of speech and constitutes impermissible "viewpoint discrimination." Bergman also alleged that in enacting this statute, the Council violated the District of Columbia Home Rule Act ("HRA"), D.C. Code §§1-201.01 *et seq.* (2007 Supp.) and the "separation of powers" doctrine by "usurp[ing] the judiciary's power to regulate the conduct of D.C. attorneys."

The trial judge rejected these contentions and granted the motions of the District and the Council Members for summary judgment. . . .

The Act makes it unlawful for "practitioner[s]" to solicit business from "a client, patient, or customer within 21 days of a motor vehicle accident with the intent to seek benefits under a contract of insurance or to assert a claim against an insured, a governmental entity, or an insurer on behalf of any person arising out of the accident." [Citation omitted.] A "practitioner" is defined as "a person, licensed to practice a profession or trade in the District, whose services are compensated either in whole or in part, directly or indirectly, by insurance proceeds." [Citation omitted.] The Act thus applies not only to lawyers, but to "all relevant practitioners (*e.g.*, attorneys, health care professionals, and others licensed to practice a profession or trade in the District)." [Citation omitted.]

The Act contains several exemptions from this twenty-one day prohibition. It permits immediate solicitation of legal business from accident victims through the mail, and the proscription against in-person solicitation does not apply if there is a preexisting relationship between the practitioner and the person solicited, or if the contact is initiated by the "potential client, patient, or customer." [Citation omitted.] The Act also provides that any release of liability executed within twenty-one days of an accident "without the assistance or guidance of legal counsel" is voidable within 14 days of the execution of such a release. [Citation omitted.] It further requires that any such release "shall contain a notice of the claimant's right to rescind conspicuously and separately stated on the release."

The Act was intended to address "an existing problem with practitioners (or their agents) soliciting accident victims." . . . The Act was passed unanimously by the Council. . . . While considering the proposed legislation, the Council received extensive information regarding the practices sought to be prohibited and the effects of these practices upon victims of accidents and their families. . . . Taken as a whole, the legislative record supports a finding that even if no overly aggressive tactics were employed — a dubious assumption — the sheer number and frequency of the telephone calls and in-person contacts to which many accident victims were subjected in the immediate aftermath of an accident could be extremely disturbing and unsettling. . . .

The judge concluded that the Act does not violate the HRA because it "does not directly affect the organization or jurisdiction of the District of Columbia courts, nor does it interfere with the Court of Appeals' authority over Bar admission or attorney discipline." She described the Act's temporary restriction on in-person solicitation as "a narrowly drawn anti-fraud criminal and consumer protection statute intended to protect against harassment of motor vehicle accident victims and the invasion of their privacy, in the immediate aftermath of an accident," and she held that the Act "does not unduly burden the Court of Appeals in the exercise of its core functions." This timely appeal followed. . . .

Bergman's claim that the Act denies him the freedom of speech guaranteed by the First Amendment raises a constitutional issue of considerable moment, for it implicates "the core values of a free society." [Citation omitted.] . . . This case, however, is not about the benign democratic ideal of opposing views competing for public acceptance. Rather, it is about practitioners aggressively seeking to secure potentially profitable business. As the Supreme Court stated in *Ohralik v. Ohio State Bar Ass'n*, 436 U.S. 447, 459, 98 S. Ct. 1912, 56 L. Ed. 2d 444 (1978), "[a] lawyer's procurement of remunerative employment is a subject only marginally affected with First Amendment concerns. It falls within the State's proper sphere of economic and professional regulation." . . .

Although Bergman depicts the issue in this case as involving a battle of ideas — fighting for the accident victim's rights against surrender of the victim's claim by settlement without the benefit of legal advice — the critical and dispositive fact is that we are dealing here with uninvited attempts to secure employment for remuneration — a classic example of a business transaction. *See Ohralik*, 436 U.S. at 459, 98 S. Ct. 1912. Nevertheless, since the First Amendment is marginally implicated, *id.*, the regulation (i.) must address a "substantial interest"; (ii.) must "directly and materially advance that interest"; and (iii.) must be "narrowly drawn." *Went For It*, 515 U.S. at 624, 115 S. Ct. 2371 (quoting *Central Hudson Gas & Elec. Corp. v. Public Serv. Comm'n of N.Y.*, 447 U.S. 557, 564-65, 100 S. Ct. 2343, 65 L. Ed. 2d 341 (1980)). In our view, the Act satisfies all of these criteria. . . .

We are satisfied that the Act addresses a substantial governmental interest, namely, the protection of consumers from unsolicited and often distressing one-on-one intrusions upon their privacy, effected for the purpose of securing their business in the immediate aftermath of an automobile accident, a time when many of them are likely to be in physical or emotional distress or in vulnerable circumstances.

In *Went For It*, which we consider dispositive of the First Amendment issue in this case, the Supreme Court held that a Florida Bar rule prohibiting "personal injury lawyers from sending targeted direct-mail solicitations to victims and their relatives for 30 days following an accident or disaster" did not violate the First Amendment (as applied to the State of Florida by the Fourteenth). [Citation omitted.] The Court so held even though solicitation by direct mail is far less intrusive than the kinds of solicitation by uninvited personal visits or unwanted telephone contacts at issue in the present appeal. The Court concluded in *Went For It* that Florida had "a substantial state interest in protecting the privacy and tranquility of personal injury victims and their loved ones against intrusive, unsolicited contact by lawyers." [Citation omitted.]

We have no doubt that the Act, even more than the Florida regulation at issue in *Went For It*, substantially advances the legitimate state interest in protecting the privacy and tranquility of accident victims and their families. In *Went For It*, the Supreme Court upheld Florida's thirty-day prohibition on direct-mail solicitation of accident victims — a far more extensive restriction than that imposed by the Act. The Court relied on various kinds of evidence, including anecdotal reports, newspaper articles, and complaints from potential clients who had received unwanted solicitations. [Citation omitted.] In this case, as in *Went For It*, the record includes articles in the media, as well as testimony from representatives of the Bar Association of the District of Columbia, the Trial Lawyers Association, and the United States Attorney's Office, regarding the mischief caused by uninvited in-person solicitation. It also contains reports from individuals describing the intrusion upon their privacy which resulted from the practices sought to be prohibited. Moreover, the Court stated in *Went For It* that "we have permitted litigants to justify [commercial] speech restrictions by reference to studies and anecdotes pertaining to different locales altogether[.]" [Citation omitted.]. Accordingly, Florida's experience and that of other jurisdictions may also be considered in assessing the constitutionality of the District's legislation. We are therefore satisfied that the legislative record regarding the effects of in-person solicitation conducted a short time after a motor vehicle accident readily satisfies the "substantial interest" prong of the *Central Hudson* standard.

Following its earlier decision in *Central Hudson*, the Supreme Court recognized in *Went For It* that a regulation limiting commercial speech must be "narrowly drawn" to focus upon the substantial interest sought to be served. [Citation omitted.] The Court explained, however, that the phrase "narrowly drawn" does not require the legislature to select the "least restrictive means" available. . . . We believe that the Act satisfies the requirement of proportionality.

The statute challenged here does not *prohibit* personal solicitation, or even *immediate* personal solicitation. On the contrary, like the more extensive regulation upheld in *Went For It*, it imposes only a brief time restriction regarding when and how such solicitation may be carried out. It applies only to the in-person solicitation of business from a limited and identifiable group of citizens, namely, accident victims and their families. The Act targets and proscribes the precise source of the kinds of problems described in the legislative record — intrusive personal solicitation by practitioners, or their agents or runners, in the immediate aftermath of an accident. The Act can therefore fairly be described as "narrowly drawn," and it deals only with the specific harm sought to be addressed. . . .

Bergman contends, however, that the Act is aimed at the content of an attorney's speech (*i.e.*, his or her encouragement of potential clients not to settle their cases immediately without legal counsel) and that it discriminates on the basis of the speaker's viewpoint. We do not agree. . . .

The Act was not aimed at the "content" of a practitioner's speech, but at the offensive behavior that often accompanies its delivery. Legislation aimed at intrusive and exploitive practices cannot reasonably be viewed as siding with insurance companies, or as seeking to inhibit the exercise by accident victims of their right to counsel. The Act does not "disapprove" any message. . . .

Bergman further invokes separation of powers principles in support of his claim. . . . Bergman contended in the trial court, and reiterates on appeal, that the Act directly conflicts with, and effectively reverses, a policy judgment made by this court promulgating Rule 7.1 of the Rules of Professional Conduct. Rule 7.1 does not impose a specific time restriction on in-person solicitation by lawyers of potential clients, but it does preclude a lawyer from engaging in in-person solicitation that involves the "use of undue influence," and it prohibits such solicitation if the "potential client is apparently in a physical or mental condition which would make it unlikely that the potential client could exercise reasonable, considered judgment as to the selection of a lawyer." *See* Rule 7.1(b)(2) & (3) of the Rules of Professional Conduct. The Rule also prohibits use of an intermediary to solicit clients in certain circumstances involving "the use of coercion, duress, compulsion, intimidation, threats, or vexatious or harassing conduct." Rule 7.1(b)(5).

The trial judge recognized that the intrusive conduct on the part of attorneys which is addressed by Rule 7.1 was also a primary focus of the Council in its consideration and eventual passage of the Act. Nevertheless, she concluded that this court's inherent and statutory authority to regulate the practice of law in the District of Columbia is not "exclusive" in the sense that it would preclude the Council from enacting legislation pursuant to its police powers that might also affect the conduct of lawyers in some respect. Even if there is an overlap between the authority of the Court of Appeals to regulate the practice of law by members of the District of Columbia Bar and the authority of the Council to enact legislation to protect against invasions of privacy and harassment of accident victims and consumers in the District of Columbia, those overlapping powers only constitute a violation of separation of powers if the intruding branch "impermissibly undermines the powers" of the other branch or "disrupts the proper balance between the coordinate branches by preventing the [allegedly intruded-on] branch from accomplishing its constitutionally assigned functions." . . . In our view, the Council's passage of the Act, in the exercise of its power to enact legislation of general applicability, does not impermissibly burden or unduly interfere with this court's authority to exercise its core functions relating to Bar admission and the discipline of attorneys. . . .

For the foregoing reasons, the judgment is affirmed.

Questions about the Case

1. What did the law specifically prohibit? Who was the law aimed at protecting? What kinds of people are subject to its restrictions?
2. What kind of conduct led to the law's being adopted? Was this similar to the conduct described in *Went For It?* In what ways was the prohibited conduct like that in *Ohralik?*
3. On what grounds did Bergman object to the law? What test did the court use to decide?
4. Thinking back to the separation of powers principles laid out in Chapter 1, what do you think about the court's holding that this law did not infringe on its inherent authority over the practice of law?

7

Fees and Client Funds

This chapter examines the ethics rules relating to financial matters in the representation of clients, including a range of issues from fees and billing to client trust funds. Chapter 7 covers:

- the various kinds of fee arrangements made with clients, including fixed fees, contingency fees, and hourly fees
- the growing use of alternative fee arrangements
- factors considered in determining if a fee is unethically excessive
- billing practices and abuses
- fee agreements with clients
- attorney's fees under fee-shifting statutes and the compensation in fee awards for paralegal time
- fee splitting and referral fees
- ethics rules prohibiting lawyers from entering into partnerships with paralegals
- duties in handling client funds and client trust accounts

A. Fee Arrangements with Clients

Several different methods are used to charge clients for legal services. The method selected depends mostly on the nature of the services being rendered. The most common methods of billing are fixed fees, contingency fees, and hourly fees.

1. Fixed Fees

Fixed fee
Fee for legal services based on a set amount

Fixed fees (also known as **flat fees**) usually are used for routine legal services, ones for which the attorney knows in advance the length of time needed to complete the work. In this instance, the client is paying for the attorney's expertise as much as for the time expended. Typical services for which a fixed or flat fee is charged are filing a default divorce, forming a corporation, and handling a simple wage-earner bankruptcy.

A variation on the fixed fee is a fee that is based on the percentage of the worth of the matter being handled, either by statute or by practice. In probate matters, for example, the fee usually is based on a percentage of the value of the estate, according to statute. It is common practice in some states for an attorney to charge a percentage of the value of a real estate transaction. Although calculated as a percentage, these kinds of fees are not to be confused with contingency fees used in civil litigation matters, in which the lawyer's fee is paid as a percentage of the recovery in the cases and the lawyer does not collect a fee if he or she loses the case.

2. Contingency Fees

Contingency fee
Fee depends on the successful outcome of a case and is based on a percentage of the recovery

Contingency fees are usually based on a percentage of the recovery in a case. Sometimes a fixed fee is made contingent on the outcome in a case, giving it the most important attribute of a contingency fee — risk. Contingency fee arrangements typically are utilized by plaintiffs' attorneys in civil litigation matters such as personal injury. The risk to lawyers who handle cases on contingency is that they will lose the case and receive no compensation for the time and effort expended.

Although the contingency fee is now well accepted in the United States (it is not utilized in England or Canada), it was resisted by American lawyers and courts until early in the twentieth century. Contingency fees were thought to stir up litigation and to encourage attorneys to engage in unethical conduct to win cases. Gradually, the bar came to recognize the value of the contingency fee as a means to provide access to legal services to those who have a legal claim but who cannot otherwise afford legal services.

Despite the widespread use of contingency fees in personal injury and medical malpractice cases, ethics rules still place some limitations on their use. Contingency fee arrangements are not permitted in any state in **criminal cases** because they are thought to encourage corruption and to discourage plea bargaining. ABA Model Rule 1.5(d)(2). Most jurisdictions also have rules prohibiting contingency fees in **marital dissolution, divorce, and separation** cases because they are thought to discourage reconciliation and settlement. In addition, a contingency arrangement in such cases may not be necessary to provide access to legal services as the court may award attorney's fees to the spouse without the means to pay them.

Other limitations on contingency fee arrangements have been codified into state ethics rules or statutes that restrict the **percentage of the fee**. For example, the Federal Torts Claims Act, 28 U.S.C.A. §2678, places the maximum fee at 25 percent. Some state statutes, including California Business and Professions Code §6146, limit the percentage that can be collected in medical malpractice cases. In recent years, more states have enacted statutes that restrict the amount that lawyers may collect in contingent matters.

The ABA Model Rules and most jurisdictions have special ethics rules relating to the communication with the client of the terms of a contingency fee arrangement. Under these rules, contingency fee agreements must be **in writing and signed** by the client even though other fee agreements are not required to be in writing. See, for example, ABA Model Rule 1.5(c). (Communication of fee agreements is discussed in the next section of this chapter.) Some states have rules requiring ads that mention contingency fees to disclose that clients are liable for costs even if they lose their case. These rules were upheld in *Zauderer v. Office of Disciplinary Counsel of the Supreme Court of Ohio*, 471 U.S. 626 (1985). Finally, contingency fees are subject to special judicial scrutiny for reasonableness and are disallowed if the percentage is considered exorbitant or the fee is well out of proportion to the work done or the risk taken by the attorney.

Contingency fees are a perpetual subject of debate within the legal profession. Some lawyers and commentators would like to prohibit them altogether or to limit the amount of fees if a case is uncontested or settles before trial. Despite the controversy, contingency fees have gained in popularity as clients explore alternative fee arrangements. For example, more corporate clients are requesting contingency arrangements in business litigation, even on the defense side. This kind of arrangement is believed to incentivize lawyers to settle or win in order to earn the fee, or a larger one if they prevail even more quickly and efficiently.

A typical contingency fee in a personal injury matter is one-third of the recovery, but many lawyers charge on a sliding scale that reflects both the amount of risk to the attorney and the time and effort expended by the attorney as the case moves forward. For example, a lawyer might charge 25 percent if the case settles before trial, one-third if it goes to trial, and 40 percent if it is appealed.

3. Hourly Fees

Hourly fees
Fees based on hourly rates and the amount of time actually expended

Hourly fees are the most common method of billing in matters other than civil litigation on the plaintiff side. Charging for time was not always so common in the legal profession but has become deeply ingrained in law practice during the past 30 years. The ABA estimates that 90 percent of lawyers charge by the hour. Most large firms bill mainly by means of hourly rates, with every lawyer and paralegal keeping close track of the time spent on client matters, usually in increments of either six or ten minutes.

Hourly rates are based on the expertise and other qualifications of the person billing, the nature and complexity of the services performed and, of course, the market. For example, a senior partner in a major law firm who handles complex securities transactions may have a billing rate of $600–900 an hour or even higher. The time of a mid-level associate with five years' experience, however, may be charged at $250–600 an hour, and that of a five-year paralegal may be charged at $85–150 an hour.

During the last 15 years, we have seen a call for the end of billing by the hour and many law firms have started to move away from hourly billing, developing alternative methods of charging for their services. Part of the impetus for this move is the increased efficiency of law firms through specialization and the use of technology. Firms that have developed highly valuable expertise and means of producing documents quickly and efficiently want to avoid being penalized for their efficiency and to be fairly compensated not just for their time but for the "value" of their services. Some commentators have decried the billable hour because they believe that it encourages lawyers to do work less efficiently and has led to widespread billing abuse and long hours that result in poor quality of life for lawyers. Studies also show that the quality of work starts to degrade after a person has worked about 40 hours in a week. Clients, especially corporate clients that use legal services extensively, want changes in the way that legal services are priced as they seek ways to lower legal fees and to structure fee agreements that allow them to plan and budget more accurately and to assess the value and productivity of the services provided.

4. Alternative Fee Arrangements

As noted above, there is a trend toward the use of alternative billing arrangements, based largely on dissatisfaction with the billable hour model. This trend has accelerated in the last few years as more big law firms have jumped on the bandwagon. Several notable large corporate clients, such as Pfizer Inc., Cisco Systems, American Express, and Pitney Bowes, have indicated publicly that they favor flat fees and discounts for volume work. Firms would rather avoid having clients question every entry on their bills and demand discounts after the work has been done. Clients find these flat fees and other alternatives attractive because they are predictable, which helps with budgeting and planning, and because it allows them to control costs. Some courts have even weighed in; for example, a Florida court cited a law firm's billable hour policies when it sanctioned a lawyer for overbilling a client by 300 hours on an alimony case. Some new firms are touting their refusal to bill by the hour as a way to interest prospective clients. One recent study of law firms showed that billing rates are negotiable, finding that nearly 80 percent of major law firms charge different rates to different clients.

Many firms are utilizing an array of alternative methods of structuring fee arrangements, such as charging a percentage of the value of a transaction, charging a premium for achieving results that are especially beneficial to a client, or charging a fixed fee that reflects the value of the services to the client without regard to the time expended. Capping of fees at a predetermined amount, discounted hourly rates or bills for major clients, blended hourly rates arrived at by averaging rates for all firm lawyers and/or paralegals, contingency fees in defense matters, and hybrids of several different billing methods are all commonly used now.

Another innovation is task-based billing, in which clients are charged an agreed-on predetermined flat rate for specific functions, such as taking a deposition or representing a client at a particular kind of hearing. Some small firms are charged for pieces of legal work as matters proceed, which is similar to the principle of "unbundling" legal work. Finally, some firms that represent start-up companies are doing legal work in exchange for a percentage interest in the new corporation's stock. This kind of fee arrangement raises a potential conflict of interest because the lawyers have a dual role as investors, but is acceptable if certain conditions are met, including informed written client consent. (See ABA Ethics Opinion 00-418 and Chapter 5 on business relationships with clients.) Most firms that engage clients using these alternative fee arrangements only do so for a relatively small proportion of their clients (estimated at 5 to 25 percent). Only a few firms have shifted entirely away from hourly billing.

5. Billing for Paralegal Time

Billing practices will continue to evolve as law practice responds to market forces and to changes in the nature of legal work and law practice. The effect on paralegals is significant: Paralegals must be proficient in technology and demonstrably efficient and productive in all their work. Paralegal managers and supervising lawyers must be certain that paralegals are well trained and are assigned to perform work that matches their degree of expertise.

It is well accepted that paralegal time may be charged directly to clients just as attorney time is. When utilized properly, paralegals are engaged in professional level work that would otherwise have to be done by a lawyer. And because paralegal time is billed to clients at lower rates than lawyer time is, the cost to the client is lower.

Guideline 8 of the ABA Model Guidelines for the Utilization of Paralegal Services (ABA Model Guidelines) provides that lawyers may charge for paralegal services. Most state guidelines also specifically endorse this customary practice, which was validated by the U.S. Supreme Court in *Missouri v. Jenkins*, 491 U.S. 274 (1989) (with regard to statutory fee awards). (Section C later in the chapter covers this topic further.)

Note that nonlawyer legal service providers who do not work under lawyer supervision are not covered by this principle. At least one state has adopted a statute that prohibits nonlawyers from receiving fees for providing legal services. Illinois's Attorney Act contains the following provision:

> No person shall receive any compensation directly or indirectly for any legal services other than a regularly licensed attorney. . . .
>
> Any person practicing, charging or receiving fees for legal services within this State, either directly or indirectly, without being licensed to practice as herein required, is guilty of contempt of court and shall be punished accordingly. . . .

Illinois Compiled Statutes, Ch. 705, S. 205/1, eff. 2000.

Similarly, the California statutes on paralegals prohibit them from collecting fees for legal services directly from clients (see Chapter 2).

6. Ethics Rules on Fees

The ethics rules covering fees prohibit fees that are **illegal, excessive, unconscionable, or unreasonable**. A fee is usually found illegal if it exceeds statutory limits such as those set by the Federal Torts Claims Act, mentioned earlier. It may also be illegal if the legal services were sought for an illegal purpose, such as a criminal enterprise. The ABA Model Rules set standards for judging whether a fee is unethical. The earlier Model Code indicated that fees were unethical if "clearly excessive" whereas the ABA Rules prohibit "unreasonable" fees; however, both contain the same eight factors used to determine whether a fee is unethically high:

(1) the time and labor required, the novelty and difficulty of the questions involved, and the skill requisite to perform the legal service properly;
(2) the likelihood, if apparent to the client, that the acceptance of the particular employment will preclude other employment by the lawyer;

(3) the fee customarily charged in the locality for similar legal services;
(4) the amount involved and the results obtained;
(5) the time limitations imposed by the client or by the circumstances;
(6) the nature and length of the professional relationship with the client;
(7) the experience, reputation, and ability of the lawyer or lawyers performing the services; and
(8) whether the fee is fixed or contingent.

ABA Model Rule 1.5(a)(1)-(8).

Some states, such as California, set the standard for excessive fees at the "unconscionable" level, which differs in degree from both the ABA Model Code and Model Rules standards.

The reasonableness of fees has been litigated extensively, mainly in cases involving statutory fee awards (discussed later in Section C). Guidelines can be drawn from litigation over fees and from disciplinary cases. Although all the factors on the ABA list are generally considered by courts and disciplinary bodies in determining if a fee is unethical, the amount of **time spent** tends to be the most important and serves as a starting point in the analysis of reasonableness of a fee. In fee dispute cases and disciplinary matters, the client's understanding of the fee agreement is also a critical factor.

Probably the most widespread ethical problem relating to fees is one that is not addressed directly by either ethics codes or case law, but nonetheless is one that paralegals are likely to face during the course of their careers. That problem encompasses several activities that constitute **billing fraud or abuse**, such as the practice of inflating the time spent on client matters that are billed by the hour.

As noted above in the discussion on the development of alternative fee agreements, the pressure to bill an ever-increasing number of hours in firms that use the hourly billing method is tremendous. The value of a fee-generating attorney or paralegal is measured largely by how much revenue that person produces for the firm. Expectations for billable hours have risen dramatically since the 1980s. In the early 1980s, 1,200 billable hours a year was common in a large firm; now, the expectation is 2,200 hours a year for associates in many large firms. This standard means that a person must do billable work at the rate of about 9 hours a day, every working day of the year. It is estimated that to bill 9 hours of time requires a work day of 11 to 12 hours.

Most of the pressure to bill falls on highly compensated associates trying to make partner. Several studies have shown that most associates believe that the pressure to bill time hurts their personal lives. Paralegals feel this pressure, too. Many large firms have strict guidelines on paralegal billable hours that require 1,500 to 1,800 hours a year. The pressure to bill creates an incentive to engage in improper billing practices, such as double billing, billing full rates for recycled work product, overbilling, overstaffing such as sending two or three lawyers to hearings unnecessarily, billing for overhead costs, padding hours, doing unnecessary work for clients, and spending excessive amounts of time on matters that do not warrant it.

An ongoing parade of cases involving lawyers who have engaged in **overbilling** and **billing of personal expenses** to clients is found in legal newspapers, periodicals, and blogs. Some cases have involved padding hourly bills in corporate, insurance defense, and criminal defense cases; others have involved charging clients for personal expenses, including clothes, travel, meals, gifts, personal phone calls, and even credit cards. In one recent case, a New York law firm charged more than $3 million in fees within six months and was sued in malpractice by its corporate client, who claimed that the lawyers spent much of their time surfing the Internet while they claimed to be doing legal work. In another, a former tax partner at a major firm was suspended for a year for charging $30,000 of private phone calls to a client. He was earning more than $1 million a year at the time. He testified at his disciplinary hearing that he was concerned what his partners would think if they knew how much time he was spending on personal matters. In a recent Pennsylvania case, a small law firm was ordered to pay a judgment of more than $5 million, including punitive damages, for intentionally overcharging homeowners who were being foreclosed on. In a New York case, a lawyer billed time amounting to more than 1,200 days in one year. In Ohio, a lawyer was recently suspended for overbilling after on three occasions submitting bills for working more than 24 hours a day.

Reported cases have involved billing for the time of nonprofessional staff such as secretaries; overcharging for legal research and driving time to an unnecessarily distant library; doubling the costs of process servers and independent contractors; billing clients more than 24 hours a day; charging fees and costs that were agreed in advance not be charged. In one case, a lawyer was told to get a car phone so that he could bill one client for travel time while he talked on the phone with another client, resulting in double billing. In another, a lawyer was found to have charged three hours of time for reading one sentence. In yet another, a firm charged eight hours of paralegal time for buying and serving lunch at a meeting. Some firms that have agreed to blended rates or another alternative form of billing have found that these forms are not profitable. A few have remedied this problem by multiplying the time spent by specific factors to ensure a profit, for example, charging 1.5 times the actual time spent.

These incidents have caused much speculation about the actual prevalence of abuses and the extent to which they can be attributed to fraud, overzealousness, or sloppy timekeeping or oversight practices. Corporate clients have taken proactive steps to prevent themselves from becoming the victims of unscrupulous billing practices and high legal bills. Many clients ask firms to make **proposals for services**, establish budgets for legal work beyond which a firm may not bill, and demand task-based billing, which provides detailed information on the cost of services from which clients can evaluate services and negotiate future billing arrangements. Many corporations also **restrict the costs** they will pay. For example, they reimburse for coach air fare and standard business accommodations only and will not pay surcharges on computerized legal research or for secretarial overtime or computer use.

An ABA formal ethics opinion that addresses billing abuses has been widely cited and followed throughout the country. The abuses highlighted in the opinion are **double billing** (that is, billing more than one client for the same hours — such as billing twice for travel time when making court appearances for more than one client in the same day), **surcharges** on services contracted with outside vendors, such as expert witnesses, and charges beyond reasonable costs for in-house services such as photocopying and computer searches. The opinion calls for **full disclosure** of the basis for charges when the fee agreement is made and subsequently when the client is billed. Further, the opinion emphasizes that the charges must also be reasonable, that is, no charges for unnecessary work or for hours not actually expended (ABA Formal Opinion 93-379). Also see California State Bar Ethics Opinion 147 (1996), which is in accord.

Lately several bar associations have publicly acknowledged the inherent hazards in judging a lawyer's or paralegal's performance solely by the amount of time billed and have pushed firms to consider the quality of life for employees of firms as well as the potential for billing abuse. One ethically dubious practice is "block billing," which consists of stating several tasks with one hourly amount, such as, "reviewed letter, talked with opposing counsel, conducted research for hearing: 6 hours." Insurance companies and many corporate clients do not allow this kind of billing and want tasks and time itemized. Another is using unrealistically large minimum units for billing. Most firms use 6- or 10-minute increments (i.e., a tenth or sixth of an hour); some use 15-minute blocks (i.e., 25 percent of an hour). This size increment is objectionable, in part, because many small routine tasks, such as a phone call or e-mail, do not take a quarter of an hour. Some courts have found the 15-minute increment unacceptable and have reduced fee awards when this was the billing unit used.

Paralegals have been implicated in some highly publicized cases. For example, paralegals in one case billed deposition summaries at the rate of four to five pages an hour, about a fourth of the average speed. In another case, a paralegal billed 43 hours in one day. In some cases, paralegal billing rates have been double the market rate or the time was billed for routine clerical work, such as copying and filing. A few well-publicized cases in the insurance industry have forced insurance defense firms to reconsider what work they assign to paralegals because their clients refuse to pay paralegal rates for work they consider to be clerical.

Billing abuses are not only dishonest and unethical but also detrimental in the long term to the law firm and its relationships with clients. Good firms do not send bills to clients without first examining them to see that the amount fairly reflects the services rendered. If the bill is excessive, the partner who is responsible for billing the client will adjust it down, "writing off" excessive time. The written-off time will be allocated back to the one who billed it and deducted from his or her total billable hours.

The firm that does not **review bills** or adjust them in this fashion is running the risk of having dissatisfied clients. Egregious abuses may result in disbarment, malpractice suits, or even criminal prosecution. Some commentators believe that excessive legal fees caused by dishonest billing practices have been a leading factor in the revolt by clients against the high cost of legal services and in the lowered esteem in which lawyers are held by the public.

Paralegals should not themselves engage in such unethical billing practices and have an obligation to report others who do to a supervising attorney. A paralegal should not continue to work in a firm that encourages such conduct. The NFPA Model Code calls attention to the proper paralegal role in billing under Canon 1.2. Ethical Considerations advise paralegals to prepare thorough, accurate, honest, and complete timekeeping and billing records and tell paralegals not to knowingly engage in fraudulent billing practices, such as inflating hours, misrepresenting the nature of the work that was done for a client, or submitting false expenses. (Also see NFPA Ethics Opinion 95-4, which discusses the ethics of billing for tasks that may be considered nonprofessional clerical work.)

Finally, paralegals should be aware of several related guidelines concerning the reasonableness of fees. One important rule is that clients cannot "agree" in advance to fees and costs that are unreasonable. Courts have found that such fee agreements are not a defense to an ethics complaint or lawsuit concerning unreasonable fees. It has also been found improper to charge clients for time spent preparing a motion to withdraw from representation and defending against a client's claim in a fee dispute or ethics complaint. Lawyers also cannot bill time spent by paralegals as though they had done the work.

B. Terms and Communication of Fee Arrangements with Clients

As soon as possible after a lawyer and client agree to representation, the lawyer should fully explain the terms of the fee agreement to the client. It is good practice — required in some cases — to put the agreement in writing.

ABA Model Rule 1.5 states that lawyers should communicate to the client, "preferably in writing," within a reasonable time after commencing representation, "the scope of representation and the basis or rate of the fee and expenses." Changes in rates and fees must also be communicated (Model Rule 1.5(b)). Contingency fee agreements must be in writing and include the method and percentage(s) by which the fee is to be calculated and provision for payment of costs (i.e., whether they are deducted before or after calculation of the fee). A written statement showing the calculations is required at the conclusion of the matter (Model Rule 1.5(c)). Some states have more stringent requirements about what kinds of fee agreements must be in writing, and many states now require all fee agreements with new clients to be in writing.

Written fee agreements are favored because they promote clear communication between the attorney and client and prevent later disputes over the fee. In addition, they protect both parties in the event of a dispute — especially the lawyers, who will have any misunderstanding about the fee arrangements construed against them. Some state bars have standard engagement forms that attorneys are encouraged to use.

As indicated in Chapter 3 on unauthorized practice of law, paralegals should be aware that they are prohibited from establishing the attorney-client relationship and setting the fee to be charged in a matter. Only the lawyer can agree to represent a client and in doing so set the appropriate fee arrangement and meet the ethical obligation to explain it fully to the client. The role of the paralegal as a liaison with the client may include answering questions about fees and costs but should not include entering into the contractual agreement with the client on the lawyer's behalf. The paralegal can, of course, relay information back and forth between the lawyer and the client concerning the representation and the fee agreement.

The ABA Model Guidelines state that **establishing a fee** is one of the few specified functions that a lawyer cannot delegate to a paralegal. Guideline 3(b) advises that a lawyer may not delegate "responsibility for establishing the amount of a fee to be charged for a legal service." The comment emphasizes the importance of attorney-client communication and cites state guidelines that also prohibit paralegals from "setting fees" or accepting cases. (See also ABA Informal Opinion 875 (1965), which provides that lay employees may not make fee arrangements or agree to undertake representation on the lawyer's behalf.) The National Association of Legal Assistants (NALA) Code of Ethics and Professional Responsibility provides in Canon 3(b) that paralegals "must not establish an attorney-client relationship [or] set fees."

Written fee agreements or engagement letters should cover:

- the scope of the firm's services
- the responsibilities of the client and the firm
- details regarding the method of determining the fee (i.e., hourly, fixed, contingency, or some other method)

- if hourly billing is used, the rates or ranges of rates of all potential billers, including paralegals, should be specified
- the costs the client is obligated to pay and when they are paid (i.e., out of the client's recovery after the attorney's fee is calculated in the case of contingency arrangements or at specified regular billings)
- termination rights and responsibilities of both parties
- method and time of fee payment
- procedure for and frequency of billings, if applicable

The agreement should contain a provision indicating that the agreement is privileged. It is also wise to include language indicating that the firm is not guaranteeing a particular result. If the client does not speak or read English proficiently, the agreement should be in a language that the client does understand. The signature clause should include an acknowledgment that the client has read and understood the terms of the agreement. The client should also be given sufficient time to read and reflect on the agreement before signing it. Fee agreements may also contain provisions about how disputes between the lawyer and client are handled (e.g., by mediation or arbitration).

Some lawyers and bar associations advocate the **"unbundling" of legal services** as a means to increase access to legal services for clients who cannot afford to have a lawyer handle all aspects of their legal matters. Some lawyers are handling divorce, small business matters, and some litigation this way. If this kind of representation is undertaken, the limits on the lawyer's role in representing the client must be very carefully and clearly laid out so that the understanding about what the lawyer will and will not do is very specifically understood. Otherwise, the client may later seek damages from the lawyer if the legal matter is not resolved to his or her satisfaction. The ABA and other bar associations have been progressive in promoting unbundling as a way to increase access to and decrease the cost of legal services. ABA Model Rule 1.2(c) allows lawyers to limit their representation as long as it is reasonable under the circumstances and the client gives informed consent.

Retainer
Nonrefundable fee paid at the commencement of agreed-on work to assure the availability of the lawyer to handle specified matters

Advance fee
Fee paid for legal services in advance, which is refundable if not earned

For some kinds of legal work, attorneys may require a ***retainer*** or ***advance fee***, which is paid at the commencement of the agreed-upon work. Although frequently called retainers, advance fees are usually refundable, in that the attorney earns the fee as the work progresses and refunds to the client whatever portion is unearned when, for whatever reason, the services stop. Retainer fees are in whole or in part nonrefundable, in essence acting as a minimum fee regardless of the amount of work done and as a guarantee that the attorney will be available to handle whatever comes up during the period covered by the retainer. A nonrefundable retainer is ethically acceptable so long as the client fully understands the arrangement and the fee is not excessive, considering the factors noted above and set forth in Model Rule 1.5. Advances must be deposited into the client trust account until earned while nonrefundable retainers may be deposited directly into a firm operating account. (Client trust accounts are discussed later in Section E.)

Hourly billing presents the potential for misunderstandings with clients because, without an estimate of the number of hours a project will take, the client will have no idea what the ultimate bill for services might be. It is good practice for the attorney to provide the client with an estimate if at all possible and to update the estimate if it changes as the matter proceeds. Care must be taken in making such projections, however. In one recent case, a small nonprofit sued a large law firm after being charged over $1 million for something that initially was projected to be billed at about $50,000.

Payment of **costs** requires special clarity in fee agreements as clients may not expect to pay or may resent paying many additional charges when they are already paying what they believe are high fees. The kind of costs billed directly to clients varies somewhat from firm to firm. As a rule, all lawyers expect clients to pay direct expenses that the firm incurs on behalf of the client by paying an entity outside the firm. These costs include filing fees with courts and government bodies, transcripts of depositions and trials, expert reports and testimony, out-of-area travel expenses, outside printing, and messengers. Most firms also charge for copying done within the firm and long-distance telephone calls. Some firms also charge clients for costs that might ordinarily be thought of as part of overhead, such as secretarial overtime, computer use, and even air conditioning, in the event the firm must work extra evening and weekend hours for a particular client. Costs should be itemized on a client's bill. (Also see Chapter 5 for conflicts of interest rules relating to advancing costs and other expenses for clients.)

Although not in widespread use, more than 30 jurisdictions permit lawyers to accept payment of legal fees by **credit card**. This practice was first approved by the ABA in its Formal Opinion 338 (1974) with several limitations, including one that the attorney not increase fees to cover expenses of participating in such a plan. Some states also permit attorneys to help clients work out financing for the payment of fees with a bank. This practice was also approved by ABA Formal Opinion 338 (1974). Some attorneys will accept property in payment of fees. When doing so, attorneys must pay special attention to the value of the property and reasonableness of the fee. **Discounting of fees** is also ethical so long as ads or coupons with discounts are honored for the relevant time frame. (See Connecticut Ethics Opinion 94-23, South Carolina Ethics Opinion 96-27, and Texas Ethics Opinion 452 (1998).)

C. Court-Awarded Attorney's Fees

As a general rule, litigants in the United States must pay their own attorney's fees. This practice is different from that in England, Canada, and most European countries, which have widespread fee shifting. In England and Canada, for example, all or part of the attorney's fees in litigation are awarded to the prevailing party.

Efforts have been made to reform the American system with court decisions, contracts, and legislation. Courts have awarded attorney's fees in cases in which a common fund that benefits persons other than the parties was created as a result of the litigation; in which the litigation resulted in a common benefit to the public or some portion of the public even though no fund was created; similarly, in which the plaintiff acted as a "private attorney general" vindicating a legal right that also benefits others and for which the plaintiff's actual damages are relatively small; and, finally, in actions for malicious prosecution, for abuse of civil process, or those taken in bad faith. This last category of fee shifting is also supported by legislation in some states. Contract provisions for attorney's fees are relatively common and are generally enforced by the courts.

Fee-shifting statute
A law that allows a court to award attorneys' fees to one of the parties

Fee-shifting statutes have proliferated, and hundreds of state and federal statutes provide for the award of attorney's fees in specified kinds of litigation. These fee-shifting statutes generally apply to the kinds of litigation that the legislature wants to encourage as a matter of public policy (for example, protecting civil rights) and award fees only to prevailing plaintiffs, not defendants. Like contingency fees, statutory fees enable plaintiffs who might not otherwise be able to afford an attorney to bring legal action to vindicate their rights. And like contingency fees, the attorney is accepting the risk of not being compensated if he or she does not prevail.

Conflicts of interest may arise in cases involving statutory fees when the interests of the client clash with the interest of the attorney in maximizing the fee award. For example, an offer to settle may satisfy the client but not include sufficient fees for the lawyer or may satisfy the lawyer as to the fee award but not the client, who wants a larger recovery. The tort reform movement cites this kind of conflict as a reason for legislating against class actions and other kinds of lawsuits, especially noting large attorney's fee awards in suits in which the members of the class get only a small sum of money or no monetary recovery at all. Lawyers must always be aware of the potential for a conflict in cases with court-awarded fees and keep the client's best interests in mind when advising whether to accept a settlement offer.

One of the most important court decisions concerning paralegals is in the area of statutory fees. The landmark decision of *Missouri v. Jenkins*, 491 U.S. 274 (1989), upheld an award of attorney fees that included compensation for paralegal time under the federal civil rights statute. The lower court had awarded fees that included compensation for paralegal time at hourly market rates. The state of Missouri contended, first, that the statute provided only for attorney's fees, not paralegal's, and second, that if paralegal time were to be compensable, it should be compensated at cost, not at a market rate that included a profit to the law firm.

In upholding the award, the Court construed the attorney's fee statute broadly, finding that it did include paralegal fees, and followed the long-standing measure of market rates as the appropriate one for setting paralegal fees. In an important recent case, *Richlin*, the U.S. Supreme Court applied *Missouri v. Jenkins* to a case brought under the Equal Access to Justice Act. In that case, the appeals court for the Federal Circuit had disallowed compensation for paralegal time at market rates by pointing to the fact that the federal statute was not the same as the one in *Missouri v. Jenkins*. Both cases are included later in this chapter, as are several other cases in which paralegal fees were at issue.

Missouri v. Jenkins was a critical case for paralegals; a court decision that had gone the other way would have acted as a disincentive to the utilization of paralegal services by firms that work on cases for which attorney's fees may be awarded and may have called into question the common practice of billing for paralegal time at market rates. Thousands of cases awarding paralegal fees as part of attorney's fee awards have been decided in state and federal trial courts since *Missouri v. Jenkins*. It was also the first U.S. Supreme Court decision in which the role of paralegals was discussed at any length and endorsed as a praiseworthy innovation and an effective means of containing the costs of legal services. Finally, this case gave guidance in what had been in dispute throughout the country; several state and some federal appeals courts had interpreted attorney's fee statutes contrary to the holding in *Missouri v. Jenkins*, some finding the statutes not to include paralegal fees at all, some applying the cost, not market measure, to calculate the award.

As a result of decisions prior to *Missouri v. Jenkins*, in which courts had denied the award of paralegal fees at market rates, several states have amended statutes and/or court rules to clarify that attorney's fee awards include paralegal fees at market rates (e.g., Alaska, Arizona, California, Florida, New Jersey, Illinois, Indiana, New York, Oklahoma, and Ohio). Most states have followed the reasoning of *Missouri v. Jenkins*. In recent years, state courts have ruled that attorney fee awards in administrative agencies may include compensation for paralegal time at market rates. See, for example, *Schroff, Inc. v. Taylor-Peterson*, 732 A.2d 719 (R.I. 1999), and *Vitac Corp. v. Workers' Compensation Appeals Board*, 854 A.2d 481 (Pa. 2004). Many state supreme courts have followed the lead of the U.S. Supreme Court in *Missouri v. Jenkins* in interpreting their own fee award statutes. See, for example, *Blair v. Ing.*, 31 P.3d 184 (Haw. 2001), and *Riemers v. State*, 2008 N.D., 188, 756 N.W.2d 344 (2008).

A few courts have also tied the award of fees to prequalifying the paralegal, such as probate courts that require paralegals to be registered with the court by providing background and certification by the supervising lawyers that the paralegal has appropriate training, education, and work experience. (See, e.g., Franklin County Probate Court, Franklin County, Ohio, Local Rule 75.8.) In a recent California case, a court determined a fee petition that included compensation for paralegal time would not cover the time of employees who did not meet the statutory minimum qualifications for paralegals. This is an important case, as you will remember from Chapter 2 that tying paralegal regulation to fee awards is one of the strategies that advocates for paralegal regulation have used. See *Sanford v. GMRI* at the end of this chapter.

Most states that disallowed compensation for paralegal time in fee awards did not object conceptually to the notion that paralegal time is compensable, but asserted that the legislature, not the courts, should make the determination of whether attorney's fees should also cover paralegal work. Further, some states have found that not all fee award statutes were intended to compensate lawyers for the time of paralegals. For example, many states have statutes that allow one or two lawyers to be appointed to handle criminal cases, particularly capital cases, at the state's expense. Some courts have held that these statutes do not authorize additional expense for paralegal time. (See, for example, *Moncier v. Ferrell*, 990 S.W.2d 710 (Tenn. 1998).)

Federal courts have interpreted most federal statutes to allow paralegal fees under *Missouri v. Jenkins*. And several **federal attorney fee statutes** have been amended to provide for the award of paralegal fees, including the Federal Bankruptcy Law (11 U.S.C. §330); the Employee Retirement Income Security Act of 1974 (29 U.S.C. §100); the Sherman Antitrust Act and Clayton Act (15 U.S.C. §1); and the Surface Mining Control and Reclamation Act of 1977 (30 U.S.C. §1270). After the decision in *Richlin*, it is doubtful that any federal courts would refuse to apply the reasoning of *Missouri v. Jenkins* to fee awards under other federal statutes.

Some federal bankruptcy courts have disallowed fees for paralegal time to bankruptcy trustees, who are entitled to compensation under the Bankruptcy Act, which compensation is capped. The most definitive case on the subject at the time of this writing is *In re Jenkins*, 130 F.3d 1335 (9th Cir. 1997), which affirmed a Bankruptcy Appeals Panel decision that bankruptcy courts may award compensation for trustee duties performed by paralegals employed by the trustee, provided that the total compensation does not exceed the statutory cap.

An important issue in statutory fee cases involves the kind of information that must be supplied to the court to justify the award of compensation for paralegal work in **fee petitions.** Some trial courts have denied paralegals' fees on the grounds that the work done by paralegals was clerical in nature and not the kind of work intended to be covered by an award of attorney's fees. Others have objected when the fee request did not contain adequate information about the qualifications of the paralegals or the nature of their work. Some have demanded more information about the customary practice of billing clients separately for paralegal time and the market rates charged for their services.

Some courts have reduced the amounts requested for paralegal fees because the petitions were not sufficiently documented, the time was duplicative or excessive, or the work was of a clerical nature. For example, one federal court considering a fee petition under the Copyright Act court reduced by 20 percent the number of hours of paralegal time spent indexing files and handling discovery, calling it, without explanation, "excessive." See *Yankee Candle Co., Inc. v. Bridgewater Candle Co.*, 140 F. Supp. 2d 111 (U.S.D.C., D. Mass. 2001).

Some statutes or court rules set forth requirements that paralegals must meet to qualify for compensation in attorney fee awards. For example, local court rules for bankruptcy courts in the Northern District of California require that the services would have to have been performed by a lawyer if not done by the paralegal and that the paralegal is "specially trained" or is a law student and "not primarily a secretary or clerical worker."

In general, documentation supplied to a court when seeking fees should include:

- **credentials and experience** of the paralegal, including college education and degrees granted; formal paralegal education; years of legal and other related work experience and nature of that experience; and certification or compliance with statutory, court rule, or bar guidelines for paralegals
- **detailed descriptions** of the work performed, including the number of hours spent and the exact nature of the work, which must be professional in nature and not clerical (i.e., would have been done by a lawyer if it were not for the paralegal)
- information on **firm and market practices and rates**, including paralegal compensation, overhead allocated to paralegals, hourly rates, and comparison data on practices and rates in the legal community

Additionally, it is preferable for a firm to have a **range of rates** for paralegals, just as they do for lawyers, depending on their experience and the level of work they are performing. As with lawyer work, not all paralegal work requires the same level of sophistication and expertise.

If these key matters are not covered in fee petitions, courts may deny the award or reduce the amount of time or fee. For example, in one case the court was not persuaded of the credentials, rates, or contribution of the paralegals and denied the compensation, giving the following explanation:

> We cannot overlook the fees granted for two legal assistants. It is not immediately apparent why a legal assistant bills $165 per hour while an associate attorney bills $150 per hour. The record before us does not divulge that these persons are lawyers or even paraprofessionals, and this is a claim for attorneys' fees. From our review of the record, legal assistant could mean secretary. If these persons were paralegals or law clerks to the firm or [the client], then they had the burden to state this on the record.

> The fees for secretarial staff are typically considered a cost of doing business and are implicit in the hourly rate charged by an attorney. Moreover, both the $165 and the $115 per hour fees are unreasonable for secretaries (or paralegals) in this locality. Additionally, there is no indication what these individuals contributed.

B-Right Trucking v. Interstate Plaza Cons., 154 Ohio App. 3d 545, 563, 798 N.E.2d 29 (2003).

Another caution concerns alternative fee agreements and statutory fee awards. A court may not allow a firm to use blended rates in its request for fees. See, for example, *Dept. of Trans. v. Robbins and Robbins, Inc.*, 700 So. 2d, 782 (Fla. App. 5 Dist. 1997). In reversing a lower court decision on a fee award, the court said:

> [T]he trial court improperly included the paralegal hours as part of the attorneys' hours to get a "blended" effective hourly rate. The trial court counted the paralegal hours and attorneys' hours to obtain the lodestar. Instead of separately awarding paralegal time, ordinarily billed at $75 per hour, the trial court mixed paralegal and attorney time, then awarded the firm more than $300 per hour for paralegal time. . . .
>
> While the trial court is required . . . to consider time expended by legal assistants when awarding attorney's fees in eminent domain proceedings, [citation omitted] this court has never held that paralegal time can be "blended" with attorney time to set a reasonable attorney rate. Further, it is not logical to use a paralegal to help on a client's case because it is cheaper for the client, then seek to recoup the paralegal time at an attorney rate. . . . Coupling that with the admission that the paralegal would not reap the benefit of this windfall shows that this "blending" is simply another method to increase the attorneys' fees in the case. Upon remand, the trial court will separate out the paralegal time . . . and multiply the number of paralegal hours by the hourly rate of $75.

Finally, a few courts have **reduced fee awards** for attorney time when the work billed at the attorney's rate could have been done by a paralegal. This line of cases demonstrates the growing appreciation within the judiciary of the contribution paralegals can make to improving the cost-effectiveness of and access to legal services. The *Music Merchants* case at the end of this chapter illustrates this trend. Also see *Interfaith Community Org. v. Honeywell Int'l, Inc.*, 336 F. Supp. 2d 270 (U.S.D.C., D.N.J. 2004), where the court said that a paralegal should not be compensated for clerical work at paralegal rates and likewise that a lawyer should not be compensated for "merely clerical tasks such a moving furniture or stacking boxes." This reasoning is being applied generally by the courts. However, in one recent decision, a court refused to reduce the fee award on this basis in a case brought under the Age Discrimination in Employment Act, reasoning that the lawyer was a sole practitioner and did not employ anyone to whom he could delegate paralegal work. See

Jordan v. CCH, Inc., 230 F. Supp. 2d 603 (U.S.D.C., E.D. Pa. 2002); *Metro Data Systems, Inc. v. Durango Systems, Inc.*, 597 F. Supp. 244 (1984); *Lipsett v. Blanco*, 975 F.2d 934 (2d Cir. 1992); and *Rodriguez-Hernandez v. Miranda-Vales*, 132 F.3d 848 (1st Cir. 1998). Also see *Jordan v. CCH, Inc.*, No. CIV.A. 01-053 (U.S.D.C., E.D. Pa. 2002), for an alternative view.

The American Bar Association has endorsed fee awards and billing for paralegal time. In 1993 the American Bar Association House of Delegates adopted a resolution "support[ing] the award of legal assistant/ paralegal fees to law firms or attorneys who represent prevailing parties in a lawsuit where statutes or current case law allow for the recovery of attorney fees." This resolution supports Guideline 8 of the ABA Model Guidelines for the Utilization of Paralegal Services, which endorses both recovery for paralegal time in statutory attorney's fee matters and the billing of clients for paralegal time.

REVIEW QUESTIONS

1. What are fixed fees? For what kinds of work are they typically used?
2. What are contingency fees? When are they usually used?
3. What are the traditional objections to contingency fees? What are the most important modern limitations on contingency fees? What is a sliding-scale contingency fee?
4. What are hourly fees? In what kinds of legal matters are they typically used?
5. What is the authority for paralegal time to be billed separately to clients? What is the advantage to the client?
6. Why are some firms starting to use alternatives to hourly billing? What kinds of new fee arrangements are being developed as firms move away from hourly billing? How do these affect paralegals?
7. What factors may be taken into account in determining if a fee is unreasonable or excessive?
8. What is an illegal fee? Give an example.
9. What kinds of billing abuses sometimes take place in law firms, and why? What are some of the risks of these abuses?
10. What is double billing? Is it ethical?
11. What kinds of expenses can be billed to clients?
12. What are a lawyer's duties relating to the fee arrangement when he or she undertakes representation?
13. Under what circumstances must a fee arrangement be in writing?
14. Can a paralegal tell a client what the firm's fees are? Can a paralegal negotiate a fee arrangement with a client? What is the paralegal role with regard to fees?
15. What is the difference between a retainer and an advance fee? How are these fees treated when received by the firm?
16. What provisions should a written fee agreement contain?

17. What is unbundling of legal services and how should it be reflected in a fee agreement?
18. What is the purpose of "fee shifting"?
19. Give some examples of fee-shifting statutes.
20. What was the holding in *Missouri v. Jenkins?* Why is this decision so important for paralegals? What was the decision in *Richlin?* Why is this decision important?
21. What information should be included in a request to the court for paralegal's fees as part of an award of attorney's fees?
22. What are three reasons that the amount for paralegal fees in a court-ordered fee might be denied or reduced?

DISCUSSION QUESTIONS AND HYPOTHETICALS

1. Do you believe that the special restrictions on contingency fees (for example, in criminal and divorce cases) are warranted? Why, or why not?
2. Do you believe the ethics rules should require all fee agreements to be in writing? Why, or why not?
3. Should the percentage of attorney's fees in contingency cases be limited by statute or ethical codes? Why, or why not? What do you think is the reason for limiting the amount of contingency fees in medical malpractice cases?
4. Do you think the trend toward using alternative methods of fee structures — for instance, task-based, value, or premium billing — in lieu of traditional hourly rates is a good one? Why, or why not?
5. What would you do if you became aware that several associates in your firm were padding their hours? What if paralegals were doing this?
6. What would you do if your firm expected you to bill 1,800 hours annually, and you knew by September of that year that your hours were going to fall short?
7. What would you do if your firm expected you to bill 1,500 hours a year, but you were not being delegated enough work to keep you busy for that many hours?
8. What would you do if you discovered that you and an associate were doing the same work on a case, and the client was being billed for the duplicative work?
9. In an article in the *ABA Journal*, lawyer-author Scott Turow said: "Whoever says to a client that my billing system on its face rewards me at your expense for slow problem solving, duplication of effort, featherbedding the workforce and compulsiveness — not to mention

fuzzy math?" Do you agree with this assessment of the hourly billing model? Why or why not?

10. What would you do if the supervising attorney in a matter continually wrote off your time as excessive, diminishing your billable hours?
11. What would you do if a client called and wanted to know the firm's hourly rates to handle certain kinds of legal work?
12. What would you do if you worked for a sole practitioner and a prospective personal injury client with a good case came into the office seeking representation and the attorney was out of town for two weeks?
13. What would you do if you discovered that an attorney was inflating the costs on clients' bills?
14. You are flying across the country for client X and en route do some work for client Y. How do you bill your time?
15. What will a court do if it sees that a lawyer did paralegal work and is requesting attorney billing rates for this time? If two paralegals did the same work and requested fees for all the time spent?
16. Would a court award paralegal fees for time spent filing documents? Organizing documents? Drafting documents? Summarizing documents?
17. Do you think the United States should have the kind of two-way fee-shifting that England and Canada have? Why, or why not?

RESEARCH PROJECTS AND ASSIGNMENTS

1. Contact five local law firms and find out:

   a. what kinds of fee arrangements they use for legal work (e.g., contingency for personal injury, fixed to form a corporation, hourly to negotiate a deal);
   b. their range of hourly rates for lawyers and paralegals;
   c. the number of billable hours per year that lawyers and paralegals are expected to record;
   d. what costs they bill directly to clients; and
   e. whether they require fee agreements to be in writing (ask if you can have a copy of a standard fee agreement or engagement letter if the firm has one).

2. In a fee dispute, the client, who does not want to pay the whole bill, refuses to pay for paralegal time as it was not covered in the fee agreement. What should the outcome be if the matter is decided by a court? For one court's opinion, see *Updike, Kelly & Spellacy v. Beckett*, 269 Conn. 813, 850 A.2d 145 (2004).

3. Outline the arguments in the *Missouri v. Jenkins* majority opinion and dissent on the award of paralegal's fees in attorney's fees awards. Which side do you find more convincing, and why? Outline the arguments for charging paralegal fees at market rate as opposed to cost. Which do you find more convincing, and why?
4. Were there cases on paralegal fees in your state and your federal circuit before *Missouri v. Jenkins?* Are these supportive of paralegal fees awards or not? Have there been any cases on paralegal fee awards in your jurisdiction since *Missouri v. Jenkins?*
5. Are there any statutes or court rules in your jurisdiction that provide for paralegal fees awards as part of attorney's fees awards? Check the Probate Code, for example.
6. If you are interested in paralegals who work in administrative practice, read the *Vitac* and *Schroff* decisions cited earlier in this chapter and brief them for the class. Do the same principles that apply in civil litigation also apply to fee awards in administrative agencies?
7. In a newsworthy case on fees, a federal district court judge has said, "Assigning two partners to prepare the same witness for deposition approaches the definition of 'chutzpah.' " For an amusing read about the ways in which courts examine fee petitions, see *Microsoft Corp. v. United Computer Resources of NJ, Inc.*, 216 F. Supp. 383 (N.J. 2002). Be sure to read footnote 13, which defines "chutzpah" and cites other famous judges who have used this Yiddish term.
8. Do you think that courts in California should require paralegals to meet statutory requirements for paralegals described in Chapter 2 for the lawyers who employ them to be awarded compensation for their time in fee awards? Read the related statutes and consider arguments both for and against.
9. Do any of the state and local bars in your jurisdiction have ethics rules on billing practices? If so, what do these opinions suggest?
10. Do you think that firms should be compensated for paralegal time that was initially volunteered? What are the arguments on both sides? For one court's opinion, see *Sundance v. Municipal Court*, 192 Cal. App. 3d 268, 237 Cal. Rptr. 269 (1987), and see if any cases have followed this decision.
11. Would a court award fees to a "paralegal" who is not working under the supervision of a lawyer? See *Gross v. Perrysburg Exempted Village School*, 306 F. Supp. 2d 716 (U.S.D.C., N.D. Ohio 2004), where the court made this distinction in a decision under the Individuals with Disabilities Act fee-shifting provision.
12. Do you think that sole practitioners who do not have paralegals should have their fees reduced in fee awards if they petition for compensation for paralegal work they have done at lawyers' rates? What are the arguments for and against? What if they cannot afford to hire paralegals? Read the relevant cases cited in this chapter where

lawyers' hourly rates were reduced because they were doing paralegal work and see what patterns you find.

13. It is said in many fee award cases that paralegal fees are recoverable only to the extent that the paralegal performs work that would otherwise have to be done by a lawyer. Do you agree with this reasoning? Why or why not? What kinds of tasks might not be strictly "lawyer" work but are not clerical either? For guidance, see *Williams v. R.W. Cannon, Inc.*, 657 F. Supp. 2d 1302 (S.D. Fla. 2009), and *Gross v. Perrysburg Exempted Village School Dist.*, 3:03 CV 7286 (U.S.D.C., N.D. Ohio 2004).
14. Lawyers who do not delegate or supervise effectively can find their fee awards reduced when there is duplicative work or excessive time spent on projects. For an example of too much time spent researching by a paralegal, see *In re Arabia*, 270 Kan. 742, 19 P.3d 113 (2001). What does this case tell you about how you need to interact with your supervisor?

D. Fee Splitting, Referral Fees, and Partnerships between Nonlawyers and Lawyers

Ethics rules in every state carefully control the way in which lawyers and nonlawyers are compensated from fees that are collected by lawyers. These rules are designed with a number of important policies in mind: to prevent the unauthorized practice of law; to guard against interference with the lawyer's independent professional judgment; and to discourage unethical direct solicitation of clients by agents of the lawyer.

Ethics codes have long limited the **splitting of fees** between or among lawyers who are not members of the same firm. ABA Model Rule 1.5(e) permits a division of fees if (1) the division is in proportion to services or the client agrees in writing and the attorneys assume joint responsibility; (2) the client agrees to the arrangement including the share that each receives and the agreement is confirmed in writing; and (3) the fee is reasonable. Some states require only that the client be informed and not object to the arrangement, which was an earlier version of the Rule.

The earlier ABA Model Code was more conservative and several states followed it, interpreting it to mean that an attorney may not pay a **referral fee** or a portion of a client's fee to another attorney simply for referring a case. Referral fees like these have long been thought to be unprofessional and to increase the cost to the client. However, a growing number of states (California, Connecticut, Kansas, Massachusetts,

Pennsylvania, and Texas, for example) have rules that permit "forwarding fees" or that exclude the requirement that the fee division be proportionate to services, thereby effectively allowing referral fees. Proponents of referral fees say that they serve the client's interests by encouraging a thoughtful referral to a competent attorney and point out that clients are protected by the part of the rule that requires the fee to be reasonable.

Referral fees involving nonlawyers are prohibited under ABA Model 7.2(b), which prohibits payment for recommending the lawyer's services except for a few narrow exceptions. All states prohibit referral fees paid to nonlawyers, including paralegals, and prohibit fee splitting between lawyers and nonlawyers, including paralegals. ABA Model Rule 5.4(a) is similar, specifically prohibiting the sharing of fees between lawyers and nonlawyers. The provision also prohibits lawyers from being influenced in making professional judgments by one who recommends their employment. Exceptions to fee splitting are allowed for lawyers to pay for the purchase of the practice of a deceased, disabled, or disappeared lawyer and for lawyers to share court-awarded fees with a nonprofit corporation that retained or recommended the lawyer.

Most important for paralegals is the provision for nonlawyer employees to be included in **compensation and retirement plans** based in whole or in part on profit sharing, found in Model Rule 5.4(a)(3). The ABA Model Guidelines follow the standard prohibitions against fee splitting with nonlawyers in Guideline 9. As noted in the comment to that guideline, virtually all states that have adopted guidelines on paralegals have acknowledged the ethics rule on fee splitting. State guidelines use different language to interpret this restriction, making some profit-sharing plans acceptable in some states and not in others. Most emphasize that retirement plans and bonuses based in part on a firm's overall profitability are acceptable. Some are more restrictive, prohibiting profit-sharing that "by advance agreement is contingent on the profitability" of the practice. This language means that a firm cannot pay a paralegal from a profit-sharing plan that was agreed on at the time of hire to include a bonus if the firm has a profitable year. These states sometimes couple this prohibition with language indicating that a paralegal may be paid a bonus based on the value of their contribution to the firm's practice. Most states are more flexible, allowing profit sharing as long as it is not tied to a specific case or the paralegal's role in bringing in the case.

An early ABA ethics opinion endorsed the inclusion of nonlawyers in profit-based compensation and retirement plans (ABA Informal Opinion 1440 (1979)). Several opinions give advice on compensation plans that are tied to profitability. For example, Mississippi Ethics Opinion 154 (1989) endorsed a bonus plan that compensated paralegals and associates whose billable hours exceeded a set minimum. Iowa Ethics Opinion 90-9 (1990) allows firms to pay paralegals a percentage of total firm income as an incentive. Virginia Ethics Opinion 885 (1987) endorses paralegal compensation based on a percentage of profits from collections plus a base salary. Virginia Ethics Opinion 806 (1986) endorsed secretarial bonuses based on annual firm profits. The Utah bar endorses compensation plans based on profit-sharing, but not with freelance paralegals (Utah Ethics Opinion 02-07). Oregon Ethics Opinion 505 (1985) and Maryland Ethics Opinion 84-103 (1984) advise that lawyers may not compensate paralegals on a contingent basis or only when fees are collected from a client. Maryland and New York warn that profit-sharing plans may not be tied to referrals or solicitation of clients (New York State Bar Association 733 (2000) and Maryland Ethics Opinion 86-57). See also Philadelphia Ethics Opinion 80-14 (1980) and Virginia Ethics Opinion 767 (1986).

Maryland Ethics Opinion 84-103 (1984) prohibits compensation calculated on a percentage of the recovery in a case. New York's Nassau County Ethics Opinion 87-38 (1987) states that a lawyer may not split fees with a paralegal who brings in clients, interviews them, and prepares legal documents under attorney supervision. The Oregon State Bar Legal Ethics Committee states that compensation may not be calculated on a contingency basis or paid only when fees are recovered (Oregon Ethics Opinion 505 (1985)).

The ethics rules and the court cases and ethics opinions interpreting them make it clear that it is not acceptable for an attorney to pay a nonlawyer for **referring a case**, by means of a direct bonus, increase in compensation, or payment of a portion of a fee received from the client. They also make it clear that an attorney may not pay a nonlawyer, under any circumstances, a percentage of a fee from a specific client or case. A "bonus" tied to a particular client or case is not acceptable. However, it is appropriate for a firm to increase compensation, to pay bonuses, and to establish a retirement or other deferred compensation plan based on the firm's *overall* profitability. This kind of arrangement breaks the direct link between the payment and a specific client, eliminating concerns about unauthorized practice and incentives to solicit clients or to settle cases even when it is not in the best interests of the client. Bonus plans are commonly used by firms to reward paralegals for their contribution to making the firm profitable. See *In re Bass* and *In re Hessinger* at the end of this chapter for examples of compensation arrangements that violate the ethics rules.

A few **exceptions** to the prohibition against fee splitting with nonlawyers do exist. As mentioned earlier, fees may be paid to the estate of a deceased lawyer. A lawyer may pay a fee to an approved lawyer referral service. Lawyer referral services are regulated by ethics rules and usually must be approved by the state bar or some other entity. Many are run by local bar associations. Lawyer referral services charge either a flat fee or a percentage of fees. Another exception is the prepaid legal plan, under which a member pays a fee for entitlement to a range of services, and the fee is divided between the lawyer and the plan sponsor. All jurisdictions permit such fee splitting when the plan is nonprofit; some specifically prohibit lawyer participation in profit-making prepaid legal services plans. Remember from Chapter 6 that some states prohibit a lawyer from using unapproved Internet services that match lawyers and clients under the principles against fee splitting.

The same theories underlying the prohibitions on fee splitting with nonlawyers form the basis for rules prohibiting lawyers from entering into **partnerships with nonlawyers**. ABA Model Rule 5.4(b) prohibits a lawyer from forming a partnership with a nonlawyer "if any of the activities of the partnership consist of the practice of law." This rule is sometimes implicated when lawyers are disciplined for aiding in the unauthorized practice of law, fee splitting, and unlawful solicitation if the arrangement with the nonlawyer looks like a partnership or business venture where the nonlawyer has an equal or greater voice in the operation of the firm. See, for example, *In re Hessinger*, at the end of this chapter.

All jurisdictions except the District of Columbia have such a rule and most states that have guidelines for the utilization of paralegals reiterate this rule. See Illinois Guideline (D), Kansas Guideline VII, Kentucky Supreme Court Rule 3.700 Sub-Rule 5, Michigan Guideline III(3), Missouri Guideline II(b), New Hampshire Supreme Court Rule 35 Sub-Rule 5, New Mexico Guideline V, North Carolina Guideline 8, and Rhode Island Guideline VIII.

Because of the changing nature of law practice and the desire of law firms, especially large law firms, to be full-service providers for their large corporate clients, a movement to modify this prohibition took off in the 1980s. The District of Columbia adopted its own version of Rule 5.4 in 1990, providing that "a lawyer may practice law in a partnership or other form of organization in which a financial interest is held or managerial authority is exercised by an individual nonlawyer who performs professional services which assist the organization in providing legal services to clients. . . ." The rule has specified limitations and the comment makes it clear that paralegals are not eligible to become partners. The comment differentiates between nonlawyer "assistants" and nonlawyer "professionals," specifically naming economists, psychologists or psychiatric social workers, lobbyists, certified public accountants, and professional managers and executive directors as examples of acceptable participants under the rule.

Multidisciplinary practice
A business model under which law firms and other professionals form partnerships to deliver legal and other related services to clients

The movement to get the ABA and state bars to endorse such arrangements, called ***multidisciplinary practice*** or MDP, had strong momentum in the 1990s but then suffered serious setbacks, in large part because of the legal and ethical scandals that surrounded the large accounting firms that were involved in the collapse of Enron. It became clear from those scandals that the accounting firms some lawyers were eager to partner with did not live by the degree of ethical integrity that lawyers are expected to have. In 2000, the ABA decisively refused to endorse this model of practicing law. Now proponents of MDP have come back, arguing that U.S. law firms will fall behind in global competitiveness if they do not practice under this model, which is allowed in the United Kingdom. Other alternatives to traditional practice are also being considered. For example, Australia allows law firms to incorporate and be publicly traded.

E. Client Funds and Property

The mishandling of client funds is one of the leading causes of disciplinary sanctions imposed on attorneys. The typical scenario is a sole practitioner with cash-flow problems who "borrows" funds from a client trust account to pay operational expenses. Sometimes, a shortfall in a client trust account is found because of sloppy bookkeeping and management practices. In either case, when the clients cannot get their money promptly, they will file a complaint with the state or local bar and maybe even the local prosecutor's office. Examples of this form of misconduct are found quite frequently in bar reports on discipline. In one recent posting, the Pennsylvania Disciplinary Board reported that 12 lawyers paid their annual fees with checks drawn on client trust accounts.

The most important ethics rule related to client funds is the requirement to keep the client's money separate from the lawyer's, in other words, not to commingle client and law firm funds. The rule against commingling also applies to funds from third parties held by the lawyer. This rule means that lawyers must have a separate bank account that contains only client funds. Some clients may warrant having their own individual ***client trust account*** if the lawyer handles large amounts of funds or transactions for them. See ABA Model Rule 1.15(a).

Client trust account
Bank account set up by a lawyer in which funds are kept that belong to one or more clients

Lawyers hold client funds for many reasons. Client trust accounts may contain estate or trust distributions, funds to be distributed at a real estate closing or on settlement of a matter, advance fees, and awards of which the attorney is owed a portion under a fee agreement.

In the case of funds that are to be divided between the client and the attorney, the funds must remain in the client trust account until they are earned by the lawyer and she or he prepares an accounting for the client, indicating how the funds are to be divided under the fee agreement. In the event a dispute over the fee arises, the amount in dispute must be kept in the client trust account until the dispute is resolved. See ABA Model Rule 1.15(c). A minority of jurisdictions allow advance fees to be deposited into a lawyer's operating account. Remember that advances are different from retainers, which are nonrefundable and paid directly to the lawyer.

Most jurisdictions have detailed guidelines or rules on handling client trust accounts, including what kinds of journals, ledgers, accounting, fee agreements, bills, registers, and other records must be maintained. The ABA has Model Rules for Client Trust Account Records, which were amended in 2010 and have been adopted by several jurisdictions.

Most states have a program under which the interest on certain client trust accounts is used to fund the bar disciplinary system, client security fund, or legal services for the poor, specified by the state's bar, legislature, or supreme court. Well over $100 million a year is raised annually through these programs, known as ***IOLTA*** (Interest on Lawyers' Trust Accounts). IOLTA programs can be mandatory, voluntary, or "opt-out." A voluntary program means that a lawyer must affirmatively decide to participate; an opt-out program means that all lawyers participate unless they affirmatively declare *not* to. The plans ordinarily cover only client funds that are too small in amount or are to be held for too brief a period to earn interest for the client. The majority of jurisdictions have voluntary or opt-out plans, or some hybrid of the two, although a growing number of plans are being converted to mandatory status.

IOLTA
Interest on Lawyers' Trust Accounts. A program under which the interest from lawyers' client trust accounts, which is too small to pay to clients, is collected by banks and used by bar associations and/or courts to fund law-related programs.

The funds collected by the states from IOLTA plans are substantial. Each state has its own rules about how these funds are expended. For example, Minnesota's plan allocates the funds to "the poor, law-related education and projects to improve the administration of justice." North Carolina designates its funds for lawyer referral services, attorney grievance and discipline, and a client security fund to reimburse clients for losses caused by the dishonest conduct of attorneys when no other recourse is available.

The constitutionality of IOLTA programs has been challenged in the courts on the grounds that clients have property rights in the interest generated in these accounts, which rights are violated when the interest income, however small, is not paid to the clients. In the most recent U.S. Supreme Court decision on this matter, *Brown v. Legal Foundation of Washington*, 123 S. Ct. 1406 (2003), the Court upheld the constitutionality of the Washington IOLTA plan. In the opinion, the Court found that there was not a "taking" under the clause of the Constitution that allows for the state to confiscate private property for public use. Further, the Court found that if there were a taking, the interest income that was "confiscated" was clearly being used for a valid public purpose. Finally, the Court went on to say that the amount of just compensation that the client should get was nothing because the amount earned on an individual deposit was either extremely small or nothing. In an earlier decision, the U.S. Supreme Court decided the narrow issue that interest on client trust accounts held in IOLTA accounts is the private property of the clients. The Court did not decide in that case the issue of the constitutionality of the "taking" of these funds. *Phillips v. Washington Legal Foundation*, 524 U.S. 156, 118 S. Ct. 1925 (1998).

Commingling of funds is a basis for disciplinary action, as is ***conversion of funds***, a much more serious breach. Commingling refers only to mixing client funds with those of the attorney and does not require any intent to harm the client or actual harm to the client. Conversion is the misappropriation of the client's funds for the attorney's or firm's use. Conversion may take place when the attorney draws funds from the client trust account for personal use or for payment of firm expenses.

Commingling of funds
The mixing of client funds with lawyers' funds

Conversion of funds
The tortious deprivation of another's property without justification or authorization

Disciplinary bodies are not sympathetic to the defenses that lawyers sometimes use in such cases, including the intention to return the funds or the actual restoration of the funds. An attorney's personal or financial problems or the mismanagement of the firm are also not legitimate excuses; in fact, they may be considered aggravating circumstances because they indicate that the lawyer could repeat this kind of conduct.

Lawyers and paralegals also have a duty to **protect client property** other than money. This duty to safeguard usually requires that property be placed in a safe deposit box. Property covered by these rules typically includes titles to real estate or valuable personal property, jewelry, and securities. If a safe deposit box is shared with other clients, the items must be identified and labeled. ABA Model Rule 1.15(a).

Lawyers have a duty to keep **accurate and complete records** of client funds and property. The ABA Model Rule provides for a specific number of years (five) that records must be kept. Model Rule 1.15(a). Several states have different periods (usually six or seven years) and more specific provisions on recordkeeping. A few jurisdictions provide for random audits of client trust accounts and some for annual certification or verification of compliance with recordkeeping rules. Many states provide for audits in conjunction with disciplinary actions.

Duties specified in the ethics rules are the **duties to notify the client of the receipt of funds** or property, **to deliver client funds or property promptly**, and **to provide a full accounting** to the client on request. ABA Model Rule 1.15(d). The duties to notify, to deliver, and to account for client funds are most often breached because of lax office procedures, but sometimes are a result of a more egregious violation, such as conversion of client funds. If a third party has a claim on client funds held by the lawyer, the lawyer may have a duty not to turn over the funds to the client until the various parties' rights are clarified. The notion of what is "prompt" delivery is sometimes an issue in disciplinary actions. The best practice certainly requires action within the month in which funds are received, if not more quickly. Regular periodic accountings to clients (monthly or quarterly) are advisable rather than accountings only on client request.

All jurisdictions also have some special rules that require attorneys to turn over papers, funds, money, and unearned advanced fees on **termination of representation**. ABA Model Rule 1.16(d) so provides, emphasizing the lawyer's obligation to protect the client's interests and extending the lawyer's duty after representation ends.

One final matter in this area is the handling of a client file after work on the matter is completed. Firms should have policies on **retention of files**, turning files over to clients, destroying files, and security for files maintained in off-site storage. In most jurisdictions, the client file is considered the property of the client; therefore, the lawyer cannot destroy old files without first informing the client and getting permission or giving the client the chance to keep the file. Destruction practices should be specified in policies, to guard against the destruction of important papers that should be retained, such as wills, deeds, securities, and tax returns, and to ensure that all copies of documents meant for destruction are in fact destroyed—a challenge when one is working with electronic documents. It is good practice to include a provision about the handling of client files in the agreement for representation. The material in client files can also protect a lawyer if a malpractice suit is filed, so the statute of limitations should guide the length of time that detailed records of the legal work are kept. Finally, converting hard copy files to electronic files such as CD-ROMs or DVDs requires the approval of the client in some jurisdictions. Care should be taken when doing this kind of conversion to preserve hard copies of critical legal documents like wills and deeds.

The rules governing the handling of client funds and property are especially important to paralegals, especially in small law firms where they often must implement instructions relating to client funds and may be delegated substantial responsibility for handling these matters. Checks or property often come directly to the attorney, who will instruct the paralegal on how to handle the money or property. In small firms, a paralegal may perform some of the bookkeeping and recordkeeping functions. Paralegals must know the rules well enough to identify improprieties and either to rectify them or to inform the supervising attorney. There is a split of authority on whether a paralegal may serve as signatory on client trust accounts; some states allow this practice and others do not. The ABA Model Rules on Client Trust Accounts require the lawyer "or a person under the direct supervision of the lawyer" to sign. (See Rule 2(a).)

It is not unusual for an attorney in trouble to blame a nonlawyer employee for poor office practice that has resulted in the mishandling of client funds or commingling of client and lawyer funds. Most courts and disciplinary bodies are unsympathetic to this defense, as lawyers are expected to supervise nonlawyers and are responsible for their conduct. And there have been reported cases of paralegals embezzling money from lawyers, including a recent case in Florida in which a lawyer, now disbarred, and his paralegal used $72,000 for personal expenses and vacations. NALA's Code does not address this area directly, but NFPA's ethics rules call on paralegals to be "scrupulous, thorough and honest" in handling client assets. NFPA Model Code of Ethics Professional Responsibility, EC 1.2(e).

REVIEW QUESTIONS

1. What are the rules about referral fees? What is the basis for these rules? Do the same rules apply to lawyers and paralegals?
2. What are the rules about fee splitting? Give several examples of payments to paralegals that violate these rules.
3. What kinds of retirement, bonus, and profit-sharing plans are permitted for paralegals under the ethics rules?
4. Why do the ethics rules prohibit lawyers from being partners with paralegals in a law practice?
5. What is the basis for the District of Columbia rules permitting nonlawyer partners? May paralegals become partners under this rule?
6. What are the duties of lawyers and paralegals regarding client funds?
7. What is a client trust account? What do the ethics rules require concerning client trust accounts?
8. What is IOLTA? What is a client security fund?
9. Describe the difference between the commingling and the conversion of funds. Which is more serious?
10. Is mishandling of client funds common? Why or why not? How does it usually arise?
11. How might a paralegal violate ethics in the handling of client funds?
12. When a lawyer receives a check for a judgment or settlement and the case was taken on contingency, what should he or she do with the check?
13. Do the facts that an attorney is very busy, has high staff turnover, and has not had a bookkeeper in months mitigate against charges of commingling of funds?
14. What are the duties with regard to client property held for client?
15. What are the duties related to handling of client funds, files, and property when representation ceases?

DISCUSSION QUESTIONS AND HYPOTHETICALS

1. Do you think the rules prohibiting fee splitting are well founded? Why, or why not? Do you think the rules should be different for lawyers and nonlawyers?
2. Do you think the rules prohibiting referral fees are well founded? Why, or why not?
3. Can a personal injury firm pay a $500 bonus for every case you bring in? Can you be paid one-third of the fee when the case settles?
4. Do you think the rule prohibiting paralegals from becoming partners in law firms is well founded? Why, or why not? Do you think this rule should be changed? Why or why not?

5. What would you do if an attorney handed you a settlement check in a contingency case and asked you to deposit it in the firm's operating account?
6. Where should you keep the deed of trust to a client's real estate? In your desk? In the client file? Under the floor board in your attic? Why, or why not? What if the property were a valuable diamond ring? Stock certificates?
7. What would you do if you found out your firm was having temporary cash-flow problems because of uncollected receivables and had borrowed from client trust accounts to make the payroll?
8. What is wrong with an attorney putting client funds in the firm's account if he or she plans to replace them in two days? Would it make any difference if the period were two weeks? If the client owed fees to the attorney? What if the attorney were doing this for the benefit of another client and did not benefit himself or herself in any way?
9. What would you do if your attorney-employer was very careful about handling client funds but kept no records other than bank reports and withdrawal slips?
10. What would you do if you discovered that a settlement check had come in and been deposited six months ago but that the client had never been notified?
11. What would you do if you found several months-old checks from clients, insurance companies, and others in the bottom of a desk drawer?

RESEARCH PROJECTS AND ASSIGNMENTS

1. Does your jurisdiction allow attorneys to pay or receive referral fees? Is it common practice?
2. Call five local law firms and find out if they have pension or profit-sharing plans for their paralegals or pay their paralegals bonuses. Ask them how the amount of bonus is determined.
3. Ask some lawyers and practicing paralegals what they think about lawyers forming partnerships with nonlawyers. Has your jurisdiction considered adopting a rule like the District of Columbia's or considered adopting rules that would allow multidisciplinary practice?
4. What kind of IOLTA does your state have — voluntary, opt-out, or mandatory? How do attorneys pay the fund? What are the funds used for? How much money is currently in the fund?
5. Does your state have a client security fund? How is it funded? How much money is in the fund? What kinds of payments have been made from the fund?
6. Draft a provision for a client engagement letter on handling of client files after the matter is closed and on storing documents electronically.

7. Does your state or local bar have an opinion on how long lawyers should retain client files? If so, what is the period?
8. Find the disciplinary reports for your jurisdiction and review them to see if any of the recently disciplined lawyers got into trouble because of unethical fee splitting, referral fees, or client trust account violations. Share these stories with your class.
9. Read and brief the case of *In the Matter of Hear*, 755 N.E.2d 579 (Ind. 2001). In this case a nonlawyer working for a lawyer with a debt collection business was disciplined when the nonlawyer embezzled funds that belonged to clients.
10. For an example of a lawyer and a paralegal who did not follow the rules on client trust accounts, see *In re Martinez*, 107 N.M., 754 P.2d 842 (1988). Read this case and brief it, paying special attention to the several ethics violations. Have any such cases been published in your jurisdiction?
11. In Chapter 3 we read *In re Morin*, which involved a lawyer who over-delegated work relating to trusts. For a case where a lawyer also engaged in this kind of work violated rules on fee splitting with nonlawyers, see *In re Flack*, 272 Kan. 465, 33 P.3d 1281 (2001). Exactly what kind of agreement is described in this case? Is this the kind of situation that the rules on fee splitting were intended to prevent? Why or why not? How does this compare with *In re Hear*, 755 N.E.2d 579 (Ind. 2001), in which the lawyer went into the debt collection business?
12. In *Sanford v. GMRI, Inc.* (also known as the Red Lobster case, found at the end of this chapter), a federal court disallowed the inclusion of paralegal time in a fee award for paralegals who did not meet the statutory requirements to use the title "paralegal." See *Hawkins v. Berkeley Unified School District*, No. C-07-4206 (U.S.D.C., N.D. Cal. 2008), for a contradictory ruling. What does the California statute (Business and Professions Code 6450, et seq.) say about paralegal fee awards? What would you argue on each side of this issue?
13. Read *Florida Bar v. Glueck*, 985 So. 2d 1052 (Fla. 2008), and compare it with *Hessinger* at the end of this chapter. Consider the relationship of lawyer to the "paralegal" involved, the number of clients affected, the seriousness of the violations, and so on. What can you learn from this comparison? What was the difference in the outcome. Why?

CASES FOR ANALYSIS

In the following landmark case, the U.S. Supreme Court held that attorney fee's awards under the Civil Rights Act may include paralegal fees at market rates. Pay close attention to both issues — the payment of fees for paralegal time and the basis on which the fee should be calculated.

Missouri v. Jenkins
491 U.S. 274 (1989)

Justice BRENNAN delivered the opinion of the Court.

This is the attorney's-fee aftermath of major school desegregation litigation in Kansas City, Missouri. We granted certiorari, 488 U.S. —, 109 S. Ct. 218, 102 L. Ed. 2d 209 (1988), to resolve two questions relating to fees litigation under 42 U.S.C. §1988. First, does the Eleventh Amendment prohibit enhancement of a fee award against a State to compensate for delay in payment? Second, should the fee award compensate the work of paralegals and law clerks by applying the market rate for their work?

I

This litigation began in 1977 as a suit by the Kansas City Missouri School District (KCMSD), the School Board, and the children of two School Board members, against the State of Missouri and other defendants. The plaintiffs alleged that the State, surrounding school districts, and various federal agencies had caused and perpetuated a system of racial segregation in the schools of the Kansas City metropolitan area. They sought various desegregation remedies. KCMSD was subsequently realigned as a nominal defendant, and a class of present and future KCMSD students was certified as plaintiffs. After lengthy proceedings, including a trial that lasted 7½ months during 1983 and 1984, the District Court found the State of Missouri and KCMSD liable, while dismissing the suburban school districts and the federal defendants. It ordered various intradistrict remedies, to be paid for by the State and KCMSD, including $260 million in capital improvements and a magnet-school plan costing over $200 million.

The plaintiff class has been represented, since 1979, by Kansas City lawyer Arthur Benson and, since 1982, by the NAACP Legal Defense and Educational Fund, Inc. (LDF). Benson and the LDF requested attorney's fees under the Civil Rights Attorney's Fees Awards Act of 1976, 42 U.S.C. §1988.[1] Benson and his associates had devoted 10,875 attorney hours to the litigation, as well as 8,108 hours of paralegal and law clerk time. For the LDF the corresponding figures were 10,854 hours for attorneys and 15,517 hours for paralegals and law clerks. Their fee applications deleted from these totals 3,628 attorney hours and 7,046 paralegal hours allocable to unsuccessful claims against the suburban school districts. With additions for post-judgment monitoring and for preparation

1. Section 1988 provides in relevant part:

In any action or proceeding to enforce a provision of sections 1981, 1982, 1983, 1985, and 1986 of this title, title IX of Public Law 92-318 [20 U.S.C. 1681 et seq.], or title VI of the Civil Rights Act of 1964 [42 U.S.C. 2000d et seq.], the court, in its discretion, may allow the prevailing party, other than the United States, a reasonable attorney's fee as part of the costs.

of the fee application, the District Court awarded Benson a total of approximately $1.7 million and the LDF $2.3 million.

In calculating the hourly rate for Benson's fees the court noted that the market rate in Kansas City for attorneys of Benson's qualifications was in the range of $125 to $175 per hour, and found that "Mr. Benson's rate would fall at the higher end of this range based upon his expertise in the area of civil rights." It calculated his fees on the basis of an even higher hourly rate of $200, however, because of three additional factors: the preclusion of other employment, the undesirability of the case, and the delay in payment for Benson's services. The court also took account of the delay in payment in setting the rates for several of Benson's associates by using current market rates rather than those applicable at the time the services were rendered. For the same reason, it calculated the fees for the LDF attorneys at current market rates.

Both Benson and the LDF employed numerous paralegals, law clerks (generally law students working part-time), and recent law graduates in this litigation. The court awarded fees for their work based on Kansas City market rates for those categories. As in the case of the attorneys, it used current rather than historic market rates in order to compensate for the delay in payment. It therefore awarded fees based on hourly rates of $35 for law clerks, $40 for paralegals, and $50 for recent law graduates. The Court of Appeals affirmed in all respects.

II

Our grant of certiorari extends to two issues raised by the State of Missouri. Missouri first contends that a State cannot, consistent with the principle of sovereign immunity this Court has found embodied in the Eleventh Amendment, be compelled to pay an attorney's fee enhanced to compensate for delay in payment. . . .

To summarize: We reaffirm our holding . . . that the Eleventh Amendment has no application to an award of attorney's fees, ancillary to a grant of prospective relief, against a State. It follows that the same is true for the calculation of the *amount* of the fee. An adjustment for delay in payment is, we hold, an appropriate factor in the determination of what constitutes a reasonable attorney's fee under §1988. An award against a State of a fee that includes such an enhancement for delay is not, therefore, barred by the Eleventh Amendment.

III

Missouri's second contention is that the District Court erred in compensating the work of law clerks and paralegals (hereinafter collectively "paralegals") at the market rates for their services, rather than at their cost to the attorney. While Missouri agrees that compensation for the cost of these personnel should be included in the fee award, it suggests that an hourly rate of $15 — which it argued below corresponded to their salaries, benefits, and overhead — would be appropriate, rather than the market rates of $35 to $50. According to Missouri, §1988 does not authorize billing paralegals' hours at market rates, and doing so produces a "windfall" for the attorney.[7]

We begin with the statutory language, which provides simply for "a reasonable attorney's fee as part of the costs." 42 U.S.C. §1988. Clearly, a "reasonable attorney's fee" cannot have been meant to compensate only work performed personally by members of the bar. Rather, the term must refer to a reasonable fee for the work product of an attorney. Thus, the fee must take into account the work not only of attorneys, but also of secretaries, messengers, librarians, janitors, and others whose labor contributes to the work product for which an attorney bills her client; and it must also take account of other expenses and profit. The parties have suggested no reason why the work of paralegals should not be similarly compensated, nor can we think of any. We thus take as our starting point the self-evident proposition that the "reasonable attorney's fee" provided for by statute should compensate the work of paralegals, as well as that of attorneys. The more difficult question is how the work of paralegals is to be valuated in calculating the overall attorney's fee.

The statute specifies a "reasonable" fee for the attorney's work product. In determining how other elements of the attorney's fee are to be calculated, we have consistently looked to the marketplace as our guide to what is "reasonable." . . . A reasonable attorney's fee under §1988 is one calculated on the basis of rates and practices prevailing in the relevant market, i.e., "in line with those [rates] prevailing in the community for similar services by lawyers of reasonably comparable skill, experience, and reputation," and one that grants the successful civil rights plaintiff a "fully compensatory fee," comparable to what "is traditional with attorneys compensated by a fee-paying client."

If an attorney's fee awarded under §1988 is to yield the same level of compensation that would be available from the market, the "increasingly widespread custom of separately billing for the services of paralegals and law students who serve as clerks" must be taken into account. All else being equal, the hourly fee charged by an attorney whose rates include paralegal work in her hourly fee, or who bills separately for the work of paralegals at cost, will be higher than the hourly fee charged by an attorney competing in the same market who bills separately for the work of paralegals at "market rates." In other words, the prevailing "market rate"

7. The Courts of Appeals have taken a variety of positions on this issue. Most permit separate billing of paralegal time. Some courts, on the other hand, have considered paralegal work "out-of-pocket expense," recoverable only at cost to the attorney. At least one Court of Appeals has refused to permit any recovery of paralegal expense apart from the attorney's hourly fee. *Abrams v. Baylor College of Medicine*, 805 F.2d 528, 535 (CA 1986).

for attorney time is not independent of the manner in which paralegal time is accounted for.[8] Thus, if the prevailing practice in a given community were to bill paralegal time separately at market rates, fees awarded the attorney at market rates for attorney time would not be fully compensatory if the court refused to compensate hours billed by paralegals or did so only at "cost." Similarly, the fee awarded would be too high if the court accepted separate billing for paralegal hours in a market where that was not the custom.

We reject the argument that compensation for paralegals at rates above "cost" would yield a "windfall" for the prevailing attorney. Neither petitioners nor anyone else, to our knowledge, have ever suggested that the hourly rate applied to the work of an associate attorney in a law firm creates a windfall for the firm's partners or is otherwise improper under §1988, merely because it exceeds the cost of the attorney's services. If the fees are consistent with market rates and practices, the "windfall" argument has no more force with regard to paralegals than it does for associates. And it would hardly accord with Congress' intent to provide a "fully compensatory fee" if the prevailing plaintiff's attorney in a civil rights lawsuit were not permitted to bill separately for paralegals, while the defense attorney in the same litigation was able to take advantage of the prevailing practice and obtain market rates for such work. Yet that is precisely the result sought in this case by the State of Missouri, which appears to have paid its own outside counsel for the work of paralegals at the hourly rate of $35.[9]

Nothing in §1988 requires that the work of paralegals invariably be billed separately. If it is the practice in the relevant market not to do so, or to bill the work of paralegals only at cost, that is all that §1988 requires. Where, however, the prevailing practice is to bill paralegal work at market rates, treating civil rights lawyers' fee requests in the same way is not only permitted by §1988, but also makes economic sense. By encouraging the use of lower-cost paralegals rather than attorneys wherever possible, permitting market-rate billing of paralegal hours "encourages cost-effective delivery of legal services and, by reducing the spiraling cost of civil rights litigation, furthers the policies underlying civil rights statutes."[10]

8. The attorney who bills separately for paralegal time is merely distributing her costs and profit margin among the hourly fees of other members of her staff, rather than concentrating them in the fee she sets for her own time.

9. A variant of Missouri's "windfall" argument is the following: "If paralegal expense is reimbursed at a rate many times the actual cost, will attorneys next try to bill separately — and at a profit — for such items as secretarial time, paper clips, electricity, and other expenses?" The answer to this question is, of course, that attorneys seeking fees under §1988 would have no basis for requesting separate compensation of such expenses unless this were the prevailing practice in the local community. The safeguard against the billing at a profit of secretarial services and paper clips is the discipline of the market.

10. It has frequently been recognized in the lower courts that paralegals are capable of carrying out many tasks, under the supervision of an attorney, that might otherwise be

Such separate billing appears to be the practice in most communities today.[11] In the present case, Missouri concedes that "the local market typically bills separately for paralegal services," and the District Court found that the requested hourly rates of $35 for law clerks, $40 for paralegals, and $50 for recent law graduates were the prevailing rates for such services in the Kansas City area. Under these circumstances, the court's decision to award separate compensation at these rates was fully in accord with §1988.

IV

The courts below correctly granted a fee enhancement to compensate for delay in payment and approved compensation of paralegals and law clerks at market rates. The judgment of the Court of Appeals is therefore

Affirmed.

Justice MARSHALL took no part in the consideration or decision of this case.

Justice O'CONNOR, with whom Justice SCALIA joins, and with whom THE CHIEF JUSTICE joins in part, concurring in part and dissenting in part.

I agree with the Court that 42 U.S.C. §1988 allows compensation for the work of paralegals and law clerks at market rates, and therefore join Parts I and III of its opinion. I do not join Part II, however, for in my view the Eleventh Amendment does not permit enhancement of attorney's fees assessed against a State as compensation for delay in payment. . . .

---

performed by a lawyer and billed at a higher rate. Such work might include, for example, factual investigation, including locating and interviewing witnesses; assistance with depositions, interrogatories, and document production; compilation of statistical and financial data; checking legal citations; and drafting correspondence. Much such work lies in a gray area of tasks that might appropriately be performed either by an attorney or a paralegal. To the extent that fee applicants under §1988 are not permitted to bill for the work of paralegals at market rates, it would not be surprising to see a greater amount of such work performed by attorneys themselves, thus increasing the overall cost of litigation.

Of course, purely clerical or secretarial tasks should not be billed at a paralegal rate, regardless of who performs them. What the court in *Johnson v. Georgia Highway Express, Inc.*, 488 F.2d 714, 717 (CA5 1974), said in regard to the work of attorneys is applicable by analogy to paralegals:

> It is appropriate to distinguish between legal work, in the strict sense, and investigation, clerical work, compilation of facts and statistics and other work which can often be accomplished by non-lawyers but which a lawyer may do because he has no other help available. Such non-legal work may command a lesser rate. Its dollar value is not enhanced just because a lawyer does it.

11. *Amicus* National Association of Legal Assistants reports that 77 percent of 1,800 legal assistants responding to a survey of the association's membership stated that their law firms charged clients for paralegal work on an hourly billing basis. Brief for National Association of Legal Assistants as *Amicus Curiae* 11.

Chief Justice REHNQUIST, dissenting.

I agree with Justice O'CONNOR that the Eleventh Amendment does not permit an award of attorney's fees against a State which includes compensation for delay in payment. Unlike Justice O'CONNOR, however, I do not agree with the Court's approval of the award of law clerk and paralegal fees made here.

Section 1988 gives the district courts discretion to allow the prevailing party in an action under §1988 "a reasonable attorney's fee as part of the costs." 42 U.S.C. §1988. The Court reads this language as authorizing recovery of "a 'reasonable' fee for the attorney's work product," which, the Court concludes, may include separate compensation for the services of law clerks and paralegals. But the statute itself simply uses the very familiar term "a reasonable attorney's fee," which to those untutored in the Court's linguistic juggling means a fee charged for services rendered by an individual who has been licensed to practice law. Because law clerks and paralegals have not been licensed to practice law in Missouri, it is difficult to see how charges for their services may be separately billed as part of "attorney's fees." And since a prudent attorney customarily includes compensation for the cost of law clerk and paralegal services, like any other sort of office overhead — from secretarial staff, janitors, and librarians, to telephone service, stationery, and paper clips — in his own hourly billing rate, allowing the prevailing party to recover separate compensation for law clerk and paralegal services may result in "double recovery."

The Court finds justification for its ruling in the fact that the prevailing practice among attorneys in Kansas City is to bill clients separately for the services of law clerks and paralegals. But I do not think Congress intended the meaning of the statutory term "attorney's fee" to expand and contract with each and every vagary of local billing practice. Under the Court's logic, prevailing parties could recover at market rates for the cost of secretaries, private investigators, and other types of lay personnel who assist the attorney in preparing his case, so long as they could show that the prevailing practice in the local market was to bill separately for these services. Such a result would be a sufficiently drastic departure from the traditional concept of "attorney's fees" that I believe new statutory authorization should be required for it. That permitting separate billing of law clerk and paralegal hours at market rates might "reduc[e] the spiraling cost of civil rights litigation" by encouraging attorneys to delegate to these individuals tasks which they would otherwise perform themselves at higher cost may be a persuasive reason for Congress to enact such additional legislation. It is not, however, a persuasive reason for us to rewrite the legislation which Congress has in fact enacted.

I also disagree with the State's suggestion that law clerk and paralegal expenses incurred by a prevailing party, if not recoverable at market rates as "attorney's fees" under §1988, are nonetheless recoverable at actual cost under that statute. The language of §1988 expands the traditional definition of "costs" to include "a reasonable attorney's fee," but it cannot fairly be read to authorize the recovery of all other out-of-pocket expenses actually incurred by the prevailing party in the course of litigation. Absent specific statutory authorization for the recovery of such expenses, the prevailing party remains subject to the limitations on cost recovery imposed by Federal Rule of Civil Procedure 54(d) and 28 U.S.C. §1920, which govern the taxation of costs in federal litigation where a cost shifting statute is not applicable. Section 1920 gives the district court discretion to tax certain types of costs against the losing party in any federal litigation. The statute specifically enumerates six categories of expenses which may be taxed as costs: fees of the court clerk and marshal; fees of the court reporter; printing fees and witness fees; copying fees; certain docket fees; and fees of court-appointed experts and interpreters. We have held that this list is exclusive. Since none of these categories can possibly be construed to include the fees of law clerks and paralegals. I would also hold that reimbursement for these expenses may not be separately awarded at actual cost.

I would therefore reverse the award of reimbursement for law clerk and paralegal expenses.

Questions about the Case

1. Do you agree that the language of the statute "[c]learly . . . cannot have been meant to compensate only work performed by members of the bar"? Is the Court's reasoning on this point persuasive?
2. Why does the Court hold that attorney's fees generally should be calculated according to prevailing market rates?
3. Do you agree with the Court that attorneys should be able to make a profit from their paralegals' work in cases like this? Why, or why not?
4. Do you agree with the Court's comment in footnote 9 about the "discipline of the market"? Why, or why not?
5. What is the most convincing argument that the Court makes for using market rates to calculate paralegal fees awards?
6. What does the Court say about the nature of paralegal work that can be compensated in fee awards? Do you think that time spent numbering documents should be compensated as paralegal time? What about organizing documents? Summarizing depositions? Inputting data into a computer?
7. Summarize the points made by the dissent. Do you think any of them are valid?

In the following case, the Supreme Court had to decide whether to adhere to its interpretation of attorney fee statutes set forth in *Missouri v. Jenkins* or to follow a different path in interpreting a different federal statute.

Richlin Security Service Co. v. Chertoff

553 U.S. 571, 128 S. Ct. 2007 (2008)

[After prevailing against the Government on a claim originating in the Department of Transportation's Board of Contract Appeals, petitioner (Richlin) filed an application with the Board for reimbursement of attorney's fees, expenses, and costs, pursuant to the Equal Access to Justice Act (EAJA). The Board concluded, *inter alia*, that Richlin was not entitled to recover paralegal fees at the rates at which it was billed by its law firm, holding that EAJA limited such recovery to the attorney's cost, which was lower than the billed rate. In affirming, the Federal Circuit concluded that the term "fees," for which EAJA authorizes recovery at "prevailing market rates," embraces only the fees of attorneys, experts, and agents. . . .]

Justice Alito delivered the opinion of the Court. . . .

The question presented in this case is whether the Equal Access to Justice Act (EAJA), 5 U.S.C. §504(a)(1) (2006 ed.) and 28 U.S.C. §2412(d)(1)(A) (2000 ed.), allows a prevailing party in a case brought by or against the Government to recover fees for paralegal services at the market rate for such services or only at their cost to the party's attorney. The United States Court of Appeals for the Federal Circuit limited recovery to the attorney's cost. 472 F.3d 1370 (2006). . . .

EAJA permits an eligible prevailing party to recover "fees and other expenses incurred by that party in connection with" a proceeding before an administrative agency. 5 U.S.C. §504(a)(1). EAJA defines "fees and other expenses" as follows:

> "[F]ees and other expenses" includes the reasonable expenses of expert witnesses, the reasonable cost of any study, analysis, engineering report, test, or project which is found by the agency to be necessary for the preparation of the party's case, and reasonable attorney or agent fees. (The amount of fees awarded under this section shall be based upon prevailing market rates for the kind and quality of the services furnished, except that (i) no expert witness shall be compensated at a rate in excess of the highest rate of compensation for expert witnesses paid by the agency involved, and (ii) attorney or agent fees shall not be awarded in excess of $125 per hour unless the agency determines by regulation that an increase in the cost of living or a special factor, such as the limited availability of qualified attorneys or agents for the proceedings involved, justifies a higher fee.) §504(b)(1)(A).

In this case, Richlin "incurred" "fees" for paralegal services in connection with its contract action before the Board. Since §504(b)(1)(A) awards fees at "prevailing market rates," a straightforward reading of the statute leads to the conclusion that Richlin was entitled to recover fees for the paralegal services it purchased at the market rate for such services.

The Government resists this reading by distinguishing "fees" from "other expenses." The Government concedes that "fees" are reimbursable at "prevailing market rates," but it insists that "other expenses" (including expenses for "any study, analysis, engineering report, test, or project") are reimbursable only at their "reasonable cost." And in the Government's view, outlays for paralegal services are better characterized as "other expenses" than as "fees." The Government observes that the second sentence of §504(b)(1)(A), which explains how to calculate awards for "fees," refers to attorneys, agents, and expert witnesses, without mentioning paralegals. From this omission, the Government infers that Congress intended to treat expenditures for paralegal services not as "fees" but as "other expenses," recoverable at "reasonable cost."

We find the Government's fractured interpretation of the statute unpersuasive. Contrary to the Government's contention, §504(b)(1)(A) does not clearly distinguish between the rates at which "fees" and "other expenses" are reimbursed. Although the statute does refer to the "reasonable cost" of "any study, analysis, engineering report, test, or project," Congress may reasonably have believed that market rates would not exist for work product of that kind. At one point, Congress even appears to use the terms "expenses" and "fees" interchangeably. . . . There is no indication that Congress, in using the term "expenses" in one place and "fees" in the other, was referring to two different components of expert remuneration.

Even if the dichotomy that the Government draws between "fees" and "other expenses" were supported by the statutory text, it would hardly follow that amounts billed for paralegal services should be classified as "expenses" rather than as "fees." The Government concludes that the omission of paralegal fees from §504(b)(1)(A)'s parenthetical (which generally authorizes reimbursement at "prevailing market rates") implies that the recovery of paralegal fees is limited to cost. But one could just as easily conclude that the omission of paralegal fees from the litany of "any study, analysis, engineering report, test, or project" (all of which are recoverable at "reasonable cost") implies that paralegal fees are recoverable at market rates. Surely paralegals are more analogous to attorneys, experts, and agents than to studies, analyses, reports, tests, and projects. . . .

But even if we agreed that EAJA limited a prevailing party's recovery for paralegal fees to "reasonable cost," it certainly would not follow that the cost should be measured from the perspective of the party's attorney. To the contrary, it would be anomalous to measure cost from the perspective of the attorney rather than the client. . . . Such an interpretation would be tough to square with the statutory language. Section 504(a)(1) provides that an agency shall award to a prevailing party "fees and other expenses *incurred by that party*." . . . That language leaves no doubt that Congress intended the "reasonable cost" . . . to be calculated from the perspective of the litigant. That being the case, we find it hard to believe that Congress, without even mentioning paralegals, intended to make an exception of them by calculating their cost from the perspective of their employer rather than the litigant. . . .

To the extent that some ambiguity subsists in the statutory text, we need not look far to resolve it, for we have already addressed a similar question with respect to another fee-shifting statute. In *Missouri v. Jenkins*, 491 U.S. 274 (1989), we considered whether litigants could recover paralegal fees under the Civil Rights Attorney's Fees Awards Act of 1976, 42 U.S.C. §1988. Section 1988 provides that "the court, in its discretion, may allow the prevailing party, other than the United States, a reasonable attorney's fee as part of the costs." We concluded that the term "attorney's fee" in §1988 "cannot have been meant to compensate only work performed personally by members of the bar." 491 U.S., at 285. Although separate billing for paralegals had become "increasingly widespread," *id.*, at 286 (internal quotation marks omitted), attorney's fees had traditionally subsumed both the attorney's personal labor and the labor of paralegals and other individuals who contributed to the attorney's work product, see *id.*, at 285. We were so confident that Congress had given the term "attorney's fees" this traditional gloss that we declared it "self-evident" that the term embraced the fees of paralegals as well as attorneys. *Ibid.*

We think *Jenkins* substantially answers the question before us. EAJA, like §1988, entitles certain parties to recover "reasonable attorney . . . fees." 5 U.S.C. §504(b)(1)(A). EAJA, like §1988, makes no mention of the paralegals, "secretaries, messengers, librarians, janitors, and others whose labor contributes to the work product for which an attorney bills her client." *Jenkins*, *supra*, at 285. And we think EAJA, like §1988, must be interpreted as using the term "attorney . . . fees" to reach fees for paralegal services as well as compensation for the attorney's personal labor. The Government does not contend that the meaning of the term "attorney's fees" changed so much between §1988's enactment in 1976 and EAJA's enactment in 1980 that the term's meaning in one statute must be different from its meaning in the other. Under the reasoning of *Jenkins*, we take it as "self-evident" that when Congress instructed agencies to award "attorney . . . fees" to certain parties prevailing against the Government, that term was intended to embrace paralegal fees as well. Since §504 generally provides for recovery of attorney's fees at "prevailing market rates," it follows that fees for paralegal services must be recoverable at prevailing market rates as well.

The Government contends that our decision in *Jenkins* was driven by considerations arising from the different context in which the term "attorney's fee" was used in §1988. At the time *Jenkins* was decided, §1988 provided for the recovery of attorney's fees without reference to any other recoverable "expenses." The Government insists that *Jenkins* found paralegal fees recoverable under the guise of "attorney's fee[s]" because otherwise paralegal fees would not be recoverable at all. Since EAJA expressly permits recovery (albeit at "cost") for items other than attorney, agent, and expert witness fees, the Government sees no reason to give EAJA the broad construction that *Jenkins* gave §1988.

The Government's rationale for distinguishing *Jenkins* finds no support either in our opinion there or in our subsequent decisions. Our opinion in *Jenkins* expressed no apprehension at the possibility that a contrary decision would leave the claimant empty-handed. This omission is unsurprising, since our decision in *Jenkins* did not rest on the conviction that recovery at market rates was better than nothing. Our decision rested instead on the proposition — a proposition we took as "self-evident" — that the term "attorney's fee" had historically included fees for paralegal services.

Indeed, the Government's interpretation of *Jenkins* was rejected by this Court just two years after *Jenkins* was handed down. . . .

The Government parries this textual and doctrinal analysis with legislative history and public policy. We are not persuaded by either. . . . We find the Government's policy rationale for recovery at attorney cost likewise unpersuasive. The Government argues that market-based recovery would distort litigant incentives because EAJA would cap paralegal and attorney's fees at the same rate. See 5 U.S.C. §504(b)(1)(A) ("[A]ttorney or agent fees shall not be awarded in excess of $125 per hour unless the agency determines by regulation that an increase in the cost of living or a special factor, such as the limited availability of qualified attorneys or agents for the proceedings involved, justifies a higher fee."). The Government observes that paralegal rates are lower than rates for attorneys operating in the same market. If EAJA reimbursed both attorney time and paralegal time at market rates, then the cap would clip more off the top of the attorney's rates than the paralegal's rates. According to the Government, a market-based scheme would encourage litigants to shift an inefficient amount of attorney work to paralegals, since paralegal fees could be recovered at a greater percentage of their full market value.

The problem with this argument, as Richlin points out, is that it proves too much. The same reasoning would imply that agent fees should not be recoverable at market rates. If market-based recovery of paralegal time resulted in excessive reliance on paralegals, then market-based recovery of agent time should result in excessive reliance on agents. The same reasoning would also imply that fees for junior attorneys (who generally bill at lower rates than senior attorneys) should not be recoverable at market rates. . . . Yet despite the possibility that market-based recovery of attorney and agent fees would distort litigant incentives, §504 unambiguously authorizes awards of "reasonable attorney or agent fees . . . [at] prevailing market rates." 5 U.S.C. §504(b)(1)(A). The Government offers no persuasive reason why Congress would have treated paralegal fees any differently. . . .

We also question the practical feasibility of the Government's interpretation of the statute. The Board in this case relied on the Internet for data on paralegal salaries in the District of Columbia, but the Government fails to explain why a law firm's cost should be limited to salary. The benefits and perks with which a firm compensates its staff come out of the bottom line no less than salary. The Government has offered no solution to this accounting problem, and we do not believe that solutions are readily to be found. Market practice provides by far the more transparent basis for calculating a prevailing party's recovery under EAJA. It strains credulity that Congress would have abandoned this predictable, workable framework for the uncertain and complex accounting requirements that a cost-based rule would inflict on litigants, their attorneys, administrative agencies, and the courts. . . .

For these reasons, we hold that a prevailing party that satisfies EAJA's other requirements may recover its paralegal fees from the Government at prevailing market rates. The Board's contrary decision was error, and the Federal Circuit erred in affirming that decision. The judgment of the Federal Circuit is reversed, and this case is remanded for further proceedings consistent with this opinion.

It is so ordered.

Questions about the Case

1. What federal fee award statute is the subject of interpretation in this case? What fee award statute was the subject of *Missouri v. Jenkins?* How does the wording of the two statutes differ? Why is this wording important in this case?
2. What did the appellate court decide about the fees? No award? Award at cost? Award at market rate?
3. Explain the argument in favor of awarding paralegal fees as "expenses." What are three reasons that the Supreme Court does not agree with this interpretation?
4. What would have been the possible consequences for paralegals and law firms if the court had upheld the appellate court decision?

In this case, the Supreme Court of Oklahoma determined that attorney's fees may also include paralegal work and addressed the issues of the proper rate for paralegal time and of the nature of the work that is compensable.

Taylor v. Chubb

1994 Okla. 47, 874 P.2d 806 (Okla. 1994)

The United States District Court for the Northern District of Oklahoma certified questions of state law to this Court under the Oklahoma

Uniform Certification of Questions of Law Act, 20 O.S. 1991 §§1601, et seq. The federal court asks two interrelated questions:

(1) Whether the phrase "attorneys fees," when used in Oklahoma statutory or case law providing for the award of costs to a prevailing party, should be interpreted to encompass all work product of an attorney, including fees for services performed by legal assistants or paralegals?
(2) If the preceding question is answered in the affirmative, whether the decision of the Oklahoma Supreme Court should be applied retroactively to provide for the award of fees in the present litigation?

. . . The Taylors' attorney fee application included time charges for services performed by a legal assistant, who was designated by the National Association of Legal Assistants as a Certified Legal Assistant and Civil Litigation Specialist. The legal assistant's services were performed under the supervision of counsel, were non-clerical in nature, and provided meaningful support to counsel in his handling of the case. The Taylors' lawyers practice in Tulsa, where the prevailing community practice is for lawyers to bill legal assistant's time to clients.

I

We first consider whether charges for legal assistants' time are included in the term "attorney fees," as that term is used in 36 O.S. 1991 §3629.B. This is a question of first impression. . . .

The parties have stipulated that the legal assistant's services were valuable to the Taylors during the litigation. They have also stipulated that the "prevailing practice in the community is for attorneys to bill legal assistant or paralegal time to clients." Under these circumstances we see no reason to ignore such charges. We believe the legislature would have said so had it intended the term "attorney fees" to except charges for the time of legal assistants in communities where the "prevailing practice" is to charge for such time.

The United States Supreme Court considered this issue in *Missouri v. Jenkins*, 491 U.S. 274, 109 S. Ct. 2463, 105 L. Ed. 2d 229 (1989). Seven of the eight justices participating agreed that hourly charges for paralegals and law clerks must be considered in setting an attorney's fee under federal civil rights statutes. . . .

Separately charging for the time of legal assistants has grown in larger communities in response to clients' desire to keep the average hourly rate as low as possible, consistent with competent handling of cases. The U.S. Supreme Court said that to the extent fee applicants for statutory attorney's fees "are not permitted to bill for the work of paralegals at market rates, it would not be surprising to see a greater amount of such work performed by attorneys themselves, thus increasing the overall cost of litigation." *Missouri v. Jenkins*, 491 U.S. at 288. . . .

There is no reason to exclude charges for the time of legal assistants in computing statutorily mandated attorney fees where such charges are customarily made to clients and the legal assistant's services are useful to the client. A contrary holding would require us to assume that the legislature intended the term "attorney fee" to mean something different from the meaning that the stipulation of the parties shows attorneys and clients give it. This we decline to do.

Our holding today, that the time of paralegals is properly includable as a component to be considered in the trial court's assessment of the total value of services rendered, is limited to charges for work performed, *which otherwise would have had to have been performed by a licensed attorney at a higher rate*. There are several charges in the Taylors' attorneys' billings, however, that apparently fail to satisfy this requirement. The billings reflect a charge for the legal assistants' time in court at the same rate, $150.00 per hour, as the licensed attorney charged for his own time. Charges were made for time spent in copying documents and in doing other secretarial tasks, rather than substantive legal work. Such charges are *not* includable in attorneys fees awarded under §3629.B. The only charges for nonlawyers' time that properly fall within the definition of "attorney fees," under §3629.B are those that are clearly shown to have been made (1) for the delegated performance of substantive legal work, that (2) would otherwise have to be performed by a lawyer, (3) at a rate higher than that charged for the nonlawyers' time. . . .

As its pattern of proof, a party seeking attorney fees must plead and prove that the charges made for non-lawyer's time covered work that a lawyer would have had to perform but for the performance of such services by a legal assistant. In addition, the total charges made for the legal assistant's services must be less than the total charges would have been, had a lawyer performed the services.

Among other tasks, a legal assistant may:

- interview clients
- draft pleadings and other documents
- carry on legal research, both conventional and computer aided
- research public records
- prepare discovery requests and responses
- schedule depositions and prepare notices and subpoenas
- summarize depositions and other discovery responses
- coordinate and manage document production
- locate and interview witnesses
- organize pleadings, trial exhibits, and other documents
- prepare witness and exhibit lists
- prepare trial notebooks
- prepare for the attendance of witnesses at trial
- assist lawyers at trials

II

. . . Here, our conclusion that the term "attorney fees" includes time charges for legal assistants represents only a clarification of the law, not a change. Our holding is supported by the overwhelming weight of authority. Thus, today's pronouncement changes no preexisting rule of Oklahoma law. We see no reason to apply it prospectively only. We therefore answer yes to Certified Question number (2).

CERTIFIED QUESTIONS ANSWERED.

Questions about the Case

1. What were the credentials of the legal assistant whose time was at issue in this case?
2. What is the prevailing practice of attorneys in Oklahoma concerning billing of paralegal time?
3. Does this court limit its decision to the particular fee award statute in this case? What other kinds of statutes have such provisions?
4. What limitations are placed by the court on compensation for paralegal time?
5. What are some of the tasks that the court acknowledges that legal assistants perform?
6. What should paralegal rates be relative to attorney rates?
7. Does the court find this decision to be a "change" in the law? How does the court describe the ruling?

In upholding an attorney's fee award that included fees for paralegal time, the Washington Appeals Court sets forth a good set of criteria that courts should look to in evaluating whether the paralegal time is compensable.

Absher Construction Co. v. Kent School District

79 Wash. App. 841, 905 P.2d 1229 (1995)

. . . The appellants sued Kent for amounts they claimed were owing under a public works contract, approximately \$205,000. Kent won on summary judgment and was awarded \$34,648.86 in fees and costs. Kent also prevailed on appeal and now seeks an additional \$36,911.54 in fees and costs. The basis for the award is RCW 39.04.240.

The fee request includes time for the following individuals:

(1) A partner in practice for 20 years billed 104.2 hours at \$225.00 per hour (\$23,445);

(2) A fourth-year associate billed 53.1 hours at $130.00 per hour ($6,903);
(3) A sixth-year associate billed 4.5 hours at $155.00 per hour ($697.50);
(4) A legal assistant billed 39.5 hours at $67.00 per hour ($2,646.50);
(5) A legal editor billed 4 hours at $62.00 per hour ($248); and
(6) A legal clerk billed 8.5 hours at $35.00 per hour ($297.50).

The latter three are not attorneys.

No case in Washington specifically addresses whether the time of non-lawyer personnel may be included in an attorney fee award.

We find persuasive the reasoning of the Arizona court in *Continental Townhouses East Unit One Ass'n v. Brockbank*, 152 Ariz. 537, 733 P.2d 1120, 73 A.L.R. 4th 921 (1986). Properly employed and supervised non-lawyer personnel can decrease litigation expense. Lawyers should not be forced to perform legal tasks solely so that their time may be compensable in an attorney fee award.

The question then becomes what sort of work performed by non-lawyer personnel is compensable. Regardless of the name given to the category of person who performs the work, we believe, as did the Arizona court, that the definition of legal assistant formulated by the American Bar Association Standing Committee on Legal Assistants provides appropriate guidance. . . .

The following criteria will be relevant in determining whether such services should be compensated: (1) the services performed by the non-lawyer personnel must be legal in nature; (2) the performance of these services must be supervised by an attorney; (3) the qualifications of the person performing the services must be specified in the request for fees in sufficient detail to demonstrate that the person is qualified by virtue of education, training, or work experience to perform substantive legal work; (4) the nature of the services performed must be specified in the request for fees in order to allow the reviewing court to determine that the services performed were legal rather than clerical; (5) as with attorney time, the amount of time expended must be set forth and must be reasonable; and (6) the amount charged must reflect reasonable community standards for charges by that category of personnel. . . .

Employing these criteria, we allow only part of the fees requested for the legal assistant's services. He has requested compensation for preparing pleadings for duplication, preparing and delivering copies, requesting copies, and obtaining and delivering a docket sheet. We do not view this time as work which falls within these guidelines. We do allow an award for time spent preparing the briefs and related work. In computing the time we allow for him, we will assume, absent any other evidence in the record, that the hourly rate of $67.00 is reasonable for this type of work. We allow an award of $2,110.50 for 31.5 hours. We allow the recovery of fees for the time claimed by the legal editor for verifying citations and quotations. We disallow the time claimed for the legal clerk, which appears to consist primarily of obtaining copies of pleadings and organizing working copies of the pleadings. . . .

In sum, we conclude that the fees of nonlawyer personnel may be properly requested as part of an attorney fee award. In this case, applying the factors and considerations listed above, we award $23,055.50 plus $1,633.74 as a reasonable attorney fee on appeal, together with $134.65 costs on appeal.

Questions about the Case

1. What were the titles, duties, and rates of the persons for whom this law firm sought compensation in this case? Which were lawyers and which were nonlawyers?
2. On what reasoning does the court rely in interpreting the statute to include paralegal time in attorney fee awards?
3. What are the criteria that a court should use in determining if the award should cover the paralegal time? Are these criteria the same as those noted in other cases in this chapter?
4. What paralegal time is allowed and disallowed in this case, and why?
5. Is the time of the "legal editor" compensated, and why?
6. What does the court decide about the time of the "legal clerk"?
7. Do the job titles of the nonlawyers in this case reflect accurately what these persons do? Are these common job titles in your community?

In the following case, defendants seek a reduction of an attorney's fee award based on several grounds pertinent to paralegals, including what is the proper rate, whether the work is professional work that should be compensated, and whether the work is duplicative.

New Mexico Citizens for Clean Air and Water v. Espanola Mercantile Co.

72 F.3d 830 (10th Cir. 1996)

. . . This is an action to enforce the Clean Water Act against defendant for unpermitted discharges and other violations at the Espanola Transit Mix Facility in Espanola, New Mexico. Plaintiff New Mexico Citizens for Clean Air and Water is an environmental group and plaintiff Pueblo of San Juan is an Indian tribe that owns the affected land. . . .

The consent decree further provided in pertinent part: "Defendant stipulates that it is not entitled to an award of attorneys fees. Plaintiffs shall submit their petition for attorneys fees within twenty (20) days after entry of this Consent Decree. Defendant agrees to pay attorney fees awarded to Plaintiffs by the Court."

After both plaintiffs submitted requests, the district court awarded $46,003.69 in fees and costs. Defendant appeals the award. . . .

The Defendant's first challenge to the amount of fees awarded concerns the district court's failure to consider whether any modification of the lodestar figure should be made based on Citizens' limited success in the action. In the district court, defendant argued that plaintiffs were not as successful as they had portrayed themselves to be in their fee petition. . . .

Defendant raises numerous other challenges to the amount of fees awarded, some of which were not specifically raised in the district court. Only three of these other objections merit consideration by the district court on remand.

The first is the defendant's contention that attorney Eric Ames improperly billed attorney rates for tasks that either could have been performed by someone other than an attorney or that are not properly compensable at any rate. Specifically, defendant objects to paying attorney rates for time spent investigating the factual basis for Citizens' claims and time spent performing what defendant characterizes as secretarial duties, e.g., copying documents, faxing documents, and filing documents.

"[W]hen a lawyer spends time on tasks that are easily delegable to non-professional assistance, legal service rates are not applicable." *Halderman ex rel. Halderman v. Pennhurst State Sch. & Hosp.*, 49 F.3d 939, 942 (3d Cir. 1995); see also *Ursic v. Bethlehem Mines*, 719 F.2d 670, 677 (3d Cir. 1983) ("Nor do we approve the wasteful use of highly skilled and highly priced talent for matters easily delegable to non-professionals or less experienced associates. . . . A Michelangelo should not charge Sistine Chapel rates for painting a farmer's barn."); *Mares*, 801 F.2d at 1204 (criticizing fees for messenger services).

Although commenting that Ames was not entitled to compensation for at least one secretarial task — organizing files — the district court's opinion does not reflect whether it carefully scrutinized some of the other seemingly secretarial work Ames performed. Further, the opinion does not reflect consideration of the defendant's argument that a paralegal or investigator could have performed much, if not all, of the factual investigation of Citizens' claims. We express no opinion as to whether any of the challenged time is properly compensable at attorney rates, but commend the matter to the district court's attention on remand.

The second matter the district court should consider is the potential duplication of effort. Defendant contends that the attendance of two attorneys for Citizens at various meetings was not necessary, and that only one attorney's time should be billed. While we have "decline[d] to require an automatic reduction of reported hours to adjust for multiple representation," we have advised district courts to "give particular attention to the possibility of duplication." *Ramos*, 713 F.2d at 554.

Here, the district court did consider whether the two attorneys properly billed for conferences with each other, but the opinion does not disclose whether the judge also considered potential duplication of effort by the attorneys when meeting with others, such as the plaintiffs, defense counsel, or the court. On remand, the district court should give attention to the possibility of duplication in these meetings as well.

Finally, defendant contends, and Citizens concedes, that the district court failed to eliminate all the time billed by counsel for communications with the press. The district court stated its intention to eliminate all time spent on press-related matters, except time spent in preparing a post-settlement press release, but the court overlooked some press-related billing entries in its reduction of counsel's fees. See *Halderman*, 49 F.3d at 942 ("[T]he proper forum for litigation is the courtroom, not the media."). On remand, the court should reduce the fee award accordingly.

The judgment of the United States District Court for the District of New Mexico is REVERSED, and the matter is REMANDED. . . .

Questions about the Case

1. What federal statute authorized the attorney's fee award in this case?
2. What does the court say about lowering the fee because the plaintiffs were not completely successful?
3. Is it proper to charge attorney rates for copying, filing, and faxing? What did the trial court decide?
4. Should a fee award include compensation for all the persons attending meetings?
5. Should a fee award cover the time spent communicating with the press?
6. What does the case tell you about how to prepare or dispute a fee petition?

In this case, brought under federal ERISA law, the attorney fee award was deemed excessive on several grounds, including the charging of lawyers' fee rates for paralegal work.

Mogck v. UNUM Life Ins. Co. of America

Case No. 99-CV-0201 LSP
(U.S.D.C., S.D. Cal. 2003)

Plaintiff Kenneth Mogck has filed a motion for attorneys' fees and costs in the above-captioned matter. The Court has considered the arguments raised in the briefs and finds the matter suitable for decision without oral argument. See S.D. Cal. Civ. R. 7.1(d)(1). . . .

The facts underlying this lawsuit arise from a March 25, 1993 motor vehicle accident in which Plaintiff sustained serious injuries. At the time of the accident, Plaintiff was insured for long term disability benefits under an insurance policy issued by Defendant UNUM Life Insurance Company of America. Defendant paid Plaintiff occupational long term disability benefits for two years, from June 25, 1993 to June 25, 1995, and then terminated payment by letter dated June 1, 1995. The letter explained that Defendant would not extend benefits past June 25, 1995 as Defendant had determined that Plaintiff no longer met the definition of disability.

After pursuing administrative remedies, Plaintiff filed suit against Defendant on February 5, 1999. Defendant contended that Plaintiff's action was untimely. The parties filed cross-motions for summary adjudication on the statute of limitations issue. Magistrate Judge Cynthia G. Aaron, finding that Plaintiff's action was contractually barred by the three-year time limitation set forth in Defendant's policy, issued an order on September 22, 2000 granting Defendant's motion for summary adjudication and denying Plaintiff's motion for partial summary adjudication. Plaintiff appealed. On June 10, 2002, the Ninth Circuit issued a published opinion reversing and remanding the case for further proceedings. See Mogck v. UNUM Life Ins. Co. of America, 292 F.3d 1025 (9th Cir. 2002). The appeals court disagreed with this Court's determination that Defendant's June 1, 1995 letter constituted an adequate "request for proof" under the policy, and found that Defendant thus "never took the steps necessary to trigger the running of the contractual time limitation under the policy." *Mogck*, 292 F.3d at 1028. Accordingly, the Ninth Circuit held that Plaintiff's action was not time-barred. Id. at 1029.

On remand, the parties participated in a Settlement Conference . . . , which resulted in a settlement agreement dated November 13, 2002. The terms of the settlement included separate lump-sum payments to Plaintiff and Plaintiff's attorneys' firm, Miller, Monson. (Settlement Agreement and Release of Claims at 1.) The parties and Magistrate Judge Stiven agreed that Plaintiff's request for statutory attorneys' fees and costs would be submitted to the Court by formal motion. . . .

The long term disability contract at issue in this case is governed by the Employee Retirement Income Security Act of 1974 (ERISA), 29 U.S.C. §1001 *et seq.* In an ERISA action, a court in its discretion may award attorneys' fees and costs to either party. . . .

Defendant did demonstrate bad faith in its handling of Plaintiff's disability claim. As Defendant points out, however, the parties never litigated the merits of Plaintiff's claim, and thus the propriety of Defendant's claims decision was never adjudicated. Accordingly, the Court does not find evidence that Defendant acted in bad faith in this matter. This factor weighs against awarding attorneys' fees to Plaintiff. . . . Defendant concedes that it has the ability to satisfy a fee award. Thus, this factor weighs in favor of awarding attorneys' fees to Plaintiff. . . .

[Deterrence as a] factor requires the Court to consider whether an award of fees against Defendant would deter others from similar conduct in the future. The Court finds that this factor weighs neither in favor of nor against an award of attorneys' fees to Plaintiff. . . . Although Plaintiff brought this suit to benefit himself, the Court agrees that Plaintiff's suit, and appeal, could benefit ERISA plan participants and beneficiaries by helping to resolve contractual statute of limitations and contractual language interpretation issues. . . . Therefore, this factor weighs in favor of awarding attorneys' fees to Plaintiff. . . . [T]his Court exercises its discretion and awards Plaintiff his reasonable attorneys' fees as set forth below. . . .

Plaintiff requests fees in the amount of $351,217.20, consisting of 175.3 hours of work by Attorney Monson at $350.00 per hour, 868.8 hours of work by Attorney Horner at $325.00 per hour, 63.6 hours of paralegal time at $65.00 per hour, and 153.1 hours of secretary time at $22.00 per hour. In addition, Plaintiff seeks additional fees for "approximately two days' work" to compensate Plaintiff for filing the reply and objections to evidence regarding the instant motion, as well as for three hours spent reviewing the papers for confidential information and resubmitting the reply brief. Defendant contends that the amount of fees sought [is] "excessive and patently unreasonable."

Attorneys' fees in ERISA actions are calculated using a hybrid lodestar/multiplier approach. [Citation omitted.] The court first determines the "lodestar" amount by multiplying the number of hours reasonably expended on the litigation by a reasonable hourly rate. The party seeking a fee award must submit evidence supporting the hours worked and the rate claimed. The court may then adjust the lodestar upward or downward using a "multiplier" based on factors not subsumed in the initial calculation of the lodestar. . . .

Plaintiff claims that his attorneys are entitled to recover the "market rates" of $350.00 per hour for Monson and $325.00 per hour for Horner. In support of his claim, Plaintiff submits declarations from eight ERISA attorneys who practice in the Ninth Circuit to demonstrate that Monson's and Horner's actual fees of $295.00 and $250.00, respectively, are below prevailing market rates. Defendant argues that Plaintiff's counsels' normal hourly rates, not the "market rates," should be used. . . .

[T]he Court finds that the rates of $350.00 per hour for Monson and $325.00 per hour for Horner are reasonable attorneys' rates in this case. Monson's and Horner's actual rates indeed appear to be *below* prevailing market rates. Although the Court recognizes that the "relevant community," when determining appropriate attorneys' rates, is generally the one in which the district court sits [citations omitted], it is appropriate to consider the declarations of attorneys in other jurisdictions because ERISA cases involve a national standard, and attorneys practicing ERISA law in the Ninth Circuit tend to practice in different districts. Furthermore, the Court observes that ERISA cases are often considered to be complex, ERISA plaintiff cases are often undesirable, and Plaintiff's attorneys possess extensive experience in ERISA law. . . .

In determining reasonable hours, the party requesting fees bears the burden of submitting detailed time records justifying the hours claimed to have been expended. [Citation omitted.] Those hours may be reduced by the court where documentation of the hours is inadequate, if the case was overstaffed and hours are duplicated, or if the hours expended are deemed excessive or otherwise unnecessary. . . .

[The court reviewed the hours to determine if they were excessive and declined to reduce the hours except for the time spent by one lawyer listening to the oral arguments. The court also denied the Defendant's request to deny fees for all "block-billed" entries.]

Defendant argues that Horner's billing of 77.8 hours to prepare a chronology of documents in this case should be billed at Miller, Monson's $65.00 per hour paralegal rate rather than Horner's attorney rate. Attorney Horner describes the preparation of the chronology as "reviewing of the documents and selecting the pertinent facts and information." The Court agrees that this is a paralegal task. "[W]hen a lawyer spends time on tasks that are easily delegable to non-professional assistance, legal service rates are not applicable." New Mexico Citizens for Clean Air and Water v. Espanola Mercantile Co., Inc., 72 F.3d 830, 835 (10th Cir. 1996). However, the Court finds that Horner spent 49.6 hours, not 77.8 hours, on the chronology. Thus, the Court reduces the fee award by $12,896.00 (49.6 hours × $260 per hour).

In addition to preparing a chronology, Horner engaged in other tasks that would have been easily delegable to either a paralegal or secretary. For example, on 9/7/00, Horner billed .1 hours to "Calendar rescheduled pre-trial conference." On 12/17/01, she billed for calling the Ninth Circuit regarding "page limit and style and cover color." And, on 11/14/01, Horner's billing entry included making "reservations for travel to Pasadena." Other paralegal/secretarial tasks billed for by Horner include creating files, reorganizing files, preparing tables of contents and tables of authorities, and preparing indexes. . . . Therefore, the Court reduces Horner's requested hours by 3%. . . .

Fees for secretarial time may be included in an award for attorneys' fees. See, e.g., D'Emanuele v. Montgomery Ward & Co., Inc., 904 F.2d 1379, 1387 (9th Cir. 1990), *overruled on other grounds by* Burlington v. Dague, 505 U.S. 557 (1992). However, like attorney time, secretarial time must be sufficiently documented. *D'Emanuele*, 904 F.2d at 1387. Miller, Monson's billing entries for secretarial time do not include any information describing the tasks performed. Although Attorney Monson provides a general description of the secretarial tasks performed, including "telephone contact[s] . . . , assisting attorneys and paralegals with finalizing and filing of motion papers, typing letters . . . , and contact with the client," this generalized description provides insufficient support for the secretarial fees requested. Thus, the Court reduces the requested secretarial fees by 25%.

Although not raised by Defendant, the Court finds that there are additional reasons to reduce Plaintiff's attorneys' bills. First, the Court finds that Monson and Horner billed an inordinate amount of time for interoffice conferences. In reviewing Miller, Monson's bills, the Court has noted numerous occasions in which Attorneys Monson and Horner consulted and coordinated with one another. Although it has been recognized that "the participation of more than one attorney does not necessarily constitute an unnecessary duplication of effort" [citation omitted], the Court believes that Monson and Horner inappropriately billed for communicating with one another and delegating tasks to office personnel. . . . This Court doubts that Miller, Monson would have charged Plaintiff for all of Monson's and Horner's consultations with one another (it is not Plaintiff's [nor Defendant's] fault that Miller, Monson chose to staff the case with two attorneys), and thus, as discussed further below, Plaintiff's requested attorney hours will be reduced accordingly.

Additionally, the Court finds that Monson's and Horner's billing entries reflect, at times, double-billing and/or a duplication of effort. For example, on 2/21/00, Monson and Horner each billed for reviewing Defendant's objection to Plaintiff's expert designation. On 6/10/02 and 6/11/02, Monson and Horner each billed for reviewing the Ninth Circuit's opinion in this case. On 11/5/02, both attorneys billed for reviewing Magistrate Judge Stiven's settlement recommendation. These entries provide further support for a reduction in Plaintiff's requested attorney hours, as these hours were not "reasonably expended." [Citation omitted.]

Finally, the Court notes that some of Plaintiff's attorneys' billing entries were vague and thus do not support the hours claimed. See, e.g., 2/10/00 billing entry for "continued work on case." See also 2/21/01 billing entry for "research of issues." Additionally, Plaintiff's attorneys billed for correcting errors previously made. See, e.g., 5/10/01 billing entry, in which Horner billed 2.1 hours for "Telephone call from Mr. Wong at 9th Circuit re: font in footnotes; call to office; review for corrections and review brief format and pagination." Defendant should not be required to pay for Plaintiff's attorneys to fix their own errors.

Pursuant to the above, the Court reduces Monson's and Horner's requested hours by 10% each. . . .

For the reasons set forth above, this Court hereby **GRANTS IN PART** Plaintiff's Motion for Attorneys' Fees and Costs. The Court awards Plaintiff $285,869.00 in attorneys' fees (151.8 hours at $350 per hour for Monson, 755.8 hours at $325 per hour for Horner, minus $12,896.00), $4,134.00 in paralegal fees (63.6 hours at $65.00 per hour), $2,525.60 in secretarial fees (114.8 hours at $22.00 per hour), and $3,246.39 in costs for a total of $295,774.99. . . .

Questions about the Case

1. How did the case get to this point? Did the plaintiffs go to trial and prevail?
2. The court initially analyzes whether attorneys' fees are appropriate. What kinds of factors does the court consider? What did it decide about the fairness of awarding fees?
3. What is the lodestar method? Did the court find the rates reasonable?
4. What tasks did the attorney Horner perform that the court found to be paralegal tasks? Do you agree with this finding? What was the consequence of this finding in terms of the fee award?
5. What does this court say about fee awards for secretarial time?
6. The court reduces the award for inter-office conferences and communications among lawyers and with staff. Do you think it is common practice to bill clients for these communications? If so, is it fair for the court to reduce the fee award given that the fees are based on market rates?
7. Do you agree that fees should not be awarded for time spent correcting the law firm's mistakes?

In this bankruptcy matter, the court lowers the rate of compensation to match the work that was performed, providing an incentive to firms to utilize the services of paralegals to do work that does not require the application of an attorney's knowledge, skill, and judgment.

In re Music Merchants, Inc.

208 B.R. 944 (9th Cir. BAP 1997)

. . . In July, 1987, Music Merchants, Inc. filed bankruptcy under chapter 11. In April, 1988, the U.S. Trustee appointed a creditors' committee, and a few weeks later, appellant T. Edward Malpass ("Malpass") was appointed its counsel. . . .

Following the hearing, by memorandum opinion entered on February 12, 1996, the trial court granted the motion for reconsideration and allowed Malpass approximately $13,000 in additional fees from the second interim and final fee applications but again denied enhancement of the award to compensate for delay in payment. . . .

Malpass timely filed a motion for alteration of the court's order, asserting that the court erred when it disallowed certain fees and refused to enhance the award to compensate for delays caused in part by Malpass's appeal of the court's erroneous ruling. The court denied this request on March 29, 1996 and Malpass filed this timely appeal. . . .

Although Malpass cites several alleged errors on the part of the trial court, he principally argues that "reasonable compensation must contain an enhancement to compensate for unreasonable delays in payment." Malpass states that "case law, including Ninth Circuit decisions . . . makes it clear that a reasonable attorney's fee is obtained only when payment is received within the time payment is normally received by similarly skilled professionals practicing in other areas of the law" and, therefore, calculation of Malpass's fee "must take into account whether payment has been delayed such that enhancement is necessary." . . .

None of the cases cited by Malpass supports his argument that enhancement is required by law. . . .

Malpass argues that the trial court erred when it deducted fees based upon Malpass's failure "to properly utilize junior associates or paralegals for less sophisticated legal tasks." Malpass claims that his firm's paralegals were not sophisticated litigation paralegals and were unable to perform the services he performed. Malpass argued below that he should not be penalized because he is a sole practitioner. Malpass also states that the trial court did not point to a specific instance in which a paralegal was available to perform particular services.

Malpass misperceives the trial court's ruling. Although the trial court reasoned that certain tasks could have been performed by a paralegal, it also stated: "Even if he did not have any other staff members capable of performing less sophisticated legal tasks, Malpass is still not entitled to bill at a partner's rate for such work." The court, therefore, reduced Malpass's hourly rate from $195 to $125 for specific tasks "which could have been performed by a paralegal or a junior associate." Although the court did not state that a paralegal could have performed the specified tasks, the court listed the amount by which it would reduce the fee request. Malpass does not argue that the court is prohibited from reducing the fee award for work that could have been performed by a lower paid professional. Therefore, Malpass has not shown that the trial court abused its discretion on this issue. . . .

Malpass has litigated for the fees requested for more than eight years. Malpass acknowledges that "the amounts involved are relatively small," but he claims that "resolution [of the appeal] involves several important issues which are apparently open in the Ninth Circuit." However, Malpass has not shown that the trial court abused its discretion when it refused to enhance Malpass's fee for delay in payment or when it denied certain requested fees. Therefore, the trial court is AFFIRMED.

Questions about the Case

1. Under what kind of statute did the court award attorney's fees in this case?
2. Does this court believe that an "enhancement" of the fee is called for? Why, or why not?

3. On what ground had the lower court deducted fees? What does this court decide about that matter?
4. Does this court require lawyers to employ paralegals?
5. How could an attorney who does not use the services of paralegals prevent a reduction in fees such as the one in this case?

This case is an example of how the federal courts examine a fee petition that includes a substantial amount of paralegal time. Note the several issues regarding the status and qualifications of the paralegal, the appropriate market rate, and the nature of work that will be compensated in a fee award.

Kooritzky v. Herman

6 F. Supp. 2d 13 (D.C. 1998)

A Memorandum and Order . . . resolved the majority of issues in plaintiff's long-pending fee application, and invited the parties to provide further information pertaining to the single outstanding issue—compensation for services provided by paralegal James Moore. . . .

Defendant continues to insist that plaintiff is not entitled to any compensation for hours worked by Moore. This issue was addressed and resolved by the Court. . . . To buttress her argument, defendant now points to a rule of the Virginia Supreme Court pertaining to court appearances by third-year law students. This rule is entirely irrelevant to the present situation, where Moore made no court appearances on behalf of the plaintiff. The record contains no indication that Moore held himself out . . . as a practicing attorney; on the contrary, plaintiff's claim . . . is that Moore provided paralegal services. The Court is not aware of any law in either Virginia or the District of Columbia which prohibits law students from working as paralegals, and accepting compensation for such work. . . .

The . . . Memorandum found that plaintiff was eligible to be compensated for the work performed by legal assistant Thomas Moore, but not at the $75 per hour rate requested in his fee petition. . . . Accordingly, an accompanying Order invited the parties to submit ". . . evidence relevant to the 'prevailing market rate' at which legal assistants working as independent contractors in the Washington, D.C. area are compensated."

. . . Moore came to Kooritzky's "team" with 30 years of service in the Department of Transportation. He had retired as Chief of the Tariff Division of the Department as a GS-15. Over those years he claims to have become "proficient and knowledgeable with the APA." . . . [S]ince Moore's retirement he has "read law" in preparation for the Virginia bar exam and in 1996 sat for it; there is no indication of the result.

Plaintiff proffers two types of evidence about the market rates of fees payable to independent contractor paralegals, as distinguished from the

$75 per hour charged by the Teras firm. First, Moore's affidavit states that he recently surveyed eight area firms which specialize in providing paralegals or consultants on a contract basis to assist with APA litigation. According to Moore, the "market rates quoted ranged between [$20 and $35] per hour depending on experience." Moore also surveyed three Washington, D.C. law firms, which were "willing to pay between [$45 and $55] per hour for a paralegal/legal assistant or consultant with a substantial knowledge of the APA and some knowledge of litigating APA cases. . . .

Second, . . . Moore was paid by his firm "to review and prepare a report on a Notice of Proposed Rulemaking issued by the Department of Transportation" at a rate of $50 per hour.

In addition, . . . plaintiff and Moore have offered several somewhat inconsistent versions of their original understanding about Moore's compensation. . . . [The range of compensation, depending on the version of the understanding, was $37 to $60 an hour.]

The defendant submits the current Register of Wage Determination . . . [which] includes four types of paralegal positions, . . . whose hourly wages range from $13.22 to $24.95. . . . Judicial notice is taken. . . .

"[A] fee applicant's burden in establishing a reasonable hourly rate entails a showing of at least three elements: . . . billing practices; . . . skill, experience and reputation; and the prevailing market rates in the relevant community. [Citation omitted.] . . .

The record does not indicate that Moore has had enough experience as an independent contractor paralegal to acquire a "reputation" within the private sector. However, his limited paralegal experience . . . is balanced by his excessive experience with agency rulemaking under the APA. . . . Thus no special adjustment to Moore's hourly rate—either upward [or] downward—is warranted. . . .

Assessing the "prevailing market rate" for Moore's services is difficult, where the market at issue—that for independent contractor paralegals—is ill-defined and unfamiliar. . . .

[T]he "prevailing market rate" for Moore's services to plaintiff appears to lie somewhere between $20.62 and $50.00 per hour. Both the pay scales offered by the government and the firm surveys by Moore suggest that the most important factor in determining the pay of any individual paralegal is experience. In this case, at the time Moore undertook his work for plaintiff, he had no previous experience as a paralegal, and thus none of the litigation support skills—e.g., organizing large numbers of documents, cite-checking, knowledge of court procedures—which command a premium. At the same time, Moore's extensive prior experience in government is not only an indicator of reliability and competence, but gave him familiarity with the Administrative Procedures Act which was undoubtedly useful in his work for plaintiff. . . . [T]he direct evidence yields a finding that Moore should be compensated at the rate of $35.00 per hour, i.e., in the middle of the range. . . .

[T]he next question is to determine the number of hours expended by Moore for which plaintiff is reasonably entitled to compensation. . . . As indicated in the . . . Memorandum, time spend on clerical tasks, including the filing of documents with the Court, does not constitute compensable legal work. . . . [The court reduced the compensable time by 63 hours for clerical tasks.]

Moore's time records were a significant focus of the evidentiary hearings. . . . In his Report & Recommendations, Magistrate Judge Kay concluded: . . .

> The Court is constrained to observe that the cavalier manner [in which] Kooritzky kept time records was equally pervasive in his claim for hours worked by Moore. . . . [H]e failed to fully cure or explain the inaccuracies that pervade even his modified request for fees. For example, . . . the claim for Moore's fees contains a request for more hours worked during a three week period than there were actual hours in that period . . . ; a bill for 29 hours worked in a single day . . . ; a bill for 48 hours of work done on a pleading that had already been filed . . . ; a bill for 21 hours in a day working on a pleading. . . .

. . . Moore disputes the "inference" . . . that he was incapable of working 20-hour days . . . and offers documents that suggest that he had a history of working long hours. . . . However, this fact alone is not sufficient to justify compensating plaintiff for all hours claimed for Moore. First, plaintiff must support his fee request with detailed information, based on "contemporaneous, completed, and standardized time records which accurately reflect the work done. . . ." [Citation omitted.] . . . [T]he claim for Moore's fees falls short of this standard, thus requiring the fact finder to discount some of the hours claimed due to insufficient documentation. Second, even if plaintiff's application were technically impeccable, and even if Moore is assumed to have worked all of the hours claimed, plaintiff would not be automatically entitled to compensation for all hours billed: the Court must still make a determination that those hours represent "time reasonably expended."

In other instances, Moore's undisputed dedication to plaintiff's case appears itself to have resulted in excess hours. . . .

Moore's hours for the period 1991 through 1995 should be reduced by the same percentage by which plaintiff's own hours were ultimately reduced: 54%.

Questions about the Case

1. What were the qualifications of the paralegal in this case? If paralegals were regulated, do you think that Moore would have qualified as a paralegal? Did Moore's status as an independent contractor make any difference to the court?

2. What were the two areas of inquiry about the fee award for the paralegal's time?
3. What evidence was provided by the parties about the compensation of paralegals in this area of the country? What kind of evidence could you provide for your locale if you were doing such a fee petition?
4. What factors did the court consider in setting the hourly rate that the plaintiff's counsel would get for Moore's time?
5. Do you think the court set the fee correctly? What was the difference in the rate requested and the rate that the firm got?
6. In what two ways did the court reduce the time for which fees would be awarded? Why? Do you agree? Was the reduction substantial?
7. How should you avoid having fees cut this way?

In the following case, the Iowa Supreme Court strikes down a cap on paralegal fees that is based on a statutory cap on fees for lawyers.

GreatAmerica Leasing v. Cool Comfort Air Conditioning and Refrigeration, Inc.

691 N.W.2d 730 (Iowa 2005)

GreatAmerica Leasing Corporation sued Cool Comfort Air Conditioning and Refrigeration, Inc., after Cool Comfort breached a lease for a telephone system. GreatAmerica was partially successful in the suit and obtained a judgment against Cool Comfort for a little less than $17,000.

Pursuant to a fee-shifting clause in the parties' written contract, GreatAmerica asked the district court to require Cool Comfort to reimburse it approximately $35,000 for attorney fees it had expended in the suit. This request included about $5000 in litigation expenses for paralegal work. In support of its motion, GreatAmerica attached a copy of a bill it had received from its law firm. The bill indicated the firm had charged GreatAmerica $80 per hour for paralegal work. Cool Comfort resisted GreatAmerica's motion for attorney fees. Cool Comfort argued GreatAmerica should not recover expenses that were unsuccessful.

The district court granted GreatAmerica almost $19,000 in attorney fees. The district court awarded GreatAmerica less than it had requested for two reasons. First, the court noted GreatAmerica was only partially successful in the suit. For this reason, the court nearly halved the award. [Citations omitted.] Second, the court subtracted an additional $1880 from the amount GreatAmerica had claimed in litigation expenses for paralegal work. The court stated it was

> troubled that regular, licensed attorneys defending felony defendants in criminal cases in Iowa are paid only $50 an hour for what can be more

> complex litigation [that requires] a license to practice law with substantial trial ability and experience. In this court's view, a paralegal fee assessed against another party should not exceed what the State of Iowa pays for indigent defense. . . . Because no evidence rebuts the necessity of the hours devoted to the case, this court will not reduce the number of hours compensated. However, the award will be at the rate of $50 per hour.

GreatAmerica appealed the district court's award of attorney fees. It challenges only the reduction in litigation expenses due to the capping of the paralegal's hourly rate. Cool Comfort did not cross-appeal and has not filed a brief in this matter. . . .

The sole issue is whether the district court abused its discretion in reducing the amount of attorney fees for GreatAmerica's litigation expenses. We begin with the Iowa Code, which provides:

> When judgment is recovered upon a written contract containing an agreement to pay an attorney's fee, the court shall allow and tax as a part of the costs a reasonable attorney's fee to be determined by the court.

Iowa Code section 625.22 (2003).

A reasonable attorney fee is not limited to the hourly fee charged by lawyers. The concept includes certain litigation expenses, including the cost of paralegals. See, e.g., *Schaffer v. Frank Moyer Constr., Inc.*, 628 N.W.2d 11, 23 (Iowa 2001) (litigation expenses, including the cost of hiring a paralegal, allowed as part of a reasonable attorney fee); [citations omitted]; cf. *Missouri v. Jenkins*, 491 U.S. 274, 284-89, 109 S. Ct. 2463, 2469-72, 105 L. Ed. 2d 229, 241-44 (1989) (construing 42 U.S.C. §1988 to permit reimbursement for paralegal expenses). The district court is considered an expert in what constitutes a reasonable attorney fee, and we afford it wide discretion in making its decision. [Citations omitted.] The district court should consider a number of factors, including:

> the time necessarily spent, the nature and extent of the service, the amount involved, the difficulty of handling and importance of the issues, the responsibility assumed and results obtained, the standing and experience of the attorney in the profession, and the customary charges for similar service.

The court also correctly recognized it was required to "look at the whole picture and, using independent judgment with the benefit of hindsight, decide on a total fee appropriate for handling the complete case." [Citation omitted.]

In its analysis, however, the district court did not consider the *Schaffer* factors nor look at the whole picture. Instead the court focused upon the fact that the State only pays some criminal defense attorneys

$50 per hour. . . . Although there is a blush of fairness in the district court's logic that paralegals should not earn more than attorneys, this analysis ignores the fact that the markets for criminal defense attorneys and paralegals in civil litigation are different. To the extent the district court adopted a per se rule capping all pay for paralegals at $50 per hour, the court abused its discretion. Iowa Code section 625.22 contains no such requirement, and to the extent the district court invented one its ruling was based on untenable grounds. Such a fixed policy is the antithesis of discretionary decision-making. [Citation omitted.]

The appropriate remedy is to reverse and remand for "a fresh consideration" of a reasonable attorney fee. [Citation omitted.] On remand, the court shall look at the whole picture and determine a reasonable amount for GreatAmerica's litigation expenses. The *Schaffer* factors, although explicitly designed for attorneys, apply by analogy. See *Cont'l Townhouses E. Unit One Ass'n v. Brockbank*, 152 Ariz. 537, 733 P.2d 1120, 1128 (Ct. App. 1986) ("The trial judge . . . may . . . consider the value of services rendered in a case by . . . paralegals, applying the same standards as are used in evaluating lawyers' time."). . . . [Citations omitted.] The fundamental question, however, is simply whether the claimed litigation expenses are reasonable and thus part of a reasonable attorney's fee. [Citation omitted.]

GreatAmerica bears the burden to prove its request was reasonable. [Citations omitted.] As framed in this case, the crux of the dispute revolves around the paralegal's hourly rate. On remand, the district court will have to determine whether $80 per hour is consistent with market rates and practices for similar work in the community. . . . [Citations omitted.] The market rate for the paralegal's services is not necessarily the rate of pay plaintiff's counsel billed its client. Billing sheets provided by the firm, although little evidence of the prevailing rate of pay for similarly situated paralegals, may be considered by the court. [Citation omitted.] In this case GreatAmerica did not offer the district court any additional evidence. While such evidence is not necessary to prevail, . . . it would have helped the court reach a decision. . . . In its absence, the district court, as an expert in calculating the local going rate, may settle matters itself. . . .

Nothing in this opinion should be construed as an endorsement or rejection of any particular rate for reimbursement of paralegal expenses.

REVERSED AND REMANDED.

Questions about the Case

1. What was the basis for the limitation on the paralegal fees in the lower court case? Do you find this reasoning about the cap to be persuasive?
2. Why did this court reverse this decision?

3. How does the lower court reasoning conflict with the principles of *Missouri v. Jenkins*?
4. Compare the reasoning of the lower court with the reasoning of the court in the *Richlin* opinion concerning the cap on lawyer fees under EAJA. Do you understand the problem posed by these caps? How would you suggest that this issue be addressed so that it does not recur?

This case demonstrates how a court handles a petition for fees with issues relating to compensation for clerical tasks, the proper role for the paralegal, and the ethics of an unusual compensation plan.

In re Bass

227 B.R. 103 (E.D. Mich. 1998)

This matter is before the Court on the Chapter 13 trustee's objection to the fee applications of the Castle Law Office filed in these cases. The trustee filed a blanket objection covering approximately 100 fee applications. The trustee also raised a separate objection relating to Castle's method of compensating legal assistants. . . .

The trustee objects to charges for clerical functions under the categories of: calendar, corrections, type petition, correspondence and remind of appointments. The items for which Castle billed include: entering of information from questionnaires and notes into bankruptcy programs, preparation and printing of documents, docketing of dates, review of file, review of Trustee notices, verification of debtor addresses, and placing notices in file.

Clerical services should be included in office overhead and not billed separately to clients. [Citation omitted.] The time entries to which the trustee objects were for services performed by legal assistants. In *In re Bank of New England Corp.*, 134 B.R. 450 (Bankr. D. Mass. 1991), *aff'd*, 142 B.R. 584 (D. Mass. 1992), the court stated:

> The Court accepts that paraprofessionals performing limited professional tasks can result in considerable savings in costs and efficiency in operations of estates. For that reason, hourly rates for such persons may be separately stated and compensated, subject to the same limitations as the fees of professionals. However it should be noted that if the service performed by a paralegal consists of typing, data entry, checking court dockets or court dates, manually assembling, collating, marking, processing, photocopying, or mailing documents the task is clerical in nature and not compensable. Such tasks are traditionally charged to overhead and included in the professionals' hourly rate. . . .

The Court finds that the preparation of the schedules, preparation and printing of documents, and corrections to schedules are professional tasks that require knowledge and expertise of the legal assistant and are thus compensable. The charges for phone calls to remind of appointments are also compensable, because in most instances, these phone calls entailed more than simply an appointment reminder. The legal assistant also answered questions for the clients and reviewed information. Likewise, the court finds reviewing trustee notices to be a compensable professional task.

However, verifying that the debtor's address is correct and placing notices and letters in the file are clerical tasks. The calendaring and docketing of dates are also clerical in nature and are not compensable. . . .

The trustee objects to the limited amount of time the attorney spends with the client and asserts that the majority of client contact is handled by the legal assistant. Castle states that it modified its practices in June of 1997 so that an attorney would meet with the client in every case prior to filing. . . . Castle's current practice is for an attorney to meet with the client at the initial consultation.

In the majority of the fee applications currently before the Court, the initial consultation took place before this Court's opinion in *Pinkins* and an attorney did not meet with the client until the signing appointment. In those circumstances, the Court finds that the legal assistants were engaged in the unauthorized practice of law. In *Pinkins*, the Court stated that "[a]lthough it is not improper for attorneys to delegate certain matters to nonlawyer members of their staff, lack of contact or a direct relationship with the client precluded proper delegation." . . . It is therefore necessary for an attorney to meet with the client at the initial consultation, before delegating matters to nonlawyer staff members. It is not sufficient for the attorney to simply meet with the client at the signing appointment. Fees for work of legal assistants in cases in which the attorney did not meet with the client until the signing appointment are therefore denied.

In the more recent cases in which an attorney met with the client at the initial consultation, the legal assistant met with the client initially to gather the client's financial information. The attorney then met with the clients and reviewed the client's paperwork, advised the client of duties under the Code, and discussed options under chapters 7, 11, 12 and 23. The attorney accomplished all of this in approximately 15-20 minutes. In most of these cases, the attorney did not meet with the client again until the meeting of the creditors. . . .

Considering the minimal contact that the attorney has with the client at the initial consultation and the fact that in most cases there is no further contact until the Section 341 hearing, the Court must conclude that the overall quality of attorney services and representation is reduced and fees should be reduced accordingly. . . .

The trustee objects to the duplication of services by the attorney and legal assistants at the signing appointments. . . . Generally, "no more than one attorney may charge the estate for interoffice conferences meetings and court appearances unless an adequate explanation is given." [Citation omitted.] However, in these cases, the Court finds that it is necessary and more cost effective for both the attorney and the legal assistant to be present at the signing appointments. Therefore, the fees for each will be allowed. . . .

Finally, the trustee contends that Castle's method of compensating its legal assistants constitutes improper fee sharing.

Castle states that it compensates its legal assistants based on the total number of weekly bankruptcy cases that Castle files. Castle's payment scale . . . reveals that legal assistants conducting initial consultations receive a base salary of $375 per week for a minimum of 15 bankruptcy cases file by Castle. Each additional filing, up to 39 filings, results in an increase in the base salary of $25 per week. A $40 bonus is given for the 25th filing, with increases in the bonus in $10 increments up to the 39th filing. The result is that if Castle files 15 cases per week, the legal assistant receives a weekly salary of $375. Thirty-nine filings per week results in the maximum salary of $1,150. . . .

Castle contends that the compensation arrangement constitutes profit-sharing, which is permitted under MRPC 5.4(a)(3). Further Castle contends that the compensation arrangement does not interfere with the professional judgment of its lawyers and does not promote the solicitation of clients. . . .

The issue of fee sharing was addressed in State Bar of Michigan Ethics Opinion RI-143, August 25, 1992. . . . The Committee found that . . . Rule 5.4(a)(3) . . . allows a law firm to include nonlawyer employees in compensation plans, even if the plan is based on a profit sharing arrangement. The Committee went on to state:

> In CI-478 we approved a lawyer's proposal to pay nonlawyer employees a set salary plus bonuses calculated on the lawyer's gross or adjusted gross income, provided that the bonus was not in any way tied to the employee's effort to solicit clients for the firm.

The Committee further noted that "the result might be different if the compensation plans were based on the fees generated from a particular case or a particular client rather than net profits of the law practice of the firm." . . .

Although Castle's compensation package for its legal assistants is not based on a percentage or share of fees received, it is directly tied to the filing of particular cases and is likely to encourage solicitation of clients or the unauthorized practice of law, two activities the prohibition against fee sharing is designed to prevent. The legal assistants who conduct initial consultations at Castle have a "vested pecuniary interest in [the] attorney's disposition of [the] case that could possibly take preeminence over [the] client's best interest." [Citation omitted.]

Although, as Castle contends, the attorney and the client make the final decision as to whether to file a petition, the legal assistants, as the first personal contact the client has with Castle, collects the client's financial information and may be motivated to present the information in a way that would more likely lead to the filing of a petition. Further compensating the legal assistants based on the number of petitions filed also encourages the legal assistant to attempt to include the client's decisions.

For these reasons, the Court finds that Castle's practice of compensating its legal assistants based on the number of petitions filed is improper. However, for several reasons, the Court concludes that it is not appropriate to reduce Castle's fees on this account. First, there were limited precedents addressing this somewhat confusing area of law, and it is apparent to the Court that Castle relied upon a good faith interpretation of those precedents. Second, the Court is confident that Castle will adjust its compensation practices as required by this opinion. . . . Third, the Court is unable to identify from the present record any connection between Castle's improper compensation practices and . . . a reasonable fee. . . .

Questions about the Case

1. What were the objections to the fee petition relating to clerical work? What did the court decide? Do you agree with the way that the court characterized the various tasks as clerical and nonclerical?
2. What was the trustee's objection about the limited amount of time spent with clients? Do you think this is a legitimate objection?
3. What was the law firm trying to do by establishing this kind of practice model? Is there a legitimate motivation here for increasing access to affordable legal services in bankruptcy? Who is the law firm competing with for these clients? (Remember the discussion of nonlawyer legal service providers earlier in the book.)
4. What did the court mandate about the role of the lawyer in meeting with the client? Did this undermine the paralegal's role?
5. What was the compensation plan for paralegals at this firm? Did it comply with the ethics rules in Michigan? Why, or why not? Do you agree with the reasoning of this court that the plan encouraged solicitation and UPL and impaired the lawyer's exercise of independent professional judgment on behalf of the client?

In this California case, a federal court refuses to award fees for paralegal time if the paralegals are not qualified under the California statute regulating paralegals.

Sanford v. GMRI, Inc.

CIV-S-04-1535 DFL CMK (E.D. Cal. 2005)

Plaintiff James Sanford ("Sanford") moves for attorneys' fees and costs in the amount of $18,268.09 following the settlement of his ADA accessibility lawsuit against defendant GMRI, Inc. ("GMRI"). GMRI challenges the reasonableness of the requested fee award. For the following reasons, the court awards $8,132.67 in attorneys' fees and costs.

Sanford, a quadriplegic, filed his lawsuit on August 5, 2004, claiming that he experienced numerous access barriers on his visits to GMRI's Red Lobster restaurant. On August 18, 2005, the parties filed a settlement agreement and the case was dismissed. Sanford released all of his equitable relief claims in exchange for $8,000 in monetary damages and GMRI's promise to remove or remedy the remaining architectural barriers. The resolution of the attorneys' fees issue was left for this motion.

The ADA provides that a court "in its discretion, may allow the prevailing party . . . a reasonable attorney's fee, including litigation expenses, and costs." 42 U.S.C. §12205. . . .

Sanford requests $18,268.09 in attorneys' fees and costs. This amount includes $11,300 in attorney and paralegal fees for 61.45 billed hours and $6,968.09 in litigation expenses and costs. The bulk of the requested litigation expenses consists of $5,513.75 in expert's fees. While conceding that Sanford is the prevailing party, GMRI challenges the hours requested on several grounds. In addition, GMRI argues that Sanford's request for expert witness fees should be denied as insufficiently documented. . . .

GMRI argues that the lodestar figure should be reduced to reflect Sanford's limited success. One of the factors courts must consider in determining the lodestar figure is the "results obtained" in the litigation, especially where a plaintiff did not succeed on some of his claims. . . . Because Hubbard's time entries cannot be easily divided between the successful and unsuccessful claims, the court reduces Sanford's fee award by one-third to account for his limited success. . . .

GMRI also challenges the appropriateness of Hubbard's requested hours, asserting that many of them are unnecessary, excessive, and/or redundant. . . . First, it argues that many of Hubbard's requested hours were unnecessary because Hubbard expended resources on claims which he knew Sanford lacked standing to pursue. However, this is already accounted for in the reduction addressed above. Second, GMRI argues that Hubbard's fees are excessive. For example, GMRI argues that Hubbard's bill for 0.80 hours for preparation of his boilerplate settlement demand letter was unreasonable. Hubbard responds that the amount of time spent drafting the settlement letter was not excessive as he also reviewed the file and associated documents. . . . GMRI makes similar arguments as to other entries, challenging a total of 2.25 hours. The court is not persuaded that these hours were excessive or unnecessary and declines to strike them. The court notes that these hours will be reduced by one third in any event.

In addition to the above charges, GMRI challenges the time billed for plaintiff's motion to compel a site inspection. . . . The court agrees with defendant that these hours were not reasonably expended and should not be awarded.

Similarly, GMRI challenges the time Hubbard took to read its responses and objections to discovery requests. It submitted the same responses and objections in the two previous cases filed against it by Hubbard, so it argues that it should have only taken 0.50 hours, not 3.65 to review the responses here. The court agrees that these hours are excessive given the repetitive nature of the litigation prosecuted by plaintiff's counsel. The court will reduce these hours to 1 hour.

Third, GMRI challenges the reasonableness of Sanford's claimed paralegal fees. Sanford seeks to recover paralegal-level rates for individuals that Hubbard has previously categorized as legal assistants. Under California Business & Professional Code §6450(c), a person is qualified as a paralegal if: (1) she possesses a certificate of completion of a paralegal program from an ABA-approved or other accredited post-secondary institution; (2) she possesses a baccalaureate degree and has completed one year of law-related experience under the supervision of a qualified attorney; or (3) she possesses a high school diploma or GED and has completed three years of law-related experience under the supervision of a qualified attorney before December 31, 2003. GMRI challenges each of the five individuals listed as paralegals.

First, it alleges that Sanford must present the court with a "written declaration . . . stating that [each individual] is qualified to perform paralegal tasks." Cal. Bus. & Prof. Code §6450(c)(3). Hubbard's declaration generally states that each of the individuals is qualified to perform paralegal tasks. Therefore, Sanford has met this requirement.

Next, GMRI challenges each of the individuals based on her failure to meet the §6450 requirements listed above. Sanford concedes that Christa Duncan will not be a qualified paralegal until she receives her certificate of completion from a paralegal program. In addition, it appears that Alisha Petras is not a qualified paralegal because: (1) she does not have a baccalaureate degree or paralegal certification; and (2) Sanford has not shown that she completed three years of law-related experience under a qualified attorney before December 2003. Finally, MeLisa Dotson and Elva Garcia hold baccalaureate degrees, but they did not complete their one year of law-related service under a qualified attorney until June of this year. Therefore, any time attributed to Dotson and Garcia before June 2005 should not have been billed at a paralegal rate.

On the other hand, GMRI's challenge to Bonnie Vonderhaar should fail. GMRI argues that Vonderhaar does not qualify because Sanford fails to present evidence that she completed one year of legal experience under the supervision of a qualified attorney. However, she satisfies §6450(c) because she holds a paralegal certificate from a NALA-approved institution. Therefore, she is a qualified paralegal in California.

In sum, Duncan and Petras should have been categorized as legal assistants for the entire case, and Dotson and Garcia should have been categorized as legal assistants for any time billed before June 2005. Sanford does not provide a proposed fee for legal assistants. Therefore, Sanford can only recover paralegal rates for Vonderhaar's time and Dotson's and Garcia's time post–June 2005. The resulting fee award is $225.00 out of the total $1,680.00 billed, or a reduction of $1,455.00. . . .

Based on the foregoing discussion, Sanford is awarded $4,957.50 for attorneys' fees, calculated as follows:

***Attorneys/Assistants	Hours	Rate	Total
Lynn Hubbard (attorney)	27.50	$250	$6,875.00
Scott Hubbard (associate)	1.90	$175	$ 332.50
Paralegals	3.00	$ 75	$ 225.00
Sub-Total:			$7,432.50
Limited Success Reduction (1/3):			$4,957.50

In addition, the court awards Sanford's requested litigation expenses and costs minus a portion of the requested expert witness fees, totaling $3,175.17. In sum, the court awards Sanford $8,132.67 in attorneys' fees and costs. . . .

Questions about the Case

1. Under what statute did the lawyer seek attorney's fees? Was there any discussion of whether or not attorneys' fees under this statute should include paralegal time at market rates?
2. What was the basis for reducing the paralegal fees?
3. Given what you learned in this chapter about fee petitions, what should the lawyer herein have done to ensure that he would get fully compensated for paralegal time?
4. Is there such a thing as a "NALA-approved" paralegal program? What does the statute really say about the entities that approve paralegal programs?
5. What message does this case send to lawyers in California who might be seeking attorneys' fees under federal statutes?

See other, related cases with the same name for additional findings about compensation for paralegal time in fee awards.

The bankruptcy business in this case engaged in practices that violated several rules covered in this chapter, including the prohibitions on partnerships between lawyers and nonlawyers, fee splitting, and excessive fees.

In re Hessinger & Associates

171 B.R. 366 (N.D. Cal. 1994)

. . . Hessinger & Associates started out as Varbel & Associates, run by Earl Cook and Duane Varbel, an Arizona lawyer. The firm started in Arizona, and then expanded into southern and northern California as well as other areas. Its mode of operation was to advertise very heavily, with high-profile radio and television advertising as well as late-night "info-mercials" touting the instant relief from debt problems and how bankruptcy was a "constitutional right" which every citizen should use to get out of debt. The advertising made heavy use of actors portraying harassed and troubled debtors.

Varbel & Associates hired a few young and inexperienced lawyers, but most of its work was performed by "paralegals" with little or no formal training. Within the firm, they were called "credit specialists." Their job was to lure the debtor into their offices, get them to sign a contract promising to pay the fee, then preparing and filing the bankruptcy papers. In the majority of cases, the debtor had no contact with a lawyer at all until the 341 meeting, when a Hessinger lawyer they had never met was present.

Varbel's main selling point, as well as its means of funneling funds to its nonlawyer principals, was to offer its services for no money down. The debtor was asked to sign a promissory note for the fees, to be paid after bankruptcy. The fees were typically set at three times the amount normally charged by lawyers for doing those types of consumer cases. After bankruptcy, the notes were transferred to numerous "finance companies" set up by Cook. Some of these companies were owned by Cook himself, or by his relatives, some by Varbel, and at least one by Hessinger. These finance companies collected the fees from the debtors. If the debtors did not pay, they were dunned and sued by the finance companies.

In early 1993, Varbel was disbarred and, in his own words, Hessinger "took over" the practice. In reality, he became the figurehead for the firm, which continued doing business in the same way as before. The firm continued to be run overall by Cook and locally by Hansen, who made all the hiring and firing decisions and exercised complete control over the day-to-day operations of the business, including the conduct of the few lawyers employed by the firm.

Hessinger first came to the attention of this court when the U.S. Trustee objected to his fees in two Chapter 7 cases, which were two or three times as high as other attorneys were charging. Further investigation revealed that all of the work in the cases had been done by nonlawyers and without supervision, and that Hessinger was selling the fee contracts to finance companies for enforcement after bankruptcy even though the promissory notes were executed before bankruptcy and clearly had been discharged. It became clear to the court that more was involved here than simple overcharging, and that ethical issues must be addressed. . . .

Hessinger & Associates is nothing more than a get-rich-quick scheme of Earl Cook. Aided by a venal and morally bankrupt lawyer, Duane Varbel, Cook set up a business to sell bankruptcies to the public and reap the rewards. Upon Varbel's disbarment, Hessinger stepped in to become the front man for the enterprise.

Hessinger maintained that he was in charge of the firm, but the evidence is absolutely overwhelming that he exercised no actual control whatsoever and that all decisions regarding all phases of the operation are made by nonlawyers.

The court was very strongly affected by the testimony of Stephanie Morris, a young lawyer in need of a job who worked for Hessinger & Associates for several months. She was hired by Cook and met Hessinger only once, at a dinner party. She was expressly told by Cook that she was to take directions from only him and his local managers, . . . neither of whom were lawyers. She was directly and expressly told by Cook that she was not to contact Hessinger for any reason.

Morris was under the direct supervision of [these nonlawyers]. On several occasions she had arguments with them over her conduct as a lawyer. They complained to her that her "sales" were considerably less than those of the paralegals who were performing the same duties as her. When she explained that she could not ethically file a bankruptcy for someone who did not need it, they told her that the firm's policy was to sign up every person who came in for an interview. They expected her to use the standard interview, called the "six-minute sell," whereby every debtor who came in was expected to be talked into signing the Hessinger fee agreement within six minutes of walking in the door.

Morris also was subject to rebuke . . . for refusing to quote every debtor a fee of $1,500.00. They told her that it was the firm's policy to charge every debtor this amount. Morris refused, on grounds that in many cases this amount was unconscionable. [Two other former employees reported "almost identical" experiences.]

Another former Hessinger lawyer . . . reported the same practices in family law cases. . . .

Despite Hessinger's lame representation that all the decisions were his, it is clear that all of the decisions were made by Cook and his non-lawyer deputies. All of the attorneys . . . state that they were hired . . . —without ever having seen Hessinger.

When [one attorney at the firm] wanted a raise in pay, he asked Cook, not Hessinger. In a declaration filed to discredit [an attorney employee and a firm paralegal] noted that he was fired by "our Administrator," not Hessinger. Morris' termination was the same. Hessinger presides over a "law firm" in which all the hiring, firing, and supervision of lawyers is done by nonlawyers who also set the fees.

No lawyer may ethically practice law under the direction of a non-lawyer. To do so violates Rule 1-600 of the California Rules of Professional Conduct, which forbids a lawyer to participate in any organization which allows any third person to interfere with the lawyer's independence or professional judgment or allows an unlicensed person to practice law. The reason for such a rule is to "prevent business relationships with non-lawyers from compromising a lawyer's independence of thought and action." G. Hazard, 2 *The Law of Lawyering* (2d Ed. 1990), 5.4:502.

By lending his name and license to an organization run by a layman, Hessinger has committed the grossest of ethical violations. He has allowed Cook to set up a system whereby nonlawyers supervise and direct lawyers and coerce them to do something not in their clients' best interests. This conduct is reprehensible beyond words. To anyone who has any degree of love for the law, it is physically revolting. . . .

The accounting of how much Cook is reaping from this operation is beyond the court's ability to investigate. However, the mechanics of it are fairly clear. First, Cook is paid a salary of $4,000.00 per month. Second, Cook is the owner of the advertising company which produces Hessinger's commercials. Third, Cook owns part or all of several of the finance companies to whom notes from clients are assigned for collection. Between all of these sources of revenue, Cook's income from Hessinger operations far outstrips that of Hessinger.

Rule 1-320 of the California Rules of Professional Conduct provides that a lawyer or law firm may not directly or indirectly share legal fees with a person who is not a lawyer. Rule 1-600 contains a similar ban. Hessinger's financial arrangements with Cook are clearly intended to circumvent these rules, and are not in any way legitimate exceptions to the rules. There is no legitimate employer-employee relationship between Hessinger and Cook. It is that latter who is the employee. The court accordingly finds a gross violation of Rule 1-320 and Rule 1-600. . . .

Rule 3-110(A) of the California Rules of Professional Conduct provides that a member shall not intentionally, recklessly, or repeatedly fail to perform legal services with competence. Hessinger has violated this rule in hundreds of cases, if not thousands.

First and foremost, the policies set by Cook and enforced by [non-lawyer administrators] were designed to maximize their income, not properly counsel clients as to whether or not they should file a bankruptcy petition. Within Hessinger, petition filings are referred to as "sales." All Hessinger employees who interviewed clients, whether attorneys or non-lawyer "credit specialists," were given specific and repeated directives to sign to a fee contract every person who came in the door within six minutes. Called the "six-minute sell," it was the official policy of Hessinger to sell every person who responded to one of their ads on filing a bankruptcy within six minutes of the start of the interview. Those attorneys who knew better and balked were criticized and let go. Nonlawyers, in addition to not having the training needed to evaluate if a bankruptcy was appropriate, had no ethical considerations to worry about.

Additionally, Hessinger regularly offered special bonuses, in the form of cash or trips, to attorneys or credit specialists who filed the most bankruptcy petitions. Hessinger's argument that these were only to "reduce the backlog" is nonsense; the bonuses were simply to encourage Hessinger employees to talk every single person whom they interviewed into filing a bankruptcy petition. The former Hessinger attorneys who have come forth have confirmed that this was the official policy of the firm.

Counseling is the fundamental function performed by consumer lawyers. By placing its interest in revenue ahead of its obligation to counsel its clients, Hessinger & Associates has acted recklessly and incompetently and has violated Rule 3-110(A). By failing to stop the practice and insure that each and every person who came into one of his offices received proper counseling, Joseph Hessinger has personally violated the rule.

Additionally, Hessinger has violated the rule by allowing nonlawyer employees, many with little or no legal training, to interview clients and prepare their bankruptcy papers without any significant (and in hundreds of cases not even insignificant) supervision by a lawyer. . . .

The incidental availability of a lawyer does not make the practice legal where the attorney exercised no actual and significant supervision over the nonlawyer. See *Glad*, supra; *In re Stone*, 166 B.R. 269 (Bankr. W.D. Pa. 1994). In *Stone*, the court held that a paralegal had been engaged in the unauthorized practice of law when he prepared bankruptcy petitions even though he had a lawyer check his paperwork for mistakes because the lawyer had no way of knowing what legal advice the paralegal had given or whether the advice was proper. 166 B.R. at 275. Here, the record shows that it was Hessinger's practice to present petitions prepared by nonlawyer "credit specialists" in large quantities for the few lawyers to sign, without even checking for obvious errors. Even if the Hessinger lawyers reviewed the credit specialists' work, Hessinger would still be guilty of aiding in the unauthorized practice of law. The fact that most of such petitions are signed without any review at all makes the offense particularly egregious. . . .

As noted above, at least two Hessinger attorneys pointed out to Cook that to charge a four-figure fee in every case is unconscionable and a violation of Rule 4-200(A) of the California Rules of Professional Conduct. Cook's response was to get rid of these lawyers. Hessinger apparently has no such qualms, and has accordingly violated this rule in hundreds or thousands of cases.

In one case now before this court, . . . the debtor had only $2300 in assets including a $1300 rental security deposit. He had no secured debt, and $14,113.00 in unsecured debt. The case was as simple as they come, at least from the information Hessinger's "credit specialist" was able to garner. Even a seasoned bankruptcy lawyer would charge no more than $500 or $600 for such a bankruptcy, after first counseling the debtor as to other alternatives because of the small total debt. Many attorneys of lesser experience would charge around $300. Hessinger's fee in the case was $1,000. . . .

From the overwhelming record supplied by the U.S. Trustee, the court has no difficulty in finding that in the vast majority of Hessinger's cases the fees are unconscionable. The fees are set by nonlawyers, with no regard for the simplicity of the case. The cases are prepared either by nonlawyers or very inexperienced and unqualified lawyers. The individuals receive no counseling, and in fact are looked upon as customers to be bilked and milked rather than clients. The court finds that by charging fees in excess of those charged by experienced practitioners and delivering services of the lowest order Hessinger has violated Rule 4-200(A). . . .

Conclusion

Although the court has found hundreds or thousands of serious violations of the California Rules of Professional Conduct, it is important to note that even one single use of the "six-minute sell" to one single client is enough justification for revoking an attorney's license to practice. Hessinger's violations of ethics are rampant and outrageous, and demand the strongest possible sanction. Accordingly, the court will order as follows:

1. Pursuant to Local Rule 110-6, an order to show cause will be issued requiring Hessinger to show cause to the district court, if he has any, why he should not be disbarred from practice in this district for the conduct set forth in this memorandum.
2. Pursuant to Local Rule 110-7, the court assesses a fine against Hessinger in the amount of $100,000.00, to be paid to the clerk of the court. Until the fine is paid in full, Hessinger and his firm will not be permitted to practice bankruptcy law in this district, nor charge any person any fee whatsoever for any bankruptcy-related service in this district. Provided, however, that any other judge in this district may modify this order as to cases pending before him or her as he or she sees fit.

Questions about the Case

1. Were the "legal assistants" in this firm properly trained and educated for their work?
2. What does the court say about who controlled the law firm operation? Which ethical rule or rules did this particular conduct breach?

3. How was the nonlawyer Cook paid? Who decided his compensation? Is this unethical fee splitting? Why, or why not?
4. Did the lawyer Hessinger perform legal services competently? Did clients get good legal advice and representation?
5. On what basis were bonuses paid to employees? Did this plan violate any ethical rules?
6. Did Hessinger supervise the "paralegals" properly? Were the paralegals doing any work that falls within the definition of unauthorized practice of law?
7. How did the firm determine how much a client would be charged for its services? Were the rates more or less than market rates? Was this method of setting fees proper?
8. Is the advertising in which this firm engaged permissible under the standards described in Chapter 6?

8

Competence

This chapter addresses the issue of competence, an essential element of ethical conduct in every profession. Lack of professional competence in legal practice is grounds for both legal remedies and disciplinary sanctions. Chapter 8 covers:

- definitions of lawyer and paralegal competence
- key components of paralegal competence, including
  - knowledge
  - skills
  - thoroughness and preparation
  - diligence and promptness
  - communication with clients
- sanctions for incompetence, including disciplinary actions and malpractice suits
- trends in malpractice, including the growth in claims against lawyers, third-party actions, and the application of consumer protection statutes
- common dilemmas confronting paralegals in the area of competence, including those related to delegation, supervision, and attorney review of work
- factors in the work environment that affect competence

A. Introduction

Lawyers are obligated to represent clients competently by both ethics codes and the common law rules of tort liability for professional negligence. A lawyer's duty to represent a client competently also makes the lawyer responsible for the work of paralegals and others in the law firm; the ultimate responsibility for the competent handling of a client matter rests with the lawyer.

Paralegals must perform competently and hold competence as one of their highest values, both because they desire professional status and treatment and because they share with the lawyer the moral and ethical responsibility for providing quality legal services. As discussed in Chapter 2, paralegals should also be mindful of their own personal tort liability because clients may name paralegals in malpractice actions against law firms.

Because competence cannot be defined or measured neatly or quantitatively and the range of incompetent acts is virtually limitless, competence may seem like an amorphous notion. As a starting point, most definitions of competence begin with legal knowledge and skill.

B. Legal Education

Legal knowledge for lawyer competence generally begins with, at a minimum, a law school education of three or four years followed by passing a bar examination, which primarily tests substantive legal knowledge and judgmental-analytical ability. As law schools have sought to make legal education more relevant to practice, clinical programs, lawyering skills, and trial techniques courses have been added to the traditional law school curriculum in most law schools. Internship and externship programs, many for course credit, are offered by virtually all schools. Testing of performance skills is included on the bar exam in many states. Periodically, there are calls for mandatory apprenticeships as a prerequisite to bar admission, but so far no state requires apprenticeship as a prerequisite to admission to the bar.

Legal knowledge and skills encompass many things not covered in school. Lawyers learn on the job from more experienced lawyers in the firms that hire them. Some of this training is informal: learning by example, through model forms and documents available in the firm, and by trial and error. Some is more formal: by means of in-house training programs and mentoring by more experienced lawyers.

Lawyers must continue to develop legal knowledge and skills throughout their careers. Formal continuing education programs are an important aspect of this; 49 U.S. jurisdictions, including territories, have mandatory continuing legal education, usually about 12 hours a year. Beyond these mandates, continuing one's professional development is a matter of commitment and integrity, driven by the sense of personal satisfaction derived from doing one's job well, appreciating the ever-changing nature of law and procedure, and valuing the important service that lawyers provide to clients and society at large.

C. Paralegal Education

Paralegals share lawyers' commitment to education and skill development. Because paralegals in most jurisdictions do not have to comply with minimum educational standards, the responsibility for achieving and maintaining competence through education and skill development rests firmly with paralegals and the lawyers who employ them.

Paralegal education programs are as new as the profession itself—a little more than 40 years old. The first programs were established around 1970, an estimated half dozen scattered across the country. At last count, there are as many as a thousand paralegal programs situated in a wide variety of institutions, including traditional two- and four-year colleges (both public and private), multidisciplinary and freestanding proprietary institutions (some of which are vocationally oriented), and correspondence and online schools.

Unlike the law school curriculum, the paralegal curriculum is not standardized, and offerings vary widely in length, content, format, level of sophistication, and degree of specialization. Good programs teach an appropriate balance of substantive law and practical job skills, have good library collections and access for students to legal research databases, well-qualified faculty, technology support, and an array of services to help students achieve their goal of finding an appropriate paralegal position upon graduation.

More than 250 paralegal programs are currently approved by the American Bar Association (ABA), having met guidelines on curriculum, admissions, faculty, administration, staff, facilities, finances, library, and support services, such as counseling and placement. ABA approval, first granted in 1975, is the only kind of specialized recognition of paralegal educational programs available. It is purely voluntary and is not formally recognized by the federal government; the ABA has never sought such recognition. The standards for paralegal education are set in the American Bar Association Guidelines for the Approval of Paralegal Education Programs. The American Association for Paralegal Education, representing more than 300 paralegal programs, also supports paralegal educators to develop and offer quality educational experiences for their students.

Formal paralegal education has become the recognized pathway for entry into the paralegal profession although firm hiring standards vary throughout the country. Some firms do not require a formal paralegal education but favor candidates who have formal training over those who do not. In some cities, a baccalaureate degree alone is the hiring standard in large law firms. Smaller firms often require previous legal work experience.

Guideline 1 of the ABA Model Guidelines for the Utilization of Paralegal Services (ABA Model Guidelines), in stating the lawyer's responsibility for the actions of paralegals, emphasizes the importance of paralegal education. The comment to the Guideline states that a lawyer should ensure that a paralegal is competent to perform assigned tasks based on the paralegal's education, training, and experience. This Guideline builds on ABA Model Rule 5.3, which requires lawyers to make reasonable efforts to ensure that the conduct of nonlawyer employees is compatible with the lawyer's professional obligations. This rule and the common law rules of tort liability are discussed in Chapter 2. It should be noted that California, which has quasi-regulatory legislation for paralegals, sets minimum educational requirements and requires continuing education. (See Chapter 2 for more details on the California law.) Several state guidelines on paralegals note that lawyers should ensure that paralegals are competent to do the work they are assigned, and some have a guideline that reflects the paralegal's duty of competence. Several states have a guideline on continuing education for paralegals. The voluntary certification programs that now exist in a few states also set requirements for entry-level and ongoing education. Guideline 10 of the ABA Model Guidelines advises lawyers to encourage continuing education for their paralegals to assure competence.

Whether or not employers require it, paralegals should acquire appropriate formal education to meet their professional obligation of competence. This education should include not only a basic paralegal education but also regular and frequent continuing education to update areas of expertise and to develop skills and higher levels of expertise. Continuing education is available to paralegals in many forms. Paralegals can take courses designed for lawyers or courses designed specifically for paralegals. Continuing education for lawyers is readily available through state and local bar associations and independent providers. Paralegal continuing education is provided by paralegal programs; local, regional, and national paralegal associations; and a few independent organizations.

Both national organizations, the National Association of Legal Assistants (NALA) and the National Federation of Paralegal Associations (NFPA), promote competence and provide continuing education to their members. NALA's Code of Ethics Canon 6 requires paralegals to maintain a high degree of competency. NALA has translated this ideal into action by offering its ***Certified Legal Assistant/Certified Paralegal*** examination and its advanced certification examinations, discussed in Chapter 2. Educational or experience requirements must be met to sit for the exams, and CLAs/CPs must meet continuing education requirements to maintain their certified status. The NFPA Model Code contains a strong statement concerning competence and education in Canon 1. It states that "[p]aralegals shall achieve and maintain a high level of

Certified Legal Assistant/Certified Paralegal
Certification for paralegals offered by NALA for passing the Certified Legal Assistant examination

competence," through education, training, and work experience. The Code also recommends that paralegals participate in a minimum of 12 hours of continuing education a year and complete all assignments promptly and efficiently. NFPA requires PACE-certified ***Registered Paralegals*** to participate in continuing education and monitors compliance. Both NALA and NFPA have annual national educational seminars and encourage their local chapters to provide frequent continuing education courses.

Registered Paralegal
Certification offered by NFPA for passing the Paralegal Advanced Competency Examination

D. A Definition of Competency

Competence cannot be defined solely in terms of formal education and professional skill. These are essential preconditions to competence, but competence has full meaning only when it is applied to the tasks at hand, to the specific legal work to be done.

The ABA Model Rules define competence in Model Rule 1.1, which states that competent representation requires "the legal knowledge, skill, thoroughness and preparation reasonably necessary for the representation." Model Rule 1.3 adds two more elements by requiring lawyers to "act with reasonable diligence and promptness." Finally, Rule 1.4 adds that lawyers must communicate competently, meaning that they must inform clients promptly when a matter requires their informed consent, must reasonably consult with clients and keep them "reasonably informed," and must "promptly comply with reasonable requests for information."

These ethics rules and the cases interpreting them can be synthesized into a list of qualities that comprise competence for lawyers and paralegals alike.

1. Knowledge

Both lawyers and paralegals must have appropriate formal education, both legal and general, that enables them to communicate well, in oral and written form; that provides them with knowledge of substantive law and procedure; that has developed their analytical and judgmental abilities; and that has provided them with the information and skills needed to resolve legal issues presented by clients.

The bodies of knowledge needed by the lawyer and the paralegal differ somewhat because the lawyer exercises independent professional judgment about how to advise and serve clients, while the paralegal participates in the practical steps both preliminary to these decisions (e.g., interviewing clients, conducting legal and factual research) and later to implement plans for handling a client matter (e.g., drafting a document). Further, lawyers represent clients as advocates in courts, which paralegals generally do not do.

Increasingly, the legal knowledge needed to be competent is highly specialized. As the law has become increasingly complex, most practitioners emphasize no more than a few areas of practice. The trend away from "general practice" is reflected in specialized certification programs offered for lawyers by most states, by the departmentalization of large firms, and by the widespread existence of "boutique" firms that devote themselves to highly specialized areas of law. Lawyers have a duty to refer highly complex, specialized cases to another attorney with appropriate expertise if they do not have the necessary expertise.

Paralegals usually specialize in one practice area, working in civil litigation, estate planning, corporate matters, or bankruptcy. Most paralegal programs' curricula, unlike law school curricula, include required specialty courses, and most paralegal continuing education programs are devoted to specialized or advanced coursework.

Orientation and formal on-the-job training have become important elements of legal training. Large law firms and government agencies often have formal in-house training programs for lawyers and paralegals, which not only orient them to the firm's "way of doing things" but also teach substantive knowledge and skills. Many firms have in-house training for paralegals on functions such as legal research, cite checking, document management, and conducting document productions.

Keeping abreast of changes in law and practice is critical in the application of technology. It is especially easy to make errors when working with technology, such as selecting the wrong electronic form; not using the correct provisions; changing some but not all names, numbers, or provisions; and misdirecting e-mail. For example, a lawyer in Kansas was recently suspended from practice for ignoring a notice that he was required to file cases electronically. (See the cases at the end of this chapter for examples of errors.)

2. Skills

Skills are acquired through formal education and through training and experience on the job. The term *skills* refers primarily to the execution of tasks and the implementation of plans for handling a client matter into action, as opposed to the mastery of a body of substantive legal knowledge. Lawyers and paralegals both apply their skills to the resolution of legal problems in carrying out their respective roles. Skills needed most by paralegals include drafting documents, analyzing documents, summarizing information, handling procedural matters, gathering information, and conducting legal and factual research. Lawyers need different skills, such as trial advocacy and negotiating. Lawyers usually retain the most complex and sophisticated tasks and delegate to paralegals duties that require organizational and oral and written communication skills.

3. Thoroughness and Preparation

In applying knowledge and skills to any legal problem, both lawyers and paralegals must be careful and thorough in their information gathering, analysis, application of judgment, and actions. Neglecting to learn all the facts, to fill out forms properly, or to be meticulous about every detail can have devastating consequences for the client. Because paralegals are especially valued for their knowledge of the facts in the cases they work on and for their attention to detail, thoroughness is one of the most critical aspects of paralegal competence.

Related is preparation. Most successful lawyers credit their success in large part to their careful and thorough preparation. Paralegals are often delegated considerable responsibility for preparation, for example, by organizing documents and other information before a trial or by drafting and organizing documents for a real estate closing. To be effective, the paralegal and attorney must work together as a team in preparation.

Examples of failure to be thorough from real cases include failure to include a bonus in calculating a spouse's legal share of the other spouse's compensation; bad tax advice on a real estate trust that led to payment of huge tax bills, including interest and penalties; and advice to settle a case that resulted in the client accepting a much smaller settlement than the case was worth. One firm was recently hit with a $16 million verdict for including the wrong provision in an agreement, as the result of a cut-and-paste error.

4. Diligence and Promptness

Legal knowledge and skills alone are worthless unless they are applied to a client's case in a timely and attentive manner. "Diligence" means persistent attention to the legal matter to ensure that it is resolved with the best possible outcome for the client. A lack of diligence or promptness is evidenced by delays that may harm a client's case or cause the client unnecessary anxiety. Examples of failure to act diligently and promptly include missing court dates and appointments, frequently needing continuances, missing a statute of limitations or other filing deadline, not pursuing discovery, or taking an unnecessarily long time to act. Implied in the duty of diligence is the necessity for firm organization and management that ensure against the missing of critical deadlines, scheduling of conflicting court dates, and so forth. Often these important organizational tasks are delegated to paralegals. (See the *Pincay* case at the end of this chapter for an instance of a missed deadline.)

5. Communication with Clients

The importance of clear communication with clients cannot be underestimated. The good work of competent lawyers and paralegals will not be recognized if clients are not kept fully informed about the status of their cases. Lawyers and paralegals must return clients' phone calls and respond to their e-mails promptly. Ongoing communication with clients is often an important duty of paralegals. Many lawyers are too busy in court and meetings to return clients' calls as promptly as clients would like and to make regular reports on how matters are proceeding. Paralegals are ideally situated to handle this kind of communication.

E. Sanctions for Incompetence

Malpractice
Improper conduct in the performance of duties by a professional, either intentionally or through negligence

Lack of competence can be fatal to a client's rights and to a lawyer's or a paralegal's career. Professional negligence in the handling of a case is the most common basis for ***malpractice*** actions against attorneys. Professional negligence is defined as the failure to exercise the standard of care commonly observed in other professionals. The remedy is compensation for the loss of the client's legal rights, in other words, damages for losing a case in which the client would have prevailed if the lawyer had acted competently. Some cases also permit recovery to third persons who are damaged by an attorney's failure to act competently (discussed in more detail in the next section). Finally, lawyers found to have been negligent can have the fees associated with the underlying matter disgorged in addition to paying damages.

As discussed in Chapter 2, paralegals may be named in malpractice actions against lawyers, including independent contractor paralegals working under the direction of a lawyer. Most lawyers carry malpractice insurance that covers the actions of their employees; such insurance is mandatory in some states. Paralegals should be certain the firm they work for has adequate malpractice coverage that covers paralegals. Malpractice insurance providers have found that the most common bases for claims are (1) substantive incompetence; (2) management incompetence such as missing deadlines and mismanaging time; (3) poor communication with clients; (4) fee misunderstandings; and (5) substance abuse and stress.

Lack of competence is also grounds for **disciplinary action.** Normally the incompetence must be severe or repeated for sanctions to be imposed. Frequently the incompetence is coupled with other ethical violations, such as commingling or conversion of client trust account funds or failure to turn over client papers after representation is terminated. Lawyers have been disciplined for competence-related violations involving paralegals, including failing to supervise paralegals properly and aiding in the unauthorized practice of law by allowing paralegals to give legal advice and to prepare legal documents without supervision or review.

Because paralegals are not subject to discipline by the bar and not usually named in malpractice suits, the most likely consequence of failing to act competently is losing one's job, reputation, and employability.

Many malpractice and disciplinary cases involving competence relate to procrastination or to a lack of promptness, thoroughness, or communication. Typical scenarios include missing statutes of limitations, failing to proceed on a client's case after agreeing to representation, and not returning phone calls for an extended period, often because the lawyer has not taken the necessary steps to address a matter. These allegations are sometimes tied to financial improprieties as well, such as not returning advanced fees, not turning over a settlement check or client's file promptly, or "borrowing" from a client trust account. Some cases of this type are the result of mismanaged law offices; some, troubled attorneys. Personal problems — such as financial, marital, substance abuse, and health problems — often interfere with an attorney's ability to function competently.

A large proportion of attorneys with disciplinary records have **alcohol or drug dependency problems** or emotional and personal problems that impair their ability to function in an ethical and effective manner. Many state bars now have programs to help attorneys with these problems. Lawyers can participate voluntarily or be required to participate as part of an agreement or sanction for violation of the ethics rules. Studies show that as many as 20 percent of lawyers have alcohol or substance abuse problems and that at least 20 percent of disciplinary matters stem from these problems. Lawyers have been found to have the highest depression rates among the professions. One of four lawyers has elevated feelings of distress, and half of lawyers feel that they do not have enough time for their families. Paralegals should be alert to the symptoms of substance abuse and addiction in colleagues so that they can intervene as needed. Among the common symptoms are missed work, lateness to work, procrastination, missed deadlines, blaming others, withdrawing from relationships at work, deterioration in appearance, memory loss, erratic behavior, and losing control in work or social settings.

Several cases involving mistakes of paralegals are found at the end of this chapter. In addition, see *Musselman v. Willoughby Corp.* in Chapter 2 and *In re Hessinger* in Chapter 7, both of which involve a lawyer's failure to exercise adequate oversight of paralegals who made substantive errors that harmed clients.

F. Current Developments in Legal Malpractice

The number and size of **malpractice claims** made against attorneys fluctuates, in part because in bad economic times people seek restitution for financial losses. Overall, lawsuits against lawyers have increased about 60 percent since the mid-1990s. Some of the increase in claims against lawyers is from ***third-party claims*** by non-clients who were harmed by the actions of clients from whom they can no longer recover. Not all states allow such third-party claims. Arizona, California, and Missouri allow them, but New York and Ohio do not recognize a duty beyond that owed to the client.

Third-party claims
Claims by nonclients against lawyers who, in representing clients, may have caused harm to the third person

Examples of third-party liability are found in corporate securities work, where additional duties to the purchasers of securities are imposed by federal law. Under securities law, attorneys may be liable if material false or misleading statements are included in offerings. Private investors in all kinds of investments see attorneys as possible defendants when promoters have misled investors or when the investors depended on opinion letters or other documents prepared by lawyers.

The principles underlying third-party liability were first broadly applied during the savings and loan crisis in the 1990s in lawsuits by the federal government against lawyers who represented failed thrift institutions. Many recent cases have involved claims against lawyers who provided opinion letters to banks about the viability of companies seeking to borrow funds. When the companies later became insolvent, the lawyers were sued. The failure of large companies such as Enron and WorldCom led to many such lawsuits, which claimed that the law firms gave legal advice that allowed these companies to defraud investors and lenders. In recent years, a multi-million-dollar verdict was rendered in a case where third parties sued lawyers who had approved an illegal tax shelter. During the economic downturn that began in 2007, bankruptcy trustees and large investors sued lawyers for fraud and for aiding and abetting breaches of fiduciary duty.

Another practice area where third-party liability is a risk is **estate planning.** When a gift to an intended beneficiary fails because of an attorney's negligence, the intended beneficiary may seek damages from the attorney, even though the attorney represented the testator, not the beneficiary. Other cases hold that a lawyer has a duty to the beneficiaries of an estate to ascertain a client's testamentary capacity. (For example, see *Moore v. Anderson Ziegler*, 109 Cal. App. 4th 1287, 135 Cal. Rptr. 2d 888 (2003); *Fickett v. Superior Court*, 27 Ariz. App. 793, 558 P.2d 988 (1976), where a lawyer was held liable not only to the guardian-client but also to his ward. Also see *Johnson v. Sandler*, 958 S.W.2d 42 (Mo. Ct. App. W.D. (1997)).)

Similar cases have held attorneys who represented sellers in **real estate transactions** liable to buyers for making misleading statements that the buyer relied on in making the purchase. (See the *Biakanja* case at the end of this chapter for an example.) In another recent case, a law firm that represented defendants in a lawsuit against its insured was held liable to the plaintiff in that lawsuit for making a fraudulent statement about coverage under the policy at issue. (See *Shafer v. Berger, Kahn*, 107 Cal. App. 4th 54, 131 Cal. Rptr. 777 (Cal. Ct. App. 2003).)

Further extensions of third-party liability are expected, especially in areas heavily regulated by the government, such as environmental and securities law. Civil lawsuits have been brought by insurance companies against the lawyers who represented their insureds and lost; the jurisdictions are split on whether such actions are permitted.

More malpractice cases are being brought against lawyers for breaches of confidentiality and **conflict of interest**, in some instances where a firm represented two clients who ultimately became adversaries. Some cases concern conflicts that arose when an attorney did business with clients or served on a corporate client's board of directors. In one recent case, a multimillion-dollar verdict was rendered against a law firm that provided bad advice in the handling of an estate and advised the client-beneficiary to make a large donation to a foundation represented by the firm. In another case, a client sued and prevailed when a conflict screen was not honored.

Malicious prosecution cases against lawyers are also on the rise. In these cases, a lawyer can be held liable civilly for initiating a lawsuit without probable cause or continuing to prosecute a case after learning that there is no probable cause.

One area of particular concern to practitioners now is the degree to which lawyers and paralegals must have the latest information available through technology. The standard of care for lawyers in doing **research** is based on what was readily available at the time the research was performed and what could be found by standard research techniques. Lawyers are expected to conduct reasonable research to identify controlling law and to make decisions based on that law. Lawyers use electronic research services that provide access to the latest opinions, which are not yet available in hard copy. Electronic research has become the "standard" that lawyers are required to meet.

Some states allow lawyers to be sued under **consumer fraud statutes** that provide for damages for deceptive practices or fraud. Such statutes may apply even where the client could not prevail in a malpractice case. Other states specifically refuse to apply such statutes to lawyers, holding to the traditional separation of powers interpretations that give exclusive authority over the practice of law to the courts. (See Chapter 1.) Of the states that do allow such actions, some apply consumer protection statutes only to the entrepreneurial or commercial aspects of law practice, such as advertising and fee setting. Louisiana, Texas, Connecticut, Washington, Colorado, and Florida allow lawyers to be sued under the statutes. (See *Reed v. Allison & Perrone*, 376 So. 2d 1067 (La. App. 4th Cir. 1979); *Heslin v. Conn. Law Clinic*, 190 Conn. 510, 461 A.2d 938 (1983); *Short v. Demopolis*, 103 Wash. 52, 691 P.2d 163 (1984); *Kelly v. Palmer, Reifler & Assoc.*, 681 F. Supp. 2d 1356 (S.D. Fla. 2010).) The states that have held that these statutes may not be used against lawyers include Illinois, New Jersey, Georgia, New Hampshire, Pennsylvania, and Delaware. (See, for example, *Rousseau v. Eshleman*, 128 N.H. 564, 519 A.2d 243 (1986);

Crowe v. Tull, 126 P.3d 196 (Colo. 2006); *Latham v. Castillo*, 972 S.W.2d 66 (Tex. 1998); *Cripe v. Leiter*, 184 Ill. 2d 185, 703 N.E.2d 100 (1998); *Jamgochian v. Prousalis*, 99C-10-022 (Del. Super. 2000); *Averill v. Cox*, 145 N.H. 328, 761 A.2d 1083 (2000); *Macedo v. Russo*, 178 N.J. 340, 840 A.2d 238 (2004); *Beyers v. Richmond*, 594 Pa. 654, 937 A.2d 1082 (2007); *State v. Hanna & Assoc.*, 287 Ga. 289 (2000).)

Providing legal information or services over the Internet creates issues about the establishment of the **attorney-client relationship**. As discussed in both Chapters 3 and 6, lawyers who give their opinions in chat rooms or on Web sites that provide "legal information" run the risk of inadvertently establishing a lawyer-client relationship that may end in a malpractice suit if the "client" is dissatisfied with the outcome of the matter.

G. Avoiding Malpractice

The cost of malpractice insurance has continued to rise over the last 30 years. About 10 percent of firms do not carry such insurance. Some are self-insured, maintaining their own fund for paying out claims should the need arise. It is worth noting that a growing number of states require malpractice coverage, and the ABA has a Model Court Rule that would require lawyers to indicate on state registration forms whether or not they carry malpractice insurance. A few states require that lawyers inform clients whether or not they are covered.

The following is a summary of advice on avoiding malpractice claims:

1. Lawyers should use carefully drafted **letters of engagement** as well as **letters terminating or declining representation**. These documents must spell out and limit the scope of representation, the expectations and responsibilities of the law firm, and those of the client. Engagement letters should clearly indicate that the lawyer is not guaranteeing a particular outcome.
2. **Clients should be selected carefully**. Difficult personalities and questionable cases should not be accepted. Lawyers should learn about the client before accepting a case, checking for a history of fraud, legal problems, changing lawyers, criminal activity, and so on.
3. Lawyers and clients should enter into complete and well-drafted **fee agreements** for each representation that cover all the terms noted in Chapter 7. Fee agreements should be entered into as soon as possible in the representation and should be followed meticulously.
4. Clients should be charged **reasonable fees** that are in accord with the fee agreements. Bills should be detailed and should be reviewed before being sent. Excessive, duplicative, or inappropriate charges

should be removed before sending bills. Billing should be prepared and sent regularly and timely.

5. Clients' **phone calls and e-mails should be returned promptly**, preferably the same day. Attorneys and paralegals should take the time to educate the client about the law and legal process and show that they care about clients' concerns. Clients should be sent copies of documents and work product. Correspondence and other materials from clients should be promptly acknowledged.
6. Lawyers and paralegals should **listen to clients** carefully and try to understand their goals and expectations. Unrealistic expectations should be addressed immediately and thoughtfully.
7. Lawyers should exercise **independent judgment** on clients' behalf and should **respect clients' decisions.**
8. Law firms should have **good management systems** and **well-trained personnel** in place, especially concerning the following matters:

   - conflicts checks and screens
   - protection of client confidentiality
   - calendaring deadlines, court dates, and the like
   - billing and time keeping
   - handling client property
   - client trust accounts

9. Lawyers and paralegals should be scrupulous in the handling of **clients' funds** in keeping with the rules set forth in Chapter 7. Client trust accounts and related records must be perfectly maintained with no commingling or other irregularities. Client files must be turned over promptly upon termination and settlements must be paid promptly after receipt.
10. If a client asks for advice on an **unsettled area of law**, the lawyer should be sure that the client understands that the area of law is unsettled and that the lawyer is making a judgment about the likely state of the law, not a guarantee.
11. Be meticulous about checking for **conflicts of interest** and, when appropriate, obtaining consents and establishing screens.
12. Lawyers and paralegals should know the **limits of their competence** and should seek guidance and consultation when in doubt about how to proceed on a matter. Lawyers should not accept cases for which they do not have the necessary expertise and should not "dabble" in these areas.
13. Firms should provide **education** for lawyers and paralegals and have mentors for employees to consult for **support** when challenged by an assignment.
14. The **culture** of the firm and its commitment to high standards can deter the kind of sloppy work that leads to malpractice actions.
15. The firm management should also be alert to employees who may have **personal or substance abuse problems** that could interfere with their work.

Paralegals can help firms avoid malpractice. Communication with clients is greatly improved when lawyers give paralegals responsibility for keeping clients informed. When clients call and the lawyer is unavailable, the paralegal can take or return calls promptly. Keeping accurate and detailed time records and alerting the lawyer to potential problems in time and billing can prevent problems with clients. Paralegals often have responsibility for monitoring deadlines and handling client funds, especially in small law firms.

H. Factors Affecting Paralegal Competence

Paralegals must be cognizant not only of the meaning of competence and how it is embodied in their work, but also of the factors that may either enhance their competence or detract from it. Because paralegals work under the direction and supervision of lawyers, they are not in a position to establish the quality standards for the firm or determine the firm culture. However, paralegals can influence firm standards and culture and can seek out firms that have high standards of quality and encourage competence and professionalism.

Paralegals face some common competence-related issues. Perhaps the most common is being asked to perform a task that the paralegal does not have the requisite knowledge or skill to perform. This scenario presents an especially difficult dilemma for paralegals, who want to do challenging, interesting work and who know their value is in relieving lawyers from tasks that they would otherwise have to perform. A new paralegal, like a lawyer just out of law school, must learn on the job. With a strong education, good research and drafting skills, self-confidence, and motivation, a paralegal can learn how to perform assigned tasks by conducting research, finding models in firm files, and consulting with a mentor or colleague in the firm. If the paralegal accepts a new and challenging assignment, the supervising lawyer should be made aware that the paralegal has not previously undertaken such a task, so that the lawyer exercises a heightened level of review.

A related concern is the proper **delegation**, supervision, and review of paralegal work by attorneys. The ethics and agency rules discussed earlier and in Chapter 2 make it clear that the lawyer is ultimately responsible for the work of the paralegal. For a variety of reasons, attorneys do not always carry out their supervisory responsibilities as well as they should. Many lawyers are not skilled delegators; they often do not give adequate information and instructions when assigning work. Many lawyers are overloaded and simply do not take the time to delegate thoughtfully and to review thoroughly. Proper delegation requires selecting the appropriately skilled person for the task and giving sufficient direction to see that the finished product meets expectations. The information that must be given to the one performing the task includes background on the matter or reference to appropriate files that contain relevant information; an exact description of the end product desired; references to sources that may be of assistance; deadline dates; and, if possible, an estimate of the time the task should take. Paralegals given assignments without this information may end up spending too much time, creating an end product that was not desired, or missing the expected due date. The paralegal who works for a poor delegator must take the responsibility for getting information and instructions necessary to complete projects correctly and on time by asking the appropriate questions, repeating back instructions to make sure that they have been understood, and reducing oral instructions to writing, which can be done in a short confirming e-mail or memorandum to the attorney.

Paralegals also find that lawyers do not always **review** their work as carefully as they should, especially when the paralegal is a long-term, trusted employee whose competence has been proven. Even if the paralegal is confident in his or her work product, the lawyer must review it. If a paralegal is aware that the lawyer is not reviewing adequately, the paralegal should discuss the matter with the lawyer to encourage more careful review. The problem of inadequate review is exacerbated when a paralegal is working for an inexperienced lawyer who does not have expertise in the relevant area of practice. If the paralegal is very experienced, the lawyer may rely too heavily or even completely on the paralegal's expertise. For an example of a nonlawyer employee not being properly supervised, read *De Vaux v. American Home Assurance Co.* at the end of this chapter.

A **heavy workload** often interferes with the performance of lawyers, paralegals, and other law firm employees. A recent ABA ethics opinion advises lawyers not to accept a court appointment if their workload is too heavy and to request to be withdrawn if the overload situation arises after the appointment. The opinion notes that many factors determine whether someone's caseload is too heavy, including not only the number of cases, but their complexity, the degree of support provided, the lawyer's ability and experience, and the lawyer's other duties. The opinion also notes the supervisor's ethical duty not to overload lawyers and staff. (ABA Formal Opinion 06-441.)

Signs of a lawyer with an unreasonably heavy workload include taking on too many cases, being poorly organized or managed, and not having adequate staff. Sometimes, especially in litigation, temporary crises occur before and during trial that require everyone involved in a case to work long hours for extended periods. Paralegals need to be assertive enough in their dealings with lawyers to avoid taking on more work than they can competently handle. Too heavy a workload causes a decline in productivity and quality and increases the likelihood of shortcuts being taken and mistakes being made. A firm that continually operates in this crisis mode is not a good place to work — the work will not be done effectively, the stress will be unhealthy, and the staff will not feel personally or professionally satisfied. Paralegals should avoid working for law firms characterized by such constant pressure caused by excessive workloads. They also should be aware of the potential problems created by a temporary heavy workload. When a project or group of projects requires long hours and creates high pressure over an extended period, measures should be taken to remedy the situation. Additional support staff and temporary paralegals to help out may alleviate the situation, making it possible for everyone to function more effectively.

Paralegals should have a realistic perception of their own level and areas of competence and, while striving to learn and develop, should not get so far ahead of their knowledge and skills that they are no longer acting competently. Continuing education, in-house training programs, and mentoring can help paralegals develop and have long and satisfying careers.

An honest **self-assessment** will identify personal characteristics that affect competence. Experienced paralegals know what talents and qualities they do and do not possess, and they optimize their strong points and compensate for their weaknesses. Paralegals should work on improving weak skill areas, strengthen their natural abilities, and seek work that matches their attributes. For example, a paralegal who is not a good writer should strive to improve those skills but should also avoid assignments that require sophisticated writing. A paralegal who works well with people should seek a position that will make use of that ability, such as one that involves supervision of others or frequent client contact.

Paralegals with personal, health, or family problems must consider how these problems affect their work. No one functions effectively when troubled, worried, or distracted. A paralegal who has difficulties outside the office must be alert to the potential for a decline in productivity and accuracy. Paralegals with problems should take special care to ensure that the quality of their work is maintained during stressful periods by double-checking work, getting support from colleagues in the office, and taking time off to address their problems. If problems are serious or ongoing, the paralegal should discuss them with a supervisor for emotional and practical support. Paralegals with substance abuse problems should seek professional help, and their colleagues and friends in the workplace should encourage them to do so.

REVIEW QUESTIONS

1. What are the elements of competence?
2. Are lawyers responsible for the conduct of their paralegals? Cite the relevant ABA Model Rule and the relevant section of the ABA Model Guidelines.

3. Because lawyers are responsible for the professional actions of their paralegals, what is the motivation for paralegals to be competent? Give as many reasons as you can.
4. Describe and compare legal and paralegal education.
5. What kinds of education do lawyers and paralegals need in addition to their formal professional education?
6. What are three good sources of paralegal continuing education?
7. What do the NALA and NFPA ethics guidelines say about competence?
8. How do the Model Rules define competence?
9. Do lawyers and paralegals need to have the same knowledge and skills to be competent? How do their knowledge and skills differ? What skills might they both need?
10. How does the trend toward increasing legal specialization affect competence?
11. What role do law firms' in-house training and orientation programs play in developing competence?
12. How does a paralegal demonstrate competence in preparing a case?
13. What does diligence mean? What is the paralegal's role in ensuring diligence?
14. Give three examples of common problems associated with a lack of diligence or promptness.
15. Why is communication with clients included in the definition of competence? What role can a paralegal play in this area?
16. What are three possible consequences of a lawyer's failure to act competently? What are the possible consequences of a paralegal's incompetence?
17. Give five examples of common grounds for malpractice claims.
18. What is third-party liability? Give two examples of third-party claims against lawyers.
19. Besides negligence, what ethical duties can form the basis for a malpractice claim?
20. What is malicious prosecution and how is it used?
21. Can lawyers be sued under consumer protection statutes?
22. Name five steps that a firm can take to prevent malpractice claims.
23. How should a paralegal respond if he or she is asked to perform a function in which he or she has no expertise?
24. What steps should a paralegal take if his or her supervising attorney gives incomplete instructions on a project?
25. What should a paralegal do if the supervising attorney is not carefully reviewing the paralegal's work?
26. What should a paralegal do if his or her workload is too heavy and cannot be handled in a timely and effective manner?
27. What might a paralegal do upon learning that another paralegal in the firm has a substance abuse problem that is affecting his or her work?

DISCUSSION QUESTIONS AND HYPOTHETICALS

1. Do you think states should set minimum levels of education for paralegals? Why, or why not?
2. What would your model of paralegal education be if you were required to set minimum standards? Consider how much college education and paralegal education should be included. How would your model look if it were an ideal, rather than a minimum?
3. Do you think paralegals should have to take a licensing exam to demonstrate their competence? Why, or why not? What should such an exam cover?
4. Are there any other elements that you think should be added to the definition of competence given in the ABA Model Rules 1.1, 1.3, and 1.4?
5. How can you tell whether a law firm encourages competence and quality?
6. What would you do if on your first day on the job, right out of paralegal school, an attorney asked you to draft an antitrust complaint for filing the next day in federal court? Assume that your specialties in school were probate and real estate.
7. What would you do if you were an independent probate paralegal and were asked to do work for an attorney who admittedly knew nothing about probate?
8. What would you do if an attorney passed you in the hall, handed you a phone message, and told you to call the client back and draft whatever documents the client asked for?
9. Describe the extent to which an attorney should review the following work:

   a. form complaint
   b. articles of incorporation
   c. a trial notebook
   d. answers to interrogatories
   e. deposition summaries
   f. abstracts of documents in a computerized retrieval system.

10. What would you do if you worked for a firm that was always in an overworked, crisis mode?
11. What would you do if you knew that attorneys in your firm frequently took shortcuts, such as not gathering facts carefully or not researching legal issues thoroughly?
12. Name three personal strengths that may help you in your career. Name three weaknesses that might interfere with your competence or success. Considering these, what should you do to maximize your strengths and minimize your weaknesses? What kind of work are you best suited for? What kind of work environment?

13. What would you do if your best paralegal friend at work was having a personal problem and asked you to cover for his or her tardiness, long personal phone calls, and so forth? What if you could see that this friend was making a lot of mistakes at work? Would it make any difference if the friend were an attorney? Your supervising attorney?

RESEARCH PROJECTS AND ASSIGNMENTS

1. Check the local ethics code in your jurisdiction to see what provisions it contains on competence.
2. Check the listings of lawyers who were recently disciplined in your jurisdiction. What kinds of competence-related issues do you see? What proportion of the sanctions relate directly to issues of competence, as opposed to other kinds of ethical breaches?
3. Call five local law firms and find out:
   a. their hiring standards for paralegals
   b. whether they have in-house orientation or training programs for paralegals
   c. whether they have a mentoring program for paralegals
   d. whether they pay the cost for their paralegals to take continuing education or other job-relevant courses.
4. Call your local paralegal association and get a listing of its continuing education programs for the upcoming year.
5. Obtain the current informational materials on NALA's CLA/CP program and NFPA's PACE program. What are the requirements to take these exams? What is tested on these exams? How many paralegals in your area are certified by one of those organizations? Ask ten paralegals who are certified why they took the exam and how it has affected their careers.
6. To what extent is legal specialization important in your area? Does your jurisdiction have a certified specialist program for attorneys? In what areas of law? How many lawyers are certified? Do most paralegals in your area "specialize"?
7. Interview five paralegals who work in five different areas of practice, asking them to list the functions that they perform and the functions that their attorney-supervisors perform. Compare the lists and look for functions in common. Is there a difference in the competence needed by lawyers and paralegals? What generalities can you draw about the differences and common elements?
8. Does your state or local bar association have a lawyer assistance program to help lawyers who have alcohol or substance abuse problems? What does it do? Does it cover nonlawyer employees such as paralegals?

9. Read *The T.J. Hooper*, 60 F.2d 737 (2d Cir. 1932), and *Whirlpool v. GN Holdings*, 67 F.3d 605 (1995), and see what support they give for the proposition that lawyers must engage in electronic legal research to meet their duty to perform competently.
10. Does your jurisdiction have any cases or statutes about a lawyer's duties to third parties? You can start with the cases cited in this chapter and see what other cases or statutes they cite. If so, what do these cases hold? Do they lean toward expanding or restricting a lawyer's duties to those who are not clients?
11. Does your jurisdiction have any cases interpreting whether consumer protection statutes apply to lawyers? Start with the cases in this chapter on this topic and see what you find. Do the decisions in your jurisdiction allow the use of these statutes as a basis to sue lawyers? Describe the bases for the conflicting interpretations about whether these statutes can be used to sue lawyers. Which position do you support and why?
12. For a case in which a former client sues a law clerk, read *Busch v. Flangas*, 837 P.2d 438 (Nev. 1992).
13. For a case where a lawyer is disciplined for failure to act competently because of the misdeeds of his secretary, see *Mahoning Cty. Bar Ass'n. v. Lavelle*, 107 Ohio St. 3d 92, 836 N.E.2d 1214 (2005). What did the secretary do with regard to each of the two clients who complained? What should the lawyer have done to guard against this conduct? What ABA Model Rule was implicated and how?

CASES FOR ANALYSIS

In this disciplinary matter, a lawyer was sanctioned for incompetence and other violations arising out of an improper relationship with nonlawyers.

In re Gillaspy

640 N.E.2d 1054 (Ind. 1994)

Respondent Joseph M. Gillaspy was charged by Verified Complaint for Disciplinary Action with numerous violations of the *Rules of Professional Conduct for Attorneys at Law*. . . . Rothfuss referred Hamilton and Hamilton's wife to James Wilson ("Wilson") of JNW Management Corporation for the purpose of filing a petition for bankruptcy, pursuant to Chapter 13 of the United States Bankruptcy Code. Like Rothfuss, Wilson was not a lawyer. On August 1, 1991, a voluntary petition for bankruptcy was filed in United States Bankruptcy Court, Southern Division, Indianapolis, on behalf of Hamilton and his wife. The petition listed

Respondent as the attorney of record, even though Wilson had prepared the paperwork relative to the petition. On November 7, 1991, Hamilton and his wife attended the first meeting of creditors, pursuant to Section 341 of the bankruptcy code. At this meeting, Hamilton met Respondent for the first time.

Hamilton did not pay Respondent for the legal services. Respondent received a check for $300.00 from Benefit Planners as payment for the legal services he rendered on behalf of Hamilton. Rothfuss, as president of Benefit Planners, signed the check. Respondent undertook to represent other individuals in bankruptcy matters under circumstances similar to those in the Hamilton bankruptcy.

The agreed facts clearly and convincingly establish that Respondent violated Ind. Professional Conduct Rule 1.4(b) since, having never even met Hamilton or his wife prior to the filing of the bankruptcy petition; Respondent did not explain matters to them to the extent reasonably necessary to permit them to make informed decisions regarding the representation. Because he abdicated the factual and legal analysis of this matter to non-lawyers Rothfuss and Wilson, Respondent failed to provide competent representation and therefore violated Prof. Cond. R. 1.1. Respondent violated Prof. Cond. R. 1.8(f) by accepting compensation from Rothfuss for representing Hamilton, while non-lawyers Rothfuss and Wilson exercised what should have been Respondent's independent professional judgment and confidential lawyer-client relationship between Respondent and the Hamiltons. By sharing fees with Rothfuss and Wilson, allowing them to direct and regulate his professional judgment in rendering legal services, and by assisting Rothfuss and Wilson in activity which constituted the unauthorized practice of law, Respondent violated Prof. Cond. R. 5.4(a), 5.4(c), and 5.5(b). . . .

We are inclined to accept the agreed sanction, noting that Respondent's fee-sharing arrangement with non-lawyers clearly threatened Respondent's independent professional judgment and competence. However, we are also cognizant of the fact that none of the bankruptcy petitioners filed grievances relating to any unprofessional or incompetent representation by Respondent; that Respondent ceased his affiliation with Benefit Planners immediately upon learning that there were ethical problems with the arrangement; and that Respondent was completely cooperative and truthful during the Commission's investigation of this matter. The Commission and Respondent characterize Respondent's dealings with Benefit Planners as resulting from professional naïveté, rather than from a willful scheme to take advantage of clients. . . .

It is, therefore, ordered that Respondent, Joseph M. Gillaspy, is suspended from the practice of law for a period of not less than ninety (90) days, beginning November 14, 1994, with automatic reinstatement to occur immediately after the conclusion of the suspension period. . . .

Questions about the Case

1. Who prepared and filed the bankruptcy? Who appeared at the hearing?
2. What functions did the lawyer Gillaspy and the nonlawyer involved perform in this legal matter? Which constituted the practice of law?
3. Why did the representation here amount to "incompetence"?
4. Who did the clients pay? How was Gillaspy paid?
5. What were the mitigating factors in setting the sanction? What was the sanction? Do you believe that it was an appropriate sanction?

A case of a missed statute of limitations illustrates how an attorney is held responsible for the acts of employees in a malpractice case. As you read, consider how a paralegal might get into a situation like this.

De Vaux v. American Home Assurance Co.

387 Mass. 814, 444 N.E.2d 355 (1983)

. . . On July 17, 1971, the plaintiff fell as she entered a Curtis Compact Store in Hanover. The plaintiff claims that she suffered a serious back injury as a result of this fall. On May 11, 1973, the plaintiff was admitted to South Shore Hospital for removal of a spinal disc.

A few days after her fall, the plaintiff called the defendant attorney's office seeking legal advice. That day a secretary in the attorney's office returned the plaintiff's call and advised her to write a letter to the store stating that she had fallen in the store and received an injury. The secretary also arranged a medical examination for the plaintiff with the store's insurance company. Finally, the secretary instructed the plaintiff to write a letter to the defendant attorney requesting legal assistance.

Following that instruction, the plaintiff personally delivered a letter to the attorney's secretary. In this letter, the plaintiff described her fall. The letter ended with the question. "Would you kindly advise me legally?" The secretary misfiled this letter. The defendant did not discover the letter until June, 1974, after the statute of limitations on the plaintiff's tort claim had run.

From the date she delivered the letter in 1971 until June, 1974, the plaintiff did not visit the defendant attorney's office or speak with him. In the interim, the plaintiff called the attorney's office a number of times. Each time, the plaintiff was told that her calls would be returned. But the attorney never returned any of her calls.

In February, 1978, the plaintiff filed a complaint in the Superior Court alleging that she retained the attorney to represent her concerning the fall at the store. In his answer, the defendant attorney denied that he was ever retained to represent the plaintiff in regard to the fall. . . . "It is the general rule that an attorney's liability for malpractice is limited to some duty owed to a client. . . . Where there is no attorney/client relationship there is no breach or dereliction of duty and therefore no liability."

On appeal, the plaintiff advances two theories in support of her claim that there was an attorney-client relationship between the plaintiff and the attorney. First, the plaintiff argues that the secretary had actual authority to take the actions that she did. Therefore, the secretary's knowledge of the plaintiff's request for legal assistance can be imputed to the attorney. When an agent acquires knowledge in the scope of her employment, the principal, here the attorney, is held to have constructive knowledge of that information. There is a question for the jury whether the secretary's actions concerning the plaintiff's request for the attorney's services were within the scope of her employment. The plaintiff argues that, because the attorney had constructive knowledge of her problem, she reasonably relied on him to provide her with legal assistance. The plaintiff asserts that, therefore, her reliance established an attorney-client relationship.

The plaintiff also contends that the secretary had apparent authority to establish an attorney-client relationship on behalf of the defendant. Apparent authority "results from conduct by the principal which causes a third person reasonably to believe that a particular person . . . has authority to enter into negotiations or to make representations as his agent." Applying the doctrine of apparent authority to this case, the plaintiff claims that the attorney placed his secretary in a position where prospective clients might reasonably believe that she had the authority to establish an attorney-client relationship. There is a question of fact for the jury whether the attorney permitted his secretary to act as she did, thereby creating the appearance of authority. . . .

We find support for both of the plaintiff's theories in the Massachusetts Canons of Ethics and Disciplinary Rules . . . particularly Canon 3, a structure against the unauthorized practice of law. The Canons can be interpreted using the Ethical Considerations of the American Bar Association, Code of Professional Responsibility and Canons of Judicial Ethics (1970). Ethical Consideration 3-6 states:

> A lawyer often delegates tasks to clerks, secretaries, and other lay persons. Such delegation is proper if the lawyer maintains a direct relationship with his client, supervises the delegated work, and has complete professional responsibility for the work product. This delegation enables a lawyer to render legal service more economically and efficiently.

The supervised use of lay persons in a legal office is intended to permit their involvement in most matters, but not in the direct practice of law. See ABA Comm. on Professional Ethics, Formal Op. 316 (1967).

Therefore an attorney should not permit lay persons even to appear to form the attorney-client relationship with a prospective client, because that is part of the practice of law. See ABA Comm. on Ethics and Professional Responsibility, Informal Op. 998 (1967) (advising against a lay employee conducting the initial interview of a client if the client does not confer with the attorney soon afterwards). It is a question for the jury whether the attorney allowed his secretary to act as she did, and whether he knew what she was doing. We believe that an attorney who places his lay employees in a position which may deceive prospective clients as to the attorney's willingness or ability to represent them may be liable for malpractice for the negligence of those employees.

Therefore, there are factual issues for the jury whether the attorney in this case put himself in a position in which he should be liable to the plaintiff. We reverse the judgment of dismissal and remand the case to the Superior Court for trial.

Questions about the Case

1. Why do you think the secretary acted as she did in this case? What ethics rules did she break? Were her functions akin to those of a legal assistant?
2. Explain the two arguments of the plaintiff about actual authority and apparent authority. What does the court decide about these theories, and why?
3. What rule covered in Chapter 3 on unauthorized practice was violated by the secretary's actions in this case?
4. How does the court dispose of this case?

The following case involves a lawyer being disciplined for the conduct of her paralegal, who had been in prison, and addresses an array of competency and supervision issues.

Mississippi Bar v. Thompson
5 So. 3d 330 (Miss. 2008)

Gail Thompson employed Robert Tubwell, a former inmate at the Mississippi State Penitentiary at Parchman, as a paralegal at the Thompson Law Firm in Tunica County. Thompson hired Tubwell based, in part, on his reputation as a successful writ writer while at Parchman, and his potential ability to generate business for Thompson's firm.

Mario McGaughy, an inmate serving a life sentence without the possibility of parole, met Tubwell while the two were at Parchman.

When McGaughy learned that Tubwell was working as a paralegal, he wrote Tubwell at Thompson's law office. McGaughy sought to hire a lawyer to file his petition for post-conviction relief. A series of communications then ensued between Tubwell and McGaughy, McGaughy's mother, and McGaughy's stepfather.

On February 1, 2002, Tubwell wrote McGaughy on Thompson Law Firm letterhead. The letter stated that Tubwell had consulted with Thompson and that she had agreed to work with him on McGaughy's case. Tubwell stated that everything would be reviewed by an attorney and quoted McGaughy a fee of $500 for the preliminary work. He also requested that McGaughy send future correspondence to his Southaven apartment address, and provided McGaughy his personal home and cellular phone numbers.

It is somewhat unclear whether the $500 payment was made, and if so, to whom such payment was directed. McGaughy stated that his father paid $550 via money order, but could not confirm whether the payment was made to the Thompson Law Firm or to Tubwell himself. Tubwell acknowledged that he received fifty dollars for travel-related expenses, but claimed that he never received the $500 money order. Thompson also denied ever receiving anything from McGaughy. Regardless, the complaint tribunal found implicitly that the $500 payment was made.

On March 18, 2002, Tubwell again wrote McGaughy on Thompson Law Firm letterhead. Tubwell advised McGaughy that he had a strong case and that there was a seventy-percent chance that this Court would reverse and grant a new trial.

Tubwell eventually obtained McGaughy's court records and mailed McGaughy his files, along with a pro se petition for post-conviction relief. Per Tubwell's instructions, McGaughy signed and had notarized the necessary documentation without realizing that he was filing pro se. This Court ultimately denied McGaughy's pro se petition for post-conviction relief.

Thereafter, Tubwell informed McGaughy that the next step would be to file a writ of habeas corpus in federal court. Tubwell later wrote McGaughy to inform him that he had begun work on filing the habeas corpus petition. But a petition for habeas corpus was never filed on McGaughy's behalf.

On November 18, 2004, McGaughy, on the belief that he had hired Thompson's law firm to represent him on his application for post-conviction relief and his federal habeas corpus petition, filed an informal complaint against Thompson with the Mississippi Bar. . . .

A hearing was held on March 14, 2006, in which Thompson testified that she was unaware of Tubwell's correspondence with McGaughy, and claimed that he had taken advantage of her. Thompson stated that she trusted Tubwell and had instructed him that any cases he was working on had to come through her office. Yet she admitted that additional safeguards should have been implemented.

In addition to the McGaughy matter, the Bar inquired about Thompson's handling of client files after she moved her law office from Oxford to Tunica in 2000, and when she closed her Tunica practice in 2003. When Thompson moved her practice from Oxford to Tunica in 2000, she left some client files in a storage facility in Oxford. She admitted that those files had been lost. In 2003, Thompson closed her Tunica office after being suspended from the practice of law for a period of eighteen months. After closing the Tunica office, Thompson kept two file drawers of client files in a storage unit in Tunica. She testified that those file drawers were later moved to the home/office of Oxford attorney Alvin Chambliss. She explained that those file drawers remain locked because she lost the keys.

After hearing testimony and arguments, the complaint tribunal issued its opinion on March 16, 2007. . . . Aggrieved by the complaint tribunal's ruling, the Bar appeals to this Court. . . .

The complaint tribunal found that Thompson failed to adequately safeguard client property by losing or misplacing client files. Rule 1.15 requires lawyers to hold the property of others with the care required of a professional fiduciary. M.R.P.C. 1.15, cmt. The loss of client files constitutes a violation of Rule 1.15. [Citations omitted.] Thompson admitted to losing client files that she had placed in an Oxford storage unit. Although Thompson said that she returned important documents to clients "most times," she could not say that she had done so every time. We find that Thompson violated Rule 1.15. . . .

The complaint tribunal found that Thompson did not violate Rule 1.6 because there was no proof that she divulged any confidential client information. With certain exceptions, Rule 1.6 generally prohibits the disclosure of information relating to the representation of a client, absent the client's informed consent. M.R.P.C. 1.6. While Thompson admitted to losing the client files in Oxford, there is no evidence that any of those files were divulged. Likewise, there is no evidence that any of the client files from her Tunica office were disclosed. We find that there is insufficient evidence to show that Thompson violated Rule 1.6.

The complaint tribunal found that Thompson had not violated Rule 1.2(a) or 1.3 because no attorney-client relationship existed between Thompson and McGaughy. The Bar contends that Tubwell, acting as an agent for Thompson, communicated Thompson's consent to act as McGaughy's lawyer, and that Thompson should have known of McGaughy's reliance. Rule 1.2(a) provides that a lawyer shall abide by a client's decisions concerning the objectives of representation and shall consult with the client as to the means by which they are pursued. M.R.P.C. 1.2(a). Rule 1.3 requires a lawyer to act with reasonable diligence and promptness in representing a client. M.R.C.P. 1.3. For either rule to be implicated, an attorney-client relationship must exist.

The existence of an attorney-client relationship depends upon the circumstances and may be a question of fact. M.R.P.C., SCOPE. The

Restatement (Third) of the Law Governing Lawyers, Section 14 (2000), states, in pertinent part . . . :

> A relationship of client and lawyer arises when:
> (1) a person manifests to a lawyer the person's intent that the lawyer provide legal services for the person; and either
> (a) the lawyer manifests to the person consent to do so; or
> (b) the lawyer fails to manifest lack of consent to do so, and the lawyer knows or reasonably should know that the person reasonably relies on the lawyer to provide the services. . . .

A lawyer's consent to represent a client need not be made by the lawyer himself. "An agent for the lawyer may communicate consent, for example, a secretary or paralegal with express, implied, or apparent authority to act for the lawyer in undertaking a representation." Restatement (Third) of the Law Governing Lawyers §14 cmt. e (2000).

Thompson hired Tubwell to do legal research and draft briefs. He was told not to independently communicate with clients. Thus, Tubwell lacked express authority to communicate Thompson's consent to represent a client. Tubwell also lacked implied authority because communicating Thompson's consent to represent a client was not "necessary, proper, and usual," in the exercise of his express duties. [Citations omitted.]

Apparent authority is "authority that the principal has by words or conduct held the alleged agent out as having." [Citation omitted.] Apparent authority requires "(1) acts or conduct of the principal indicating the agent's authority, (2) reasonable reliance on those acts, and (3) detrimental change in position as a result of reliance." [Citations omitted.] A principal is "bound if the conduct of the principal is such that persons of reasonable prudence, ordinarily familiar with business practices, dealing with the agent might rightfully believe the agent to have the power he assumes to have."

The Bar cites *De Vaux v. American Home Assurance Co.*, 387 Mass. 814, 444 N.E.2d 355 (1983), for support. In *De Vaux*, an individual called the attorney's office seeking legal advice. The attorney's secretary returned this person's phone call and rendered some legal advice, arranged for a medical examination, and instructed the person to write a letter requesting the attorney's assistance. This person delivered a letter to the attorney's office, but the secretary misfiled the letter. As a result, the attorney failed to discover the letter until after the statute of limitations had expired. The person then filed a malpractice suit against the attorney based, in part, on a theory that the secretary had apparent authority to establish an attorney-client relationship on behalf of the attorney. The plaintiff claimed that the attorney had placed the secretary in a position in which prospective clients might reasonably believe that she had the authority to establish an attorney-client relationship. The Supreme

Judicial Court of Massachusetts held that "[i]t is a question for the jury whether the attorney allowed his secretary to act as she did, and whether he knew what she was doing."

Thompson stated that Tubwell had not been given authority independently to communicate with clients and had been instructed not to sign any letters. She told Tubwell that any cases he worked on had to come through her office. Thompson included Tubwell's name on the law firm letterhead, but identified him as a paralegal. Furthermore, she disclaimed any knowledge of Tubwell's correspondence with McGaughy or his work on McGaughy's case. We find insufficient evidence to support that Thompson, by her words, actions, or conduct, indicated that Tubwell had authority to communicate her consent to undertake the representation of a client.

We also find that no attorney-client relationship was established by Thompson's failure to communicate her lack of consent to represent McGaughy. Thompson had no knowledge of McGaughy's case or Tubwell's correspondence with McGaughy, and therefore, could not reasonably have known about McGaughy's reliance on her services. Because no attorney-client relationship existed, we find that Thompson did not violate Rules 1.2(a) and 1.3. . . .

The complaint tribunal found that Thompson had violated Rule 5.3 by failing to implement adequate safeguards to give reasonable assurance that Tubwell's conduct complied with the professional obligations of a lawyer. The tribunal concluded that Thompson's lack of supervision had permitted Tubwell to engage in the unauthorized practice of law.[10]

Rule 5.3 provides that a lawyer with managerial authority in a law firm "shall make reasonable efforts to ensure that the firm has in effect measures giving reasonable assurance that the [non-lawyer's] conduct is compatible with the professional obligations of the lawyer. . . ." Thompson testified that she had total control of the firm's post office box and that she reviewed all mail that came into the firm, including any letters addressed to Tubwell. McGaughy stated that every letter he wrote to Tubwell was addressed to the Thompson Law Firm in Tunica. While it is unclear from the record exactly how many letters McGaughy sent to Tubwell, six letters from Tubwell to McGaughy acknowledged, either directly or implicitly, the receipt of an earlier letter from McGaughy. Nevertheless, Thompson said she could not recall seeing any letters from McGaughy.

While Thompson set forth some general instructions and procedures, she admitted that she had not done enough. When asked what steps

10. "The practice of law includes the drafting or selection of documents, the giving of advice in regard to them, and the using of an informed or trained discretion in the drafting of documents to meet the needs of the person being served. So any exercise of intelligent choice in advising another of his legal rights and duties brings the activity within the practice of the legal profession." [Citations omitted.].

she had put into place to ensure that Tubwell was not independently working on cases that he had handled while in prison, Thompson answered:

> Other than trusting him and, you know, telling him that any cases that, you know, we have, any cases that you have that you're working on, it's got to come through my office. . . . And, you know, had I — I guess had the foresight or just had — [he] didn't give me any reason to distrust him. You know, I wouldn't have — you know, I would have put other, I guess, precautions in place.

Furthermore, while she knew about Tubwell's armed robbery conviction at the time she hired him, she was unaware of his prior conviction for forgery until she read his deposition in this matter.

We find that Thompson violated Rule 5.3 by failing to make sufficient efforts to supervise Tubwell's work. This is especially true in light of Tubwell's criminal past and Thompson's awareness of the fact that Tubwell might have continued to work on cases from his earlier days as a writ writer. While Thompson's ill-advised choice of an untrustworthy paralegal may bear upon the degree to which she could foresee Tubwell's actions, it does not excuse her violation of the rules of professional conduct. [Citation omitted.].

The complaint tribunal held that there was insufficient evidence to find that Tubwell had violated Rule 5.5(b). The tribunal determined that there was not enough evidence to show that Thompson knew or should have known that Tubwell was holding out himself or her firm as attorneys for McGaughy. The Bar, however, asserts that a lawyer can assist a non-lawyer in the unauthorized practice of law by giving him all the necessary resources to practice law, and then failing to supervise him.

Rule 5.5(b) prohibits a lawyer from assisting a non-lawyer in the unauthorized practice of law. While a lawyer may employ paralegals and delegate duties to them, the lawyer must supervise the delegated work and retain responsibility for it. The Bar cites *In re Gaff*, 272 Ga. 7, 524 S.E.2d 728 (2000), to support its argument that a Rule 5.5 violation can occur as a result of a lawyer's failure to supervise. In *In re Gaff*, Gaff opened a second law office in another town and allowed a disbarred attorney, Ellis, to work there unsupervised as a paralegal. *Gaff*, 524 S.E.2d. at 728. Gaff failed to implement procedures to insure that Ellis did not have contact with Gaff's clients. Ellis engaged in forgery, theft, and met with and assisted clients on his own. The Supreme Court of Georgia held that Gaff had assisted Ellis in the unauthorized practice of law by failing to supervise him and failing to establish precautionary policies and procedures. . . .

While Tubwell took advantage of his position in Thompson's firm and engaged in the unauthorized practice of law without her direct knowledge, her failure to supervise and enforce necessary precautions allowed his actions to go unnoticed. . . . Accordingly, we find that Thompson assisted Tubwell in the unauthorized practice of law by giving him the position and resources necessary to practice law, and then failing to adequately supervise him. Therefore, we find that Thompson violated Rule 5.5(b). . . .

Rule 8.4(a), (d), provides that it is professional misconduct to violate or to attempt to violate the rules of professional conduct and to engage in conduct that is prejudicial to the administration of justice. M.R.P.C. 8.4(a), (d). Whenever there is a violation of any other rule, there will always be a violation under Rule 8.4. [Citation omitted.]. Having found that Thompson violated Rules 1.15, 5.3, and 5.5(b), we necessarily find that she violated Rule 8.4(a) as well. Furthermore, Thompson's conduct was prejudicial to the administration of justice, because McGaughy was deprived of his right to file a habeas corpus petition and paid for non-existent representation. Therefore, we find that Thompson violated Rule 8.4(a), (d). . . .

In imposing the retroactive, one-year suspension, the complaint tribunal failed to examine the nine factors that are required to be considered in attorney disciplinary matters. Those factors are:

> (1) The nature of the misconduct involved; (2) the need to deter similar misconduct; (3) the preservation of dignity and reputation of the legal profession; (4) the protection of the public; (5) sanctions imposed in similar cases; (6) the duty violated; (7) the lawyer's mental state; (8) the actual or potential injury resulting from the misconduct; and (9) the existence of aggravating or mitigating factors. [Citations omitted.]

The Bar contends that this case merits a harsher penalty than a one-year, retroactive suspension. . . . Thompson's conduct reflects a continuing pattern of neglect as to her professional responsibilities. Her neglect ultimately caused severe prejudice to McGaughy. While Thompson acknowledged her wrongdoing and gave some indication that she has learned from her mistakes, the public maintains an interest in proper and prompt discipline. . . . Neither the passage of time nor subsequent developments have lessened such public interest in this case. . . . [12]

We affirm the complaint tribunal with regard to its finding that Thompson violated Rules 1.15, 5.3, and 8.4(a), (d). We find that Thompson also violated Rule 5.5(b), and therefore, reverse the complaint tribunal's finding as to that issue. . . . [W]e reverse the one-year, retroactive suspension and remand this case to the tribunal for consideration of the appropriate sanction(s) in light of these factors.

12. The record indicates that Thompson has a history of disciplinary violations. In addition to her aforementioned eighteen-month suspension for mishandling client funds in 2003, Thompson was privately reprimanded in 1997 and 2002, and publicly reprimanded in 2002. Thompson's prior disciplinary conduct should be considered as an aggravating factor on remand.

Questions about the Case

1. What was the relationship of the lawyer Thompson and her paralegal Tubwell? Why did she hire Tubwell? Was he qualified to work as a paralegal? What kinds of background checks or conditions should lawyers insist on when hiring a paralegal?
2. What were the ways in which Tubwell acted unethically or incompetently in this case? What should Thompson have done to prevent these breaches?
3. What did you learn about protecting the records of clients? What other ethical issues are raised by Thompson's conduct concerning the files?
4. Do you agree with the court's analysis about apparent authority? Do you think that the facts here are substantially different from those in *DeVaux?*
5. Do you agree that Thompson aided in UPL? Why or why not? What was the UPL? Could Thompson have prevented it?
6. Given the factors to be considered in setting the sanction, as cited in the case, what do you think is an appropriate sanction?

In this disciplinary matter, a lawyer fails to supervise a paralegal and is held accountable for her many errors.

People v. Smith

74 P.3d 566 (Colo. O.P.D.J. 2003)

During the relevant time period from 1999 to 2001, Smith was a sole practitioner. He handled a large-volume practice with approximately half of the practice devoted to domestic law. Jeanette Ross ("Ross") worked as Smith's legal assistant from 1996 to 2001. During the period of her employment, Smith put measures in place to assure that all communications, oral and written, were brought to his attention. Ross was required to receive, open and sort mail and record telephone messages. Ross would review incoming mail and place matters requiring prompt attention on Smith's desk with the client file. Less critical communication was placed in sorted stacks for Smith's review. Smith would then review his mail or telephone messages and instruct Ross what action to take on a given case. It was Smith's practice to review all court orders. Smith did not utilize computer software to track deadlines in cases. Smith and Ross did, however, manually record dates on two calendars. In addition, Smith allowed Ross to prepare form pleadings, prepare and send correspondence, docket court appearances, communicate with clients by phone, and handle settings with the court. Smith periodically reviewed case files to determine if cases were properly advancing.

Smith did not give Ross permission to sign his name to pleadings. Ross was permitted to write checks on Smith's operating account and utilize his signature stamp on operating account checks without prior authorization from Smith. Ross testified that she signed Smith's name to routine pleadings. Ross's testimony that Smith permitted her to sign his name to pleadings was not credible. . . .

In late 1998, Roy Reynolds, Jr. ("Reynolds") retained Smith to represent him in an uncontested divorce and paid him $800. . . . On January 27, 1999, Smith filed Reynolds' Petition for Dissolution of Marriage together with a Summons for Dissolution of Marriage or Legal Separation and Temporary Injunction. . . . On the same day, the court issued a form order entitled "Domestic Case Management and Delay Reduction Order" requiring that Smith take specified actions by a date certain. The order required Smith to provide a copy to Mrs. Reynolds. Although Smith did not see the order, he was fully aware of the routine procedure in uncontested divorces and knew what deadlines were imposed by the court as a matter of course. Smith did not set a Temporary Orders Hearing or engage in the pre-hearing conference as required by the court's order. Smith knew that Mrs. Reynolds was pregnant and he felt it necessary to wait for the birth of the child before requesting that the court enter child support orders. Smith did not file a plan for alternative dispute resolution by the stated deadline due to his unconfirmed belief Reynolds' desired to forestall the divorce.

Thereafter, Mrs. Reynolds, who resided in Kansas, signed a Waiver and Acceptance of Service and Affidavit with Respect to Financial Affairs prepared by Smith, and returned both documents to Smith's office. Mrs. Reynolds did not obtain counsel at that time.

Between January and May, Smith and Reynolds were in communication. In May 1999, Smith drafted a Settlement Agreement and gave it to Reynolds to review. Reynolds took the Separation Agreement prepared by Smith to Kansas for Mrs. Reynolds to sign, and she signed it on June 16, 1999, had it notarized and gave it back to Reynolds. Reynolds gave it back to Ross shortly thereafter. Reynolds failed to sign it. Smith was unaware that Reynolds had returned the Separation Agreement to his office.

On May 20, 1999, Ross filed a Notice to Set regarding a hearing on Permanent Orders. Ross affixed Smith's signature to the Notice to Set. Thereafter, she neglected to call the court at the appointed time to set the hearing.

On June 7, 1999, the court issued a form Status Order notifying the parties that the Reynolds case would be dismissed unless Smith took certain specific actions. Smith did not see the Status Order, did not take any of the actions the court directed him to take, and did not provide a copy of the Order to the parties. Smith believed that the case was proceeding on course and that he was waiting for a return of the signed Separation Agreement by the parties.

Ross, in an effort to cover her failure to follow through on the Notice to Set, filed another Notice to Set on June 10, 1999. Smith signed the notice but did not confirm with Ross that she set the hearing. A hearing was not set.

Ross attempted to contact Reynolds but was unable to do so. Smith told Ross to send a letter to Reynolds and advise him that the case may be dismissed if the Separation Agreement was not filed. Smith believed Ross did so, but did not check the file to confirm that she had. Ross did not send a letter to Reynolds.

During July and August 1999, Reynolds attempted to contact Smith several times but was able to only speak to Ross. The calls were not routed to Smith, and Smith was not advised that Reynolds was attempting to reach him.

On August 11, 1999, the court dismissed the case on the grounds that the parties had not complied with the court's June 7, 1999 Status Order and required Smith to provide a copy of the order to the parties. Smith did not see the order and therefore did not comply with it. Smith continued to believe that Reynolds had lost interest in pursuing the divorce.

In October, Ross contacted the court to set the matter for a Permanent Orders hearing. It was at this point that she discovered the case had been dismissed. She determined to conceal this fact from Smith. On October 25, 1999, without Smith's knowledge or approval, Ross filed a Notice to Set Uncontested Permanent Orders, an Affidavit With Respect to Financial Affairs and the Separation Agreement both of which Mrs. Reynolds had signed on June 16, 1999. Ross hoped that the court would reopen the case. Nothing further occurred . . . in [the] [c]ase. . . .

In early 2000, due to the lack of communication with Smith, Reynolds came to Smith's office to inquire about the status of his case. Reynolds never spoke directly with Smith; rather, he believed at the time that Ross was his lawyer. Reynolds confronted Ross with the court order dismissing the case in August 1999 which he first saw when he reviewed the court file at the courthouse. Ross told Reynolds the court had lost the paperwork and it would be necessary to file a new case. Ross did not tell Smith about Reynolds' visit to the office.

On March 6, 2000, without Smith's knowledge or approval, Ross commenced a new action on behalf of Reynolds by filing a Summons for Dissolution of Marriage and Temporary Injunction in Arapahoe County District Court. . . . Ross affixed Smith's signature to the documents. Ross falsely notarized a Waiver and Acceptance of Service and affixed Mrs. Reynolds' signature without her knowledge or authority.

The next day, without informing Smith, Ross sent a letter to Reynolds enclosing financial affidavits, a Separation Agreement and Child Support Worksheets. After receiving these documents, Reynolds came to the office and was angry with Ross. Ross did not inform Smith that

Reynolds had visited the office. Smith believed the case was closed because Reynolds had not signed the Separation Agreement. Smith had no communication with Reynolds in 2000.

On March 20, 2000, Ross filed a Petition for Dissolution of Marriage and affixed Smith's name to the pleading.

In July 2000, Mrs. Reynolds believed the divorce had been finalized. She contacted Smith's office and spoke to Ross numerous times and to Smith once, asking for a copy of the decree. Ross informed her she would inquire into the status of the case and get back to her. Later Ross told Mrs. Reynolds she was not sure why there was no decree and that there was some confusion in Smith's office. After receiving a call from Mrs. Reynolds' father, Smith asked Ross about the status of the case. Ross said that Reynolds came in to sign the Separation Agreement and that they were waiting to receive a decree from the court. Smith then told Mrs. Reynolds that he was waiting for a decree from the court and that he would get back to her. Smith did not get back to Mrs. Reynolds.

On July 15, 2000, Ross drafted a second Separation Agreement. She affixed the signatures of Smith as counsel for Reynolds, Mrs. Reynolds, and the attorney's name who shared Smith's office as counsel for Mrs. Reynolds. Ross notarized the signatures stating that she witnessed the signatures in Adams County, even though Mrs. Reynolds continued to reside in Kansas. Ross filed it with the court. Neither Smith, Mrs. Reynolds nor the attorney who was purportedly signing as counsel for Mrs. Reynolds knew that Ross had affixed their signatures to the document. Ross knew at the time that Smith would not condone her drafting the Separation Agreement and affixing signatures to it.

In August 2000, Ross filed an Affidavit for Decree Without Appearance of Parties with the court. She affixed the signatures of Smith and the attorney who shared Smith's office as counsel for Mrs. Reynolds without their knowledge or approval. Ross knew the court would rely on the document as containing valid signatures and knew at the time she filed the document that she was making a false statement to the court.

Finally, in the spring of 2001, Mrs. Reynolds hired an attorney in Kansas to commence a new divorce proceeding at a cost of $1,500. On April 3, 2001, Ross sent a letter to Mrs. Reynolds' attorney in Kansas stating that the dissolution of marriage action in Arapahoe County had not been dismissed. She wrote the letter on behalf of Smith and affixed his signature to the letter without his knowledge. On the same date, she notified the clerk of the district court in Shawnee County, Topeka, Kansas, that the matter had not been dismissed, and again affixed Smith's name to the letter without his knowledge.

On April 12, 2001, a Decree of Dissolution of Marriage issued from Arapahoe District Court in [the second case]. The Magistrate entered the Decree unaware that it had been presented by Ross with falsified signatures of the attorneys and parties.

Shortly thereafter, the divorce proceeding in Kansas was completed and Mrs. Reynolds obtained a decree.

Smith acknowledged that he was responsible for Ross's actions, but also believed that his actions were based on his belief that Reynolds had decided not to go forward with the divorce. Smith also believed that were it not for Ross's actions as an "intervening cause," he would have been aware of the court's orders and of Reynolds' communication with Ross.

Both parties suffered harm as a result of the delay in obtaining the divorce: Mrs. Reynolds applied for but could not obtain financial aid because she was required to include Mr. Reynolds' income on her application, and she paid additional attorneys' fees to resolve the divorce. Mr. Reynolds was required to resolve child support issues in another jurisdiction. Both parties suffered personal inconvenience and stress for over one and one half years.

Smith refunded the $800 Reynolds paid to him.

The Complaint filed in this matter alleges that Smith's conduct violated Colo. RPC 1.3 (an attorney shall act with reasonable diligence and promptness in representing a client) in claim one; Colo. RPC 1.4(a) (an attorney shall keep a client reasonably informed about the status of a matter and promptly comply with reasonable requests for information) and Colo. RPC 1.4(b) (an attorney shall explain a matter to the extent reasonably necessary to permit the client to make informed decisions regarding the representation) in claim two; Colo. RPC 5.3(a) (partner in a law firm shall make reasonable efforts to ensure that the firm has in effect measures giving reasonable assurance that the person's conduct is compatible with the professional obligations of the lawyer) and Colo. RPC 5.3(b) (a lawyer having direct supervisory authority over the non-lawyer shall make reasonable efforts to ensure that the person's conduct is compatible with the professional obligations of the lawyer) in claim three, and Colo. RPC 1.16(d) (upon termination an attorney take steps to the extent reasonably practicable to protect a client's interests) in claim four.

Colo. RPC 5.3 provides:

> With respect to a non-lawyer employed or retained by or associated with a lawyer:
>
> (a) a partner in a law firm shall make reasonable efforts to ensure that the firm has in effect measures giving reasonable assurance that the person's conduct is compatible with the professional obligations of a lawyer;
>
> (b) a lawyer having direct supervisory authority over the non-lawyer shall make reasonable efforts to ensure that the person's conduct is compatible with the professional obligations of the lawyer. . . .

Smith entered into an attorney/client relationship with Reynolds, thereby forming an obligation to perform the agreed-upon professional services, including obtaining a divorce for Reynolds through the entry of permanent orders. By agreeing to perform the requested services, Smith inherently agreed that he would perform the services in accordance with the Colorado Rules of Professional Conduct. The Complaint alleges that Smith did not have measures in place which would give reasonable assurance that Ross's conduct was compatible with the obligations of a lawyer. The evidence presented, however, revealed that Smith did have measures in place to reasonably assure that all communications with his office were promptly brought to his attention and that Ross would conduct herself in such a manner as was compatible with his professional responsibilities. Ross didn't follow those measures. Since such measures were in place, the charged violation of Colo. RPC 5.3(a) is dismissed.

The charged violation of Colo. RPC 5.3(b) requires a different consideration. Colo. RPC 5.3(b) focuses upon whether the attorney having direct supervisory authority over a non-lawyer adequately supervises that individual. Smith had direct supervisory authority over Ross in this case. He delegated substantial responsibility to her and failed to review her work. Indeed, although the client file was in his office for the entire period of time the events were unfolding, he did not review that file to determine if Ross was, in fact, attending to the case as she described to him. Smith's failure to adequately supervise Ross allowed her to conceal the court's orders requiring that Smith take specific action on Reynolds' behalf, including setting a temporary orders hearing, engaging in alternative dispute resolution or informing the court that none was necessary, calendaring all deadlines set by the court, confirming that Smith's office was in contact with the client, and confirming the correct status of the case. A simple examination of the Reynolds file would have disclosed Ross's activities and alerted Smith of the problems developing in the case.

Smith's failure to adequately supervise Ross resulted in her engaging in the unauthorized practice of law. Smith's acting as Ross's direct supervisor but failing to fulfill his professional obligations with regard to that supervision violated Colo. RPC 5.3(b). Allowing a non-lawyer assistant to engage in the unauthorized practice of law by failing to supervise the non-lawyer is grounds for discipline. *People v. Reynolds*, 933 P.2d 1295, 1298-99 (Colo. 1997); *People v. Stewart*, 892 P.2d 875, 877-78 (Colo. 1995).

Smith argues that but for Ross's failing to advise him of Reynolds' attempts to contact him, her failing to provide him with the court's orders, and her failing to advise him that the case had been dismissed, he would not have neglected the client's case. Smith's argument is without merit.

Other jurisdictions have examined this issue. The Restatement (Third) of Law Governing Law. §11 (2003) concerning a lawyer's duty of supervision, provides:

Supervision is a general responsibility of a principal. A . . . lawyer with authority to direct the activities of another lawyer or nonlawyer employee of the firm is such a principal. Appropriate exercise of responsibility over those carrying out the tasks of law practice is particularly important given the duties of lawyers to protect the interests of clients and in view of the privileged powers conferred on lawyers by law. The supervisory duty, in effect, requires that such additional experience and skill be deployed in reasonably diligent fashion.

Lack of awareness of misconduct by another person, either lawyer or nonlawyer, under a lawyer's supervision does not excuse a violation of this Section. To ensure that supervised persons comply with professional standards, a supervisory lawyer is required to take reasonable measures, given the level and extent of responsibility that the lawyer possesses. Those measures, such as an informal program of instructing or monitoring another person, must often assume the likelihood that a particular lawyer or nonlawyer employee may not yet have received adequate preparation for carrying out that person's own responsibilities. . . .

After initially pursuing the Reynolds matter and drafting a separation agreement, Smith lost contact with Reynolds and failed to inform himself of the status of the case. He failed to comply with the court's January 27, 1999 and June 7, 1999 orders. Even if as Smith asserts he did not see the court orders and therefore could not comply with them, he was fully aware of the procedures and deadlines set forth by the court in a divorce proceeding. Smith failed to make every effort to locate the client and acquire his signature on the Separation Agreement, and failed to take adequate measures to confirm the status of the case. Instead, he relied on Ross to oversee the file. Smith's failing to take the required steps to resolve the Reynolds matter constitutes neglect in violation of Colo. RPC 1.3.

Although Smith's conduct clearly constitutes neglect, it does not, however, rise to the level of abandonment. To find abandonment rather than mere neglect, the evidence must objectively indicate that counsel deserted, rejected, and/or relinquished his professional responsibilities. In the present case, although Smith should have taken measures to locate Reynolds, Ross did not inform Smith that Reynolds had come to the office inquiring about the status of the case. Smith continued to believe that Reynolds had lost interest in pursuing the divorce. Ross fostered Smith's lack of awareness of Reynolds' numerous attempts to contact him. He did not, therefore, desert, reject or relinquish his professional responsibilities. Smith's actions did not terminate the attorney client relationship with Reynolds and the provisions set forth in Colo. RPC 1.16(d) were not triggered. Accordingly, claim four alleging a violation of Colo. RPC 1.16(d) is dismissed.

Initially, for approximately the first four months of representation, Smith stayed in adequate contact with Reynolds and kept him informed of the case status. Thereafter, however, for a period of a year and a half, Smith violated Colo. RPC 1.4(a) by failing to keep Reynolds reasonably informed about the status of the divorce proceeding. Smith violated

Colo. RPC 1.4(b) by failing to explain the procedural status of the case to Reynolds to the extent reasonably necessary to permit the client to make informed decisions. His failure to inform himself of the status of the case does not abrogate his responsibility to keep the client reasonably informed.

Smith's conduct regarding the Reynolds matter resulted in injury to Reynolds: his divorce matter was dismissed, both parties suffered considerable distress not knowing whether they were divorced over a considerable period of time, and Reynolds must suffer the inconvenience of pursuing his legal rights in another jurisdiction.

MATTHEW S. SMITH . . . is suspended from the practice of law for a period of nine months. . . . Smith shall pay the costs in conjunction with this matter. . . .

Questions about the Case

1. Make a list of all the mistakes that the paralegal made in this case. Sort them as failing to meet standards of competence and intentional acts.
2. On what basis did the court find the lawyer Smith responsible for the paralegal's actions?
3. Did the court find that the paralegal had committed UPL? On what basis, and under what definition of the practice of law? Was the lawyer held responsible for aiding in the unauthorized practice?
4. What should the lawyer have done to avoid this situation? Did he "over-delegate"?
5. What could the paralegal have done?
6. Was there a basis here for a malpractice action against Smith and Ross?
7. Was the sanction appropriate?

The mistake in this appeal was the result of a paralegal's not calendaring a deadline properly.

Pincay v. Andrews

389 F.3d 853 (9th Cir. 2004)

This appeal represents a lawyer's nightmare. . . .

The underlying dispute began in 1989 when Laffit Pincay, Jr. and Christopher McCarron (Pincay) sued Vincent S. Andrews, Robert L. Andrews, and Vincent Andrews Management Corp. (Andrews) for financial injuries stemming from alleged violations of the Racketeer Influenced and Corrupt Organizations Act (RICO) and California law. In 1992, a jury returned verdicts in Pincay's favor on both the RICO and the California counts. Pincay was ordered to elect a remedy, and he chose to pursue the RICO judgment. This judgment was reversed on appeal on the ground that the RICO claim was barred by the federal statute of limitations. [Citation omitted.] On remand, Pincay elected to pursue the remedy on his California law claim. Judgment was entered in his favor on July 3, 2002.

Andrews's notice of appeal was due 30 days later, but a paralegal charged with calendaring filing deadlines misread the rule and advised Andrews's attorney that the notice was not due for 60 days, the time allowed when the government is a party to the case. *See* Fed. R. App. P. 4(a)(1)(B). Andrews's counsel learned about the error when Pincay relied upon the judgment as being final in related bankruptcy proceedings, and Andrews promptly tendered a notice of appeal together with a request for an extension within the 30-day grace period. By that time the matter had been in litigation for more than 15 years. Everyone involved should have been well aware that the government was not a party to the case, and any lawyer or paralegal should have been able to read the rule correctly. The misreading of the rule was a critical error that, had the district court viewed the situation differently, would have ended the litigation then and there with an irreparably adverse result for Andrews. The district court, however, found the neglect excusable and granted the motion for an extension of time to file the notice of appeal.

Pincay appealed to this court, and a majority of the three-judge panel concluded that Andrews's attorney had improperly delegated the function of calendaring to a paralegal, and held that the attorney's reliance on a paralegal was inexcusable as a matter of law. *Pincay v. Andrews*, 351 F.3d 947, 951-52 (9th Cir. 2003). It ordered the appeal dismissed. The dissent would have applied a more flexible and deferential standard and affirmed the district court. *Id.* at 952-56. . . .

A majority of the active non-recused judges of the court voted to rehear the case en banc to consider whether the creation of a per se rule against delegation to paralegals, or indeed any per se rule involving missed filing deadlines, is consistent with the United States Supreme Court's leading authority on the modern concept of excusable neglect. [Citation omitted.] . . . The *Pioneer* decision arose in the bankruptcy context and involved the "bar date" for the filing of claims. The Court in *Pioneer* established a four-part balancing test for determining whether there had been "excusable neglect" within the meaning of Federal Rule of Bankruptcy Procedure 9006(b)(1). The Court also reviewed various contexts in which the phrase appeared in the federal rules of procedure and made it clear the same test applies in all those contexts. The *Pioneer* factors include: (1) the danger of prejudice to the non-moving party, (2) the length of delay and its potential impact on judicial proceedings, (3) the reason for the delay, including whether it was within the reasonable control of the movant, and (4) whether the moving party's conduct was in good faith. 507 U.S. at 395, 113 S. Ct. 1489.

In this case, the district court analyzed each of the *Pioneer* factors and correctly found: (1) there was no prejudice, (2) the length of delay was small, (3) the reason for the delay was carelessness, and (4) there was no evidence of bad faith. It then concluded that even though the reason for the delay was the carelessness of Andrews's counsel, that fact did not render the neglect inexcusable. . . .

Because the panel majority decided the case in part on the issue of delegation of calendaring to a paralegal, we consider that issue first. This issue was not presented to the district court, and it was raised sua sponte by the three-judge panel.

In the modern world of legal practice, the delegation of repetitive legal tasks to paralegals has become a necessary fixture. Such delegation has become an integral part of the struggle to keep down the costs of legal representation. Moreover, the delegation of such tasks to specialized, well-educated non-lawyers may well ensure greater accuracy in meeting deadlines than a practice of having each lawyer in a large firm calculate each filing deadline anew. The task of keeping track of necessary deadlines will involve some delegation. The responsibility for the error falls on the attorney regardless of whether the error was made by an attorney or a paralegal. *See* Model Rules of Prof'l Conduct R. 5.5 cmt. 2 (2002) ("This Rule does not prohibit a lawyer from employing the services of paraprofessionals and delegating functions to them, so long as the lawyer supervises the delegated work and retains responsibility for their work."). We hold that delegation of the task of ascertaining the deadline was not per se inexcusable neglect.

The larger question in this case is whether the misreading of the clear rule could appropriately have been considered excusable. Resolution of that question requires some effort to try to distill any principles that have evolved in the 10 years since *Pioneer*. In *Pioneer* itself, the Court adopted a broader and more flexible test for excusable neglect. A narrower test existed in many circuits before *Pioneer* that limited excusable neglect to situations that were beyond the control of the movant for an extension as, for example, the messenger being hit by a truck on the way to the court clerk's filing desk. *See Pioneer*, 507 U.S. at 387-88 & n. 3, 113 S. Ct. 1489.

The district court followed our decision in *Marx*, where we acknowledged that *Pioneer* had worked a change in our circuit's law as to what constitutes excusable neglect. 87 F.3d at 1053-54. As we explained in *Marx*, our "strict standard," which required both a showing of extraordinary circumstances that prevented timely filing and injustice resulting from denying an extension gave way to an equitable determination that involves consideration of the four *Pioneer* factors. We therefore affirmed the district court's grant of an extension of time to file a notice of appeal in *Marx* because the district court correctly considered the *Pioneer* factors. . . .

Our court, in other cases, has also described *Pioneer*'s flexible approach, saying, for example, "we will ordinarily examine all of the circumstances involved rather than holding that any single circumstance in isolation compels a particular result regardless of the other factors." [Citations omitted.]

We seemed to take a more narrow approach in *Kyle v. Campbell Soup Co.*, 28 F.3d 928 (9th Cir. 1994). In that case our court reversed the district court's finding of excusable neglect. We emphasized the fact that the attorney had made a mistake in interpreting rules that were not ambiguous and we focused on the particular facts of *Pioneer*, including a "dramatic ambiguity" in the notice of the filing deadline at issue.

Our circuit's confusion is not isolated. The authorities interpreting *Pioneer* in a number of circuits are in some disarray. In fact, the confusion begins with *Pioneer* itself, and various subsequent circuit opinions have cited similar portions of *Pioneer* to support their respective but differing conclusions. . . .

In this case the mistake itself, the misreading of the Rule, was egregious, and the lawyer undoubtedly should have checked the Rule itself before relying on the paralegal's reading. Both the paralegal and the lawyer were negligent. That, however, represents the beginning of our inquiry as to whether the negligence is excusable, not the end of it. The real question is whether there was enough in the context of this case to bring a determination of excusable neglect within the district court's discretion.

We therefore turn to examining the *Pioneer* factors as they apply here. The parties seem to agree that three of the factors militate in favor of excusability, and they focus their arguments on the remaining factor: the reason for the delay. Appellee Andrews characterizes the reason for the delay as the failure of a "carefully designed" calendaring system operated by experienced paralegals that heretofore had worked flawlessly. Appellant Pincay, on the other hand, stresses the degree of carelessness in the failure to read the applicable Rule.

We recognize that a lawyer's failure to read an applicable rule is one of the least compelling excuses that can be offered; yet the nature of the contextual analysis and the balancing of the factors adopted in *Pioneer* counsel against the creation of any rigid rule. Rather, the decision whether to grant or deny an extension of time to file a notice of appeal should be entrusted to the discretion of the district court because the district court is in a better position than we are to evaluate factors such as whether the lawyer had otherwise been diligent, the propensity of the other side to capitalize on petty mistakes, the quality of representation of the lawyers (in this litigation over its 15-year history), and the likelihood of injustice if the appeal was not allowed. Had the district court declined to permit the filing of the notice, we would be hard pressed to find any rationale requiring us to reverse.

We are also mindful that Rule 4 itself provides for leniency in limited circumstances. It could have been written more rigidly, allowing for no window of opportunity once the deadline was missed. Many states' rules provide for an extension of the time for filing a notice of appeal under few, if any, circumstances. . . .

We understand several of our sister circuits have tried to fashion a rule making a mistake of law per se inexcusable under Rule 4. [Citations omitted.] . . . We agree that a lawyer's mistake of law in reading a rule of procedure is not a compelling excuse. At the same time, however, a lawyer's mistake of fact, for example, in thinking the government was a party to a case and that the 60-day rule applied for that reason, would be no more compelling.

We are persuaded that, under *Pioneer*, the correct approach is to avoid any per se rule. *Pioneer* cautioned against "erecting a rigid barrier against late filings attributable in any degree to the movant's negligence." There should similarly be no rigid legal rule against late filings attributable to any particular type of negligence. Instead, we leave the weighing of *Pioneer*'s equitable factors to the discretion of the district court in every case.

We hold that the district court did not abuse its discretion in this case. Therefore, the district court's order granting the defendant's motion for an extension of time to file the notice of appeal is AFFIRMED. . . .

KOZINSKI, Circuit Judge, with whom Judges RYMER and MCKEOWN join, dissenting . . .

At bottom, what the sophisticated-calendaring-system excuse comes down to is that the lawyer didn't bother to read the rule; instead, he relied on what a calendaring clerk told him. While delegation may be a necessity in modern law practice, it can't be a lever for ratcheting down the standard for professional competence. If it's inexcusable for a competent lawyer to misread the rule, it can't become excusable because the lawyer turned the task over to a non-lawyer. Errors made by clerks performing lawyerly functions are probably less excusable than those made by the lawyer himself; they certainly can't be more so.

The majority may be right that any competent lawyer or clerk should have been able to read the rule correctly, but that is quite different from saying that a lawyer and a non-lawyer would be equally likely to *mis* read the rule. Studying and practicing law develops certain skills and habits of mind that, one hopes, make lawyers more careful than non-lawyers about reading rules. When a lawyer turns this function over to a non-lawyer, it increases the likelihood an error will be made. Had the lawyer in this case read the rule himself, rather than relying on what a clerk told him, he doubtless would have gotten it right. Indeed, the 30-day rule for appeals in federal court is so well known among federal practitioners that, had the lawyer but *thought* about the rule, rather than relying entirely on the calendaring clerk's representation, he would surely have realized that the 60-day period is wrong. Instead, the lawyer delegated the calendaring issue to the calendaring "system," which is made up entirely of non-lawyers. If turning large chunks of law practice over to para-professionals can itself be an excuse for misreading rules, then we'll probably see more such delegation and misreading. It is the cold logic of the marketplace that conduct that is rewarded will be repeated. . . .

I would hold that the error here — whether made by the lawyer, the calendaring clerk or the candlestick-maker — is inexcusable and dismiss the appeal as untimely. . . .

Questions about the Case

1. What was the paralegal's error? Did the work that the paralegal was doing require a sophisticated knowledge of the law? What competencies mentioned in this chapter did it require?
2. What did the court say about establishing a rule for mistakes made by paralegals? Is this good or bad for paralegals?
3. What is "excusable neglect"? Was the neglect here found to be excusable? If so, why?
4. What should the lawyer and the paralegal have done to prevent this error?
5. What might have been the consequences if the decision had gone the other way?
6. What do you think about the dissent's opinion?

Tegman v. Accident & Medical Investigations

107 Wash. App. 868, 30 P.3d 8 (2001)

. . . Between 1989 and 1991, plaintiffs Maria Tegman, Linda Leszynski, and Daina Calixto were each injured in separate and unrelated automobile accidents. After their accidents, each plaintiff retained G. Richard McClellan and Accident & Medical Investigations, Inc. (AMI) for legal counsel and assistance in handling their personal injury claims. McClellan and AMI purported to represent each plaintiff in seeking compensation from insurance companies for their injuries. Each plaintiff signed a contingency fee agreement with AMI, believing that McClellan was an attorney and AMI a law firm. McClellan has never been an attorney in any jurisdiction.

McClellan and AMI employed Camille Jescavage and Lorinda Noble, both licensed attorneys. Jescavage and Noble learned that McClellan entered into contingency fee agreements with AMI's clients and that McClellan was not an attorney. They settled a number of cases for AMI, and learned that McClellan processed settlements of AMI cases through his own bank account. Noble resigned from AMI in May 1991, after working there approximately six months.

In July 1991, McClellan hired Deloris Mullen as a paralegal. Mullen considered Jescavage to be her supervising attorney though Jescavage provided little supervision. Jescavage resigned from AMI in the first week of September 1991. McClellan told Mullen that her new supervising attorney would be James Bailey. Mullen did not immediately contact Bailey to confirm that he was her supervising attorney. He later told her he was not.

While at AMI, Mullen worked on approximately 50-60 cases, including those of plaintiffs Tegman, Leszynski and Calixto. Mullen was aware of some of McClellan's questionable practices and knew that there were substantial improprieties involved with his operation. Mullen stopped working at AMI on December 6, 1991, when the situation became personally intolerable to her and she obtained direct knowledge that she was without a supervising attorney. When she left, she did not advise any of the plaintiffs about the problems at AMI.

After Mullen left, McClellan settled each plaintiff's case for various amounts without their knowledge or consent, and deposited the funds in his general account by forging their names on the settlement checks.

In 1993, Calixto, Leszynski, and Tegman each individually sued McClellan, AMI, Mullen and Jescavage. Tegman also sued Noble. Their complaints sought damages on various theories. The cases were consolidated. Discovery took place between 1993 and 1998. In the interim, McClellan pleaded guilty to mail fraud in United States District Court in 1997 and was sentenced to two years imprisonment. Also, this court affirmed a judgment by the same trial court in another case where McClellan settled a client's case without authorization and stole the proceeds. *Bullard v. Bailey*, 91 Wn. App. 750, 959 P.2d 1122 (1998). That judgment apportioned 20-percent fault to attorney James Bailey who, like Noble and Jescavage, had associated himself with AMI and failed to warn his clients of McClellan's improprieties.

In the present matter, the court entered summary judgment against McClellan and AMI on the issue of liability. After a six-day trial, the court held Mullen, Noble, and Jescavage liable for negligence and legal negligence, and awarded damages. Only Mullen and Noble appeal. Their appeals have been consolidated. . . .

Mullen, a paralegal, contends the court erred in finding her negligent. To establish the elements of an action for negligence, a plaintiff must show: (1) the existence of a duty owed, (2) breach of that duty, (3) a resulting injury, and (4) a proximate cause between the breach and the injury. [Citation omitted.]

Non-attorneys who attempt to practice law will be held to the same standards of competence demanded of attorneys and will be liable for negligence if these standards are not met. *Bowers v. Transamerica Title Insurance Company*, 100 Wn. 2d 581, 586-89, 675 P.2d 193 (1983); *Hogan v. Monroe*, 38 Wn. App. 60, 65, 684 P.2d 757 (1984) (realtor who drafted addendum that substantially altered the rights of property buyers held to the standard of care of a reasonably prudent attorney).

In *Bowers*, sellers sold property to buyers who had persuaded a non-attorney escrow agent to prepare an unsecured promissory note in favor of the sellers. After the deed was delivered to the buyers, the sellers learned the significance of the fact that the note was unsecured. . . . The sellers sued the escrow agent and obtained summary judgment on liability for negligence. Our Supreme Court affirmed, holding the escrow agent to an attorney's standard of care. The escrow agent breached a duty to inform the sellers of the advisability of obtaining independent counsel. *Bowers*, 100 Wn. 2d at 590. That duty was owed because the escrow agent, by preparing the closing documents, was engaging in the practice of law.

The "practice of law" clearly does not just mean appearing in court. In a larger sense, it includes "legal advice and counsel, and the preparation of legal instruments and contracts by which legal rights are secured." *In re Droker and Mulholland*, 59 Wn. 2d 707, 719, 370 P.2d 242 (1962). *See also Bowers*, 100 Wn. 2d at 586; *Washington State Bar Ass'n v. Great West. Union Fed. Savings & Loan Ass'n.*, 91 Wn. 2d 48, 54, 586 P.2d 870 (1978); *State v. Hunt*, 75 Wn. App. 795, 801-02, 880 P.2d 96 (1994).

Mullen contends that her status as a paralegal precludes a finding that she was engaged in the practice of law. She argues that a paralegal is, by definition, someone who works under the supervision of an attorney, and that it is necessarily the attorney, not the paralegal, who is practicing law and owes a duty to the clients. Her argument assumes that she had a supervising attorney. The trial court's determination that Mullen was negligent was dependent on the court's finding that Mullen knew, or should have known, that she did not have a supervising attorney over a period of several months while she was at AMI. "Had Mullen been properly supervised by an attorney at all times during her employment with AMI, plaintiffs presumably would have no case against her. Rather, her supervising attorney would be responsible for any alleged wrongdoing on her part."

We agree with the trial court's observation. The label "paralegal" is not in itself a shield from liability. A factual evaluation is necessary to distinguish a paralegal who is working under an attorney's supervision from one who is actually practicing law. A finding that a paralegal is practicing law will not be supported merely by evidence of infrequent contact with the supervising attorney. As long as the paralegal does in fact have a supervising attorney who is responsible for the case, any deficiency in the quality of the supervision or in the quality of the paralegal's work goes to the attorney's negligence, not the paralegal's.

In this case, Mullen testified that she believed James Bailey was her supervising attorney after Jescavage left. The court found Mullen was not justified in that belief. Mullen assigns error to this finding, but the evidence supports it. Mullen testified that she had started to distrust McClellan before he informed her that Bailey would be her supervising attorney. Mullen also testified that she did not contact Bailey to confirm that he was supervising her. Bailey testified at a deposition that he did not share Mullen's clients and she did not consult him regarding any of her ongoing cases. He also said that one of the only conversations he remembers having with Mullen with respect to AMI is one where he told her that he was not her supervising attorney after she raised the issue with him. This testimony amply supports the trial court's finding that Mullen was unjustified in her belief that Bailey was her supervising attorney.

In *Hunt*, a paralegal appealed a criminal conviction for the unauthorized practice of law based on his conduct in running a claim settlement company. Among other things, Hunt failed to inform his clients of his activities, did not inform clients of the full amount of settlements, reached settlements without consulting his clients, and filed incomplete or improper documents in court. In a constitutional challenge to the unauthorized practice of law statute, RCW 2.48.180, Hunt argued that his status as a paralegal prevented a finding that he was engaged in the practice of law. The Court of Appeals disagreed and affirmed his conviction: " 'It is the nature and character of the service performed which governs whether given activities constitute the practice of law, not the nature or status of the person performing the services' ". Hunt, 75 Wn. App. at 802 (citing in part *WSBA*, 91 Wn. 2d at 54). As in Hunt, Mullen's status as a paralegal did not preclude the trial court from concluding that Mullen had engaged in the practice of law.

Contrary to Mullen's argument, such a conclusion does not require evidence that the paralegal called herself an attorney, entered appearances, or charged fees. Mullen testified that she negotiated settlements on behalf of the plaintiffs. She sent a letter rejecting, without Tegman's knowledge, a settlement offer made to Tegman. She continued to send out demand and representation letters after Jescavage left AMI. Letters written by Mullen before Jescavage's departure identify Mullen as a paralegal after her signature, whereas letters she wrote after Jescavage's departure lacked such identification. Even after Mullen discovered, in late November 1991, that Bailey was not her supervising attorney, she wrote letters identifying 'this office' as representing the plaintiffs, neglecting to mention that she was a paralegal and that no attorney was responsible for the case. This evidence substantially supports the finding that Mullen engaged in the practice of law.

Mullen contends that she cannot be held liable for negligence because the statute that prohibits the unauthorized practice of law was not in effect at the time she worked for AMI. The trial court dismissed the plaintiffs' claims that were based on the alleged statutory violation, but this does not prevent Mullen from being liable on the negligence claim.

Under *Bowers*, the duty arises from the practice of law, not from the statute. Mullen points out that an attorney-client relationship is an element of a cause of action for legal malpractice. [Citation omitted.] The trial court did not find that she had an attorney-client relationship with any of the plaintiffs, and she contends that as a result it is illogical to hold her to the standard of care of an attorney.

Mullen, because she is not an attorney, could not have attorney-client relationships. Nevertheless, as *Bowers* demonstrates, a layperson can logically be held to the standard of care of an attorney in a negligence action. The duty arises from the attempt to engage in the practice of law rather than from the professional status of the defendant. The trial court, covering all bases, held Mullen liable both for negligence and legal negligence. While the "legal negligence" label may have been incorrect, any such error is immaterial because the negligence theory produces the same result and, as the trial court observed, for practical purposes the allegations are the same.

Accordingly, we conclude the trial court did not err in following *Bowers* and holding Mullen to the duty of an attorney. The duty of care owed by an attorney is that degree of care, skill, diligence, and knowledge commonly possessed and exercised by a reasonable, careful, and prudent lawyer in the practice of law in Washington. [Citation omitted.]

Mullen challenges, as unsupported by the evidence, the trial court's key finding as to the duties that Mullen owed and breached. The court found that the standard of care owed by an attorney, and therefore also by Mullen, required her to notify the plaintiffs of: (1) the serious problems concerning the accessibility of their files to persons who had no right to see them, (2) the fact that client settlements were not processed through an attorney's trust account, but rather McClellan's own account, (3) the fact that McClellan and AMI, as non-lawyers, had no right to enter into contingent fee agreements with clients and receive contingent fees, (4) the fact that McClellan was, in fact, engaged in the unlawful practice of law, and that, generally, (5) the clients of McClellan and AMI were at substantial risk of financial harm as a result of their association with AMI. Mullen breached her duty to her clients in all of these particulars.

The finding rests on the testimony of attorney Charles Nelson Berry III, an expert witness for the plaintiffs. The trial court found Berry's testimony to be "thoughtful and well-considered" and significantly, unrebutted.

Mullen argues that the finding must be stricken because Berry improperly derived the standard of care from the Rules of Professional Conduct. In testifying that an attorney's conduct violated the legal standard of care, an expert witness may base an opinion on an attorney's failure to conform to an ethics rule, and may testify using language found in the Rules of Professional Conduct, as long as the jury is not led to believe that the ethical violations were actionable. [Citation omitted.] Berry's testimony, phrased in terms of breach of the standard of care, stayed within this constraint. We conclude the finding is supported by substantial evidence. Accordingly, the trial court did not err in concluding that Mullen was negligent. . . .

All three plaintiffs testified that they hired McClellan and AMI to legally represent them and believed that McClellan was an attorney whom they trusted and relied upon to handle their respective claims.

They found out that he was not an attorney only after their claims had been settled. Mullen did not advise any of the plaintiffs that McClellan was not a lawyer; that AMI was not a law firm; that she, as a paralegal, had no real supervision; or that client funds did not go through a trust account. These omissions by Mullen sufficiently link her to the plaintiffs' later injury to establish cause in fact. It was reasonable for the trial court to infer that if Mullen had properly advised the plaintiffs of the problems at AMI, more likely than not they would have withdrawn their cases from AMI in time to avoid being harmed by McClellan's fraudulent acts.

Legal causation turns on a policy question of how far the consequences of a defendant's acts should extend. [Citations omitted.] Mullen contends that her connection to the plaintiffs' injuries is too remote because she did not render direct legal advice and that it is unjust to hold her, an employee paralegal, responsible for the criminal, intentional acts of her employer. The *Bullard* court rejected a similar argument asserted by Bailey, an attorney who allowed himself to become associated with McClellan. . . .

Although Mullen was a paralegal, she is held to an attorney's standard of care because she worked on the plaintiffs' cases during a period of several months when she had no supervising attorney. The fact that she did not render legal advice directly does not excuse her; in fact, her failure to advise the plaintiffs of the improper arrangements at AMI is the very omission that breached her duty. Under these circumstances it is not unjust to hold her accountable as a legal cause of the plaintiffs' injuries.

As all the elements of negligence have been established, we affirm the judgment against Mullen.

The trial court entered judgment against Mullen and Noble, McClellan, and AMI jointly and severally for compensatory damages. . . . The court entered judgment against McClellan and AMI for substantial additional sums, including attorney fees, for criminal profiteering and Consumer Protection Act violations. Mullen and Noble object to being held jointly liable for the compensatory damages. They ask that the judgments be revised so that they are responsible for only that portion of the compensatory damages corresponding to the percentages of fault the trial court attributed to them. . . .

[T]he trial court determined that Mullen was 10 percent at fault in each of the three cases; attorney Jescavage was 10 percent at fault in each of the three cases; and Noble was five percent at fault in Tegman's case. The court determined that McClellan and AMI had the remaining percentages in each case. The court then concluded that each of the plaintiffs was not at fault, and held all defendants jointly as well as severally liable in accordance with the statute. . . .

The judgments are affirmed.

[*Postscript:* On appeal, the Washington Supreme Court held that "Noble is jointly and severally liable only for those damages caused by 'fault' of the defendants, and to this extent she is jointly and severally liable with all the defendants. She is not, however, liable for damages that result from intentional acts or omissions. We remand for segregation of that part of the damages due to intentional conduct from those damages due to negligence." See *Tegman v. Investigations, Inc.*, 150 Wash. 2d 102, 75 P.3d 497 (2003).]

Questions about the Case

1. What specifically did the paralegal do that the court construed as being negligent?
2. To what standard of care was she held? Why?
3. What should the paralegal have done to avoid malpractice?
4. Did the paralegal also engage in UPL? What effect does the finding have on the outcome of the case?
5. What was the issue relating to the expert witness? How did the court decide?
6. What proportion of the damages did the paralegal have to pay?
7. Under what act was the principal of the company convicted of a crime? What does this chapter say about the application of similar statutes to lawyers?

In the following case, a paralegal's clerical error makes its way to the California Supreme Court.

Zamora v. Clayborn Contracting Group, Inc.

28 Cal. 4th 249, 121 Cal. Rptr. 2d 187, 47 P.3d 1056 (2002)

. . . Pablo Zamora (Zamora), doing business as Creative Engineering and Fabrication, filed suit against Clayborn Contracting Group, Inc. (Clayborn), alleging breach of contract and other related claims. The complaint alleged that Clayborn failed to pay for road signs produced and supplied by Zamora and sought approximately $143,000 in damages plus attorney fees. Clayborn answered and filed a cross-complaint. Although the cross-complaint did not specify the amount of damages sought, Clayborn sent Zamora an invoice for approximately $157,000 before filing the cross-claim.

Less than two months before trial, Zamora's counsel mailed Clayborn a section 998 offer. Although Zamora apparently intended to offer to settle for a judgment in his favor in the amount of $149,999, the actual offer sent to Clayborn stated: "Plaintiff Pablo Zamora aka Pablo Iniguez dba Creative Engineering and Fabrication hereby offers to have judgment *taken against himself and for* defendant Clayborn Contracting Group, Inc. . . . pursuant to Section 998 of the Code of Civil Procedure for the sum of $149,999. . . ."

Clayborn filed a notice of acceptance of the offer approximately three days after reviewing it. One week later and two days after learning about the mistake in the offer, Zamora's counsel advised the court of his intention to file a motion to set aside "the judgment based on mistake, inadvertence and excusable neglect." After obtaining an order shortening the time for hearing the motion, Zamora filed a motion to set aside the section 998 offer or to vacate entry of judgment pursuant to the discretionary relief provision of section 473, subdivision (b).

In support of the motion, Zamora submitted declarations from himself, his counsel, the legal assistant who typed the section 998 offer and other litigants in related cases. Zamora averred that he *only* authorized his attorney to settle for a judgment in his favor in the amount of $149,999 and never authorized his attorney to agree to any judgment in favor of Clayborn.

Zamora's counsel declared that he, by phone, instructed his legal assistant to prepare a document offering to settle for a judgment against Clayborn in the amount of $149,999 pursuant to section 998. Zamora's counsel, per office policy, authorized his legal assistant to send the document with his stamped signature even though he had not reviewed it, because he was out of town and time was of the essence. He further stated that, before making this offer, Zamora had never offered to settle the matter for less than $150,000 *from* Clayborn. His legal assistant largely corroborated his story and claimed that she "mistakenly typed the word 'against' as opposed to the phrase 'in favor of' Pablo Zamora."

Zamora's counsel also stated that, after accepting the section 998 offer, Clayborn unilaterally cancelled depositions and took pending motions to coordinate this action with other actions and to amend the cross-complaint off calendar without informing Zamora or other interested parties. A declaration from another litigant involved in the coordination motion corroborated these statements.

In opposition, Clayborn submitted declarations claiming that it acted in good faith and believed the offer was correct as written. Clayborn claimed that the proposed amount of the settlement—$149,999—was consistent with the amount stated in its latest invoice to Zamora—approximately $157,000. Clayborn's counsel further stated that he had told Zamora's counsel that Clayborn would not give Zamora any money and had suffered significant damages due to Zamora's conduct. Finally, Clayborn identified two tax levies against Zamora for approximately $31,000, as grounds for its failure to question the validity of the offer.

After a hearing, the trial court found that Zamora's counsel made a ministerial or clerical error and granted the motion to set aside the judgment pursuant to the discretionary relief provision of section 473, subdivision (b). The Court of Appeal affirmed. After ordering the trial court to "enter judgment, nunc pro tunc as of February 17, 2000, pursuant to the section 998 offer filed that date," the court concluded that: (1) Section 473, subdivision (b) permitted relief from a judgment entered in accordance with a section 998 settlement for "mistake, inadvertence, surprise, or excusable neglect"; and (2) the trial court did not abuse its discretion by granting Zamora relief from the section 998 settlement. . . .

As relevant here, the discretionary relief provision of section 473, subdivision (b) provides that: "The court may, upon any terms as may be just, relieve a party or his or her legal representative from a judgment, dismissal, order, or other proceeding taken against him or her through his or her mistake, inadvertence, surprise, or excusable neglect." According to Clayborn, this provision applies only to involuntary judgments or dismissals; therefore, Zamora could not obtain relief from the voluntary judgment. . . . We disagree.

Our analysis begins with the statutory language. [Citation omitted.] The discretionary relief provision of section 473, subdivision (b) applies to *any* "judgment, dismissal, order, or other proceeding." Ostensibly, this statutory language does not limit the application of the discretionary relief provision to involuntary judgments or dismissals. Indeed, our courts have interpreted the provision in this manner for over a century.

The Legislature first enacted the discretionary relief provision found in section 473, subdivision (b) in 1872, and the language of this provision has not changed appreciably since then. [Citations omitted.] . . . Since 1872, California courts have consistently applied the discretionary relief provision of section 473 to voluntary judgments or dismissals. For example, as early as 1901, this court affirmed an order setting aside a voluntary dismissal entered pursuant to a settlement agreement. In holding that the trial court had authority to do so under the discretionary relief provision of section 473, this court rejected Clayborn's very contention and held that a party who "consented to the dismissal to his injury, under a mistake of fact, excusable under the terms of the statute, . . . is not barred of relief." (*Palace Hardware Co. v. Smith* (1901) 134 Cal. 381, 384.) [Citations omitted.]

Palace Hardware was not an aberration. California courts have long held that "[e]ven after a voluntary dismissal with prejudice has been filed, the trial court *has jurisdiction* to vacate the judgment of dismissal under Code of Civil Procedure section 473 where it has been entered as a result of the plaintiff's 'mistake, inadvertence, surprise, or excusable neglect.' " [Citations omitted.] . . . In accordance with these principles, California courts have consistently held that parties may obtain relief from judgments, dismissals, or stipulations voluntarily entered into pursuant to a voluntary agreement through the discretionary relief provision of section 473. In fact, Clayborn cites no majority decision to the contrary.

Indeed, this longstanding interpretation of the discretionary relief provision of section 473 comports with its underlying purpose. . . . "It is well settled that appellate courts have always been and are favorably disposed toward such action upon the part of the trial courts as will permit, rather than prevent, the adjudication of legal controversies upon their merits." [Citation omitted.] Thus, "the provisions of section 473 of the Code of Civil Procedure are to be liberally construed and sound policy favors the determination of actions on their merits." [Citation omitted.] By applying the discretionary relief provision of section 473 to judgments entered pursuant to section 998, subdivision (b)(1), we simply remain faithful to these venerable principles.

In doing so, we reject Clayborn's contention that the statutory phrase "taken against" limits the discretionary relief provision to *involuntary* judgments or dismissals. . . .

The recent addition of a mandatory relief provision to section 473 for attorney fault also does not dictate a contrary result. . . . In enacting this exception, the Legislature, however, made no changes to the discretionary relief provision of section 473, and the legislative history indicates no intent to alter the scope of this provision. Indeed, the Legislature has *never* substantively altered the statutory language at issue here despite the long line of California cases permitting discretionary relief from judgments entered pursuant to a settlement agreement . . . even though it has amended section 473 many times. Thus, the Legislature has apparently adopted this longstanding interpretation of the provision. [Citation omitted.]

Having established that Zamora may avail himself of the discretionary relief provision of section 473, subdivision (b), we now consider whether the trial court properly applied it. "A ruling on a motion for discretionary relief under section 473 shall not be disturbed on appeal absent a clear showing of abuse." [Citation omitted.] . . . "A party who seeks relief under section 473 on the basis of mistake or inadvertence of counsel must demonstrate that such mistake, inadvertence, or general neglect was excusable because the negligence of the attorney is imputed to his client and may not be offered by the latter as a basis for relief." [Citation omitted.] In determining whether the attorney's mistake or inadvertence was excusable, "the court inquires whether 'a reasonably prudent *person* under the same or similar circumstances' might have made the same error.' " [Citation omitted.] In other words, the discretionary relief provision of section 473 only permits relief from attorney error "fairly imputable to the client, i.e., mistakes anyone could have made." [Citation omitted.] "Conduct falling below the professional standard of care, such as failure to timely object or to properly advance an argument, is not therefore excusable. To hold otherwise would be to eliminate the express statutory requirement of excusability and effectively eviscerate the concept of attorney malpractice."

The party seeking relief under section 473 must also be diligent. [Citation omitted.] Thus, an application for relief must be made "within a reasonable time, in no case exceeding six months, after the judgment, dismissal, order, or proceeding was taken." (§473, subd. (b).)

Where the mistake is excusable and the party seeking relief has been diligent, courts have often granted relief pursuant to the discretionary relief provision of section 473 if no prejudice to the opposing party will ensue. [Citations omitted.] In such cases, the law "looks with [particular] disfavor on a party who, regardless of the merits of his cause, attempts to take advantage of the mistake, surprise, inadvertence, or neglect of his adversary." [Citation omitted.] Here, the trial court reasonably concluded that the mistake made by Zamora's counsel was excusable. The erroneous substitution of the word "against" for the phrase "in favor of" is a clerical or ministerial mistake that could have been made by anybody. While counsel's failure to review the document before sending it out was imprudent, we cannot say that his imprudence rendered the mistake inexcusable under the circumstances. Indeed, appellate courts have routinely affirmed orders vacating judgments based on analogous mistakes made by an attorney or his or her staff. For example, courts have set aside judgments where: (1) The attorney mistakenly checked the "with prejudice" box instead of the "without prejudice" box; (2) an associate misinterpreted the instructions of the lead attorney and gave incorrect information at a hearing; and (3) the attorney's secretary lost the answer to be filed. [Citations omitted.]

In addition, Zamora was diligent in seeking relief, and Clayborn suffered no apparent prejudice. Finally, the record suggests that Clayborn took unfair advantage of the mistake. We find it hard to believe that Clayborn had no inkling that the section 998 offer was a mistake when the uncontroverted record established that: (1) Zamora's complaint sought over $140,000 in damages; (2) Zamora had never offered to settle for less than $150,000 from Clayborn prior to making the offer; (3) the section 998 offer proposed to settle the matter for almost the same amount ($149,999) as Clayborn's entire claim for damages (approximately $157,000); and (4) Clayborn knew Zamora was having financial difficulties and had failed to pay approximately $31,000 in tax levies. Clayborn's rush to get approval of the settlement and its abrupt cancellation of depositions and hearings on pending motions with no notice to the parties involved cast further doubt on its claim of innocence. Under these facts, the trial court did not abuse its discretion by granting relief to Zamora pursuant to section 473, subdivision (b). . . .

Finally, in reaching this holding, we do not offend the public policies favoring the private resolution of civil disputes. Although the law favors settlements [Citation omitted], it only favors *authorized* settlements. . . .

Our holding also does not circumvent longstanding principles of contract law. Even if, as Clayborn contends, Zamora was limited to the contractual defense of unilateral mistake, ample evidence supports the trial court's decision. As noted above, the undisputed facts strongly suggest that Clayborn "had reason to suspect that a mistake had been made." [Citation omitted.] Moreover, even assuming Clayborn had no knowledge of Zamora's mistake, enforcement of the section 998 settlement would still arguably be unconscionable. . . . Thus, requiring Zamora to file a separate action in order to rescind his section 998 offer would not promote the sanctity of contract law. It would only waste judicial resources.

In any event, we are confident trial courts will exercise this discretionary power to vacate judgments entered pursuant to a settlement agreement both carefully and sparingly. . . . Indeed, courts have been exercising this power for over a century with no apparent ill effects. Most cases still settle, and courts rarely set aside settlement agreements. Our holding today should not change that.

We affirm the judgment of the Court of Appeal.

Questions about the Case

1. What was the error that the paralegal made in this case? How did the lawyer compound the error?
2. What did the opposing counsel do in response to the error? What should he have done? (See Chapter 9 for duties in litigation for more background.) Could the opposing counsel have been sanctioned for this conduct?
3. What was the basis for the court's decision?
4. How does the California Supreme Court's analysis of "excusable neglect" in this case compare with that of the U.S. Court of Appeal in the *Pincay* case above?
5. What system could be put into place in a law firm to prevent this kind of mistake from being made?

In the following case, a nonlawyer makes a serious error in preparing a legal document for a client. The plaintiff, a third party, is damaged and sues the nonlawyer for the amount of damages. Think about how this case might be used in situations in which a "legal technician" acts incompetently.

Biakanja v. Irving

49 Cal. 2d 647, 320 P.2d 16 (1958)

Plaintiff's brother, John Maroevich, died, leaving a will which devised and bequeathed all of his property to plaintiff. The will, which was prepared by defendant, a notary public, was denied probate for lack of sufficient attestation. Plaintiff, by intestate succession, received only one-eighth of the estate, and she recovered a judgment against defendant for the difference between the amount which she would have received had the will been valid and the amount distributed to her.

Defendant, who is not an attorney, had for several years written letters and prepared income tax returns for Maroevich. The will was typed in defendant's office and "subscribed and sworn to" by Maroevich in the presence of defendant, who affixed his signature and notarial seal to the instrument. Sometime later Maroevich obtained the signatures of two witnesses to the will, neither of whom was present when Maroevich signed it. These witnesses did not sign in the presence of each other, and Maroevich did not acknowledge his signature in their presence.

An attorney who represented Maroevich's stepson in the probate proceedings testified that he had a telephone conversation with defendant shortly after Maroevich's death, in which defendant said he prepared the will and notarized it. According to the attorney, defendant, in discussing how the will was witnessed, "admonished me to the effect that I was a young lawyer, I'd better go back and study my law books some more, that anybody knew a will which bore a notarial seal was a valid will, didn't have to be witnessed by any witnesses."

The court found that defendant agreed and undertook to prepare a valid will and that it was invalid because defendant negligently failed to have it properly attested. The findings are supported by the evidence.

The principal question is whether defendant was under a duty to exercise due care to protect plaintiff from injury and was liable for damage caused plaintiff by his negligence even though they were not in privity of contract. In *Buckley v. Gray* (1895), 110 Cal. 339 142 P. 900, 52 Am. St. Rep. 88, 31 A.L.R. 862, it was held that a person who was named as a beneficiary under a will could not recover damages from an attorney who negligently drafted and directed the execution of the will with the result that the intended beneficiary was deprived of substantial benefits. The court based its decision on the ground that the attorney owed no duty to the beneficiary because there was no privity of contract between them. *Mickel v. Murphy*, 147 Cal. App. 2d 718 [305 P.2d 993], relying on *Buckley v. Gray*, supra, held that a notary public who prepared a will was not liable to the beneficiary for failing to have it properly executed. When *Buckley v. Gray*, supra, was decided in 1895, it was generally accepted that, with the few exceptions noted in the opinion in that case, there was no liability for negligence committed in the performance of a contract in the absence of privity. Since that time the rule has been greatly liberalized, and the courts have permitted a plaintiff not in privity to recover damages in many situations for the negligent performance of a contract. . . .

The determination whether in a specific case the defendant will be held liable to a third person not in privity is a matter of policy and involves the balancing of various factors, among which are the extent to which the transaction was intended to affect the plaintiff, the foreseeability of harm to him, the degree of certainty that the plaintiff suffered injury, the closeness of the connection between the defendant's conduct and the injury suffered, the moral blame attached to the defendant's conduct, and the policy of preventing future harm. Here, the "end and aim" of the transaction was to provide for the passing of Maroevich's estate to plaintiff. Defendant must have been aware from the terms of the will itself that, if faulty solemnization caused the will to be invalid, plaintiff would suffer the very loss which occurred. As Maroevich died without revoking his will, plaintiff, but for defendant's negligence, would have received all of the Maroevich estate, and the fact that she received only one-eighth of the estate was directly caused by defendant's conduct.

Defendant undertook to provide for the formal disposition of Maroevich's estate by drafting and supervising the execution of a will. This was an important transaction requiring specialized skill, and defendant clearly was not qualified to undertake it. His conduct was not only negligent but was also highly improper. He engaged in the unauthorized practice of the law, which is a misdemeanor in violation of section 6126 of the Business and Professions Code. Such conduct should be discouraged and not protected by immunity from civil liability, as would be the case if plaintiff, the only person who suffered a loss, were denied a right of action.

We have concluded that plaintiff should be allowed recovery despite the absence of privity, and the cases of *Buckley v. Gray* and *Mickel v. Murphy*, are disapproved insofar as they are in conflict with this decision.

The judgment is affirmed.

Questions about the Case

1. Why do you think the defendant prepared the will? What was the mistake in preparing the will that caused it to be invalid?
2. Explain who the plaintiff is in this case. What is privity of contract? How does it apply here?
3. What was the rule on third-party recovery in such cases prior to this decision?
4. What factors will the court consider in future cases to determine whether to allow third-party liability?
5. How is this ruling relevant to the increase in malpractice claims by non-clients?

9

Special Issues in Advocacy

This chapter describes the many ethical dilemmas that paralegals face when working in litigation. Chapter 9 covers:

- the role of the attorney and paralegal in litigation
- the duty to represent clients zealously
- rules about unmeritorious claims, delay, and abuse of discovery
- prohibitions on disruptive courtroom tactics
- sanctions for ethics violations before courts
- duties of candor and honesty
- prohibited relationships and communications with judges
- prohibited contact with jurors
- restrictions on contact with represented parties and unrepresented persons
- contact with witnesses
- rules on trial publicity
- special rules for prosecutors and their paralegals

A. Introduction

The trial lawyer arguing for a client in front of a judge and jury is the commonly held image of what a lawyer does. In fact most lawyers are not litigators who regularly appear in court. The majority of lawyers in this country do not litigate matters, either civil or criminal, and many lawyers never represent a client in an adversarial proceeding. Areas of practice that do not emphasize litigation include corporate, tax, business transactions, real estate, estate planning, probate, environmental law, entertainment law, intellectual property, and trademark and copyright. Increasingly, even lawyers who practice in areas that are within the purview of the courts, such as family law, resolve matters through negotiation, mediation, and other alternative means that avoid resolution by way of a trial.

Nonetheless, the legal profession is often accused of promoting a culture that is "too litigious." People do look to the courts to handle disputes that would not have been resolved by lawyers and judges 50 or 60 years ago. Some commentators believe that there is a litigation explosion; others argue that this claim is not borne out by empirical research. Politicians blame the rising cost of health care and insurance on the growth in litigation against doctors and hospitals. Punitive damage awards have been vigorously attacked. Plaintiff lawyers disagree with this characterization and contend that resolving disputes in court is often the only way to get justice for persons who have been injured and to force reluctant corporations to change the way they do business. A review of American legal history supports this contention.

Court dockets are crowded and the wheels of justice often seem to grind slowly. However, reforms have streamlined litigation by encouraging alternate dispute resolution, limiting discovery, creating fast-track processes of certain kinds of disputes, and instituting more effective trial procedures.

Litigation paralegals must be diligent in their efforts to meet high standards of competence and ethics and keep up with the ever-changing ethics rules and court decisions that govern conduct in litigation.

Unlike lawyers, the majority of paralegals, about 75 percent, work in civil litigation. Although lawsuits culminate in a trial, most of the work in litigation is done out of court, before trial, in the preparation of a case. The role of paralegals in litigation is expansive, including fact gathering, interviewing clients and witnesses, drafting pleadings and motions, conducting legal research, drafting discovery requests and motions and responding to discovery, preparing for trial by organizing documents, managing databases of documents, overseeing e-discovery, locating and preparing expert witnesses, and preparing demonstrative evidence. Many litigation paralegals serve on a team with the lawyers, accompanying them to court and assisting in court by taking notes, making observations about jurors' reactions to the proceedings, handling logistics and emergencies, and doing last-minute research. As the discovery experts in a case, paralegals must have a mastery of the facts and evidence. Litigators greatly value the contribution that paralegals make to the team effort that is needed to win. Paralegals are often the ones who find a "smoking-gun" document. Finally, paralegal work enables lawyers to concentrate their full attention on presenting the case, examining and cross-examining witnesses, and making objections.

Because paralegals have such an expansive role in litigation, they need a deep understanding of the ethics rules governing advocacy. Violations of litigation-related rules sometimes occur when a lawyer acts through someone else, such as a paralegal. Related rules have already been covered in this book — paralegals may not make court appearances or give clients legal advice, must disclose to courts and clients their identity as nonlawyers, must avoid conflicts of interest in litigation, and must protect privileged information and material in litigated matters.

The rules on advocacy start with the basic premise that attorneys must represent clients zealously. The ABA Model Rule of Professional Conduct 1.3 calls on lawyers to exercise "reasonable diligence and promptness," and comment [1] describes this duty further as "zeal in advocacy. . . ." **Zealous representation** entails exercising one's best efforts on the client's behalf within the boundaries of law and ethics. The duty to represent clients zealously has special meaning in the context of the lawyer's role as an advocate. This duty must be exercised within the constraints created by other ethical duties, legal obligations, and moral imperatives, such as the lawyer's duties of candor to the court, the administration of justice, client confidentiality, and the search for the truth. The following sections address the ethics rules on advocacy, with emphasis on the rules that affect paralegals most directly.

B. Unmeritorious Claims, Delay, and Discovery Abuse

Both the ABA Model Code and ABA Model Rules have provisions that prohibit lawyers from bringing **unmeritorious claims and defenses**. ABA Model Rule 3.1 states that lawyers shall not make a claim or defense unless it has a basis in law and fact. This provision allows for the situation where the lawyer is arguing in good faith for an extension, modification, or reversal of the law. Actions that violate this rule are typically called "frivolous."

Violations of this rule most commonly occur when an attorney brings an unwarranted action to gain some advantage over the opposition, to force a party to expend funds to defend the action, or simply to earn fees. A lawyer who brings an action based on inaccurate information supplied by a client, without conducting any investigation, may be in breach of this rule. If the action is in fact unmeritorious, the attorney may be found to have violated ethics rules, court rules, and/or related statutes for failing to investigate. Many courts have held the attorney to a duty to make a reasonable inquiry unless immediate action is necessary to protect the client's interests; others have found that the attorney may proceed in reliance on the truth of a client's story. Another example of an unmeritorious claim is a plaintiff who sues a competitor without proper grounds under the law merely for the purpose of driving him or her out of business.

Related to unmeritorious claims are **abuses of the discovery process**. Conducting excessive or unnecessary discovery has been employed as a strategy to delay litigation, to burden the opposing counsel, to raise the cost to the opposition and, generally, to wear down the opposing party and counsel. Manipulation of discovery rules to gain tactical advantage is common, but this tactic carries the risk of alienating the judge. Courts have addressed discovery abuse through rules that strictly circumscribe discovery, expedite the pretrial stage, and discourage excessive and unnecessarily lengthy discovery. Such rules set limits on the number of interrogatories that can be served on others, establish strict deadlines for completion of discovery, and mandate alternative dispute resolution and pretrial settlement procedures. Recently adopted rules on e-discovery address some concerns about the issues related to cost and protection of privileged communications in electronic files, but this kind of discovery has greatly complicated trial preparation and increased the time and money required to prepare a case.

ABA Model Rule 3.4(d) specifically forbids making frivolous pretrial discovery requests and failing to comply with proper discovery requests. Violations of this rule occur, for example, when an attorney requests discovery that is beyond the scope of the case, perhaps by flooding the opposition with irrelevant interrogatories; giving incomplete answers to interrogatories; requesting discovery of confidential, sensitive, or embarrassing information; or making unfounded objections to discovery. Lawyers have been known to provide many more documents than requested, seeking to hide a damaging document. Examples of recent ethics violations involving discovery include a major corporation and its lawyers who were recently sanctioned for removing 2,300 documents from 81 boxes of documents that were ordered produced. In another, the failure to produce a key letter from a doctor in a case involving a disability led to the dismissal of the case.

ABA Model Rule 3.2 requires lawyers to "make reasonable efforts to expedite litigation consistent with" clients' interests. The comment to this rule cites as improper delays made for a lawyer's convenience or made to deliberately frustrate the opposition's legitimate goals or to realize financial gain. Unethical delays for which attorneys have been sanctioned include refusing to respond to communications of opposing counsel; repeated failure to appear at hearings, settlement conferences, or depositions; unnecessary delays in filing motions to disqualify counsel; and failing to complete discovery in accordance with court rules, court orders, or statutes. Violations of this rule may also have implications for the lawyer's duty to act competently because timeliness in handling client matters is an element of competence.

The most common way that these ethical breaches are addressed is in the underlying court action by means of a sanction against the lawyer. Discipline by state disciplinary authorities for bringing frivolous actions or defenses, abusing discovery, or causing unnecessary delays is relatively rare. When it does occur, it is usually in a particularly egregious case, such as lawyer who has filed several frivolous lawsuits or when the ethical violation is coupled with other violations such as incompetence or failure to obey a court order.

In the recent flurry of litigation involving foreclosures, two law firms were sanctioned with six-figure fines for incorrectly claiming in a bankruptcy filing that their client owned a mortgage that had in fact been reassigned. In another case, a prominent New York firm was sanctioned for bringing a "ridiculous frivolous" lawsuit on behalf of a billionaire client concerning his former father-in-law's estate. The court said that no competent lawyer could have concluded that a lawsuit could be brought upon reading the testamentary documents.

One important remedy available to the victims of such conduct is a civil suit against the client, the lawyer, or both for ***malicious prosecution*** or ***abuse of process***. Grounds for malicious prosecution exist when a civil lawsuit or criminal prosecution has been brought, without probable cause and with malice, after the defendant prevails in the action. Limited immunity for attorneys exists if it is shown that the lawyer acted in good faith. An abuse of process action may be brought when the legal process is misused to achieve other than legitimate legal purposes, such as filing a criminal complaint to force the defendant to pay a debt.

Malicious prosecution/abuse of process
Improper use of a civil or criminal process

The courts impose sanctions against lawyers who violate the ethics rules and related statutes and court rules under their **contempt power**. This power can be exercised for virtually any lawyer misconduct in a matter before a court, including disobeying a court order (including a discovery order) or acting in a manner that disrupts the proceedings. Contempt is covered in more detail in Section C.

Courts can impose **monetary sanctions**. Under federal statutes and procedural rules and under state court rules or statutes, courts have authority to impose sanctions against lawyers, clients, or both for actions that are unwarranted, delaying, or harassing. The most frequently used rule in federal court is Federal Rule of Civil Procedure 11, which provides for sanctions against attorneys, clients, or both for filing unwarranted or other objectionable pleadings and papers. Rule 11 is supplemented by Federal Rule of Civil Procedure 37, which provides for sanctions for failure to make or cooperate in discovery. These rules parallel the ethics rules, specifically requiring filings to be well grounded in fact, and warranted by existing law or a good-faith argument for the extension, modification, or reversal of existing law. Filings for an improper purpose, such as to harass or to cause unnecessary delay or needless expense, are also prohibited. Possible sanctions include payment of expenses and attorney's fees to the opposing party or parties. Courts may also order attorneys, clients, or both to pay fines. The most severe sanction, rarely exercised, is the dismissal of an action with prejudice.

Rule 11, adopted to alleviate unnecessary delays and paperwork, has been widely used by federal judges. Monetary sanctions can be substantial. Examples of some kinds of cases in which sanctions have been awarded under Rule 11 are using abusive language in a motion, filing an action unwarranted by law for purely political reasons, asking for an inflated amount of damages, delaying the production of specific documents without adequate explanation for an extended period, filing a motion to disqualify counsel purely to delay the proceedings, and lying about the existence of documents sought through discovery.

Rule 11 contains provisions designed to make the application of sanctions uniform and fair. The imposition of sanctions is discretionary, not mandatory. Parties are usually given time to remedy conduct after notification that sanctions will be sought. Nonmonetary sanctions that will deter the wrongful conduct are favored. Law firms, not just individual attorneys, can be held responsible for violations. States have comparable rules and statutes authorizing sanctions, and case law recognizes the inherent authority of a court over its proceedings as the basis for imposing sanctions. See the *Bonda* case at the end of this chapter for an example of sanctions imposed by a trial judge for delays and failure to pursue discovery.

C. Disruption in the Courtroom and Disobeying Court Orders

Trial lawyers are bound by ethics rules to conduct themselves with decorum, according to the Model Rules. A lawyer may not "engage in conduct intended to disrupt" proceedings (ABA Model Rule 3.5(d)).

A tension exists between this rule and the duty to advocate zealously. Lawyers who are charged with disruptive conduct usually contend that they are just doing their utmost to represent their clients. Sometimes unacceptable conduct in court is designed to influence the jury or to throw the opposing counsel off track. Some examples of **disruptive conduct** and **dirty tricks** in the courtroom are raising an unfounded objection to break opposing counsel's train of thought; making faces or gestures to the judge or the jury; asking a question that alludes to evidence known to be inadmissible; insulting the judge or opposing counsel, for example, by calling them names or accusing them of collusion, racism, incompetence, or bias; referring to the proceedings in an insulting or rude manner; making unsupportable, inflammatory, or prejudicial side remarks to the jury; and asking questions of a witness after the judge has warned that the questions are prohibited.

In a highly publicized Florida case, a judge slashed attorney's fees in a case where the plaintiff's lawyers, who prevailed in the case, had been "overzealous." These "hardball" litigators refused to shake hands with the opposing counsel and were verbally abusive to them. During trial, they frequently rolled their eyes, looked at the ceiling, and flailed their arms. They started each day with statements such as "Let's kick some ass" and "Let the pounding begin." In a California case, all the lawyers in a defense firm were required to take an ethics course by a judge who found that the lawyers had repeatedly misstated the record, made frivolous objections, and mischaracterized the law. The court may also sanction lawyers for written comments. In a recent Oklahoma case, a lawyer was ordered to write an article on civility after he wrote to opposing counsel to "sit quietly in the corner," "be like a potted plant," "spare me your phony sermons," and "please stop the charade," among other insults. A Texas judge found a lawyer guilty of contempt and sentenced him to 90 days in jail after he made a lewd gesture in a criminal proceeding. A Tennessee lawyer was suspended from federal court practice and fined after he repeatedly interrupted or talked over a judge who was questioning him. And a prominent California lawyer was suspended for three years for disruptive conduct, including repeatedly asking identical inadmissible questions, being sarcastic or snide to witnesses, badgering witnesses, and personally attacking opposing counsel.

Disobeying a court order is also an ethical breach and sanctionable. ABA Model Rule 3.4(c). Violations of this rule most often arise when a lawyer does not comply with a discovery order issued by the court. For example, in a Texas case, a lawyer agreed to pay more than $1 million in fines for violating a court order by failing to produce records from a former client for more than two and a half years. In another case, a California court granted summary judgment when a lawyer failed to participate meaningfully in judicial arbitration.

Acts that reflect disrespect for the court may subject an attorney to disciplinary action, but they are more likely to elicit an immediate response from the judge. Judges may hold an attorney in ***contempt*** for offensive courtroom conduct. Their contempt power is reserved for situations in which the administration of justice and orderly proceedings are immediately and substantially threatened. Generally, the court will warn a lawyer, sometimes repeatedly, before holding the lawyer in contempt. Contempt can be punishable by jail time and is reported to the disciplinary authorities, which may give rise to disciplinary proceedings.

Contempt
An act that obstructs the administration of justice, impairs the dignity of the court, or shows disrespect for the authority of the court

Judges have imposed the contempt sanction on attorneys for many kinds of disruptive conduct such as the ones described above.

Other examples are continued argument on a point on which the court has ruled; continued mention of inadmissible evidence or prohibited arguments; absence from or tardiness for scheduled court dates; presentation of false evidence; the use of abusive, vulgar, and obscene language; disrespectful, irrelevant, or unjustified criticism of the court. Insults, sarcasm, and the like can be punishable by contempt if they disrupt the proceedings.

Most paralegals do not find themselves in situations in which they would have the opportunity to engage in unethical conduct in court, but issues can arise when they accompany their lawyer-supervisors to court. Many paralegals working in civil litigation and criminal practice attend court proceedings and therefore must be aware of and abide by these rules. NFPA Model Code EC-1.3(a) calls on paralegals to refrain from "conduct that offends the dignity and decorum" of courts.

D. Candor and Honesty

The ABA Model Rules contain several provisions calling for lawyers to be **honest** in their representation of clients. Candor in communications with the court does not, however, obligate the lawyer to disclose evidence that is prejudicial to the client unless such information is not privileged and is requested through proper discovery or the lawyer is so obligated by some special rule of law, such as the duty of prosecutors to disclose exculpatory evidence.

The ethics rules specifically prohibit a lawyer from making a **false statement of law or fact**, ABA Model Rule 3.3(a)(1); offering **false evidence,** Rule 3.3(a)(3); and **not disclosing adverse controlling authority** when opposing counsel fails to do so, Rule 3.3(a)(2). The Rules further require an attorney who later discovers that false evidence has been submitted to **correct the fraud** on the court under Model Rule 3.3(a)(1) and (b). A nonclient's fraud on the court must be promptly revealed to the court by the lawyer.

Model Rule 3.4 prohibits lawyers from **obstructing access** to evidence; **altering**, destroying, or **concealing evidence**; and **falsifying or allowing others to falsify evidence**. (See the section later on witnesses for more on false testimony by witnesses.) See *Eaton v. Fink* at the end of this chapter, about a paralegal who reveals that false evidence was admitted in a case.

Some examples of violations of the ethics rules on honesty with tribunals may be instructive. In one disciplinary case, an attorney was censured for failing to disclose to arbitrators that a doctor had changed his diagnosis of the condition of the client. In another case, a court ordered a default judgment against a defendant whose attorney refused to produce a witness that had avoided service. A federal court ordered a default in a high-profile race discrimination case against a corporate defendant for altering and destroying key documents, leaving critical information out of affidavits, blocking access in court to relevant information, and intimidating a witness. Other cases have involved a lawyer requesting that his client be released from custody to attend his mother's funeral after it had been held; an attorney providing false information on the value of a client's property; a lawyer failing to provide the names of more than 20 known witnesses in a case; and a lawyer conveying property with the intent to defraud a creditor. In a major case against an automobile manufacturer, lawyers were held to be acting improperly for allowing false testimony of an employee several times over a period of years. In a recent case, defense lawyers were sanctioned for failing to produce relevant reports that the plaintiff's counsel obtained from a federal agency.

Perjury
Criminal offense of making false statements under oath

Client ***perjury*** is a difficult and complex ethical dilemma for lawyers. The courts have not been uniform in their handling of this area, and ethics rules and their interpretations also vary from one jurisdiction to the next. As a general rule, in a civil case, the lawyer who knows that his or her client intends to commit perjury should not call the client to testify. Most courts recommend or mandate withdrawal from representation or disclosure to the court if the client testifies dishonestly.

Criminal cases in which a client lies present even more serious problems because of the client's right to testify and to be represented by competent counsel. The U.S. Supreme Court has held that withdrawal is the appropriate action (*Nix v. Whiteside*, 475 U.S. 157 (1986)). However, withdrawal may not be allowed at the time of trial if the court finds that withdrawal would interfere with a speedy trial and the administration of justice. Authorities are split on whether a lawyer who is not permitted to withdraw should disclose the intended perjury. Some courts endorse allowing the defendant to testify in narrative form without the attorney's help. After the perjury has occurred, most courts require the lawyer to seek withdrawal. If withdrawal is not granted, some courts require disclosure of the perjury. Both narrative testimony and withdrawal during trial signal to the jury that the defendant was lying, highlighting the conflict between duties of zealous representation and candor to the court.

Some commentators believe that client and witness perjury is widespread. Judges have accused parties of perjury in several high-profile cases. Some examples are: relatives testifying falsely as alibi witnesses; spouses hiding assets in marital dissolution cases; and police lying under oath about the circumstances of an arrest, a search and seizure, or an informant. In one Silicon Valley case, a defendant in a patent case falsified a notebook that was said to contain his notes on an invention. A paralegal in the case noticed differences in two versions of the same notebook, which the court ultimately found to have been falsified. The client in this case was prosecuted for obstruction of justice and perjury.

The **duty of candor** also applies to legal research and use of precedent in documents filed with a court. A paralegal who finds adverse controlling authority while conducting legal research must report the authority to the supervising attorney, who should include it in relevant documents filed with the court. (See Model Rule 3.3(a)(1), which prohibits lawyers from making a "false statement of law," and 3.3(a)(2), which requires lawyer to disclose adverse controlling authority.) Of course, paralegals and lawyers drafting briefs and motions can cite the adverse authority and seek to distinguish it legally or factually or argue for a change in the law. The *Massey* case later in this chapter illustrates one possible result of controlling adverse authority not being cited. Lawyers who do not follow this rule find themselves being sanctioned and reported to disciplinary authorities.

Remedies for destroying, altering, or suppressing evidence imposed by disciplinary bodies and the courts are supplemented by **obstruction of justice** statutes, at both state and federal levels. In addition to criminal charges being brought against the attorney, client, or both, statutes provide for sanctions in the pending case, including fines, dismissal, award of legal fees and costs, and civil causes of action by the injured party. Destruction of evidence may also give rise to a civil cause of action for ***spoliation,*** in which the injured party can collect damages for substantial interference with the ability to prove a claim or defense because the evidence is no longer available. In some states, courts allow an adverse inference to be drawn from a party's failure to produce the evidence.

Spoliation
Destruction of evidence that may result in a civil cause of action for damages for interference with the ability to prove a claim or defense

REVIEW QUESTIONS

1. Why do paralegals need to know about the rules governing advocacy?
2. What is zealous representation, and what other ethics rules constrain a lawyer's unfettered zeal in representing a client?
3. Define two kinds of unmeritorious claims or defenses, and give an example of each.
4. Under what circumstances can a lawyer make a claim that is not warranted under existing law?
5. Does a lawyer have a duty to investigate a client's story before filing an action?
6. Give three examples of abuses of the discovery process.
7. Give an example of an unethical delay. What other ethics violations might be involved in an unnecessary delay?
8. Name four kinds of remedies or sanctions that might result from bringing unmeritorious claims, abusing discovery, or causing unnecessary delays.
9. Under what circumstances may an action for malicious prosecution be brought? Abuse of process?

10. What kinds of sanctions may a court impose for unwarranted, delaying, or harassing actions? On whom are they imposed?
11. Give three examples of actions by lawyers that would be disruptive in the courtroom. What do the ethics rules prohibiting such disruptions say? For what reasons might a lawyer be disruptive?
12. What is the most immediate remedy for disruptive conduct in the courtroom or disobedience of a court order?
13. What kinds of actions are prohibited by a lawyer's duty of candor?
14. What must a lawyer do if he or she discovers that false testimony has been given by a non-client witness? What if the false testimony is given by a client in a civil case? In a criminal case?
15. What should a paralegal do if he or she discovers adverse controlling authority in the course of research?
16. What are three things that might happen if a lawyer presents false evidence or permits false testimony in court?

DISCUSSION QUESTIONS AND HYPOTHETICALS

1. Why are there proportionately more paralegals in litigation than there are lawyers working in litigation?
2. Are you surprised that lawyers have duties that temper their duty to represent clients zealously? Did you know that a lawyer's highest duty is not just to win? Discuss the tension between the sometimes conflicting sets of duties and discuss whether the courts and ethics authorities seem to have found the right balance.
3. What would you do if you interviewed a client who told you a story that you did not fully believe and your supervising attorney told you to draft a complaint on the client's behalf based solely on the client's story?
4. How would you respond if your supervising attorney asked you to prepare an involuntary bankruptcy petition that you knew was unwarranted and designed solely to stop a foreclosure proceeding against your client?
5. What would you do if a supervising attorney asked you to prepare requests for continuances in virtually every case he or she handled? What if you knew it was because the attorney was unprepared and behind in his or her work? What if you knew it was because your client was ill and the attorney was trying to avoid going to trial before the client's death?
6. How would you handle it if the supervising attorney asked you to prepare 300 interrogatories in a case that you knew warranted only 50?
7. What would you do if the supervising attorney asked you to give nonresponsive or incomplete answers to interrogatories? Asked you

not to produce certain documents that you believe were requested in a proper document production?

8. How would you react if you were asked to draft interrogatories about the opposition's personal affairs, which had no relationship to the case? What about interrogatories requesting information that you knew to be privileged?
9. Why are court-imposed sanctions such a powerful remedy for abuses in pleading and discovery?
10. Suppose you are responsible for handling the discovery in a case, and the supervising lawyer tells you to disregard a court order to complete discovery. What do you do?
11. Suppose you are a litigation paralegal who is accompanying a lawyer to court for an important trial. What would you do if the supervising lawyer kept whispering to you during opposing counsel's examination of witnesses? What if you knew that this conduct was intended to distract the jury?
12. How would you respond if the supervising lawyer asked you to shred documents that you knew were discoverable?
13. How would you use adverse authority in a brief if you believed the authority was not controlling in your jurisdiction?
14. What steps would you take if you knew that a client was planning to lie during testimony? What if you knew a non-client witness was planning to lie? Would your answer depend on whether the supervising attorney knew too?
15. Do you believe that the adversary system encourages perjury? Contact the local federal and/or state prosecutors and interview several lawyers for their opinion on this issue. Ask them how many prosecutions for perjury have been brought in recent years.

RESEARCH PROJECTS AND ASSIGNMENTS

1. Find the rules of civil procedure, court rules, and ethics rules in your jurisdiction about frivolous and unwarranted claims and contentions. How do these rules compare with each other and with the ABA Model Rules? What interesting recent cases have been decided on the basis of these rules? Have any of them involved paralegals?
2. For an interesting high-profile case involving a professional basketball player, see *Sprewell v. Golden State Warriors*, 231 F.3d 520 (2000), in which the federal appellate court upholds the lower court's decision to dismiss the case and sanction the lawyers for conduct discussed in this chapter. Read and brief this case for the class.
3. What are your state's rules on e-discovery? Have the courts in your jurisdiction decided any cases interpreting them? What do they say about destroying e-mails and other electronic evidence?

4. New York's trial judges have adopted Uniform Rules Relating to the Conduct of Depositions to promote ethical and civil behavior in taking depositions. Does your jurisdiction have any such rules? Interview five trial lawyers and ask them if bad conduct in depositions is a problem.
5. Read *In re Thomas Consolidated Ind., Inc.*, 456 F.3d 719 (7th Cir. 2006), in which the appellate court upholds the dismissal of a case for failure to comply with court orders for discovery and for lying to a court about it. Compare this case with *Hoag v. Amex Assurance Co.*, 953 A.2d 713 (Del. 2008), in which the court upheld a dismissal after the plaintiff failed to comply with four court orders for discovery over a period of three years.
6. In *Wade v. Soo Line Railroad Corp.*, 06-1878 (7th Cir. 2007), the judge dismissed a case and sanctioned a lawyer for concealing documents in several different ways. Read and brief this case to see what the appeals court decided.
7. For a case addressing the extent and cost of e-discovery, see *Zubulake v. UBS Warburg*, 216 F.R.D. 280 (S.D.N.Y. 2003).
8. For an exceptionally contentious case involving discovery, which contains allegations of bribes and a request for the judge to recuse himself, see *Sentis Groups v. Shell Oil,* 559 F.3d 888 (8th Cir. 2009). In this case, the judge was the one who was accused of inappropriate language, directing profanities at the plaintiffs' counsel more than 15 times.
9. Making frivolous claims in appeals is also sanctionable. For an interesting case, see *In re White,* 121 Cal. App. 4th 1453, 18 Cal. Rptr. 3d 444 (2004). In this case involving three appeals, the lawyer was found to be operating a habeas corpus writ mill in which he aided in the unauthorized practice of law and failed to supervise nonlawyers. The appeals he filed were found to be frivolous and he was ordered to refund fees to clients and pay a sanction.

E. Relationships and Communications with Others

As discussed in Chapters 3 and 6, paralegals must take care to disclose their status as a paralegal. Paralegals who communicate with persons outside their own law firms may easily be mistaken for lawyers. A third person who mistakenly assumes that a paralegal is a lawyer may believe that the paralegal intended this impression, giving rise to a claim that the paralegal held himself or herself out as a lawyer. This rule is critical in litigation practice because paralegals communicate frequently with courts, opposing counsel, co-counsel, clients, third parties, and witnesses.

1. Judges

As mentioned in Section C, inappropriate **criticism of judges** in court may give rise to disciplinary action, although it is not ordinarily grounds for contempt proceedings because of free speech considerations. Ethics rules also prohibit lawyers from making false statements about the "qualifications or integrity of a judge. . . ." ABA Model Rule 8.2(a). Lawyers are protected from liability for derogatory statements about a judge unless made with knowledge of the statement's falsity or with reckless disregard (*Garrison v. Louisiana*, 379 U.S. 64, 85 S. Ct. 209 (1964)). In most jurisdictions, the courts have held that the First Amendment does not protect lawyers from disciplinary action for criticizing judges inappropriately because of the strong state interest in protecting public officials and in maintaining respect for the courts. However, in a minority of jurisdictions, discipline of lawyers who publicly and harshly criticized judges has been struck down on appeal. In one case, the lawyer called a judge an anti-Semite and a drunk. In the other, the lawyer called a local judge "a midget among giants" in a letter to a newspaper. A Tennessee lawyer was recently given a two-year suspension for saying that a judge "disgrace[d] his judicial office" and that his decision was "a stench in the nostrils of the nation." An Illinois lawyer was suspended for six months recently for criticizing a judge, calling him at one point "a narcissistic, maniacal mental case." And in a highly publicized case in Michigan, a well-known lawyer was brought before the state grievance commission for repeatedly using obscenities in courts and calling justices "three jackass court of appeals judges" and "Nazis."

Ethics rules prohibit lawyers from attempting to **influence judges**. Model Rule 3.5(a) prohibits a lawyer from seeking to influence a judge by any illegal means, for example, ***bribery***. Bribery is also a crime punishable under state law. Rule 8.4(f) also prohibits knowingly assisting a judge in violating the law or the rules of judicial conduct. Implying or stating that one can influence a public official, including a judge, is prohibited by Model Rule 8.4(e). It should be noted that judges are governed by their own ethics canons and rules of conduct in every jurisdiction and that these rules parallel those already stated.

Bribery
The crime of giving or receiving something of value as payment for an official act

Paralegals must also be mindful of rules relating to ***ex parte*** communications with judges. To ensure fairness in the adversarial process, lawyers are prohibited from having contact with the judge in a case without the presence of the opposing counsel. Such secret communications might give the communicating party an unfair advantage or give an appearance of influence or favoritism. The ethics rules that prohibit ex parte communications with judges are set forth in Model Rule 3.5(b). Exceptions to these rules are made for special ex parte proceedings that do not require opposing counsel's presence, such as petitions for a temporary restraining order. The NFPA Model Code calls attention to the rules regarding ex parte communications in EC-1.2(a) and (b).

Ex parte
Action taken by or on behalf of a party without the presence of the opposing party

2. Jurors

Seeking to influence or having **ex parte communications with jurors** or prospective jurors, before and during trial, is expressly prohibited by ethics rules to prevent influence and bribery. ABA Model Rule 3.5(a) and (b). Lawyers are prohibited from such communications even if they are not involved in the case at issue. A lawyer may not circumvent these rules by using an agent, such as the client or a paralegal.

In addition to disciplinary action for such conduct, a ***mistrial*** is likely to be declared if ex parte communications with jurors come to light. The lawyer's intent or lack of intent to influence the juror or jurors is not relevant in such cases. A lawyer's research on prospective jurors by using an investigator to contact them and ask them questions from a standard questionnaire has been held impermissible and, in one case, led to the criminal conviction and disbarment of the lawyer. Even simple socializing during a break in the proceedings has been held to be grounds to declare a mistrial. See the *Omaha Bank* case at the end of this chapter for an illustration of what can happen when a lawyer has contact with a juror outside the courtroom. Some courts have also disqualified counsel for such improprieties.

Mistrial
Trial terminated and declared void prior to the return of a verdict

Jury tampering is, of course, a crime in every jurisdiction and under federal laws. For example, 18 U.S.C. §§1503 and 1504 make it a crime to attempt to influence a juror or judge.

Communicating with jurors after a trial is forbidden in some states. Other states do not prohibit post-trial communications, which attorneys may desire to evaluate their presentation, to find out what influenced the jurors, and to ascertain whether the jury deliberated appropriately. ABA Model Rule 3.5(c) allows communication after the jury is discharged unless prohibited by law or court order; if the juror has made known a desire not to communicate; or if the communication involves misrepresentation, coercion, harassment, or duress. General harassment of jurors is also prohibited by the general provision on respect for the rights of third persons, found in Model Rule 4.4.

Finally, some states have a rule that obligates lawyers to reveal improper conduct toward or among jurors to the court, although no comparable provision exists in the Model Rules.

3. Parties and Unrepresented Persons

Lawyers are prohibited from communicating directly with **parties who are represented by counsel** and may communicate only with the person's lawyer unless authorized by law or a court order or with the other lawyer's consent. ABA Model Rule 4.2. This rule is based primarily on concerns about overreaching conduct that may disrupt the trust between the attorney and client or influence the client against the client's interest. Clients are more vulnerable when their counsel is not present and may be more easily persuaded to give information or settle a case against their own interest. Unethical solicitation is also a concern, as described in Chapter 6.

Rules prohibiting communication with represented parties do not apply when represented parties are not truly adverse, are seeking a second opinion or new counsel, or are dissatisfied with their lawyers over the representation or fees and are considering taking action against the lawyer. This prohibition does not restrict the actions of the *parties*, who are free to speak to each other, although most lawyers warn their clients not to do so because of the potential for such conversations interfering with the representation and strategy in the case. The *Crane* case at the end of this chapter illustrates how a lawyer might break this rule and what consequences might follow. When a violation of this ethics rule takes place during proceedings, remedies include suppression of evidence and disqualification of counsel. Disciplinary sanctions may follow, especially if the conduct involved dishonesty.

It should be noted that the rules prohibiting lawyers from communicating with represented parties apply to federal prosecutors. For some time in the 1990s, the U.S. Attorney General argued otherwise, but in 1998 Congress passed a law holding federal prosecutors to the state ethics rules, which prohibit such contacts in all jurisdictions (28 U.S.C. §530B). Subdivision (a) of this statute states, "An attorney for the Government shall be subject to State laws and rules, and local Federal court rules, governing attorneys in each State where such attorney engages in that attorney's duties, to the same extent and in the same manner as other attorneys in that State."

Ethics rules also restrict the communications a lawyer may have with a **party not represented by counsel**. ABA Model Rule 4.3 prohibits a lawyer from stating or implying that the lawyer is "disinterested," requires a lawyer to clear up any misconception that an unrepresented person may have about the lawyer's role, and prohibits the lawyer from giving legal advice to the unrepresented person. The only advice that the lawyer can give such a person is to secure counsel. Paralegals who conduct investigations and talk to prospective witnesses should be keenly aware of these restrictions.

In the corporate setting, determining who a lawyer or paralegal may communicate with during litigation is sometimes difficult. Most cases hold that a lawyer may speak to unrepresented former employees of a corporation on the opposing side of litigation unless the employees were privy to privileged information. Current employees may be classified as "represented persons" if the corporation provides counsel to them. Members of a class in a class action are also considered to be represented parties. A recent ABA opinion addresses the issue of whether a lawyer can communicate with in-house counsel when the corporation is represented by outside counsel. In holding that such communications generally do not require advance approval of outside counsel, the opinion does prohibit such a communication if the lawyer is a party to the matter (ABA Formal Opinion 06-443).

Because a lawyer may not circumvent the rules on communications by using an agent, a paralegal should not engage in improper ex parte communications when working in litigation or other areas of practice. Paralegals frequently have contact with clients, opposing counsel, and witnesses. They must refrain from communicating with persons represented by counsel and from misleading persons not represented by counsel about their interest in a matter. An earlier ABA ethics opinion makes it clear that a lawyer is responsible for the improper ex parte contacts of nonlawyers. In the scenario posed by the ABA, a lawyer is responsible for the violations of this rule by an investigator under his or her supervision who made improper contacts, which the lawyer either did not try to prevent, told the investigator to make, or failed to instruct the investigator not to make once the contact came to light (ABA Formal Opinion 95-396). See *In re Ositis* at the end of this chapter for an example of a case in which a lawyer was disciplined for directing his investigator to pose as a journalist to interview a potential party. Many but not all states follow this interpretation and prohibit lawyers from allowing their agents to "pretext" in investigations.

The ABA Guidelines on the Utilization of Paralegal Services and most state guidelines do not make specific reference to paralegals' communicating with third parties. The Pennsylvania Bar in its ethics opinion on paralegals is the exception, reminding lawyers to caution paralegals not to communicate with represented persons. Penn. Bar Ass'n Formal Opinion 98-75.

4. Witnesses

A few special rules govern lawyers' contact with witnesses. A lawyer is forbidden from advising or causing a witness to **flee the jurisdiction or to hide to avoid testifying**. ABA Model Rule 3.4(a) and (f). In addition to violating ethics rules, such conduct constitutes obstruction of justice and violates statutes that make it a crime to tamper with a witness or to delay, hinder, or prevent a witness from testifying.

An attorney may not advise a witness to **testify falsely** or offer an inducement to testify falsely. ABA Model Rule 3.4(b). Giving false testimony under oath constitutes perjury, and counseling a witness to do so constitutes the crime of ***subornation of perjury***.

Subornation of perjury
Criminal offense of encouraging another to commit perjury

Lawyers and paralegals interview witnesses in depth to ascertain as exactly as possible the content of the witnesses' testimony, their credibility, and their consistency. Witnesses sometimes change or are unclear about their stories, providing the opposing counsel with a chance to impeach the credibility of the witness.

Ethics rules do not prohibit lawyers from **preparing witnesses**, including clients, to testify effectively. A witness who is familiar with deposition and courtroom procedure and who knows the kinds of questions that counsel and opposing counsel will ask is more likely to be consistent and clear and less likely to be confused by opposing counsel. Lawyers and paralegals who handle witness preparation must be careful not to encourage witnesses to give false testimony or to over-coach witnesses so that their testimony seems "prepared" and they lose credibility.

Unethical coaching of witnesses surfaces on occasion in high-stakes cases. In one large asbestos case, the plaintiffs' lawyers prepared a detailed memorandum to their clients telling them how to testify, including what to say about their injuries. When the defense counsel was inadvertently given a copy of this memorandum, the firm stopped sending it to the plaintiffs and blamed an overzealous paralegal for writing it. The judge reported the matter to the state bar but no action was taken against the lawyers involved. In seeking the death penalty in a criminal case against a terrorist, a veteran U.S. attorney coached witnesses and gave them copies of trial transcripts in contravention of a court order, causing the judge to sanction the lawyer and to exclude key witnesses and other evidence.

Paralegals must be mindful of the line between preparing witnesses to give their testimony effectively and encouraging them to testify untruthfully. Perjury is hard to prove, especially when the witness is also the client; but judges have little tolerance for over-coaching witnesses and juries are usually very perceptive about the veracity of witnesses.

General rules about the treatment of third persons serve to prohibit the **harassment of witnesses**, both inside and outside the courtroom. ABA Model Rule 4.4 prohibits lawyers from engaging in any conduct the only purpose of which is to "embarrass, delay, or burden a third person."

Related to these ethics prohibitions are statutes that prohibit the **recording** of a person without his or her permission. Federal statutes provide criminal and civil remedies for interception and disclosure of wire, oral, or electronic communications and prohibit their use as evidence in court. But not all jurisdictions prohibit secret tape recording of conversations, and some states have actually endorsed the practice. An ABA advisory opinion recommends against secret tape recording on ethical grounds (ABA Formal Opinion 74-331). It is advisable to consult state statutes and rules before engaging in such conduct.

Lawyers may **pay witnesses for expenses** related to their testifying. The usual and permissible expenses are travel and lost wages. Payment may be made for time spent in preparation, such as meetings with lawyers and paralegals; however, witnesses must not be paid for the value or efficacy of their testimony. The agreement to pay the witness should meet the standards of the ethics rules and should not be kept secret from the court.

Expert witnesses may also be paid a reasonable fee for their professional services. No witness, including experts, may be paid a fee or bonus that is contingent on the outcome of a case, as this would obviously provide an incentive for false testimony. ABA Model Rule 3.4(b) prohibits attorneys from offering an illegal "inducement" to a witness.

As discussed in Section D earlier, with regard to client perjury, a lawyer has special duties to prevent the introduction of false testimony and to take corrective measures if a witness gives false testimony. A lawyer who knows that a witness intends to testify falsely should advise the witness not to do so and should refuse to call the witness if he or she persists in intending to commit perjury. Once false testimony is given by a witness, the lawyer must inform the court. ABA Model Rule 3.3(a)(3).

F. Trial Publicity

Balancing **the right of free expression and the right to a fair trial** is sometimes challenging. The public interest in criminal and civil cases and the pervasiveness of the modern media have frequently clashed with the smooth administration of the court system and assurance of a fair trial, especially in criminal cases and cases where a jury is involved. This conflict has most noticeably presented itself in sensational cases, especially those in which the press sought to have cameras in the courtroom or in which a judge issued a ***gag order***. Lawyers sometimes meet daily with the media in high-profile cases and are often accused by opposing counsel of "trying the case in the press."

Gag order
Court-imposed order that restricts information or comment about a case

The original ABA Model Code provisions on trial publicity were challenged in court as unconstitutional. At least three appellate courts found that they interfere with free speech although the U.S. Supreme Court did not decide the matter. Model Rule 3.6 contains a general admonition against extrajudicial statements if "the lawyer knows or reasonably should know [that the statement] will be" publicly disseminated "and will have a substantial likelihood of materially prejudicing an adjudicative proceeding." Additional provisions list the basic items of information that a lawyer can state publicly in any case. Lawyers are also specifically permitted to make statements to mitigate adverse publicity not generated by the lawyer or the client. All lawyers in a firm involved in a case are covered.

All states have a rule on trial publicity, but the details of the rules vary from jurisdiction to jurisdiction. Some states have retained the rule from the old Model Code, but most have adopted some version of Model Rule 3.6. A few have established a more permissive standard, prohibiting only statements that create a danger of "imminent and substantial harm" of prejudicing the adjudicative proceeding.

Although disciplinary actions against lawyers for violations of these provisions are relatively rare, they do occur, usually in sensational cases that are closely covered by the media. For example, the lawyer representing criminal underworld figure John Gotti was held in contempt for statements made in his media campaign, particularly for statements intended for potential jurors. The defense lawyers in the O. J. Simpson murder prosecution were investigated for statements made to the media about a frame and cover-up of a frame of their client, but no ethics charges were brought. As already noted, some courts issue gag orders to prevent lawyers from making any statements, in the interests of a fair trial, but when challenged these gag orders are sometimes struck down as unconstitutional prior restraints on speech.

The debate over lawyer relations with the media in high-profile cases related not only to legal ethics but to the impact of lawyer conduct on public opinion of lawyers. Polls have shown that the public views lawyers negatively in part because of their conduct in heavily reported, often scandalous, cases.

ABA Model Rule 3.6(d) prohibits associates in the same firm from commenting on a case but does not specifically refer to nonlawyer "employees"; however, the general provision in the ABA Model Rules covering a lawyer's responsibility for acts of employees extends the reach of this rule to paralegals (ABA Model Rule 5.3).

G. Special Rules for Prosecutors

As representatives of the government and "the people," prosecutors have a special duty of truth and fairness in the administration of justice. Prosecutors must not seek only to convict but also to **seek justice** and to ensure that all citizens are afforded their rights. A separate rule (Model Rule 3.8) sets forth these obligations, and local laws frequently impose additional obligations.

One critical duty of the prosecutor is not to institute unsupported criminal charges or to continue to pursue an unsupported action. **Probable cause** is required. ABA Model Rule 3.8(a). This limitation also prevents prosecutors from abusing their discretion in prosecuting cases by singling someone out for prosecution. Prosecutors are also required to **disclose information** that tends to negate or mitigate guilt or to reduce punishment. ABA Model Rule 3.8(d).

The ABA Model Rules contain additional provisions that require prosecutors to make reasonable efforts to see that the accused **knows of the right to counsel** and has had an opportunity to secure counsel, ABA Model Rule 3.8(b); **not to obtain a waiver** of rights from an unrepresented accused, ABA Model Rule 3.8(c); and to exercise reasonable care to prevent employees and others involved with the prosecution from making extrajudicial statements that would "heighten public condemnation of the accused," ABA Model Rule 3.8(f). Finally, ABA Model Rule 3.8(e) limits a prosecutor's right to subpoena a lawyer to testify about a client or former client. A prosecutor may subpoena a lawyer only if the information sought is not privileged, is essential to the case and not otherwise available, and the prosecutor has prior judicial approval. For additional guidance on ethical issues in the criminal area, see the ABA Standards for Criminal Justice, which include separate sections on the prosecutorial and defense functions.

In addition to disciplinary sanctions for violations of these rules, courts may impose remedies in a pending case if the defendant's constitutional rights have been violated. For example, a court may **reverse a conviction, suppress evidence, dismiss charges, or order a new trial**. In several recent cases, convictions have been reversed for prosecutorial conduct. For example, a murder conviction was reversed on appeal when the appellate court found extensive prosecutorial misconduct, including misrepresenting the law and the facts and intimidating witnesses. In another case, the prosecutor in closing arguments misstated the defendant's testimony and said that the defendant had been "programmed" and "counseled" to lie. In a 2008 case, the district attorney in Durham, North Carolina, was disbarred after it came to light that he had made untrue accusations, influenced the police investigation, attempted to manipulate witnesses, and refused to hear exculpatory evidence in a highly publicized case involving Duke University lacrosse players charged with sexual assault. In this case, the charges against the students were ultimately dropped. In two recent cases in California, prosecutors were suspended for ethics violations relating to failure to disclose exculpatory evidence after the defendants in question were convicted. In 2009 a U.S. District Court judge in Massachusetts wrote a 42-page opinion charging the U.S. Attorney there with engaging in a pattern of misconduct by failing to disclose exculpatory evidence.

REVIEW QUESTIONS

1. What are the three main ethics rules governing lawyers' relationships with judges?
2. What do the ABA Model Rules say about lawyers influencing judges? What crime occurs when a lawyer tries to influence a judge?
3. Can a lawyer give a judge a gift? What if they are good friends?
4. Why are lawyers and their employees prohibited from having ex parte communications with judges?
5. What kinds of contact with jurors are prohibited by the ethics rules and why? What crime might be involved when a lawyer or paralegal tries to influence a juror?

6. What are the general rules about lawyers and their agents having contact with persons who already have a lawyer? Why? What are the exceptions?
7. What is the general rule about contact with persons who are not represented by counsel?
8. Do federal prosecutors have to follow state ethics rules, such as those prohibiting contact with represented persons? Under what authority?
9. What is prohibited by the ethics rules in lawyers' contact with witnesses? What crimes might such actions constitute?
10. What contact can lawyers or paralegals have with witnesses? What kinds of things do they need to be careful about when they talk to witnesses?
11. What are the ethical and practical concerns when lawyers and paralegals talk to employees and other lawyers in the corporate setting?
12. What actions might constitute harassing a witness? What crime (or crimes) might be committed in addition to violations of ethics rules?
13. May a lawyer pay a witness to testify? What are the applicable restrictions?
14. May a lawyer pay an expert witness? May the amount be based on the outcome in the case?
15. What two important constitutional interests are being balanced in the ethics rules on trial publicity?
16. What kinds of extrajudicial statements are generally permitted by ethics rules? What kinds are prohibited?
17. May a lawyer have a paralegal speak to the press and reveal information about a pending case that the lawyer could not under the ethics rules? Why, or why not?
18. Why are prosecutors bound by additional ethics rules? Name four ethical duties that prosecutors have that other lawyers do not have.
19. What sanctions and remedies may be imposed for prosecutorial misconduct?

DISCUSSION QUESTIONS AND HYPOTHETICALS

1. What would you do if your attorney-employer asked you to invite a judge who was serving on one of your cases to a social event you were planning?
2. Can you ask a judge who is a friend of yours questions about a pending case?
3. Do you think lawyers and their employees should be prohibited from giving campaign contributions to judges? Why or why not? What restrictions, if any, might mitigate the potential for harm?

4. What would you do if your supervisor asked you to give a sealed note to a juror during a recess?
5. Why are lawyers not involved in a case prohibited from talking to jurors about the case?
6. Suppose you work for the U.S. Attorney General's office. You are asked to call a person who is being investigated in a major organized crime case. You know that the person is likely to be indicted and is already represented by counsel. What do you do? Do you think that federal prosecutors should be exempt from state ethics rules? Why, or why not?
7. What would you do if the supervising attorney asked you to contact the opposing party in a divorce case to see if the spouses could meet without the lawyers present to work out an amicable settlement?
8. What would you do if a co-plaintiff who was not represented by your firm contacted you to discuss changing lawyers? What if the party wanted to discuss the merits of the case? The performance of his or her lawyer?
9. What would you do if you were interviewing a potential witness who did not have an attorney, and you suddenly realized that he seemed to believe that you and your firm were representing him?
10. Suppose that one of your duties as a litigation paralegal is to prepare witnesses for trial. What would you do if you were preparing a witness and his or her story kept changing? What if the witness seemed to be changing his or her version of the facts to be more favorable to your side? Suppose the witness, although generally favorable to your client, has some information that is adverse to your client. What do you tell the witness about how to handle this information while he or she is on the stand?
11. What would you do if you discovered that a client was sending anonymous threatening letters to a witness who planned to testify against her? Would it make any difference if you knew the witness's testimony would be false?
12. What would you do if your firm paid a witness, who was not an expert, a witness fee that was three times his normal salary?
13. Review the rules governing a lawyer's handling of client perjury. Do you think a lawyer should be bound to tell the court if her client commits perjury? Would you answer differently in criminal and civil cases? What does your jurisdiction's ethics rule say? Are there any cases on the issue in your jurisdiction?
14. What would you do if your supervising attorney asked you to leak information to the press that you know is prohibited by ethics rules? Would it make any difference if you were certain that without press coverage of this information your client would be unfairly convicted of a serious crime?
15. Suppose you work for the local prosecuting attorney. What would you do if you uncovered information that proved a criminal

defendant in a case was innocent? What if you went to the supervising attorney and he refused to drop the charges or to turn over the exculpatory evidence to the defendant's counsel?

16. What would you do if your supervisor, the prosecuting attorney, asked you to obtain a statement from a recently arrested person, and in doing so you discovered that the person had not been advised of her right to counsel? What if the accused had been advised of her right to counsel but had not yet been able to reach an attorney?

RESEARCH PROJECTS AND ASSIGNMENTS

1. Read, brief, and compare these three interesting cases about lawyers who were disciplined for criticizing judges: *Standing Committee v. Yagman*, 55 F.3d 1430 (9th Cir. 1995); *In re Green*, 11 P.3d 1078 (Colo. 2000); and *In re Koven*, 134 Cal. App. 4th 262, 35 Cal. Rptr. 3d 317 (2005).
2. Read and brief the following case on tape recording by a lawyer and compare it with ABA Ethics Opinion 74-331 mentioned in this chapter: *Mississippi Bar v. Attorney ST*, 621 So. 2d 229 (Miss. 1993).
3. Read and brief the case of *Dayton Bar Association v. O'Brien*, 103 Ohio St. 3d 1 (2004), in which a lawyer implies to a client in a criminal matter that he could bribe a judge.
4. Does your state have ethics rules that govern communication with jurors after trial? Do you think lawyers should be able to interview jurors after a trial is over? Why, or why not?
5. For a case applying the rules about communicating with unrepresented persons in a corporate setting, read *Snider v. Superior Court*, 113 Cal. App. 4th 1187, 7 Cal. Rptr. 3d 119 (2003), in which an order disqualifying a lawyer is vacated on appeal.
6. Does your jurisdiction have a statute that prohibits or limits the tape recording of conversations? What does it say about getting permission from the party or parties? About the admissibility of illegally tape-recorded conversations?
7. What does your jurisdiction's ethics code say about extrajudicial statements or trial publicity? Do you think the rule strikes the right balance between free speech and fair trial? Have any lawyers in your jurisdiction been disciplined under the rule?
8. Obtain a copy of your state judicial canons and compare the relevant provisions to those for lawyers covered in this chapter.
9. Prosecutors were suspended for ripping pages out of opposing counsel's notebook during a deposition so that they could get a handwriting sample. To find out the rest of the facts and see what happened to the lawyers, read and brief *In re Winkler*, 834 N.E.2d 85 (Ind. 2005).

10. For a leading case on pretexting, see *Midwest Motor Sports v. Arctic Sales, Inc.*, 347 F.3d 693 (8th Cir. 2003). This case interprets Model Rule 8.4(c), concerning conduct involving dishonesty, fraud, deceit and misrepresentation, and finds the conduct in this case unethical and the evidence inadmissible.
11. For an interesting case involving a juror and a lawyer, see *Colosimo v. Pennsylvania Elec. Co.*, 486 A.2d 1378 (Pa. 1984). In this case, the lawyer represented a juror in another, unrelated matter.
12. A California court found that a lawyer did not violate ethics rules when he used an investigator to interview employees who were potential witnesses in a sexual harassment case prior to the time the lawsuit was filed and when none of those interviewed was represented by counsel. *Jorgensen v. Taco Bell Corp.*, 50 Cal. App. 4th 1398, 58 Cal. Rptr. 2d 178 (1996). Do you agree with this ruling? Why or why not? Is there potential for ethics violations in this scenario?

CASES FOR ANALYSIS

In the following case, the court dismisses the complaint of a litigant who failed to move forward with this case. As you read, consider what conduct by a litigant might warrant this harsh sanction.

Bonda Industrial (HK) Co., Ltd. v. Talbot Group, LLC

08 Civ. 5507 (PKL) (U.S.D.C., S.D.N.Y. 2009)

Bonda initiated this action . . . in New York State Supreme Court alleging breach of contract, conversion, promissory estoppel, and unjust enrichment. Bonda's claims are based upon defendants' alleged failure to pay Bonda for certain clothing Bonda manufactured. Defendants removed the case to this Court. . . .

In their amended answer, defendants denied the majority of plaintiff's allegations and asserted counterclaims against Bonda and Wong for breach of contract, breach of warranty, conversion, and trademark infringement in connection with the promotion, marketing, and distribution of clothing using defendants' trademark.

As this Court explained during the . . . order to show cause hearing, to date, Bonda and Wong have not filed a reply to the counterclaims, due in large part to the fact that their attorney, Dwane Smith, Esq., cannot file pleadings on his clients' behalf as he is neither admitted to this Court, nor admitted to try this particular case *pro hac vice*. In addition, plaintiff has otherwise neglected to prosecute its claims, as demonstrated by its failure to respond adequately to, or to serve, discovery requests, or to otherwise advance this case.

Plaintiff's failure to prosecute is exacerbated by Mr. Smith's repeated misrepresentations to this Court as to his intentions to move the case forward. Time after time, the Court gave Mr. Smith and his client the benefit of the doubt, granting numerous extensions to allow Bonda and Wong time to file a reply to the counterclaims, and to otherwise demonstrate an intent to prosecute plaintiff's claims. As far back as July 21, 2008, Mr. Smith informed the Court by letter that he intended to seek admission *pro hac vice*, and he assured the Court that he would be following up on his application in the upcoming week. Based on this representation, the Court so ordered the parties' stipulation, granting plaintiff an additional twenty (20) days to respond to the counterclaims and for Mr. Smith to appear in the action. Plaintiff's requests for extensions were again granted . . . based upon the Court's understanding that Mr. Smith was trying to gain admission to this Court.

Mr. Smith's representations were not limited to written communications. At both the September . . . and November . . . pre-trial conferences, Mr. Smith assured the Court that he would promptly submit a *pro hac vice* application, and that his client intended to pursue its claims. On both occasions, the Court cautioned Mr. Smith that plaintiff's failure to prosecute this case would be grounds for dismissal under Rule 41(b) and pursuant to the Supreme Court's decision in Link v. Wabash R.R. Co., 370 U.S. 626 (1962), and its progeny.

In a purported effort to address Mr. Smith's failure to gain admission to this Court, on November 10, 2008, Bonnie Mohr, Esq. filed a notice of appearance in this action. The notice provides, "Please take notice that the undersigned hereby appears in the above captioned action as counsel to the Law Offices of Dwane Smith PLLC." Notably, Ms. Mohr did not appear on behalf of Bonda and Wong. Prior to the November 25, 2008 pre-trial conference, Ms. Mohr informed the Court that she would be assisting Mr. Smith with electronic filing, as she was admitted to the Southern District of New York, but that Mr. Smith would continue to represent Bonda and Wong in the case. Ms. Mohr's notice of appearance was not accompanied by an application for Mr. Smith's *pro hac vice* admission, nor did her assistance impact plaintiff's lack of effort in the case.

By order to show cause, Talbot Group and Potamus Holding ask the Court to dismiss the case pursuant to Rule 41(b). Specifically, defendants contend that Mr. Smith's inability to gain admission to this Court or to move his client's case forward in any manner warrants dismissal. In the alternative, Talbot Group and Potamus Holding seek a default judgment against Bonda and Wong for their failure to respond to the counterclaims.

In opposition to defendants' motion, plaintiff's counsel emphasize that plaintiff has not missed any conferences, has not submitted any vexatious or burdensome filings to the Court, and that it is unlikely that defendants have suffered economic loss by plaintiff's delays. In addition, plaintiff's counsel submitted notice of a cross-motion, seeking leave of the

Court to extend time to December 12, 2008, to allow Bonda and Wong to serve and file an answer to the counterclaims, to serve supplemental discovery responses, and to serve discovery demands. Moreover, Mr. Smith and Ms. Mohr submitted a signed consent to substitute Ira Meyerowitz, Esq. as attorney of record for Bonda and Wong.

As proposed substituted counsel, Mr. Meyerowitz attended the December 17, 2008 hearing. After reviewing plaintiff's abysmal record in this case, the Court specifically asked Mr. Meyerowitz whether he was prepared to get involved in this case in its current posture. Mr. Meyerowitz informed the Court that he was reluctant to get involved in this "hornet's nest" unless the Court was prepared to consider his participation a "clean break from the past."

Federal Rule of Civil Procedure 41(b) allows a district court to dismiss an action if a plaintiff fails to prosecute the case or fails to comply with orders of that court. The Second Circuit has outlined five factors that a district court must consider to determine whether dismissal pursuant to Rule 41 is appropriate, including: (1) the duration of plaintiff's failure to prosecute the case and/or comply with court orders; (2) whether plaintiff was on notice that further delay and/or continuing to disregard court orders would result in dismissal; (3) whether defendants would likely be prejudiced by further delay; (4) a balancing of the court's interest in managing its docket with plaintiff's right to an opportunity for a day in court; and (5) whether there are other lesser sanctions available to the court to remedy the situation. [Citations omitted.] . . .

In balancing these five factors, the Court is mindful that involuntary dismissal of a plaintiff's case is "a harsh remedy to be utilized only in extreme situations." [Citations omitted.] . . .

The first factor — the duration of plaintiff's delay and/or disregard of Court orders — favors dismissing plaintiff's case pursuant to Rule 41(b). Here, plaintiff's inexcusable behavior provides the Court with two alternative grounds to dismiss: (1) plaintiff and its counsel have failed to comply with specific orders of this Court for an unreasonable amount of time; and (2) there has been a complete lack of prosecution of this case for more than six months.

Without offering a reasonable excuse, plaintiff has failed to comply with the orders of this Court. At the September 4, 2008 pre-trial conference, the Court specifically instructed Mr. Smith to gain admission before this Court and to promptly move plaintiff's case along. The Court reiterated these directives at the November 25, 2008 pre-trial conference. Both orders were completely ignored until defendants brought the instant motion. In opposition to defendants' motion, plaintiff's only explanation for its failure to comply with this Court's orders is that Mr. Smith's financial constraints, the demands of his practice as a solo practitioner, and personal issues he faced impeded his ability to gain admission to this Court and to otherwise proceed with this case. Mr. Smith was responsible for bringing these facts to the Court's attention, rather than misrepresenting his intentions and ignoring the Court's directives. . . . While sympathetic to Mr. Smith's purported difficulties, the Court is not satisfied that Bonda has demonstrated any good faith efforts to comply with the orders that would excuse counsel's behavior. [Citation omitted.]

Moreover, while plaintiff's counsel argued to this Court that he is exclusively to blame for plaintiff's inactivity in this case, it is well established that a client is bound by the actions of his counsel. [Citations omitted.] Further, Bonda has not presented any evidence that its intention to pursue its claims was inhibited by its counsel's neglect. Rather, it appears that plaintiff put its head in the sand, allowing its counsel to file notices of appearance and substitution of counsel, but ignoring the fact that discovery was not served, that the counterclaims were not answered, and that there was no indication plaintiff's claims were progressing. In fact, Mr. Smith's only representations to this Court as to his clients' participation in this case indicate difficulties he encountered in getting information from his client due to the fact that he contacted Wong too late, she was traveling, needed more time, and had laser surgery. As defendants argue . . . in opposing this motion to dismiss, Bonda had the opportunity to state clearly its intention to prosecute this case. Bonda's opposition, however, does not demonstrate that counsel's failures alone are to blame for the lack of progress in this suit.

Alternatively, plaintiff's claims must be dismissed because plaintiff has failed to prosecute this case since it has been pending before this Court. [Citation omitted.] For more than six months after the case was removed to this Court, plaintiff has failed to demonstrate any intent to advance its claims, or to defend against the counterclaims. Failing to prosecute these claims for more than six months is unreasonable, and grounds for dismissal. [Citations omitted.]

The Second Circuit has instructed district courts to consider whether plaintiff received notice that its failure to comply with Court orders and/or additional delays would result in dismissal. The Court finds that this factor supports dismissal. This Court emphasized at both the September and November pre-trial conferences that there is clear precedent allowing the Court to dismiss a case when plaintiff fails to prosecute its claims. The Court also reminded Mr. Smith that it was completely unacceptable for him to ignore his duty to gain admission to this Court. At both conferences, the Court cautioned that if plaintiff and its counsel continue to ignore their obligations, plaintiff's claims would be dismissed. As such, only after plaintiff disregarded these explicit warnings did the Court consider dismissing plaintiff's claims. [Citation omitted.] Moreover, the fact that the Court invited defendants to make this motion to dismiss by order to show cause demonstrates that plaintiff was on notice that the Court was contemplating dismissal. [Citations omitted.]

The third factor the Court considers in assessing whether plaintiff's claims should be dismissed is whether defendants would be prejudiced by further delay. Where, as here, delay is unreasonable, prejudice may be presumed as a matter of law. [Citations omitted.] Such a presumption is generally warranted because "delay by one party increases the likelihood that evidence in support of the other party's position will be lost and that discovery and trial will be made more difficult." [Citation omitted.]

While defendants need not show prejudice in this case, in considering this factor, the Court notes that defendants have offered uncontested evidence of the prejudice they have suffered because of plaintiff's behavior. In particular, defendants offered uncontroverted evidence that Wong knew that defendants were trying to finalize a business arrangement, but that the ongoing stalemate in this litigation was preventing the deal [from closing]. . . .

The fourth factor requires the Court to strike a "balance between [its] calendar congestion and the plaintiff's right to an opportunity to be heard." [Citation omitted.] The Court is always reluctant to deprive a plaintiff of a chance to litigate its claims, but finds that this case is an example of a "rare occasion" where such deprivation is warranted. [Citation omitted.] Because of plaintiff's lack of prosecutorial activity in this case, this Court was forced to consider several requests for extensions and to hold three pre-trial conferences discussing plaintiff's failures. Thus, the Court devoted significant time and resources to this case. At no time, however, did plaintiff demonstrate its intent to comply with Court orders or illustrate that it was not burdening this Court's docket with a case that it did not intend to prosecute. [Citation omitted.]

Moreover, plaintiff could have avoided this dismissal if it made any attempt to comply with the orders of this Court and advance this case. Instead, plaintiff's right to its day in court is diminished by plaintiff's and plaintiff's counsel's recalcitrance. [Citations omitted.]

In evaluating the fifth and final factor, the Court considers the appropriateness of alternative sanctions. . . . After considering the option of sanctioning the attorneys and/or plaintiff directly, the Court finds that such sanction would be insufficient to remedy this situation. . . .

Despite Mr. Smith's assurances to the contrary, plaintiff provided no evidence to indicate that it was not complicit in counsel's failures. . . . This Court will not ignore six months of inactivity, misrepresentations, and disregard of Court orders to the defendants' detriment.

The Court is mindful of the fact that sanctioning lawyers directly might be a more appropriate sanction when the delay is occasioned by plaintiff's counsel's disregard of their obligations rather than by plaintiff's own behavior or strategy. [Citation omitted.] Here, however, plaintiff's counsel's egregious behavior in the face of the Court's repeated warnings, coupled with the lack of any evidence of good faith efforts by plaintiff to advance its claims, leaves dismissal as the only possible remedy. [Citation omitted.] This Court will not penalize defendants for plaintiff's failures. [Citation omitted.]

For the foregoing reasons, defendants' motion to dismiss is hereby GRANTED, and plaintiff's claims are DISMISSED with prejudice.

Plaintiff's cross-motion for leave of this Court for additional time to supplement discovery responses and to serve discovery demands is DENIED AS MOOT, to the extent those requests pertain to plaintiff's claims. This decision does not, however, dismiss or otherwise limit defendants' counterclaims. To the extent defendants intend to pursue their counterclaims, the parties are ordered to appear before this Court for a pre-trial conference. . . .

Questions about the Case

1. How long was the delay in pursuing this case? Does that seem like a long time to you?
2. What were the five factors that the court considered in deciding whether to dismiss? Which were the most compelling in this case?
3. What does *pro hac vice* mean? What were the roles of the other two lawyers who were involved on the plaintiff's side in this case? Why was their involvement not sufficient to save the case from dismissal?
4. Does the plaintiff have a cause of action against this lawyer? What did this court say about the plaintiff's role in the dismissal?

In the following case, the lawyers on both sides missed the controlling legal authority at the trial court and the matter had to be corrected after an incorrect ruling was made.

Massey v. Prince George's County
907 F. Supp. 138 (D. Md. 1995)

. . . Plaintiff Willie Massey alleges that in the early morning hours of November 4, 1992 he was sleeping in a vacant or abandoned building in Cheverly, Maryland. He contends that all of a sudden he was awakened by Prince George's County police officers who, without warning, set their police dog upon him. Massey says that although he offered no resistance, the animal proceeded to bite him and inflict painful and permanent injury all over his body. In his Third Amended Complaint before the Court, Massey has sued the individual officers for assault and battery under Maryland law and for deprivation of his Fourth Amendment rights, i.e., for use of excessive force, under 42 U.S.C. §1983. The officers have denied liability, claiming that Massey was warned about the dog in a loud voice and that he resisted their efforts to arrest him.

Earlier in these proceedings, Defendants filed a fifteen page Motion for Summary Judgment to which excerpts from depositions of Plaintiff and various officers were appended. With regard to the Section 1983 claims, Defendants argued that their seizure of Plaintiff and the force used by them were reasonable as a matter of law. After citing general Supreme Court law regarding such claims, defense counsel invited the Court's attention to the case of *Robinette v. Barnes*, 854 F.2d 909 (6th Cir. 1988), in which the U.S. Court of Appeals for the Sixth Circuit concluded that the use of a trained police dog in circumstances comparable to those in the case at bar was reasonable as a matter of law. . . .

In the present case, Plaintiff's Response to Defendants' Motion for Summary Judgment consisted of a single page, his Statement of Material Facts in Dispute barely more than two. In these, Plaintiff's counsel cited one case and one alone, namely the *Robinette* case already cited by defense counsel, which Plaintiff's counsel did no more than attempt to distinguish on its facts.

When the matter came on for oral argument, defense counsel again argued the applicability of *Robinette* to the present case, while Plaintiff's counsel again tried to distinguish *Robinette* on its facts, offering no further citation to authority.

At the conclusion of oral argument, largely on the strength of *Robinette*, the Court announced its decision to dismiss the two counts of excessive force, finding the officers' actions reasonable as a matter of law. What remained open, however, was the issue of whether Plaintiff's state law cause of action for assault and battery could survive in the face of the Court's ruling with regard to the two federal constitutional torts. . . .

Defense counsel has now submitted a one-page letter brief in conformity with the Court's request. Plaintiff's counsel has submitted a six-page letter which, while it comports with the Court's directive in part, in effect invites the Court to reconsider its dismissal of the two federal constitutional counts. Plaintiff seems to understand that his request for reconsideration is out of order at this time, but there is a feature of counsel's letter that cannot go unremarked even now. The critical feature is that for the first time Plaintiff's counsel cites legal authority directly on point to the case at bar. The case, *Kopf v. Wing*, 942 F.2d 265 (4th Cir. 1991), is not only an excessive force case involving a police dog, but is the controlling law in this Circuit. As the Court will discuss presently, that case clearly mandates denial of Defendants' Motion for Summary Judgment, which is to say reinstatement of the excessive force claims the Court recently dismissed. But the fact that *Kopf* has been cited for the first time by Plaintiff's counsel in a supplemental letter—well after the filing of his threadbare initial response to Defendants' Motion for Summary Judgment and his equally scant oral argument on the motion—is a cause for considerable concern. At the same time, the fact that this case has never been cited by defense counsel in his initial pleadings, in oral argument or indeed to this day, gives cause for even greater concern. . . .

The parallels between *Kopf* and the case at bar are striking and need little elaboration. The Court accepts without question that, on the authority of *Kopf*, Plaintiff ought to have prevailed as against Defendants' Motion for Summary Judgment. Notwithstanding this, neither Plaintiff's nor Defendants' counsel brought the case to the Court's attention even through oral argument. Thereafter, only Plaintiff's counsel, never defense counsel, cited the case, and then only because the Court had directed briefing on another point of law. . . .

One must assume that had Plaintiff's counsel, in preparing his initial Opposition to the Motion for Summary Judgment, exhibited the same degree of diligence that ultimately permitted him to locate the case in untimely fashion, he could have located the case in timely fashion. Instead, counsel offered only the sketchiest statement of grounds, reflecting a bare minimum of legal research, showing every sign of having been dictated on the run. The net effect of this truncated effort was to consume valuable court time in oral argument and the preparation of supplemental briefs (not to mention preparation of the present Opinion), all of which could have been avoided by earlier diligence on counsel's part. Counsel appears to have forgotten two of the most fundamental rules of professional conduct. First, Rule of Professional Conduct 1.1 provides that:

> [a] lawyer shall provide competent representation to a client. Competent representation requires the legal knowledge, skill, thoroughness and preparation reasonably necessary for the representation. . . .

The other Rule of Professional Conduct counsel has apparently misplaced is Rule 1.3 which holds that "[a] lawyer shall act with reasonable diligence and promptness in representing a client." Failure to pursue applicable legal authority in timely fashion may well constitute a violation of this rule.

The action of defense counsel in this case raises a far more serious concern. It is possible that defense counsel also overlooked the *Kopf* precedent, but if he did, the oversight was glaring and extremely troublesome. *Kopf* not only deals with a claim of excessive force against police where a police dog was involved; individual Prince George's County police officers and the County itself were defendants in that case. Indeed, at least one attorney for Prince George's County in *Kopf*, as shown in the reported case, was an individual, whom the Court judicially notices, was still in the County Attorney's office at the time of the filing of the present Motion for Summary Judgment.

The regrettable inference is that defense counsel in the instant case may in fact have deliberately failed to disclose to the Court directly controlling authority from this Circuit. If so, the action would constitute a clear violation of the Rules of Professional Conduct.

Thus, Rule 3.3(a)(3) provides that "a lawyer shall not knowingly . . . fail to disclose to the tribunal legal authority in the controlling jurisdiction known to the lawyer to be directly adverse to the position of the client and not disclosed by opposing counsel." In federal court, the "controlling jurisdiction" is the circuit in which the district court sits.

Hazard & Hodes, op. cit. §3.3.207. Particularly disturbing is the type of case encountered here — a litigant who was an unsuccessful party to a directly relevant adverse precedent who has failed to cite that precedent to the court. (Citations omitted.) . . .

Under the circumstances, the Court will direct defense counsel to show cause to the Court in writing within thirty (30) days why citation to the *Kopf* case was omitted from his Motion for Summary Judgment, oral argument, and indeed from any pleading or communication to date.

The Court also recollects that in the last several months counsel for Prince George's County was before the Court in at least one other police dog excessive force case in which a Motion for Summary Judgment in favor of the County was granted. It may be that *Kopf* was omitted from the pleading in that proceeding as well. Accordingly, the Court directs defense counsel and the Office of the Prince George's County attorney, within sixty (60) days to disclose to the Court the status of that case and any and all police dog excessive force cases involving Prince George's County that were pending as of August 9, 1991, the date *Kopf* was decided by the Fourth Circuit, or that have been filed from that date to the present. The Court's Show-Cause Order, entered simultaneously with this Opinion, spells out the information that is to be provided. Any further sanctions that may be imposed by the Court will depend on the County's showing of cause pursuant to this directive.

Enough has been said for now. No formal Motion for Reconsideration need be filed by Plaintiff's counsel since, as indicated, *Kopf* clearly dictates reinstatement of the excessive force claims. In consequence, the state court claim for assault and battery also remains in the case. . . .

Questions about the Case

1. What was the disposition of the case at the hearing on the summary judgment? On what case did the court rely and what did it hold?
2. What was the correct statement of the law? What happened to the case as a result of this ruling?
3. Why does it appear that the plaintiff's counsel did not cite the case? Why did the defense not cite the case?
4. What are the possible ethical violations of both the lawyers involved? Which is most egregious?
5. What remedy is the court likely to impose on the lawyers if they cannot justify their actions? What disciplinary sanction do you think might be appropriate? Why do courts disapprove of this particular ethical violation so strongly?

In the following case, sanctions were imposed on attorneys who knowingly failed to cite adverse controlling authority. Consider why the attorneys might have done this and how the trial judge reacted when he discovered the omitted cases.

Jorgenson v. County of Volusia

846 F.2d 1350 (11th Cir. 1988)

Per Curiam:

The appellants, attorneys Eric Latinsky and Fred Fendt, were sanctioned by the district court pursuant to Fed. R. Civ. P. 11 for failing to cite adverse, controlling precedent in a memorandum filed in support of an application for a temporary restraining order and a preliminary injunction. In the appellants' initial appeal to this court, the case was remanded to the district court because the court had failed to notify the attorneys in advance that it was considering sanctions, and did not give them an opportunity to respond. *Jorgenson v. County of Volusia*, 824 F.2d 973 (11th Cir. 1987) (unpublished opinion). On remand, the district court reaffirmed the imposition of sanctions, and the attorneys appeal. . . .

Appellants filed an application in the district court for a temporary restraining order and a preliminary injunction on behalf of their clients, who own and operate a lounge known as "Porky's." In support of the application, appellants filed a memorandum of law which challenged the validity of a Volusia County ordinance prohibiting nude or semi-nude entertainment in commercial establishments at which alcoholic beverages are offered for sale or consumption. The memorandum failed to discuss or cite two clearly relevant cases: *City of Daytona Beach v. Del Percio*, 476 So. 2d 197 (Fla. 1985), and *New York State Liquor Authority v. Bellanca*, 452 U.S. 714, 101 S. Ct. 2599, 69 L. Ed. 2d 357 (1981). We find that this failure supports the imposition of Rule 11 sanctions in the circumstances of this case.

The field of law concerning the regulation of the sale and consumption of alcohol in connection with nude entertainment is a narrow and somewhat specialized field. Prior to the opinion of the Supreme Court of Florida in *Del Percio*, the critical question of whether the state of Florida had delegated its powers under the Twenty-First Amendment to counties and municipalities had gone unanswered. In some circles, that decision was long-awaited. If the state had delegated the authority, local ordinances regulating the sale or consumption of alcohol would be entitled to a presumption in favor of their validity which is conferred by the Twenty-First Amendment. See *Bellanca*, 452 U.S. at 718, 101 S. Ct. at 2601. If the state had not delegated the authority, the ordinances would be subject to the stricter review applicable to exercises of the general police power. See *Krueger v. City of Pensacola*, 759 F.2d 851, 852 (11th Cir. 1985).

The question regarding Florida's delegation of its powers under the Twenty-First Amendment was answered by the Supreme Court of Florida in *Del Percio*, a case in which one of the appellants, Latinsky, participated. The court held that the powers had been delegated.

Less than one year later, on or about January 13, 1986, Latinsky and an associate brought the instant suit seeking a declaration that a similar ordinance was unconstitutional and requesting a temporary restraining order and a preliminary injunction. In their presentation to the court, the appellants cited a number of cases describing the limits on the exercise of the general police power. However, they did not advise the court in any way that *Del Percio* had been decided, despite the fact that *Del Percio* required that the validity of the ordinance be judged in light of powers retained under the Twenty-first Amendment rather than the general police power.

The appellants purported to describe the law to the district court in the hope that the description would guide and inform the court's decision. With apparently studied care, however, they withheld the fact that the long-awaited decision by the Supreme Court of Florida had been handed down. This will not do. The appellants are not redeemed by the fact that opposing counsel *subsequently* cited the controlling precedent. The appellants had a duty to refrain from affirmatively misleading the court as to the state of the law. They were not relieved of this duty by the possibility that opposing counsel might find and cite the controlling precedent, particularly where as here, a temporary restraining order might have been issued ex parte.

In this court, appellants argue that the cases were not cited because they are not controlling. We certainly acknowledge that attorneys are legitimately entitled to press their own interpretations of precedent, including interpretations which render particular cases inapplicable. It is clear, however, that appellants' attempts to show that *Del Percio* and *Bellanca* are not controlling are simply post hoc efforts to evade the imposition of sanctions. Neither the original complaint nor the memorandum of law filed by appellants in the district court reflect or support the arguments they now raise. Indeed, it is likely that the arguments were not raised previously because they are completely without merit. In the circumstances of this case, the imposition of Rule 11 sanctions by the district court was warranted. The judgment of the district court is affirmed.

Questions about the Case

1. What ethics rules did the attorneys violate in this case?
2. What cases should the attorneys have cited, and why?
3. Is it possible that the attorneys did not know about these cases?
4. What were the attorneys intending to do by not citing these cases?
5. Did the opposing attorneys cite the cases in question? Why did the court say that it made no difference whether the opposing attorneys did or didn't cite the cases?
6. Are the cases in question controlling? How does the court treat this matter?

7. On whom was the sanction imposed in this case? Should it also have been imposed on the client? Why, or why not?
8. Under what rule was the sanction imposed? Might the attorneys also be disciplined for an ethics violation? Under what rule?
9. Why does the court react so strongly to having the law misrepresented? What if the court wrote a decision based on an inaccurate statement of the law?

The following case illustrates how the advocacy rules may apply even when there is no lawsuit pending. The attorney who is being disciplined in this case engages in more than one kind of the prohibited conduct discussed in this chapter. He claims that nonlawyers in his office were partly responsible.

Crane v. State Bar of California

30 Cal. 3d 117, 635 P.2d 163,
177 Cal. Rptr. 670 (1981)

. . . 1. *The Mercury Case*

Representing the sellers of a residence, in April 1978 petitioner sought and obtained from Mercury Savings and Loan Association (Mercury), the beneficiary under a first trust deed, a beneficiary statement describing the status and indebtedness of the underlying loan. Without either the consent or knowledge of Mercury, he then "crossed out" certain printed material included in the statement by Mercury. The deleted language gave notice that Mercury intended to enforce an acceleration clause in the note and deed of trust unless it received an assumption agreement executed by any purchaser of the premises. Petitioner subsequently forwarded the altered statement to the escrow company handling the sale, describing it as "the Beneficiary Statement from the . . . lender on your escrow," and without notifying that company that the deletions were made by him and were wholly unauthorized.

The State Bar Court found petitioner's conduct in this regard to be [willful], improper and a dishonest act under the statute.

2. *The Robinson Case*

In December 1978 petitioner communicated with counsel for Mr. and Mrs. Robinson both by telephone and by mail in connection with the unrecorded claim of petitioner's client to real property which was subject to a trust deed then being foreclosed by the Robinsons. Both orally and in writing, the Robinsons' attorney specifically advised petitioner that he represented the Robinsons. Thereafter, petitioner's office sent two letters directly to the Robinsons without notifying their lawyer. The first—which apparently was a "follow-up" to a still earlier letter sent to the Robinsons before petitioner had been contacted by their lawyer—repeated a request for a beneficiary statement on their trust deed and offered to "waive" the $100 statutory penalty if it was received promptly. The second, sent seven days later, demanded that the Robinsons forward "forthwith" the $100 and the beneficiary statement. It stated further that if the statement was not received within five days, an action would be commenced against the Robinsons to recover both damages and the forfeiture, and that "the Department of Savings and Loan and the Attorney General's office will be requested to assist us in solution." A notation on the last letter indicated that copies were being sent to a named commissioner of the Department of Savings and Loan and to a named deputy attorney general. The letters were on petitioner's legal stationery and purported to be signed by him.

The State Bar Court found that petitioner's direct communication with the Robinsons despite his knowledge that they were represented by a lawyer was a clear violation of rule 7-103 of the Rules of Professional Conduct, and that his final letter to them constituted an impermissible threat in violation of rule 7-104.

Discussion

With respect to the Mercury matter, petitioner admits both his unauthorized alteration of the beneficiary statement and his failure to advise the escrow company that the deletion was his, and not that of the beneficiary or trustee under the trust deed. He denies, however, that he was "dishonest," arguing that he had no intent to deceive the escrow company, but merely sought to prevent Mercury from improperly interfering with the prospective sale by asserting demands which Mercury had no right to make in the beneficiary statement.

We reject petitioner's disavowal of any dishonest intent. Even if we assume for purposes of argument that Mercury endangered the successful closing of escrow by asserting a right which it did not have, any such risk could be removed or minimized *only* if the reader of the statement believed the acceleration language was deleted by Mercury itself. The circumstances of petitioner's unauthorized unilateral alteration were deceptive and known by him to be so. . . .

In the Robinson matter, petitioner also admitted in a stipulation of facts filed with the State Bar Court his "technical violation" of rule 7-103 of the Rules of Professional Conduct by communicating directly with the Robinsons despite his awareness that they were represented by counsel. He now contends, however, that the letters to the Robinsons requesting, and then demanding, the beneficiary statement and statutory penalty, and threatening suit and action by state officials, were not "upon a subject of controversy" and that his client and the Robinsons were not "adverse parties" within the meaning of that rule.

There was substantial evidence to the contrary, however, including testimony of the Robinsons' lawyer that he had discussed with petitioner the adverse interest of the parties in connection with the foreclosure of the trust deed, and beyond that evidence, the contents of the letters themselves belie petitioner's claims.

We similarly reject petitioner's asserted excuse that any violation of rule 7-103 was inadvertent and precipitated by members of his staff. Acknowledging negligence in failing properly to prevent direct contact with represented parties by correspondence on his letterhead and over his purported signature, petitioner contends that the discipline proposed for that negligence is unduly severe. Petitioner's attempt to avoid the blame for his violation of the Rules of Professional Conduct is unconvincing. An attorney is responsible for the work product of his employees which is performed pursuant to his direction and authority. The legal onus for the violation of rule 7-103 rests upon petitioner alone. . . .

Accordingly, it is ordered that Fred R. Crane be suspended from the practice of law in this state for a period of one year. . . .

Questions about the Case

1. Describe the acts that constituted breaches of ethics in the *Mercury* and *Robinson* cases. What ethical principles presented in this chapter do these acts offend?
2. What was attorney Crane's defense in the *Mercury* matter? How did the court handle this defense?
3. What were Crane's defenses in the *Robinson* case? How did the court handle them?
4. Was Crane aware of the correspondence with the Robinsons? Would it have made any difference whether he knew it or not?
5. What sanction was imposed? Do you think it was appropriate?

In the *Omaha Bank* case that follows, an appellate court examines the decision of a lower court that refused to replace a juror after the juror had contact with the defendant's attorneys outside the courtroom. As you read, consider whether this incident might also give rise to a disciplinary action.

Omaha Bank v. Siouxland Cattle Cooperative

305 N.W.2d 458 (Iowa 1981)

Siouxland Cattle Cooperative (Siouxland) appeals from an adverse judgment on its damage claim in a law action for fraud against Omaha Bank for Cooperatives (Omaha Bank) and Robert Zuber, a bank officer, and from the trial court's order for a sheriff's deed to the bank in a foreclosure action. Siouxland claims that the trial court erred in failing to replace a juror with an alternate, in its instructions to the jury, and in ruling that Siouxland has lost a right of redemption from the foreclosure sale. . . .

After a day at trial on March 3, 1980, Omaha Bank's lawyers, Robert J. Banta and Gerald P. Laughlin, stopped for dinner in Merrill, Iowa. After finishing dinner, they entered the bar portion of the restaurant to pay their bill. Juror Adamson was seated at the bar. He offered to buy the lawyers a drink and they declined. Adamson was insistent and offered again. The lawyers then sat at a booth near the bar and received a drink, courtesy of Adamson. Adamson introduced the lawyers to other patrons and they all conversed about various subjects. There is no evidence that the pending trial was discussed.

On March 6 attorney Laughlin informed the court, in the presence of lawyers for other parties, of the contact with juror Adamson. We do not have a transcript of the meeting but apparently the trial court concluded that nothing improper had occurred.

On March 11 Siouxland's attorney, Steven A. Carter, reported to the court that he had advised his client to move for a mistrial because of the misconduct. Carter also stated that Siouxland did not want a mistrial and wanted to proceed with the jury. Because Siouxland would not follow Carter's advice to move for a mistrial, Carter requested the court, before the case was submitted to the jury, to remove Adamson and replace him with an alternate juror under Iowa R. Civ. P. 189, as then in effect. The trial court denied the request, stating, "I said at the time there was nothing wrong with it and found that, and I do now." The court also indicated that a motion for a mistrial was the only proper procedure to follow.

After the jury returned a verdict for the bank and Zuber, Siouxland moved for a new trial because of misconduct by juror Adamson, who had become foreman of the jury. Iowa R. Civ. P. 244(b). The trial court overruled the motion primarily because Siouxland had not moved for a mistrial during trial.

The juror's offer of drinks and the lawyers' acceptance was clearly misconduct by all of them. Adamson, in speaking to the lawyers and offering and buying them drinks, violated the standard admonition given by the court to refrain from contact with the lawyers involved in the case. The bank's lawyers violated their ethical obligation prohibiting communication with a juror during trial unless it is in the course of official proceedings. Iowa Code of Professional Responsibility DR 7-108(B) and (C).

Omaha Bank and Zuber apparently concede that the contact was misconduct but argue that Siouxland has waived any claim for a new trial. The waiver argument is based on Siouxland's refusal to move for a mistrial after discovering the misconduct. A party learning during trial of misconduct by a juror must complain to the trial court rather than wait for the outcome and then move for a new trial after losing.

Siouxland declined to move for a mistrial during trial. The record does not indicate, however, that Siouxland elected to wait until the adverse verdict before complaining to the court about the misconduct. Rather, before the case was submitted for jury decision, Siouxland requested the court to replace Adamson with an available alternate. Iowa R. Civ. P. 189, The Code 1979. We conclude that Siouxland adequately made its record to the court by requesting that an alternate replace the offending juror. . . .

In this case, we conclude that the trial court abused its discretion because there is not substantial evidence to support a finding that the contact was not prejudicial to Siouxland. Adamson and the lawyers did not merely meet and exchange greetings, but rather had an extended conversation. [Citations omitted.] The lawyers accepted a drink and participated with the juror in the gathering in the bar. The circumstances surrounding the contact are the only bases upon which to determine whether the contact may have influenced the juror or the jury.

In addition, we conclude that the fraud claim must be retried to "zealously [guard] the utter independence of jurors." *State v. Carey*, 165 N.W.2d 27, 29 (Iowa 1969). We simply cannot allow a foreman of a jury to purchase drinks during trial for lawyers representing a party. In cases of such gross impropriety, even if the meeting were unintentional, we are not only concerned with injustice to particular litigants but also with the appearance of impropriety that casts doubt on our jury system. Attempts to ingratiate one side to a juror by extended conversation and acceptance of drinks must be condemned. . . .

Questions about the Case

1. What ethics rule did the attorneys violate in this case? Could their acts have been grounds for discipline?
2. Exactly what contact did the bank's attorneys have with the juror Adamson? Who instigated the contact? Did they discuss the case? Does it matter? Why, or why not?
3. Why wasn't a mistrial declared when the trial judge discovered the contact? Why wasn't the juror replaced? When was the trial judge informed of this conduct?
4. As the juror and attorneys did not discuss the case, what is the potential prejudice to the other party?
5. What reasons does the court give for reversing the decision of the lower court? With which court do you agree? Why?

This case arises from civil litigation in which a paralegal claims that false evidence was admitted. The court explains how a paralegal has the same duties as a lawyer to prevent false evidence from being admitted in a case and protects the paralegal who revealed the unethical actions of her employer.

Eaton v. Fink

697 N.E.2d 490 (Ind. Ct. App. 1998)

Mark Van Eaton filed a Complaint for Damages for Defamation against Donna Fink. . . .

. . . This suit arises from statements made by Fink in connection with another case, *Kirchoff v. Selby*. . . . Fink worked as a legal assistant for attorney Dean Richards, who represented the Selbys. Attorney Patrick Shoulders represented the Kirchoffs. A jury awarded the Selbys $730,000.00. Before the trial court entered the judgment on the verdict, Fink informed Shoulders that she had manufactured an exhibit on behalf of the Selbys, at Richards' request, in order to rehabilitate Van Eaton's testimony. She also stated that Van Eaton had testified falsely when he claimed, on rebuttal, that he had made notes regarding the differences between Exhibit 10 and Exhibit 12 prior to trial. In addition, Fink claimed that she has assisted Richards in the fabrication of Exhibit 61, a Stock Exchange and Subscription Agreement. After her sworn statement was taken before a notary, Fink sent a copy via facsimile to Richards.

The Kirchoffs filed a motion to correct error based on newly discovered evidence. . . . The trial court granted the Kirchoffs' motion and ordered a new trial. Cross appeals were filed, and we affirmed the trial court's judgment. . . . [T]he case is now pending before our supreme court. . . .

On the same day the Kirchoffs filed their motion to correct error, Van Eaton filed this defamation suit against Fink. Fink responded that her statements were privileged and filed a motion for judgment on the pleadings. . . . The court agreed and granted Fink's motion for summary judgment.

Indiana law affords absolute privilege to statements made in the course of a judicial proceeding. . . . We hold that the rule also applies to communications subsequent to a judicial proceeding, provided that the communication is related to the proceeding, made in good faith and in contemplation of further proceedings before the trial court or on appeal.

Here, although the *Kirchoff v. Selby* trial had ended, the trial court's judgment was not yet final. Fink's statement to Shoulders, which contained allegations that she had falsified a document at the direction of Richards during trial and that Van Eaton had lied regarding the falsified document during cross-examination, was made in contemplation that the Kirchoffs would request a new trial based on that information. Thus, Fink's statement to Shoulders is entitled to absolute privilege.

Fink concedes that the separate defamation that occurred when she separately published the statement via facsimile to Richards is not entitled to absolute privilege. Instead she maintains that qualified privilege applies.

The doctrine of qualified privilege protects "communications made in good faith on any subject matter in which the party making the communication has an interest or in reference to which he has a duty, either public or private, either legal or moral, or social, if made to a person having a corresponding interest or duty." [Citation omitted.] . . .

The defendant has the burden to establish the existence of a privileged occasion for the publication by proof of a recognized public or private interest which would justify the utterance of the words. Once the existence of the privilege is established, the burden shifts to the plaintiff to prove that the defendant abused the privilege. Abuse is shown when: (1) the communicator was primarily motivated by ill will . . . ; (2) there was excessive publication . . . ; or (3) the statement was made without belief or grounds for belief in its truth. [Citation omitted.]

Here, as Richards' legal assistant, Fink was required to conform to the same standards as an attorney. See Rule of Professional Conduct, Guideline 9.10(j) (legal assistant shall be governed by the American Bar Association Model Code of Professional Responsibility and American Bar Association Model Rules of Professional Conduct). An attorney shall not unlawfully obstruct another's parties access to evidence or unlawfully alter, destroy or conceal a document or other material having potential evidentiary value. Ind. Prof. Con. R. 3.4. A lawyer shall not counsel or assist another person to do any such act. Id. A lawyer shall not knowingly make a false statement of material fact to a tribunal or offer evidence the lawyer knows to be false. Ind. Prof. Con. R. 3.3(a)(1) and (2). Fink's statement contained allegations that she and Richards had falsified evidence presented to the court at the trial. Assuming that Fink and Richards had engaged in the conduct described by Fink, Fink and Richards would have corresponding legal, moral and social duties to correct the injustice that resulted from their behavior. . . .

Still, Van Eaton contends that Fink abused her qualified privilege because her statement was motivated primarily by ill will and without belief in its truth. In support of his contention, Van Eaton directs us to the one-paragraph supplemental affidavit of Richards and claims that it demonstrates that Fink made her statements in an attempt to extort money from the Selbys. The affidavit states:

> That during an argument [Richards] had with Donna Fink . . . she stated that she was going to [accuse Richards and an associate] of raping her and . . . manufacturing false documents. She named numerous documents . . . that she felt could have been manufactured. . . . [S]ome of

> the documents were Exhibit 12 . . . and Exhibit 61. She mentioned numerous other exhibits that were admitted at the trial. She stated that Mark Van Eaton, Jeff and Diane Selby, Richards [and others] would be in serious trouble.

Van Eaton mischaracterizes the supplemental affidavit. Although the affidavit shows that Fink was upset with Richards, it does not demonstrate that she attempted to extort money from anyone. Further, we cannot infer from the affidavit that Fink's statement was motivated by "ill will" or that she did not believe in the truth of her statements. Rather the supplemental affidavit indicates that she believed that the documents were manufactured. . . . [W]e conclude that the trial court properly granted summary judgment in favor of Fink.

Affirmed.

Questions about the Case

1. What kind of false evidence was presented in this case? If the paralegal Fink is telling the truth, what were the roles of the lawyer Richards, the witness Van Eaton, and herself in this matter?
2. When in the case did Fink raise the issues of the false evidence and testimony? Why does this matter?
3. What happened to the parties to the case where the false evidence was presented?
4. What ethics rules were violated? What could happen to the lawyer? To Fink? To Van Eaton?
5. What was cited by the court in holding that Fink had a duty relating to the false evidence?
6. Why is this case important for paralegals?

In this case, a lawyer is disciplined for directing a nonlawyer, his investigator, to pose as a journalist to interview an unrepresented person likely to be named as an adverse party.

In re Ositis

333 Or. 366, 40 P.3d 500 (2002)

. . . In 1989, the accused represented Hickey, who bought and sold animals for medical research, in proceedings before the United States Department of Agriculture. Hickey's business had been targeted by animal rights activists, and Hickey felt that he was in some personal danger. The accused introduced Hickey to Stevens, a private investigator, who initially was hired to provide security for Hickey and his wife at [a] . . . hearing.

After the hearing, Settlemier, who owned a farm that was directly adjacent to Hickey's business, spoke to television news reporters, and her statements were later televised. Hickey and the accused knew Settlemier, and knew that she strongly opposed Hickey's business. Hickey and the accused believed that Settlemier was permitting animal rights activists to use her property as a base of operations for observing and "raiding" Hickey's facilities. . . .

[O]n November 7, 1989, Stevens, the private investigator, telephoned Settlemier, introduced himself as a reporter for the International News Services, and asked if Settlemier would answer some questions about Hickey's animal research supply business. . . .

Settlemier agreed to the interview, and Stevens questioned her at length about the factual basis for her comments to the news reporters . . . to the effect that Hickey's business was involved in animal abuse and pet theft. Stevens tape-recorded his conversation with Settlemier without her knowledge and permission. He never informed Settlemier that he was gathering information for Hickey and the accused.

After the interview, Stevens shared what he had learned from Settlemier with the accused. Several years later, Settlemier's tape-recorded statements were used as impeachment evidence in a defamation action that Hickey brought against her. Settlemier's lawyer later complained to the Bar that the accused had violated his ethical duties by participating in a scheme to obtain information from Settlemier by deceitful means. The present disciplinary proceedings against the accused followed. . . .

[Ositis] contends, specifically, that DR 1-102(A)(3) [which says that lawyers may not engage in conduct involving dishonesty, fraud, deceit, or misrepresentation] should not be interpreted to apply to misrepresentations made directly or indirectly by a lawyer that go solely to the lawyer's identity and purpose and that are made for the purpose of gathering information from potential adversaries before the institution of a legal action.

The accused's arguments in that regard focus on the same concerns that this court considered in *In re Gatti*, 330 Or. 517, 8 P.3d 966 (2000). That is, the accused argues that use of this limited sort of misrepresentation is a common and longstanding practice among lawyers, that an exception from the broad disciplinary rule prohibiting misrepresentation is necessary if lawyers are to succeed in discovering and rooting out wrongful conduct, that legal scholars and other jurisdictions have concluded that such limited deception is not unethical, and that the Bar's enforcement practices strongly suggest that identical conduct by government lawyers is ethical. This court rejected those arguments in *Gatti*, noting that ". . . the wording of DR 1-102(A)(3) . . . , and this court's case law does not permit recognition for an exception for any lawyer." . . .

[T]he evidence clearly and convincingly shows that . . . the accused had the undisclosed facts of Stevens's purpose and connection in mind and knew that those facts were material to Settlemier's decision to be interviewed. The ruse was a misrepresentation by nondisclosure. . . .

The accused argues, however, that, even if certain of Stevens's action would—if committed by a lawyer—violate DR 1-102(A)(3), the trial panel erred in concluding that any of Stevens's representations to Settlemier can be attributed to him. In that regard, the accused denies that Stevens was working for him when Stevens interviewed Settlemier or that he otherwise controlled Stevens's actions with regard to the interview. . . .

DR 1-102(A)(1) . . . expands the realm of accountability: It makes lawyers accountable not only if their **own** acts violate the rules, but also if they violate a rule "through the acts of another." . . .

[W]e conclude that the evidence clearly and convincingly shows that the accused made misrepresentations to Settlemier "through the acts of another." . . . Our conclusion arises . . . out of the undisputed fact that the accused suggested a particular line of inquiry to Stevens, knowing that Stevens intended to represent himself to Settlemier as a reporter, not as a private investigator. . . .

The accused is reprimanded.

Questions about the Case

1. Is it clear who the investigator Stevens was working for—the lawyer or the client? Did it make a difference to the outcome?
2. Was the status of the investigator similar to that of a paralegal who might contact a possible adversary?
3. What ethics rules were violated? What is the equivalent rule in the Model Rules?
4. Are there other rules that may have been violated, for example, contact with unrepresented persons?
5. The lawyer seems to think that what he did was a standard investigative technique. Do you agree? What about his claim that lawyers need to be able to use ruses such as this one to investigate thoroughly?
6. Do you think that the tape recording in the case may have been illegal? Why did the court not consider this?

10 Professionalism

This chapter addresses issues relating to professionalism in the legal field and outlines some of the challenges facing paralegals. Chapter 10 covers:

- the image of the legal profession in our society
- where paralegals "fit" in the legal profession
- definitions and elements of professionalism for paralegals
- current issues for paralegals, including
  - regulation of the paralegal profession
  - title and definition of legal assistant/paralegal
  - paralegal education
  - utilization of paralegal services
  - overtime compensation
  - gender and bias issues
- paralegal participation in pro bono activities

A. The State of Professionalism in the Legal Field

A poor **public image** has plagued the legal profession for more than 50 years. In the last third of the twentieth century and into the twenty-first, the legal profession has fallen dramatically in the estimation of the general public. The lack of esteem can be traced to the dishonest and manipulative conduct of White House lawyers during the Watergate scandal. The notion that lawyers engage in unscrupulous behavior has been reinforced in succeeding decades by media attention focusing on individual lawyers whose outrageous misconduct has shocked and embarrassed the profession. Film and television images of lawyers are often very negative and frequently depict lawyers as inept or dishonest, ranging from the image of the lawyer as a pathological liar to a television commercial that advertises "lawyer-free zones." Lawyer jokes feed the frenzy.

During this period, society has become more litigious. Lawyers — and what many people consider an oversupply of them — have been blamed for the increase in litigation. The public looks to the law to solve many of its problems, sometimes social and personal ones, which prior to the 1960s would have been dealt with in other ways or not dealt with at all. The press jumps on the filing of frivolous lawsuits; it rarely reports when those suits are thrown out.

Public opinion polls consistently show that lawyers rate well below most other occupations in several areas, including honesty and integrity. An ABA survey conducted earlier this decade showed that people perceive lawyers to be greedy, manipulative, and corrupt. Those polled told stories of "lawyers who misrepresent their qualifications, over-promise, are not up front about their fees, charge too much for their services, take too long to resolve matters, and fail to return client phone calls." The poll also showed that Americans believe lawyers have too close a connection to politics, government, and big business and are not effective at policing themselves. Less than one in five surveyed were extremely or very confident in lawyers. Most thought lawyers are more interested in winning and making money than in justice. Despite these general opinions, more than half of the respondents were very satisfied with the quality of services provided by their own lawyers, and many more believe that we have the best justice system in the world (Public Perceptions of Lawyers, Consumer Research Findings, April 2002).

The high salaries paid to lawyers — especially new lawyers right out of law school — shock many Americans, who cannot hope ever to achieve such salaries. The high legal fees generated in major litigation have likewise added to the perception of lawyers as overpaid and greedy. Many large law firms pay lawyers salaries and bill clients at rates that the public regards as astronomical. Some top-tier specialized lawyers charge more than $1,500 an hour. Law firms that base fees on billable hours create great pressure on lawyers to bill for an unrealistically high number of hours. As noted in Chapter 7, this pressure can lead lawyers to inflate or pad bills. Overbilling drives clients away, creating a cycle of competitiveness and ever-higher billable hour requirements. Loyalty within law firms is not high in this environment; 35 years ago, most law school graduates went with a firm and stayed there for their entire career. Lawyers now commonly move three or four times before they stick with a firm. Even name partners in large firms have left for more attractive situations. The overwhelming sense of law practice as a business first and a profession second has caused great turnover and instability in firms, which themselves dissolve and merge frequently.

The public perception is that lawyers manipulate the legal process, finding clever ways to circumvent the law to prevail. This goal of winning at all costs has made many lawyers seem like devious and overzealous abusers of the system. Many citizens believe that lawyers use "technicalities" to get criminal defendants off. Lawyers' involvement in highly publicized criminal cases and business-related scandals have validated public opinion that lawyers' knowledge and skills are for sale to the highest bidder and that lawyers will not hesitate to use their talents to line their client's or their own pockets, whatever the cost to the public. A related client complaint is that lawyers are too chummy with one another; some clients complain when their lawyers extend professional courtesies such as extensions to opposing counsel.

The competitiveness and zeal of lawyers has led to abuses of the system, such as those described in Chapter 9 on trial advocacy. Admittedly, some lawyers view the litigation process as a game where tactics and strategy are more important than merit and substance. Bringing frivolous cases and motions, flooding an opponent with irrelevant and unwarranted discovery, and behaving discourteously and disrespectfully to other lawyers and even to judges have become the daily method of operation for some lawyers. In addition to common abuses of the system, highly visible misconduct in litigation undermines the image and status of lawyers.

An unrelenting series of high-profile scandals involving lawyers support these impressions. For example, in the 1990s tobacco industry lawyers were found to have suppressed evidence of the harmful effects of smoking. The country's leading plaintiff securities class action law firm was indicted for illegal conduct in handling its cases, and more recently its two top partners pleaded guilty to paying kickbacks to plaintiffs and were sentenced to prison and disbarred. In the past two decades lawyers serving high-tech corporate clients have been found guilty of backdating stock options, law firms have misused consumer protection statutes and the ADA to extort fees and damages from small businesses, and lawyers representing Enron and WorldCom were found to have acted improperly, contributing to the losses of employees and investors. We now enter a new decade, and the economic recession and related investment collapses and foreclosure crisis have revealed new forms of lawyer misconduct.

One New York investment lawyer has been charged with stealing nearly $400 million from hedge funds and investors through fake investment devices. Two Florida lawyers who set up a Ponzi scheme have been charged with bilking investors of $800 million. Lawyers representing banks in foreclosures have been found responsible for some of the internal practices that led to improperly documented and sometimes invalid foreclosures. Worse yet, lawyers have defrauded thousands of desperate homeowners seeking loan modifications. These law firms advertise heavily, using names such as "U.S. Loan Auditors" and "U.S. Foreclosure Relief." They collect fees from vulnerable clients for loan modification and forensic audit services and rarely do anything to help people keep their homes. Dozens of these unethical practitioners have been charged criminally, sued civilly, and disbarred in California alone in the last year.

The positive side of the legal profession rarely makes the daily newspaper, blogs, or the evening news. In fact, lawyers who engage in the conduct that gives the legal profession a bad name are few. Most lawyers are honest and ethical and devote themselves to representing their clients as conscientiously as they can. Many lawyers take on cases at discounted fees and do extensive pro bono and public service work. They are regular volunteers in their communities. Studies show that about two-thirds of lawyers engage in pro bono and community service work. Lawyers have collectively created vast programs of support for underrepresented populations and have banded together in times of crisis to help victims of disasters like 9/11 and Hurricane Katrina. The profession has often been a lone voice protecting constitutional rights against a wave of public opposition, such as the lawyers representing detainees at Guantanamo. The images of Perry Mason and Atticus Finch still powerfully project what society wants a lawyer to be — courageous, smart, and steadfast in the quest for justice and fairness.

Snitch rules
Rules requiring lawyers to report unethical conduct

Whistleblower statutes
Laws that protect employees who report violations of law from being retaliated against by employers

Historically, lawyer misconduct is usually uncovered and reported to authorities by clients, not other lawyers. Instances where lawyers report misconduct are few despite the ***"snitch rules"*** that are contained in most states' ethics rules. Firms usually handle ethical breaches internally and as privately as possible. This silence has been broken by major scandals in recent years. Some courts have found that attorneys who report violations as required by the codes cannot be fired for these actions and have an action for retaliatory discharge if they are fired. However, not all states have decided this issue and at least one, Illinois, holds that lawyers who report ethical violations and then get fired do not have a cause of action for retaliatory discharge (*Jacobson v. Knepper & Moga*, 185 Ill. 2d 372, 706 N.E.2d 491 (1998)). A few states also have ***whistleblower statutes*** that protect employees from being discharged in retaliation for reporting violations. It should be noted that the NFPA Model Code requires paralegals to report ethical and legal violations.

The organized bar at the national, state, and local levels has developed initiatives relating to **professionalism**. Disciplinary systems have been reformed and operate more efficiently and openly. Court rules and statutes limit discovery and provide for severe sanctions against lawyers for abuse. Bar associations have launched public relations campaigns to improve their image and have encouraged lawyers to engage in pro bono work and to support local charities and community activities.

More than a hundred state and local bar associations, and some courts, have adopted codes of professional courtesy and civility or litigation guidelines, which advise lawyers on how to conduct themselves. The general courtesy or professionalism guidelines typically cover client relations (including communicating frequently, advising mediation, resolving matters expeditiously, not overcharging); relations with other lawyers and parties (including acting courteously, not engaging in delay or unmeritorious tactics, cooperating in scheduling and resolving disputes, not disparaging other lawyers, not harassing the opposition); relations with courts (including advocating vigorously but with civility, being punctual, being honest with the court); and duty to the public and the profession (including keeping current in practice areas, supporting the profession, and upholding the profession's image). Litigation guidelines usually contain rules covering continuances, extensions, service of process, communication with adversaries, discovery, and motions. They specify conduct that is courteous, honest, and not designed to harass or unduly burden opponents.

A strong correlation exists between lawyer disciplinary actions and substance abuse or emotional problems. Some studies estimate that at least half the lawyers disciplined for misconduct are "impaired" by some type of substance abuse or mental health problem such as depression. Lawyers are more likely than persons in most other occupations to be alcoholics or chemically dependent. Bar associations have been proactive in developing programs to identify and help lawyers who are impaired before the impairment leads to unethical and destructive conduct. Called "legal assistance" programs, these programs are staffed by professional therapists and peer counselors and provide confidential assistance and referrals. Programs to address lawyer impairment are now offered in every jurisdiction. Paralegals should be alert to the signs of mental health and substance abuse problems in themselves and their colleagues, such as arriving to work late or leaving early, missed appointments, last-minute cancellations, irritability, inability to work with others, hostility or avoidance, missed deadlines, and poor judgment. And firms should take action to deal with these issues before they lead to serious breaches of duty to clients or worse.

Among the other recommendations to address concerns about declining professionalism and ethics are requirements to teach ethics and professionalism across the curriculum in law school, more aggressive judicial intervention in litigation, and more pro bono and public service or public interest work. Some local bars offer client relations programs that attempt to alter lawyers' attitudes toward and treatment of clients.

Many ethicists and bar leaders have called on lawyers to examine the ethical and moral content of their actions and to avoid separating their values and beliefs as persons from their conduct as lawyers. Increasingly heard are proposals for law firms to end use of billable time as the primary method of setting legal fees. Lawyers who are sanctioned for unethical conduct are often required to attend "ethics school" as part of their penalty.

Dissatisfaction among lawyers is also high. Many lawyers leave the legal profession because of the problems that characterize law practice today. Some surveys show that as many as half the lawyers in practice would not become lawyers if they had it to do all over again. Firms deal with quality of life issues by creating counseling programs for troubled lawyers, providing part-time and flexible scheduling options, encouraging sabbaticals, increasing pro bono work, and establishing a firm culture that values collegiality and gives staff more time for their lives outside law practice. Many firms have designated an in-house ethics guru or a committee to help lawyers with ethical dilemmas and have established one-on-one or small group mentoring for new lawyers to mitigate the negative effects of working in isolation and to build collegiality and trust.

Burnout and stress are recognized factors in lawyer misconduct. The pressures of the billable hours, the competitive environment of the legal world, the lack of loyalty among clients and law firms, the constant work of meeting other peoples' needs, and the feeling of not having control all contribute to burnout, detachment from relationships with others, loss of job satisfaction, and even chronic anger and anxiety. The long hours alone make the job of a lawyer challenging, especially now that lawyers make themselves available 24-7 through technologies that enable them to work wherever they are and at any time of the night or day.

Working in this milieu presents paralegals with both challenges and great opportunities. The concerns about the integrity of the legal profession, voiced both by the public and within the profession, affect the way in which paralegals are viewed and view themselves. Paralegals are not immune from engaging in unethical conduct. In the last few years there have been several high-profile cases of paralegal misconduct, including a New Jersey paralegal who was part of a real estate fraud scheme and who pleaded guilty to making false statements to the Department of Housing and Urban Development; a Canadian paralegal found guilty of embezzling more than $1 million from trust and other counts; and a Connecticut paralegal who pleaded guilty to embezzling $600,000 by paying her bills out of the firm accounts and falsifying accounting records. An Ohio paralegal continued the law practice of a retired lawyer, and a California paralegal "bought" the law practice of an elderly and impaired lawyer for $20 and also persuaded him to make the paralegal and his family the beneficiaries of his estate plan.

Paralegals can be part of the problem — working for firms that utilize their talents to abuse the legal process and to accumulate wealth — or part of the solution—working for firms that utilize their talents to improve efficiency, to perform work competently and ethically, and to lower the cost of legal services. In the coming years, as the problems plaguing the profession and the proposals to solve them begin to shape new models of practicing law, paralegals can contribute to the creation of a profession that is characterized by integrity and honor.

B. Professionalism and the Paralegal

Paralegals are in a sometimes difficult and ambiguous position in the legal profession. Because they are not lawyers, they may not legally engage in certain activities carved out exclusively for the lawyer. But they do engage in substantive legal work that otherwise would have to be done by lawyers and that is paid for by the client. The line between permissible and impermissible conduct is not always clear. Although paralegals are part of the professional staff engaging in legal work, not part of the support staff, they can never be full and equal members of the professional team as partners in the firm. And, because the paralegal profession is a relatively new occupation, the parameters of job responsibilities remain unclear, continue to evolve, and differ according to the assignment and the supervisor. Also, because of the relative youth of the occupation, the paralegal's role is not universally understood either by those in the legal profession or by the general public. Paralegals frequently must explain what they do to laypersons and must develop their own job descriptions and their role in the legal environment. The dilemma posed by this ambiguity has many ramifications for the daily work lives of paralegals. The overriding question it raises is how paralegals can forge a role for themselves—a professional role that holds them to high standards of ethics and performance while affording them the opportunity for long, satisfying, and challenging careers. Defining professionalism is an essential first step in this process.

Surveys of employers in all industries consistently reflect the impression that workers are less prepared for work than they used to be. Employers complain that workers lack oral and written communication skills, critical thinking capacity, and the ability to work both independently and with others as a team. Most also point to declining professionalism, especially in appearance, work ethic, attitude, and an apparent sense of entitlement. Loyalty to the employer and a sense of responsibility to the collective are also found to be lacking.

Dictionaries define **"profession"** as an occupation that involves a special education and requires mental rather than manual labor. Sociologists define the term as an occupation whose members have the exclusive right to engage in certain activities that are intellectual in nature and require special education; professions are bound by codes of ethics

Paraprofessional
A person who works within a profession in a subordinate position but with special training and a degree of independence in carrying out duties

and are generally self-regulating. Philosophers tend to define a profession as a calling that requires a special commitment to public service.

Paralegals usually are classified as ***paraprofessionals***, performing legal work under the supervision of a lawyer, but having special education and sharing in the societal prestige of the lawyer. Analogous are the many paraprofessionals in health care, such as physical therapists, nurse practitioners, and dental assistants. However, it is noteworthy that the health care field has very well-delineated educational and licensing requirements for paraprofessionals, something that is missing from the legal field.

Limited research has been done on the paralegal occupation. In their excellent book *Paralegals: Progress and Prospects of a Satellite Occupation*, Quintin Johnstone and Martin Wenglinsky analyze how the paralegal occupation fits the sociologist's definition of a profession, emphasizing three main characteristics—**collegiality**, **occupational prestige**, and **overtraining**. Although the first edition is now more than 20 years old, this book provides a useful framework for analyzing the development of the paralegal profession.

The authors found many inconsistencies in the paralegal profession, which reinforce the ambiguity that paralegals typically feel about their role. For example, many law firms do not require formal paralegal training, creating inconsistent and sometimes low hiring standards in the field. On the other hand, paralegals who have a formal education, frequently a baccalaureate degree and postgraduate certificate, find themselves "overtrained" for many of the tasks that they perform. Prestige for paralegals is found mainly in the reflected, and sometimes shared, prestige of the lawyers with whom paralegals work. This status may be enhanced by the law firm's treatment of paralegals, affording them a meaningful career path and appropriate perquisites and treating them with respect.

Collegiality also presents dichotomies. Not all paralegals feel a common bond with and loyalty to their paralegal colleagues, not having had a shared educational experience, like lawyers have, and not possessing a common exclusive grant to engage in certain work. Aggravating this lack of bond is the fact that many paralegals view themselves as competitors within the firm for the most interesting work and highest pay. Thus, they often express their primary loyalty to the firm or to their supervising attorney, not to their occupation. Many paralegals work in small or midsized firms where they may be the only paralegal, lending to their feelings of isolation from other paralegals. On the other hand, paralegal associations have been quite successful in building a strong sense of camaraderie and shared interests and responsibilities among their members. However, it is estimated that only about 20 percent of the paralegals in the country belong to such as an organization. See Q. Johnstone & M. Wenglinsky, *Paralegals: Progress and Prospects of a Satellite Occupation*, pp. 183 et seq. (1985).

Another interesting analysis of the paralegal occupation traces its evolution from an occupation to a profession, as defined by sociologists who study occupations. Green, Snell, Corgiat, and Paramanith,

The Professionalization of the Legal Assistant: Identity, Maturation States and Goal Attainment, 7 J. Paralegal Educ. & Prac. 35 (1990). This article cites five stages in the **development of a profession**: diffusion, education, associations, agitation and self-regulation, and formulation of a professional code. The authors found in 1990 that the paralegal field was advancing, although not smoothly, in the second stage (education) and recommended a strengthened and standardized paralegal curriculum.

Since that time, substantial progress has been made in the "professionalization" of the paralegal occupation. Levels of education, both general and specialized paralegal education, are rising, and more law firms are requiring college and paralegal-specific education. Paralegal work has grown and become more sophisticated. It includes more client contact and requires higher levels of organizational and communication skills. Billing rates and salaries continue to rise. Both national associations promote voluntary certification, and several statewide voluntary certification programs have been established, perhaps a precursor to real regulation. Paralegal associations are strong and are having an impact on important issues like certification, regulation, and attorney's fees. Given the history and future of the paralegal field, professionalism for paralegals might be viewed as having the following elements.

1. Commitment to Public Service

Paralegals should always remember that their highest goal is to assist in the delivery of legal services to the public, legal services that are delivered ethically, competently, and efficiently. In addition to being reflected in their daily work lives, this commitment also requires paralegals to engage in activities that improve access to legal services, such as pro bono programs. See Section D later in this chapter.

2. Commitment to Education

Fulfilling this commitment includes participating in formal education, continuing education, and on-the-job learning that enhance knowledge and skills and continually develop the paralegal's potential. Education heightens the paralegal's ability to deliver quality legal services and enriches long-term career satisfaction.

3. Commitment to the Highest Standards of Ethical Conduct

Paralegals should know the rules of ethics that bind lawyers and understand how these rules apply to them. Further, they should internalize the values reflected in these rules and seek to develop their own personal standards of ethics and morality that reach beyond the minimums imposed by law. Paralegals must be scrupulously honest in their relations with clients, courts, attorneys, co-workers, and others in their professional world.

4. Commitment to Excellence

Paralegals should set high standards of performance for themselves and seek to meet those standards in all the work they undertake. They should approach each task with an attitude of seriousness and apply diligently their knowledge, skill, and talent to accomplish their work.

5. Commitment to the Paralegal Profession

Paralegals are part of a distinct profession within the legal field, with interests and goals that are shared by other paralegals. They should support paralegal activities organized through professional associations, bar associations, and alumni associations. They should also engender collegiality among their colleagues, mentoring new paralegals and acting as a role model and source of information for those who aspire to the paralegal profession.

6. Commitment to a Strong Work Ethic

Paralegals should strive to do their best on every task and to serve clients diligently. They should be meticulous and thorough, organized, prompt in meeting deadlines, and always do more than the minimum. They should take pride in their work and always do work that merits that pride.

7. Commitment to Acting with Integrity and Honor

Paralegals should be courteous, respectful, and fair in their dealings with lawyers, other paralegals, support staff, clients, and others both within and outside their firm. They should demonstrate maturity, patience, and thoughtfulness in their actions, avoiding gossip, undue criticism of others, prejudice, and favoritism. This commitment means being sensitive to the needs and talents of others, valuing the differences in people's backgrounds, and recognizing others' achievements.

8. Commitment to Balance as a Person

Paralegals should not become so consumed by their work that they neglect other aspects of their lives, such as family, friends, health, and personal interests and activities. They should seek to be well rounded and should have a variety of interests. Commitment to a profession need not prevent paralegals from leading a full life; in fact, paralegals who narrow their interests to work only will not be as effective in relations with others and can lose the sense of proportion and balance needed to fulfill their commitments as professionals.

9. Commitment to Good Judgment, Common Sense, and Communication

Paralegals should strive to understand and work well with others. They should listen to others carefully and communicate, both orally and in writing, clearly and persuasively.

C. Current Issues in Professionalism

A number of important issues face the paralegal profession. One issue that has always been central to the debate about the evolution of the paralegal field is **regulation**. Discussed in Chapter 2, regulation is a complex question that will not be resolved easily. The debate has raised many difficult questions:

- Is there a need for regulation, i.e., what purposes would regulation serve?
- Who should be regulated?
- Who should do the regulating?
- Should regulation be mandatory?
- What level of regulation is appropriate?
- What educational requirements should be established?
- What kind of examination, if any, should be required?
- What, if any, tasks should paralegals be authorized to perform?
- Do paralegals need their own ethics rules?
- Should paralegals be required to meet continuing education requirements?

Resolution of the regulation issue will determine the future of the career; the extent to which it becomes an independent, self-regulated profession; and the nature and character of the paralegal role and the work that paralegals do.

A related issue has been the use of **the titles "paralegal" and "legal assistant"** to identify persons working in a paralegal capacity. For many years the two titles were used interchangeably, although there were some regional preferences for one title or the other. Some paralegals advocated for one uniform title and definition, which they believed would advance the profession. In the 1990s, many lawyers started to give the title "legal assistant" to personnel who previously would have been called legal secretaries. This enhancement of title for their assistants created conflict with paralegals, who often have specific educational credentials and do billable work for clients. At the same time, a growing number of states have started to reserve both titles for "true" paralegals. Many firms and educational programs have moved away from title legal assistant to paralegal. Local associations affiliated with NFPA all use "paralegal," and NALA gives those who pass its certification examination the option of using Certified Legal Assistant or Certified Paralegal. The recently adopted state certification programs also use "paralegal" instead of legal assistant in their titles. In 2003 the ABA changed the name of its entity on paralegals from the Standing Committee on Legal Assistants to the Standing Committee on Paralegals.

The movement toward one title also has ramifications for the **definition of paralegal**, i.e., whether the term *paralegal* should include nonlawyer legal service providers who do not work under lawyer supervision. Note that the definitions cited in Chapter 2 endorse the view that this title belongs to those persons who work under the supervision of a lawyer. This limitation on the use of the title has been reinforced in states from Maine to California that have statutes and court rules that prohibit the use of the title by persons who act as nonlawyer legal services providers. As noted in Chapter 2, some states give other titles to nonlawyers who provide legal services directly to the public, like Legal Document Assistant and Legal Document Preparer.

Education is another important issue for paralegals. The lack of consistency in hiring standards and the lack of uniformity in the paralegal curriculum have prevented paralegals from having a shared body of knowledge and a shared educational experience, two important characteristics of a profession. The lack of common educational experience also inhibits the development of collegiality among paralegals. However, the diversity within paralegal education offerings and the variety of ways that one can enter the field have allowed the paralegal profession to flourish. Paralegals have a continuously expanding bank of job responsibilities, unhindered by a standardized, limiting education that trains everyone to perform the same tasks. The diverse work and life experiences that are brought to the profession by the wide variety of people who become paralegals have enriched both the career possibilities and the legal profession itself. Whereas the ABA and the American Association for Paralegal Education endorse a minimum of two years of college for entry into the paralegal field, the International Paralegal Management Association, representing corporate counsel offices and large law firms, favors a four-year degree. As noted earlier, levels of educational attainment among paralegals are rising.

The ambiguity that comes with a relatively new and evolving profession creates problems for paralegals. Even now, 40 years after the advent of the modern American paralegal, **utilization of paralegal services** is not universal. Some lawyers do not hire paralegals at all; others are unclear on how to utilize their talents and skills or reluctant to delegate anything more than routine or repetitive work to them. Although all large law firms and many midsized ones employ paralegals, the majority of sole practitioners and small firms do not use paralegal services. Some lawyers and law firms treat their paralegals poorly — by not compensating them fairly, not providing appropriate working conditions and clerical support, or not giving them recognition when deserved — but still expect professional work and loyalty. Nor surprisingly, this kind of treatment results in high turnover. Many paralegals leave the profession after a few years, dissatisfied with their treatment, compensation, and the nature of their work.

One important question about the status and treatment of paralegals was resolved in the last decade: whether paralegals should be classified as **exempt or nonexempt** employees. Nonexempt employees are entitled to overtime compensation under the Fair Labor Standards Act and similar state laws. When the Department of Labor adopted new Wage and Hour Rules and Regulations in 2004, it established the rule that paralegals are not generally exempt from overtime under the category of exempt "learned professional." The Department cited accurate evidence that a four-year degree is not required for entry into the profession, which is considered a minimal prerequisite for classification of an occupation as exempt. The new provision does permit exempt status for paralegals who "possess advanced specialized degrees," such as engineers, and other provisions of the rules allow exempt status for managers and supervisors (see 29 CFR 541.301(e)(7)).

Prior to the adoption of this rule, paralegals were divided on the question of overtime. Some believed that their classification as nonexempt undermines their professional work and status. Others appreciate that they receive higher compensation when paid for overtime work. It appears that most firms are honoring the rules. Some large law firms have career paths that classify the lower rungs of the ladder as nonexempt and the top level or levels as exempt, based on the qualifications of the paralegals, the nature and complexity of specific responsibilities, the degree of independence exercised by the paralegal, and the involvement of the paralegal in management or supervisory work.

Finally, the paralegal career continues to be a **female-dominated occupation** that serves a still male-dominated profession. Other traditionally female-dominated professions such as nursing and teaching have struggled very hard — not always successfully — to achieve parity in status and recognition, fair treatment, good working conditions, and compensation that is based on the value, nature, and difficulty of their work. Women are entering law school in numbers equal to men and now make up about one-third of the lawyers in this country. However, women lawyers have not yet broken through the glass ceiling into the ranks of partners and judicial officers in proportion to their overall numbers in the profession.

Women lawyers and paralegals continue to experience harassment and discrimination. Several high-profile lawsuits have been won by women lawyers and support staff. Surveys show that 50 percent of the women lawyers believe they have been harassed and almost as many believe that they have been discriminated against in the allocation of work and in salary and promotion decisions. Many women leave the practice of law or leave traditional law firms to move in house or to start their own firms.

Bias against lawyers on the basis of racial/ethnic background, sexual orientation, and disability also plagues the legal profession. Minority lawyers make less money, are less likely to make partner, are less likely to be appointed to the bench, and are systematically excluded from key firm committees and prestigious practice areas. Some law firms have not been proactive in hiring lawyers from underrepresented groups, and others do not create a climate that is conducive for the success of minority lawyers. Several jurisdictions have anti-bias rules that make it an ethical violation to discriminate in the operation of a practice and/or to disparage or humiliate someone on the basis of race, national origin, sex, sexual orientation, religion, age, or disability. For example, see California Rules of Professional Conduct 2-400 and Florida Rule 4-8.4. The Americans with Disabilities Act has added protection for disabled employees and other persons in their interactions with law firms. Diversity pipeline projects at the national and local levels seek to bring more underrepresented groups into the legal profession and to support efforts to achieve fairness and parity in law practice.

D. Pro Bono Work

The legal needs of the vast majority of Americans are not being met by our current system. Study after study has proven that most Americans — including poor and moderate-income persons — do not have access to a lawyer when they need one. Most Americans cannot afford a lawyer; many who actually can afford one believe that they cannot. Most would not know how to go about finding a lawyer.

Pro bono
For free

To cope with this problem, the organized bar has encouraged individual lawyers to engage in ***pro bono*** work and has sponsored a wide variety of pro bono programs to which lawyers can contribute their time and expertise. Many states and some local bars have aspirational guidelines for lawyers, usually for 50 hours of pro bono work a year. Only a few have rules mandating pro bono work, which can be fulfilled by making a donation in lieu of doing the work. Two states, Florida and Maryland, require lawyers to report the amount of time they devote each year to pro bono work. Some law schools have a requirement for public service or pro bono work, and many law firms have policies that encourage their attorneys to engage in such activities.

The last two decades have seen an increase in voluntary pro bono work being done by lawyers and law firms. However, the need for legal services has increased during this time despite these efforts, which cannot hope to close the huge access gap. Paralegals have an opportunity to help. Participating in pro bono activities as part of one's professional commitment also increases career satisfaction. A recent survey of paralegals showed that more than 40 percent participate in some kind of pro bono work, usually through a program with their employer or a paralegal association.

Guideline 10 to the ABA Model Guidelines for the Utilization of Paralegal Services (ABA Model Guidelines) and several states' guidelines encourage lawyers to facilitate paralegal participation in pro bono activities. Lawyers have a duty to provide pro bono services under ABA Model Rule 6.1 and Canon 2 of the ABA Model Code, and the ABA has called on lawyers to fulfill this duty by aspiring to do 50 hours of pro bono work annually.

Many law firms that do pro bono work include paralegals in these activities. Paralegals who do not have an opportunity to become involved in pro bono work through their jobs should seek out activities on their own. Local bar associations and paralegal associations have pro bono projects on which paralegals can work. Legal aid organizations and law clinics are always in need of volunteers.

Pro bono programs have been established in many specialized areas of law, affording paralegals a chance either to exercise their expertise or to develop it in a new area. Examples of the areas some of the programs cover are court-appointed special advocates in juvenile; facilitators or mediators in family law; consumer and landlord–tenant matters; major public interest litigation (e.g., housing or employment discrimination, elder abuse, and children's rights); immigration; mental health advocacy; domestic violence counseling; AIDS; and homeless projects.

Paralegals who do pro bono work often find themselves working more independently than they do in their law firms, engaged in challenging tasks that they would not be delegated on their jobs. Paralegals in legal aid settings very often have extensive client contact, handling intake interviews and helping clients directly with matters not requiring a lawyer. They sometimes advocate for clients before administrative agencies, conduct in-depth research, and draft documents and memoranda.

Besides skill development and growth, paralegals who do pro bono work derive the ultimate satisfaction of helping someone who needs help and might not otherwise have gotten that help. Usually the assistance needed and provided is of the most critical kind — for instance, keeping someone from losing a home or welfare benefits—and is a matter of survival to the clients.

The National Federation of Paralegal Associations Model Code of Ethics and Professional Responsibility and Guidelines for Enforcement, Canon 1.4, states that paralegals "shall serve the public interest by contributing to the improvement of the legal system and delivery of quality legal services, including pro bono publico legal services." In the accompanying Ethical Consideration 1.4(d), the Federation asks its members to aspire to contribute at least 24 hours of pro bono services annually. Excellent materials on paralegal involvement in pro bono activities are available through local bar associations, the National Federation of Paralegal Associations, and the National Association of Legal Assistants, and their local chapters and affiliates.

REVIEW QUESTIONS

1. Give five reasons why the public image of lawyers is so poor. Is this image warranted?
2. What are lawyers doing to improve their public image?
3. What is a code of professional courtesy? What kinds of conduct does it require?
4. What can a paralegal do to improve professionalism and the public image of the legal field?
5. Why are paralegals in a somewhat ambiguous position in the legal environment? Give at least three reasons.
6. How is "profession" defined?
7. What is a paraprofessional?
8. What is collegiality? Why is collegiality difficult for legal assistants to have?
9. To what extent are paralegals over-trained?
10. Describe the nine professional commitments that paralegals should make.
11. Name and discuss three issues facing today's paralegals.
12. What are the issues related to the title and definition of paralegal/legal assistant?
13. What is the basis for classifying a paralegal as an exempt or nonexempt employee? What is the law currently?
14. Does the fact that paralegals are predominately female affect the career? How?
15. What is the current state of legal services for poor and middle-income Americans?
16. Have pro bono activities increased or decreased in the last decade?
17. What kinds of pro bono activities do lawyers and paralegals do?
18. What are the benefits to a paralegal of doing pro bono work?
19. How can a paralegal get involved in pro bono work?

DISCUSSION QUESTIONS AND HYPOTHETICALS

1. Do you think the legal profession deserves its poor public image? Why, or why not?
2. How can the legal profession overcome its poor image?
3. Do you think lawyers' salaries are disproportionately high? Why, or why not?
4. Do you think lawyers' increased mobility is a good or bad thing? Why?
5. What are some of the signs of substance abuse or mental health problems that may affect performance and ethics?
6. Do you think paralegals are professionals or paraprofessionals? Is this distinction important to you? Why?
7. Do you think Johnstone and Wenglinsky's three characteristics (collegiality, overtraining, and prestige) are instructive in evaluating the paralegal occupation as a profession? Why, or why not?
8. Do you think standardization in paralegal education would be good or bad for the career? Why?
9. How can paralegals build collegiality? Why is it important?
10. Do you think voluntary certification is good for paralegals? Why, or why not? What about mandatory regulation? Why, or why not?
11. Looking at the five stages toward professionalization presented by the Green article, where do you think the paralegal occupation fits?
12. Do you agree with the nine professional commitments for paralegals? Why, or why not? How would you prioritize their relative importance? What would you add or delete?
13. Do you think regulation of paralegals would enhance their professional status? Why, or why not?
14. How can paralegals help overcome lawyers' reluctance to utilize their services? How can paralegals encourage lawyers to utilize their services more effectively and fully?

RESEARCH PROJECTS AND ASSIGNMENTS

1. Read the newspaper every day for a month and clip out all the articles that mention lawyers. How many are favorable? What image do they present?
2. Read the legal newspaper for a month and see how many articles are about lawyers engaged in unprofessional conduct or are about good work that lawyers are doing. Does this information align with the information in this chapter? Report to the class.
3. Does your local bar association or court have a code of professional courtesy? Do you think a nonbinding code such as this is appropriate

for a court or bar association to have? Why, or why not? Should such a code be binding? Why, or why not? Do such codes derogate the lawyer's duty of zealousness? Do they contribute to lawyers' "clubbiness"? Do they work?

4. Contact your local paralegal association and get salary surveys that ask about job satisfaction, career paths, pro bono work, and exempt or nonexempt status.
5. Contact five paralegals at local law firms and ask them:

   a. if they regard their paralegal career as a profession;
   b. if they are treated as professionals by their employers;
   c. if they plan to continue as a paralegal indefinitely, and if not, what they plan to do and why they are leaving the career;
   d. if they are members of the local paralegal association;
   e. if their firm does pro bono work;
   f. if they do pro bono work;
   g. if their education and training are well utilized;
   h. if they are paid overtime;
   i. if they have experienced discrimination.

6. Does your state or local bar association have a program to provide assistance to impaired lawyers? How does it work? How many lawyers participate in it? Does the bar have an estimate of how many lawyer disciplinary programs are associated with substance abuse?
7. Does your state or local bar association undertake activities to promote diversity in the legal profession? Find out if the bar can give you statistics on the underrepresented groups and women in the legal profession. What kinds of activities does it undertake to promote diversity? Is your paralegal class at school more or less diverse than the local bar? Than the general population?
8. Contact the local bar and paralegal associations and find out what kinds of pro bono opportunities are available to you.

A

NALA Code of Ethics and Professional Responsibility

Each NALA member agrees to follow the canons of the NALA Code of Ethics and Professional Responsibility. Violations of the Code may result in cancellation of membership. First adopted by the NALA membership in May of 1975, the Code of Ethics and Professional Responsibility is the foundation of ethical practices of paralegals in the legal community.

A paralegal must adhere strictly to the accepted standards of legal ethics and to the general principles of proper conduct. The performance of the duties of the paralegal shall be governed by specific canons as defined herein so that justice will be served and goals of the profession attained. (See Model Standards and Guidelines for Utilization of Legal Assistants, Section II.)

The canons of ethics set forth hereafter are adopted by the National Association of Legal Assistants, Inc., as a general guide intended to aid paralegals and attorneys. The enumeration of these rules does not mean there are not others of equal importance although not specifically mentioned. Court rules, agency rules and statutes must be taken into consideration when interpreting the canons.

Definition: Legal assistants, also known as paralegals, are a distinguishable group of persons who assist attorneys in the delivery of legal services. Through formal education, training and experience, legal assistants have knowledge and expertise regarding the legal system and substantive and procedural law which qualify them to do work of a legal nature under the supervision of an attorney.

In **2001**, NALA members also adopted the ABA definition of a legal assistant/paralegal, as follows:

A legal assistant or paralegal is a person qualified by education, training or work experience who is employed or retained by a lawyer, law office, corporation, governmental agency or other entity who performs specifically delegated substantive legal work for which a lawyer is responsible. (Adopted by the ABA in 1997.)

Canon 1

A paralegal must not perform any of the duties that attorneys only may perform nor take any actions that attorneys may not take.

Canon 2

A paralegal may perform any task which is properly delegated and supervised by an attorney, as long as the attorney is ultimately responsible to the client, maintains a direct relationship with the client, and assumes professional responsibility for the work product.

Canon 3

A paralegal must not: (a) engage in, encourage, or contribute to any act which could constitute the unauthorized practice of law; and (b) establish attorney-client relationships, set fees, give legal opinions or advice or represent a client before a court or agency unless so authorized by that court or agency; and (c) engage in conduct or take any action which would assist or involve the attorney in a violation of professional ethics or give the appearance of professional impropriety.

Canon 4

A paralegal must use discretion and professional judgment commensurate with knowledge and experience but must not render independent legal judgment in place of an attorney. The services of an attorney are essential in the public interest whenever such legal judgment is required.

Canon 5

A paralegal must disclose his or her status as a paralegal at the outset of any professional relationship with a client, attorney, a court or administrative agency or personnel thereof, or a member of the general public. A paralegal must act prudently in determining the extent to which a client may be assisted without the presence of an attorney.

Canon 6

A paralegal must strive to maintain integrity and a high degree of competency through education and training with respect to professional responsibility, local rules and practice, and through continuing education in substantive areas of law to better assist the legal profession in fulfilling its duty to provide legal service.

Canon 7

A paralegal must protect the confidences of a client and must not violate any rule or statute now in effect or hereafter enacted controlling the doctrine of privileged communications between a client and an attorney.

Canon 8

A paralegal must disclose to his or her employer or prospective employer any pre-existing client or personal relationship that may conflict with the interests of the employer or prospective employer and/or their clients.

Canon 9

A paralegal must do all other things incidental, necessary, or expedient for the attainment of the ethics and responsibilities as defined by statute or rule of court.

Canon 10

A paralegal's conduct is guided by bar associations' codes of professional responsibility and rules of professional conduct.

B

National Federation of Paralegal Associations, Inc.

Model Code of Ethics and Professional Responsibility and Guidelines for Enforcement

Preamble

The National Federation of Paralegal Associations, Inc. ("NFPA") is a professional organization comprised of paralegal associations and individual paralegals throughout the United States and Canada. Members of NFPA have varying backgrounds, experiences, education and job responsibilities that reflect the diversity of the paralegal profession. NFPA promotes the growth, development and recognition of the paralegal profession as an integral partner in the delivery of legal services.

In May 1993 NFPA adopted its Model Code of Ethics and Professional Responsibility ("Model Code") to delineate the principles for ethics and conduct to which every paralegal should aspire.

Many paralegal associations throughout the United States have endorsed the concept and content of NFPA's Model Code through the adoption of their own ethical codes. In doing so, paralegals have confirmed the profession's commitment to increase the quality and efficiency of legal services, as well as recognized its responsibilities to the public, the legal community, and colleagues.

Paralegals have recognized, and will continue to recognize, that the profession must continue to evolve to enhance their roles in the delivery of legal services. With increased levels of responsibility comes the need to define and enforce mandatory rules of professional conduct. Enforcement of codes of paralegal conduct is a logical and necessary step to enhance and ensure the confidence of the legal community and the public in the integrity and professional responsibility of paralegals.

In April 1997 NFPA adopted the Model Disciplinary Rules ("Model Rules") to make possible the enforcement of the Canons and Ethical Considerations contained in the NFPA Model Code. A concurrent determination was made that the Model Code of Ethics and Professional Responsibility, formerly aspirational in nature, should be recognized as setting forth the enforceable obligations of all paralegals.

The Model Code and Model Rules offer a framework for professional discipline, either voluntarily or through formal regulatory programs.

§1. NFPA Model Disciplinary Rules And Ethical Considerations

1.1 A Paralegal Shall Achieve and Maintain a High Level of Competence.

Ethical Considerations

EC-1.1(a) A paralegal shall achieve competency through education, training, and work experience.

EC-1.1(b) A paralegal shall aspire to participate in a minimum of twelve (12) hours of continuing legal education, to include at least one (1) hour of ethics education, every two (2) years in order to remain current on developments in the law.

EC-1.1(c) A paralegal shall perform all assignments promptly and efficiently.

1.2 A Paralegal Shall Maintain a High Level of Personal and Professional Integrity.

Ethical Considerations

EC-1.2(a) A paralegal shall not engage in any ex parte communications involving the courts or any other adjudicatory body in an attempt to exert undue influence or to obtain advantage or the benefit of only one party.

EC-1.2(b) A paralegal shall not communicate, or cause another to communicate, with a party the paralegal knows to be represented by a lawyer in a pending matter without the prior consent of the lawyer representing such other party.

EC-1.2(c) A paralegal shall ensure that all timekeeping and billing records prepared by the paralegal are thorough, accurate, honest, and complete.

EC-1.2(d) A paralegal shall not knowingly engage in fraudulent billing practices. Such practices may include, but are not limited to: inflation of hours billed to a client or employer; misrepresentation of the nature of tasks performed; and/or submission of fraudulent expense and disbursement documentation.

EC-1.2(e) A paralegal shall be scrupulous, thorough and honest in the identification and maintenance of all funds, securities, and other assets of a client and shall provide accurate accounting as appropriate.

EC-1.2(f) A paralegal shall advise the proper authority of non-confidential knowledge of any dishonest or fraudulent acts by any person pertaining to the handling of the funds, securities or other assets of a client. The authority to whom the report is made shall depend on the nature and circumstances of the possible misconduct, (e.g., ethics committees of law firms, corporations and/or paralegal associations, local or state bar associations, local prosecutors, administrative agencies, etc.). Failure to report such knowledge is in itself misconduct and shall be treated as such under these rules.

1.3 A Paralegal Shall Maintain a High Standard of Professional Conduct.

Ethical Considerations

EC-1.3(a) A paralegal shall refrain from engaging in any conduct that offends the dignity and decorum of proceedings before a court or other adjudicatory body and shall be respectful of all rules and procedures.

EC-1.3(b) A paralegal shall avoid impropriety and the appearance of impropriety and shall not engage in any conduct that would adversely affect his/her fitness to practice. Such conduct may include, but is not limited to: violence, dishonesty, interference with the administration of justice, and/or abuse of a professional position or public office.

EC-1.3(c) Should a paralegal's fitness to practice be compromised by physical or mental illness, causing that paralegal to commit an act that is in direct violation of the Model Code/Model Rules and/or the rules and/or laws governing the jurisdiction in which the paralegal practices, that paralegal may be protected from sanction upon review of the nature and circumstances of that illness.

EC-1.3(d) A paralegal shall advise the proper authority of non-confidential knowledge of any action of another legal professional that clearly demonstrates fraud, deceit, dishonesty, or misrepresentation. The authority to whom the report is made shall depend on the nature and circumstances of the possible misconduct, (e.g., ethics committees of law firms, corporations and/or paralegal associations, local or state bar associations, local prosecutors, administrative agencies, etc.). Failure to report such knowledge is in itself misconduct and shall be treated as such under these rules.

EC-1.3(e) A paralegal shall not knowingly assist any individual with the commission of an act that is in direct violation of the Model Code/Model Rules and/or the rules and/or laws governing the jurisdiction in which the paralegal practices.

EC-1.3(f) If a paralegal possesses knowledge of future criminal activity, that knowledge must be reported to the appropriate authority immediately.

1.4 A Paralegal Shall Serve the Public Interest by Contributing to the Improvement of the Legal System and Delivery of Quality Legal Services, Including Pro Bono Publico Services.

Ethical Considerations

EC-1.4(a) A paralegal shall be sensitive to the legal needs of the public and shall promote the development and implementation of programs that address those needs.

EC-1.4(b) A paralegal shall support efforts to improve the legal system and access thereto and shall assist in making changes.

EC-1.4(c) A paralegal shall support and participate in the delivery of Pro Bono Publico services directed toward implementing and improving access to justice, the law, the legal system or the paralegal and legal professions.

EC-1.4(d) A paralegal should aspire annually to contribute twenty-four (24) hours of Pro Bono Publico services under the supervision of an attorney or as authorized by administrative, statutory or court authority to:

1. persons of limited means; or
2. charitable, religious, civic, community, governmental and educational organizations in matters that are designed primarily to address the legal needs of persons with limited means; or
3. individuals, groups or organizations seeking to secure or protect civil rights, civil liberties or public rights.

The twenty-four (24) hours of Pro Bono Publico services contributed annually by a paralegal may consist of such services as detailed in this EC-1.4(d), and/or administrative matters designed to develop and implement the attainment of this aspiration as detailed above in EC-1.4(a) or (c), or any combination of the two.

1.5 A Paralegal Shall Preserve All Confidential Information Provided by the Client or Acquired from Other Sources Before, During, and After the Course of the Professional Relationship.

Ethical Considerations

EC-1.5(a) A paralegal shall be aware of and abide by all legal authority governing confidential information in the jurisdiction in which the paralegal practices.

EC-1.5(b) A paralegal shall not use confidential information to the disadvantage of the client.

EC-1.5(c) A paralegal shall not use confidential information to the advantage of the paralegal or of a third person.

EC-1.5(d) A paralegal may reveal confidential information only after full disclosure and with the client's written consent; or, when required by law or court order; or, when necessary to prevent the client from committing an act that could result in death or serious bodily harm.

EC-1.5(e) A paralegal shall keep those individuals responsible for the legal representation of a client fully informed of any confidential information the paralegal may have pertaining to that client.

EC-1.5(f) A paralegal shall not engage in any indiscreet communications concerning clients.

1.6 A Paralegal Shall Avoid Conflicts of Interest and Shall Disclose any Possible Conflict to the Employer or Client, as Well as to the Prospective Employers or Clients.

Ethical Considerations

EC-1.6(a) A paralegal shall act within the bounds of the law, solely for the benefit of the client, and shall be free of compromising influences and loyalties. Neither the paralegal's personal or business interest, nor those of other clients or third persons, should compromise the paralegal's professional judgment and loyalty to the client.

EC-1.6(b) A paralegal shall avoid conflicts of interest that may arise from previous assignments, whether for a present or past employer or client.

EC-1.6(c) A paralegal shall avoid conflicts of interest that may arise from family relationships and from personal and business interests.

EC-1.6(d) In order to be able to determine whether an actual or potential conflict of interest exists a paralegal shall create and maintain an effective record keeping system that identifies clients, matters, and parties with which the paralegal has worked.

EC-1.6(e) A paralegal shall reveal sufficient non-confidential information about a client or former client to reasonably ascertain if an actual or potential conflict of interest exists.

EC-1.6(f) A paralegal shall not participate in or conduct work on any matter where a conflict of interest has been identified.

EC-1.6(g) In matters where a conflict of interest has been identified and the client consents to continued representation, a paralegal shall comply fully with the implementation and maintenance of an Ethical Wall.

1.7 A Paralegal's Title Shall be Fully Disclosed.

Ethical Considerations

EC-1.7(a) A paralegal's title shall clearly indicate the individual's status and shall be disclosed in all business and professional communications to avoid misunderstandings and misconceptions about the paralegal's role and responsibilities.

EC-1.7(b) A paralegal's title shall be included if the paralegal's name appears on business cards, letterhead, brochures, directories, and advertisements.

EC-1.7(c) A paralegal shall not use letterhead, business cards or other promotional materials to create a fraudulent impression of his/her status or ability to practice in the jurisdiction in which the paralegal practices.

EC-1.7(d) A paralegal shall not practice under color of any record, diploma, or certificate that has been illegally or fraudulently obtained or issued or which is misrepresentative in any way.

EC-1.7(e) A paralegal shall not participate in the creation, issuance, or dissemination of fraudulent records, diplomas, or certificates.

1.8 A Paralegal Shall not Engage in the Unauthorized Practice of Law.

Ethical Considerations

EC-1.8(a) A paralegal shall comply with the applicable legal authority governing the unauthorized practice of law in the jurisdiction in which the paralegal practices.

Last revised 2006.

[The Guidelines for the Enforcement of the Model Code of Ethics and Professional Responsibility are not included in this Appendix.]

Glossary

Abuse of process The improper use of a civil or criminal process.

Administrative agency A government body responsible for the control and supervision of a particular activity or area of public interest.

Advance fee A fee paid by a client to a lawyer in advance of the work being done, which is earned by the lawyer as the work is done.

Associate A lawyer in a law firm who is not a partner but is an employee.

Attorney-client privilege The rule of evidence that protects confidential communications between a lawyer and client made in the course of the professional relationship.

Barratry The common law crime of stirring up lawsuits and disputes.

Bribery The crime of giving or receiving something of value as payment for an official act.

Certification A form of recognition of an occupation based on a person's having met specified qualifications.

Certified Legal Assistant Certification for paralegals offered by NALA for passing the Certified Legal Assistant examination.

Champerty An old common law agreement between a lawyer and client under which the lawyer undertakes representation and pays costs and is reimbursed and paid a fee out of the recovery; such agreements were outlawed in most states.

Chinese wall An antiquated term for a screen. See **Screen/screening.**

Class action suit A lawsuit brought by a representative of a group of persons on behalf of the group.

Client security fund A fund set aside to reimburse clients whose funds have been converted or misappropriated by lawyers.

Client trust account A bank account set up by a lawyer in which funds are kept that belong in whole or in part to the client.

Commingling The mixing of the funds of a fiduciary, including a lawyer, with those of a client.

Cone of silence The silence imposed on a person with a conflict of interest when a screen is erected to protect against breaches of confidentiality.

Confidentiality agreement An agreement entered into between a law firm and an employee or other agent in which the employee or agent agrees to keep client information confidential.

Contempt An act that obstructs the administration of justice, impairs the dignity of the court, or shows disrespect for the authority of the court.

Contingency fee A fee that is contingent on the successful outcome of a case and based on a percentage of the recovery.

Control group test The test applied by some courts to determine whether communications in a corporate setting are covered by the attorney-client privilege; under this test, communications are privileged only if they are made with the management and board members.

Conversion The tortious deprivation of another's property without justification or authorization.

Court facilitators Persons employed by the courts to assist laypersons who are representing themselves in their own court matters. Typically employed in family law courts.

Deposition A method of pre-trial discovery that consists of a witness statement taken under oath in a question-and-answer format and recorded.

Disbarment The rescinding of a lawyer's license to practice law.

Disclaimers A statement denying a person's claim or right.

Discovery Pre-trial procedures designed for the parties to gain information in order to narrow the issues of fact and law.

Document production A form of discovery under which one party must provide copies of specified documents to the other side.

Ethics opinions Written opinions promulgated by bar associations in which the association interprets the relevant ethical precedents in the context of a specific ethical dilemma posed to it.

Ex parte An action taken by or on behalf of a party without the presence of the opposing party.

Extra-judicial An act that takes place outside the presence of the judge or jury.

Fee-shifting statute A law that allows a court to award attorneys' fees to one of the parties.

Fixed fees A fee for legal services based on a set amount, usually used for standardized routine work.

Forwarding fee A fee paid by a lawyer to another lawyer for referring a case.

Freelance paralegals Legal assistants who work as independent contractors providing services to lawyers on an as-needed basis.

Gag order A court-imposed order that restricts information or comment about a case.

Hourly fees Fees for legal services based on hourly rates and the amount of time actually expended in rendering the services.

Imputed conflict/disqualification A conflict of interest involving one person that is attributed vicariously to the entire law firm, which is disqualified from representing the party at issue.

In camera Proceedings held in the judge's chambers without the jury or public present; the examination of documents to determine if there is privileged information is conducted "in camera."

Independent paralegals A term sometimes used by nonlawyer legal service providers and sometimes used by freelance paralegals. See both these terms in this glossary.

Integrated bar A bar association in which the mandatory and voluntary aspects of bar activities are combined, and membership is required.

Inter vivos During life.

IOLTA Interest on Lawyers' Trust Accounts. A program under which the interest from lawyers' client trust accounts, which is too small to pay to clients, is collected by banks and used by bar associations and/or courts to fund law-related programs.

Issue conflict The situation that arises when a lawyer argues opposing sides of a legal issue, the result of which may be that one client's interests are harmed, even though that client is not a party to the matter.

Jailhouse lawyers Prison inmates who assist other prisoners in preparing writs and lawsuits.

Legal document assistants/preparers Nonlawyer legal service providers who assist persons in preparing legal documents without giving legal advice under California statutes or Arizona court rules.

Legal malpractice Improper conduct in the performance of duties by a legal professional, either intentionally or through negligence.

Legal technicians A term used by some nonlawyer legal service providers.

Licensing Mandatory governmental regulation of a profession requiring that the members meet specified qualifications.
Lien An encumbrance or claim on the property of another as security for a debt or charge.

Malicious prosecution An action to recover damages resulting from an unsuccessful criminal or civil action which was instituted without probable cause and with malice.
Malpractice Improper conduct in the performance of duties by a professional, either intentionally or through negligence.
Mistrial A trial terminated and declared void prior to the return of a verdict, often because of a jury deadlock.
Multidisciplinary practice A business model under which law firms and other professionals form partnerships to deliver legal and other related services to clients.
Multijurisdictional practice Engaging in the practice of law in more than one state.

Nonlawyer legal service providers Laypersons who provide legal services directly to the public.

Paraprofessional A person who works within a profession in a subordinate position but with special training and a degree of independence in carrying out duties.
Perjury The criminal offense of making false statements under oath.
Pleading Statements in written legal form that set forth the plaintiff's cause of action and the defendant's grounds of defense.
Probation A procedure under which someone found guilty of an offense is subjected to certain conditions and oversight by the entity involved and is released from a more serious sanction.
Pro bono For free.
Professional negligence Improper conduct in the performance of duties by a professional, either intentionally or through negligence.
Pro hac vice The permission granted by a court to an out-of-state lawyer to appear in a particular case as though admitted to practice in that jurisdiction.
Pro per A nonlawyer representing himself or herself in a legal matter.
Pro se A nonlawyer representing himself or herself in a legal matter.

Real estate closing The consummation of the sale of real estate by payment of the purchase price, delivery of the deed, and finalizing collateral matters, such as mortgage, insurance, and taxes.
Registered Paralegal Certification offered by NFPA for passing the Paralegal Advanced Competency Examinations.

Reprimand A warning; the least serious sanction that can be placed on a lawyer for unethical conduct; it may be public or private.

Reproval Another word for reprimand, used in some states.

Retainer A fee for legal services paid to assure the availability of the lawyer to handle specified matters whether or not any such matters arise during the retainer period.

Runners and cappers Agents of lawyers who solicit clients in violation of ethics rules.

Screen/screening The isolation of a person from participation in a matter through the timely imposition of procedures within a firm that are reasonably adequate under the circumstances to protect information that the person is obligated to protect under the ethics rules or the attorney-client privilege.

Self-representation The act of representing oneself in legal proceedings before a tribunal.

Simultaneous representation The representation of clients in current legal matters that involve a conflict of interest.

Snitch rules Rules requiring lawyers to report unethical conduct.

Solicitation Direct unrequested contact with a prospective client for the purpose of obtaining employment.

Spoliation Destruction of evidence that may result in a civil cause of action for damages for interference with the ability to prove a claim or defense.

Subject matter test The test applied by some courts to determine whether communications in a corporate setting are covered by the attorney-client privilege; under this test, communications with corporate employees are privileged if they related to the legal matter being discussed.

Subornation of perjury The criminal offense of encouraging another to commit perjury.

Successive representation The representation of clients in a conflict of interest situation involving a current matter and a former client whose interests conflict.

Suspension The temporary removal of a lawyer's license to practice law for a stated period.

Testamentary Through a will.

Testimonial advertisements Ads in which a client or person acting as a client explains how valuable the lawyer's services were.

Third-party claims Claims by nonclients against lawyers who, in representing clients, may have caused harm to the third person.

Unconscionable So unreasonable as to render a contract unenforceable, usually because the terms are so favorable to one party.

Unlawful detainer cassistant Title granted by the California legislature to persons who provide legal-clerical services to persons representing themselves in matters relating to evictions.

Vicarious disqualification The imputation of a conflict to others in a firm so that the entire firm is disqualified from undertaking the representation.

Whistleblower statutes Statutes that protect and/or reward persons who reveal unlawful practices.

Will execution The formal process of signing and witnessing of a will.

Work product rule The rule of evidence that protects the work done by a lawyer and his/her employees and agents in the process of representing a client in litigation.

Table of Cases

Principal cases are in italics.

Index